Get more out of your textbook with the FREE Book Companion Site.

Created to help you master key themes and concepts and build skills, the activities in this free resource help you test and broaden your knowledge.

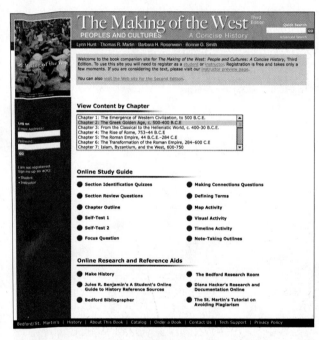

bedfordstmartins.com/huntconcise

Online Study Guide. Get immediate feedback on your progress with Self-Tests and Defining Terms activities designed to check your understanding of chapter concepts and key terms. Other resources, such as map and visual activities, note-taking outlines, and more, help reinforce concepts and ideas presented in the textbook.

Make History. Access our online database with thousands of images, maps, Web links, and documents. Browse by topic, date, or resource type.

Online Research and Reference Aids. Research guides, models for documenting sources, plagiarism tutorials, and other resources provide you with the support you need to refine your research skills, effectively evaluate sources, and organize your findings.

THIRD EDITION

The Making of the West

Peoples and Cultures

A Concise History

Volume I: To 1740

Lynn Hunt
University of California, Los Angeles

Thomas R. Martin
College of the Holy Cross

Barbara H. Rosenwein
Loyola University Chicago

Bonnie G. Smith
Rutgers University

Bedford / St. Martin's
Boston ■ *New York*

For Bedford / St. Martin's

Publisher for History: Mary Dougherty
Director of Development for History: Jane Knetzger
Developmental Editor: Danielle Slevens
Senior Production Editor: Rosemary R. Jaffe
Senior Production Supervisor: Dennis J. Conroy
Executive Marketing Manager: Jenna Bookin Barry
Editorial Assistant: Robin Soule
Production Assistants: Alexis Biasell, Samuel S. Jones, and Alexandra Leach
Senior Art Director: Anna Palchik
Text Designer: Lisa Buckley
Copyeditor: Barbara Jatkola
Proofreaders: Linda McLatchie and Stella Gelboin
Indexer: Leoni Z. McVey
Photo Researcher: Gillian Speeth
Cover Designer: Donna Lee Dennison
Cover and Title Page Art: A Fête at Vermondsey, c. 1570, Joris Hoefnagel (1542–1600). Hatfield
    House, Hertfordshire, UK/The Bridgeman Art Library International.
Cartography: Mapping Specialists, Ltd.
Composition: MPS Limited, A Macmillan Company
Printing and Binding: RR Donnelley and Sons

President: Joan E. Feinberg
Editorial Director: Denise B. Wydra
Director of Marketing: Karen R. Soeltz
Director of Editing, Design, and Production: Marcia Cohen
Assistant Director of Editing, Design, and Production: Elise S. Kaiser
Managing Editor: Elizabeth M. Schaaf

Library of Congress Control Number: 2009924677

Copyright © 2010, 2007, 2003 by Bedford/St. Martin's

All rights reserved. No part of this book may be reproduced, stored in a retrieval system, or transmitted in any form or by any means, electronic, mechanical, photocopying, recording, or otherwise, except as may be expressly permitted by the applicable copyright statutes or in writing by the Publisher.

Manufactured in the United States of America.
4   3   2   1   0
f   e   d   c   b

For information, write: Bedford/St. Martin's, 75 Arlington Street, Boston, MA 02116 (617-399-4000)

ISBN 10: 0-312-55458-3 ISBN 13: 978-0-312-55458-3 (combined edition)
ISBN 10: 0-312-55459-1 ISBN 13: 978-0-312-55459-0 (Vol. I)
ISBN 10: 0-312-55460-5 ISBN 13: 978-0-312-55460-6 (Vol. II)

Credits and copyrights appear at the back of the book on page G-8, which constitutes an extension of this copyright page.

Preface

THE DRAMATIC EVENTS OF THE LAST DECADE have pushed us to look at the history of the West in new ways. The terrorist attacks of September 11, 2001, the subsequent wars in Afghanistan and Iraq, and a global financial and economic crisis all have roots in the past. Digging down to those roots helps us make better sense of the present, and at the same time gives us a better appreciation of how the past differs from the present. We welcome the challenge of incorporating and explaining these momentous events and believe that our project's basic goal and approach are well suited to meeting the challenge presented by them. From the very beginning, we have insisted on an expanded vision of the West that includes the United States, fully incorporates eastern Europe, and emphasizes Europe's relationship with the rest of the world, whether through trade, colonization, migration, cultural exchange, or religious and ethnic conflict. This approach enables us to explain how globalization can seem both promising and problematic, now and in the past.

Textbooks, even very good ones, must constantly evolve. New developments, whether in the form of events or historical approaches, require new efforts at synthesis. This observation applies not just to the recent past, where change is evident at every level, but also to all the other epochs in history, right back to what has been called "prehistory." New archaeological discoveries and techniques for studying the remains of the past continually produce fresh evidence, even about peoples who lived before the invention of writing. Contrary to popular opinion, the past never stands still, and so authors of textbooks must constantly gather up the new evidence, consider the new approaches, and rewrite history accordingly. We relish the opportunity and take seriously the responsibility of providing a coherent narrative of the West that will enable students to understand the world they live in now.

Central Themes and Approach

Our title, *The Making of the West: Peoples and Cultures, A Concise History* makes three enduring points about our themes and approach: (1) that the history of the West is the story of a process that is still ongoing, not a finished result with only one fixed meaning; (2) that "the West" includes many different peoples and cultures; that is, that there is no one Western people or culture that has existed from the beginning until now. To understand the historical development of the West and its position in the world today, it is essential to place the West's emergence in a larger, global context that reveals the cross-cultural interactions fundamental to the shaping of Western identity. Finally, (3) that a "concise" approach is ideally suited to meet the needs of instructors who wish to assign additional supplementary readings, who need to cover the entire introduction to Western civilization in a single semester, or who find a comprehensive textbook too detailed and daunting for their students. By reworking, condensing, and combining thematically related sections throughout the text ourselves, we've created a brief edition that preserves the narrative flow, balance, and power of our full-length work. We've also provided for maximum flexibility by publishing *A Concise History* in an electronic format (see below) and three print versions. Volume I extends from the beginning of civilization to 1740; Volume II picks up at 1340, for courses on Europe from the Renaissance to the present; and a one-volume softcover edition treats the whole of Western history.

We know from our own teaching that introductory students need a solid chronological framework, one with enough familiar benchmarks to make the material readily digestible, but also one with enough flexibility to incorporate the new varieties of historical research. That is one reason we present our account in a straightforward, chronological manner. Each chapter treats all the main events, people, and themes of a period in a common context; thus students are not required to learn about political events in one chapter, and then backtrack to concurrent social and cultural developments in the next. The chronological organization also accords with our belief that it is important, above all else, for students to see the interconnections among varieties of historical experience—between politics and cultures, between public events and private experiences, between wars or economic crisis and everyday life. Our integrated approach allows students to appreciate these relationships; it captures the spirit of each age and sparks students' historical imaginations. For teachers, our chronological approach ensures a balanced account, allows the flexibility to stress themes of one's own choosing, and perhaps best of all, provides a text that reveals history not as a settled matter but as a process that is constantly alive, subject to pressures, and able to surprise. Our task as authors, moreover, is to integrate the best of social and cultural history with the enduring developments of political, military, and economic history, offering a clear, compelling narrative that sets all the key events and stages of the West's evolution in a broad, meaningful context.

In writing *The Making of the West: Peoples and Cultures, A Concise History,* it has been our aim to communicate the vitality and excitement as well as the fundamental importance of history. If we have succeeded in conveying some of the vibrancy of the past and the thrill of historical investigation, we will be encouraged to start rethinking and revising—as historians always must—once again.

Textual Changes

Unlike most scholarly books, a textbook offers historians the rare chance to revise the original work, to keep it fresh, and to make it better. It has been a privilege to bring our own scholarship and teaching to bear on this rewriting. In this third edition, we have kept our emphasis on a strong central story line that incorporates the best of new research, but we have worked to make the narrative even more concise, focused, and accessible.

In this edition, we have further highlighted thematic coverage to help students discern major developments. Coverage of the Renaissance and Reformation has been revised thoroughly, with more on Renaissance art and architecture, the Ottomans' influence on the West, and a consolidated treatment of the European Reformation. We have worked to make key developments clearer in other chapters as well. Changes to this end include refocused sections on Pompey and Julius Caesar in Chapter 4 and Romanization in Chapter 5; a new section on the political transformation of the Roman Empire in Chapter 6; a reorganized treatment of Islam and Byzantium in Chapter 7; a consolidated discussion of the medieval papacy and lay piety in Chapter 10; newly consolidated coverage of the scientific revolution in Chapter 12; refocused sections on the execution of Louis XVI in Chapter 16 and nineteenth-century social reform in Chapter 17; and consolidated and strengthened coverage of Robespierre and Napoleon in Chapter 16, and of industrialization in Chapter 17.

We have also added new material and drawn on new scholarship on topics such as the emergence of civilization, in light of recent findings in Turkey (Chapter 1); the origins of the Black Death (Chapter 11); the Atlantic system and the creation of a new public sphere (Chapter 14); and the conflict in the Middle East, the effects of increasing globalization, and the global economic crisis (Chapter 24).

A final way we have chosen to help students identify and absorb major developments is by adding and refining "signposts" to guide students' reading. New chapter-opening focus questions, posed at the end of the opening vignettes, encapsulate the essence of the era covered in the chapter and guide students toward each chapter's core message. To help students as they read, we have worked hard to ensure that chapter and section overviews outline the central points of each section clearly, and that section headings are as clear and strong as possible. We have also condensed some material to better illuminate key ideas, resulting in a textbook that is a good deal shorter than the previous edition, and—we hope—a clearer, more accessible read for students.

Pedagogy and Features

More and more is required of students these days, and not just in Western Civilization courses. We know from our own teaching that students need all the help they can get in assimilating information, acquiring skills, and learning about historical debate. With these goals in mind, we retained the class-tested learning and teaching aids that contributed to the previous edition, but we have also added more such features.

Each chapter begins with a *vivid anecdote* that draws readers into the atmosphere and issues of the period and raises the chapter's main themes, supplemented by a full-page illustration that echoes the anecdote and similarly reveals the temper of the times. A *new Chapter Focus Question* provides students with an overarching theme to help guide their reading. *Review questions* strategically placed at the end of each major section help students check their comprehension of main ideas. Bolded key terms in the text are defined in the **Glossary of Key Terms** at the end of the book. A list of author-selected **Suggested References**, now present in every chapter, directs students to print and online resources for further investigation. Each chapter closes with a **new graphical Timeline**, which enables students to see the sequence and overlap of important events in a given period, and two **Chapter Review Questions** that encourage their analysis of chapter material.

The map program of *A Concise History* has been widely praised as the most comprehensive of any brief survey text. In each chapter we offer a set of three types of maps, each with a distinct role in conveying information to students. On average, three to four **full-size maps** show major developments; one to three **"spot" maps**—small maps that emphasize a detailed area from the discussion—aid students' understanding of specific but crucial issues; and a **Mapping the West** summary map at the end of each chapter provides a snapshot of the West at the close of a transformative period and helps students visualize the West's changing contours over time. In addition to the **more than 160 maps**, numerous charts and graphs visually support the narrative, including innovative **Taking Measure** features, which highlight a chart, table, graph, or map of historical statistics that illuminates an important political, social, or cultural development.

It has been our intention to integrate art as fully as possible into the narrative and to show its value for teaching and learning. **Over 260 illustrations**, carefully chosen to reflect this edition's broad topical coverage and geographic inclusion, reinforce the text and show the varieties of visual sources from which historians build their narratives and interpretations. All artifacts, illustrations, paintings, and photographs are contemporaneous with the chapter; there are no anachronistic illustrations—no fifteenth-century peasants tilling fields in a chapter on the tenth century! We know that today's students are very attuned to visual sources of information, yet they do not always receive systematic instruction in how to "read" or think critically about such visual sources. Our substantive captions for the maps and art help them learn how to make the most of these informative materials, and we have frequently included specific questions or suggestions for comparisons that might be developed. Specially designed visual exercises in the *Online Study Guide* supplement this approach.

Supplements

We have taken great care in revising and augmenting the comprehensive and well-integrated set of print and electronic resources for students and instructors that support the third edition of *The Making of the West: A Concise History*.

FOR STUDENTS

Print Resources

Sources of THE MAKING OF THE WEST, Third Edition—Volumes I (to 1740) and II (since 1500)—by Katharine J. Lualdi, University of Southern Maine. This companion sourcebook provides written and visual sources to accompany *The Making of* *the West: A Concise History.* Political, social, and cultural documents offer a variety of perspectives that complement the textbook and encourage students to make connections between narrative history and primary sources. A correlation guide showing how the documents align with each textbook chapter appears in *Sources of THE MAKING OF THE WEST* and on the *Book Companion Site.* The reader is available free when packaged with the text.

The Bedford Series in History and Culture. Over one hundred titles in this highly praised series combine first-rate scholarship, historical narrative, and important primary documents for undergraduate courses. Each book is brief, inexpensive, and focused on a specific topic or period. Package discounts are available.

Rand McNally Atlas of Western Civilization. This collection of over fifty full-color maps highlights social, political, and cross-cultural change and interaction from classical Greece and Rome to the post-industrial Western world. Each map is thoroughly indexed for fast reference. The Atlas is available for $3.00 when packaged with the text.

The Bedford Glossary for European History. This handy supplement for the survey course gives students historically contextualized definitions for hundreds of terms—from Abbasids to Zionism—that students will encounter in lectures, reading, and exams. The Glossary is available free when packaged with the text.

Trade Books. Titles published by sister companies Farrar, Straus and Giroux; Henry Holt and Company; Hill and Wang; Picador; St. Martin's Press; and Palgrave Macmillan are available at a 50 percent discount when packaged with Bedford/St. Martin's textbooks. For more information, visit bedfordstmartins.com/tradeup.

New Media Resources

THE MAKING OF THE WEST: A CONCISE HISTORY e-Book. This electronic version of *The Making of the West: A Concise History* offers students unmatched value—the complete text of the print book, with easy-to-use highlighting, searching, and note-taking tools, at a significantly reduced price.

FREE *Online Study Guide* at bedfordstmartins.com/huntconcise. The popular *Online Study Guide for THE MAKING OF THE WEST: A CONCISE HISTORY* is a free learning tool to help students master the themes and information presented in the textbook and improve their historical skills. Assessment quizzes help students to evaluate their comprehension, a flashcard activity tests students' knowledge of key terms, and a wide range of further quizzing, map, and primary document analysis activities provides them with the opportunity for further study. Instructors can monitor students' progress through the online *Quiz Gradebook* or receive e-mail updates.

Jules R. Benjamin's A Student's Online Guide to History Reference Sources at bedfordstmartins.com/huntconcise. This Web site provides links to history-related databases, indexes, and journals, plus contact information for state, provincial, local, and professional history organizations.

Bedford Bibliographer at bedfordstmartins.com/huntconcise. This simple but powerful Web-based tool assists students with the process of collecting sources and generates bibliographies in four commonly used documentation styles.

Diana Hacker's Research and Documentation Online at bedfordstmartins.com/huntconcise. This Web site provides clear advice on how to integrate primary and secondary sources into research papers, how to cite sources correctly, and how to format in MLA, APA, *Chicago,* or CBE style.

The St. Martin's Tutorial on Avoiding Plagiarism at bedfordstmartins.com/huntconcise. This online tutorial reviews the consequences of plagiarism and explains what sources to acknowledge, how to keep good notes, how to organize research, and how to integrate sources appropriately. The tutorial includes exercises to help students practice integrating sources and recognizing acceptable summaries.

FOR INSTRUCTORS

Print Resources

Transparencies. This set of full-color acetate transparencies includes all maps and many images from the parent textbook to help instructors prepare lectures and teach students important map-reading skills. A correlation guide showing how the transparencies align with the brief text appears in the *Instructor's Resource Manual* and on the *Book Companion Site.*

New Media Resources

Instructor's Resource Manual at bedfordstmartins.com/huntconcise/catalog. This manual by Dakota Hamilton, Humboldt State University, offers both experienced and first-time instructors tools for presenting textbook material in exciting and engaging ways. It includes an outline of main chapter topics, annotated chapter outlines, lecture strategies, ways to start class discussions, answer guidelines for questions in the book, tips for discussing the documents and working with visual sources, mapping exercises, suggestions for in-class activities (including using film, video, and literature), and take-home essay questions. Each chapter concludes with a guide to all the chapter-specific supplements available with *The Making of the West: A Concise History.* The manual also features essays on approaches to the Western Civilization course.

Instructor's Resource CD-ROM. This disc provides instructors with ready-made and customizable PowerPoint multimedia presentations built around chapter outlines, maps, figures, and selected images from the textbook, plus jpeg versions of all maps, figures, and selected images. Outline maps are provided in PDF format for quizzing or handouts. Also included are chapter questions formatted in PowerPoint and MS Word for use with i>clicker, a classroom response system.

Computerized Test Bank. The test bank, by Joseph Coohill, Pennsylvania State University at New Kensington, and Frances Mitilineos, Loyola University Chicago, offers over eighty exercises per chapter, including multiple-choice, fill-in-the-blank, short-answer, primary-source analysis, and essay questions. The answer key includes textbook page numbers and correct answers for all questions except the essays. Instructors can customize quizzes, add or edit both questions and answers, and export questions to a variety of formats, including WebCT and Blackboard.

Book Companion Site at bedfordstmartins.com/huntconcise. The companion Web site gathers all the electronic resources for the text, including the *Online Study Guide* and *Quiz Gradebook,* at a single Web address, providing convenient links to lecture, assignment, and research materials such as PowerPoint chapter outlines and the digital libraries at *Make History.*

Make History at bedfordstmartins.com/huntconcise. Comprising the content of our five acclaimed online libraries—*MapCentral, The Bedford History Image Library, DocLinks, HistoryLinks,* and *PlaceLinks*—*Make History* provides one-stop access to relevant digital content including maps, images, documents, and Web links. Students and instructors can browse this free, easy-to-use database by course, topic, date, or resource type and can download the content they find. Instructors can also create entire collections of content and store them online for later use or post their collections to the Web to share with students.

Content for Course Management Systems. A variety of student and instructor resources developed for this textbook is ready for use in course management systems such as Blackboard, WebCT, and other platforms. This e-content includes nearly all of the offerings in the book's *Online Study Guide,* as well as the book's *Test Bank.*

Videos and Multimedia. A wide assortment of videos and multimedia CD-ROMs on various topics in European history is available to qualified adopters. Contact your Bedford/St. Martin's sales representative for more information.

Acknowledgments

In the vital process of revision, the authors have benefited from repeated critical readings by many talented scholars and teachers. Our sincere thanks go to the following instructors, as well as three anonymous reviewers, whose comments often challenged us to rethink or justify our interpretations and who always provided a check on accuracy down to the smallest detail.

Marjorie Berman, *Red Rocks Community College*

Scott G. Bruce, *University of Colorado at Boulder*

Tamara Chaplin, *University of Illinois at Urbana*

Stephanie Christelow, *Idaho State University*

Marcus Cox, *The Citadel*

Jason Coy, *College of Charleston*

Cara Delay, *College of Charleston*

Gillian Hendershot, *Grand Valley State University*

David Hudson, *Texas A&M University*

Geoffrey Jensen, *University of Arkansas*

Brian Nance, *Coastal Carolina University/American Academy in Rome*

Ian Petrie, *Saint Joseph's University*

Craig Pilant, *County College of Morris*

James Sack, *University of Illinois at Chicago*

Jim Slocombe, *Champlain Regional College*

Charles Steinwedel, *Northeastern Illinois University*

Matthew Stith, *University of Arkansas*

David Tengwall, *Anne Arundel Community College*

Victor Triay, *Middlesex Community College*

Kirk Tyvela, *Sinclair Community College*

Rachelle Wadsworth, *Florida Community College at Jacksonville*

Janet Walmsley, *George Mason University*

Many colleagues, friends, and family members have helped us develop this work as well. They know how grateful we are. We also wish to acknowledge and thank the publishing team at Bedford/St. Martin's who did so much to bring this revised edition to completion: president Joan Feinberg, editorial director Denise Wydra, publisher for history Mary Dougherty, director of development for history Jane Knetzger, editor Danielle Slevens, freelance editors Jim Strandberg and Debra Michals, editorial assistant Robin Soule, executive marketing manager Jenna Bookin Barry, managing editor Elizabeth Schaaf, senior production editor Rosemary Jaffe, art researcher Gillian Speeth, permissions manager Sandy Schechter, and senior art director Donna Dennison. Our students' questions and concerns have shaped much of this work, and we welcome all our readers' suggestions, queries, and criticisms. Please contact us at our respective institutions or via history@bedfordstmartins.com.

Brief Contents

Contents

Chapter 1

The Emergence of Western Civilization, to 500 B.C.E. *3*

Chapter 3

From the Classical to the Hellenistic World, 400–30 B.C.E. *85*

Chapter 4

The Rise of Rome, 753–44 B.C.E. *119*

Chapter 5

The Roman Empire, 44 B.C.E.–284 C.E.   *155*

Chapter 6

The Transformation of the Roman Empire, 284–600 C.E. *197*

Chapter 7
Islam, Byzantium, and the West, 600–750 *237*

Chapter 8

Emperors, Caliphs, and Local Lords, 750–1050 *271*

Chapter 9

The Flowering of the Middle Ages, 1050–1200 *311*

Chapter 10

The Medieval Search for Order, 1200–1340 *353*

Chapter 12

Struggles over Beliefs, 1500–1648 435

Chapter 13

State Building and the Search for Order, 1648–1690 *481*

Chapter 14

The Atlantic System and Its Consequences, 1690–1740 *521*

Maps and Figures

MAPS

FIGURES

Authors' Note
The B.C.E./C.E. Dating System

WHEN WERE YOU BORN?" "What year is it?" We customarily answer questions like these with a number, such as "1991" or "2008." Our replies are usually automatic, taking for granted the numerous assumptions Westerners make about how dates indicate chronology. But to what do numbers such as 1991 and 2008 actually refer? In this book the numbers used to specify dates follow a recent revision of the system most common in the Western secular world. This system reckons the dates of solar years by counting backward and forward from the traditional date of the birth of Jesus Christ, over two thousand years ago.

Using this method, numbers followed by the abbreviation B.C.E., standing for "before the common era" (or, as some would say, "before the Christian era"), indicate the number of years counting backward from the assumed date of the birth of Jesus Christ. B.C.E. therefore indicates the same chronology marked by the traditional abbreviation B.C. ("before Christ"). The larger the number following B.C.E. (or B.C.), the earlier in history is the year to which it refers. The date 431 B.C.E., for example, refers to a year 431 years before the birth of Jesus and therefore comes earlier in time than the dates 430 B.C.E., 429 B.C.E., and so on. The same calculation applies to numbering other time intervals calculated on the decimal system: those of ten years (a decade), of one hundred years (a century), and of one thousand years (a millennium). For example, the decade of the 440s B.C.E. (449 B.C.E. to 440 B.C.E.) is earlier than the decade of the 430s B.C.E. (439 B.C.E. to 430 B.C.E.). "Fifth century B.C.E." refers to the fifth period of 100 years reckoning backward from the birth of Jesus and covers the years 500 B.C.E. to 401 B.C.E. It is earlier in history than the fourth century B.C.E. (400 B.C.E. to 301 B.C.E.), which followed the fifth century B.C.E. Because this system has no year "zero," the first century B.C.E. covers the years 100 B.C.E. to 1 B.C.E. Dating millennia works similarly: the second millennium B.C.E. refers to the years 2000 B.C.E. to 1001 B.C.E., the third millennium to the years 3000 B.C.E. to 2001 B.C.E., and so on.

To indicate years counted forward from the traditional date of Jesus's birth, numbers are followed by the abbreviation C.E., standing for "of the common era" (or "of the Christian era"). C.E. therefore indicates the same chronology marked by the traditional abbreviation A.D., which stands for the Latin phrase *anno Domini* ("in the year of the Lord"). A.D. properly comes before the date being marked. The date A.D. 1492, for example, translates as "in the year of the Lord 1492," meaning 1492 years after the birth of Jesus. Under the B.C.E./C.E. system, this date would be written as 1492 C.E. For dating centuries, the term "first century C.E." refers to the period from 1 C.E. to 100 C.E. (which is the same period as A.D. 1 to A.D. 100). For dates C.E, the smaller the number, the earlier the date in history. The fourth century C.E. (301 C.E. to 400 C.E.) comes before the fifth century C.E. (401 C.E. to 500 C.E.). The year

312 C.E. is a date in the early fourth century C.E., while 395 C.E. is a date late in the same century. When numbers are given without either B.C.E. or C.E., they are presumed to be dates C.E. For example, the term *eighteenth century* with no abbreviation accompanying it refers to the years 1701 C.E. to 1800 C.E.

No standard system of numbering years, such as B.C.E./C.E., existed in antiquity. Different people in different places identified years with varying names and numbers. Consequently, it was difficult to match up the years in any particular local system with those in a different system. Each city of ancient Greece, for example, had its own method for keeping track of the years. The ancient Greek historian Thucydides, therefore, faced a problem in presenting a chronology for the famous Peloponnesian War between Athens and Sparta, which began (by our reckoning) in 431 B.C.E. To try to explain to as many of his readers as possible the date the war had begun, he described its first year by three different local systems: "the year when Chrysis was in the forty-eighth year of her priesthood at Argos, and Aenesias was overseer at Sparta, and Pythodorus was magistrate at Athens."

A Catholic monk named Dionysius, who lived in Rome in the sixth century C.E., invented the system of reckoning dates forward from the birth of Jesus. Calling himself *Exiguus* (Latin for "the little" or "the small") as a mark of humility, he placed Jesus's birth 754 years after the foundation of ancient Rome. Others then and now believe his date for Jesus's birth was in fact several years too late. Many scholars today calculate that Jesus was born in what would be 4 B.C.E. according to Dionysius's system, although a date a year or so earlier also seems possible.

Counting backward from the supposed date of Jesus's birth to indicate dates earlier than that event represented a natural complement to reckoning forward for dates after it. The English historian and theologian Bede in the early eighth century was the first to use both forward and backward reckoning from the birth of Jesus in a historical work, and this system gradually gained wider acceptance because it provided a basis for standardizing the many local calendars used in the Western Christian world. Nevertheless, B.C. and A.D. were not used regularly until the end of the eighteenth century. B.C.E. and C.E. became common in the late twentieth century.

The system of numbering years from the birth of Jesus is far from the only one in use today. The Jewish calendar of years, for example, counts forward from the date given to the creation of the world, which would be calculated as 3761 B.C.E. under the B.C.E./C.E. system. Under this system, years are designated A.M., an abbreviation of the Latin *anno mundi,* "in the year of the world." The Islamic calendar counts forward from the date of the Prophet Muhammad's flight from Mecca, called the *Hijra,* in what is the year 622 C.E. The abbreviation A.H. (standing for the Latin phrase *anno Hegirae,* "in the year of the Hijra") indicates dates calculated by this system. Anthropology commonly reckons distant dates as "before the present" (abbreviated B.P.).

History is often defined as the study of change over time; hence the importance of dates for the historian. But just as historians argue over which dates are most significant, they disagree over which dating system to follow. Their debate reveals perhaps the most enduring fact about history—its vitality.

About the Authors

LYNN HUNT (Ph.D., Stanford University) is Eugen Weber Professor of Modern European History at University of California, Los Angeles. She is the author or editor of several books, including most recently *Inventing Human Rights* (2007) and *Measuring Time, Making History* (2008). She has in press a co-authored work on religious toleration in early eighteenth-century Europe.

THOMAS R. MARTIN (Ph.D., Harvard University) is Jeremiah O'Connor Professor in Classics at the College of the Holy Cross. He is the author of *Sovereignty and Coinage in Classical Greece* (1985) and *Ancient Greece* (1996, 2000) and is one of the originators of *Perseus: Interactive Sources and Studies on Ancient Greece* (www .perseus.tufts.edu). He is currently conducting research on the career of Pericles as a political leader in classical Athens as well as on the text of Josephus's *Jewish War.*

BARBARA H. ROSENWEIN (Ph.D., University of Chicago) is professor of history at Loyola University Chicago. She is the author or editor of several books, including *A Short History of the Middle Ages* (2001, 2004, 2009) and *Emotional Communities in the Early Middle Ages* (2006). She is currently working on a general history of the emotions in the West.

BONNIE G. SMITH (Ph.D., University of Rochester) is Board of Governors Professor of History at Rutgers University. She is the author or editor of several books, including *Ladies of the Leisure Class* (1981); *The Gender of History: Men, Women and Historical Practice* (1998); and *The Oxford Encyclopedia of Women in World History* (2007). Currently she is studying the globalization of European culture and society since the seventeenth century.

THIRD EDITION

The Making of the West

Peoples and Cultures

A Concise History

The Emergence of Western Civilization

To 500 B.C.E.

THE MESOPOTAMIAN *EPIC OF CREATION* explains that war between the gods created the universe. The goddess Tiamat, furious over her husband's destruction, threatened to destroy the other gods. Her enemies swore to make the male god Marduk their king if he protected them. Marduk—"four were his eyes, four were his ears; when his lips moved, fire blazed forth"—crushed Tiamat and her army of snaky monsters. He then created human beings from the blood of her fiercest monster to be the gods' servants.

Gold Bull's Head Decoration for a Musical Instrument from Ancient Iraq

This bull's head, made of gold leaf and lapis lazuli (a semiprecious stone prized for its vivid blue color), decorated a lyre—a stringed instrument similar to a harp. It was found in a tomb in the royal cemetery at Ur, in what is today southern Iraq, and was probably made in the period 2650–2550 B.C.E. The scenes below the beard, carved from mother of pearl, show animals walking upright like human beings and a mythological figure who appears to be a combination of a man and perhaps a scorpion. The donkey shown just above him is playing a lyre like this one. The meaning of the bull's head and the scenes remains a mystery. (© *University of Pennsylvania Museum [image #SR-142913].*)

This myth explained a belief—there is a divine world more powerful than the human—that goes back to the time before **civilization**, when people lived as hunter-gatherers to find food instead of farming. When a period of global warming that began about ten to twelve thousand years ago led to the invention of agriculture and then eventually to the emergence of civilization around 4000–3000 B.C.E. in the cities of Mesopotamia (the region between the Euphrates and Tigris rivers, today Iraq), religious beliefs remained strong. Historians define civilization as life based on agriculture and increased trade, with cities containing large buildings for political and religious purposes; the technology to produce metals, textiles, pottery, and other manufactured objects; and the knowledge of writing.

Civilization arose at different times in different places, but always with a religious core. In Mesopotamian civilization, rulers believed that the gods held them responsible for maintaining order on earth and honoring

3

the gods. Egyptian civilization, which began about 3100–3000 B.C.E., showed its religious dedication by building enormous temples and pyramids. Civilizations emerged starting about 2500 B.C.E. in India, China, and the Americas. By 2000 B.C.E., civilizations had appeared in Anatolia (today Turkey), on islands in the eastern Mediterranean Sea, and in Greece.

The peoples of Mesopotamia, Egypt, the eastern Mediterranean, and Greece created Western civilization by interacting with each other. Building on concepts from their Near Eastern neighbors, the Greeks originated the idea of the West as a region with its own type of civilization. They identified Europe as the West (where the sun sets) and considered it to be different from the East (where the sun rises). The peoples of Europe made Western civilization by exchanging ideas, technologies, and objects with other peoples through trade, travel, and war. The making of the West depended on cultural, political, and economic interaction among diverse groups. The West remains a constantly evolving concept, not a fixed region with unchanging borders and members.

The process of different peoples learning from one another and adapting the knowledge and the beliefs of others for their own purposes produced intended and unintended consequences. The spread of metallurgy (using high heat to extract metals from ores), for example, created better tools and weapons but also increased social differences among people. **Hierarchy** (status differences among people), like the ranking among the gods that myth described, became an enduring characteristic of human civilization.

CHAPTER FOCUS QUESTION   What changes did early Western civilization bring to human life?

From the Stone Age to Civilization and Empire in Mesopotamia, to 1200 B.C.E.

Important patterns of life that developed in the time before civilization have persisted ever since. About four hundred thousand years ago, people whose brains and bodies resembled ours appeared first in Africa. Called *Homo sapiens* ("wise human beings") by scientists, they were the immediate ancestors of modern human beings. Spreading out from Africa, they gradually populated the rest of the earth. Anthropologists call this time before civilization the Stone Age because people made tools and weapons from stone as well as bone and wood; they did not yet know how to work metals. The Stone Age is divided into two periods: the earlier part is the Paleolithic (Old Stone), and the more recent is the Neolithic (New Stone), beginning around 10,000 to 8000 B.C.E.

The most important change in the patterns of human life in ancient times occurred during the Stone Age. People originally lived as hunter-gatherers in the Paleolithic Age. They usually roamed to find food, hunting and gathering in the wild. The shift from Paleolithic to Neolithic patterns of life was supremely important because climate change that altered the patterns of plant growth allowed hunter-gatherers slowly to learn to farm, domesticate animals, and, in the end, establish permanent settlements that grew into cities. This change had such radical consequences for human life that historians call it the Neolithic Revolution,

Another great change took place when people learned to work metals by smelting copper ore. They then invented bronze, a metal alloyed from copper and tin that could be shaped into durable tools, sharp weapons, and lustrous jewelry. Archaeologists call the period from approximately 4000 to 1000 B.C.E. the Bronze Age. The rulers of Bronze Age Mesopotamian cities battled one another for glory, territory, and especially access to copper and tin. The drive to acquire metal ores pushed the Akkadians (named after Akkad, their capital city on the Tigris River) to create the first **empire**, a gigantic political state under a single ruler controlling formerly independent territories.

From Paleolithic Life to the Neolithic Revolution, 400,000–4000 B.C.E.

The most significant Stone Age developments were the evolution of hierarchy and the Neolithic Revolution. Paleolithic hunter-gatherers perhaps originally lived in egalitarian societies (meaning all adults enjoyed a rough equality in making decisions for the group). They roamed in groups of twenty to fifty, hunting animals, catching fish and shellfish, and gathering plants, fruits, and nuts. Women with young children mostly foraged to gather plants close to camp; they provided the group's most reliable supply of nourishment. Men did most of the hunting of dangerous wild animals far from camp, although recent archaeological evidence shows that women also participated, especially in hunting with nets. Objects from distant regions found in burials show that hunter-gatherer bands traded with one another. Trade spread knowledge—especially technology, such as techniques for improving tools, and art for creating beauty and expressing beliefs—that changed lives. Using fire for cooking was a major innovation because it allowed people to eat wild grains that they could not digest raw.

Evidence from graves shows that hierarchy, a persistent characteristic of human society, eventually emerged in Paleolithic times. Some Paleolithic burials contain weapons, tools, animal figurines, ivory beads, seashells, and bracelets alongside the corpses, which indicate that some dead persons had greater status and wealth than others. Hierarchy probably emerged as men acquired prestige from bringing back meat from long hunts and fighting in wars. (The many traumatic wounds seen in male skeletons show how frequent warfare was.) Older women and men also earned hierarchical status based on their experience and longevity at a time when illness and accidents killed most people before age thirty. The decoration of corpses with red paint and valuable objects suggests that Paleolithic people wondered about the mystery of death and perhaps believed in an afterlife. Paleolithic artists also sculpted statuettes of human figures, probably for religious purposes.

Climate and geography—the fundamental features of the natural environment—defined a new way of life for human beings some twelve thousand years ago. This very gradual process started when a climate change in the late Paleolithic period brought warmer temperatures and more rainfall. This change in the weather increased

Prehistoric Venus Figurine
Archaeologists have discovered small female figures, like this one from Romania, at many late Paleolithic and Neolithic sites in Europe. They predate writing, so we cannot be sure of their significance, but many scholars assume that their hefty proportions are meant to signal a special concern for fertility. These female figures may represent prehistoric people's vision of rare good fortune: having enough food to become fat and produce healthy children. The statuettes are called Venus figurines after the Roman goddess of love. (Erich Lessing/Art Resource, NY.)

the amount of wild grains people could gather in the foothills of the Near East's Fertile Crescent, an arc of territory that curved up from what is today the Jordan valley in Israel, through eastern Turkey, and down into the foothills and plains of Iraq and Iran (Map 1.1).* This more plentiful food supply led Paleolithic hunter-gatherers to settle where wild grains grew most abundantly and animals such as gazelles grazed in large numbers. Recent archaeological excavation in Turkey suggests that around eleven thousand years ago, such groups organized to erect stone monuments to worship gods believed to help people find food. The more reliable supply of food allowed them to raise more children, and the increased social organization promoted larger settlements. The more hungry mouths that were born, however, the greater the need for food became.

---

*The meanings of the terms *Near East* and *Middle East* have changed over time. Both originally reflected a European geographic point of view. During the nineteenth century, *Middle East* usually meant the area from Iran to Burma, especially the Indian subcontinent (then part of the British Empire); *Near East* meant the Balkan peninsula (today the countries of Croatia, Slovenia, Bosnia-Herzegovina, Macedonia, Yugoslavia, Albania, Greece, Bulgaria, Romania, and the European portion of Turkey) and the eastern Mediterranean. The term *Far East* referred to the Asian lands that border the Pacific Ocean. Today, *Middle East* usually refers to the area encompassing the Arabic-speaking countries of the eastern Mediterranean region, Israel, Iran, Turkey, Cyprus, and much of North Africa. Ancient historians, by contrast, commonly use the term *ancient Near East* to designate Anatolia (also called Asia Minor), Cyprus, the lands around the eastern end of the Mediterranean, the Arabian peninsula, Mesopotamia (the lands north of the Persian Gulf, today Iraq and Iran), and Egypt. Some historians exclude Egypt from this group on strict geographic grounds because it is in Africa (the rest of the region lies in Asia). In this book, we observe the common usage of the term *Near East* to mean the lands of southwestern Asia and Egypt.

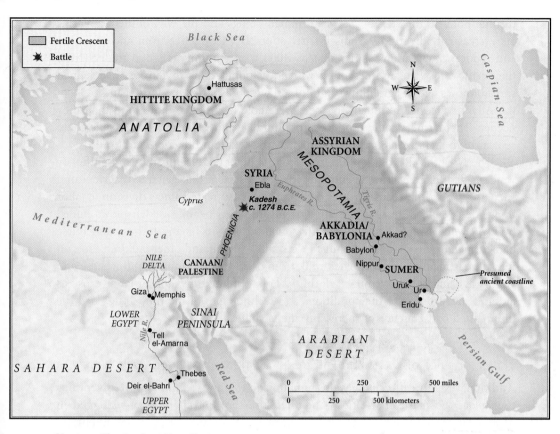

Map 1.1 The Ancient Near East, 4000–3000 B.C.E.
The large region we call the ancient Near East included a variety of landscapes, climates, peoples, and languages; monarchy was the usual form of government. Trade by land and sea for natural resources, especially metals, kept the peoples of the region in constant contact with one another, as did the wars of conquest that the region's kings regularly launched.

The Neolithic Revolution began when, after thousands of years of trial and error, people in the Fertile Crescent invented agriculture by sowing seeds from wild grains to produce regular harvests. Since women had more experience gathering plants than men, they probably played the major role in developing farming, while men continued to hunt. Recent research suggests that people also learned to domesticate animals about the same time that they began to farm. By some nine thousand years ago, keeping herds for food was widespread in the Near East, which was home to wild animals that could be domesticated, such as sheep, goats, pigs, and cattle.

Historians call agriculture and the domestication of animals the "farming package" that defines the Neolithic Revolution. The change in the way people got their food had revolutionary effects on human life because it produced many permanent settlements and surpluses of food. Some Neolithic people lived as pastoralists (herders moving around to find grazing land for their animals), but farmers had to reside in a settled location to raise crops year after year. Fixed settlements marked a turning point in the relation between human beings and the environment as farmers increasingly diverted streams for irrigation. DNA evidence from ancient bones and modern populations shows that by 4000 B.C.E., immigrants and traders from the Fertile Crescent, by interacting with local populations in Europe, had helped spread knowledge of agriculture and domestication as far as the European shores of the Atlantic Ocean. Eventually, farmers were able to produce more food than they needed. That farmers could produce agricultural surpluses meant other people could specialize in architecture, art, crafts, metalwork, textile production, and trade.

The Neolithic Revolution led to more hierarchy because positions of authority were needed to supervise the complex irrigation system that generated agricultural surpluses, and also because greater economic activity created a new division of labor by gender. Men began to dominate agriculture when heavy wooden plows pulled by oxen were invented, sometime after 4000 B.C.E. Not having to bear and nurse babies, men also took over long-distance trade. Women and older children took on new domestic tasks as they turned milk from domesticated animals into cheese and yogurt and made their families' clothing. This gendered division of labor arose as an efficient response to the conditions and technologies of the time, but it had the unintended consequence of increasing men's status.

The Emergence of Cities and Empire in Mesopotamia, 4000–1200 B.C.E.

Additional significant changes in human society and technological inventions took place when the first cities—and therefore the first civilization—emerged in Mesopotamia about 4000–3000 B.C.E. in the plains bordering the Tigris and Euphrates rivers (Map 1.1, page 7). Cities developed there because the climate and the land could support large populations. Mesopotamian farmers operated in a challenging environment: temperatures soared to 120 degrees Fahrenheit and little rain fell, yet the rivers flooded unpredictably. They maximized agricultural production by devising the technology and administrative arrangements necessary to irrigate the arid flatlands with water channeled from the rivers. A vast system of canals controlled flooding and turned the former desert green with food crops. The need to construct and maintain a system of irrigation canals in turn led to the centralization of authority in Mesopotamian cities, which controlled the farmland and irrigation canals lying outside their fortified walls. This political arrangement—an urban center exercising control over the nearby countryside—is called a **city-state**. Mesopotamian city-states were independent communities competing with each other for land and resources.

The people of Sumer (southern Mesopotamia) established the earliest city-states. Unlike other Mesopotamians, the Sumerians did not speak a Semitic language (the group of languages from which Hebrew and Arabic came); the origins of their language remain a mystery. By 3000 B.C.E., the Sumerians had created twelve independent city-states, such as Uruk, Eridu, and Ur, which repeatedly battled each other for territory. By 2500 B.C.E., these cities had expanded to twenty thousand residents or more. The rooms in Sumerians' mud-brick houses surrounded open courts. Large homes had a dozen rooms or more.

Agricultural surpluses and trade in commodities and manufactured goods made these cities prosperous. Sumerians bartered grain, vegetable oil, woolens, and leather with one another, and they acquired metals, timber, and precious stones from foreign trade. Traders traveled as far as India, where the cities of Indus civilization emerged about 2500 B.C.E. The invention of the wheel for use on transport wagons around 3000 B.C.E. strengthened the Mesopotamian economy. Temples and the rulers' families dominated the Sumerian economy because they controlled large farms and gangs of laborers, but some private households also became rich.

Increasingly rigid forms of hierarchy evolved in Sumerian society. Slaves, owned by temples and by individuals, had the lowest status. People became slaves by being captured in war, by being born to slaves, by voluntarily selling themselves or their children (usually to escape starvation), or by being sold by their creditors when they could not repay loans (debt slavery). Children whose parents dedicated them as slaves to the gods could rise to prominent positions in temple administration. In general, however, slaves existed in near-total dependence on other people and were excluded from normal social relations. They usually worked without pay and lacked almost all legal rights. They could be bought, sold, beaten, or even killed by their masters because they were considered property.

Slaves worked in domestic service, crafts production, and farming, but scholars dispute whether they or free laborers were more important to the economy. Free persons performed most government labor, paying their taxes with work rather than with money, which was measured in amounts of food or precious metal (coins were not invented until much later). Most slaves had little chance of becoming free, although owners sometimes liberated slaves in their wills, and slaves could purchase their freedom from earnings that some owners let them keep.

Hierarchy became so strong in Mesopotamian society that it led to the political system—monarchy—that became the most widespread form of government in the ancient world. In monarchies, the king was at the top of the hierarchy, like the ruler of the gods. His male descendants inherited his position. To display their exalted status, royal families lived in elaborate palaces that served as administrative centers and treasure-houses. Archaeologists excavating royal graves in Ur have revealed the rulers' dazzling riches—spectacular possessions crafted in gold, silver, and precious stones. These burials also have yielded grisly evidence of the top-ranking status of the king and queen: servants killed to look after their royal masters after death.

Patriarchy—domination by men in political, social, and economic life—already existed in Mesopotamian city-states, probably as an inheritance from the development of hierarchy in Paleolithic times. A Sumerian queen was respected because she was the king's wife and the mother of the royal children, but her husband held supreme power. The king formed a council of older men as his advisers, but he publicly acknowledged the gods as his rulers; this concept made the state a theocracy (government by gods) and gave priests and priestesses public influence. The king's greatest responsibility was to keep the gods happy and to defeat attacks from rival cities. The king demanded taxes from the working population to support his family, court, palace, army, and officials. The kings, along with the priests of the large temples, regulated most of the economy in their kingdoms by controlling the exchange of food and goods between farmers and crafts producers in a system known as a **redistributive economy**.

In religion, Mesopotamians continued earlier traditions by practicing **polytheism**: worshipping many gods who were thought to control different aspects of life, including the weather, fertility, and war. People believed that their safety depended on the goodwill of the gods, and each city-state honored one deity as its special protector. To please their gods, city dwellers offered sacrifices and built ziggurats (temple towers) soaring as high as ten stories. Mesopotamians believed that if human beings angered the gods, divinities such as the sky god Enlil and the goddess of love and war Inanna (also called Ishtar) would punish them by sending disease, floods, famine, and defeats in war.

Myths told in long poems such as the *Epic of Creation* and the *Epic of Gilgamesh* expressed Mesopotamian ideas about the challenges and violence that human beings faced in struggling with the natural environment and creating civilization. Gilgamesh was a legendary king of Uruk who longed to cheat death. He forced the young men of Uruk to labor like slaves and the young women to sleep with him. When his subjects begged the mother of the gods to grant them a protector, she created Enkidu, "hairy all over . . . dressed as cattle are." A week of sex with a prostitute tamed this brute, preparing him for civilization: "Enkidu was weaker; he ran slower than before. But he had gained judgment, was wiser." After wrestling Gilgamesh to a draw, Enkidu became his friend, and they defeated Humbaba, the ugly giant of the Pine Forest, and the Bull of Heaven. The gods doomed Enkidu to die soon after these triumphs. Depressed about the human condition, Gilgamesh sought the secret of immortality, but a thieving snake ruined his quest. He decided that the only immortality for mortals was winning fame for deeds. Only memory and gods could live forever.

Mesopotamian myths, living on in poetry, song, and art, greatly influenced other peoples. A late version of the Gilgamesh story recounted how the gods sent

The Ziggurat of Ur in Sumer
King Ur-Nammu and his son Shulgi built this huge temple to honor the gods in their city of Ur, in what is today southern Iraq, in the early twenty-first century B.C.E. It had three massive terraces, one above another, connected by stairways. The mud-brick core of the structure was covered with baked bricks held in place with tar. The walls were more than seven feet thick to support the enormous weight of the terraces. The total height is uncertain, but the first terrace alone soared some forty-five feet above ground level. (Hirmer Fotoarchiv, Munich, Germany.)

a huge flood over the earth. They warned one man, instructing him to build a boat. He loaded his vessel with his relatives, workers, possessions; domesticated and wild animals; and "everything there was." After a week of torrential rains, they left the boat to repopulate the earth and regenerate civilization. This story recalled the frequent floods of the Mesopotamian environment and looked ahead to the later biblical account of the great flood covering the globe and Noah's ark.

The invention of the technology of writing in Mesopotamia transformed the way people exchanged stories and ideas. Sumerians originally invented this new technology to do accounting. Before writing, people drew small pictures on clay tablets to keep count of objects or animals. Writing developed when people created symbols instead of pictures to represent the sounds of speech. Sumerian writing did not use an alphabet (a system in which each symbol represents the sound of a letter), but rather a system of wedge-shaped marks pressed into clay tablets to represent the sounds of syllables and entire words (Figure 1.1). Today this form of writing is called **cuneiform** (from *cuneus*, Latin for "wedge"). For a long time, writing was a professional skill for accounting mastered by only a few men and women known as scribes.

The possibilities for communication over time and space exploded when people began writing down nature lore, mathematics, foreign languages, and literature. In the twenty-third century B.C.E., Enheduanna, the daughter of King Sargon of the city of Akkad, composed the oldest written poetry whose author is known.

					SAG Head
					NINDA bread
					GU₇ eat
					AB₂ cow
					APIN plough
					SUHUR carp
c. 3100 B.C.E.	c. 3000 B.C.E.	c. 2500 B.C.E.	c. 2100 B.C.E.	c. 700 B.C.E. (Neo-Assyrian)	Sumerian reading + meaning

Figure 1.1 Cuneiform Writing
The earliest known form of writing developed in different locations in Mesopotamia in the late 3000s B.C.E., when meaning and sound were associated with signs such as these. The scribes who mastered the system used sticks or reeds to press dense rows of small wedge-shaped marks into damp clay tablets or chisels to engrave them on stone. Cuneiform was used for at least fifteen Near Eastern languages and continued to be written for three thousand years.

A Cuneiform Letter in Its Envelope
Written about 1900 B.C.E., this cuneiform text records a merchant's complaint that a shipment of copper contained less metal than he had expected. His letter, written on a clay tablet several inches long, was enclosed in an outer clay shell marked with the sender's private seal. This envelope protected the inner text from tampering or breakage. (© Copyright The Trustees of The British Museum.)

Written in Sumerian, her poetry praised the life-giving goddess of love, Inanna: "the great gods scattered from you like fluttering bats, unable to face your intimidating gaze . . . knowing and wise queen of all the lands, who makes all creatures and people multiply." Later princesses who wrote love songs, lullabies, dirges, and prayers continued the Mesopotamian tradition of royal women becoming authors.

Metallurgy was another technology that generated life-altering change in this period. Bronze, a new invention, could be sharpened into deadly swords and spearheads. Rich men found a new way to display their status by paying artisans to decorate their weapons with ornate engravings and inlays, as on costly guns today. Metal weapons also differentiated men's and women's roles in society by highlighting the masculine role of warrior.

The development of metallurgy helped lead to the world's first empire, in Akkadia (Map 1.1, page 7). Because Mesopotamian kings craved a reliable supply of metals to support their royal status, those who had no ore in their territory had to get it by trade or by conquest. The first empire arose about 2350 B.C.E., when King Sargon launched invasions seeking metals and glory. His violent campaigns conquered lands from Sumer all the way to the Mediterranean Sea, creating the world's first political superpower (a state able to dominate others). These conquests also spread Mesopotamian literature and art throughout the Near East. Although the Akkadians spoke a Semitic language, not Sumerian, after conquering Sumer they adopted much of the defeated land's religion, literature, and culture. Other peoples later conquered by the Akkadians were thus exposed to Sumerian beliefs and traditions, which they in turn adapted to their own purposes. In this way, war had the unintended consequence of promoting cultural interaction between peoples.

The Akkadian Empire's great size did not preserve it. Neighboring hill peoples, the Gutians, defeated it around 2200 B.C.E. A Mesopotamian poet offered a religious explanation for this defeat: King Naram-Sin, enraged at the god Enlil when his capital's prosperity waned, reduced Enlil's temple to "dust like a mountain mined for silver." Enlil then punished the Akkadians by sending the Gutians swooping down from their "land that rejects outside control, with the intelligence of human beings but with the form and stumbling words of a dog." This account reflects the Mesopotamians' deep-seated belief that the gods held ultimate power over human destiny.

Commerce, Law, and Learning in Mesopotamia, 2200–1200 B.C.E.

Mesopotamian innovations in private commerce, law, and learning influenced later Western civilization. These innovations took place in two kingdoms, Assyria and Babylonia, which emerged in the second millennium B.C.E. after the fall of the Akkadian Empire. The Assyrians, a Semitic people descended from the Akkadians, lived in northern Mesopotamia (Map 1.1, page 7). By becoming middlemen in the long-distance trade between Anatolia and southern Mesopotamia, the Assyrians became the Near East's leading merchants. They produced woolen textiles to exchange for Anatolian copper, silver, and gold, which they sold throughout Mesopotamia. In earlier Mesopotamian societies, the kings and priests had directed a largely state-run redistributive economy. This tradition never totally disappeared, but by 1900 B.C.E., the Assyrian kings were allowing private individuals to trade with other city-states and regions on their own. Assyrian investors sought profits by financing donkey caravans to travel hundreds of rocky and dangerous miles to Anatolia.

The expansion of private, profit-based commerce set an enduring precedent for later times, especially in the need to create binding contracts, which in turn required laws. It was the king's sacred duty to render justice in commercial disputes as well as for crimes. The record of the king's decisions is today called a law code. King Hammurabi (r. c. 1792–1750 B.C.E.) of Babylon, a great city on the Euphrates River, instituted the most famous set of early laws. Hammurabi proclaimed he was showing Shamash, the Babylonian sun god and god of justice, that he was fulfilling a king's responsibility: "So that the powerful may not oppress the powerless, to provide justice for the orphan and the widow . . . let the victim of injustice see the law which applies to him, let his heart be put at ease."

Hammurabi's code divided society into a three-part hierarchy: free persons, commoners, and slaves. We do not know what made the first two categories different, but free persons outranked commoners in the hierarchy of Babylonian society. An attacker who caused a pregnant woman of the free class to miscarry, for example, paid twice the fine levied for the same offense against a woman of the commoner class. A member of the free class who killed a commoner was fined instead of executed. For social equals, the code specified "an eye for an eye."

Widespread participation characterized the Babylonian justice system. People assembled as courts to determine most cases. The laws primarily concerned the king's interests as a property owner who leased innumerable tracts of land to tenants in return for rent or services. For offenses against property, the laws imposed severe penalties, including mutilation or a gruesome death for crimes as varied as theft, wrongful sales, and careless construction. In this patriarchal society, women had limited legal rights, but they could make business contracts and appear in court. A wife could divorce her husband for cruelty; a husband could divorce his wife for any reason. However, divorced wives were entitled to recover the property they had brought to the marriage.

Hammurabi's laws reveal much about urban life in Bronze Age Mesopotamia. Burglary and assault apparently plagued city dwellers. Marriages were arranged by the groom and the bride's father and sealed with a legal contract. Laws about surgery inform us about the work of doctors. Mesopotamian medicine included magic as well as potions and specific diets. Magicians treated illness by interpreting signs, such as the patient's dreams or hallucinations, and casting spells. Archaeological excavations and cuneiform records reveal that Mesopotamian cities had numerous wineshops, often run by women proprietors, offering drinks and a place to relax. Residents also found relief from the odors and crowding through open spaces set aside as parks. The world's oldest known map, an inscribed clay tablet showing the outlines of the Babylonian city of Nippur about 1500 B.C.E., indicates that a sizable section of the city was parkland.

Mesopotamians made especially influential achievements in mathematics and astronomy. Mathematicians used algebra to solve complex problems and knew how to derive the roots of numbers. They invented positional notation (the system of writing numbers in which each position is related to the next by a fixed multiple of value, as in our system based on a multiple of ten) and a system of reckoning based on sixty, still used in our division of a circle into hours, minutes, and degrees. Mesopotamians' skill in describing the paths of the stars and planets probably arose from a desire to make predictions about the future, based on the astrological belief that the movements of celestial objects affect human life. The charts and tables compiled by Mesopotamian stargazers laid the foundation for later advances in astronomical knowledge.

REVIEW   How did life change for people in Mesopotamia when they began to live in cities?

The Emergence of Egyptian and Hittite Civilization, 3100–1200 B.C.E.

Africa was home to the second great civilization to shape the West: Egypt. Egyptians created a wealthy, deeply religious, and strongly traditional civilization ruled by kings. Unlike Mesopotamia, Egypt was politically united under a strong central authority. The Egyptian kings' desire for immortality in the afterlife led them to build some of the largest tombs in history, the pyramids. Egyptian architecture and art inspired later Mediterranean peoples, especially the Greeks.

The height of Egyptian power came under the New Kingdom (c. 1569–1081 B.C.E.),* when the Hittite kingdom in Anatolia became Egypt's most aggressive rival (Map 1.1, page 7). The Hittites had become a powerful people by about 1750 B.C.E. They flourished because they inhabited the fertile upland region of Anatolia and controlled trade there and southward into the Levant** (today Syria, Lebanon, Israel, and Jordan), the commercial crossroads of the eastern Mediterranean and the persistent site of conflict among Near Eastern powers.

*Every date in Egyptian history is approximate and controversial, and different scholars use different dates because the evidence is often contradictory. Those used here are taken from the articles and "Egyptian King List" in *The Oxford Encyclopedia of Ancient Egypt*, edited by Donald B. Redford (2001).

**The name *Levant*, French for "rising (sun)"—that is, the East—reflects the European perspective on the area's location.

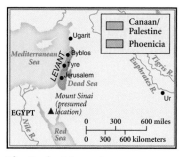

The Ancient Levant

Life in Old Kingdom Egypt, 3100–2190 B.C.E.

Geography propelled Egyptian history. Egypt's people lived mainly in farming villages in a narrow band of land along both sides of the Nile. Their irrigated farms extended several miles away from the river's banks. The Nile overflowed its banks once every year for several weeks, when melting snow from the mountains of central Africa gradually swelled its flow. This predictable and gentle flood enriched the soil near the river with nutrients from silt and diluted harmful deposits of mineral salts. Unlike the random deluges in Mesopotamia, the Nile's flood occurred at the same time every year and benefited the land. Trouble came only if dry weather in the mountains kept the river from overflowing. Deserts east and west of the Nile protected Egypt from invasion, except through the Nile delta in the north and on the southern frontier with Nubia. Deposits of metal ores, trade by sea, and lush agriculture made Egypt prosperous, but it had fewer and smaller cities than Mesopotamia. From their ample supplies of grain, the Egyptians made bread and beer, the most popular beverage.

Egypt's population included a diversity of people, whose skin color ranged from light to very dark. The modern controversy over whether Egyptians were people of color is anachronistic; ancient Egyptians presumably identified themselves by geography, language, religion, and social traditions and not by race. Later peoples, especially the Greeks, admired Egyptian civilization for its great antiquity and religious devotion. Some nineteenth-century historians minimized Egypt's contribution to Western civilization, but ancient peoples did not. Like everyone else in history, ancient Egyptians learned from other peoples. For example, they probably learned the technology of writing from the Sumerians, but they developed their own scripts rather than adopting cuneiform. To write formal and official texts, they used an ornate, picture-based script known as hieroglyphs (Figure 1.2).

The first large-scale Egyptian state emerged about 3100–3000 B.C.E., when King Menes united Upper (southern) Egypt and Lower (northern) Egypt.* By around 2687 B.C.E., the kings following Menes had forged a centralized state, known today as the Old Kingdom, which lasted until around 2190 B.C.E. (Map 1.2). By traveling and trading southward, Egyptians learned that the Nubians had already built extensive settlements and produced complex art by Menes' time. At places such as Afyeh, near the Nile's First Cataract, a Nubian social elite lived in dwellings much grander than the small huts housing most of the population. Egyptians constantly

---

*Upper and Lower refer to the direction in which the Nile River flows—from south of Egypt northward to the Mediterranean Sea.

Hieroglyph	Meaning	Sound value
	vulture	glottal stop
	flowering reed	consonantal I
	forearm and hand	ayin
	quail chick	W
	foot	B
	stool	P
	horned viper	F
	owl	M
	water	N
	mouth	R
	reed shelter	H
	twisted flax	slightly guttural
	placenta (?)	H as in "loch"
	animal's belly	slightly softer than h
	door bolt	S
	folded cloth	S
	pool	SH
	hill	Q
	basket with handle	K
	jar stand	G
	loaf	T

Figure 1.2 Egyptian Hieroglyphs Ancient Egyptians developed their own system of writing about 3100 B.C.E., using pictures such as these. Because this formal script was used mainly for religious inscriptions on buildings and sacred objects, Greeks referred to it as *ta hieroglyphica* (the sacred carved letters), from which comes the modern term *hieroglyphs*. Egyptian hieroglyphs employ around seven hundred pictures in three categories: ideograms (signs indicating things or ideas), phonograms (signs indicating sounds), and determinatives (signs clarifying the meaning of the other signs). Eventually (the chronology is unsure), Egyptians also developed the handwritten cursive script called *demotic* (Greek for "of the people"), a much simpler and quicker form of writing.

interacted with Nubians while trading for raw materials such as gold, ivory, and animal skins, and Nubia's hierarchical organization perhaps influenced the development of centralized authority in Egypt's Old Kingdom. Eventually, however, Egypt's power overshadowed that of its southern neighbor.

The strength or weakness of the central authority determined Egyptian political history. When the kings were strong, as during the Old Kingdom, the country was

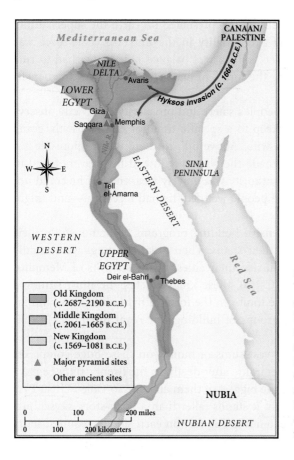

Map 1.2 Ancient Egypt
The Nile River, closely embraced by arid deserts, provided Egyptians with water to irrigate their fields and a highway for traveling north to the Mediterranean Sea and south to Nubia. The only easy land route into and out of Egypt lay through the Nile delta into the northern Sinai peninsula and on into the coastal area of the Levant. Egyptian kings therefore always fought to control these areas to secure the safety of their land.

stable, and trade flourished with the Levant and other Mediterranean areas. However, political instability resulted when regional governors or prominent priests, whose status was second only to that of the royal family, refused to support the king. The king's success depended on his properly fulfilling his religious duties. Egyptians worshipped many gods, often depicted as creatures with both human and animal features, such as the head of a jackal or a bird atop a human body. They did not worship animals; rather, they believed that each god had a particular animal to serve as the bearer of the god's divine soul. A picture or statue of a divinity had to include the animal so the image would include the soul. Egyptian religion told lively stories about the passion-filled lives of the gods to explain their powers. Deities were associated with powerful natural objects, emotions, qualities, and technologies. Examples include the sun god Re; Isis, goddess of love and fertility; and Thoth, god of wisdom and the inventor of writing.

Egyptians regarded their king as a god in human form, but they recognized that the man on the throne was mortal, seeing a difference between the individual king's human existence and the divine origin of his rule. As a system of government, monarchy was regarded as divine because it represented on earth the supernatural, eternal force that created harmony and stability in the universe. This force was called *maat* (meaning "truth," "justice," or "correct balance"). The king had to rule by promoting maat, thereby keeping the forces of nature in balance for the benefit of his people.

An Egyptian king ensured his people's safety and prosperity by strictly observing ritual. For example, he had to keep to a specific time for taking a bath, going for a walk, or having sex with his wife. Above all, the king was responsible for summoning the divine power that made the Nile overflow. If his prayers failed to make the flood occur, his political authority was gravely weakened. If he could not produce annual floods and keep the people well fed, he had lost maat—and might lose his kingdom.

Old Kingdom rulers used expensive building programs to demonstrate their devotion to the gods and proclaim their status. Their great buildings were mainly the temples or tombs constructed outside their cities. In the suburbs of Memphis, the first capital (south of modern Cairo), these kings erected the most stunning proofs of their piety and status: huge tombs in the form of pyramids. These monuments formed the centerpieces of groups of buildings for royal funerals and religious ceremonies.

The Old Kingdom rulers spent vast sums of money on these huge complexes because Egyptians had a strong belief in life after death. In the twenty-sixth century B.C.E., King Cheops commissioned the biggest of them all—the so-called Great Pyramid at Giza. At about 480 feet high, it stands taller than a forty-story skyscraper. Covering over thirteen acres and extending 760 feet on each side, it required more

The Pyramids at Giza in Egypt
The kings of Old Kingdom Egypt constructed enormous stone pyramids for their tombs. Pyramids were the centerpieces of large complexes of temples and courtyards stretching to the banks of the Nile or along a canal leading to the river. The burial chambers lay at the end of long, narrow tunnels snaking through the pyramids' interiors. The largest pyramid, shown here, is the nearly five-hundred-foot-high Great Pyramid of King Cheops, erected in the twenty-sixth century B.C.E. (© John Lawrence/SuperStock.)

than two million blocks of limestone, some of which weighed fifteen tons apiece. Quarried in the desert, the stone was floated to the site on river barges and dragged on rollers and sleds up earthen ramps into position. A prayer from about 2300 B.C.E. expresses the royal hopes for the pyramids: "O divine Atum, put your arms around King Neferkare Pepy II, around this construction work, around this pyramid. . . . May you guard lest anything evil happen to him throughout the course of eternity." So the royal family would be comfortable in their new existence, they packed their tombs with gilded furniture and luxury items. Archaeologists have uncovered two full-size cedar ships buried next to the Great Pyramid, meant to carry King Cheops on his voyage into eternity.

Their need to manage the labor and expenses for their mammoth projects led Old Kingdom rulers to centralize their administration and strengthen the social hierarchy. The king and queen topped the social order. Brothers and sisters in the royal family could marry each other, perhaps because such matches were believed necessary to preserve the purity of the royal line or to imitate the marriages of the gods. The priests, royal administrators, regional governors, and commanders of the army ranked next in the hierarchy. The common people, who did all the manual labor, made up the great majority of free people in Egypt. (Slaves became more common after the Old Kingdom.) Free workers had heavy obligations to the state. For example, although they were not slaves, they were required to work on the pyramids. On occasion they received wages, but mostly their labor was a way of paying taxes. Rates of taxation reached 20 percent on the produce of free farmers.

Women generally had the same legal rights as men. They could own land and slaves, inherit property, pursue lawsuits, transact business, and initiate divorces. Old Kingdom portrait statues display the equal status of wife and husband: each figure is the same size and sits on the same kind of chair. Men dominated public life, while women devoted themselves mainly to private life, managing their households and property. When their husbands went to war, however, women often took on men's work: some women held government posts, served as priestesses, managed farms, and practiced medicine.

The formal, even rigid appearance of Egypt's art illustrates how much its people valued religion, order, and predictability. Almost all sculptures and paintings were made for tombs or temples. Old Kingdom artists excelled in stonework, from carved ornamental jars to massive portrait statues of kings and queens. These statues represent the person either standing stiffly with the left leg advanced or sitting on a chair or throne, stable and poised. Concern for appropriate behavior also appears in the Old Kingdom literature the Egyptians called instructions, known today as wisdom literature. These texts told high officials how to act. In the *Instruction of Ptahhotep*, for example, the king advises his minister Ptahhotep to tell his son, who will follow him in office, not to be arrogant or overconfident just because he is well educated and to seek advice from ignorant people as well as from the wise.

Life in Middle Kingdom and New Kingdom Egypt, 2190–1200 B.C.E.

The Old Kingdom's stability disintegrated when temporary climate change shrank the annual Nile flood. This disaster caused starvation, which triggered civil unrest, which in turn discredited the kings. By 2190 B.C.E., regional governors seized and held on to power until a strong king finally restored central authority, initiating what historians call the Middle Kingdom (c. 2061–1665 B.C.E.). Judging from the period's abundant literature, this restoration of the monarchy gave Egyptians pride in their homeland. The Egyptian narrator of *The Story of Sinuhe,* for example, reports that he lived luxuriously during a forced stay in Syria but still dreamed of returning: "Whichever deity you are who ordered my exile, have mercy and bring me home! . . . Nothing is more important than that my body be buried in the country where I was born!" The Middle Kingdom fell apart, however, around 1665 B.C.E., when irregular Nile floods again undermined royal power.

The weakening of the king's authority led to a foreign takeover. A Semitic people from the Syria-Palestine region, whom the Egyptians called the Hyksos, gained control of Lower Egypt around 1664 B.C.E. (Map 1.2, page 17). As with the foreign wars of the Akkadians, the Hyksos' takeover of Egypt generated cultural interchange. The Hyksos transplanted elements of foreign culture to Egypt by introducing bronze-making technology, horses and war chariots, more powerful bows, new musical instruments, humpbacked cattle, and olive trees.

The New Kingdom of Egypt (c. 1569–1081 B.C.E.) formed when leaders of Thebes in southern Egypt defeated the Hyksos rulers. Its kings used diplomacy and war to advance Egypt's interests. Known as pharaohs (meaning "the Great House," that is, the royal palace and estate), New Kingdom rulers rebuilt central authority by restricting the power of regional governors. They earned the title "warrior-pharaohs" by invading Nubia and the Sudan to the south, in search of gold and other precious materials, and by fighting in Palestine and Syria to control trade routes. As before, religion remained the kings' most important activity. The principal festivals of the gods, for example, involved lavish public celebrations. A calendar based on the moon governed the dates of religious ceremonies. (The Egyptians also developed a calendar for administrative and fiscal purposes that had 365 days divided into twelve months of thirty days each, with the extra five days added before the start of the next year. Our modern calendar comes from it.)

The New Kingdom kings and queens built most of Egypt's magnificent temples, whose sculpted columns set a precedent for later Greek architecture. Queen Hatshepsut in the fifteenth century B.C.E., for example, erected a massive sanctuary at Deir el-Bahri near Thebes. After her husband (who was also her half brother) died, Hatshepsut proclaimed herself "female king" and co-ruler with her young stepson. To observe Egyptian political traditions, which did not include a queen ruling on her own, she had official artists portray her as a man sporting a king's beard and male clothing.

A dispute over religion threatened the stability of the New Kingdom in the fourteenth century B.C.E., when the pharaoh Akhenaten changed traditional practice. He made the cult of Aten, the shining disk of the sun, the centerpiece of royal worship and excluded

Queen Hatshepsut as Pharaoh Offering *Maat*
This eight-and-a-half-foot-tall granite statue shows the New Kingdom queen Hatshepsut dressed as a male pharaoh and wearing a ceremonial beard. She is performing her royal duty of offering *maat* (the divine principle of order and justice) to the gods. Egyptian religion taught that the gods "lived on maat" and that the land's rulers were responsible for providing it. Hatshepsut had this statue and many others placed in a huge temple she built outside Thebes in Upper Egypt. (The Metropolitan Museum of Art, Rogers Fund, 1929 [29.3.1]. Photography by Schechter Lee. Photograph © 1986 The Metropolitan Museum of Art.)

other deities and their supporters. Akhenaten's reforms did not aim at pure **monotheism** (belief in the existence of only one god, as in Judaism, Christianity, and Islam), as some scholars assert, because they did not change the divine status of the king. His wife, Queen Nefertiti, tried to restrain him when she realized the hostility that his changes had created in the priesthood and the general population, but he kept on, even neglecting the defense of Egypt to devote himself to religion. His religious reform died with him; during the reign of his successor, Tutankhamun (r. 1355–1346 B.C.E.), famous today as a result of the discovery of his unlooted tomb in 1922, the traditional solar cult of Amun-Re reclaimed its leading role.

Most Egyptians' daily lives focused on manual labor and religion. Working as farmers or crafts producers, ordinary people devoted much attention to deities outside the royal cults, especially to gods they believed protected them. They venerated Bes, for instance, a dwarf with the features of a lion, as a protector of the household. They carved his image on amulets, beds, headrests, and the handles of mirrors. Magic also played a large role in people's lives. They used spells and charms to ward off demons, smooth the course of love, take revenge on enemies, and find relief from disease and injury. Egyptian doctors made medicinal use of herbs, knowledge that was passed on to later civilizations, and they could perform surgeries, including opening the skull.

Like royalty, ordinary people prepared for the afterlife. Those who could afford it arranged to have their bodies mummified and their tombs outfitted with all the goods needed for the journey to their new existence. A mummy's essential equipment included a copy of the *Book of the Dead*—a collection of magic spells to ward off danger and gain a successful verdict from the divine jury that put every soul on trial. To avoid experiencing death a second time, the *Book* instructed, dead people had to convince the jury of gods by sworn statements such as "I have not committed crimes against people; I have not mistreated cattle; I have not robbed the poor; I have not caused pain." Souls who received positive judgments experienced a mystical union with the god Osiris, the head judge of the dead.

Life in the Hittite Kingdom, 1750–1200 B.C.E.

The greatest external threat to the safety of New Kingdom Egyptians came from the aggressive wars of the Hittite kingdom, which emerged about 1750 B.C.E. in Anatolia (Map 1.1, page 7). The Hittites spoke an Indo-European language from the family of languages that eventually spread over most of Europe. The original Indo-European speakers had migrated as separate groups into Anatolia and Europe from somewhere in western Asia. Recent archaeological discoveries there of women buried with weapons suggest that Indo-European women originally occupied positions of leadership alongside men; the prominence of Hittite queens in official documents perhaps sprang from that tradition.

Hittite kingship was based on religion—the worship of Indo-European gods and local Anatolian deities. The king served as high priest of the storm god and had to maintain strict purity. His drinking water, for example, was always strained, and his water carrier was executed if so much as a hair was found in a drink. Like other Near Eastern rulers, Hittite kings felt responsible for maintaining divine goodwill toward their subjects. One of them, King Mursili II (r. 1321–1295 B.C.E.), issued a set of prayers begging the gods to end a plague: "What is this, o gods, that you have done? Our land is dying. . . . O gods, whatever sin you behold, either let a prophet come forth to identify it . . . or let us see it in a dream!"

The Hittite rulers launched long-range military campaigns to acquire metals and control trade routes. The Hittites did not owe their success in war to a special knowledge of making weapons from iron, as was once thought, because iron weapons did not become common until after 1200 B.C.E. They did excel in the use of war chariots, however. Hittite kings particularly wanted to dominate the lucrative trade from Mesopotamia and Egypt. In 1595 B.C.E., therefore, their army raided as far as Babylon, overthrowing that kingdom.

They also invaded the Levant, the principal crossroads leading to Egypt. Previously, independent Canaanite city-states, such as the bustling ports of Ugarit, Byblos, and Tyre, had dominated the Levant. There, the interaction of traders and travelers from different cultures created about 1600 B.C.E. a supremely important innovation in writing technology: the alphabet. In this new system, a simplified picture—that is, a letter—stood for only one sound in the language. This offered a dramatic improvement in ease of writing over cuneiform and hieroglyphic scripts. The Canaanite alphabet later became the basis for the Greek and Roman alphabets, from which came modern Western alphabets.

REVIEW   How did religion guide the lives of people in Egyptian and Hittite civilization?

From the Sea Peoples to the Reemergence of Empires in the Near East, 1200–500 B.C.E.

Widespread attacks, generated by invasions of separate bands of shipborne raiders known as the Sea Peoples (their origins remain uncertain), wiped out or weakened many states in the eastern Mediterranean region from about 1200 to 1000 B.C.E. The depopulation and economic collapse that resulted in many areas, as well as our dim knowledge of what happened, has led historians to talk of the "Dark Age." Egypt lost its international power forever during this troubled period when the New Kingdom fell apart about 1081 B.C.E.

In the Near East, recent archaeological excavation suggests that this period lasted only about a century, with empire then once again emerging as the system of government. The constant striving for imperial wealth and territory kept the Near East on the same violent political and military path—monarchy and empire—as in the past. By 900 B.C.E., the Neo-Assyrian (New Assyrian) Empire ruled the region. First the Neo-Babylonian Empire and then the Persian Empire, the greatest the world had ever seen, followed.

Hebrew (or Israelite) civilization, centered in the southern Levant, lost its independence to these Near Eastern empires, but its religion—Judaism—became influential in Western civilization. The Hebrews' religion, originally reflecting influences from their polytheistic Canaanite neighbors, took a long time to develop into monotheism. Eventually, however, the Hebrew ideas of belief in one god and basing a religion on scripture became essential concepts for major religions that deeply influenced Western civilization.

From Neo-Assyrian to Babylonian to Persian Empire, 900–500 B.C.E.

The collapse of the Egyptian and Hittite kingdoms allowed the aggressive Neo-Assyrian rulers to build an empire by 900 B.C.E. by seizing supplies of metal and controlling trade routes. Their armies drove westward until they punched through to the Mediterranean coast (Map 1.3). Neo-Assyrian monarchs constantly pursued foreign expansion, and for the first time their armies made foot soldiers, instead of cavalry, the principal striking force. Trained infantrymen excelled in the use of military technology such as siege towers and battering rams; archers rode in chariots. Campaigns against foreign lands brought back plunder to supplement the kingdom's agriculture and long-distance trade. Conquered peoples had to pay annual tribute to the Assyrians, supplying raw materials and luxury goods such as incense, wine, dyed linens, glass, and ivory.

Neo-Assyrian kings treated conquered peoples brutally to keep order. They herded large numbers of people from their homelands to Assyria, forcing them to build temples and palaces. This merciless policy had an unintended cultural consequence: so many Aramaeans were deported from Canaan to Assyria that Aramaic largely replaced Assyrian as Assyria's native, everyday language. When not waging war, Neo-Assyrian men loved to hunt, and the more dangerous the animal, the better. The king hunted lions as proof of his vigor and power. Although the Neo-Assyrian imperial administration preserved countless documents in its archives, literacy apparently mattered less to the kingdom's males than war, hunting, and practical technology. Ashurbanipal (r. 680–626 B.C.E.) was the only king to proclaim his scholarly accomplishments: "I have read complicated texts, whose versions in Sumerian are obscure and in Akkadian hard to understand. I do research on the cuneiform texts on stone from before the Flood." Women of the social elite probably

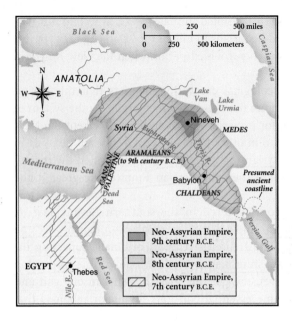

Map 1.3 Expansion of the Neo-Assyrian Empire, c. 900–650 B.C.E.
Like their Akkadian, Assyrian, and Babylonian predecessors, the Neo-Assyrian kings dominated a vast region of the Near East to secure a supply of metals, access to trade routes on land and sea, and imperial glory. They built the largest empire the world had yet seen. Also like their predecessors, they treated disobedient subjects harshly and intolerantly to try to prevent their diverse territories from rebelling.

learned to read, but they were excluded from the male dominions of hunting and war. Public religion, which included deities adopted from Babylonia, also reflected the prominence of war in Assyrian culture. Even the Assyrian cult of Ishtar (the Babylonian name for Inanna), the goddess of love and fertility, glorified warfare.

The Neo-Assyrian kings' harshness made their own people, especially the social elite, dislike their rule. Rebellions were common, and in the seventh century B.C.E. they crippled the kingdom. The Medes, an Iranian people, and the Chaldeans, a seminomadic Semitic people who had driven the Assyrians from Babylonia, combined forces to destroy the Neo-Assyrian capital at Nineveh in 612 B.C.E. and end the kings' imperial power.

The Chaldeans established the Neo-Babylonian Empire, which became the most powerful empire in Babylonian history. King Nebuchadnezzar II (r. 605–562 B.C.E.) spent lavishly to turn Babylon into an architectural showplace, rebuilding the great temple of its chief god, Marduk; creating the famous Hanging Gardens (so named because lush plants drooped over its terraced sides); and constructing a dazzling city gate dedicated to the goddess Ishtar. Blue-glazed bricks and lions molded in yellow, red, and white decorated the gate's walls, which soared thirty-six feet high.

The Chaldeans adopted traditional Babylonian culture and preserved much ancient Mesopotamian literature, such as the *Epic of Gilgamesh*. They also created many new works of prose and poetry, which educated people often read aloud publicly for the enjoyment of the many illiterate members of the population. Particularly popular were fables, proverbs, essays, and prophecies that taught morality and proper behavior. This wisdom literature, a Near Eastern tradition going back at least to the Egyptian Old Kingdom, greatly influenced the later religious writings of the Hebrews.

The Chaldeans' advances in astronomy became so influential in the ancient Mediterranean world that the word *Chaldean* became the Greeks' word for "astronomer." People's main reason for observing the stars was the belief that the gods communicated their will to humans through events in nature, such as eclipses and the movements of the stars and planets, abnormal births, smoke curling upward from a fire, and the trails of ants. The interpretation of these events as messages from the gods was characteristic of the mixture of science and religion in ancient Near Eastern thought, which so deeply influenced the Greeks.

The Persian Empire, the Near East's last and greatest empire, began when Cyrus (r. 559–530 B.C.E.) overthrew Median rule in Persia (today Iran) by conquering Babylon in 539 B.C.E. A rebellion there by Marduk's priests, provoked when the king had promoted a different deity, had weakened the Chaldean dynasty. Cyrus profited from this religious crisis by promising to restore traditional Babylonian religion, thereby winning local support. According to an ancient inscription, he proclaimed: "Marduk, the great lord, caused Babylon's generous residents to adore me."

Later Persian kings expanded their rule by following Cyrus's principles of military strength and cultural tolerance. Darius I (r. 522–486 B.C.E.) greatly extended Cyrus's conquests by pushing Persian power eastward to the Indus valley and westward to Thrace (Map 1.4). Organizing this vast territory into provinces, Darius assigned each region taxes payable in the form best suited to its local economy—precious metals, grain, horses, or slaves. He required each region to send soldiers to staff the royal army. A network of roads and a courier system for royal mail aided communication among the far-flung provincial centers. The Greek historian Herodotus reported that neither snow, rain, heat, nor darkness slowed the couriers from completing their routes as swiftly as possible (an achievement later transformed into the U.S. Postal Service motto). The kings' belief in their divine right to rule everyone, everywhere would provoke great conflicts—above all, the war between Persians and Greeks that would break out around 500 B.C.E.

The revenues flowing into the imperial treasury made the Persian king wealthy beyond imagination and supported the royal hierarchy. So special was the monarch that servants held their hands before their mouths in his presence so that he would not have to breathe the same air. In sculpture adorning the immense palace at Persepolis, artists carved royal figures larger than other people. The king's purple robes were more splendid than anyone else's, and no other person could walk on the red carpets spread before him. To show that he used his gargantuan resources to help his loyal subjects, the king often provided meals for fifteen thousand nobles, courtiers, and other followers at one sitting—although he himself ate hidden from his guests' view. The king punished lawbreakers and rebels harshly, mutilating their bodies and executing their families. Greeks, in awe of the Persian monarch's power and luxury, referred to him as "the Great King." So long as his subjects—numbering in the millions and of many different ethnicities—remained peaceful, the king let them live and worship as they pleased.

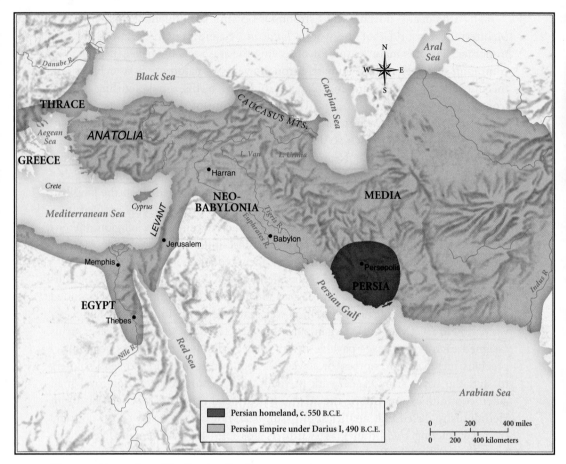

Map 1.4 Expansion of the Persian Empire, c. 550–490 B.C.E.
Cyrus (r. 559–530 B.C.E.) founded the Persian Empire, which his successors expanded to be even larger than the Neo-Assyrian Empire, which it replaced. By the later years of Darius's reign (r. 522–486 B.C.E.), the Persian Empire had expanded east as far as the western edge of India; to the west, it reached Thrace, the eastern edge of Europe. Persian kings, unlike their imperial predecessors, won their subjects' loyalty with tolerance and religious freedom, although they treated rebels harshly.

Ruling as absolute autocrats with the power to make the rules for everyone else, the Persian kings believed they were superior to all humans. They regarded themselves not as gods but as the agents of Ahura Mazda, the supreme god of Persia. As Darius said in his autobiography, which was carved into a mountainside in three languages, "Ahura Mazda gave me kingship . . . by the will of Ahura Mazda the provinces respected my laws."

Persian religion, based on the teachings of the legendary prophet Zarathustra (and called Zoroastrianism from the Greek name for this holy man), made the god Ahura Mazda the center of worship. It seems, however, not to have been pure monotheism. Its most important doctrine was a moral dualism: perceiving the

The Great King of Persia
Like their Assyrian predecessors, the Persian kings decorated their palaces with large relief sculptures emphasizing royal dignity and success. This one from Persepolis shows officials and petitioners giving the king proper respect when entering his presence. To symbolize their elevated status, the king and his son, who stands behind the throne, are depicted as larger than everyone else. **For more help analyzing this image, see the visual activity for this chapter in the Online Study Guide at** bedfordstmartins.com/huntconcise. (Courtesy of the Oriental Institute of the University of Chicago.)

world as the arena for an ongoing battle between good and evil. Ahura Mazda's two children, according to Persian belief, made different moral choices: one chose the way of the truth, and the other chose the way of the lie. Humans were also free to choose: Zoroastrianism promised salvation to those following the way of the truth and damnation to those taking the way of the lie. The Persian religious emphasis on ethical behavior had a lasting influence on others, especially the Hebrews.

The Development of Hebrew Monotheism, to 539 B.C.E.

The Hebrews' enduring impact on Western civilization comes from the book that became their sacred Scriptures, the Hebrew Bible (known to Christians as the Old Testament), and their monotheistic religion. The Hebrew Scriptures deeply affected the formation of not only Judaism but also Christianity and, later, Islam. Unfortunately, no source provides clear information on the origins of the Hebrews or their religion. The Bible tells stories to explain God's moral plan for the universe, not the full history of the Hebrews, and archaeology has not yielded a clear picture.

The traditional version of the early history of the Hebrews places them in Mesopotamia. From there, Abraham, in about 1900 B.C.E., led his followers to ancient Palestine, at the southeast corner of the Mediterranean Sea, where the Canaanites ruled (Map 1.1, page 7). Supposedly divided into twelve tribes, the Hebrews never formed a political state in this period. The biblical story of Joseph bringing Hebrews to Egypt may belong between 1600 and 1400 B.C.E., during the time of Hyksos rule.

By the thirteenth century b.c.e., the pharaohs had conscripted the male Hebrews into labor gangs for farming and construction work.

The biblical narrative then relates the central event in Hebrew history: the sealing of a covenant between the Hebrews and their deity, Yahweh, at Mount Sinai after Yahweh instructed Moses to lead the Hebrews on an exodus out of bondage in Egypt about 1250 b.c.e. This agreement declared that if the Hebrews promised to worship Yahweh as their only God and to live by his laws, Yahweh would make them his chosen people and lead them into a promised land of safety and prosperity. This binding arrangement demanded human obedience to divine law and promised punishment for unrighteousness. As God described himself, he was "compassionate and gracious, patient, ever constant and true . . . forgiving wickedness, rebellion, and sin, and not sweeping the guilty clean away; but one who punishes sons and grandsons to the third and fourth generation for their fathers' iniquity" (Exodus 34:6–7). The religious and moral code that bound the Hebrews was written down in the Ten Commandments and the Pentateuch (the first five books of the Hebrew Bible), or Torah.

Many of the laws in the Pentateuch recalled earlier Mesopotamian rules, such as those of Hammurabi, but Hebrew law differed because it applied the same rules and punishments to everyone, regardless of their social position. Hebrew law also ruled out vicarious punishment—a Mesopotamian tradition ordering, for example, that a rapist's wife be raped. Hebrew women had less extensive legal rights than men, such as in seeking a divorce. Crimes against property never carried the death penalty, as they frequently did in other Near Eastern societies, and Hebrew law protected slaves against glaring mistreatment.

Many uncertainties cloud our understanding of how the Hebrews acquired their monotheism. It seems that it took much longer to develop monotheism than the biblical account suggests. In the time of Moses, Yahweh-religion was not yet monotheistic because it did not deny the existence of other gods, such as Baal of Canaan. Fully developed Hebrew monotheism did not emerge until well after 1000 b.c.e., by which time the first Hebrew kingdom had formed. Solomon (r. c. 961–922 b.c.e.) brought the united nation to the height of its prosperity, largely as a result of trade. He displayed his wealth by building in Jerusalem a temple to Yahweh that was richly decorated with gold leaf; it became the center of Hebrew religion.

After Solomon, the monarchy split into two kingdoms: Israel in the north and Judah in the south. The Neo-Assyrians conquered Israel in 722 b.c.e. and deported its population to Assyria. In 597 b.c.e., the Neo-Babylonians conquered Judah; ten years later, they destroyed Solomon's temple and sent most of the Hebrews into exile in Babylon. When the Persian king Cyrus overthrew the Babylonians in 539 b.c.e., he permitted the Hebrews to return to Palestine, which was called Yehud from the name of the southern Hebrew kingdom, Judah. From this geographical term came the name *Jews,* a designation for the Hebrews after their Babylonian exile. In keeping with the policy of cultural tolerance, Cyrus allowed them to rebuild their temple in Jerusalem and practice their religion. After returning from exile, the Jews in the ancient world remained a people subject to the political domination of various

Near Eastern powers, except for a period of independence during the second and first centuries B.C.E.

Jewish prophets, both men and women, preached that the Hebrews' defeats were divine punishment for neglecting the Sinai covenant and mistreating the poor. Some prophets also predicted the end of the present world following a great crisis, a judgment by Yahweh, and salvation leading to a new and better world. Yahweh would save the Hebrew nation, the prophets thundered, only if Jews learned to observe divine law strictly. This **apocalypticism** ("uncovering" of the future), which recalled Babylonian prophetic wisdom literature, would later influence Christianity.

Jewish religious leaders developed strict regulations requiring people to maintain ritual and ethical purity in all aspects of life. Ethics applied not only to obvious crimes but also to financial dealings. Jews had to pay taxes and offerings to support Yahweh's temple, and they had to forgive debts every seventh year. Jews therefore created laws based on ethics as the focus of the world's first monotheism. They retained their cultural identity by following their religious laws, regardless of where they lived. In this way, Jews who did not return to their homeland could maintain their identity while living among foreigners. Over time, the Diaspora (dispersion of population) came to characterize the history of the Jewish people.

Hebrew monotheism made the preservation and understanding of a sacred text, the Hebrew Bible, the key to a religious life. Making scripture central to religion became a crucial development in the history of Judaism, as well as in Christianity and Islam, because these later religions placed their own sacred texts, the Christian Bible and the Qur'an, respectively, at the center of their beliefs and practices. The Hebrews thus passed on ideas that have endured to this day, such as the belief in monotheism, the importance of scripture in religion, and a commitment to a covenant between God and a people who are promised salvation if they obey divine will.

> **REVIEW** How did religion affect the history of the Near East from 1200 to 500 B.C.E.?

The First Greek Civilization, 8000–750 B.C.E.

Early Greek civilization developed through the interaction of peoples inhabiting islands and coastal areas in the middle Mediterranean region. By 8000 B.C.E., settlements of Indo-European speakers dotted the mountainous Greek mainland and the islands of the Aegean Sea. By 7000 B.C.E., Anatolian peoples had migrated to the large island of Crete, southeast of the Greek mainland (Map 1.5). The type of language spoken by these early Cretans, called Minoans, remains uncertain, but they created the first civilization in this part of the world in the late 2000s B.C.E. Eventually, they lost their preeminence and power to their warlike neighbors on the mainland, the Mycenaeans. When Mycenaean civilization was destroyed during the extended warfare that affected the eastern Mediterranean from about 1200 to 1000 B.C.E., the Dark Age of depopulation and poverty that followed almost ended Greek civilization.

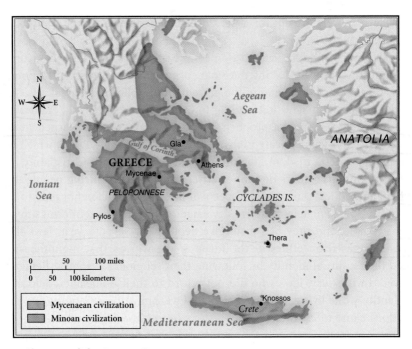

Map 1.5 Greece and the Aegean Sea, c. 1500 B.C.E.
Mountains, islands, and sea defined the geography of Greece. The rough terrain and seasonally stormy sailing made travel a chore. The distance from the mainland to the largest island in this region, Crete, where Minoan civilization arose, was sufficiently long to keep Cretans isolated from the turmoil of most of later Greek history. **For more help analyzing this map, see the map activity for this chapter in the Online Study Guide at** bedfordstmartins.com/huntconcise.

Minoan and Mycenaean Civilization, 2200–1000 B.C.E.

Crete offered a fine home for settlers because it had fertile plains, adequate rainfall, and sheltered ports for fishing and seaborne trade. By 2200 B.C.E., the inhabitants of Crete created what scholars call a palace society, referring to the many-chambered buildings that were both the residences of the rulers and the centers of political, economic, and religious administration. The palaces seem to have been independent; no one ruler controlled Crete. We call this civilization Minoan because a prominent archaeologist who excavated there believed that its greatest ruler was King Minos, famous in Greek myth because his wife gave birth to the half-man, half-bull Minotaur (Minos's bull).

Minoan farmers developed Mediterranean polyculture—growing olives, grapes, and grain on the same farm, which became the hallmark of agriculture in the region ever after. This innovation made the best use of agricultural labor because these crops' different growing cycles allowed the same laborers to take care of them all. Farmers could thus produce valuable and versatile products such as olive oil and wine. This combination of crops provided a healthy way of eating (today called the Mediterranean diet) that stimulated population growth. Minoans also developed deep-hulled sailing ships that promoted long-distance trade in commodities by sea.

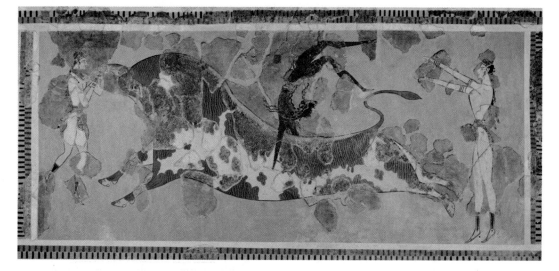

Minoan Wall Painting from Knossos, Crete
Minoan artists painted with vivid colors on plaster to enliven the walls of buildings. This painting from the palace at Knossos depicts an acrobatic performance in which a youth leaped in an aerial somersault over the back of a charging bull. Some scholars speculate this dangerous jump was a religious ritual instead of just a circus act. Unfortunately, time and earthquakes have severely damaged most Minoan wall paintings, and the versions we see today are largely reconstructions, painted around surviving fragments of the originals. (© National Archaeological Museum, Athens, Greece/The Bridgeman Art Library.)

Minoan rulers enforced a redistributive economic system. The Knossos palace, for example, held hundreds of gigantic jars holding 240,000 gallons of olive oil and wine. The rulers evidently decided how much each farmer or crafts producer had to contribute to the palace storehouse and how much of those contributions would then be redistributed to each person in the community for basic subsistence or as an extra reward.

Independent rulers on the mainland also controlled redistributive economies. This civilization, called Mycenaean from the hilltop site of Mycenae in the Peloponnese (the large peninsula forming southern Greece), emerged in the centuries after 2000 B.C.E. By 1400 B.C.E., Mycenae had a fortified settlement with a palace and rich tombs. Because mountainous Greece had little fertile land but many useful ports, settlements tended to arise near the coast. Greeks always depended on the sea: for food, for trade with one another and with foreign lands, and for naval raids on rich targets.

Seaborne commerce strongly promoted cultural interaction, as underwater archaeology reveals. Off Uluburun in Turkey, for example, divers discovered a late-fourteenth-century B.C.E. ship carrying such a mixed cargo and varied personal possessions—from Greece, Egypt, Canaan, Cyprus, Babylon, and elsewhere in the Near East—that attaching a single "nationality" to this vessel makes no sense.

Connections by sea brought Minoans and Mycenaeans into close contact. Many objects found on the mainland display designs clearly inspired by Cretan traditions. At the same time, the two peoples remained different in important ways.

The Mycenaeans burned sacrifices to the gods; the Minoans did not use fire in this way. The Minoans distributed sanctuaries across the landscape in caves, on mountaintops, and in country villas; the Mycenaeans kept their sanctuaries inside their palaces. When the Mycenaeans started building palaces in the fourteenth century B.C.E., unlike the Minoans they designed them around rooms with prominent ceremonial hearths and thrones for the rulers.

Mycenaeans eventually achieved dominance over Crete, possibly in a war over international trade. Later Greeks recalled this conquest of Crete with the myth describing how Theseus of Athens defeated the Minotaur: when Minos forced the Athenians to send youths for the creature to devour in his labyrinth, Theseus slew the monster and found his way out of the maze by backtracking along the thread that the king's daughter Ariadne, who had fallen in love with the handsome hero, told him to leave to mark his path.

By the time Mycenaeans ruled Crete, war at home and abroad was the principal concern of well-off Mycenaean men. Contents of Bronze Age tombs in Greece reveal that no wealthy man went to his grave without his war equipment. Their warlike spirit, however, probably ruined the Mycenaeans during the Sea Peoples period (c. 1200–1000 B.C.E.). At this time, the palace settlements of eastern Greece constructed such massive defensive walls that later Greeks believed giants had built them. The fortifications of coastal sites would have protected coastal palaces against invading Sea Peoples, but the great wall around the palace at Gla, far inland where foreign sea raiders could not easily reach, suggests fear of a land-based threat, too. Archaeologists therefore speculate that local warfare among Mycenaeans, made worse by earthquakes, led to what is called "systems collapse," destroying the Mycenaean states by about 1000 B.C.E. The disappearance of the redistributive economic system devastated Mycenaeans who did not have farms, as they depended on their rulers' system for their subsistence. The catastrophic fall of Mycenaean civilization brought on the Greek Dark Age.

The Greek Dark Age, 1000–750 B.C.E.

Greek civilization almost ended in the Dark Age (1000–750 B.C.E.). Political systems collapsed, the economy contracted, and the population shrank. Conditions were so depressed that Greeks even lost the technologies of writing and of illustrating people and animals in art. They did preserve their traditional divisions into groups speaking different dialects of the same language, namely Ionians, Dorians, and Aeolians. They regarded themselves as sharing a Greek identity because they worshipped the same gods.

The conditions of the Dark Age eventually led to new social values. When the palace-based rulers of Mycenaean Greece fell, competition for leadership in society became wide open. The men and women who proved themselves excellent in action, words, and religious knowledge became the new social elite. Excellence became a competitive value: individuals earned high social status by outdoing others. The new emphasis on individualism shows up in burial practices, as cremation replaced inhumation and graves housing multiple corpses. Men displayed excellence through achievement in war and persuasiveness in speech, while women displayed excellence by managing a household of children, slaves, and the family's storerooms. Members of the elite accumulated wealth by controlling agricultural land, which people of lower status farmed for them as tenants or slaves.

The rebuilding of Greek life after the Dark Age required the establishment of social and political values that recognized both individual excellence and justice in a community. Tension between these two ideals was inevitable. The poems of Homer and Hesiod express these ideas so powerfully that later Greeks regarded them as the foundational literature of Greek identity.

Later Greeks believed that Homer was an eighth-century B.C.E. blind poet from Ionia (today Turkey's western coast) who composed the epic poems *The Iliad* and *The Odyssey*. The stories in these poems explore the consequences of making individual excellence the principal social value. *The Iliad* tells the story of the Greek army attacking the Anatolian city of Troy. (The Trojan War was one of the many wars of the Sea Peoples period.) The manliest Greek hero is Achilles, who displays his surpassing excellence in *The Iliad* by choosing to die gloriously in battle rather than return home safely but without glory. *The Odyssey* describes the hero Odysseus's ten-year adventure finding his way home to his family in Greece after the fall of Troy. It also describes the struggle of his wife, Penelope, to protect their household while her husband is missing. Penelope proves herself the best of women, showing her excellence by outwitting treacherous neighbors and preserving her family's prosperity.

The Iliad and *The Odyssey* reveal how the quest for individual excellence could produce both wondrous accomplishments and brutal inhumanity. In *The Iliad*, after Achilles kills Hector, the prince of Troy, he mutilates his body. When Hecuba, the queen of Troy and Hector's mother, sees this outrage, she bitterly shouts, "I wish I could sink my teeth into his liver in his guts to eat it raw." Homer's poems suggest that the gods could promote reconciliation, but they also reveal that the level of suffering in the human condition means excellence comes at a supremely high price.

Hesiod's poetry stresses the value of justice supported by a community. Like Homer a poet of the eighth century B.C.E., Hesiod tells stories influenced by Near Eastern myths, such as the Mesopotamian *Epic of Creation.* His poems explain that existence, even for deities, entails sorrow and violence. They also show that justice is part of the divine order of the universe. In *Works and Days,* Hesiod identifies Zeus, king of the gods, as the source of justice: "Zeus ordained that fishes and wild beasts and birds should eat each other, for they have no justice; but to human beings he has given justice, which is far the best." Hesiod emphasizes that men from the elite should demonstrate excellence in their relations to their social inferiors by promoting justice through persuasion instead of force: "When his people in their assembly get on the wrong track, [a good leader] gently sets matters right, persuading them with soft words." Hesiod proclaims that the divine origin of justice should be a warning to "bribe-devouring chiefs" who impose "crooked judgments." By the end of the Dark Age, the outrage that ordinary people felt at not receiving just treatment was producing pressure for a new form of social and political organization in Greece.

New technology as well as new values came to Dark Age Greece. Contacts with the Near East retaught Greeks how to write, this time learning the alphabet from Phoenician traders from Canaan. Eastern art inspired Greeks once more to include lively figures in their paintings. Trade also brought to Greece the new technology of iron metallurgy. Because iron ore was available in Greece, iron was cheaper than bronze. The relatively low cost of iron tools helped revive farming, which in turn rebuilt the population. By the eighth century B.C.E., Greece was emerging from its Dark Age.

REVIEW What were the consequences of the Greek Dark Age?

Remaking Greek Civilization, 750–500 B.C.E.

Beginning in the eighth century B.C.E., Greeks gradually remade their civilization on new social and political principles, inventing citizenship based on freedom and the sharing of power in city-state government. The Greeks' contacts with Egypt and the Near East had helped them emerge from the Dark Age, but they now created their own version of the city-state, striking out in new directions in politics, art, literature, philosophy, and science.

The best evidence of a revival of a sense of Greek identity is the founding of the Olympic Games, traditionally dated to 776 B.C.E. Every four years, the games took place as part of a religious festival at Olympia, in the northwest Peloponnese, in a huge sanctuary dedicated to Zeus. There, male athletes from elite families from communities all over Greece competed in sports based on activities needed for war: running, wrestling, jumping, and throwing. Horse and chariot racing were added to the program later, but the main event remained a two-hundred-yard sprint. Women were barred on pain of death, but they had their own separate Olympic festival on a different date in honor of Hera, queen of the gods; only unmarried women could compete.

Historians date the end of the Greek Dark Age and the beginning of the Archaic Age (750–500 B.C.E.) near the time when the Olympics began. The Archaic Age gave birth to the Greek city-state (**polis**) as an independent community of citizens inhabiting a city and the countryside around it. Greece's geography, dominated by mountains and islands, promoted the creation of city-states that remained fiercely independent communities (Map 1.6). The ancient Greeks never constituted a united nation. During the Archaic Age, Greeks established settlements around the Mediterranean in a process traditionally called colonization. This modern term, however, is misleading because it implies that governments originated and administered colonies in foreign lands. In reality, individual entrepreneurs' desire for profit from trade,

Map 1.6 Archaic Greece, c. 750–500 B.C.E.

The Greek heartland lay in and around the Aegean Sea, in what is today the nation of Greece and the western edge of the nation of Turkey (ancient Anatolia). The "mainland," where Athens, Corinth, and Sparta are located, is the southernmost tip of the mountainous Balkan peninsula. The many islands of the Aegean area were home mainly to small city-states, with the exception of the large islands just off the western Anatolian coast, which were home to populous ones.

especially in raw materials such as metals, and from acquiring farmland on foreign shores drove the founding of most new settlements. By about 580 B.C.E., Greeks had settled in Spain, present-day southern France, southern Italy and Sicily, North Africa, and along the Black Sea. Greek settlements in the east were fewer, perhaps because the monarchies there restricted foreign immigration.

Citizenship and Freedom in the Greek City-State

The Greek city-state was a new form of political organization because all free inhabitants were considered citizens, and all male citizens could usually participate in governing. Some historians argue that the Greeks modeled their city-states on the older city-states on the island of Cyprus and in Phoenicia in the Levant, but this conclusion seems flawed because those city-states were ruled by kings and were not based on the concept of free citizens sharing power in governing. The most famous ancient analyst of Greek politics and society, the philosopher Aristotle (384–322 B.C.E.), insisted, "Humans are beings who by nature live in a city-state." Anyone who existed outside such a community, Aristotle concluded, must be either a simple fool or superhuman. Greeks founded more than a thousand separate city-states, most with populations ranging from several hundred to several thousand citizens.

Citizenship was a new concept because it assumed a basic level of political and legal equality—above all, the expectation of equal treatment under the law for citizens regardless of their social status or wealth. Women had the protection of the law, but they were barred from participation in politics on the assumption that female judgment was inferior to male. The most dramatic indication of political equality in a Greek city-state was the right of all adult male citizens to vote on laws and policies in a political assembly. Not all city-states reached this level of power sharing and participation, however. In some, the social elite kept a stranglehold on politics, with a small group or, more rarely, a single person or family dominating. Greeks called rule by a small elite group oligarchy, and rule by one person tyranny.

Although the Greeks' ideas of citizenship and equality before the law remained imperfect by modern Western standards, the fact that they developed these concepts at all is remarkable because legal inequality between rich and poor in the free population was the rule in the ancient Near East and in Greece itself before the polis came into existence. Given the lack of precedent, how and why the poor in Greece gained citizenship and equality before the law remains a mystery. The greatest population increase in the late Dark Age and in the Archaic Age occurred in the ranks of the poor. These families raised more children to help farm more land, which otherwise would have lain idle because of the depopulation brought on by the worst of the Dark Age. There was no precedent for extending even limited political and legal power to this growing segment of the population, but most Greek city-states did so.

For a long time, historians attributed the general widening of political and legal rights to a so-called hoplite revolution, but recent research undermines this theory. Hoplites were infantrymen who wore metal body armor, carrying a large shield in one hand and wielding a spear in the other. They constituted the main strike force of the volunteer militia that defended each city-state. In the eighth century B.C.E., a growing number of men could afford to buy hoplite equipment (the use of iron had cut its cost). It seems likely that the new hoplites believed they were entitled to a say in politics because they bought their own equipment and voluntarily trained hard to defend their communities. According to the hoplite revolution theory, the new hoplites forced the social elite to share political power by threatening to refuse to serve in the militia. The problem with that theory is that hoplites were not poor. How, then, did poor men, too, win political rights, especially the vote in the assembly? It is perhaps possible that modern historians underestimate the military importance of the poor men who fought in the army as unarmed fighters, disrupting the enemy's infantry by hurling barrages of rocks, and that the poor earned the vote for this service. Whatever the reason for the designation of poor men as citizens with roughly the same rights as the rich, this unprecedented decision constituted the most innovative feature of the transformation of Greek society in the Archaic Age.

A Hoplite's Breastplate
This bronze armor protected the chest of a sixth-century B.C.E. hoplite. It had to be fitted to his individual body; the design is meant to match the musculature of his chest and symbolize his manliness. The Greek soldier would have worn a cloth or leather shirt underneath to prevent the worst chafing, but such a heavy and hot device could never be comfortable, and soldiers often removed them despite the danger. A slave would have carried the soldier's armor for him until the moment of battle, when he would have donned his protective gear just before facing the enemy. (Olympia Museum © Archaeological Receipts Fund.)

As the notion of the citizen's freedom became stronger, the practice of slavery—the opposite of freedom—became ever more widespread in Archaic Age Greece. Individual Greeks and the city-states themselves owned slaves. Public slaves sometimes lived on their own, performing specialized tasks such as detecting counterfeit coins. Temple slaves "belonged" to the deity of the temple, for whom they worked as servants. Private slaves totaled perhaps a third of the population by the fifth century B.C.E. They did all sorts of jobs, from household chores to crafts production to farm labor. Their masters controlled their lives and could punish them or demand sexual favors at will. Most owners did not brutalize their slaves because that damaged their human property. Slaves lacked any right to family life and had no property or legal rights. As Aristotle put it, slaves were "living tools." Sometimes owners let slaves earn money to purchase their freedom, or promised freedom at a future date to encourage hard work. Slaves who gained their freedom did not become citizens but instead joined the population of noncitizens officially allowed to live in the city-state. Despite the bitter nature of their existence, Greek slaves rarely revolted on a large scale except in Sparta, perhaps because elsewhere they were of too many different origins and nationalities to organize. No Greek is known to have called for the abolition of slavery.

Women, like slaves, lacked the right of political participation in the city-state. Freeborn women, however, counted as citizens, enjoyed the protection of the laws, and—in a crucial role respected by everyone—performed numerous religious functions. Citizen women had recourse to the courts in disputes over property, although

A Greek Woman at an Altar
This vase painting from the center of a large drinking cup shows a woman in rich clothing pouring a libation to the gods onto a flaming altar. In her other arm, she carries some sort of religious object. This scene illustrates the most important and frequent role of women in Greek public life: participating in religious ceremonies, both at home and in community festivals. This painting style is called red figure because the picture's details are painted over the reddish color of the baked clay, which shows through to depict the surfaces of the figures, such as skin or clothing. (The Toledo Museum of Art, Toledo, Ohio. Purchased with funds from the Libbey Endowment, Gift of Edward Drummond Libbey [1972.55].)

they usually had to have a man speak for them. Before marriage, a woman's father served as her legal guardian; after marriage, her husband did. The paternalism of Greek society—men acting as "fathers" to regulate the lives of women and safeguard their interests as men defined them—demanded that all women have male guardians to protect them physically and legally.

The expansion of slavery in the Archaic Age added new responsibilities for women by increasing the size and complexity of households. While their husbands farmed, participated in politics, and met with their male friends, wives managed the household by raising children, supervising the cooking, keeping the family's financial accounts, making clothing, directing the slaves, and tending them and other family members when they were ill. Poor women also worked outside the home, tilling gardens and selling produce and small goods such as ribbons and trinkets in the market found at the center of every settlement. Women rich and poor attended funerals, state festivals, and public rituals, and they controlled cults reserved exclusively for female worshippers. Their religious functions gave them freedom of movement and prestige. At Athens, for example, by the fifth century B.C.E. elite women officiated as priestesses for more than forty different deities and enjoyed benefits such as salaries paid by the state.

Greek patriarchy allowed men to control human reproduction and therefore the inheritance of property. Families arranged marriages, and everyone was expected to marry and produce children. The bride brought to the marriage a dowry of property (land yielding an income, if she was wealthy) that her children would inherit. Her husband was legally obligated to preserve this dowry and to return it to his wife if they divorced. A husband could divorce his wife at will. Legally, a wife could leave her husband on her own initiative to return to the guardianship of her male relatives, but her husband could force her to stay if her family refused to help her. Except in certain cases in Sparta, monogamous marriage was the rule in Greece, as was a nuclear family (that is, husband, wife, and children living together without other relatives in the same house). Citizen men could have sexual relations without penalty with slaves, foreign concubines, female prostitutes, or willing preadult citizen males. Citizen women, single or married, had no such freedom. Sex between a married woman and anyone other than her husband carried harsh penalties for both parties.

Sparta was the Greek city-state that went the farthest in supporting community values. Spartans placed obedience and discipline above individual desires because Sparta's survival was threatened by rebellion from its economic foundation: the great mass of slaves called helots, who were owned by the community and did almost all the work. Helots were Greeks from neighboring towns and regions that the Spartans had conquered. The helots greatly outnumbered Sparta's citizens, so Spartans had to spend their lives training to defend against the helots as well as foreign enemies. Helots toiled as farmers and servants so that Spartan men and women would not have to stoop to manual labor. Spartan men wore their hair very long to show that they were "gentlemen" warriors, not laborers.

Sparta's helots faced constant violence and humiliation. Every year Spartan officials formally declared war on them so that a citizen could kill without penalty any helot thought to be disobedient or dangerous. Spartans devoted their lives to constant preparation for war. Boys left home at age seven to live in barracks, drilling and eating together to learn discipline. Any youth unable to complete the harsh training fell into disgrace and lost citizen rights. Adolescent boys in Sparta often were involved in homosexual relationships with older men. A boy would be chosen as a special favorite by a man to promote love for a fellow soldier at whose side he would one day march into battle; their relationship could include sex. The elder partner was supposed to help educate the young man in politics and community values and not just exploit him for physical pleasure. Both were expected to marry women. Homoerotic sex between adult males was considered disgraceful, as it was between women of all ages (at least according to the reports of men).

Sparta and the Peloponnese, c. 750–500 B.C.E.

Spartan women were known throughout the Greek world for their various freedoms, including property ownership and being able to exercise in public in short outfits. Citizen women were expected to use their liberty from manual labor to stay fit so they could bear healthy children to sustain the Spartan population. They could own property, including land. Women also were expected to teach their children Spartan values. One mother became legendary for handing her son his shield on the eve of battle and sternly telling him, "Come back with it—or on it!"

Athens exemplified a greater concern for the value and values of the individual. During the Archaic Age, it took the first steps toward democracy, a new system of government that gave equal political and legal rights to all male citizens, and toward an economy based on international trade by sea. In 594 B.C.E., an economic crisis that pitted rich against poor unexpectedly promoted change when Solon, appointed as a mediator, outlawed debt slavery and created a council to guide the legislative work of the assembly. The council's members were chosen by lottery and could serve only two annual terms (not in succession), ensuring wide participation. Equally important was Solon's decision to empower any citizen to bring charges in court on behalf of any victim and to appeal any magistrate's judgments to the assembly. These reforms gave ordinary citizens a real share in the administration of justice. Finally, Solon convinced the Athenians to improve the economy by exporting olive oil.

Some elite Athenians vehemently opposed Solon's political reforms because they wanted oligarchy. The unrest they caused opened the door temporarily to tyranny in Athens, and the family of Peisistratus held power from 546 to 510 B.C.E. by championing the interests of the poor. A rival elite family finally got the tyranny overthrown by denouncing it as unjust and inducing the Spartans, the self-proclaimed defenders of Greek freedom, to "liberate" Athens. Cleisthenes, an ambitious politician, found that he could win prominence only by promising greater democracy to the masses. Beginning in 508 B.C.E., he delivered on his promises and came to be remembered as "the father of Athenian democracy" for his reforms. His complex political reorganization achieved its goal of promoting participation in governance by as many male citizens as possible. It would take another fifty years of controversy before Athens's democracy reached its full form, but Cleisthenes' changes opened the way to an unprecedented way of life based on people persuading, not compelling, each other to achieve common goals. Athenian citizens believed in the rule of law, but they chose individual freedom and responsibility for themselves (though not for their slaves) over forced social regimentation like that in Sparta.

New Ways of Thought and Expression

A spirit of intellectual change spread across Greece in the late Archaic Age that corresponded to the political idea that persuasion, not force or social status, should motivate people's decisions. In city-states all over the Greek world, new ways of thought inspired artists, poets, and philosophers. Ongoing contacts with the Near East exposed the Greeks to traditions from which to learn and create something new. Artists became expert at rendering increasingly realistic three-dimensional figures. Sculptors made their statues less stiff and more varied, from gracefully clothed young women to muscular male nudes, and made them come alive with gleaming paint.

Poets expanded the Near Eastern tradition of expressing personal emotions in poetry by developing lyric poetry, a new type of verse similar to popular songs

Archaic Age Sculpture of a Dead Warrior

This Athenian marble statue dating from about 530–520 B.C.E. shows the stiff posture and smiling expression that Archaic Age Greek sculptors used for "heroic nudes" portraying dead young men. These statues had a striding stance recalling the style of Egyptian art and were painted in bright colors. This one, standing six feet four inches tall, retains traces of red paint. An inscription on its base addressed people passing by: "Stand and weep at this monument of Croesus, now dead. Raging Ares [the Greek war god] destroyed him battling in the front line." (The Art Archive/National Archaeological Museum Athens/Dagli Orti.)

and stressing individual feelings. Composed in diverse rhythms and performed to the music of a lyre (a kind of harp that gives its name to the poetry), Greek lyric poems could be short and for one singer, or long and for a chorus. Archilochus of Paros, who lived in the early 600s B.C.E., became infamous for his unheroic lines about throwing down his shield in battle so he could flee to save his life: "Oh, the hell with it; I can get another one just as good." Sappho, a lyric poet from Lesbos born about 630 B.C.E., became famous for her love poems, writing, "Some would say the most beautiful thing on our dark earth is an army of cavalry, others of infantry, others of ships, but I say it's whatever a person loves." In this poem Sappho was expressing her longing for a woman she loved, who was far away.

Greek philosophers in the Archaic Age developed radically new explanations of the nature of the universe and the role of the gods. Most of these thinkers came from Ionia. This location placed them in close contact with Near Eastern knowledge, especially astronomy, mathematics, and myth. Because there were no formal schools, pupils who studied privately with these philosophers helped spread the new ideas. Inspired by Babylonian astronomy, Ionian Greek philosophers expressed the bold idea that laws of nature, not the whims of individual gods, governed the universe. Pythagoras, who emigrated from the island of Samos to the Greek city-state Croton in southern Italy about 530 B.C.E., taught that patterns and relationships of numbers explained the entire world and promoted the systematic study of mathematics and its relation to music.

**Ionia and the Aegean,
c. 750–500 B.C.E.**

Ionian philosophers insisted that they could discover the workings of the universe because nature was not random but in fact determined by what we today call the laws of physics or laws of nature. They named the universe *cosmos,* meaning an orderly arrangement that is beautiful. The order of the cosmos encompassed not only the motions of stars and planets but also the weather, the growth of plants and animals, human health, and so on. Because the universe was ordered, it could be understood, and its events could be explained by thought and research. Early Greek philosophers, therefore, looked for the first or universal cause of things, a problem that scientists still pursue. The philosophers who taught these ideas about the cosmos believed they needed to give reasons for their conclusions and to persuade others by arguments based on evidence. That is, they used logic. This mode of thought, called **rationalism,** was a crucial first step toward science and philosophy as these disciplines exist today. The rule-based explanation of the causes of things developed by these philosophers contrasted sharply with the traditional mythological explanation that the gods' wishes controlled the universe. Naturally, many people had difficulty accepting such a startling change in their understanding of the world, and the older tradition explaining events as the will of different gods lived on alongside the new idea, which did not deny the existence of the divine but insisted that discoverable truths determined the course of events.

The Ionian philosophers' most important achievement was the idea that people must give reasons to justify their beliefs, rather than just make assertions that others must accept without evidence. This insistence on logic as the key to understanding the world gave people hope that they could improve their lives through their own efforts. As Xenophanes from Colophon (c. 580–480 B.C.E.) put it, "The gods have not revealed all things from the beginning to mortals, but, by seeking, human beings find out, in time, what is better." This saying well expressed the value Archaic Age Greek philosophers attached to intellectual freedom, a new idea corresponding to the value given to the new ideals of the individual citizen's freedom and legal equality as guaranteed in the community of the city-state.

REVIEW   How did Greek life change in the Archaic Age?

Conclusion

In a sense, civilization emerged as an <u>accident of climate change</u>. Stone Age people existed for a long time before the features of life that historians associate with civilization slowly developed when global warming made agriculture and domestication of animals possible (the so-called Neolithic Revolution). That, in turn, led to vastly growing populations and settled farming communities, which led to the formation of cities and political states. Eventually some of the states in the Near East became imperial giants, while others, especially the later Greek city-states, remained small. Most ancient states were ruled as monarchies, perhaps reflecting the religious belief that a king ruled the gods and that this was therefore the proper form for rule. Political diversity nevertheless developed when some Greeks decided to be governed as citizens in democracies, an unprecedented decision stressing individual values that created a kind of egalitarian society (at least for citizen men) not seen since early Paleolithic times. Intellectual diversity also emerged in Greece with the creation of rationalism to explain the world and its workings based on reason and persuasion rather than myth. Religious change

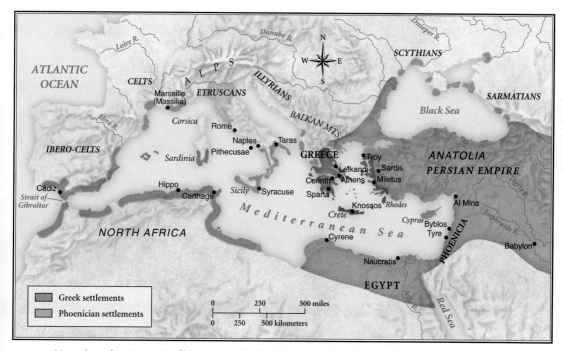

Mapping the West Mediterranean Civilizations, c. 500 B.C.E.
At the end of the sixth century B.C.E., the Persian Empire was far and away the most powerful civilization touching the Mediterranean. Its vast territory and riches gave it resources that no Phoenician or Greek city could match. The Phoenicians dominated economically in the western Mediterranean, while the Greek city-states in Sicily and southern Italy rivaled the power of those in the heartland. In Italy, the Etruscans were the most powerful civilization; the Romans were still a small community struggling to replace monarchy with a republic.

came with the creation of monotheism by the Hebrews (perhaps influenced by Persian Zoroastrianism). The Hebrews' development of a scripture-based monotheistic religion was a development second to none in its consequences for later history.

Some patterns of life that dated back to the Stone Age persisted after the emergence of civilization, especially the importance of social hierarchy, religion, trade, and war. Long-distance trade grew when private commerce developed, and commercial exchange was a powerful mechanism for cultural interchange. Both ideas and technologies, from writing to metallurgy, were spread among diverse peoples by trade and also by the unintended consequences of war. Although people may not have always intended to share their knowledge, their desires for the goods that trade and conquest could win and for the excitement that travel and foreign adventure could generate led to the depth and breadth of interchange and interaction that created the first stages of Western civilization.

CHAPTER REVIEW QUESTIONS
1. How did life in the Greek city-state differ from that in earlier Mesopotamian and Egyptian civilization?
2. How were the ideas of Ionian philosophers different from mythic traditions?

For practice quizzes and other study tools, see the Online Study Guide at bedfordstmartins.com/huntconcise.

For primary-source material from this period, see Chapters 1 and 2 of *Sources of THE MAKING OF THE WEST*, Third Edition.

TIMELINE

(Scale changes to 500 years starting with 4000 B.C.E.)

C. 10,000–8000 B.C.E. Neolithic Revolution (the development of agriculture and domestication of animals)

C. 4000–3000 B.C.E. First cities established and writing developed in Mesopotamia

■ 2500S B.C.E. Great Pyramid built in Egypt

10,000 B.C.E.	4000 B.C.E.	3500 B.C.E.	3000 B.C.E.	2500 B.C.E.

C. 4000–1000 B.C.E. Bronze Age in southwestern Asia, Egypt, and Europe

Suggested References

*Primary sources are indicated with an asterisk.

Archaeological excavation is our best resource for understanding the long period of history from the Stone Age to the rise of the Greek city-state.

Ancient Olympic Games: http://www.perseus.tufts.edu/Olympics/

*Barnes, Jonathan. *Early Greek Philosophy*. 1987.

Brosius, Maria. *Women in Ancient Persia (559–331 B.C.)*. 1996.

Bryce, Trevor. *The Kingdom of the Hittites*. 1998.

*Dalley, Stephanie, trans. *Myths from Mesopotamia: Creation, the Flood, Gilgamesh, and Others*. 1991.

Ehrenberg, Margaret. *Women in Prehistory*. 1989.

Hodos, Tamar. *Local Responses to Colonization in the Iron Age Mediterranean*. 2006.

Moore, A. M. T. *Village on the Euphrates: From Foraging to Farming at Abu Hureyra*. 2000.

Nigosian, S. A. *The Zoroastrian Faith: Tradition and Modern Research*. 1993.

Osborne, Robin. *Greece in the Making, 1200–479 B.C.* 1996.

Szapakowska, Kasia. *Daily Life in Ancient Egypt: Recreating Lahun*. 2008.

Virtual Museum of Nautical Archaeology (including the Uluburun shipwreck): http://ina.tamu.edu/vm.htm

- **776 B.C.E.** Traditional date of first Olympic Games in Greece
- **C. 900 B.C.E.** Neo-Assyrians create an empire
- **C. 2200 B.C.E.** Earliest Minoan palaces on Crete
- **C. 1000–750 B.C.E.** Greece's Dark Age
- **C. 2350 B.C.E.** Sargon establishes the first empire in Akkadia
- **C. 1200–1000 B.C.E.** Sea Peoples period
- **C. 1400 B.C.E.** Mycenaeans take over Minoan Crete

2000 B.C.E.	1500 B.C.E.	1000 B.C.E.	500 B.C.E.

- **C. 1792–1750 B.C.E.** Reign of Hammurabi, king of Babylon, in Mesopotamia
- **C. 1750 B.C.E.** Beginning of Hittite kingdom in Anatolia
- **775–500 B.C.E.** Greeks establish many new settlements around the Mediterranean
- **C. 750 B.C.E.** Greeks begin to create city-states
- **559 B.C.E.** Cyrus founds the Persian Empire
- **508 B.C.E.** Cleisthenes strengthens Athenian democracy

2

The Greek Golden Age

THE PROSPERITY AND INDEPENDENCE that Greece had achieved in the Archaic Age (750–500 B.C.E.) almost came to an abrupt end. In 507 B.C.E., the Athenians, fearing a Spartan invasion, sent ambassadors to the Persian king, Darius I (r. 522–486 B.C.E.), to request a protective alliance. The Persian Empire was then the greatest power in the ancient world. The diplomats met with one of the king's governors in the western region of the empire, an area in Anatolia (modern Turkey) inhabited by Greeks. After the royal administrator heard their plea, he replied, "But who in the world are you and where do you live?" This incident hints at the dangers that threatened Greece at the time. First, the two major powers of mainland Greece—Athens and Sparta—were hostile to each other. Second, the Persian kingdom was expanding westward and had already conquered the Ionian Greeks in Anatolia. Yet neither the Persians nor the mainland Greeks knew much about each other. This mutual ignorance sparked a bloody conflict between Persia and Greece that we call the Persian Wars (499–479 B.C.E.), which were then followed by decades of war between the Greek city-states throughout the rest of the fifth century B.C.E.

This century of almost continuous war became the period of Greece's most enduring cultural and artistic achievements, which raises the question of the direct and indirect effects of war on civilization. Athenian political, social, and cultural accomplishments in the fifth century B.C.E. had such a lasting impact that historians call this period the Golden Age. This Golden Age opens the Classical Age of Greek history, a modern title that covers the period from about 500 B.C.E. to the death of Alexander the Great in 323 B.C.E.

A Greek Warrior Leaves Home for Battle

This vase, made about 450 B.C.E. to hold wine, shows a well-armed Greek infantryman (hoplite) leaving for battle. The vase painter portrayed the warrior in full armor to make the scene more dramatic. In real life, a slave would have carried the nearly seventy pounds of metal armor to the battlefield, where the soldier would have put it on at the last minute. The warrior holds a thrusting spear, his main battle weapon, but also wears a sword from a strap over his shoulder for close-in fighting. The man on the left is probably the warrior's father, his age indicated by his cane. The woman is probably his wife, who is ready both to pour a libation to the gods for her husband's safety and to give him a last drink before he leaves home on his dangerous mission.

(© Copyright The Trustees of The British Museum.)

Athenians in the Golden Age created Greece's leading state, developing a "radical" democracy at home while establishing a regional empire. They achieved economic prosperity and produced artistic and cultural accomplishments that dazzled the Greek world. While other commercially oriented city-states also became prosperous in this period, it was Golden Age Athens that created innovations in drama, art, architecture, and thought that have deeply influenced Western civilization up to the present. Some of these changes angered Greeks at the time, however, because they conflicted with traditional ideas, especially people's religious fear that abandoning their ancestors' beliefs and practices would anger the gods and bring down divine punishment.

The Peloponnesian War, a bitter struggle between Athens and Sparta that dragged on from 431 to 404 B.C.E., ended the Golden Age. This period of cultural blossoming therefore both began and finished with destructive wars, with Greeks standing together in the first one and tearing each other apart in the concluding one.

CHAPTER FOCUS QUESTION What were the direct and indirect consequences of war on Athens in the fifth century B.C.E.?

The Persian Wars, 499–479 B.C.E.

Bad diplomacy sparked the Persian Wars. At their meeting with the Persian regional governor, the Athenian ambassadors accepted the Persian terms for an alliance: formally submitting to Persian authority by presenting symbolic tokens of earth and water. Although the Athenian assembly became angry when they discovered that their diplomats had submitted to a foreign power, they never informed the Persian king Darius that they were rejecting the alliance. He therefore continued to believe that Athens remained an obedient ally. This misunderstanding eventually led to two Persian invasions of Greece, the so-called Persian Wars.

Since the Persian Empire dwarfed the city-states of Greece in every resource, from gold to soldiers, war between this huge empire and these usually small communities was like a fight between an elephant and a pack of undersized dogs. Making the situation grimmer was the Greek city-states' tendency to fight one another instead of cooperating. Greek victory in such a mismatch seemed unthinkable.

The Ionian Revolt and the Battle of Marathon, 499–490 B.C.E.

The Persian Wars began in 499 B.C.E., when the Ionian Greek city-states tried to regain their independence by revolting against Persia. Athens sent troops to aid the rebels, but a Persian counterattack sent them fleeing and crushed the revolt by 494 B.C.E. (Map 2.1). King Darius erupted when he learned that the Athenians had aided the Ionian Revolt: not only had they dared attack his kingdom, but they had done it, as far as he knew, after submitting to his authority. To remind himself to punish these traitors, Darius ordered a slave to say to him three times at every meal, "Master, remember the Athenians."

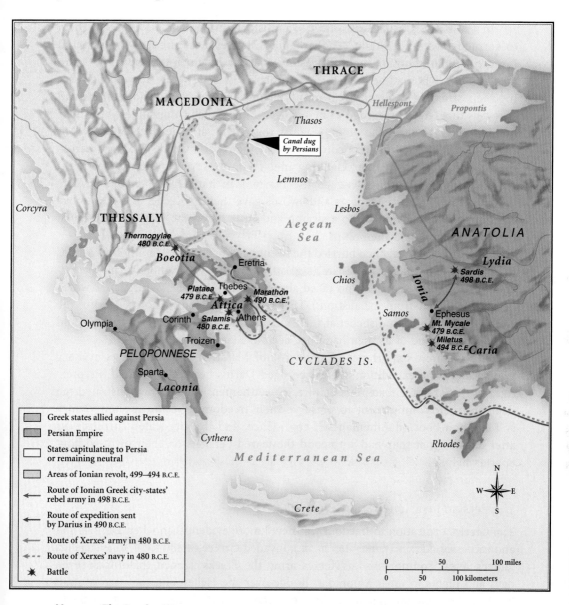

Map 2.1　The Persian Wars, 499–479 B.C.E.

The Persian Wars originated in the failed revolt (499–494 B.C.E.) of the Greek city-states in Ionia against Persian control. To punish the Greeks, the Persian king Darius (r. 522–486 B.C.E.) first sent an expedition by sea, whose infantry the Athenians defeated on the Marathon plain in 490 B.C.E. Darius's son Xerxes (r. 486–465 B.C.E.) then led a mammoth invasion of Greece, starting from Sardis in Ionia. The Persians' unexpected naval defeat at Salamis (480 B.C.E.) and their defeats on land at Plataea and Mycale (479 B.C.E.) ended the Persians' attempt to extend their empire into Europe. Compare the relative sizes of Greece and the Persian Empire to get an idea of how bold it was for Greeks to attack Persians in Asia.

In 490 B.C.E., Darius sent a fleet to punish the Athenians; he expected them to surrender without a fight. The Athenians, however, confronted the imperial invaders at Marathon, on the northeastern coast of Athenian territory. The Athenian soldiers, who had never before encountered Persians, grew nervous just seeing their strange (to Greek eyes) outfits—pants instead of the short tunics and bare legs that Greeks regarded as manly dress. The Greek commanders sent their hoplites (heavily armed infantry) against the enemy at a dead run, to shorten the time that Persian archers could shoot at them. The Greeks stomped across the Marathon plain in their clanking metal armor (seventy pounds per man) under a hail of arrows to engage the Persians in hand-to-hand combat. The Greeks' heavier thrusting spears and swords gave them the edge, and they drove their opponents backward into a swamp and slaughtered the Persians who failed to splash their way to their ships.

The Athenian army then hurried the twenty-six miles from Marathon to Athens to guard the city against a Persian naval attack. (Today's marathons recall the legendary run of a messenger who raced ahead to announce the victory, after which he dropped dead from exhaustion.) The Persians then sailed home, leaving the Athenians to rejoice in disbelief at their victory. The greatest honor a family could claim was that one of its men had once been a "Marathon fighter."

The symbolic importance of the battle of Marathon outweighed its military significance. The expedition's defeat enraged Darius because it injured his prestige, but it did not threaten his empire. The Athenians' success demonstrated the depth of their commitment to preserve their freedom. The unexpected victory at Marathon boosted Athenian self-confidence, and the city-state's citizens ever after boasted that they had withstood the feared Persians on their own, without Sparta's help.

The Persian Invasion of 480–479 B.C.E.

The Greeks' dedication to freedom was never more evident than when Darius's son and successor, Xerxes (r. 486–465 B.C.E.), invaded Greece in 480 B.C.E. to avenge his father's defeat. So immense was Xerxes' army, the Greeks claimed, that it took seven days and nights to cross a pontoon bridge over the Hellespont, the narrow strait between Anatolia and mainland Greece. Xerxes expected the Greek city-states to surrender immediately once they learned the size of his forces. Some did, but thirty-one city-states united to fight the Persians. This alliance, known as the Hellenic League, accomplished the incredible: protecting their independence from the world's superpower.

The united Greeks chose Sparta as their leader because of its famous hoplite army. The Spartans demonstrated their courage when three hundred of their men held off Xerxes' huge army for several days at the narrow pass called Thermopylae (warm gates) in central Greece. A warrior summed up Spartan bravery with his response to a remark that the Persian archers were so numerous that their arrows darkened the sky in battle. "That's good news," he said. "We'll get to fight in the shade." The Spartans died holding their position.

Luck and courage characterized Athenian participation in the war. The fortunate discovery of rich silver ore in their territory a few years earlier gave the Athenians the money to build a fleet of two hundred warships. The state claimed mineral rights, and the commander, Themistocles, persuaded the democratic assembly to vote to spend the mining revenue for national defense instead of making payments to citizens. Courage and a dedication to freedom led the Athenians to evacuate their city instead of surrendering when the Persians marched on Athens. Themistocles then tricked the other, less aggressive Greek leaders into facing the larger Persian navy in a sea battle in the narrow channel between the island of Salamis and the west coast of Athenian territory. The narrowness of the channel prevented the Persians from using all their ships at once and let the heavier Greek ships, each rowed into battle by a crew of 170, win by ramming the flimsier Persian vessels. When Xerxes observed that his most aggressive naval commander appeared to be the one woman among the admirals, Artemisia, ruler of Caria in Anatolia, he shouted, "My men have become women, and my women, men." In 479 B.C.E., the Greek infantry, headed by the Spartans, defeated the remaining Persian land forces at Plataea (Map 2.1, page 49).

The victory in the Persian Wars produced social and political consequences

A Persian Royal Guard
This life-size panel formed part of the decoration of a courtyard in a palace built by the Persian king Darius I. The warrior shown here perhaps represents one of the elite royal guards known as "immortals." An inscription records that the craftsmen who made these panels came from Babylon in Mesopotamia, which was part of the far-flung Persian Empire. (The Granger Collection, NY.)

in Athens. The war effort had cut across social and economic divisions because the city-state's forces included not only the social elite and hoplites but also the thousands of poorer men who rowed Athens's warships. The pride and confidence

REVIEW   What factors led to and determined the outcome of the Persian Wars?

these men earned from their military service led them to expect greater influence in Athenian society and democracy.

Athenian Empire and Democracy in the Golden Age, 479–431 B.C.E.

Following the Persian Wars, Athens became the most famous Greek city-state by establishing the so-called Athenian Empire, a modern label for the regional alliance that Athens dominated, and by creating what modern scholars call **radical democracy**, meaning that male citizens participated actively in governing and voted not only to elect leaders but also to set policy and enforce justice. The growth of Athens's international power, along with its silver mines, brought in greatly increased revenues that the Athenian assembly voted to spend on public buildings, art, and festivals.

The Establishment of the Athenian Empire, 479–460 B.C.E.

The Athenian Empire arose following the Persian Wars when Sparta and Athens became enemies instead of allies. Sparta already headed an alliance of Greek city-states called the Peloponnesian League, and Athens needed similar support to rival the power of Sparta and also be ready to face the Persians if necessary. (The Persian Empire remained potent and could strike back at any time.)

In 477 B.C.E., therefore, Athens allied with city-states whose locations exposed them to possible Persian retaliation—in northern Greece, on the islands of the Aegean Sea, and along the western coast of Anatolia. Most of the allies started out with strong navies, and all solemnly swore never to desert the coalition. The alliance, called the **Delian League** because its treasury was originally located on the island of Delos, also had an assembly. At this point, every ally had an equal say in making decisions.

The special arrangements for financing the alliance's naval operations allowed the Athenians in time to dominate the alliance and thus establish an "empire." Each ally paid annual "dues" based on its size and prosperity. Because they were required, these dues were actually "tribute." Larger member states supplied triremes (the premier warships) with rowers and their pay (Figure 2.1); smaller states shared the cost of a ship and crew or contributed cash instead. Over time, more and more members paid cash because they found it too demanding to build warships and train crews. (The modern construction and launching in Greece of a full-size, operating trireme rowed by volunteers has demonstrated the enormous skill and

The Delian and Peloponnesian Leagues

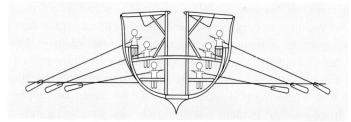

Figure 2.1 Triremes, the Foremost Classical Greek Warships
Innovations in military technology and training fueled a naval arms race in the fifth century B.C.E., when Greek shipbuilders devised larger and faster ramming ships called triremes. The boats were powered by 170 rowers seated in three rows, one above the other as shown in the illustration of the rowers from behind (top). These ships' radical new design with triple banks of oars made them expensive to build and required extensive crew training. Only wealthy and populous city-states such as Athens could afford to maintain large fleets of triremes. No ancient trireme survives to show exactly how such a warship was built, but this relief sculpture (bottom) found on the Athenian acropolis and dating from about 400 B.C.E. gives a glimpse of what a trireme looked like from the side when being rowed into battle. Sails were used to power the ship only when not in combat. (The Art Archive/Acropolis Museum Athens/Dagli Orti.)

practice required.) Athens, far larger than most league members, possessed the necessary shipyards as well as many poorer men eager to earn pay as rowers.

The Delian League turned into the Athenian Empire because most Delian League allies stopped furnishing triremes and paid Athens to build ships for the alliance. With no navies of their own, they could not defend themselves against Athens if they disagreed with league policy or wanted to stop paying tribute. As the Athenian historian Thucydides observed, rebellious allies "lost their independence," and the Athenians became "no longer as popular as they used to be." This unpopularity was the price Athenians paid for making themselves the leading naval power in the eastern Mediterranean. They insisted that their dominance of the Delian League was justified because it kept the alliance strong enough to protect Greece from the Persians, and they were right about the alliance's effectiveness. By 460 B.C.E., their fleet had driven the enemy from the Aegean Sea region, quashing any Persian threat to Greece for the next fifty years.

The consequences of their surprising success in war led the Athenians to experience an inflation of their expectations. A sea-based empire proved irresistible. Crucially, it allowed Athens to defend the trade routes needed to import the food necessary to feed a growing population that could no longer be supported by local agriculture. In addition, Athenians acquired riches by plundering Persian outposts, exacting tribute from allies, and collecting taxes from the commerce in grain, olive oil, wine, pottery, sculpture, metals, and slaves that thrived across the Mediterranean Sea. Other city-states, such as Megara and Corinth, also flourished as a result of maritime trade in this period, but Athens grew richer than them all. The Athenian assembly, made up of male citizens over age eighteen, decided how to spend the city-state's increasing revenues. Poor and rich alike therefore had a stake in keeping the fleet active and the league members paying for it. The poor men who rowed the ships came to depend on the pay they earned on league expeditions. Members of the social elite enhanced their social status by commanding campaigns and spending their portion of the plunder on public festivals and buildings to win public recognition, which they craved more than wealth. Debates over policy in the assembly concerned how Athens should spend the money it was taking in, not whether it was just to compel formerly free allies to remain tribute-paying subjects of the empire.

Radical Democracy and Pericles' Leadership, 461–445 B.C.E.

The establishment of Athenian empire led to radical democracy because the poorer men who rowed the Athenian navy, recognizing their essential role in securing Athens's security and prosperity, gained more political power by voting for leaders who supported their demands. The first change they demanded was making the judicial system of Athens just as democratic as the process of passing laws in the assembly. Members of the elite led this initiative, whether because they believed it was the people's just reward or because they wanted the esteem bestowed on leaders—or perhaps for both these reasons. Pericles (c. 495–429 B.C.E.), one of Athens's most socially prominent citizens, became the leading Golden Age politician by supporting the popular desire for greater democracy.

Government in Golden Age Athens gradually became so thoroughly shared by male citizens that today it is called radical democracy. Its principles were clear: equal protection under the law for all citizens regardless of wealth; direct and widespread participation in the assembly to make laws and policy by majority rule; random selection and rotation of jurors, most officials, and the members of the Council of 500 (which prepared the agenda for the assembly); and punitive rules against corruption. There was no written constitution and no protection for minority rights; the assembly could make any decision it desired. The need for competence and excellence at the highest level of government was recognized in two ways: first, by filling the top public offices—the ten "generals," who managed the city-state's military and financial affairs—not by a lottery but by election to an annual term;

second, by not setting a limit on how many terms a man could serve. The generals' power, however, remained subject to constant democratic scrutiny: any citizen could demand a full investigation of a general's conduct in office.

Reforming the justice system was essential to creating radical democracy. Ever since Cleisthenes' reforms at the end of the sixth century B.C.E., certain officials and ex-officials had rendered most judicial verdicts. Although these officials were now chosen annually by lottery to make their selection democratic, they were still susceptible to bribery and pressure from the social elite. Since even democratically enacted laws meant little if applied unfairly, the masses demanded reforms to halt unfair or corrupt judgments.

The opportunity for change arose in 461 B.C.E., when a prominent member of the elite sought the people's political support by sponsoring a reformed court system based on randomly selected juries. His reforms made it nearly impossible to bribe or pressure jurors. They were chosen by lottery from male citizens over thirty years old, the selection was made only on the day of the trial, all trials were concluded in one day, and juries were large (from several hundred to several thousand). No judges presided; only one official was present—to stop fistfights. Jurors voted after hearing speeches from the accuser and the accused, who had to speak for themselves, although they could pay someone else to compose their speeches and ask others to speak in support. A majority vote of the jurors ruled, and no appeals were allowed.

Majority rule was the operative principle for enforcing accountability in Athenian radical democracy. The most striking example of this principle was the procedure called **ostracism** (from *ostracon,* meaning a "piece of broken pottery," the material used for casting ballots). Once a year, all male citizens could scratch on a ballot the name of one man they thought should be ostracized (exiled for ten years). If at least six thousand ballots were cast, the man who received the most "votes" was expelled from Athenian territory. He suffered no other penalty, and his family and property remained behind undisturbed. Ostracism was not a criminal penalty, and ostracized men recovered their citizen rights after their exile.

Ostracism was meant to protect radical democracy; a man could, therefore, be ostracized if the majority perceived his prominence as a threat to their interests. An anecdote about the famous politician Aristides illustrates this possibility. He was nicknamed "the Just" because he had proved himself so fair-minded in setting the tribute amounts for Delian League members. On the day of the ostracism, an illiterate farmer handed Aristides a pottery fragment and asked him to scratch the name of the man's choice on it.

"Certainly," said Aristides. "Which name shall I write?"

"Aristides," replied the countryman.

"All right," replied Aristides as he proceeded to inscribe his own name.

"But tell me, why do you want to ostracize Aristides? What has he done to you?"

"Oh, nothing," sputtered the man. "I don't even know him. I just can't stand hearing everybody refer to him as 'the Just.'"

True or not, this tale demonstrates that Athenians assumed that the right way to protect democracy was always to trust the majority vote of freeborn, adult male citizens, without any restrictions on a man's ability to decide what he thought was best for democracy. It also shows that men seeking political success in Athenian democracy had to be ready to pay the price that jealousy or spite could exact.

Pericles became the most influential politician of the Golden Age by devising innovations to strengthen the egalitarian tendencies of Athenian government. Brilliant at public speaking—the most important skill for a politician in radical democracy—Pericles repeatedly persuaded the assembly to pass laws increasing its political power. In return, he gained such popularity that he was regularly elected as a general, at one point fifteen years in a row. Pericles' most important democratic innovation was pay for service in public jobs filled by lottery. This allowed poorer men to leave their regular work to serve in government. Early in the 450s B.C.E., he convinced the assembly to use state revenues to pay a daily stipend to men who served on juries, in the Council of 500, and in numerous other posts. The amount was approximately what an unskilled worker could earn in a day. The generals received no pay because the prestige of their position was considered its own reward.

Another Periclean innovation strengthened citizen identity, which was a source of pride and profit under radical democracy. In 451 B.C.E., Pericles sponsored a law making citizenship more exclusive by mandating that it would be given only to children whose mother and father were both Athenian by birth. Thereafter, men less often married foreign women (previously common among the elite), which in turn raised the social status of citizen women.

Finally, Pericles supported the interests of poorer men by recommending frequent naval attacks against enemies in Greece and against Persian control of Cyprus, Egypt, and the eastern Mediterranean. The assembly's confidence reached such a fever pitch that they voted to wage war on three different fronts simultaneously. The Athenians' ambitions at last exceeded their resources, however, and by 450 B.C.E., they had to pull back from the eastern Mediterranean and stop fighting against the Peloponnesian League. In the winter of 446–445 B.C.E., Pericles engineered a peace treaty with Sparta designed to freeze the balance of power in Greece for thirty years and thus preserve Athenian control of the Delian League. Pericles dropped his aggressive foreign policy because he realized that preserving radical democracy at home depended on Athens not losing its power over its allies.

The Urban Landscape of Golden Age Athens

The empire strengthened Athens by promoting seaborne trade from all around the Mediterranean, and the profits helped finance glorious public architecture, art, and religious festivals in the city. This splendor contrasted with the simplicity of people's homes in both the city and the countryside. In town, houses were wedged tightly against one another along narrow, winding streets. Their bedrooms, storerooms, and dining rooms were arranged around an open-air courtyard. People only rarely decorated their rooms with paintings or art, and furniture was scarce. Toilets usually consisted of a pit dug outside the front door, which was emptied by collectors paid to dump the excrement outside the city at a distance set by law. Poorer people rented small apartments.

Wealthy citizens were expected to spend money to enrich everyone's life in the city-state. Generals who became rich by raiding Persian settlements in the eastern Mediterranean used this wealth to beautify the city, not to build themselves mansions. They paid for public landscaping that included shade trees, running tracks for exercise, and gathering places that included stoas (narrow buildings open along one side whose purpose was to provide shelter from sun or rain). One successful general's family built the Painted Stoa in the heart of the city, on the edge of the **agora**, the central market square. The crowds that came to the agora daily to shop and chat about politics would cluster inside this shelter. There they could gaze at its bright paintings, which depicted the glorious exploits of the general's family and thus publicized the family's dedication to the city-state. The rich also paid for other major public expenses, such as equipment for warships and entertainment at city festivals. This custom was essential because Athens, like most Greek city-states, had no regular direct taxes on income or property.

The most prominent new architectural monuments in Golden Age Athens were huge buildings, especially temples, paid for with public funds. These building projects made a statement about the Athenians' pride in their success and their expectations for the future. Pericles persuaded the assembly to build the city's most expensive project ever on the rocky hill at the center of the city called the *acropolis* (Map 2.2). The centerpieces were a new temple of Athena on the crest of

Map 2.2 Fifth-Century B.C.E. Athens

The urban center of Athens with the agora and acropolis at its heart measured about one square mile, surrounded by a stone wall with a perimeter of some four miles. Fifteen large gates flanked by towers and various smaller doors allowed traffic in and out of the city; much of the Athenian population lived in the many villages (demes) of the surrounding countryside. Most of the city's water supply came from wells and springs inside the walls, but, unusually for a Greek city, Athens also had water piped in from outside. The Long Walls provided a protected corridor connecting the city to its harbor at Piraeus, where the Athenian navy was anchored and grain was imported to feed the people.

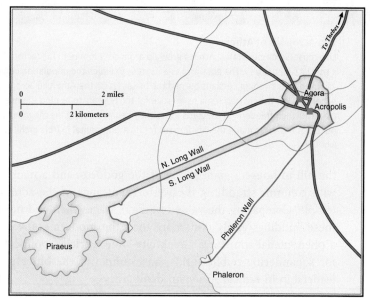

The Acropolis of Athens
Like most Greek city-states, Athens grew up around a prominent hill (acropolis), whose summit served as a special sanctuary for the gods and as a fortress to which the population could retreat when an enemy attacked. The invading Persians burned the buildings on the Athenian acropolis in 480 B.C.E. The Athenians left the charred remains in place for thirty years to remind themselves of the sacrifice they had made for their freedom. In the 440s B.C.E., they began erecting the magnificent temples and other public buildings that have made the city famous for its monumental marble architecture. (© akg-images, London/ John Hios.)

the hill to house a giant statue of the goddess, and a mammoth entrance building with columns straddling the western entrance of the acropolis on the way to the temple. Comparing the value of a day's wages then and now, we can calculate that these buildings easily cost more than the modern equivalent of a billion dollars, a phenomenal sum for a Greek city-state. Pericles' political rivals denounced him for squandering public funds, an example of the bitter political competition for leadership in radical Athenian democracy.

The vast new temple built for Athena—the Parthenon (the house of the virgin goddess)—was started in 447 B.C.E. and became Greece's most famous building. The Parthenon honored Athena as the divine champion of Athenian military power. Inside the temple stood a gold and ivory statue nearly forty feet high depicting the goddess in battle armor, holding in her outstretched hand a six-foot statue of Victory (*Nike* in Greek). Like all Greek temples, the Parthenon was built to be a house for its divinity, not as a gathering place for worshippers. Only priests and priestesses could usually enter the temple; public religious ceremonies took place out front. Its design followed standard temple architecture: a rectangular box on a raised platform, a plan the Greeks probably derived from Egyptian temples. Columns on a raised porch surrounded the box on all sides. The Parthenon's columns were carved in the simple style called Doric, in contrast to the more elaborate Ionic and Corinthian styles, all of which are often imitated in modern buildings (Figure 2.2).

The Parthenon, highly visible and extremely expensive, proclaimed the self-confidence of Golden Age Athens. Constructed from twenty thousand tons of Attic marble, it stretched nearly 230 feet in length and 100 feet wide. Its massive size conveyed an impression of power. The temple's sophisticated architecture demonstrated the Athenians' ability to construct order that was both apparent and real: because perfectly rectangular shapes in large-scale architecture appear curved to the human eye, subtle curves and inclines were built into the Parthenon to produce an illusion of completely straight lines and to emphasize its massiveness.

The elaborate sculptural frieze of the Parthenon announced the temple's most innovative and confident message: Athens's citizens possessed the special goodwill

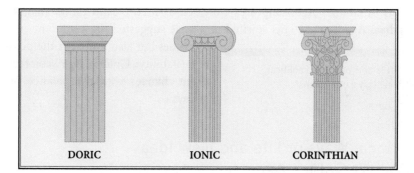

DORIC   **IONIC**   **CORINTHIAN**

Figure 2.2 Styles of Greek Capitals
The Greeks decorated the capitals, or tops, of columns in these three styles to fit the different architectural "canons" (their word for precise mathematical systems of proportions) that they devised for designing buildings. The "pillow" atop Doric columns evolved into the Ionic style sporting "ears" (volutes). Corinthian capitals with their elaborately carved leaves were a later outgrowth of Ionic. These styles were widely imitated in later times, as on many U.S. state capitols and the U.S. Supreme Court Building in Washington, D.C.

of the gods. The frieze, a continuous band of figures, was carved in relief around the top of the walls inside the porch that ran along all four sides of the building. This sort of decoration usually appeared only on Ionic-style buildings. Adding it to a Doric-style temple was a striking departure meant to attract attention. The Parthenon's frieze portrayed Athenian men, women, and children in a parade in the presence of the gods. Depicting the procession in motion, like a filmstrip in stone, the frieze included youths riding spirited horses and women carrying sacred implements. As usual on Greek temples, brightly colored paint and shiny metal attachments enlivened the figures of people and animals.

The Parthenon frieze made a unique statement about how Athenians perceived their relationship to the gods. No other city-state had ever gone beyond the traditional function of temples—glorifying and honoring the community's protector gods—by adorning a temple with representations of its citizens. A temple adorned with pictures of citizens being viewed by the gods amounted to a claim of special closeness between the city-state and the gods. This assertion reflected the Athenians' interpretation of their success in helping turn back the Persians, in achieving leadership of a powerful naval alliance, and in amassing wealth that made Athens richer than all its neighbors in mainland Greece. Their success, the Athenians believed, proved that the gods were on their side.

Like the Parthenon frieze, the changes that Golden Age artists made in freestanding sculpture broke with tradition. Archaic male statues had only one pose: arms pressed to their sides and left leg striding forward, imitating the unchanging posture of Egyptian statuary. This style gave them an appearance of stability; even a hard shove seemed unlikely to budge them. By the time of the Persian Wars, Greek sculptors began to express motion in their art. Male statues could have bent arms and the body's weight on either leg. Female statues, too, had more relaxed poses and clothing that hung in a way that hinted at the shape of the curves underneath. The faces of Golden Age sculptures were self-assuredly calm rather than smiling like Archaic Age figures. This spirited new style suggested the confident energy of the times but also hinted at the possibility of instability: Golden Age sculptors took more chances with the balance of their statues.

REVIEW   What factors prompted political change in fifth-century B.C.E. Athens?

Traditional Ways of Life and New Ideas in Athens's Golden Age

Traditional beliefs about the importance of religion in public and personal life remained strong in Golden Age Athens, as did traditional expectations about the lives of women, slaves, and resident foreigners. New ideas, however, attracted great attention in education, philosophy, history, and medicine. The appearance of teachers called **Sophists** and the ethical views of the philosopher Socrates created special controversy and tension. The most visible reflection of the tension was the growing popularity of state-funded drama, tragedies and comedies whose plots explored the problems that pride, lack of vision, and unanticipated bad luck could bring to human beings.

Traditional Public and Personal Religion

Since Greeks believed that their well-being depended on divine goodwill, religion played a central role in public life. Each city-state honored a particular god or goddess, such as Athena at Athens, as its protector and patron, while also worshipping many other deities. The community showed its religious devotion by sacrificing animals and holding festivals paid for with public funds. Individuals could find a personal relationship with the gods in the rituals of **hero cults** and **mystery cults**. The twelve most important gods were envisioned assembling for banquets atop Mount Olympus, the highest peak in mainland Greece. Zeus headed this immortal pantheon; joining him were Hera, his wife; Aphrodite, goddess of love; Apollo, sun god; Ares, war god; Artemis, moon goddess; Athena, goddess of wisdom and war; Demeter, goddess of agriculture and fertility; Dionysus, god of pleasure, wine, and disorder; Hephaestus, god of fire and technology; Hermes, messenger god; and Poseidon, sea god.

Like the peoples of the ancient Near East, the Greeks believed that humans must honor the gods to thank them for blessings received and to receive blessings in return. This idea of reciprocity between gods and humans underlay the Greeks' understanding of the nature of the gods. Deities did not love humans, though in some mythological stories they took earthly lovers and produced half-divine children. Rather, they helped humans who paid them honor and did not anger them. Gods offended by humans could punish them by sending calamities such as famine, earthquakes, epidemic diseases, or defeat in war. Greeks did not expect to achieve paradise at some future time when evil would finally be vanquished forever.

Sacrifice was the most important religious activity. As an Athenian official remarked, "Our ancestors handed down to us the most powerful and prosperous community in Greece by performing the prescribed sacrifices. It is therefore fitting for us to offer the same sacrifices they did, for the sake of the success that those rites have brought us." Each god's cult—the set of prayers and rituals for worshipping a particular divinity—had its own traditions. Sacrificing large animals such as cattle and sheep provided occasions for the community to assemble and reaffirm its ties to the divine world, and for individual worshippers to benefit from the community's relationship with the gods by sharing the roasted meat from the sacrifice. People who were not rich—the great majority of the population—particularly loved the feasting that followed a large-animal sacrifice because meat was too costly for them to buy regularly. Sacrifices could also be bloodless offerings—fruits, vegetables, and small cakes.

Public religious festivals brought the community together for worship and entertainment. Some religious occasions were for women only, such as the three-day festival for wives held to honor Demeter. Other celebrations and rituals were for everyone, featuring sacrifices and festivals with parades, plays, musical performances, and athletic competitions. Athens boasted of having the most festivals, with nearly half the days of the year featuring one. Its great festival in honor of Dionysus, the god of wine, sex, and ecstatic joy, attracted an international audience to see tragedies and comedies performed in an outdoor theater seating fifteen thousand. People all over the Greek world worshipped Dionysus for his power to bring happiness and also the knowledge of the harsh consequences of going too far in drinking and sexual activity.

Greek religion also encouraged personal devotion. Greeks believed that people received divine protection as a reward for appropriate action in worship, not just for belief. They had to perform sacrifices, pray and sing hymns praising the gods, and undergo ritual purification. Preserving these religious traditions mattered deeply to most people because they offered a safeguard against the precarious conditions of human life in a world in which early death from disease, accident, or war was commonplace. Families marked significant moments such as birth, marriage, and death with prayers, rituals, and sacrifices. They honored their ancestors with offerings made at their tombs, consulted seers about the meanings of dreams and omens, and sought out magicians for spells to improve their love lives or curses to harm their enemies.

Hero cults and mystery cults were especially important for personal religion. Hero cults were rituals performed at the tomb of an extraordinarily famous local man or woman. People believed that dead heroes could reveal the future through oracles, heal illnesses and injuries, and provide protection in battle. The only hero to whom cults were established all over the Greek world was the strongman Heracles (or Hercules, as his name was later spelled by the Romans). His superhuman feats gave him an appeal as a protector in many city-states.

Mystery cults had a special appeal because they offered the hope of protection from dangers in this life and of a better fate in the afterlife. The Athenian mystery cult of Demeter and her daughter Kore (also called Persephone), headquartered in the village of Eleusis, attracted men and women from all over the Mediterranean world. Its central rite was the Mysteries, a series of initiation ceremonies into the secret knowledge of the cult. The proof of how seriously people took these Mysteries is that no one ever revealed their secret throughout the thousand years during which the rites were celebrated.

Women, Slaves, and Metics in Traditional Society

Traditional expectations of behavior governed women's lives. Women were not confined to their homes, as scholars used to claim, but they were expected to avoid close contact with men who were not family members or good friends. In the home, women dressed and slept in rooms set aside for them that men could not enter without permission. The rooms opened onto a walled courtyard where women could walk in the open air, talk, supervise the family's slaves, manage the family's supply of food and other essentials, and interact with other members of the household and visitors, male and female. Here in her "territory," a woman would spin wool for clothing, converse with women friends, play with her children, and give her opinions on various matters to the men of the house whenever she felt like it. Rich women maintained pale complexions because they stayed out of the sun. This paleness was much admired as a sign of a life free of hard work outdoors, and women regularly used cosmetics made of powdered white lead to give themselves the desirable paleness. (People believed that this level of exposure was not dangerous; even today, no one knows precisely how much contact with lead is toxic.) Poor women had little time for socializing because they, like their husbands, sons, and brothers, had to leave their homes—usually crowded rental apartments—to work. They often set up small stalls to sell bread, vegetables, simple clothing, or trinkets.

Athenian life offered many occasions for women to go out: religious festivals, funerals, births at the houses of relatives and friends, and trips to workshops to buy shoes or other domestic articles. Sometimes her husband escorted her, but more often a woman was accompanied only by a slave and could act independently. Many upper-class women most likely viewed their limited contact with men outside the household as a badge of superior social status. In a gender-segregated society such as that of upper-class Athens, a woman's primary personal relationships were probably with her children and other women.

Men restricted women's freedom of movement partly to reduce uncertainty about the paternity of their children and to protect their daughters' virginity from seducers and rapists. Since citizenship guaranteed the city-state's political structure and a man's personal freedom, Greeks felt it crucial to ensure that a boy truly was his father's son and not the child of a foreigner or a slave. Women who bore legitimate children earned higher status and greater freedom in the family, as an Athenian man explained in this excerpt from a court case:

> When I decided to marry and had brought a wife home, at first my attitude towards her was this: I did not wish to annoy her, but neither was she to have too much of her own way. . . . I kept an eye on her as was proper. But later, after my child had been born, I came to trust her, and I handed all my possessions over to her, believing that this was the greatest possible proof of affection.

Citizen women, like men, could own property, including land (the most valued possession in Greek society), and they were supposed to preserve it to hand down to their children. A daughter's share in her father's estate usually came to her as her dowry (the money and property a woman brought to her marriage). Husband and wife co-owned the household's common property. The husband was legally responsible for preserving the dowry and using it for the support and comfort of his wife and children. At her death, her children inherited the dowry. In a divorce, the wife got her property back.

Athenian laws concerning heiresses reveal the society's goal of enabling males to establish and maintain households. If a father died leaving only a daughter, his

Vase Painting of a Woman Buying Shoes
Greek vases were frequently decorated with scenes from daily life instead of mythological stories.
Here, a woman is being fitted for a pair of custom-made shoes by a craftsman and his apprentice.
Her husband has accompanied her on the expedition and, to judge from his gesture, is participating in the discussion of the purchase. This vase was painted in so-called black-figure technique, in
which the figures are rendered as black outlines, with their details incised into a background of red
clay. Painters later reversed this technique on red-figure vases so that they could draw pictures with
greater precision and elegance of line. **For more help analyzing this image, see the visual activity for
this chapter in the Online Study Guide at** bedfordstmartins.com/huntconcise. (Henry Lillie Pierce Fund.
Photograph © 2011 Museum of Fine Arts, Boston [01.8035].)

property went to her, but she could not dispose of it as she pleased. Instead, the
law required her father's closest male relative—her official guardian after her father's
death—to marry her, with the aim of producing a son. This child inherited the
property when he reached adulthood. This law applied regardless of whether the
heiress was already married (without any sons) or whether the male relative already
had a wife. The heiress and the male relative were both supposed to divorce their
present spouses and marry each other to preserve the father's line and keep the
property in his family. Bearing male children brought special honor to a woman
because sons meant security for parents. Sons could appear in court in support of
their parents in lawsuits and protect them in the streets of Athens, which for most
of its history had no police force. By law, sons were required to support elderly
parents. So intense was the pressure to produce sons that stories of women who
smuggled in male babies born to slaves and passed them off as their own were
common. Such tales, whose truth is hard to gauge, were credible because husbands
customarily stayed away at childbirth.

Women remained barred from political participation, which meant that men might overlook women's contributions to the city-state. In his play *Medea* of 431 B.C.E., the Athenian dramatist Euripides had his heroine insist that women who bear children are owed at least as much respect as hoplites: "People say that we women lead a safe life at home, while men have to go to war. What fools they are! I would much rather fight in the army three times than give birth to a child even once." Medea's claim seems persuasive, given the high risks of childbirth under the medical conditions of antiquity. In any case, ancient sources confirm that many women remained engaged and interested in issues affecting the city-state as a whole. They often had strong opinions on politics and public policy, but they had to express their views privately to their husbands, children, and relatives.

A small number of Athenian women were able to ignore traditional restrictions on their public behavior because they gave up the usual expectations of marrying or were too rich to care what others thought. The most talked-about women of the former category were called companions. Often foreigners, they were physically attractive, witty in conversation, and educated to sing and play musical instruments. They often entertained at **symposia** (dinner parties for men only), and sometimes they sold sexual favors for a high price. Their independent lives set companions apart from citizen women, as did the freedom to control their own sexuality. Equally distinctive was their skill in conversing with men in public. Companions charmed men with their witty, joking conversation. Their characteristic skill at clever remarks and verbal jabs allowed companions a freedom of speech denied to "proper" women.

Some companions lived precarious lives subject to exploitation and even violence at the hands of their male customers, but the most skillful could attract lovers from the highest levels of society and live in luxury on their own. The most famous companion was Aspasia from Miletus, who became Pericles' lover and bore him a son. She dazzled Athens's upper-class males with her brilliant conversation and confidence. Ironically, Pericles' own law restricting citizenship to children of two Athenian parents meant that their own child was not a citizen.

Only the wealthiest citizen women could speak to men openly with the frankness of companions. One such was Elpinike, a member of a superrich Athenian family of great military distinction. She once publicly criticized Pericles for having boasted about the Athenian conquest of a rebellious ally. When some other Athenian women praised Pericles for his success, Elpinike sarcastically remarked so all could hear, "This really is wonderful, Pericles, . . . that you have caused the loss of many good citizens, not in battle against Phoenicians or Persians, like my brother Cimon, but in suppressing an allied city of fellow Greeks."

In contrast to citizen women, slaves and **metics** (immigrants who were granted permanent residency in Athens in exchange for paying taxes and serving in the military) were truly "outsiders" living inside city-state society. Individuals and the city-state alike owned slaves, who could be purchased from traders or bred in the household. Unwanted newborns abandoned by their parents (a practice

Vase Painting of a Symposium

Upper-class Greek men often spent their evenings at symposia—drinking parties that always included much conversation and usually featured music and entertainers. Wives were not included. The discussions could range widely, from literature to politics to philosophy. Here, a female musician, whose nudity shows she is a hired prostitute, entertains the guests, who recline on couches, as was customary. The man on the right is about to fling the dregs of his wine, playing a messy game called *kottabos*. (Reproduction by permission of the Syndics of the Fitzwilliam Museum, Cambridge. Master and Fellows of Corpus Christi College, Cambridge.)

called infant exposure) were often picked up by others and raised as slaves. Athens's commercial growth in this period increased the demand for slaves to provide manual labor. Slaves probably made up 100,000 or more of the city-state's estimated 250,000 residents in Pericles' time. (This population made Athens an extraordinarily large city-state.) Slaves worked in homes, on farms, in crafts shops, and, if they were truly unfortunate, in the cramped and dangerous silver mines, whose riches boosted Athens's prosperity. Unlike Sparta's helots, Athens's slaves never rebelled, probably because they originated from too many different places to be able to unite.

Golden Age Athens's wealth and cultural vitality attracted many metics, who worked in Athens as traders, crafts producers, entertainers, and laborers. By the start of the Peloponnesian War in 431 B.C.E., these immigrants made up perhaps half the free population. Metics had to pay for the privilege of working in Athens through a special foreigners' tax and military service. Citizens valued metics' contributions to the city's prosperity but only rarely offered them citizenship.

Metics sometimes found themselves forced into making a living outside the mainstream, especially as prostitutes. Men, unlike women, were not penalized for sexual activity outside marriage. "Certainly you don't think men beget children out of sexual desire?" wrote the upper-class author Xenophon. "The streets and the brothels are swarming with ways to take care of that." Men could have sex with female or male slaves, who could not refuse their masters, or they could have sex with various classes of prostitutes, depending on how much money they wanted to spend.

Traditional Education and the New Ideas of the Sophists

Tradition dictated the course of education in Golden Age Athens until the time of radical democracy in the mid-fifth century B.C.E., when the appearance of a new kind of teacher with disturbing ideas created high tensions. All education was private. Well-to-do families paid private tutors to teach their sons to read, write, and perhaps sing or play a musical instrument. They also hired trainers to instruct the boys in athletics. Physical fitness was considered vital for men because it was thought to be ugly and disgraceful to be out of shape, and because all male citizens and metics ages eighteen to sixty could be called up for military service. Men exercised daily in public, open-air facilities called gymnasia, paid for by wealthy families. The daughters of upper-class families usually learned to read, write, and do arithmetic; a woman with these skills would be better prepared to manage a household and help her future husband run their estate. Poorer girls and boys learned a trade and perhaps a bit of reading and arithmetic by assisting their parents in their daily work. If they were fortunate, they would become apprentices learning from skilled crafts producers. It is uncertain how many people could read and write; most people probably could not. The predominance of oral rather than written communication meant that people usually absorbed information by ear. Songs, speeches, narrated stories, and lively conversations were central to Greek life.

Young men from prosperous families traditionally acquired the skills to become successful participants in Athenian democracy by observing their fathers, uncles, and other older men as they debated in the Council of 500 and the assembly, served as public officials, and made speeches in court. In many cases, an older man would choose an adolescent male as his special favorite to educate. The younger man would learn about public life by spending his time in the company of the older man and his adult friends. During the day, the youth would observe his mentor talking politics in the agora, help him perform his duties in public office, and work out with him in a gymnasium. The evening would be spent at a symposium, where the entertainment ranged from serious political and philosophical discussion to riotous partying fueled by endless cups of wine.

This type of relationship could lead to sexual relations between the youth and the older male, who would normally be married. Although both male homosexuality between adults and female homosexuality in general were regarded as wrong throughout the Greek world, sexual relations between older mentors and younger favorites were considered acceptable in many, though not all, city-states. These differing attitudes about homosexual behavior reflected the complexity of Greek ideas of masculinity—of what made a man a man and what unmade him. For one thing, in Greek eyes a man had to be the one who took the lead in sex and never submitted to the control of another. In any case, a mentor was not supposed to exploit

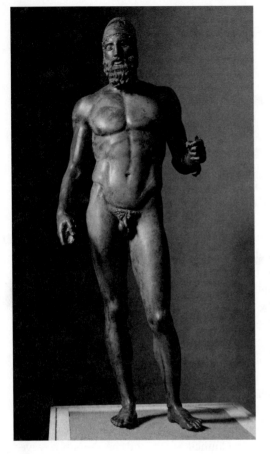

The Masculine Ideal
This bronze statue of a male warrior-athlete made in the mid-fifth century B.C.E. was found in an ancient shipwreck off the coast of southern Italy. The figure's relaxed pose displays the asymmetry—the head looking to one side, the arms in different positions, the torso tilted—that characterized the change in the style of art from the Archaic Age to the Classical Age. The body shows the physical ideal that Greek men worked to achieve through daily workouts. (Eric Lessing/Art Resource, NY.)

his younger partner just for sex or neglect his political education. Athenian society accepted the relationship as part of a complicated range of types of male bonding.

A new type of teachers called Sophists (wise men) came to Athens from elsewhere in Greece around the mid-fifth century B.C.E., at about the time that democracy became "radical." Sophists, who offered expensive instruction in public speaking, alarmed many people because what they taught seemed to threaten the stability of the democracy. Now, rich young men eager to become skilled political speechmakers no longer needed to learn from their family elders but could study with these foreign experts in the techniques of persuasion. People feared the techniques Sophists taught because charismatic public speakers could sway the assembly and the juries of radical democracy. Since codes of proper behavior, moral standards, and religious ideals were handed down in speech from generation to generation, a persuasive speaker could potentially wield as much power as an army of warriors. Sophists made people anxious especially because political leaders, such as Pericles, flocked to hear them and because the high tuition they charged restricted their knowledge to the wealthy.

The worry about Sophists was not just that their techniques taught speakers how to be dangerously persuasive; it was also that their ideas undermined traditional beliefs about religion and morality. One especially controversial Sophist was Protagoras, who arrived in Athens around 450 B.C.E. His ideas proved extremely upsetting, especially his agnosticism (the belief that human beings cannot know anything about the divine). When he said, "I cannot discover whether the gods exist, nor what their form is like, for there are many barriers to knowledge, [such as] the difficulty of the subject and the short span of human life," people worried that these ideas might provoke the gods' anger against Athens.

Equally controversial was Protagoras's denial of any absolute standard of truth: he asserted that every issue had two, irreconcilable sides. For example, he argued, if one person feeling a breeze thinks it warm, whereas another person thinks it cool, neither judgment can be absolutely correct because the wind simply is warm to one and cool to the other. Protagoras summed up his **subjectivism**—the belief that there is no absolute reality behind and independent of appearances—in the much-quoted opening of his work *Truth:* "Man is the measure of all things, of the things that are that they are, and of the things that are not that they are not." "Man" (*anthropos* in Greek, hence our word *anthropology*) in this passage refers to the individual human, male or female. Protagoras made the individual the sole judge of his or her own impressions.

This new way of thinking seemed to indicate that traditional human institutions and values were only matters of convention, custom, or law (*nomos*), not products of nature (*physis*), and that speakers should argue either side of a question with equal persuasiveness because truth was subjective. The combination of these two conclusions, many people worried, amounted to moral relativism, meaning that there were no absolute moral values. If this was true, then there could be no more shared public values. Protagoras tried to overcome such objections by insisting that his doctrines were not hostile to democracy, arguing that every person had an innate capability for "excellence" and that human survival depended on the rule of law based on a sense of justice. Members of the community, he explained, must be persuaded to obey the laws not because they are based on absolute truth, which does not exist, but because it was advantageous for people to live by them. A thief, for example, would have to be persuaded that the law forbidding theft was to his advantage because it protected his own property and the city-state in which he, like others, had to live in order to survive.

Other Sophists taught other disturbing ideas. One, for example, another friend of Pericles', offended believers in traditional religion by arguing that the sun was nothing more than a lump of flaming rock, not a god. Another Sophist invented an atomic theory of matter to explain how change was constant. Everything, he argued, consisted of tiny, invisible particles in eternal motion. Their random collisions caused them to combine and recombine in an infinite variety of forms. This physical explanation of the source of change, like the theory about the sun, implied that traditional religion, which explained events as the outcome of divine forces, was invalid. All of this made many people afraid that traditional ideas—and the success and stability that they seemed to have produced—were being destroyed.

Socrates and New Ideas on Ethics

The unique ideas of Socrates of Athens (469–399 B.C.E.), the most famous philosopher of the Golden Age, added to the tension that the appearance of the Sophists had provoked. Socrates was not a Sophist—he did not teach for money—but his views became well known because he devoted his life to spreading them through conversation. He rejected the notion that justice should be equated with the power to impose one's will on others. His passionate concern to discover valid guidelines for leading a just life and to prove that justice is better than injustice under all circumstances gave a new direction to Greek philosophy: an emphasis on ethics. Although other thinkers before him, especially poets and dramatists, had dealt with moral issues, Socrates was the first to make the ethics and morality of the individual a central concern for philosophy.

Socrates lived a life that attracted attention. He paid so little notice to his physical appearance and clothes that he seemed eccentric. Sporting a stomach, in his words, "somewhat too large to be convenient," he wore the same cheap cloak

Statuette of the Philosopher Socrates
The controversial Socrates, the most famous philosopher of Athens in the fifth century B.C.E., joked that he had a homely face and a bulging stomach. This small statue is an artist's impression of what Socrates looked like; we cannot be sure of the accuracy. Socrates was famous for his irony, and he may have purposely exaggerated his physical unattractiveness to show his disdain for ordinary standards of beauty, which valued a fit body, and his own emphasis on the quality of the soul as the true measure of a person's worth.
(© Copyright The Trustees of The British Museum.)

summer and winter and went barefoot in all weather. His tirelessness as a hoplite and his ability to outdrink anyone at a symposium amazed his companions. Unlike the Sophists, he lived in poverty and disdained material possessions, somehow managing to support a wife and several children. He may have inherited some money, but he certainly received gifts from wealthy admirers.

Socrates spent his time talking: conversing (and drinking) at symposia, strolling in the agora, or watching young men exercise in gymnasia. He wrote nothing; our knowledge of his ideas comes from others' writings, especially those of his pupil Plato (c. 428–348 B.C.E.). Plato portrays Socrates as a relentless questioner of his fellow citizens, foreign friends, and leading Sophists. Socrates' questions aimed at making his conversational partners examine the basic assumptions of their ways of life. Giving few answers, Socrates never directly instructed anyone; instead, he led them to draw conclusions in response to his probing questions, which picked apart their unexamined assumptions. Teaching this way is today called the **Socratic method**.

Socrates' indirect method of searching for the truth often made people unhappy because he forced them to conclude that they were ignorant of what they had assumed they knew very well. He argued that normal careers—pursuing success in politics or business or art—were excuses for avoiding genuine virtue. Socrates insisted that he was ignorant of the best definition of virtue, but that his wisdom consisted of knowing that he did not know. He vowed that he was trying to improve, not undermine, people's beliefs in morality, even though, as a friend put it, a conversation with Socrates made a man feel numb—just as if he had been stung by a stingray. Socrates especially wanted to use reasoning to discover universal standards justifying individual morality. He fiercely attacked the Sophists, who dismissed traditional morality as "chains that bind nature." This idea, he protested, equated human happiness with power and "getting more."

Socrates passionately believed that being just was more advantageous for people than being unjust and that morality was priceless because it guaranteed happiness. Essentially, he argued that just behavior, or virtue, was identical to knowledge, and that a true knowledge of justice would inevitably lead people to choose good over evil. They would therefore live truly happy lives, regardless of how rich or poor they were. Since Socrates believed that moral knowledge was all a person needed for the good life, he argued that no one knowingly behaved unjustly and that behaving justly was always in the individual's interest. It was simply ignorant to believe that the best life was the life of unlimited power to pursue whatever one desired. The most desirable human life was focused on virtue and guided by reason, not by dreams of personal gain.

Socrates' effect on many people was as disturbing as were the Sophists' doctrines questioning traditional morality. Socrates' attacks on his fellow citizens' ideas about the importance of wealth and public success made some men extremely upset because his ideas seemed to mean that people should not bother thinking about the community, only about their individual virtue. Unhappiest of all were the fathers whose sons, after listening to Socrates reduce someone to utter bewilderment, came home to try the same technique on their parents by arguing that the public accomplishments their family worked for were wrongheaded, even worthless. Men who experienced this reversal of the traditional educational hierarchy—fathers were supposed to educate sons—felt that Socrates was undermining the stability of society by making young men question Athenian traditions. The ancient sources fail to reveal what Athenian women thought of Socrates, or he of them. His thoughts about human capabilities and behavior could be applied to women as well as to men, and he probably believed that women and men both had the same basic capacity for justice.

People's worry that Socrates presented a danger to traditional society inspired the playwright Aristophanes to write his comedy *Clouds* (423 B.C.E.). He portrayed Socrates as a cynical Sophist operating a "thinking shop," who for a fee offered instruction in Protagoras-like techniques of making the weaker argument the stronger. When Socrates' curriculum transforms a youth into a public speaker arguing that a son has the right to beat his parents, his father burns down Socrates' school. None of these plot details were real; what was genuine was the fear that Socrates' uncompromising views on individual morality endangered the traditional practices of the community at a time when new ways of thought were angering many Athenians. Some people even believed that Socrates was an enemy of Athens's radical democracy, despite his serving heroically in the army, because some of the young men who associated with him were open supporters of oligarchy as the best form of government.

New Ideas in History and Medicine

One especially significant new idea that emerged in the Golden Age was to see the goal of history as the description and interpretation of the past based on a critical analysis of sources. Herodotus of Halicarnassus (c. 485–425 B.C.E.) and Thucydides of Athens (c. 455–399 B.C.E.) became Greece's most famous historians and established Western civilization's tradition of history writing. Herodotus wrote his groundbreaking work *Histories* (meaning "inquiries" in Greek), probably finishing it in the 420s B.C.E. It explained the Persian Wars as a clash between East and West; by Roman times he had been christened "the Father of History." Herodotus achieved an unprecedented depth in his book by giving it an investigative approach to evidence, a wide interest in human diversity, and a lively story. Herodotus searched for the origins of the Persian-Greek conflict both by delving deep into the past and by examining the cultural traditions of all the peoples involved. He recognized the relevance and the delight of studying other cultures as a component of historical investigation.

Thucydides wrote contemporary history influenced by what today is called realism in political science. His *History of the Peloponnesian War* (the generation-long war between Athens and Sparta that ended the Golden Age) made power politics, not divine intervention, the primary force in history. Deeply affected by the war's brutality, he used his personal experiences as a politician and military commander to make his history vivid and frank in describing human moral failings. His insistence that historians should spare no effort in seeking out the most reliable sources and evaluating their testimony with objectivity set a high standard for later writers.

Equally innovative and influential were the medical doctrines of Hippocrates of Cos, a fifth-century B.C.E. contemporary of Thucydides, who became Greece's most famous physician. He is remembered today in the oath bearing his name that doctors swear at the beginning of their professional careers. Hippocrates made great strides in putting medical diagnosis and treatment on a scientific basis. Earlier medicine had depended on magic and ritual. Hippocrates viewed the human body as an organism whose parts must be understood in relation to the whole. Hippocrates taught that the physician's most important duty was to base his knowledge on careful observation of patients and their response to remedies. Clinical experience, not theory, he insisted, was the best guide to effective treatments. Although various cults in Greek religion offered healing to worshippers, Hippocratic medical doctrine apparently made little or no mention of any role for the gods in illnesses and their treatments. Some attributed to him the view, profoundly influential in later times, that four humors (fluids) made up the human body: blood, phlegm, black bile, and yellow bile. This intellectual system corresponded to philosophers' division of the physical world into four parts: the elements earth, air, fire, and water. Health therefore depended on keeping the proper balance among them; being healthy was to be "in good humor."

Tragedy and Comedy as New Forms of Drama

The development of tragic drama was Golden Age Athens's most influential cultural innovation. By presenting shocking stories exploring tensions in the city-state, tragic plays inspired their large audiences to ponder the danger that arrogance, ignorance, and violence presented to Athens's democratic society. Following the tradition of Homer and Hesiod, Golden Age playwrights treated themes ranging from individual freedom and responsibility in the polis to the underlying nature of good and evil.

Tragedies were plays with plots presenting fierce conflicts among fiercely proud characters whose lives ended in disaster. These dramas were written in verse and used solemn language; they were often based on stories about the violent consequences of interactions between gods and humans told in myth. The plots often ended with a resolution to the trouble—but only after great suffering and death.

A successful tragedy presented a vivid spectacle. The actors wore rigid masks, dressed in striking costumes, and used broad gestures and booming voices to reach the upper tier of seats. A powerful voice was crucial to a tragic actor because words represented the heart of a tragedy, in which dialogue and long speeches were far more common than physical action. A chorus sang in unison between scenes of dialogue and performed intricate dance routines. Special effects were part of the spectacle. For example, a crane allowed actors playing the roles of gods to fly suddenly onto the stage.

The performance of Athenian tragedies took place over three days at an annual religious festival held during the daytime in a large outdoor theater sacred to Dionysus. In keeping with the competitive spirit characteristic of many events honoring the gods, Athens's government held a competition to choose three authors to present four plays each: three tragedies in a row (a trilogy), followed by a semicomic play. So important was a first-rate actor to a successful tragedy that performers were assigned by lottery to the playwrights to give all three an equal chance to have the finest cast. A great protagonist (the most important actor in a play) could become an international celebrity.

The prizes awarded to the authors, actors, and producers in the tragedy competition were modest, but the fame was enormous. As citizens, playwrights also fulfilled the normal military and political obligations of Athenian men. The best-known Athenian tragedians—Aeschylus (525–456 B.C.E.), Sophocles (c. 496–406 B.C.E.), and Euripides (c. 485–406 B.C.E.)—either served in the army or held public office at some point in their careers, or did both.

Theater of Dionysus at Athens
Tragedies and comedies produced at this theater in daytime festivals riveted the city's attention. The theater held about fifteen thousand spectators. In the Classical period, the seating, stage, and scenery were not yet permanent installations; the seating and stone stage building foundations are remnants of much later changes. What qualities do you think would have been most important in an actor under these conditions? (John Elk III/Bruce Coleman/Photoshot.)

Athenian tragedy was a public art form. Its performances were subsidized with public funds, and its plots explored the ethical problems of humans in conflict with the gods and with one another in a city-state. Even though most tragedies were based on stories that referred to a legendary time before city-states existed, such as tales of the Trojan War, the moral issues the plays explored always concerned the society and obligations of citizens in a city-state. To take only a few examples: In his trilogy *Oresteia* (458 B.C.E.), Aeschylus explains the importance of democratic Athens's court system by reworking the story of how the gods stopped the murderous violence in the family of Orestes, son of the Greek leader against Troy. The plays suggest that human beings have to learn by suffering but that the gods will provide justice in the long run. Sophocles' *Antigone* (441 B.C.E.) presents the pitiful story of the family of Oedipus of Thebes as a drama of harsh conflict between a courageous woman, Antigone, who insists on her family's moral obligation to bury its dead in obedience to divine command, and her uncle Creon, the city-state's stern male leader, who defends the need to preserve order and protect community values by prohibiting the burial of traitors. In a horrifying story of anger and suicide centered on one of the most famous heroines of Western literature, Sophocles deliberately exposes the right and wrong on each side of the conflict. His play offers no easy resolution to the possible conflict between divine and human laws. Euripides' *Medea* (431 B.C.E.) implies that the political order of a city-state depends on men treating their wives and families with honor and trust: when Medea's husband betrays her for a younger woman, she takes revenge by destroying their children and the community's political leadership with her magical powers.

Tragedies certainly appealed to audiences because they were entertainment, but they also had an educational function: to remind citizens that success created complex moral problems that could not be solved arrogantly or thoughtlessly. Spectators would have been aware that the central characters of the plays were figures who fell into ruin from positions of power and prestige like those enjoyed by the citizens of Athens at the head of its powerful "empire." The characters' reversals of fortune came about not because they were absolute villains but because, as humans, they could fail through a lethal combination of error, ignorance, and **hubris** (violent arrogance). Thoughtful spectators, we can imagine, thought about the warning implied by these plays that Athens's current power and prestige, managed as they were by humans, were hostage to the same forces that controlled the fates of the heroes and heroines of tragedy. The plays taught that Athenians needed to remember not to go too far in their pride in their city-state's political, social, and cultural accomplishments.

Golden Age Athens also developed comedy as another innovative form of public art. Written in verse and performed at religious festivals, comedies made direct comments about public policy, criticized current politicians and intellectuals by name, and devised plots and scenes of outrageous fantasy to make their points. An actor could fly to the gods on a giant beetle, for example, or the dancers in the chorus could dress as talking birds or dancing clouds.

Statuettes of Comic Actors
These little statues portray comic actors wearing the kinds of masks and costumes that became popular after Aristophanes and his contemporaries wrote their comedies in the fifth century B.C.E., and they give a vivid sense of the slapstick acting that characterized Greek comedy. In Aristophanes' day, the grotesque unreality of comic costumes would have been even more striking because attached below the waists of the male actors were large leather phalluses, which were props for all sorts of sex-related jokes. (Bildarchiv Preussischer Kulturbesitz/Art Resource, NY.)

The immediate goal of a comic playwright was to win the award for the festival's best comedy by creating beautiful poetry, raising laughs with constant jokes and puns, and mocking prominent men. Much of the humor concerned sex and bodily functions, described with explicit and imaginative profanity. Well-known male citizens were targeted for insults as cowardly or sexually effeminate. Women characters who were made fun of, however, seem to have been fictional.

Comedy's remarkable freedom of speech promoted frank, indeed brutal, commentary on current issues and personalities. Even during the Peloponnesian War, comic playwrights presented plays that criticized the city-state's policy, for example by recommending an immediate peace settlement. It was no accident that this energetic, critical dramatic form emerged in Athens at the same time as radical democracy, in the mid-fifth century B.C.E. The principle that all voters should have a stake in determining government policies evidently fueled a passion for using biting humor to keep the community's leaders from becoming arrogant and aloof. Athenian comedies often blamed particular political leaders for government policies that had been approved by the assembly, similar to the way ostracism singled out individuals for punishment. As the leading politician of radical democracy, Pericles came in for fierce criticism in comedy. Comic playwrights mocked his policies, his love life, and his looks ("Old Turnip Head" was a favorite insult).

The most remarkable of Aristophanes' comedies are those in which the main characters are powerful women who force the men of Athens to change their policy to preserve family life and the city-state. Most famous is *Lysistrata* (411 B.C.E.), named after the female lead character of the play. In it, the women of Athens and Sparta unite to force their husbands to end the Peloponnesian War. To make the men agree to a peace treaty, they first seize the acropolis, where Athens's financial reserves are kept, to prevent the men from spending them on the war. They then beat back an attack on their position by attacking the old men who have remained in Athens while the younger men are away from home fighting. When their husbands return from battle, the women refuse to have sex with them. This strike, which is portrayed in a series of overtly sexual episodes, finally coerces the men of Athens and Sparta to agree to a treaty.

Lysistrata presents women acting bravely and aggressively against men who seem bent on destroying traditional family life by staying away from home for long stretches while on military campaigns and ruining the city-state by prolonging a pointless war. Lysistrata insists that women have the intelligence and judgment to make political decisions: "I am a woman, and, yes, I have brains. And I'm not badly off for judgment. Nor has my education been bad, coming as it has from my listening often to the conversations of my father and the elders among the men." Her old-fashioned training and good sense allow her to see what needs to be done to protect the community. Like the heroines of tragedy, Lysistrata is a reactionary; she wants to put things back the way they were. To do that, however, she has to act like an impatient revolutionary. That irony well sums up the challenge that Golden Age Athens faced in trying to balance its faith in tradition with the energy of the period's innovation in so many areas.

> **REVIEW** How did new ideas threaten cherished traditions in the Golden Age?

The End of the Golden Age, 431–403 B.C.E.

A war between Athens and Sparta that lasted a generation (431–404 B.C.E.) ended the Athenian Golden Age. Today called the Peloponnesian War because it pitted Sparta's Peloponnesian League against Athens's Delian League, the war arose at least in part as a result of Pericles' policies. When in the 430s B.C.E. Sparta gave Athens an ultimatum—stop mistreating our allies—Pericles convinced the Athenian assembly to reject the demand as unfair because Sparta refused arbitration. In this way, the relations of Athens and Sparta with lesser city-states propelled the two powers over the brink into war.

The Peloponnesian War, 431–404 B.C.E.

The Peloponnesian War was so destructive because it lasted so many years; it was the longest war in Greek history. It took place above all because Spartan leaders feared that the Athenians would use their superior long-distance offensive weaponry—the

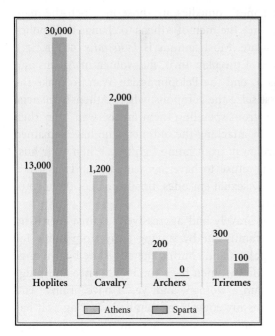

Taking Measure **Military Forces of Athens and Sparta at the Beginning of the Peloponnesian War**

These figures give estimates of the comparative strengths of the military forces of the Athenian side and the Spartan side when the Peloponnesian War broke out in 431 B.C.E. The numbers come from ancient historical sources—above all, the Athenian general and historian Thucydides, who fought in the war. The bar graphs reveal the different characteristics of the competing forces: Athens relied on its navy of triremes and its archers (the fifth-century B.C.E. equivalent of artillery and snipers). Sparta was preeminent in the forces needed for land battles—hoplites (heavily armed infantry) and cavalry (shock troops used to disrupt opposing infantry). These differences dictated the strategies and tactics of each side. Athens tried to launch surprise raids from the sea, and Sparta tried to force decisive confrontations on the battlefield.

naval forces of the Delian League—to destroy Spartan control over the Peloponnesian League (see "Taking Measure"). The duration of the struggle reflected the unpredictability of war and the consequences of the repeated refusal of the Athenian assembly to negotiate lasting peace terms when they had the chance.

Thucydides dramatically revealed the absolute refusal of the Athenians to find a compromise solution with these words of Pericles to the assembly:

> If we do go to war, never think that you went to war over a trivial affair. For you this trifling matter is the assurance and the proof of your determination. If you yield to their demands, they will immediately confront you with some larger demand, since they will think that you only gave way on the first point out of fear. But if you stand firm, you will show them that they have to deal with you as equals. . . . When our equals, without agreeing to arbitration of the matter under dispute, make claims on us as neighbors and state those claims as commands, it would be no better than slavery to give in to them, no matter how large or how small the claim may be.

Pericles convinced the Athenians to send their navy to raid enemy lands but to avoid all battles with the Spartan infantry, even when this meant abandoning the countryside and their rich properties there to be ravaged by enemy invasions. In the end, he predicted, the superior finances of Athens would enable it to win in a war of attrition. With his unyielding leadership, this strategy might have prevailed, but an unexpected disaster struck Athens soon after the start of the war.

An epidemic disease decimated the population for four years, killing thousands, including Pericles. The Athenians fought on, but they lost the clear vision for sacrificing their expectations of gain that Pericles' strategy had required; no one else was up to the task of leading Athens in the changed and unanticipated circumstances of a prolonged war. The generals after him followed increasingly risky plans, culminating in an overambitious campaign against Sparta's allies in Sicily, far to the west. Dazzling the assembly in 415 B.C.E. with the dream of conquering that rich island, Alcibiades, the most innovative and brashest commander of the war, persuaded the Athenians to launch their largest naval expedition ever by appealing to their expectations of victory and profit. His political rivals got him recalled from his command, however, and the invasion force suffered a catastrophic defeat in 413 B.C.E. (Map 2.3).

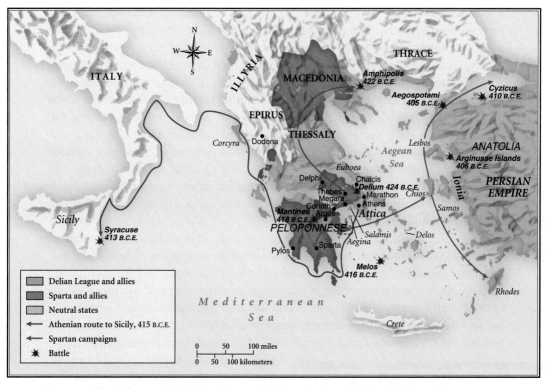

Map 2.3 The Peloponnesian War, 431–404 B.C.E.
During the first ten years of the war, most of the battles took place in mainland Greece. Sparta, whose armies usually avoided long-distance campaigns, shocked Athens with successful attacks against Athenian forces in northeastern Greece. In the war's next phase, Athens stunned the Greek world by launching a naval expedition against Spartan allies in Sicily. In the last ten years of the war, the action moved to the east, on and along the western coast of Anatolia and its islands. This was the western boundary of the Persian Empire, which helped the Spartans build a navy to defeat the Athenian fleet and win the war. **For more help analyzing this map, see the map activity for this chapter in the Online Study Guide at** bedfordstmartins.com/huntconcise.

The Spartans then launched the final phase of the war by establishing a permanent base of operations in the Athenian countryside for year-round raids. The agricultural economy was devastated, and revenues fell drastically when twenty thousand slave workers crippled production in Athens's publicly owned silver mines by deserting to the enemy. Distress over the war's losses led to a group of antidemocratic citizens briefly overturning the democracy in 411 B.C.E., but other citizens soon restored democratic government. Athens fought on. The end came when Persia sent money to help the Spartans finally build a strong navy. Aggressive Spartan action at sea forced Athens to surrender in 404 B.C.E. After twenty-seven years of near-continuous war, the Athenians were at the mercy of their enemies.

The Rule of the Thirty Tyrants, 404–403 B.C.E.

The aftermath of the war revealed that the accomplishments of Golden Age Athens had hidden a vicious disagreement over radical democracy. Following their victory, the Spartans went home after installing a regime of oligarchy-favoring Athenians to rule the city-state. Members of the social elite, they became known as the Thirty Tyrants because they murderously suppressed democratic opposition during an eight-month period of terror in 404–403 B.C.E. The speechwriter Lysias, for example, reported that the tyrants' thugs seized his brother for execution as a way of stealing the family's valuables, down to the gold earrings ripped from the ears of his brother's wife. Some of the oligarchs now terrorizing their neighbors were friends of Socrates, and people's belief that Socrates had taught these men to reject democracy created anger against him, even though he had refused to follow the orders of the tyrants to arrest a fellow citizen for execution. A resistance movement soon arose, violently expelled the Thirty Tyrants in 403 B.C.E. in a series of bloody street battles, and restored democracy.

This civil war made Athenians so angry at each other that continuing violence threatened to tear the community apart even after the restoration of democratic government. The assembly therefore proclaimed the first amnesty in Western history, a truce forbidding any official charges or revenge for crimes committed during the rule of the Thirty Tyrants. Athens's government was once again a functioning democracy, but its financial and military strength was shattered. Worse, its society harbored bitterness that no amnesty could fully dissolve. The end of the Golden Age left Athenians anxiously wondering how to remake their lives and restore the luster that their city-state's innovative accomplishments had produced in that wondrous period.

REVIEW What events and decisions contributed most to the outcome of the Peloponnesian War?

Conclusion

Two very long and very different wars framed the Greek Golden Age in the fifth century B.C.E. Twenty years of war against the Persians led to stunningly surprising Greek victories that produced significant long-term consequences: Sparta and

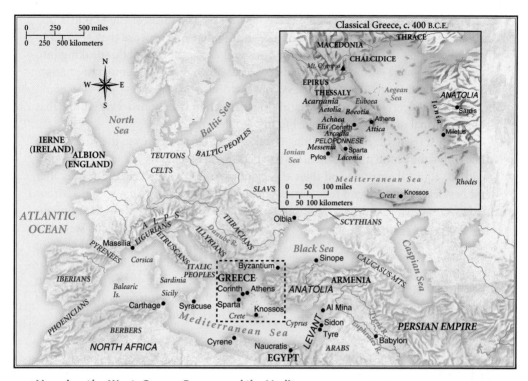

Mapping the West Greece, Europe, and the Mediterranean, c. 400 B.C.E.
No single power controlled the Mediterranean region at the end of the fifth century B.C.E. In the west, the
Phoenician city of Carthage and the Greek cities of Sicily and southern Italy were rivals for the riches to
be won by trade. In the east, the Spartans, made ambitious by their victory over Athens in the Peloponnesian War, tried to become an international power outside the mainland for the first time in their history by
sending campaigns into Anatolia and, they hoped, even farther east. This aggressive action aroused stiff
opposition from the Persians because it was a threat to their westernmost imperial provinces.

Athens, previously allies united to defend Greek freedom, became enemies; Athens
displaced Sparta as the leading city-state; and Athens, by dominating at sea militarily and commercially, reached a height of prosperity, international power, and proud
expectations unimaginable at the beginning of the century. The consequences of
this war against foreigners were beneficial for rich and poor alike because Athens
turned its naval empire into a profit-making enterprise when its allies lost the will
to defend themselves and the sea, swept clear of Persians, brought trade to Athens
from every corner of the Mediterranean. The recognition that the masses—meaning
the adult male citizens who rowed the imperial warships—gained through their war
service achieved political reality when elite leaders such as Pericles helped make
Athenian democracy "radical," motivated perhaps by a combination of genuine faith
in majority rule and the desire for the glory that popular leadership could bring.

The riches of Golden Age Athens, which financed glorious monuments proclaiming Athenian gratitude to the gods who favored them, attracted people as well

as commerce, and with new people came new ideas. The ideas of the Sophists disturbed the buoyant and confident mood of the Golden Age because they seemed to threaten to bring down the wrath of the gods and to transform public speaking into a weapon that men with bad intentions could use to seduce the democratic masses into corruption. Even Socrates' endless conversations about justice—and who could be against justice?—seemed infuriating because they questioned everything that seemed normal and pleasant about life in a golden age.

Nearly three decades of war pitting Greek against Greek destroyed the Golden Age at the end of the century. The Athenians had become so accustomed to success that they could not adjust their pride and their expectations to the changed circumstances after their best leader's death, and they overextended themselves in the war, with disastrous consequences. The outcome of the Peloponnesian War made the playwrights seem like prophets who had warned about hubris in their tragedies and comedies. It is no wonder that these works of literature remain the most thought-provoking achievements of the Greek Golden Age.

CHAPTER REVIEW QUESTIONS
1. What were the most significant differences between Greece in the Archaic Age and Greece in the Golden Age?
2. What did Greeks in the Golden Age believe it was worth spending public funds to pay for and why?

TIMELINE

- **404 B.C.E.** Athens surrenders to Sparta, ending the Peloponnesian War
- **450 B.C.E.** Sophist Protagoras comes to Athens
- **411 B.C.E.** Aristophanes presents the comedy *Lysistrata*
- **458 B.C.E.** Aeschylus presents the trilogy *Oresteia*
- **420S B.C.E.** Herodotus finishes the *Histories*
- **461–451 B.C.E.** Judicial, political, and legal reforms lead to radical democracy
- **469–399 B.C.E.** Life of Socrates

| 505 B.C.E. | 470 B.C.E. | 435 B.C.E. | 400 B.C.E. |

- **499–494 B.C.E.** Ionian Revolt against Persian control
- **490 B.C.E.** Battle of Marathon
- **480 B.C.E.** Battles of Thermopylae and Salamis
- **477 B.C.E.** Athens forms the Delian League
- **447 B.C.E.** Construction begins on the Parthenon in Athens
- **446–445 B.C.E.** Athens and Sparta sign a peace treaty meant to last thirty years
- **431 B.C.E.** Peloponnesian War between Athens and Sparta begins
- **404–403 B.C.E.** Thirty Tyrants suspend democracy at Athens but are soon overthrown in a civil war; Athenian democracy is restored but weakened economically

For practice quizzes and other study tools, see the Online Study Guide at bedfordstmartins.com/huntconcise.

For primary-source material from this period, see Chapter 3 of *Sources of THE MAKING OF THE WEST,* Third Edition.

Suggested References

A major challenge in studying the Greek Golden Age is to understand how the period's nearly constant wars affected every part of life.

Blundell, Sue. *Women in Ancient Greece.* 1995.

Camp, John M. *The Archaeology of Athens.* 2001.

*Dillon, John, and Tania Gergel. *The Greek Sophists.* 2003.

*Grene, David, and Richmond Lattimore, eds. *The Complete Greek Tragedies.*

*Herodotus. *The Histories.* Trans. Aubrey de Sélincourt. Revised by John Marincola. New ed. 1996.

Lincoln, Bruce. *Religion, Empire, and Torture: The Case of Achaemenian Persia.* 2007.

Parker, Robert. *Athenian Religion: A History.* 1996.

Parthenon: http://www.perseus.tufts.edu/cgi-bin/vor?x=16&y=13&lookup=parthenon

Patterson, Cynthia B. *The Family in Greek History.* 1998.

*Strassler, Robert B., ed. *The Landmark Thucydides. A Comprehensive Guide to the Peloponnesian War.* 1996.

Thorley, John. *Athenian Democracy.* 2004.

Wees, Han van, ed. *War and Violence in Ancient Greece.* 2000.

3

From the Classical to the Hellenistic World

ABOUT 255 B.C.E., AN EGYPTIAN CAMEL TRADER (his name is lost) working abroad in Syria paid a scribe to write a letter to his Greek employer, Zeno, back in Egypt, to complain about his mistreatment by his foreman, Krotos, also a Greek:

Solving the Mystery of Egyptian Writing

The three kinds of writing on this stone found by Napoleon's army in 1799 C.E. near Rosetta, in Egypt's Nile River delta, unlocked the thousand-year mystery of how to read ancient Egyptian hieroglyphs. The three bands of text repeat the same message (praise for King Ptolemy V of Egypt decreed by priests in 196 B.C.E.) in three different scripts: at the top, hieroglyphs (Egypt's oldest writing system, c. 3100–3000 B.C.E.), then demotic (a cursive form of Egyptian invented around 600 B.C.E.), and finally Greek. Scholars in the nineteenth century C.E. deciphered the hieroglyphs by comparing them to the Greek version, which they could read. Most Egyptians, like the mistreated camel trader stranded in Syria, could not read Greek, and most Greeks living in Egypt under the rule of the Ptolemaic kings could not read Egyptian, so bilingual texts such as the Rosetta stone were necessary to reach the widest possible audience in Hellenistic Egypt. *(Art Resource, NY.)*

You know that when you left me in Syria with Krotos I followed all your instructions concerning the camels and behaved blamelessly towards you. But Krotos has ignored your orders to pay me my salary; I've received nothing despite asking him for my money over and over. He just tells me to go away. I waited a long time for you to come, but when I no longer had enough to live on and couldn't get help anywhere, I had to run away to keep from starving to death. . . . I am desperate summer and winter. . . . They have treated me with contempt because I am not a Greek. I therefore beg you, please, command them to pay me my salary so that I won't go hungry just because I don't know how to speak Greek.

The camel trader's situation—needing to beg for help from a foreigner who held power in his homeland—reflected the changes that had taken place in the eastern Mediterranean world as it moved from the Classical Age (500–323 B.C.E.) to the Hellenistic Age (323–30 B.C.E.). These changes resulted from the large-scale immigration of Greeks into the Near East and the resulting interaction between local ways of life and the newcomers' ways of life. War started these changes. Following the Peloponnesian War (431–404 B.C.E.), the Greek city-states fought each other to exhaustion, allowing the kingdom of Macedonia to dominate them. When the Macedonian king Alexander the Great (356–323 B.C.E.) conquered the Persian Empire, he settled Greeks in colonies from Egypt to Afghanistan to help administer his conquests. The movements of people that Alexander caused led to the changes characterizing the Hellenistic Age.

Scholars use the term **Hellenistic** to designate the period of Greek and Near Eastern history from Alexander's death in 323 B.C.E. to the death of Cleopatra VII, the last Macedonian queen of Egypt, in 30 B.C.E. *Hellenistic* indicates the mixed nature of the political, social, and cultural changes that Alexander set in motion. These consequences of his conquests brought Greek and Near Eastern traditions together. In politics, kingdoms became the greatest powers in the Greek world, dominating the city-states. Hellenistic kings hired Greeks to fill royal offices, man their armies, and run businesses throughout their Near Eastern territories. Immigrant Greeks, such as Zeno in Egypt, formed a social elite.

A new, multicultural society emerged in the eastern Mediterranean region as people combined Greek and Near Eastern traditions. Locals married Greeks, shared their religious traditions with the newcomers, taught them their agricultural and scientific knowledge, and learned Greek to win administrative jobs. Social tension between immigrants and locals never disappeared, but the blending of traditions and royal financial support promoted innovations in art, science, and religion. Philosophers developed new ideas as guides to life in a world seemingly dominated by chance.

The complex interaction of peoples and ideas that occurred in the Hellenistic period greatly influenced the Romans and later Western civilization. Hellenistic religious developments, for example, provided the background for Christianity. Hellenistic cultural achievements remained influential long after the glories of Greece's Golden Age had faded away.

CHAPTER FOCUS QUESTION   What were the major political and cultural changes in the Hellenistic Age?

War and Disunity in Classical Greece, 400–350 B.C.E.

In the first half of the fourth century B.C.E., the Greek city-states continually fought one another to keep any one from becoming powerful enough to dominate. This international disunity exhausted the resources of even the richest city-states, especially because they were also internally fragmented. In Athens, the economy had gradually recovered after the Peloponnesian War, but greater prosperity did not reduce the hatred that democratic Athenians felt about the Thirty Tyrants' violent rule. This bitterness led to the execution of Socrates in 399 B.C.E. Outraged at Socrates' fate,

Plato and Aristotle created Greece's most famous philosophies about right and wrong and how human beings should live. The Spartans tried to turn their city-state into an international power, but their decision to collaborate with the Persian king stirred up fierce resistance. Ultimately, war and disunity made the Greeks too weak to prevent the expansion of their northern neighbor, the kingdom of Macedonia.

Postwar Athens and the Trial of Socrates

Athens in the early fourth century B.C.E. recovered some of its Golden Age prosperity but not its sense of confidence and unity. Economic conditions gradually improved as households and business owners revived trade and the production of goods in their homes and in small shops, such as metal foundries and pottery workshops. Businesses, usually family run, were small; the largest known was a shield-making company owning 120 slaves. The Peloponnesian War changed gender roles in the workforce because so many men who had been the family breadwinner died during the war. Without male providers, many war widows had to find work outside the home. It was in this postwar period that women and men began working together in commercial production for the first time, when weaving shops sprang up. Previously, only women had made cloth and had done so at home. Some women also carved out careers in the arts, especially painting and music.

Some families found ways to profit from women's skills. Socrates' friend Aristarchus, for example, became poverty-stricken supporting several widowed sisters, nieces, and female cousins. Socrates reminded his friend that his relatives knew how to make cloaks, shirts, capes, and smocks, "the work considered the best and most fitting for women." The women had been making clothing only for family members; Socrates suggested that they sell it for profit. The plan succeeded financially, but the women complained that Aristarchus was the only member of the household who ate without working. Socrates advised his friend to reply that the women should think of him as sheep viewed a guard dog—earning his food by keeping the wolves away.

Even in the improved postwar economy, most workers earned just enough to feed and clothe their families. They customarily ate two meals a day, a light lunch in midmorning and a heavier evening meal. Bread baked from barley provided the main part of their diet; only rich people could afford wheat bread. A family bought its bread from small bakery stands, often run by women, or made it at home. Most people ate greens, beans, onions, garlic, olives, fruit, and cheese with their bread; they had meat only at animal sacrifices paid for by the state. Everyone drank wine, diluted with water. Water was fetched from public fountains in jugs by women or slaves. All but the poorest families owned at least one or two slaves to do household chores and to look after the children.

The restored stability in the everyday lives of Athenians did not erase their memories of the murderous rule of the Thirty Tyrants and the civil war of 404–403 B.C.E. Socrates became the best-known victim of this hatred dividing Athenians when

Vase Painting of Women Fetching Water
This painting shows a scene from everyday Greek life: women filling water jugs at a covered public fountain to take back to their homes. Few Greek homes had running water, so it was the duty of freeborn and slave women in a household to gather water for drinking, cooking, washing, and cleaning. Prosperous cities built attractively decorated fountain houses, such as the one shown here, where a regular supply of fresh water was available from springs or was piped in through aqueducts. These fountains were popular spots for women's conversations outside the house. The women in this scene wear the long robes and hair coverings characteristic of the time. (William Francis Warden Fund. Photograph © 2011 Museum of Fine Arts, Boston [61.195].)

he was blamed for the violent crimes of his follower Critias, one of the tyrants. In fact, Socrates had put himself at risk by refusing to cooperate with the tyrants, but some prominent Athenians believed his philosophy had turned Critias into a traitor because Socrates questioned accepted ideas of what was proper behavior and was therefore believed to be hostile to democracy. Many Athenians apparently believed that Socrates' ideas that people should devote themselves to individual excellence and justice above any other concern meant that they should abandon their commitment to the city-state. Since the amnesty agreement blocked prosecution for offenses during the civil war, Socrates' opponents indicted him on a charge of impiety in 399 B.C.E. At his trial they accused him of not believing in the city-state's gods and of introducing new divinities, and also of turning young men away from Athenian moral traditions. When Socrates spoke in his own defense, he repeated his unyielding dedication to goading his fellow citizens into examining their unexamined assumptions about individual virtue. He vowed to remain their stinging gadfly. Socrates accepted his death sentence calmly because, as he put it, "nothing evil can happen to a good man, either in life or in death." He was executed in the customary way, with a poisonous drink concocted from powdered hemlock. Later sources report that many Athenians soon came to regret the execution of Socrates as a tragic mistake and a severe blow to their reputation as fair-minded citizens participating in a stable democracy.

The Philosophy of Plato and Aristotle

Tormented by anger and grief over Socrates' execution, his younger friend Plato (c. 429–348 B.C.E.) turned his back on marriage and a public career to become a philosopher. Plato felt driven to understand the nature of a world in which an evil fate could befall such a good man as Socrates. Plato's ideas on ethics and politics have remained central to philosophy and political science since his day, making him the most famous philosopher in Western civilization.

Plato established a philosophical "school," the Academy, in Athens around 386 B.C.E. that remained open for nine hundred years. The Academy was an informal association of educated people—mostly men but also including women—who studied philosophy, mathematics, and theoretical astronomy. Plato presented his ideas in written dialogues that read like plays instead of textbooks; he wanted them to make readers reflect thoughtfully on difficult philosophical questions. His views apparently changed over time—nowhere did he present a consistent set of doctrines.

Mosaic of Plato's Academy

This mosaic from the Roman period portrays philosophers (identified by their beards) at Plato's school in Athens holding discussions among themselves. Founded around 386 B.C.E., this school, called the Academy, became one of Greece's most famous and long-lasting organizations, attracting scholars and students until it closed around 530 C.E. The columns and tree express the Academy's harmonious blend of the natural and built environments, a setting meant to promote pleasant and productive discussions. (Erich Lessing/Art Resource, NY.)

Nevertheless, he always maintained one essential idea: moral virtues are universal and absolute, not relative.

To support this idea, Plato argued that virtues such as Goodness, Justice, Beauty, and Equality existed as realities he called Forms (or Ideas). He explained that the Forms are invisible, invariable, and eternal entities located in a higher realm beyond human existence. According to Plato, the Forms are the only true reality; what we experience through our senses in everyday life are only imperfect representations of these flawless realities, as if, he said, we were watching their shadows cast on the wall of a cave. His theory of Forms made **metaphysics**—the consideration of the ultimate nature of reality beyond the reach of the human senses—into a central issue for philosophers then and through the ages.

Plato's idea that humans possess immortal souls distinct from their bodies established the concept of **dualism**, a separation between spiritual and physical being. This notion influenced much of later philosophical and religious thought. Plato believed the proper goal for humans is to seek order and purity in their own souls by using reason to control their irrational desires, which are harmful. The desire to drink wine to excess, for example, is irrational because the drinker devalues the pain of the hangover that comes the next day. Finally, because the soul is immortal and the body is not, our present, impure existence is only one part of our true existence.

Plato presented the most famous version of his ideal society in his dialogue *The Republic*. This work, whose Greek title means "system of government," primarily concerns the nature of justice and the reasons people should be just. According to Plato, justice is impossible in a democracy and requires hierarchy. The trial of Socrates convinced Plato that most citizens are incapable of rising above ignorant self-interest. Plato ranked people in his ideal society by their ability to grasp the truth of the Forms. Women could rank as high as men because they possess the same virtues. To minimize distraction, the highest-ranking members of Plato's utopia are allowed to have neither private property nor individual families. These men and women are to live together in barracks, eat in mess halls, and exercise in the same gymnasia. They are to have sexual relations with various partners so that the best women can mate with the best men to produce the best children, who will be raised in a common environment by special caretakers. Those who achieve the highest level of knowledge in Plato's ideal society qualify to rule over it as philosopher-kings. Plato did not think such a society was truly possible, but he did believe that imagining it was important in teaching people to live justly. For this reason above all, he passionately believed the study of philosophy mattered to human life.

Plato was also influential because he trained an extremely famous pupil, Aristotle (384–322 B.C.E.). Aristotle created a practical philosophy for living a happy life and founded his own world-famous "school" in Athens in 335 B.C.E. There, he lectured with dazzling intelligence on nearly every branch of learning: biology, medicine, anatomy, psychology, meteorology, physics, chemistry, mathematics, music, metaphysics, rhetoric, political science, ethics, and literary criticism.

Aristotle's vast writings made him one of the most influential philosophers and scientists in Western civilization. His reputation rests on his development of rigorous systems of logical argument and his scientific investigation of the natural world. Creating a sophisticated system of logic, Aristotle established rules to tell the difference between a logically proven argument and a merely persuasive one. Furthermore, Aristotle insisted on explanations based on common sense rather than metaphysics. He denied the validity of Plato's theory of Forms, for example, on the grounds that the separate, unverifiable existence Plato asserted for them did not make sense. In scientific investigation, Aristotle believed that the best way to understand objects and beings was to observe them in their natural settings. The first scientist to try to collect all available information on animals, Aristotle recorded facts about more than five hundred different species, including insects. His recognition that whales and dolphins are mammals, which later writers on animals overlooked, was not rediscovered for another two thousand years.

Like Plato, Aristotle criticized democracy because it allowed uneducated instead of "better" people to control politics. Some of Aristotle's views justified inequalities characteristic of his time. He regarded slavery as natural, arguing that some people were by nature meant to be slaves because their souls lacked the rational part that should rule in a human. He also concluded, based on faulty notions of biology, that women were by nature inferior to men.

In ethics, Aristotle emphasized the need to develop habits of just behavior and not just good intentions. People should achieve self-control by training their minds to win out over instincts and passions. Self-control did not mean denying human desires and appetites; rather, it meant striking a balance between suppressing and heedlessly indulging physical yearnings, of finding "the mean." Aristotle claimed that the mind should rule in finding this balance because the intellect is the finest human quality and the mind is the true self—indeed, the godlike part of a person. Greek poets and dramatists had always emphasized the theme of moderation and humility as essential to human well-being, but Aristotle gave Western civilization the philosophical basis for achieving and valuing self-control in every individual.

The Fatal Weakening of Greece

The wars between city-states in the fifty years following the Peloponnesian War reduced Greece to a fatal state of weakness. In the 390s to 370s B.C.E., the Spartans did the most to provoke this fatal disunity by trying to conquer other city-states. Thebes, Athens, Corinth, and Argos responded by forming an anti-Spartan coalition because Spartan aggression threatened their interests at home and abroad. The Spartans counterbalanced the alliance by making a treaty with the Persian king. Abandoning their commitment to defend Greek freedom, the Spartans acknowledged the Persian ruler's right to control the Greek city-states of Anatolia—in return for permission to pursue their own power in Greece without Persian interference. This notorious treaty of 386 B.C.E., called the King's Peace, deprived the Anatolian Greeks of the freedom won in the Persian Wars. The Athenians rebuilt their military strength to combat Sparta. By 377 B.C.E., Athens had again become the leader of a naval alliance. This time, league members insisted that their rights be specified in writing to prevent any imperialistic Athenian behavior.

The Thebans became Greece's main land power in the 370s B.C.E. Attacking the Spartan homeland, they destroyed Sparta's power forever by freeing many helots. This Theban success so frightened the Athenians that they made a temporary alliance with the Spartans. Their combined armies confronted the Thebans in the battle of Mantinea in the Peloponnese in 362 B.C.E. Thebes won the battle but lost the war when its best general was killed and no capable replacement could be found.

The battle of Mantinea left the Greek city-states in powerless disunity. As the contemporary historian Xenophon said, "Everyone had supposed that the winners of this battle would be Greece's rulers and its losers their subjects; but there was only more confusion and disturbance in Greece after it than before." By the 350s B.C.E., then, the Greek city-states' struggle for domination over one another had left them in an impotent stalemate. This weakness opened the way for the rise of a new power—the kingdom of Macedonia, which threatened the Greeks' traditional independence.

REVIEW   How did daily life, philosophy, and the political situation change in Greece in the half-century following the Peloponnesian War (400–350 B.C.E.)?

Macedonia and Alexander the Great, 359–323 B.C.E.

Philip II, king of Macedonia (r. 359–336 B.C.E.), and his son and successor, Alexander the Great (r. 336–323 B.C.E.), took advantage of the Greek city-states' disunity to seize the leadership of Greece. That they transformed their previously weak kingdom into a superpower and conquered the Persian Empire ranks as one of the greatest achievements of leadership in ancient history. Their conquests marked the end of the Classical Age and propelled the cultural interactions of the Hellenistic Age.

Philip II and the Rise of Macedonian Power

The Macedonians' power sprang from the characteristics of their society and their ethnic pride. The Macedonian people demanded the freedom to tell their monarchs what needed to be changed, and a king could govern effectively only as long as he maintained the support of the other Macedonian men heading powerful families, who were the king's social equals and controlled large bands of followers. Fighting, hunting, and heavy drinking were these men's favorite pastimes. The king was expected to excel in these activities to prove he was capable of ruling. Queens and royal mothers received respect in this male-dominated society because they came from powerful families.

Macedonians thought of themselves as Greek by blood and took pride in their identity. They had their own language, but wealthy Macedonians learned to

Dancing Figures on a Gilded Bowl from Macedonia
Archaeologists discovered this large metal wine bowl, made of bronze plated with gold, in Macedonia. Its artistic style dates it to the 330s B.C.E. Wealthy Macedonian men at a Greek-style drinking party (symposium) used these expensive bowls to dilute wine so they could drink large amounts of it. The excited conditions of the two figures—a satyr (a half-man, half-horse creature) and a female worshipper of Dionysus, the god of wine and pleasure—express the ecstasy that the partygoers hoped to achieve. Since erect penises were shown frequently in Greek and Macedonian art associated with Dionysus, representing hopes for fertility and sexual pleasure, pictures like this were not regarded as obscene. (Thessaloniki, Archaeological Museum, © Archaeological Receipts Fund.)

speak Greek. Macedonians looked down on Greeks as being soft, but Greeks in turn scorned them as unsophisticated. The famed Athenian orator Demosthenes (384–322 B.C.E.) blasted Philip II as "not only not a Greek nor related to the Greeks, but not even a barbarian from a land worth mentioning; no, he's a plague from Macedonia, a region where you can't even buy a slave worth his salt."

Rivalry between kings and important families in Macedonia made it impossible to field a strong army until Philip became king. Indeed, kings so feared violence from their rivals that they stationed bodyguards outside the royal bedroom.

A military disaster brought Philip to the throne. The Illyrians, hostile neighbors to the north, had slaughtered the previous Macedonian king and four thousand troops. Philip restored the army's confidence by teaching the infantry an unstoppable new tactic. Arming his infantry with thrusting spears sixteen feet long and arranging them in a precisely aligned block formation (phalanx), he created dense rectangles of soldiers bristling with outstretched spears like a lethal porcupine. Using cavalry to disrupt the enemy's battle line and protect his own infantry's flanks, Philip smashed the Illyrians with his revived army.

Philip used diplomacy, bribery, and military action to turn Macedonia into an international power. A Greek contemporary said Philip "was never satisfied, extravagant—he did everything in a hurry . . . he never spared the time to reckon up his income and expenses." Philip found in Greek history the justification for making himself the leader of Greece: attack Persia to take revenge for the Persian Wars. Demosthenes complained that Greeks who did not resist the Macedonian king's plans were acting "as if Philip were a hailstorm, praying that he would not come their way, but not trying to do anything to head him off." Finally, Athens, Thebes, and some allies tried to block Philip, but in 338 B.C.E. the king and his Greek allies trounced the alliance's forces at the battle of Chaeronea in Boeotia. The defeated city-states were supposed to retain their internal freedom while becoming members of a military league under Philip's leadership. The course of later events showed the battle of Chaeronea to be a turning point in Greek history; although Philip promised the league city-states freedom from interference in their internal affairs, they had to yield to him their power to decide foreign policy. As it turned out, Greeks would never again regain the freedom to make such decisions on their own without some outside ruler looking over their shoulder.

Expansion of Macedonia under Philip II, r. 359–336 B.C.E.

The Conquests of Alexander the Great, 336–323 B.C.E.

Alexander III became king in 336 B.C.E. at age twenty, when an angry subordinate assassinated Philip II. Unconfirmed rumors speculated that Alexander's mother had arranged the murder. Alexander immediately killed potential rivals for the kingship and then quickly defeated Macedonia's enemies to the west and north. Next he forced the Greek city-states that had defected from the Macedonian-led league after Philip's death to rejoin. To demonstrate the price of disloyalty, in 335 B.C.E. he destroyed Thebes for rebelling.

In 334 B.C.E. Alexander launched the most astonishing military campaign in ancient history by leading a Macedonian and Greek army against the Persian

Empire to fulfill his father's dream of avenging Greece. Alexander's astounding success in conquering everything from Turkey to Egypt to Uzbekistan while still in his twenties earned him the title "the Great" in later ages and inspired countless legends. His greatness as a leader came from his ability to inspire his men to follow him into unknown lands, his genius in inventing solutions to difficult challenges on the battlefield, and his unlimited bravery. Alexander regularly rode his warhorse into the heart of the enemy's front line, sharing the danger of the common soldier. No one could miss him in his plumed helmet, vividly colored cloak, and armor polished to reflect the sun. He upset his principal adviser by giving away nearly all his property to create new landowners who would furnish troops. "What," the adviser asked, "do you have left for yourself?" "My hopes," Alexander replied. Those hopes came from his dream of becoming a warrior as splendid as Achilles in Homer's *Iliad;* he always slept with a copy of the epic and a dagger under his pillow.

Mosaic of Alexander the Great at the Battle of Issus
This large mosaic, which served as a floor in an upscale Roman house, was a copy of a famous earlier painting of the battle of Issus of 333 B.C.E. It shows Alexander the Great on his warhorse (at left) confronting the Persian king Darius in his chariot. Darius reaches out in horrified compassion for his warriors, who are sacrificing themselves to protect him. The original artist was an extremely skilled painter. Notice the dramatic foreshortening of the horse directly in front of Darius and the startling effect of the face of the dying warrior reflected in the polished shield just to the right of the horse. Alexander usually wore a helmet; why do you think the artist portrayed him bareheaded? (Erich Lessing/ Art Resource, NY.)

Alexander displayed his heroic ambitions as his army advanced eastward through Persian territory (Map 3.1). In Anatolia, he visited Gordion, where an oracle had promised the lordship of Asia to whoever could untie a seemingly impenetrable knot of rope tying the yoke of an ancient chariot preserved in the city. The young king, so the story goes, cut the Gordian knot with his sword. When Alexander defeated the Persian king at the Battle of Issus in 333 B.C.E. and forced him to flee, leaving behind his wives and daughters, the Macedonian king treated the captured women with honor. Alexander's polite behavior toward the Persian royal women, showing that he wanted to behave like a noble ruler, won him respect from the peoples of the Persian Empire.

Alexander was a brilliant innovator in warfare. When Tyre, a fortified city on an island off the coast of the Levant, refused to surrender in 332 B.C.E., he built a massive stone pier as a platform for armored battering rams and catapults flinging boulders to breach the walls of the city. The capture of Tyre demonstrated to walled

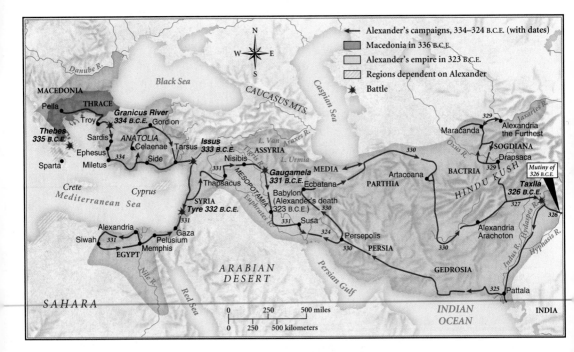

Map 3.1 Conquests of Alexander the Great, r. 336–323 B.C.E.

The huge extent of Alexander's military campaigns in Asia made him a legend. From the time he led his army out of Macedonia and Greece in 334 B.C.E. until his death in Babylon in 323 B.C.E., he never stopped fighting. His careful intelligence gathering, combined with his charismatic and brilliant generalship, produced an unbroken string of victories. His skillful choice of regional administrators, his founding of garrison cities and colonies, and his preservation of local governing structures kept his conquests stable after he moved on. **For more help analyzing this map, see the map activity for this chapter in the Online Study Guide at** bedfordstmartins.com/huntconcise.

city-states that they could no longer hold out indefinitely against a siege and should simply surrender to Alexander immediately.

Alexander had a clear strategy for ruling a vast empire: establish colonies of Greeks and Macedonians in conquered territory but keep each area's traditional administrative system. The first new colony he established, in 331 B.C.E., was a city in Egypt on the Mediterranean coast to the west of the Nile River. He named it Alexandria, after himself. In Persia, he proclaimed himself king of Asia but left the existing Persian administrative system in place, even retaining some high-ranking Persian officials. That a Macedonian was now king of Persia hardly changed the lives of the local populations. They continued to send the same taxes to a still remote master, whom they rarely if ever saw.

Alexander's goals seem to have included becoming a legend by marching to the ends of the world. He led his forces northeast into lands previously unknown to Greeks (today Afghanistan and Uzbekistan) and even founded a city named Alexandria the Furthest to show that he had penetrated deeper into this region than any Persian king. When it proved impossible to capture the fast-moving locals, however, Alexander settled for an alliance sealed by his marriage to the local princess Roxane. He then headed east into India. Seventy days of marching through monsoon rains extinguished his soldiers' passion for conquest. In the spring of 326 B.C.E., they mutinied in western India and forced Alexander to turn around. A difficult march brought them back to Persia by 324 B.C.E. Alexander immediately began planning an invasion of the Arabian peninsula and, after that, North Africa.

Alexander's conquests changed him. He broke Philip's promise to the Greek city-states to respect their internal freedom when he ordered them to give citizenship to the many war-created exiles whose status as wandering, stateless persons was creating unrest. Even more startling was his announcement that he wished to receive the honors due a god. At first bewildered by these instructions, most Greek city-states soon complied by sending honorary religious delegations to him. A Spartan expressed the only prudent position on Alexander's deification: "If Alexander wishes to be a god, then we'll agree that he be called a god." Personal rather than political motives best explain Alexander's wish. He almost certainly had come to believe he was actually the son of Zeus; after all, Greek mythology contained many stories of Zeus mating with human females and producing children. Alexander's feats exceeded the bounds of human possibility, demonstrating that he had achieved godlike powers and therefore must be a god himself. Alexander's plans for more conquest ended when he died unexpectedly of an illness, made worse by heavy drinking, in Babylon in 323 B.C.E. Roxane gave birth to a child a few months after Alexander's death, but Alexander had made no plans for who should succeed him. The story goes that when his commanders asked him on his deathbed to whom he bequeathed his kingdom, he replied, "To the most powerful."

Historians disagree about almost everything concerning Alexander's character and goals. At one extreme is the opinion that he was a bloodthirsty monster interested only in endless conquest, while at the other is the claim that he was a visionary aiming to create a multiethnic world open to all cultures. The ancient sources suggest that Alexander had interlinked goals: the conquest and rule of the known world and the exploration and possible colonization of new territory beyond. Conquest through military action was a time-honored pursuit for Macedonian leaders and suited his restless, ruthless, and incredibly energetic nature. He included non-Macedonians in his administration and army because he needed their skills. His explorations benefited numerous scientific fields, from geography to botany, because he took along experts to collect and catalog the new knowledge they acquired; he regularly sent reams of new scientific information to his old tutor Aristotle. The far-flung cities that Alexander founded served as outposts to warn him about local uprisings. They also created new opportunities for trade in valuable goods such as spices that were not produced in the Mediterranean region.

An Athenian summed up the stunned reaction of many people to Alexander's deeds: "What strange and unexpected event has not occurred in our time? The life we have lived is no ordinary human one, but we were born to be an object of wonder to later ages." This prediction was accurate: stories of fabulous deeds attributed to Alexander became popular folktales throughout the world, reaching even distant regions where Alexander had never set foot, such as southern Africa. His legend as a warrior-hero lasted into later ages because his achievements seemed incredible. The most significant effect of his career was to bring the peoples of Greece and the Near East into closer interaction than ever before.

REVIEW   How were Philip II and his son Alexander able to establish such a vast empire?

The Hellenistic Kingdoms, 323–30 B.C.E.

The political, economic, and cultural changes of the Hellenistic period arose from the interaction of Greek and Near Eastern civilizations. These changes created tension between conquerors and subjects and had greater effect in some areas than in others. Greek ideas and practices had their biggest impact on the urban populations of Egypt and southwestern Asia. The many people who farmed in the countryside had much less contact with Greek ways of life.

The greatest political change came with the rise of new kingdoms, which turned many formerly independent Greeks into royal subjects. Commanders from Alexander's army created these kingdoms by seizing portions of his empire for themselves after his death and declaring themselves kings. Twenty years of war followed, until they finally established their families as dynasties ruling newly created Hellenistic kingdoms.

The Structure of the Hellenistic Kingdoms

Three major Hellenistic kingdoms arose from the division of Alexander's empire after his death (Map 3.2): Antigonus (c. 382–301 B.C.E.) took over in Anatolia, the Near East, Macedonia, and Greece; Seleucus (c. 358–281 B.C.E.) reigned in Babylonia

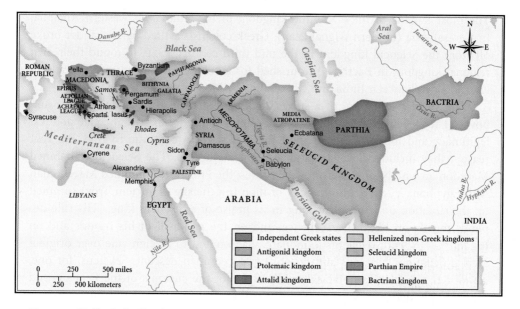

Map 3.2 Hellenistic Kingdoms, c. 240 B.C.E.
Monarchy became the dominant political system during the Hellenistic period in the areas of Alexander's former conquests. The Greek city-states kept their internal independence, but the kings controlled international policy. The biggest territorial changes to the three major kingdoms originally established by Alexander's successors were that by the mid-third century B.C.E., the Seleucids had given up their easternmost territories and the Attalid kingdom had carved out an independent local reign in western Anatolia.

and the East as far as India; and Ptolemy (c. 367–282 B.C.E.) controlled Egypt. These new rulers—historians call them the **successor kings** because they succeeded Alexander—had to create new kingdoms because they did not inherit their positions legitimately: they were self-declared monarchs with neither blood ties to any traditional royal family line nor any personal relationship to a particular territory. For this reason, historians characterize their rule as "personal monarchy."

By the middle of the third century B.C.E., these three kingdoms reached a balance of power. The Antigonid kingdom had been reduced to ruling Macedonia and controlling mainland Greece, whose city-states had to follow Antigonid foreign policy even though they retained certain internal freedoms. The Seleucid kingdom ruled in Syria and Mesopotamia but had lost Persia to the Parthians, a northern Iranian people, and the territory east of there to an Indian king. The Ptolemaic kingdom still ruled Egypt.

Conflicts frequently arose over contested border areas. The armies of the Ptolemaic and Seleucid kingdoms, for example, periodically battled over the Levant, just as the Egyptians and Hittites had done a thousand years earlier. The wars between the major kingdoms left openings for smaller, regional kingdoms to establish themselves.

The most famous of these was the kingdom of the Attalids in western Anatolia. In Central Asia (modern Afghanistan), Greek colonists settled by Alexander broke off from the Seleucid kingdom in the mid-third century B.C.E. to found their own regional kingdom in Bactria. It flourished for a century as a result of the trade in luxury goods between India and China and the Mediterranean world.

The success or failure of a successor king rested on his personal ability and power. The Hellenistic kings outside Macedonia realized they had to create political legitimacy and local support if their families were to continue to rule. For that reason, they included local traditions in their kingship. The Seleucids combined Macedonian with Near Eastern royal customs; the Ptolemies combined Macedonian with Egyptian. A letter from the city of Ilion (on the site of ancient Troy) summed up the situation of a successor king in its praise of a Seleucid king: "His rule depends mostly on his own excellence, and on the goodwill of his friends and on his forces." In truth, Hellenistic monarchy amounted to foreign rule over original local populations by kings and queens of Macedonian descent. Seleucus, for one, claimed this right as a universal truth: "It is not the customs of the Persians and other people that I impose upon you, but the law which is common to everyone, that what is decreed by the king is always just."

The survival of Hellenistic dynasties depended on their ability to create strong armies, effective administrations, and cooperative urban elites. Hellenistic armies and navies provided security against internal unrest as well as external enemies. To develop their forces, the Seleucid and Ptolemaic kings vigorously promoted immigration by Greeks and Macedonians, who received land grants in return for service as professional soldiers. When this source of manpower dried up, the kings had to employ more local men as troops. Military expenses eventually became a problem because the kings faced continual pressure to pay large numbers of mercenaries and because military technology had become so expensive. To compete effectively, a Hellenistic king had to build a fleet of warships propelled by hundreds of rowers and pay for giant artillery, such as catapults capable of flinging a projectile weighing 170 pounds a distance of nearly two hundred yards.

Hellenistic kings had to create large administrations to collect the revenues they needed. They recruited immigrant Greeks and Macedonians to be their top officials. Local men who wanted jobs as lower officials bettered their chances if they learned to read and write Greek in addition to their native language. This bilingualism qualified them to communicate official orders, especially tax laws, to farmers and crafts producers. Since Greeks and Macedonians generally saw themselves as too superior to mix with the locals, Greeks and non-Greeks tended to live in separate communities.

Agriculture and trade generated the wealth of the kingdoms, with cities as their economic and social hubs. Many Greeks and Macedonians lived in new cities founded by Alexander and his successors in Egypt and the Near East, but they also moved to old cities. Hellenistic kings promoted this urban emigration to build communities supportive of their rule. These rulers adorned their new cities with the traditional features of classical Greek city-states, such as gymnasia and theaters. Although these cities often had the political institutions of a city-state, such as councils and assemblies for citizen men, the requirement to follow royal policy limited their freedom. The kings treated the cities considerately because they needed the Greek and Macedonian urban elites to keep order and ensure a steady flow of tax revenues. Wealthy people had the crucial responsibility of collecting taxes from the surrounding countryside, as well as from their city, and sending the money on to the royal treasury. In turn, the kings honored and flattered members of the cities' social elites.

The kings' reliance on local elites led them to establish close relationships with well-to-do non-Greeks living in the old cities of Anatolia and the Near East, such as Sardis, Tyre, and Babylon. In addition, non-Greeks and non-Macedonians from eastern regions began moving westward to the new Hellenistic Greek cities in increasing numbers. Jews in particular moved from Palestine to Anatolia, Greece, and Egypt. The Jewish community eventually became an influential minority in Egyptian Alexandria, the most important Hellenistic city.

All the Hellenistic kingdoms eventually fell to the Romans. The Ptolemaic kingdom survived the longest. The end came when Queen

Hellenistic Architecture in the Jordanian Desert
This decorative front for a structure carved into a sheer rock cliff in probably the first century B.C.E. stands at the entrance to the ancient settlement of Petra, the capital of the Nabatean Arabs (in what is today Jordan). This desert people grew rich by controlling caravan trade from Asia across the deserts to the Mediterranean coast. In the Hellenistic spirit of cultural interaction, they took Greek architectural models and adapted them to express their own style. For example, this carved front has Greek triangular pediments but also includes a round gazebo to provide a break in the upper pediment. What do you think the visual effect of this innovation might have been as the sun moved through the day? (Z. Radovan, www.BibleLandPictures.com.)

Cleopatra VII, a descendant of Ptolemy and the last Macedonian to rule Egypt, chose the losing side in the Roman civil war between Mark Antony, her lover at the time, and the future emperor Augustus in the late first century B.C.E. In 30 B.C.E., an invading Roman army ended her reign and three centuries of Hellenistic monarchy.

Hierarchy in Hellenistic Society

Hierarchy became stronger in the Seleucid and Ptolemaic kingdoms. The royal family and the king's friends ranked highest. The Greek and Macedonian elites of the major cities ranked next. Just under them came the non-Greek wealthy elites of the cities, the leaders of large minority urban populations, and the traditional lords and princes of local groups who maintained their ancestral control over rural regions. Lowest of the free population were the masses of small merchants, artisans, and laborers. Slaves had no social status.

The growth of the kingdoms increased the demand for slave labor throughout the eastern Mediterranean. The centrally located island of Delos established a market where up to ten thousand slaves were bought and sold daily. The fortunate ones would become servants at court and live physically comfortable lives; the luckless ones would dig, and soon die, in the mines. Enslaved children often were taken far from home and put to work. A sales contract from 259 B.C.E. shows that Zeno, to whom the camel trader wrote, bought a girl about seven years old named Sphragis (Gemstone) to work in an Egyptian textile factory. This was not her first job. Originally from Sidon in the Levant, she had previously been the slave of a Greek mercenary soldier employed by Toubias, a Jewish cavalry commander in the Transjordan region.

The majority of the population continued to live in small villages. Most farmers were forced tenants on royal land who were not allowed to move away or stop working. Free peasants still worked their own small plots as well as the farms of wealthy landowners. Perhaps 80 percent of all adult men and women had to work the land to produce enough food to sustain the population. Men could also work as deckhands on the merchant ships that sailed the Mediterranean Sea and Indian Ocean. In the cities, the poor worked as small merchants, peddlers, and artisans.

The welfare of the masses depended on the generosity of the rich; without democracy, the poor had no political power to demand support. This strongly hierarchical arrangement reflected the top-down structure of Hellenistic society. Kings and queens intermittently helped the poor with distributions of food, and the wealthy increasingly followed their example. On the island of Samos, for example, rich citizens funded a foundation to distribute free grain. Many cities also began sponsoring doctors. Donor-sponsored schools sprang up in various cities, and sometimes girls as well as boys could attend.

Women's lives in the Hellenistic world depended on their social status. Hellenistic queens enjoyed enormous riches and high honor. Because the Ptolemaic

Egyptian-Style Statue of Queen Arsinoe II

Arsinoe II (c. 316–270 B.C.E.), daughter of King Ptolemy I and widow of the Macedonian successor king Lysimachus, married her brother Ptolemy II to unify the monarchy. Hailed as Philadelphoi (Brother-Loving), the couple set a precedent for brother-sister marriages in the Ptolemaic dynasty. One of the most remarkable women of the Hellenistic period, Arsinoe was the first Ptolemaic ruler whose image was placed in Egyptian temples as a "temple-sharing goddess." This eight-foot-tall, red granite statue portrays her in the traditional sculptural style of the pharaohs. (© Vatican Museums.)

royal family observed the Egyptian royal tradition of brother-sister marriage, daughters could rule alongside sons. For example, Arsinoe II (c. 316–270 B.C.E.), the daughter of Ptolemy I, first married the Macedonian successor king Lysimachus, who gave her four towns as her personal domain. After Lysimachus's death she married her brother Ptolemy II and exerted at least as much influence on Egyptian policy as he did. The virtues publicly praised in a queen reflected traditional Greek values for women. When the city of Hierapolis around 165 B.C.E. passed a decree honoring Queen Apollonis of the Attalid kingdom, for example, it praised her piety toward the gods, her reverence toward her parents, her distinguished conduct toward her husband, and her harmonious relations with her "beautiful children born in wedlock." Not all children were as fortunate as hers. Greeks continued to abandon infants they could not or would not raise—girls more often than boys, although Egyptians and Jews did not practice exposure (abandonment) of babies. Exposure differed from infanticide because the parents expected someone else to find the child and raise him or her, usually as a slave.

Some women achieved greater control over their own lives in the Hellenistic kingdoms. A woman of exceptional wealth could now enter public life by making donations or loans to her city and be rewarded with an official post in local government. In Egypt, women acquired greater say in the family because marriage contracts, the standard procedure, gradually evolved from an agreement between the groom and the bride's parents to one in which the bride made her own arrangements with the groom.

REVIEW What were the biggest challenges the Hellenistic kings faced in creating and running new states?

Hellenistic Literature, Art, Science, Philosophy, and Religion

Hellenistic literature, art, philosophy, science, and religion all reflected three principal characteristics of the age: the effects of royal wealth, the tendency of ordinary people to focus on private matters more than public life, and the increased interaction of diverse peoples. In keeping with the era's increasing hierarchy, the kings determined cultural developments by deciding which fields and which scholars and artists to support financially. The kings' status as sole rulers and the source of all law meant that authors and artists did not have freedom to criticize public policy and thus concentrated on individual emotions and aspects of private life. Nevertheless, royal support did produce an expansion and diversification of knowledge. Cultural interaction between Greek and Near Eastern traditions happened most prominently in language and religion. These developments greatly influenced the Romans; in this way, "captive Greece captured its fierce victor," the Roman poet Horace (65–8 B.C.E.) wrote, expressing the effect of Hellenistic culture on his own.

Patronage and Emotion in Literature and Art

The Hellenistic kings served as patrons financing writers and artists on a vast scale, competing with one another to lure the best ones to their capitals with magnificent salaries and benefits. The kings paid for many intellectual innovations but little technology, except for that which could be put to military use. The Ptolemies turned Alexandria into the Mediterranean's leading center of the arts. There they established the first scholarly research institute. Its massive library had the ambitious goal of trying to collect all the books (that is, manuscripts) in the world; it grew to hold half a million scrolls. Linked to it was a building in which the scholars dined together and produced encyclopedias of knowledge, such as *The Wonders of the World* and *On the Rivers of Europe* by Callimachus, a learned prose writer as well as a poet. The name of this building, the Museum (meaning "place of the Muses," the Greek goddesses of learning and the arts), is still used to designate institutions that preserve and promote knowledge. The output of the Alexandrian scholars was huge. The champion researcher was Didymus (c. 80–10 B.C.E.), nicknamed "Brass Guts" for having written nearly four thousand books; it is a sad commentary on the loss of ancient sources that not a single one has survived.

The writers and artists whom Hellenistic kings paid had to please their employers with their works. The poet Theocritus (c. 300–260 B.C.E.), for example, relocated from his home in Syracuse to the Ptolemaic court. In a poem praising his employer, the king, he spelled out their professional relationship: "The spokesmen of the Muses [that is, poets] celebrate King Ptolemy II in return for his benefactions." Theocritus and other poets succeeded by avoiding political subjects and stressing the division in society between the intellectual elite—to which the kings belonged—and the uneducated masses. Their poetry centered on individual emotions and broke new ground in demanding great intellectual effort, as well as emotional engagement, from the audience. Only people with a deep literary education could appreciate the allusions and complex references to mythology that these poets included in their elegant poems.

Theocritus was the first Greek poet to express the divide between town and countryside that was becoming a Hellenistic reality. The *Idylls,* his pastoral poems, emphasize the discontinuity between the elegant environment of the city and the simple life in the country, reflecting the fundamental social division of the Ptolemaic kingdom between the food consumers of the towns and the food producers of the countryside. He presented a city dweller's idealized dream that country life must be peaceful and stress-free; this fiction deeply influenced later literature.

Women poets made important contributions to literature in the Hellenistic period, apparently without any royal support. They excelled in writing **epigrams**, short poems originally meant for tombstones. Elegantly worded poems written by women from diverse regions of the Hellenistic world—Anyte of Tegea in the Peloponnese, Nossis of Locri in southern Italy, Moero of Byzantium—still survive. Women, from "companions" to respectable matrons, figured as frequent subjects in their work and expressed a wide variety of personal feelings, love above all. Nossis's poem on the power of "Eros" (Greek for "love"), for example, proclaimed, "Nothing is sweeter than Eros. All other delights are second to it—from my mouth I spit out even honey. And this Nossis says: whoever Aphrodite has not kissed knows not what sort of flowers are her roses." No Hellenistic literature presents the depth of human emotion better than the epigrams of the women poets.

Hellenistic drama mainly presented plays centered on individual emotions; writers no longer expressed open criticism of politics or contemporary leaders. Comic playwrights such as Menander (c. 342–289 B.C.E.), the most famous Hellenistic dramatist, composed plays with timeless plots concerning the trials and tribulations of fictional lovers. These comedies of manners, as they are called, proved enormously popular because, like modern situation comedies, they offered a humorous view of situations and feelings that occurred in daily life, cleverly made fun of social conditions, and usually had happy endings to resolve the troubles that energized the plot. Recent papyrus finds have allowed us to recover almost complete plays written by Menander and to appreciate his skill in depicting personality. No tragedies written in this period have survived intact, but we know that their plots could involve the interaction among peoples and cultures. Ezechiel, for example, a Jew living in Alexandria, wrote *Exodus,* a tragedy in Greek about Moses leading the Hebrews out of captivity in Egypt.

Hellenistic sculptors and painters also stressed human emotions. Classical-era artists had given their subjects' faces a serenity that represented an ideal rather than reality. Hellenistic artists portrayed individual emotions more naturally in a variety of types. In portrait sculpture, Lysippus's widely copied bust of Alexander the Great captured the young commander's passionate dreaminess. A sculpture by an unknown artist commemorated the third-century B.C.E. Attalid victory over the plundering Gauls (one of the Celtic peoples, called Galatians by the Greeks) by showing a defeated Gallic warrior stabbing himself after killing his wife to prevent her enslavement by the victors. A large-scale painting of Alexander battling the Persian

Dying Barbarians
Hellenistic artists excelled in portraying deeply emotional scenes such as this one of a Gallic warrior committing suicide after killing his wife to prevent their capture by the enemy after defeat in battle. The Gauls were one of the Celtic peoples, called Galatians by Greeks. Celtic women followed their men to the battlefield and willingly exposed themselves to the same dangers. The original statues (these are Roman imitations) were in bronze, forming part of a large sculptural group that Attalus I, king of Pergamum from 241 to 197 B.C.E., set up to commemorate his victory around 230 B.C.E. over the Gauls, who had moved into the region to conduct raids. Why do you think Attalus celebrated his victory by erecting a monument that portrayed the defeated enemy as brave and noble? **For more help analyzing this image, see the visual activity for this chapter in the Online Study Guide at** bedfordstmartins .com/huntconcise. (Erich Lessing/ Art Resource, NY.)

king Darius portrayed Alexander's intense concentration and Darius's horrified expression of concern for his dying men (see the illustration on page 95). The artist, probably either Philoxenus of Eretria or a Greek woman from Egypt named Helena (one of the first female artists known), used foreshortening and strong contrasts between shadows and highlights to increase the picture's emotional impact.

Hellenistic art differed from classical art in its social context. Works of classical art had been paid for by the city-states or by wealthy individuals to be displayed in public. Now sculptors and painters created their works primarily for royalty and the urban elites, who wanted to show they had artistic taste like the royal family.

A new diversity of subjects emerged in this Hellenistic art, showing humans in a wide variety of poses, mostly from private life. Hellenistic sculptors portrayed subjects never before shown: foreigners, drunkards, battered athletes, wrinkled old people. The female nude became a particular favorite. A statue of Aphrodite, which Praxiteles sculpted completely nude as an innovation in portraying this goddess, became so famous as a religious object and tourist attraction in the city of Cnidos that a foreign king offered to pay off the citizens' entire public debt if they would give him this work of art. They refused.

Innovation in Science

Scientific investigation of the physical world expanded so aggressively in the Hellenistic period that historians have dubbed it the Golden Age of ancient science. Various factors contributed to this flourishing of thought and discovery: Alexander's expedition had encouraged curiosity and increased knowledge about the extent and differing features of the world, royal wealth supported scientists financially, and the concentration of scientists in Alexandria paid by the Ptolemaic kings increased the exchange of ideas.

The greatest advances came in geometry and mathematics. Euclid, who taught in Alexandria around 300 B.C.E., made revolutionary progress in the analysis of two- and three-dimensional space. The usefulness of Euclidean geometry continues today. Archimedes of Syracuse (287–212 B.C.E.) was a mathematical genius who calculated the approximate value of pi and devised a way to manipulate very

Tower of the Winds
This forty-foot octagonal tower, built in Athens about 150 B.C.E., made use of scientific knowledge developed in Hellenistic Alexandria to tell time and predict the weather. Eight sundials, now missing, were carved on the wall to display the time year-round; a huge interior water clock showed hour, day, and phase of the moon; and a vane on the top showed wind direction. The carved figures represent the winds. Each figure's clothing reflects the typical weather coming from that direction, with the cold northern wind wearing boots and a heavy cloak, while the mild southern wind has bare feet and gauzy clothes. (The Art Archive/Dagli Orti.)

large numbers. He also invented hydrostatics (the science of the equilibrium of a fluid system) and mechanical devices, such as a screw for lifting water to a higher elevation. Archimedes' shout of delight—"I have found it" (*heureka* in Greek)—when he solved a problem while soaking in his bathtub lives on in the modern expression "Eureka!"

The sophistication of Hellenistic mathematics affected other fields that also required complex computations. About 280 B.C.E., Aristarchus of Samos became the first to propose the correct model of the solar system: the earth revolves around the sun, which is far larger and far more distant than it appears. Later astronomers rejected Aristarchus's heliocentric model in favor of the traditional geocentric one (with the earth at the center) because calculations based on the orbit he calculated for the earth failed to correspond to the observed positions of the planets. Aristarchus had made an unfortunate mistake: assuming a circular orbit instead of an elliptical one. Eratosthenes of Cyrene (c. 275–194 B.C.E.) pioneered mathematical geography. He calculated the circumference of the earth with astonishing accuracy by simultaneously measuring the length of the shadows of widely separated but identically tall structures.

The ideas and procedures of Hellenistic researchers gave Western scientific thought an important start toward the principle scientists now take for granted: the need to verify theory through observation and measurement in experiments. Hellenistic scientists maintained a spirit of discovery despite the difficulties imposed by technical limitations. Many experiments were not possible because no technology existed for the precise measurement of very short intervals of time. Measuring tiny quantities of matter was also next to impossible. The science of the age was as quantitative as it could be given these limitations. Ctesibius of Alexandria (b. c. 310 B.C.E.), a contemporary of Aristarchus's, invented the scientific field of pneumatics by creating machines operated by air pressure. He also built a working water pump, an organ powered by water, and the first accurate water clock. A later Alexandrian, Hero, continued the Hellenistic tradition of mechanical ingenuity by building a rotating sphere powered by steam. As in most of Hellenistic science, these inventions did not lead to uses in daily life. The scientists and their royal supporters were more interested in new theoretical discoveries than in practical results, and the metallurgical technology to produce the pipes, fittings, and screws needed to build powerful machines did not yet exist.

Military technology was the one area in which Hellenistic science produced practical inventions. The kings hired engineers to design powerful catapults and wheeled siege towers many stories high to batter down the defenses of walled cities. The most famous large-scale application of technology for nonmilitary purposes was the construction of a lighthouse three hundred feet tall (the Pharos) for the harbor at Alexandria. Using polished metal mirrors to reflect the light from a large bonfire, the lighthouse shone many miles out at sea. Grateful sailors regarded it as one of the wonders of the world.

Medicine also benefited from the Hellenistic desire for new knowledge. Increased contact between Greeks and people of the Near East made the medical knowledge of the ancient civilizations of Mesopotamia and Egypt better known in the West and promoted the study of human health and illness. Around 325 B.C.E., Praxagoras of Cos discovered the value of measuring the pulse in diagnosing illness. A bit later, Herophilus of Chalcedon (b. c. 300 B.C.E.), working in Alexandria, became the first scientist in the West to study anatomy by dissecting human cadavers and, it was rumored, the bodies of condemned criminals while they were still alive; he had this gruesome opportunity because the king authorized his research. Some of the anatomical terms Herophilus invented are still used. Other Hellenistic advances in understanding anatomy included the discovery of the nerves and nervous system.

As in science, however, Hellenistic medicine was limited by its inability to measure and observe things not visible to the naked eye. Unable to see what really occurred under the skin in living patients, for example, doctors thought many illnesses in women were caused by displacements of the womb, which they wrongly believed could move around in the body. These mistaken ideas could not be corrected because the technology to evaluate them did not yet exist.

New Personal Philosophies

New philosophies arose in the Hellenistic period asking the same question: what is the best way for humans to live? They recommended different paths to the same answer: individual humans must find personal serenity so that they feel free of the turbulence caused by forces beyond their control, especially chance. Greeks felt the need for a personal philosophy that would help them exist in a world in which they no longer had freedom because their fates ultimately rested in the hands of distant, unpredictable kings. It therefore seemed urgent, at least for those wealthy enough to spend time philosophizing, to look for personal, private solutions to the disturbing new conditions of life in the Hellenistic Age. More women than ever before joined in this philosophical quest.

Hellenistic philosophers concentrated not on metaphysics but on **materialism**, a doctrine explaining that only things made up of matter truly exist. It denied the concept of soul that Plato described and ignored any suggestion that nonmaterial phenomena could exist. Hellenistic philosophy was regularly divided into three related areas: *logic,* the process for discovering truth; *physics,* the fundamental truth about the nature of existence; and *ethics,* the way humans should achieve happiness and well-being as a consequence of logic and physics. The era's philosophical thought greatly influenced Roman thinkers and many important Western philosophers who followed them.

One of the two most significant new philosophical schools of thought was **Epicureanism**, named after its founder, Epicurus (341–271 B.C.E.). Epicurus admitted not only women but also slaves as regular members of his group. His lover, the "companion" Leontion, became well known for her treatise criticizing the views of Aristotle's most famous pupil, Theophrastus. Epicurus taught that people should above all be free of the fear of death because all matter consists of microscopic atoms in random movement and death is therefore nothing more than the painless separating of the body's atoms. Moreover, he insisted, human knowledge must be empirical—that is, derived from experience and perception. Despite what people say, he explained, the gods do not cause thunder, drought, and other natural events. The gods live far away in perfect peacefulness, paying no attention to human affairs. People, therefore, have no reason to fear the gods.

Epicurus believed people should pursue pleasure, but his notion of true pleasure had a special definition: the "absence of disturbance" from pain and everyday troubles, passions, and desires. A calm life spent with friends apart from the cares of the world could best provide this essential peace of mind. His teaching represented a serious challenge to the traditional ideal of Greek citizenship, which required men of means to participate in local politics and citizen women to engage in public religious cults.

The other important new Hellenistic philosophy, **Stoicism**, did not call for people to retire from public life. Its name derived from the Painted Stoa in Athens, where Stoic philosophers discussed their doctrines. Zeno (c. 333–262 B.C.E.), from Citium on Cyprus, founded Stoicism, but Chrysippus (c. 280–206 B.C.E.), from Cilicia in Anatolia, did the most to make it a complete guide to life. Stoics believed that life is fated but that people should still pursue virtue as their goal. Virtue, they said, consists of putting oneself in harmony with the divine, rational force of universal Nature by developing the virtues of good sense, justice, courage, and moderation. These doctrines applied to women as well as men. In fact, the Stoics advocated equal citizenship for women and doing away with marriage and families. Zeno even proposed unisex clothing as a way to obliterate unnecessary distinctions between women and men.

The belief that fate determines everything created the question of whether humans truly have free will. Employing some of the subtlest reasoning ever applied to this fundamental issue, Stoic philosophers concluded that purposeful human actions do have significance. Nature, itself good, does not prevent evil from occurring because virtue would otherwise have no meaning. What matters in life is the striving for good, not the result. A person should therefore take action against evil by, for example, participating in politics. To be a Stoic also meant to shun desire and anger while enduring pain and sorrow calmly, an attitude that yields the modern meaning of the word *stoic*. Through endurance and self-control, followers of Stoicism attained personal serenity. They did not fear death because they believed that people live over and over again infinitely, in a fashion identical to their present lives.

Numerous other philosophies emerged in the Hellenistic period to compete with Epicureanism and Stoicism. Some of them carried on the work of famous earlier thinkers such as Plato and Pythagoras. Still others struck out in new directions. Skeptics, for example, aimed at the same state of personal serenity as did Epicureans and Stoics, but from a completely different assumption about reality. Their ideas were influenced by the ascetic wise men (magi) encountered on Alexander the Great's expedition to India. Skeptics believed that secure knowledge about anything is impossible because the human senses yield contradictory information about the world. All people can do, they insisted, is depend on appearances while withholding judgment about their reality, hence our term *skeptical*.

The philosophers called Cynics boastfully rejected every convention of ordinary life, especially wealth and material comfort. They believed that humans should aim for complete self-sufficiency. Whatever is natural is good, they said, and can be done without shame before anyone. According to this idea, public defecation and fornication were acceptable, and women and men alike were free to have sex however and whenever they pleased. Above all, Cynics rejected traditional human behavior as ridiculous. The most famous early Cynic, Diogenes (d. 323 B.C.E.), from Sinope on the Black Sea, had a reputation for wearing borrowed clothes and sleeping in a giant storage jar. Almost as notorious was Hipparchia, a Cynic of the late fourth century B.C.E. She once bested an obnoxious philosophical opponent named Theodorus the Atheist with the following argument: "That which would not be considered wrong if done by Theodorus would also not be considered wrong if done by Hipparchia. Now if Theodorus strikes himself, he does no wrong. Therefore, if Hipparchia strikes Theodorus, she does no wrong." The name Cynic, which literally means "like a dog," reflects the ancient evaluation of this unconventional way of life. Our word *cynical* recalls the Cynics' biting criticism of what others regarded as normal.

Hellenistic philosophy reached a wider audience than ever before. Although the working poor had neither the leisure nor the money to attend philosophers' lectures, affluent members of society studied philosophy in growing numbers. Greek settlers took their interest in philosophy with them, even to the most remote Hellenistic cities. Archaeologists excavating a Hellenistic city located thousands of miles from Greece on the Oxus River in Afghanistan, for example, turned up a Greek philosophical text.

Hellenistic Religions

Religious ideas changed in the Hellenistic Age to reflect people's desire for a more personal experience. Sharing these new ideas became easier because a simplified version of Greek called **Koine** (meaning "shared" or "common") had become the international language of the eastern Mediterranean region; this was why the Egyptian camel trader stranded in Syria had to communicate in Greek. The most striking evidence of this development comes from Afghanistan. There, King Ashoka (r. c. 268–232 B.C.E.), who ruled most of the Indian subcontinent, used Greek as one of the languages in his public inscriptions introducing his subjects to Buddhist traditions of self-control, such as not eating meat. Local languages did not disappear in the Hellenistic kingdoms, however. In one region of Anatolia, people spoke twenty-two different languages.

The diversity of Hellenistic religions reflected the effects of cultural interaction between Greeks and local peoples in the Near East. The traditional cults of Greek religion remained popular and even spread farther, but new cults also arose in response to changing political and social conditions. As always in polytheistic religions, people could worship in both old and new cults. Those that had previously had only local significance, such as that of the Greek healing god Asclepius or the mystery cult of the

Egyptian goddess Isis, grew prominent all over the Hellenistic world. In many cases, Greek cults and local cults from the eastern Mediterranean influenced each other. Their beliefs meshed well because these cults shared many assumptions about how to remedy the troubles of human life. In other instances, local cults and Greek cults existed side by side, with some overlap. The inhabitants of villages in the Fayum district of Egypt, for example, continued worshipping their traditional crocodile god and mummifying their dead according to the old ways but also worshipped Greek deities.

New cults picked up a prominent theme of Hellenistic thought: anxiety about the relationship between individuals and the unpredictable power of chance (or luck). Although Greek religion had always been concerned with the unpredictability of life, the chaotic course of Greek history since the Peloponnesian War had made human existence seem more uncertain than ever. Since advances in astronomy had revealed the mathematical precision of the heavens, religion now had to address the seeming disconnect between that celestial uniformity and the shapeless chaos of life on earth. One increasingly popular approach to bridging that gap was to rely on astrology for guidance derived from the movement of the stars and planets, thought of as divinities. Another very common choice was to worship Tychê (Chance) as a god in the hope of securing good luck in life.

The most revolutionary approach in seeking protection from the unpredictable tricks of Tychê (Chance) was to pray for salvation from a king or queen regarded as a god, worshipped in what are known as **ruler cults**. Various populations established these cults to honor royal benefactors. The Athenians, for example, deified the Macedonians Antigonus and his son Demetrius as savior gods in 307 B.C.E., when these commanders liberated the city and bestowed magnificent gifts on it. Like most ruler cults, this one expressed both spontaneous gratitude and a desire to flatter the rulers in the hope of obtaining additional favors. Many cities in the Ptolemaic and Seleucid kingdoms created ruler cults for their kings and queens. An inscription put up by Egyptian priests in 238 B.C.E. describes the qualities appropriate to a divine king and queen:

> King Ptolemy III and Queen Berenice, his sister and wife, the Benefactor Gods, . . . have provided good government . . . and [after a drought] sacrificed a large amount of their revenues for the salvation of the population, and by importing grain . . . they saved the inhabitants of Egypt.

As these words make clear, the Hellenistic rulers' tremendous power and wealth gave them the status of gods among the ordinary people who depended on their generosity and protection in times of danger. The idea that a human being could be a god, present on earth to be a "savior" delivering people from evils, was firmly established and would prove influential later in Roman imperial religion and Christianity.

Healing divinities offered another form of protection to anxious individuals. People's faith in divine healing gave them hope that they could overcome the

Underground Labyrinth for Healing

This underground stone labyrinth formed part of the enormous healing sanctuary of the god Asclepius at Epidaurus in Greece. Patients traveled to the site from all over the Mediterranean world. They climbed down into the labyrinth, which was covered and dark, as part of their treatment, which in-volved reaching a trance state to receive dreams that provided instructions for their healing and, sometimes, miraculous surgery. (The Art Archive/Dagli Orti.)

constant, unpredictable danger from disease. The cult of the god Asclepius, who offered cures for illness and injury at his many shrines, spread widely during the Hellenistic period. Suppliants seeking Asclepius's help would sleep in special dor-mitories at his shrines to await dreams in which he prescribed healing treatments. These prescriptions emphasized diet and exercise, but numerous inscriptions set up by grateful patients also testified to miraculous cures and surgery performed while the sufferer slept. The following example is typical:

Ambrosia of Athens was blind in one eye. . . . She . . . ridiculed some of the cures [described in inscriptions in the sanctuary] as being incredible and impossible. . . . But when she went to sleep, she saw a vision; she thought the god was standing next to her. . . . He split open the diseased eye and poured in a medicine. When day came she left cured.

Mystery cults that promised secret knowledge as a key to salvation during life and after death grew even more popular. The cults of the Greek god Dionysus and, in particular, the Egyptian goddess Isis gained many followers in this period. The popularity of Isis, whose powers extended over every area of human life, received a boost from King Ptolemy I, who established a headquarters for her cult in Alexandria. He also promoted the cult of the Egyptian deity Sarapis, Isis's consort, as his dynasty's protector; Sarapis reportedly performed miracles of rescue from shipwreck and illness. The cult of Isis, who became the most popular female divinity in the Mediterranean, involved extensive rituals and festivals mixing features of Egyptian and Greek religion. Followers of Isis hoped, in return for a virtuous life, to gain the goddess's help against the demonic influence of Tychê (Chance); they also expected she would reward them with a happier fate after death. That an Egyptian deity such as Isis could achieve enormous popularity among Greeks (and Romans in later times) alongside the traditional gods of Greek religion is the best evidence of the cultural cross-fertilization characteristic of the Hellenistic world.

The history of Judaism in the Hellenistic period shows especially strong evidence of cultural interaction. King Ptolemy II had the Hebrew Bible translated into Greek (the Septuagint) in Alexandria in the early third century B.C.E. Many Jews, especially those living in the large Diaspora communities that had grown up in Hellenistic cities outside Palestine, adopted the Greek language and many aspects of Greek culture. Nevertheless, these Hellenized Jews largely retained the ritual practices and habits of life that defined traditional Judaism, and they did not worship Greek gods. The more traditional Jewish community in Palestine was controlled militarily and politically first by the Ptolemies and then by the Seleucids. Both kingdoms allowed the Jews to live according to their ancestral laws under the leadership of a high priest in Jerusalem.

Internal conflicts among Jews erupted in second-century B.C.E. Palestine over the amount of Greek influence that traditional Judaism could accept. The Seleucid king Antiochus IV (r. 175–163 B.C.E.) intervened in the conflict in support of the Jerusalem Jews who were most Greek-like in their ways. In 167 B.C.E., Antiochus converted the main Jewish temple there into a Greek temple and outlawed the practice of Jewish religious customs, such as circumcision and observing the Sabbath. A revolt led by Judah the Maccabee eventually won Jewish independence from the Seleucids after twenty-five years of war. The most famous episode of this revolt was the retaking of the Jerusalem temple and its rededication to the worship of the Jewish god, Yahweh—a triumphant moment celebrated by Jews ever since on the holiday of Hanukkah. That Greek culture attracted some Jews in the first place, however, provides a striking example of the transformations that affected many—though far from all—people of the Hellenistic world. By the time of the Roman Empire, one of those transformations would be Christianity, whose beliefs had roots in the cultural interaction of Hellenistic Jews and Greeks and their ideas on religion.

REVIEW What were the main cultural changes that took place during the Hellenistic Age?

Conclusion

The transition in Greek history from the Classical Age to the Hellenistic Age produced changes just as significant as those that had taken place earlier during the transition from the Archaic Age to the Classical Age. New ideas emerged, new political systems arose, a leader of legendary fame shocked the world, and, most important, a new level of interaction between people in Greece and the Near East changed society and culture in those regions at a fundamental level. The uncertainty of the times stimulated creativity as well as anxiety.

Some of these changes were intended; others were not. As before, war and its unpredictable consequences had a tremendous influence extending far beyond simply who won on the battlefield. The aftermath of the protracted Peloponnesian

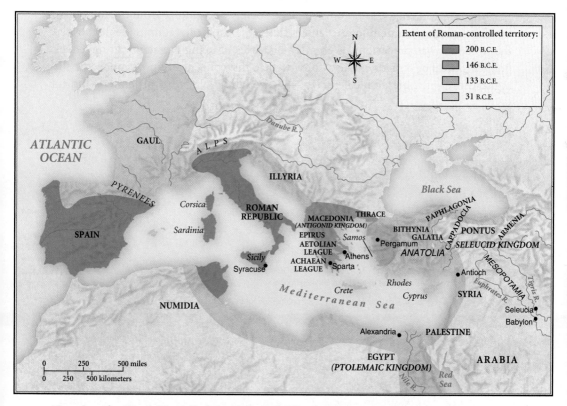

Mapping the West   The Fall of the Hellenistic Kingdoms, to 30 B.C.E.
By 30 B.C.E. (the death of Cleopatra VII, the last Ptolemaic monarch of Egypt), the Roman republic had conquered or absorbed the Hellenistic kingdoms of the eastern Mediterranean. Competition for the tremendous wealth that Romans captured in this expansion helped fuel bitter and divisive feuds between Rome's most ambitious generals and political leaders. The territories of the former Hellenistic kingdoms became the main part of the eastern half of the Roman Empire.

War eroded the confidence and prosperity that had characterized the fifth century B.C.E. and left many people, especially in Athens, feeling angry about wartime atrocities and nostalgic for the supposedly golden days of the past. Later Western civilization benefited, however, because thinkers, especially Plato and Aristotle, responded to the troubles of the times by creating philosophical and scientific knowledge that was essential to understanding and dealing with the human condition.

Philip II, the Macedonian king, certainly intended to take advantage of the disunity of the Greek city-states to make his formerly insignificant land strong enough to topple the world's superpower, the Persian Empire. Alexander, however, was the one whose unsurpassed leadership allowed him to fulfill his father's dream of glory, winning lasting fame—still to be known as "the Great" more than two thousand years later!—without ever fully disclosing why he did what he did. By installing Greeks as administrators and guards all over the Near East, he set in motion the process that created the multicultural world of the Hellenistic Age.

The new Hellenistic kingdoms changed society and culture from the top down. To Greeks, these undemocratic and strictly hierarchical regimes demonstrated that freedom was precarious, even after centuries of being the standard for Greek political life. The kingdoms also showed that the concentration of money at the highest level of a hierarchical society—in the hands of the royal family—and its

TIMELINE

306–304 B.C.E. Alexander's successors declare themselves kings

323 B.C.E. Alexander dies in Babylon

331 B.C.E. Alexander founds Alexandria in Egypt

334 B.C.E. Alexander leads an army of Greeks and Macedonians against the Persian Empire

335 B.C.E. Aristotle founds his philosophical school in Athens

30 B.C.E. Death of Cleopatra VII and takeover of the Ptolemaic kingdom by Rome

400 B.C.E.   275 B.C.E.   150 B.C.E.   25 B.C.E.

399 B.C.E. Trial and execution of Socrates in Athens

167 B.C.E. Jewish revolt in Jerusalem

386 B.C.E. Sparta makes peace with Persia, ceding control of the Anatolian Greek city-states; Plato founds the Academy in Athens

362 B.C.E. Greek city-states weakened by fighting one another at battle of Mantinea

338 B.C.E. Philip II, Macedonian king, defeats Greek alliance at Chaeronea to become the leading power in Greece

336 B.C.E. Philip II murdered; Alexander becomes king

expenditure to finance research and art could vigorously push those activities in new, though not always freely chosen, directions. The kings and queens of the period also had a lasting effect on religion by creating the cult of the ruler as protector and savior, a doctrine that combined the human with the divine in a new way that would have a long history.

Philosophy remained more independent of the new political systems than any other activity, and its diversity reflects the sense of possibility, as well as the sense of unease, that characterized the Hellenistic Age. Tychê (Chance) seemed as powerful as Zeus or Isis, a view that made the world seem more open, more unpredictable, and more dangerous. Many people therefore turned to the new ideas of Hellenistic philosophers to find a personal guide to life.

> **CHAPTER REVIEW QUESTIONS**
> 1. What were the central political, social, and cultural developments of the Hellenistic world?
> 2. Compare life for people of all social classes in the Hellenistic kingdoms with that of people living in the Classical Greek city-states.

For practice quizzes and other study tools, see the Online Study Guide at bedfordstmartins.com/huntconcise.

For primary-source material from this period, see Chapter 4 of *Sources of THE MAKING OF THE WEST*, Third Edition.

Suggested References

Research on the transition from the Classical to the Hellenistic Mediterranean world focuses on the imaginative ways in which rulers, thinkers, and artists combined the old and the new, the familiar and the foreign, in the multicultural environment that emerged from the conquests of Alexander the Great.

*Aristotle. *Complete Works*. Ed. Jonathan Barnes. 1985.

Chaniotis, Angelos. *War in the Hellenistic World*. 2005.

Empereur, Jean-Yves. *Alexandria: Jewel of Egypt*. 2002.

Evans, J. A. S. *Daily Life in the Hellenistic Age: From Alexander to Cleopatra*. 2008.

Mikalson, Jon D. *Religion in Hellenistic Athens*. 1998.

*Plato. *The Collected Dialogues*. Ed. Edith Hamilton and Huntington Cairns. 1963.

*Plutarch. *The Age of Alexander*. Trans. Ian Scott-Kilvert. 1973.

Pollitt, J. J. *Art in the Hellenistic Age*. 1986.

Ptolemaic Egypt: http://www.houseofptolemy.org/

Rogers, Guy MacLean. *Alexander: The Ambiguity of Greatness*. 2004.

Sharples, R. W. *Stoics, Epicureans, and Sceptics: An Introduction to Hellenistic Philosophy*. 1996.

Snyder, Jane M. *The Woman and the Lyre: Women Writers in Classical Greece and Rome*. 1989.

4

The Rise of Rome

753–44 B.C.E.

ROMANS TREASURED LEGENDS about Rome's transformation from an isolated village in central Italy to the greatest power in the Western world. They especially loved stories about their first king, Romulus, because they remembered him as a dynamic leader. According to the legend known as the rape of the Sabine women, Romulus's Rome was a tiny settlement without enough women to bear children to work the fields and defend the community in war. The king therefore begged nearby peoples to allow Romans to intermarry with them. Everyone turned him down out of disrespect for Rome's poverty and weakness. Enraged, Romulus invited the neighboring Sabines to a religious festival and told Rome's men to kidnap the unmarried Sabine women. The kidnappers immediately married the women, promising to cherish them as beloved wives and new citizens. When the Sabine men then attacked Rome, the brides rushed into the bloody battle, yelling at their brothers, fathers, and new husbands to stop the slaughter by either laying down their weapons or killing all the women. The men immediately made peace and united their populations under Roman rule.

This legend taught that Rome had grown stronger by absorbing outsiders into its citizen body—sometimes violently, sometimes peacefully. Rome's growth became the ancient world's largest expansion of population and territory, as a people originally housed in a few huts slowly grew to a state that, after centuries of war and diplomacy, governed most of Europe, North Africa, Egypt, and the eastern Mediterranean. The social, cultural, political, legal, and economic traditions that the Romans developed forged closer connections among the diverse peoples of this vast region than ever existed before or since. Not even Alexander the Great equaled the

The Wolf Feeding Romulus and Remus

This bronze statue illustrates the legend that a she-wolf nursed the twins Romulus and Remus, the sons of the war god Mars and the founders of Rome. Romans treasured this story because it meant that Mars favored them so much that he sent a wild animal to save their founders after a tyrant forced the boys' mother to abandon them. The legend also reminded Romans of the violence of their origins: Romulus killed Remus in an argument over who would be Rome's leader. The wolf here is an Etruscan sculpture made in the fifth century B.C.E. The infants were added in the Renaissance. *(Scala/Art Resource, NY.)*

Romans in affecting the course of Western civilization. The history of Europe and its colonies, including the United States, has deep roots in Rome.

Roman culture originated in the traditions of ancient Italy's many peoples, but Greek literature, art, and thought deeply influenced Rome. Of course, Romans did not just passively absorb other civilizations' traditions or change them only in superficial ways, such as giving Latin names to Greek gods. Whatever Romans took over from others they adapted to their own purposes. The cultural interaction that so greatly influenced Rome was a kind of competition in innovation, rather than an "advanced" Greek culture improving a "primitive" Roman one.

Kings ruled Rome at first (c. 753–509 B.C.E.), but the majority of Roman history comes in two later periods of about five hundred years each—the republic and the empire. These terms refer to the system of government in each period. Under the republic (founded 509 B.C.E.), an oligarchy (the social elite) governed a limited democracy. Under the empire (founded after civil war in the late first century B.C.E.), monarchs (the Roman emperors) once again ruled.

Rome's greatest expansion came during the republic. Roman values under the republic emphasized service to the community, individual honor and public status, religion, the importance of laws, and shared decision making led by the elite. By the first century B.C.E., however, tension between these values had erupted into civil war because powerful individuals disagreed over how to govern the republic, and some placed their personal interests ahead of the common good.

CHAPTER FOCUS QUESTION How did traditional Roman values affect the rise and then the fall of the Roman republic?

Roman Social and Religious Traditions

One reason for Rome's amazing growth came from its citizens' belief that the gods wanted them to rule the world by military might and law and improve it through social and moral values. Romans therefore regulated their lives by traditional values stressing personal connections, social hierarchy, education for public service, and religious duties. Just as Greeks had emphasized excellence as a social value, Romans believed that men and women should show courage in all aspects of life. In public life, Roman men connected with one another as patron or client, each with obligations to the other. In private life, men as the heads of households held power over their children and slaves, but most wives lived independently of their husbands' control. In religion, the gods' power over human life meant that everyone had to pray for divine favor to protect the family and the community.

Values from the Past

Since Romans believed that their ancestors had handed down their values from ancient times, they referred to these values as **mos maiorum**, "the way of the ancestors." For Romans, "old-fashioned" meant "good because tested by long experience," while "new" suggested "dangerous because not tested by experience." They believed that the keys to Roman greatness lay in preserving and cherishing the ways of the past. Abandoning tradition was, they thought, equivalent to cultural suicide.

Roman tradition made honor the reward for right conduct, which required uprightness, faithfulness, and respect for others. Uprightness defined how a person related to others. In the second century B.C.E., the poet Lucilius defined it as "virtue":

> Virtue is to know the human relevance of each thing,
> To know what is humanly right and useful and honorable,
> And what things are good and what are bad, useless, shameful, and
>   dishonorable. . . .
> Virtue is to pay what in reality is owed to honorable status,
> To be an enemy and an opponent to bad people and bad values
> But a defender of good people and good values. . . .
> And, in addition, virtue is putting the country's interests first,
> Then our parents' interests, with our own third and last.

Faithfulness meant to keep one's obligations, no matter the cost. Failing to meet an obligation offended the community and the gods. Faithful women remained virgins before marriage and avoided adultery afterward. Faithful men kept their word, paid their debts, never had sex with another man's wife, and treated everyone justly—which did not mean treating everyone the same, but rather treating people appropriately according to whether they were equals, superiors, or inferiors.

Faithfulness was linked to the value of respect. Respect meant devotion to the gods, to one's own dignity, and to one's family, especially elders. Honoring the gods required worship, prayer, and sacrifices performed with strict purity. Respect for one's self meant maintaining self-control and displaying only limited emotion. So strict was this expectation that not even wives and husbands could kiss in public without seeming emotionally out of control. Respect also required never giving up, regardless of difficulties. Standing firm and overcoming all obstacles to do one's duty were fundamental Roman values.

Honor was the Romans' reward for living by those values. Women earned honor especially by bearing legitimate children and educating them morally. Honor for upper-class men brought concrete rewards: public recognition and, perhaps, election to government office. A man regarded as especially honorable commanded so much respect that others would obey him regardless of whether he held formal power over them. A man earning this much status was said to possess "authority."

Finally, Romans believed that family background influenced a person's values. Being born in an elite family was therefore a two-edged sword. It automatically carried greater status, but at the same time it imposed a stricter demand to behave morally. Originally, wealth had nothing to do with Roman moral virtue. Over time, however, it became overwhelmingly important to the elite to spend money in displays of conspicuous consumption, social entertainments, and gifts to the community. By the later centuries of the **Roman republic**, ambitious men required vast fortunes to buy honor, and they became willing to abandon other values to acquire riches.

The Patron-Client System

The hierarchy of Roman society depended on the **patron-client system**, a network of two-way personal relationships linking Romans to one another legally and morally. A patron was a man of superior status who was obliged to provide benefits to certain men of lower status, who paid special attention to him. These were his clients, who in return owed him duties. Both sets of obligations involved financial and political help. The network had multiple levels: a patron of others was often himself the client of a more distinguished man. A thoughtful patron would greet a social inferior as "my friend," not as "my client." A client, however, showed respect by addressing his superior as "my patron."

Benefits and duties made the relationship two-way. A patron provided benefits for his clients by giving gifts or loans in hard times, supporting them when they started political careers, and speaking for them in lawsuits. Clients paid duties to their patrons by lending money when patrons needed it to pay for public works or their daughters' expensive dowries, or by soliciting votes for their campaigns to be elected to public office. Since it was a mark of great status for a patron to have numerous clients crowding around him like a swarm of bees, he expected them to gather at his house early in the morning and accompany him to the forum, the city's public center. Prominent Romans needed a large house to accommodate a crowd of clients and to entertain social equals. A house crowded with visitors indicated social success.

These mutual obligations endured over generations. Ex-slaves, for example, who automatically became the clients of the masters who freed them, passed on this relationship to their children. Wealthy Romans could acquire clients among foreigners, sometimes even entire communities. By stressing duty and permanence, the patron-client system reflected the Roman idea that society depended on people faithfully keeping their obligations to one another.

The Roman Family

The family was the bedrock institution of Roman society because it taught values and determined the ownership of property. Men and women shared the duty of teaching values to their children, though by law the father possessed the ***patria potestas*** (power of a father) over his children of any age and over his slaves. This power gave him legal ownership of all the property acquired by his dependents. As long as he was alive, no son or daughter could own anything, accumulate money, or possess any independent legal standing—in theory. In actual life, adult children controlled personal property and money, and favored slaves might accumulate savings. Fathers also held legal power of life and death over these members of their households, but they

Sculpted Tomb of a Family of Ex-Slaves
The husband and wife sculpted on this tomb, which perhaps dates to the first century B.C.E., started life as slaves but gained their freedom and thus became Roman citizens. Their son, in the background holding a pet pigeon, was a free person. One of the remarkable features of Roman civilization, and a source of its demographic strength, was that it granted citizenship to ex-slaves. This family had done well enough financially to afford an expensive grave marker. The tablets the man is holding and the carefully groomed hairstyle of the woman are meant to show that their family was educated and stylish. What do you think it means that the couple are shown holding hands? (German Archeological Institute/Madeline Grimoldi.)

rarely exercised it on anyone except unwanted or deformed newborns. "Exposure"— abandoning babies so that they would die, be adopted, or be raised as slaves by strangers—was an accepted practice to control the size of families and dispose of physically imperfect infants. Baby girls probably suffered this fate more often than boys, as a family enhanced its power by investing its resources in its sons.

As the Roman value of shared decision making required, fathers regularly conferred with others on important family issues. Each Roman man identified a circle of friends and relatives, his "council," that he always consulted before making important decisions. A man considering whether to execute an adult member of his household, for example, would never have made the decision on his own. His council would recommend this violent exercise of a father's power only in the most extreme circumstances, as in 63 B.C.E. when a father had his son executed because the youth had committed treason by joining a conspiracy to overthrow the government.

Patria potestas did not allow a husband to control his wife because "free" marriages—in which the wife formally remained under her father's power for as long as he lived—eventually became common. Many Roman wives were relatively independent because their fathers were dead, and their husbands did not legally control their lives (four out of five parents died before their children reached age thirty). Legally, a woman needed a male guardian to conduct business for her, but guardianship became an empty formality by the first century B.C.E. As one legal expert said about Roman women's freedom of action, "The common belief, that because of their instability of judgment women are often deceived and that it is only fair to have them controlled by the authority of guardians, seems more false than true. For women of full age manage their affairs themselves." Upper-class women could express their opinions publicly. In 195 B.C.E., for example, they blocked Rome's streets for days until the men ended a wartime law meant to reduce tensions between rich and poor by limiting the amount of gold jewelry and fine clothing women could wear and where they could ride in carriages.

Roman women had to grow up fast to assume their duties as teachers of values to children and managers of their family's resources. Tullia, daughter of the famous first-century B.C.E. politician Marcus Tullius Cicero, was engaged at twelve, married at sixteen, and widowed by twenty-two. As a married Roman woman of wealth, she oversaw the household slaves, including wet nurses for infants; kept account books for the property she personally owned; and accompanied her husband to dinner parties—something Greek wives never did.

Sculpture of a Woman Running a Store
This relief sculpture shows a woman selling food from behind the counter of a shop while customers make purchases or converse with each other. Roman women could own property, so the woman may be the store owner. The man immediately to her right behind the counter could be her husband or a servant. Market areas in Roman towns were packed with small family-run stores that sold everything imaginable, much like the malls of today. (Art Resource, NY.)

Roman mothers won public honor for managing their households well and shaping their children's moral outlook. Cornelia, an aristocrat of the second century B.C.E., won extraordinary fame after her husband died by refusing an offer of marriage from the Ptolemaic king of Egypt so she could instead oversee the family estate and educate her surviving daughter and two sons. (Her other nine children had died.) The boys, Tiberius and Gaius Gracchus, grew up to be among the most influential and controversial officials of the late republic. Wealthy women such as Cornelia wielded political influence, if only indirectly, by expressing their opinions to the male members of their families. Marcus Porcius Cato, a famous second-century B.C.E. political leader, remarked on the behind-the-scenes reality of women's power: "All mankind rule their wives, we rule all mankind, and our wives rule us."

Women accumulated property both through inheritance and entrepreneurship. Recent archaeological discoveries suggest that by the late republic some women owned large businesses. Poor women, like poor men, toiled to help support their families by selling vegetables and trinkets from stands. More prosperous families crafted furniture or clothing at home, the location of most Roman production, with the men cutting, fitting, and polishing the wood, leather, and metal. The poorest women could earn money only as prostitutes, which was legal but disgraceful. Prenuptial agreements to outline the rights of both partners in marriage were common, and divorce was a simple matter, with fathers usually keeping the children.

Education: From Reading to Rhetoric

Education for both women and men aimed to make them supporters of traditional values and, for different purposes, effective speakers. Women learned the legends of Roman history so they could instill values in their children and speak well at dinner parties, and men so they could make effective speeches in court or political meetings, if they were rich enough to spend their time there. Most children were homeschooled; only the rich could afford to pay teachers. Wealthy parents bought literate slaves to teach their children. Often they chose Greek slaves so their children could be taught to speak Greek and read Greek literature. Elite Romans wanted to be bilingual and read Greek drama, philosophy, and history in the original language. They wanted to understand fully the lessons of Greek culture, which they respected for its great age and insight into the human condition. Repetition was the usual teaching technique. Teachers slapped and hit students to keep them attentive.

In upper-class families, both daughters and sons learned to read. Girls studied literature and perhaps music. Boys focused on physical training, fighting with weapons, and courageous actions. The highest level of an upper-class boy's education was rhetoric—skill in persuasive public speaking based on Greek models adapted to Roman purposes. Rhetorical training was crucial to a successful public career. A boy would accompany his father to trials and political gatherings. By listening to speeches, he would learn to imitate winning techniques. Cicero, Rome's most famous orator, agreed with his brother's advice that a young man must learn "to become an excellent public speaker. This is the way to control men at Rome, winning them over to your side and keeping them from harming you. You really have power when you are a man who can cause your rivals the greatest fears of meeting you [as a speaker] in a trial."

Religion in Public and Private

Romans worshipped many divinities that corresponded with Greek gods. Romans viewed their chief god, Jupiter (the equivalent of the Greek god Zeus), as a powerful, stern father. Juno (Greek Hera), queen of the gods, and Minerva (Greek Athena), goddess of wisdom, joined Jupiter as the three central gods of Rome's official public religion. These three gods shared Rome's most famous temple on the Capitoline hill at the center of the city.

The goal of Roman public religion was to preserve Rome's safety and prosperity. Priests were supposed to ensure the gods' goodwill toward the state, a crucial relationship the Romans called the *pax deorum* (peace of or with the gods). Men from the top of the social hierarchy served as priests by conducting sacrifices and presiding at festivals and other rituals conforming to ancestral tradition. They were not professionals who devoted their lives solely to religious activity, but rather citizens who performed a public service. The most important official, the *pontifex maximus* (highest priest), served as the head of state religion and the ultimate authority on religious matters affecting government. Rome's most prominent men sought this priesthood for its political influence.

Every official action was preceded by "taking the auspices"—seeking Jupiter's approval by observing natural "signs" such as the direction of the flights of birds, their eating habits, or the presence of thunder and lightning. Officials who made mistakes in this process were punished. Naval commanders, for example, "took the auspices" by feeding sacred chickens on their ships: if the birds ate energetically before a battle, Jupiter was thought to favor the Romans, and the battle could begin. Once during a fierce third-century B.C.E. sea battle, the commander Publius Claudius Pulcher grew frustrated when his chickens, probably seasick, refused to eat. Convinced that the gods nevertheless wanted him to attack, he finally hurled the birds overboard in a rage, sputtering, "Well then, let them drink!" When he suffered a huge defeat, he was fined very heavily.

Many official prayers requested the gods' help in growing crops, preventing disease, and spurring healthy reproduction for animals and people. In times of crisis, Romans brought in foreign gods to help them, such as the healing god Asclepius from Greece or the fertility goddess Cybele, the "Great Mother," from Asia Minor (the Roman term for Anatolia).

Romans supported many other cults with special guardian responsibilities. The shrine of Vesta, goddess of the hearth and a protector of the family, housed the official eternal flame of Rome, which Romans believed guaranteed the state's permanent existence. The Vestal Virgins—six unmarried women who were sworn to chastity at ages six to ten for terms of thirty years—kept the flame from going out. Their chastity symbolized Roman family values and thus the preservation of the republic itself. As Rome's only female priesthood, the Vestals earned high status and freedom from their fathers' control. If the flame went out, the Romans assumed that one of the women had broken her vow of chastity, and the disgraced Vestal was buried alive.

Romans performed many public and private rituals to seek divine help and also reinforce traditional values. For example, during the Lupercalia festival in February (the festival's name recalled the wolf, *luper* in Latin, that legend said had reared Romulus), naked young men streaked around the Palatine hill, lashing any women they met with strips of goatskin. Women who had not yet borne children would run out to be struck, believing this would make them fertile. At home, families maintained small shrines housing statuettes of their Penates (spirits of the household) and Lares (spirits of the ancestors), protectors of their well-being and moral traditions. Upper-class families hung death masks of famous ancestors in the main room of their homes and wore them at funerals to express the current generation's responsibility to live up

Household Religious Shrine from Pompeii
This colorfully painted shrine stood inside the entrance to a house at Pompeii known as the House of the Vettii, from the name of its owners. Successful businessmen, they spared no expense in decorating their home: with 188 frescoes (paintings done by applying pigments to damp plaster) adorning its walls, the interior blazed in a riot of color. This type of shrine for family religion, found in every Roman home, is called a lararium because it housed the Lares (spirits of the ancestors), who are shown here flanking a central figure representing the spirit (*genius*) of the father of the family. The snake, ready to drink from a bowl probably holding milk set out for it, also symbolizes a protective force. The scene sums up the role Romans expected their gods to play: providing protection and preventing bad luck. Why do you think Romans regarded snakes as symbols of divine protection? (Scala/Art Resource, NY.)

to the family's traditions. The Saturnalia festival in December turned the social order upside down to release tensions caused by the inequalities between masters and slaves. As a Roman author described the occasion, "People joyfully hold feasts all through the country and the towns, each owner acting as a waiter to his slaves." This temporary reversal of roles in fact emphasized slaves' ties to their owners by symbolizing patrons' benefits, which slaves were expected to repay with faithful service.

Social tradition, not religious belief, was the source of Roman morality. The shame of losing status by tarnishing one's reputation, and not the fear of divine punishment, was the reason to avoid immoral behavior. Romans gave human moral actions a religious dimension by representing their values, such as faithfulness or piety, as divinities with temples and cults. The principal Roman gods were more connected to national security and prosperity than to human morality, as Cicero explained: "We call Jupiter the Best (*Optimus*) and Greatest (*Maximus*) not because he makes us just or sober or wise but, rather, healthy, unharmed, rich, and prosperous."

> **REVIEW**   How did traditional values affect Roman society and beliefs?

From Monarchy to Republic, 753–287 B.C.E.

Rome's astounding growth from a tiny settlement into the Mediterranean's greatest power took centuries. During this slow process, the Romans reinvented their government and seized vast territories to provide land and revenues for a growing population. Rome's first government was a monarchy, the most common type of government in the ancient world. This rule by kings lasted from 753 to 509 B.C.E., when members of the social elite overthrew it in anger at the royal family's violent behavior. The elite then created a new political system—the republic—that lasted until almost the end of the first century B.C.E. The Roman republic, from the Latin *res publica* (meaning "the people's thing" or "the public business"), was based on male citizens making political decisions as a group and electing officials in assemblies organized by social hierarchy. Rome acquired land and population by winning aggressive wars and by absorbing other peoples. Its economic and cultural growth depended on contact with peoples around the Mediterranean.

Rule by Kings, 753–509 B.C.E.

Legend taught that kings ruled Rome from 753 to 509 B.C.E., but little reliable evidence exists for this period. The kings probably created the Senate, a body of advisers chosen from the city's leading men to serve as the ruler's council, in keeping with the Roman principle that decisions should be made in a group. The Senate advised Rome's leaders for two thousand years, as the government changed from a monarchy to a republic and back to a monarchy under the empire.

Rome's policy of making conquered outsiders into citizens or allies produced tremendous expansion, promoted ethnic diversity, and contrasted sharply with the exclusionary citizenship policies of Greek city-states. Another important Roman policy—also different from Greek tradition—was to grant citizenship to freed slaves. These freedmen and freedwomen, as ex-slaves were called, became clients of their former owners. They were barred from elective offices or military service but in all other ways possessed full civil rights, such as legal marriage. Their children enjoyed citizenship without any limitations. By the late republic, many Roman citizens were descendants of freed slaves.

Geography and contact with other cultures, especially Greek, drove Rome's initial growth. The city lay at the natural center of both Italy and the Mediterranean world. As the first-century B.C.E. historian Livy, our source for the heroic legends of early Rome, expressed it, "Gods and men chose this site for good reasons: all its advantages make it the best place in the world for a city destined to grow great." Those advantages were fertile farmland, control of a river crossing on the major north-south route in the peninsula, a nearby harbor on the Mediterranean Sea, and easy access to the surrounding areas in Italy. Most important, Rome was ideally situated for contact with the outside world. The Italian peninsula stuck out so far into the Mediterranean that east-west ship traffic naturally stopped in its ports (Map 4.1).

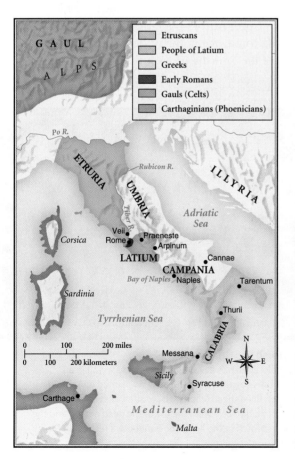

Map 4.1 Ancient Italy, c. 500 B.C.E. When the Romans ended the monarchy to found a republic in 509 B.C.E., they inhabited a relatively small territory in central Italy between the west coast and the mountain range that runs down the peninsula from north to south. Numerous different peoples lived in Italy at this time. The most prosperous occupied fertile agricultural land and sheltered harbors on the peninsula's west side. The early republic's most urbanized neighbors were the Etruscans to the north and the Greek city-states to the south and on the island of Sicily.

Ancient Italy was home to a diverse population, and the Romans' contact with their neighbors profoundly influenced their cultural development. The people of the region around Rome were poor villagers like the Romans and spoke the same Indo-European language, an early form of Latin. Flourishing Greek city-states dotted Italy to the south, however, and contact with them had the greatest effect on Rome. Greeks had established colonies in southern Italy from the 700s B.C.E. These settlements grew rich thanks to their ideal location for participating in international trade. Romans developed a love-hate relationship with Greeks, admiring their literature and art but despising their lack of military unity.

The Etruscans, a people north of the Tiber River, also influenced the Romans. They lived in prosperous, independent towns nestled on central Italian hilltops. Bright Etruscan wall paintings in tombs portray funeral banquets and games testifying to their society's splendor. Etruscans crafted fine artwork, jewelry, and sculpture, but they also imported luxury items from Greece and other Mediterranean lands. Most of the intact Greek vases known today, for example, were found in Etruscan tombs. The Etruscans' international contacts encouraged cultural interaction. Gold tablets inscribed in Etruscan and Phoenician reveal that in about 500 B.C.E., the Etruscans dedicated a temple to the Phoenician goddess Astarte, whom they had learned about by trading with Carthage. That city, founded in western North Africa (modern Tunisia) by Phoenicians around 800 B.C.E., dominated seaborne commerce in the western Mediterranean and by the third century B.C.E. had become the Romans' greatest rival.

Banquet Scene Painted in an Etruscan Tomb
Painted about 480–470 B.C.E., this brightly colored fresco at Tarquinia decorates a wall in an Etruscan tomb (known today as the Tomb of the Leopards, from the animals painted just above this scene). Wealthy Etruscan men and women filled their tombs with pictures such as these, which simultaneously represented the funeral feasts held to celebrate the life of the dead person and the social pleasures experienced in this life and expected in the next. The banqueters recline on their elbows in Greek style. (Scala/Art Resource, NY.)

The extent of Etruscan influence on Rome remains controversial. Until recently, scholars believed that the Etruscans conquered Rome and dominated it politically in the sixth century B.C.E. The Etruscans were also seen as more culturally refined, mainly because so much Greek art has been found at Etruscan sites. Etruscans were therefore assumed to have reshaped Roman culture during this period of supposed domination. New research, however, has revealed the independence of Romans in developing their own cultural traditions. They borrowed from Etruscans (as from Greeks) whatever appealed to them and adapted it to fit their local circumstances. Romans took over the Etruscans' procedures for religious rituals and adopted their magistrates' elaborate garments. They also learned Etruscan divination techniques for discovering the gods' will by identifying clues in the shapes of the internal organs of slaughtered animals. Romans may also have adopted from Etruscan society the tradition of wives joining husbands at dinner parties.

Many features of Roman culture previously thought to be the results of Etruscan influence were probably part of the ancient Mediterranean's shared cultural environment. The organization of the Roman army, a citizen militia of heavily armed infantry troops fighting in formation, reflected not just Etruscan tradition but also that of other peoples. The Romans' alphabet, which they first learned from the Etruscans, was Greek; the Greeks had acquired it through their contact with the Levant. The engineering necessary to urbanize Rome, once seen as exclusively Etruscan, did not come from one superior culture "instructing" another, less-developed one. Rather, at this time in Mediterranean history, similar cultural developments were under way in many places. The Romans, like so many others, found their own way in navigating this common cultural sea.

The Early Roman Republic, 509–287 B.C.E.

The social elite's hatred for kings created the Roman republic. Their belief that monarchy always turned into tyranny was expressed in Livy's story of the rape of Lucretia, the most famous legend about the creation of the republic. The assault on Lucretia, a chaste wife in the social elite, took place when the swaggering son of King Tarquin the Proud violently raped her to demonstrate his superior power. Despite pleas from her husband and father not to blame herself, she committed suicide after identifying her attacker.

Declaring themselves Rome's liberators from tyranny, her relatives and friends, led by Lucius Junius Brutus, expelled Tarquin in 509 B.C.E. They then created the republic, to ensure the sharing of power by the elite and to block rule by one man or family. Thereafter, the Romans prided themselves on living under a freer political system than that of their neighbors. The legend of the warrior Horatius at the bridge, for example, advertised the republic's dedication to national freedom. As Livy told the story, Horatius single-handedly blocked the Etruscan army's march on Rome when they wanted to put a king back in charge of the city. While hacking at his opponents, Horatius cursed them as slaves who had lost their freedom because they were ruled by arrogant kings. Horatius's legend made clear that Romans created the republic to prevent a leader from abusing power by ruling alone.

Conflict over which groups would control the republic persisted for over two hundred years after 509 B.C.E., in a process called the **struggle of the orders**. "Orders" refers to the two main divisions of the republic's social hierarchy, the patricians (a limited group of elite families) and the plebeians (the rest of Rome's citizen population). Patricians inherited their status by being born into one of the about 130 wealthy families controlling important religious activities. Some plebeians, however, were also rich, and they resented the patricians' arrogance in monopolizing elections to public office, banning intermarriage with plebeians, and advertising their social superiority by wearing special red shoes (later they changed to black footwear adorned with a shiny metal crescent). Above all, rich plebeians insisted they deserved the same influence in politics as patricians.

Economic and social discontent also inflamed the struggle. Poor plebeians demanded relief from crushing debts and a redistribution of farmland controlled by large landowners. To pressure the patricians, plebeians periodically took the extreme step of leaving the city (secession) and refusing to serve in the army. This tactic worked because they made up the majority of Rome's military. A secession provoked by a patrician's violence against a plebeian woman led to the earliest Roman laws, called the Twelve Tables from the bronze tablets on which they were engraved for display around 450 B.C.E. In Livy's words, these laws prevented the patrician government officials who judged most legal cases from "arbitrarily giving the force of law to their own preferences." So important did the Twelve Tables become as a symbol of the Roman commitment to justice for all citizens that for the next four hundred years, children were required to memorize them.

The Twelve Tables were only a first step toward greater sharing of legal and political power; that process occurred mainly by establishing the different and overlapping responsibilities of Rome's assemblies. At these outdoor meetings, adult male citizens elected officials, passed laws, decided government policies, and held some trials. Assemblies were only for voting, not discussion, but every session was preceded by a public gathering to hear speeches. Everyone, including women and noncitizens, could listen to these addresses. The crowd loudly expressed its agreement or disagreement by applauding or hissing. Speakers therefore had to pay close attention to public opinion in forming the proposals that they put before the male citizens who then voted them up or down in the assemblies. As a result, assemblies brought some democracy to the government of the Roman republic.

Assemblies were divided into voting groups according to the social hierarchy of status and wealth. Each group, not each individual, had a vote. A small group had the same vote as a large group (as in the U.S. Senate, in which each state has two votes regardless of size). The hierarchy of the voting groups in the Centuriate Assembly, which elected the major officials (consuls and praetors), reflected the organization of the army: it confined the huge population of men too poor to afford military weapons, the **proletarians**, to one group that cast only one out of the total of 193 votes.

The Plebeian Assembly excluded patricians and was grouped into thirty-five tribes based on where voters lived; it elected special officials (tribunes) responsible for protecting plebeians. It also passed resolutions called **plebiscites**, which were originally not recognized as law by patricians. The struggle of the orders finally ended in 287 B.C.E., when patricians agreed that plebiscites would have the status of laws. In a third grouping, the Tribal Assembly, patricians joined plebeians as voters grouped by residence. The Tribal Assembly, in which plebeians greatly outnumbered patricians, eventually became the republic's most important government institution for making policy, passing laws, and, until separate courts were created in the second century B.C.E., conducting trials.

Annually elected officials administered the republic's government. They served in groups, numbering from two to more than a dozen. The highest officials were consuls. Two consuls were elected each year, and their most important duty was commanding Rome's army. Winning a consulship was the greatest political honor a Roman man could achieve, and it bestowed high status on his descendants forever, entitling them to be called nobles. To be elected consul, a man traditionally had to work his way up the **ladder of offices**. After ten years of military service beginning at about age twenty, he would seek election as a quaestor, a financial administrator. Continuing to climb the ladder, he would next be elected to the board of aediles, officials overseeing the city's streets, sewers, aqueducts, temples, and markets. Each rung up the ladder was more competitive, and few men reached the next office, that of praetor, which performed judicial and military command duties. The most successful praetors then tried for the consulship. Ex-consuls could also compete to become one of the censors, prestigious senior officials elected every five years to conduct censuses of the citizen body and select new members of the three-hundred-man Senate, which advised the consuls (as it had the kings). The special role of the Senate in the republic's government made clear the Roman principle of making decisions through group agreement. The Senate had no authority to pass laws; it could only give advice. But its prestige was so enormous that no high official or assembly would disregard the senators' advice, unless they wished to start a political crisis. Following the Roman tradition that status should be visible, the senators wore special black high-top shoes and robes embroidered with a broad purple stripe.

The struggle of the orders also changed the balance of power among elective offices. The patricians tried to monopolize the highest ones, but through violent struggle from about 500 to 450 B.C.E., the plebeians forced them to yield a crucial concession: the creation of a special panel of ten annually elected officials called tribunes. Tribunes had the responsibility of blocking actions that would harm the plebeians and their property. The tribunate's purpose made it stand apart from regular ladder offices. Tribunes, who had to be plebeians, based their power on the sworn oath of the other plebeians to protect them against all attacks. This protected status, called sacrosanctity, allowed tribunes the right to use a veto (from the Latin meaning "I forbid") to stop the actions of officials, suspend elections, and even disregard the advice of the Senate. The tribunes' extraordinary power to halt government action sometimes made them the sources of bitter political disputes.

In the early republic, Roman values motivated men to compete for honor, not money, in pursuing a public career. By 367 B.C.E., the plebeians had forced their way fully into this competition by requiring that at least one consul every year must be a plebeian. Only well-off men could run for election because officials earned no salaries. On the contrary, they were expected to spend large sums to win popular support by entertaining the electorate with, for example, spectacles featuring gladiators (trained fighters) and wild beasts (such as lions imported from Africa). Once elected, magistrates from aediles to consuls were expected to benefit the people by paying for public works, such as roads, aqueducts, and temples. When Rome later won control of more and more overseas territory through warfare, the desire for the status that money could buy overcame the values of faithfulness and honesty. By the second century B.C.E., military officers could enrich themselves by seizing booty from enemies in successful foreign wars and by extorting bribes from the local people while administering conquered territory. They could then use their personal profits from war to finance the public works that promoted their political careers at home. In this way, acquiring money became more important in the late republic than winning honor through selfless public service.

Outrage over corrupt officials dismissing complaints about each other's conduct led to the creation of a court system with jury trials in the second century B.C.E. Since most officials were also senators, the Senate self-interestedly tried to have these juries be manned only by its members, while nonsenators agitated to be included. Both accusers and accused had to speak for themselves in court or have friends speak for them. Prominent men, usually senators with legal knowledge, played a central role as advisers in the Roman judicial system. These jurists, as they were called (from the Latin *jus, juris,* "law"), operated as private citizens, not official judges, in providing legal advice. This reliance on jurists reflected the Roman tradition of consulting a group of advisers to reach decisions. Roman law developed over centuries, sometimes adapting laws from other peoples, and became the basis for many later European legal codes still in use today.

These centuries of conflict between the orders produced overlapping political and judicial institutions. Several different assemblies voted on laws, while the Senate offered opinions that guided lawmaking. Legal cases could be decided by high-ranking magistrates, assemblies, or juries. Rome had no highest judicial authority, such as the U.S. Supreme Court, to resolve disputes about conflicting laws or verdicts. The republic's stability therefore depended on observing tradition, the mos maiorum. This reliance on tradition ensured that the most socially prominent and the richest Romans dominated government and society—because they defined the "way of the ancestors."

REVIEW   What issues fueled the struggle of the orders?

Roman Imperialism, Fifth to Second Centuries B.C.E.

During the fifth, fourth, and third centuries B.C.E., Rome fought war after war to expand in Italy until it became the most powerful state on the peninsula. In the third and second centuries B.C.E., Romans fought wars far from home in the west, the north, and the east, but above all they battled Carthage to the south. Their victories in these foreign wars won Rome an empire in Italy, Sicily, Sardinia, Corsica, Spain, North Africa, Greece, Asia Minor, and southern Gaul (France).

Rome's imperialist expansion transformed its culture and society. Astonishingly, Romans had no literature before about 240 B.C.E. Cultural interaction with others during overseas expansion stimulated Romans to write their first history and poetry and deeply influenced their art, especially portraits. Endless military campaigns far from home created stresses on family life and small farmers in the army, while the novel demands of ruling conquered territory undermined the government's stability. The importation of huge numbers of war captives to work as slaves on the estates of the rich put free laborers out of work. The conquests and spoils of war from Rome's great victories in the third and second centuries B.C.E. thus turned out to be a two-edged sword: they brought expansion and wealth, but their unexpected social and political consequences disrupted traditional values and the community's stability.

Roman Expansion in Italy

Fear, ambition, and need motivated Roman imperialism. Worries about national security made the senators recommend preemptive attacks against peoples perceived as enemies of Rome, and everyone longed to win plunder in war. Poorer soldiers hoped their gains would pull their families out of poverty. The elite longed to increase their riches and acquire glory as commanders, to promote their public careers. Finally, a growing population needed more land because the basis of the economy remained agriculture.

The Romans believed they were successful militarily because they respected the will of the gods. Cicero claimed, "We have defeated all the nations of the world, because we have realized that the world is directed and governed by the gods." Believing that the gods supported defensive wars as just, the Romans always insisted they fought only in self-defense, even when they attacked first. A devastating sack of Rome in 387 B.C.E. by Gauls (Celts) from beyond the Alps to the north proved only a temporary military setback. Celts were a

Rome and Central Italy, Fifth Century B.C.E.

diverse group of peoples living in what is today west-central Europe. Famously warlike, Celtic bands grew prosperous from raiding and control of trade routes north of Italy.

Population growth forced some of them to look for new territory south of the Alps, and the Romans feared them as potential invaders.

By around 220 B.C.E., Rome controlled all of Italy south of the Po River. The Romans sometimes forced defeated opponents to give up large amounts of land or even enslaved them, but they also often struck generous peace terms with former enemies. Some defeated Italians even became Roman citizens, and no conquered Italian peoples had to pay taxes to Rome. All, however, had to send soldiers for future wars. These new allies then received a share of the booty, chiefly slaves and land, from victorious campaigns against a new crop of enemies. In this way, the Romans used the sharing of the profits of conquest to turn former opponents into partners, an arrangement that only made Rome more powerful.

To strengthen Italy's security, the Romans planted colonies of citizens and constructed roads up and down the peninsula to allow troops to march faster. These roads also connected the diverse peoples of Italy, speeding the creation of a more unified culture dominated by Rome. Latin, for example, became the common language.

Aqueduct at Nîmes in France
Like the Greeks, the Romans supplied fountains and public baths in their towns with water by constructing aqueducts. They excelled at building complex systems of tunnels, channels, and bridges to move water over great distances. One of the best-preserved sections of a major aqueduct is the so-called Pont du Gard near present-day Nîmes in France, erected in the late first century B.C.E. to serve the flourishing town of Nemausus. Built of stones fitted together without clamps or mortar, the span soars 160 feet high and is 875 feet long, carrying water from thirty-five miles away in a channel constructed to fall only one foot in height for every three thousand feet in length, so that the flow would remain steady but gentle. What sort of social and political organization would be necessary to construct such a system? (© Hubertus Kanus/Photo Researchers, Inc.)

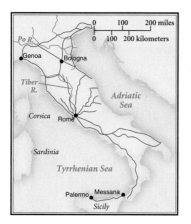

Roman Roads, c. 110 B.C.E.

The wealth flowing from Rome's first two centuries of expansion in Italy attracted hordes of people to the city because these riches financed new aqueducts to provide fresh running water—a rarity in the ancient world—and a massive building program employing poor laborers. By around 300 B.C.E., perhaps 150,000 people lived within Rome's walls. Outside the city, about 750,000 free Roman citizens inhabited various parts of Italy on land taken from local peoples. Much conquered territory was declared public land, open to any Roman to use for grazing herds of cattle.

Roman Expansion outside Italy

The Romans' victories in three wars against the wealthy North African city of Carthage began their overseas empire. Also governed as a republic, Carthage by the third century B.C.E. controlled its own empire stretching across the northwest African coast, part of Libya, Sardinia, Corsica, Malta, and the southern portion of Spain. Geography therefore ensured that an expanding Rome would bump up against Carthage's interests, which depended on the sea. The Carthaginians had a strong fleet but had to hire mercenaries to field a sizable infantry. To Romans, Carthage seemed a dangerous rival, as well as a fine prize because of its riches. Roman hostility was also fueled by horror at the Carthaginian tradition of sacrificing infants in times of trouble in the belief that this would placate their gods.

The three wars with Carthage took Roman troops outside Italy and across the sea for the first time. They are called the Punic Wars, from the Roman term *Punici,* meaning "Phoenicians" (the ancestors of the Carthaginians). The First Punic War lasted for a generation (264–241 B.C.E.). Its bloody battles revealed why the Romans consistently conquered their rivals. In addition to being able to draw on the Italian population for reserves of manpower, they were prepared to lose as many troops, vote as much money, and fight as long as necessary to win. Previously unskilled at naval warfare, they spent vast sums to build warships to combat Carthage's experienced navy; they lost more than five hundred ships and 250,000 men while learning how to win at sea. (See "Taking Measure," page 138.)

Victory in the First Punic War made the Romans masters of Sicily, where they set up their first province (a foreign territory ruled and taxed by Roman officials). This innovation proved so profitable that they created another province by seizing the islands of Sardinia and Corsica from Carthage's control. Acquiring these foreign territories whetted the Romans' appetite for more, and they also feared a renewal of Carthage's power (Map 4.2). They therefore made alliances with local peoples in Spain, where the Carthaginians were expanding.

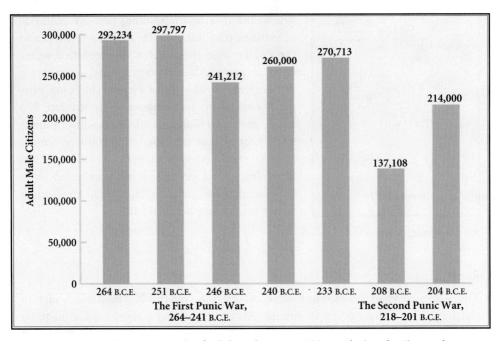

Taking Measure Census Records of Adult Male Roman Citizens during the First and Second Punic Wars

Livy (59 B.C.E.–17 C.E.) and Jerome (c. 347–420 C.E.) provided these numbers from Roman censuses conducted during and between the first two wars against Carthage. Only adult male citizens (the men eligible for Rome's regular army) were counted. The drop in the total for 246 B.C.E., compared with the total for 264 B.C.E., reflects losses in the First Punic War. The low total for 208 B.C.E. reflects losses in battle and defections by communities such as Capua in 216 B.C.E. Because the censuses did not include the Italian allies fighting on Rome's side, the numbers understate the wars' total casualties. Scholars estimate that the first two Punic Wars took the lives of nearly a third of Italy's adult male population—perhaps a quarter of a million soldiers.

The Senate's harsh warning to Carthage not to expand any further convinced the Carthaginians that another war was inevitable, so they decided to strike first. In the Second Punic War (218–201 B.C.E.), the Carthaginian general Hannibal shocked the Romans by marching troops and war elephants over the snowy Alps into Italy. After slaughtering a Roman army at the battle of Cannae in 216 B.C.E.—thirty thousand men died in the bloodiest defeat in Roman history—Hannibal tried to convince Rome's Italian allies to come over to his side. Disastrously for him, most Italians remained loyal to Rome. Hannibal's alliance with King Philip V of Macedonia forced the Romans to fight on a second front in Greece (their first presence in that region), but they refused to crack despite Hannibal's ravaging Italy for fifteen years before retreating to Africa in 203 B.C.E. The Romans finally won by invading the Carthaginians' homeland. Their general Scipio trained his soldiers to keep formation and then swivel out of the way of Hannibal's war elephants, even when facing dozens of the beasts charging so hard they shook the earth. The Romans punished the Carthaginians by forcing them to eliminate

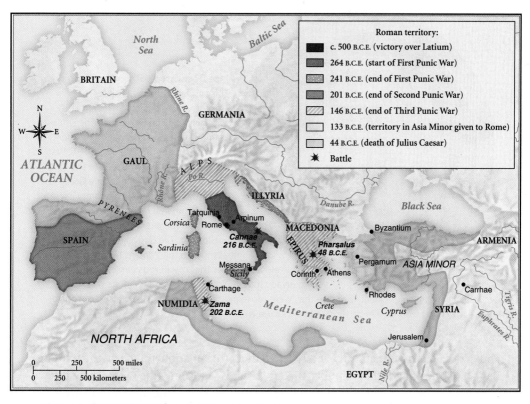

Roman territory:

- ■ c. 500 B.C.E. (victory over Latium)
- ■ 264 B.C.E. (start of First Punic War)
- ▨ 241 B.C.E. (end of First Punic War)
- ▨ 201 B.C.E. (end of Second Punic War)
- ▨ 146 B.C.E. (end of Third Punic War)
- □ 133 B.C.E. (territory in Asia Minor given to Rome)
- □ 44 B.C.E. (death of Julius Caesar)
- ✳ Battle

Map 4.2 Roman Expansion, c. 500–44 B.C.E.
During the first two centuries of its existence, the Roman republic used war and diplomacy to extend its power north and south in the Italian peninsula. In the third and second centuries B.C.E., conflict with Carthage to the south and west and with the Hellenistic kingdoms to the east extended Roman power far outside Italy and led to the creation of provinces from Spain to Greece. The first century B.C.E. saw the conquest of Syria by Pompey and of Gaul by Julius Caesar. **For more help analyzing this map, see the map activity for this chapter in the Online Study Guide at** bedfordstmartins.com/huntconcise.

their navy, pay huge fines for fifty years, and hand over their rich territory in Spain, which became Roman provinces, valuable for their mines.

The Third Punic War (149–146 B.C.E.) broke out when the Carthaginians, who had revived financially, attacked an aggressive Roman ally in North Africa. After defeating Carthage for a third time, the Romans followed Cato's brutal advice: "We must destroy Carthage." After tearing down the city, they converted its territory into a province. This disaster did not obliterate Carthaginian language and culture, however, and under the Roman Empire this part of North Africa became renowned for its economic and intellectual vitality, which emerged from a combination of Roman and Punic traditions.

Rome's conquests in the Punic Wars led to the extension of Roman power to Greece and Asia Minor. After defeating King Philip for revenge and to prevent any threat of his invading Italy, the Romans proclaimed the "freedom of the Greeks" in 196 B.C.E. to show respect for Greece's traditional independence. The Greek cities

Plate Decorated with a War Elephant
This third-century B.C.E. plate from southern Italy depicts an Indian elephant followed by her calf. The adult animal carries on her back a fortified compartment for holding archers. War elephants were introduced to the Mediterranean after Alexander the Great fought against them in his campaign in India. Commanders used them to frighten and confuse the enemy with their size and loud bellowing. The Carthaginian general Hannibal shocked the Romans by bringing elephants over the treacherous passes of the Alps to invade Italy, but most of them died on the way. Armies eventually gave up on elephants because they were too expensive to feed and too difficult to control when panicked or wounded in battle. (Scala/Art Resource, NY.)

and federal leagues naturally interpreted the proclamation to mean they could behave as they liked; they thought that as "friends" of Rome, they were truly independent. They misunderstood. The Romans meant them to behave as clients and follow their new patrons' advice. Trouble developed because the two sides failed to realize that common and familiar words such as *freedom* and *friends* could carry very different meanings in different societies. To make the Macedonians and Greeks observe their obligations as clients, the Romans repeatedly sent armies to the region. Frustrated by continuing resistance, the Senate in 146 B.C.E. ordered the destruction of Corinth for asserting its independence and converted Macedonia and Greece into a province. In 133 B.C.E., the Attalid king of Pergamum boosted Roman power with an astonishing gift: he left his rich Asia Minor kingdom to Rome in his will. In 121 B.C.E., when the Greek city of Massilia on the southern coast of Gaul asked for protection against local Celts, the Romans made the lower part of Gaul across the Alps (modern France) into a province. By this date, then, Rome governed and profited from two-thirds of the Mediterranean region; only the easternmost Mediterranean lay outside its control (Map 4.2, page 139).

Greece's Influence on Rome's Literature, Philosophy, and Art

The wars that took Roman armies to Greece brought increased Greek cultural influence on Rome. In about 200 B.C.E., the first Roman historian used Greek to compose an account of Rome's foundation and the Punic War. Greece also directly inspired the earliest literature in Latin: an adaptation of Homer's *Odyssey* by a Greek ex-slave, written sometime after the First Punic War.

Actors in a Comedy
This relief sculpture dating to the first century B.C.E. shows actors portraying characters in one of the various kinds of comedies popular during the Roman republic. In this variety, which derived from Hellenistic Greek comedies, the actors wore exaggerated masks designating stock personality types and performed broad, slapstick skits. The plots ranged from comic versions of famous legends to stereotypes of common family problems. Here, on the right, an irresponsible son returns home after a night of drinking, supported by his slave and preceded by a hired female musician. On the left, his enraged father is restrained by a friend from beating the prodigal son with his cane. (Scala/Art Resource, NY.)

Many of the most famous early Latin authors were not native Romans, coming from all over Italy and also North Africa. Their widespread origins reveal the mixing of cultures under the republic. They all found inspiration in Greek literature. Roman comedies, for example, took their plots and standard characters from Hellenistic Greek comedies, which raised laughs by portraying family life and stereotyped personalities such as the boastful warrior and the obsessed lover.

Not all Romans applauded Greek influence. Cato, although he studied Greek himself, insisted that the "feeble" Greeks were corrupting the "sturdy" Romans. In the mid-second century B.C.E., he established Latin as an appropriate language for prose by publishing a history of Rome, *The Origins,* and instructions for running a large farm, *On Agriculture.* He glumly predicted that if the Romans ever became infected with Greek literature, they would lose their power. In fact, as is usual in cultural interactions, early Roman authors employed foreign models to express their own values in new ways. The epic poet Ennius, for example, adapted the traditions of Homer to compose his *Annals,* a long poem describing Roman history, but Ennius praised ancestral Roman tradition, as a much-quoted line demonstrates: "On the ways and the men of old rests the Roman commonwealth."

Later Roman writers also took inspiration from Greek literature. Lucretius (c. 94–55 B.C.E.), for example, published a long poem titled *On the Nature of Things* to argue that people should have no fear of death, which only inflamed "the running sores of life." His work's content followed closely the "atomic theory" of the nature of existence of the Greek philosopher Epicurus and described matter as composed of tiny, invisible particles. The poem explained that death meant only that the atoms temporarily forming a person's body once again separated, without pain or suffering. There could be no eternal punishment—or reward—after death because a person's soul, itself made up of atoms, dissolved along with the body.

Hellenistic Greek authors inspired Catullus (c. 84–54 B.C.E.), whose witty poems satirized prominent politicians for their sexual behavior and revealed his own disastrous love life. His most notorious erotic poems detailed his passion for a married woman named Lesbia, whom he begged to think only of immediate pleasures: "Let us live, my Lesbia, and love; the gossip of stern old men is not worth a cent. Suns can set and rise again; we, when once our brief light has set, must sleep one neverending night. Give me a thousand kisses, then a hundred, then a thousand more."

Cicero composed many essays on philosophy, ethics, theology, and political science that adapted Greek philosophy to Roman life. Retiring temporarily from active politics after Julius Caesar's victory in the civil war that destroyed the republic, Cicero in 45–44 B.C.E. wrote about his doctrine of **humanitas** (meaning "humanness" or "the quality of humanity"). This set of ideas expressed an ideal standard of human behavior based on the generous and honest treatment of others, a recognition of the uniqueness of each human being, and an abiding commitment to morality derived from natural law (the right that exists for all people by nature, independent of the differing laws and customs of different societies). Cicero's humanitas ideal has continued to influence thinkers to this day.

Greece also influenced Rome in art and architecture, from the style of sculpture and painting to the design of public buildings. As always, Romans adapted Greek models to their own purposes, especially in portrait sculpture. Hellenistic artists had pioneered the sculpting of realistic statues that showed the damage old age and stress did to the human body. These Greek statues, however, portrayed human stereotypes ("the old man" or "the drunken woman"), not specific people. Greek portrait sculpture, however, presented real individuals in the best possible light, much like a retouched photograph today.

Roman artists in the later republic transferred the Greek tradition of realistic sculpture to portraits. Roman sculptures of specific men did not conceal unflattering features such as protruding noses, receding chins, deep wrinkles, bald heads, and careworn eyes. Because either the men shown in the portraits or their families paid for their statues, they must have wanted the faces sculpted realistically—showing the toll of age and effort—to emphasize how hard the men had worked to serve "the people's thing" that was the republic. Portraits of women, however, were more idealized, perhaps to represent the traditional vision of a happy marriage. Portraits of children were not popular during the republic, perhaps because offspring were not seen as contributing to public life until they were grown.

Imperialism's Consequences for Republican Society

Rome's long wars abroad had the unintended consequence of disrupting Roman agriculture and creating social unrest. The years of conquest created hard times because a farmer absent on prolonged military expeditions had only two choices: relying on a hired hand or slave to manage his crops and animals, or having his wife take on what was traditionally men's work in the fields in addition to her usual domestic tasks. The story of the consul Regulus in the First Punic War reveals the severe problems a man's absence could cause. When the man who managed his four-acre farm died while the consul was away fighting Carthage, a hired hand ran off with all the farm's tools and livestock. Regulus begged the Senate to send a general to replace him so he could return home to save his wife and children from starving. Instead, the senators saved Regulus's family and property from ruin because they wanted to retain him as a commander in the field.

Ordinary soldiers received no such special aid, and these troubles hit poorer families particularly hard when in the second century B.C.E., for reasons that remain unclear, there was no longer enough farmland to support their children from generation to generation. Scholars have usually concluded that the rich had deprived the poor of land, but recent research suggests that the problem stemmed from a rapid growth in the population of young people. Not all regions of Italy suffered as severely as others, and some impoverished farmers and their families managed to remain in the countryside by working as day laborers for others. Whatever the cause of the rising number of people with no way to make a living, this change created a social crisis by the late second century B.C.E. Many homeless people migrated to Rome, where the men looked for work as menial laborers and the women sought piecework making cloth but were often forced into prostitution.

This influx of desperate, landless people swelled the poor population in Rome and created political conflict as ambitious politicians competed for their votes by promising welfare benefits. Fearing violent riots by the growing number of hungry poor in the capital, the government took on the task of importing food to calm them. By the late second century B.C.E., Rome was importing massive amounts of grain from abroad to support the city's masses. Their demand for rations of low-priced (and eventually free) grain distributed at the state's expense became one of the most explosive issues in late republican politics.

At the other end of the social hierarchy, Rome's elite reaped abundant rewards from imperialism. The increased need for commanders to lead overseas military campaigns allowed successful generals to enrich themselves and their families. By using their gains to finance public buildings, the elite enhanced their reputations while benefiting the general population. Building new temples, for example, was thought to increase everyone's security by pleasing the gods.

The financial troubles of small farmers enriched big landowners because they could buy bankrupt plots to create larger estates. They also illegally occupied public land carved from the territory of defeated peoples. The rich worked their large estates, called *latifundia,* with slaves as well as free laborers. Many free but poor

Bedroom in a Rich Roman House
This bedroom from about 40 B.C.E. was in the home of a wealthy Roman family near Naples. It was buried and preserved by the eruption of the volcano Vesuvius in 79 C.E. The bright paintings included a wide variety of outdoor scenes and architecture. The stone mosaic floor helped keep the house cool in the summer. (Image copyright © The Metropolitan Museum of Art/Art Resource, NY.)

Romans now found it hard to get work as laborers because the rich had acquired slave workers from the many people taken captive during the foreign wars. The growing size of the slave crews working on latifundia was a mixed blessing for their wealthy owners because the presence of so many slaves in one place led to periodic revolts, which required the army to suppress them.

The elite also profited from Rome's expansion by filling government offices in the new provinces, where they could enrich themselves if they ignored the traditional value of uprightness. Since Roman provincial officials ruled by martial law, no one in the provinces could curb a greedy governor's appetite for extracting money from the province's local peoples. Not all governors were corrupt, but some did use their unsupervised power to extort everything they could. Until jury trials were created, such offenders escaped punishment because in the Senate they and their colleagues would routinely excuse one another's crimes.

A new desire for luxury, financed by the fruits of expansion abroad, fractured the traditional values of moderation and frugality. Before, a general such as Manius Curius in the third century B.C.E. represented the ideal: despite his glorious military victories, legend said that he boiled turnips for his meals in a humble hut. Now, the elite acquired showy luxuries, such as large country villas for entertaining friends and clients, to proclaim their social superiority. Money had become more valuable to them than the good of "the people's thing."

> REVIEW What were the intended and unintended consequences of Rome's creation of an empire?

The Destruction of the Republic, 133–44 B.C.E.

Ambitious leaders from the Roman elite destroyed the republic in civil war. The conflict had two main causes: fierce disagreements among these leaders about how much political influence and government support ordinary citizens should receive, and rivalry for individual glory. The tribunes Tiberius and Gaius Gracchus agitated for reforms to help poor Romans, whom they pitied for their bitter poverty and whose potential for rioting they feared. The brothers' opponents in the Senate resorted to murder to stop them. When Gaius Marius opened army service to the poor to boost his personal status, his creation of "client armies" undermined faithfulness to the republic. When the people's unwillingness to share citizenship with Italian allies sparked a war in Italy and the clashing ambitions of the "great men" Sulla, Pompey, and Julius Caesar burst into civil war, the republic shattered beyond repair.

The Gracchus Brothers and Political Violence

The brothers Tiberius and Gaius Sempronius Gracchus, sons of a famous elite family, won political support from poor citizens by promising a much higher level of government subsidies for them. Tiberius, the elder brother, spoke bluntly about the horrible lives of the landless poor, according to his second-century C.E. biographer Plutarch:

> The wild beasts that roam over Italy have their dens. . . . But the men who fight and die for Italy enjoy nothing but the air and light; without house or home they wander about with their wives and children. . . . They fight and die to protect the wealth and luxury of others; they are called masters of the world, and have not a lump of ground they call their own.

Tiberius was elected tribune for 133 B.C.E. Motivated by both compassion for these impoverished citizens and worry about their potential to use violence to try to improve their living conditions, he proposed reforms to give them financial support. The Senate strongly rejected his proposals. Tiberius then broke tradition by having the Plebeian Assembly pass laws contrary to the Senate's advice. He also violated tradition by running for reelection as tribune in consecutive years. In response,

Tiberius's own cousin led a band of senators and their clients in an ambush against him to, as they shouted, "save the republic." When they clubbed the tribune and many of his followers to death, their assault marked a turning point in the republic: murder now became a political tool.

Gaius, elected tribune for 123 B.C.E. and, in a dramatic break with tradition, for the following year as well, also pushed reforms that outraged the elite: land redistribution, subsidized grain prices, public works projects throughout Italy to provide employment for the poor, and colonies abroad to provide farms for the landless. Gaius's most revolutionary proposals were to grant Roman citizenship to many Italians and to establish new courts that would try senators accused of corruption as provincial governors. The new juries would be manned not by senators but by *equites* (equestrians, or knights). These were landowners from outside the city, wealthy businessmen whose choice of commerce over a public career set them apart from senators. Because they did not serve in the Senate, equestrians could convict corrupt senators without fear of peer pressure. Gaius's proposal marked the emergence of the equestrians as a political force in Roman politics and angered the Senate. When the senators blocked his plans, Gaius assembled an armed group to threaten them. They responded by instructing the consuls "to take all measures necessary to defend the republic," meaning violence. To escape execution, Gaius had one of his slaves cut his throat; the senators and their followers then murdered hundreds of Gaius's supporters.

The violent deaths of the Gracchus brothers and so many other citizens created a crisis in Roman politics. From then on, members of the elite divided themselves into two groups: "supporters of the common people" (*populares*) or "supporters of the best people" (*optimates*). Some identified with one side or the other based on genuine allegiance to its policies; others supported whichever side better promoted their own political advancement.

Gaius Marius and the First Client Armies

This crisis allowed a new kind of leader to arise: men from the elite but with no consul among their ancestors. Such men relied on sheer ability to force their way to fame, fortune, influence, and—their ultimate goal—election as consul. The most controversial of them was Gaius Marius (c. 157–86 B.C.E.), an equestrian from central Italy. Ordinarily, a man with his background had no chance of cracking the nobles' hold on the consulships. When Marius succeeded as a general against a rebel in Africa where nobles had failed, however, the people elected him consul for 107 B.C.E. In Roman terms, this election made him a "new man"—that is, the first man in the history of his family to become consul. Marius's further successes in great crises, especially against German tribes that attacked southern France and then Italy, led the people to elect him consul for six terms, including consecutive service. His career overturned Roman political tradition.

Marius became so famous that the Senate voted him a triumph, Rome's highest—and rarest—military honor. On the day of the ceremony, the general paraded through Rome in a chariot. His face was painted red for reasons Romans no longer remembered. Huge crowds cheered him, while his army teased him with off-color jokes to avert the evil eye at this moment of supreme glory. For a similar reason, a slave rode with him to keep whispering in his ear, "Look behind you, and remember that you are a mortal."

Ordinary citizens loved Marius for his reform of military service. Previously, only men with property were usually allowed to enroll as soldiers. Marius completed a growing trend by opening enlistment to proletarians, men who owned almost nothing. For them, serving in the army meant an opportunity to better their lot by acquiring plunder and a land grant to retire on.

This change created armies more tied to their commanders than to the community. Proletarian troops felt loyalty to commanders who led them to victory and then generously divided the plunder with them. Poor soldiers thus began to behave like an army of clients following their general as their patron and supporting his ambitions. Later generals used client armies in the political and personal disputes that destroyed the republic.

Sulla and Civil War

The first commander to do this was a noble named Lucius Cornelius Sulla (c. 138–78 B.C.E.). His opportunity came when Rome's Italian allies rebelled from 91 to 87 B.C.E. in frustration at their being denied citizenship. The Italians lost the war and 300,000 men, but they won the political battle: Romans granted citizenship to all freeborn peoples of Italy south of the Po River. Sulla's successful command in the war won him election as consul, and he then marched his client army against Rome to force the Senate to make him the commander in Asia Minor, to put down a serious rebellion there. The campaign would mean unimaginable plunder because Asia Minor had many wealthy cities. All Sulla's officers except one deserted him in horror, but his soldiers united behind him. Capturing Rome, Sulla murdered or exiled his opponents and let his men rampage through the city. He then led them off to Asia Minor, ignoring a summons to stand trial.

When Sulla returned victorious from Asia Minor, he devised a merciless procedure called proscription—posting a list of those supposedly guilty of treasonable crimes so that anyone could kill them without a trial. Because the property of those proscribed was confiscated, Sulla's followers listed the names of all those whose wealth they desired. The Senate in terror appointed Sulla dictator—an emergency office supposed to be held only temporarily—without any limitation of term. He reorganized the government in the interest of "the best people," his social class, by making senators the only ones allowed to judge cases against their colleagues and forbidding tribunes to offer legislation on their own or hold any other office after their terms.

Sulla died soon thereafter, but his bloody career revealed the sad fate of the traditional values of the republic. First, the definition of success in war had long ago changed from defending the community to acquiring profits for commanders and common soldiers alike. Second, the patron-client system had mutated to make poor soldiers feel stronger ties of obligation to their generals than to the republic. Finally, the traditional desire to win honor could now create political instability when a leader's desire for prestige and wealth overcame his desire to provide public service.

Pompey "the Great" and the First Triumvirate

The career of Gnaeus Pompey (106–48 B.C.E.) shows how weak the traditional restraints on a leader's power became after Sulla. Only twenty-three years old, Pompey gathered a private army from his father's clients to fight for Sulla. His spectacular victories made it impossible for Sulla to refuse his demand for a triumph. Awarding the supreme honor to such a young man, who had not held a single public office, shattered tradition, but as Pompey told Sulla, "People worship the rising, not the setting, sun."

By claiming the credit (the real victor was Marcus Licinius Crassus) for stopping a massive slave rebellion led by Spartacus, a fugitive gladiator who had terrorized southern Italy for two years and defeated consuls with his army of 100,000 escaped slaves, Pompey won election to the consulship in 70 B.C.E. without climbing the ladder of offices or reaching the legal age of forty-two. Three years later, he received unlimited powers to eradicate the pirates infesting the Mediterranean. He smashed them in a matter of months. This success made him wildly popular with the urban poor, who depended on a steady flow of imported grain; with wealthy shippers, who depended on safe sea-lanes; and with coastal communities that had suffered from the pirates' raids. Next he won the first Roman victories in the Levant and made Syria a province in 64 B.C.E., thereby ending the Seleucid kingdom and extending Rome's power to the eastern edge of the Mediterranean.

Pompey's victories were so amazing that people compared him to Alexander the Great and referred to him as *Magnus* (the Great). He boasted that he had increased Rome's provincial revenues by 70 percent and distributed plunder equal to twelve and a half years' pay to his soldiers. He treated foreign policy as his personal business. In the east he operated on his own and ignored the tradition of commanders consulting the Senate to decide on new political arrangements for conquered territories. He explained his attitude when replying to some foreigners who had objected to his actions as unjust: "Stop quoting the laws to us," he told them. "We carry swords."

Pompey's rivals in Rome tried to gain support by proclaiming their concern for the common people. By the 60s B.C.E., Rome's population had soared to over half a million, as farmers unable to make a living off the land flocked to the capital looking for day labor and government-provided food. Hundreds of thousands lived crowded together in shabby, multistory apartment buildings no better than slums and depended on subsidized grain as the basis of their meals. Work was hard to find. Danger haunted the crowded streets because the city had no police force. Even the propertied class was in trouble. Sulla's confiscations had produced a credit crunch and caused land values to crash by flooding the real estate market with properties for sale. Overextended investors were trying to borrow their way back to financial health, with no success.

In 60 B.C.E. Pompey joined his fiercest political rivals, Crassus and Julius Caesar, in an unofficial power-sharing arrangement called the **First Triumvirate** (a coalition of three men). They formed the alliance because none of them was strong enough to defeat the other two; by joining together, each could get at least part of what he wanted in political and military power. The triumvirate had no governing philosophy except self-interest; the arrangement's only cohesion came from personal connections. To cement his bond with Pompey, Caesar married his daughter, Julia, to Pompey in 59 B.C.E., even though she had been engaged to another man. Pompey then ordered his own daughter, who also had been engaged, to marry Julia's jilted fiancé. Through these marital connections, the two powerful rivals now had a common interest: the well-being of Julia, Caesar's only daughter and Pompey's new wife. (Pompey had earlier divorced his second wife after Caesar had allegedly seduced her.) Pompey and Julia apparently fell deeply in love, and as long as Julia lived, Pompey's affection for her restrained him from an outright break with her father.

The Rise and Fall of Julius Caesar

Julius Caesar (100–44 B.C.E.), born to one of Rome's oldest families and claiming the goddess Venus as his ancestor, had a brilliant military career that outshone even Pompey's. Most famously, in the 50s B.C.E. he achieved nearly ten years of victories—and swift recovery from defeats—against the fearsome Gauls in what is today France, which Caesar made into a Roman province. He awed his troops with his daring by crossing the channel to campaign even in Britain. His political enemies in Rome dreaded him even more as his military successes mounted, and the bond linking him to Pompey vanished in 54 B.C.E. when Julia died in childbirth. With Caesar's followers agitating to win the masses' support for his return to the capital, the two sides' rivalry exploded into violence. By the mid-50s B.C.E., political gangs of young men roamed the alleys of Rome in search of opponents to assault or murder. Street fighting reached such a level of violence in 53 B.C.E. that it prevented elections; no consuls could be chosen until the year was half over. The triumvirate completely dissolved that same year with the death of Crassus in battle in northern Mesopotamia. A year later, Caesar's enemies took the extraordinary step of having Pompey appointed sole consul. The traditions of republican government had crumbled.

When the Senate ordered Caesar to surrender his command and thus open himself to prosecution by his enemies, he led his army against Rome. As he crossed the Rubicon River, the official northern boundary of Italy, in early 49 B.C.E., he uttered the famous words signaling that he had chosen civil war: "The die is cast." Caesar's advance caused Pompey and most senators to flee to Greece to prepare to fight back. When Caesar led his army to Greece in 48 B.C.E., he nearly lost the war as his supplies ran out, but his soldiers remained loyal even when they were reduced to eating bread made from roots. When Pompey saw what his opponent's troops were willing to live on, he cried, "I am fighting wild beasts."

Coin Portrait of Julius Caesar

Julius Caesar (100–44 B.C.E.) was the first living Roman to have his portrait appear on a Roman coin. The images and words stamped on the front and back of Roman republican coins changed annually, chosen by the officials in charge of minting. Tradition mandated that only persons who had died could be shown (the same rule applies to U.S. currency), but after Caesar won the civil war in 45 B.C.E., he broke that tradition, as he did many others, to show that he was Rome's supreme leader. Here, he wears the laurel wreath of a conquering general. The realistic portrait conforms to late republican style. Caesar's wrinkled neck and careworn expression emphasize the suffering he endured—and imposed on others—to reach the pinnacle of success. Do you think a portrait is more impressive if it shows the person's blemishes or if it is idealized? **For more help analyzing this image, see the visual activity for this chapter in the Online Study Guide at** bedfordstmartins.com/huntconcise. (Bibliothèque nationale de France.)

Caesar defeated Pompey and then invaded Egypt, where he restored Cleopatra VII (69–30 B.C.E.) to the Egyptian throne. As intelligent as she was ruthless, Cleopatra charmed the invader into sharing her bed and supporting her rule. This attachment shocked Caesar's friends and enemies alike: they believed Rome should seize power from foreigners, not yield it to them. Still, so effective were Cleopatra's powers of persuasion that Caesar maintained the love affair and guaranteed her rule over a rich land that his army otherwise would have plundered.

By 45 B.C.E., Caesar had won the civil war but faced the problem of how to govern a shattered republic: only a popular leader ruling alone seemed capable of ending the cycle of violence, but the oldest tradition of the republic's elite was its hatred of monarchy. The second-century B.C.E. senator Cato, notorious for his advice in favor of destroying Carthage, had best expressed this feeling. "A king," he said, "is an animal that feeds on human flesh." Caesar's solution was to rule as king in everything but name. First, he had himself appointed dictator in 48 B.C.E.; by 44 B.C.E. he had become "dictator for an indefinite term," a startling break with tradition for an office meant to be short-term only. "I am not a king," he insisted, but the distinction was hard to recognize. Elections for offices continued, but Caesar controlled the results by recommending candidates to the assemblies, which his supporters dominated.

Acting as a sole ruler while carefully avoiding calling himself a monarch, Caesar introduced changes that he hoped would strengthen Rome and prevent violent unrest: a moderate cancellation of debts; a limitation on the number of people eligible for subsidized grain; a large program of public works, including the construction of public libraries; colonies for his veterans in Italy and abroad; the rebuilding of Corinth and Carthage as commercial centers; and a revival of the ancient policy of giving citizenship to non-Romans, such as the Gauls on the Italian side of the Alps. He also admitted non-Italians to the Senate when he expanded its membership from six hundred (the expanded size established by Sulla) to nine hundred.

Caesar prided himself on his clemency, the recipients of which were, by Roman custom, bound to be his grateful clients. In return, he received unprecedented honors, such as a special golden seat in the Senate house and the renaming of the seventh month of the year after him (July). He also regularized the Roman calendar by having each year include 365 days, a calculation based on an ancient Egyptian calendar that forms the basis of our modern one.

Julius Caesar's career and ideas made him the most popular and adored ruler among ordinary people in Roman history. What sort of government and society Rome would have developed if Caesar had lived longer is one of the most fascinating what-if questions in ancient history. But he was murdered soon after becoming "dictator for an indefinite term" because his rule outraged "the best people." They resented being dominated by one of their own, a "traitor" who had deserted to "the common people's" side. A band of senators formed a conspiracy, led by Caesar's former close friend Marcus Junius Brutus and inspired by the legend about Brutus's ancestor Lucius Junius Brutus having led the violent expulsion of Rome's original monarchy. They cut Caesar to pieces with daggers in the Senate house on March 15 (the Ides of March on the Roman calendar), 44 B.C.E. When his friend Brutus stabbed him, Caesar, according to some ancient reports, gasped his last words—in Greek: "You, too, my son?"

The "liberators," as the assassins called themselves, had no specific plan for reviving the republic. They apparently believed that it would automatically spring back to life, overlooking the horrible political violence of the previous forty years and the distortion of Roman values that it had brought. Panicked by the loss of their patron, the masses rioted at Caesar's funeral to vent their anger against the elite that had robbed them of their benefactor. Failing to form a united front, the elite resumed their feuds with one another. By 44 B.C.E., the republic was lost beyond recovery.

REVIEW How did the actions and policies of individual leaders destroy the republic?

Conclusion

From its beginnings in 509 B.C.E., the Roman republic flourished because its traditional values stressed the common good, it absorbed outsiders, and its small farmers produced agricultural surpluses. These surpluses supported a growing population, which supplied soldiers for a strong army that won an empire. Romans' willingness to endure tremendous losses of life and property—the proof that they valued faithfulness—helped make them unbeatable: Rome might lose battles but never wars. Because warfare brought profits, peace seemed a wasted opportunity. Elite commanders craved victories because they brought glory and riches to raise their status in Rome's social hierarchy.

Rome's long wars abroad had unexpected and harmful consequences at home. Many of Italy's rural poor farmers now found it impossible to make a living on the land. When desperate people flocked to Rome, they created political and social instability, especially with demands for food paid for with public money. Members of the elite disagreed over how to solve the problem and also increased their competition with each other for the career opportunities presented by constant war. These rivalries became unmanageable when successful generals began to extort advantages for themselves by acting as patrons to their client armies. In this hypercompetitive environment, violence became the ultimate action in political disputes. But violent actions provoked violent responses; community values were drowned in the blood of civil war. No reasonable Roman could have been optimistic about the chances for an enduring peace in the aftermath of Caesar's assassination in 44 B.C.E. That a sole ruler would forge such a peace less than fifteen years later would have seemed an impossible dream.

CHAPTER REVIEW QUESTIONS

1. Compare the political and social values of the Roman republic with those of the Classical Greek city-state.
2. What were the positive and negative consequences of war for the Roman republic?

For practice quizzes and other study tools, see the Online Study Guide at bedfordstmartins.com/huntconcise.

For primary-source material from this period, see Chapter 5 of *Sources of THE MAKING OF THE WEST*, Third Edition.

TIMELINE

■ **44 B.C.E.** Caesar appointed "dictator for an indefinite term" and then assassinated

■ **45–44 B.C.E.** Cicero writes his philosophical works on humanitas

■ **49–45 B.C.E.** Civil war, with Caesar the victor

■ **60 B.C.E.** First Triumvirate (Caesar, Pompey, and Crassus)

■ **91–87 B.C.E.** War between Rome and its Italian allies

■ **C. 450 B.C.E.** Creation of the Twelve Tables, Rome's first written law code

509–287 B.C.E. Struggle of the orders

■ **509 B.C.E.** Roman republic established

760 B.C.E.	520 B.C.E.	280 B.C.E.	40 B.C.E.

■ **753 B.C.E.** Traditional date of Rome's founding

264–241 B.C.E. First Punic War

218–201 B.C.E. Second Punic War

■ **Mid-second century B.C.E.** Cato writes *The Origins*, the first history of Rome in Latin

149–146 B.C.E. Third Punic War

■ **146 B.C.E.** Destruction of Carthage and Corinth

■ **133 B.C.E.** Tiberius Gracchus elected tribune and then assassinated

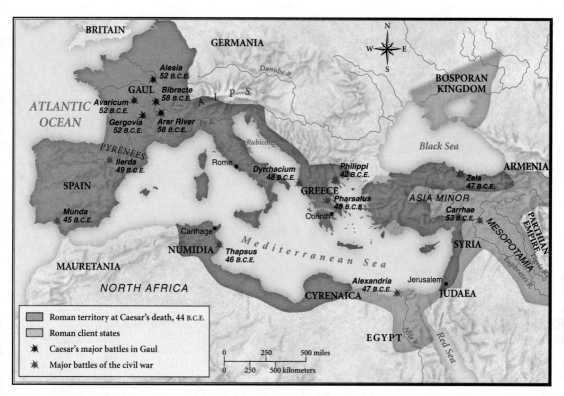

Mapping the West The Roman World at the End of the Republic, c. 44 B.C.E.
Upon Julius Caesar's assassination in 44 B.C.E., the territory that Rome would control during the coming centuries was almost complete. Caesar's young relative Octavian (the future Augustus) would conquer and add Egypt in 30 B.C.E. Geography and distance were the primary factors preventing further expansion, which Romans never stopped thinking of as desirable even when practical difficulties made this goal only a dream. The deserts of Africa and the Near East worked against expansion southward or eastward, and trackless forests and fierce resistance from local inhabitants made expansion into central Europe and the British Isles impossible to sustain.

Suggested References

Our knowledge of the political and economic changes in the Roman republic is being revised by archaeological research linked to close study of the ancient literary sources.

Ashton, Sally-Ann. *Cleopatra and Egypt.* 2008.

Beard, Mary, et al. *Religions of Rome.* 2 vols. 1998.

Bradley, Keith. *Slavery and Society at Rome.* 1994.

*Caesar. *The Civil War.* Trans. John Carter. 1997.

*Cicero. *On the Good Life.* Trans. Michael Grant. 1971.

Daily life (and more): http://www.vroma.org/~bmcmanus/romanpages.html

Earl, Donald. *The Moral and Political Tradition of Rome.* 1967.

Gardner, Jane. *Women in Roman Law and Society.* 1986.

Goldsworthy, Adrian. *The Punic Wars.* 2000.

Lancel, Serge. *Carthage: A History.* Trans. Antonia Nevill. 1995.

Strong, Donald. *Roman Art.* 2d ed. 1988.

I N 203 C.E., VIBIA PERPETUA, wealthy and twenty-two years old, nursed her infant in a Carthage jail while awaiting execution for refusing to participate in traditional sacrifices for the Roman emperor's health and safety. One morning, the jailer dragged her off to see the local Roman governor, and Perpetua described in her journal what happened next:

Executing a Criminal in Public
This mosaic shows a convicted criminal being killed by a leopard at a public execution. Romans believed that serious criminals deserved disgraceful deaths before crowds of spectators. Martyrs charged with treason, like Perpetua, often were executed by being "condemned to the beasts." Here the prisoner is tied to a stake on a chariot so the handlers can push him into the face of the leopard to provoke an angry leap; wild animals frequently would not attack without such provocation. Dated to about Perpetua's time, c. 200 C.E., the mosaic covered a villa floor in North Africa, in what is today Libya. The villa's owner perhaps ordered this subject for his floor to show visitors that he had paid for the expensive spectacle that included this grisly execution. (© Roger Wood/Corbis.)

My father came carrying my son, crying "Perform the sacrifice; take pity on your baby!" Then the governor pleaded, "Think of your old father; show pity for your little child! Offer the sacrifice for the health of the emperor's family." "I refuse," I answered. "Are you a Christian?" asked the governor. "Yes." When my father would not stop trying to change my mind, the governor ordered him thrown to the ground and whipped with a rod. I felt sorry for my father; it seemed they were beating me. I pitied his pathetic old age.

The governor, reluctantly it seems, had Perpetua executed by being gored by a bull and stabbed by a gladiator. She died still proclaiming her faith in the new Christian religion and rejecting Rome's traditional religion of the imperial cult.

Perpetua's fate illustrates the continuing importance of tradition in Roman history after the fall of the republic. She died a criminal because she refused to observe "the way of the ancestors" by submitting to the demand that she prove her loyalty to Rome's government by making a sacrifice. Her refusal to act according to traditional values, though motivated by different reasons, recalled the refusal of Roman commanders in the late republic to value the community's needs over their personal ambitions. Their civil wars created a bloodbath following Julius Caesar's assassination in 44 B.C.E. After seventeen years of Roman fighting Roman, Augustus (63 B.C.E.–14 C.E.) restored peace in 27 B.C.E. by inventing a disguised monarchy, the **principate**, which claimed to restore traditional values. His new political and social system opened the pivotal period in Western civilization that we call the Roman Empire.

Romans welcomed the two centuries of relative peace that the principate brought, a period that historians call the **Pax Romana** (Roman peace). In the third century C.E., however, rivalry over who would be emperor reignited civil war, leading to economic crisis. By the 280s C.E., the Roman imperial government again desperately needed to transform its political system to restore traditional values of loyalty and public service. Diocletian, a military commander from the provinces, would begin that process by winning rule over the Roman world in 284 C.E.

CHAPTER FOCUS QUESTION How did Augustus's new political system successfully keep the "Roman peace" for two centuries, and why did it fail in the third century?

Creating the "Roman Peace"

Inventing tradition takes time. Augustus developed his new political system gradually; as the biographer Suetonius said, Augustus "made haste slowly." The principate produced two centuries of peace, although its rulers periodically waged war to expand imperial territory, suppress rebellions, and repel invaders. Augustus succeeded in reinventing monarchy as an effective form of Roman government because he won the civil war and, during his long rule, found new ways to inspire loyalty by cashing in on the name bestowed on him by the Senate, "Father of His Country."

From Republic to Principate, 44–27 B.C.E.

The principate was born in blood. Julius Caesar's assassination in 44 B.C.E. set off another civil war between generals. The leading opponents were Mark Antony and Octavian (the future Augustus), Caesar's eighteen-year-old grandnephew, who by Caesar's will became his adopted son and heir. Octavian won the loyalty of Caesar's soldiers by taking his new father's name, making him a member of the Julian family, and by promising them rewards from their murdered general's wealth. Marching these veterans to Rome in 43 B.C.E., the teenager forced his election as consul without ever having been elected to any post on the ladder of offices, as tradition required.

Octavian, Antony, and a general named Lepidus then joined forces to eliminate rivals, especially Caesar's assassins. In late 43 B.C.E., the three formed the Second Triumvirate, which they forced the Senate to recognize as an official emergency panel for "rebuilding the state." With no checks on their power, they began to murder their enemies and confiscate the murdered men's property. Octavian and Antony soon forced Lepidus into retirement. Too ambitious to cooperate for long, especially because Antony thought the much younger Octavian should defer to him as his elder, they began a civil war with each other.

Antony made the eastern Mediterranean his base, joining forces with Cleopatra VII (69–30 B.C.E.), the Ptolemaic queen of Egypt who had earlier allied with Caesar. Enchanted by Cleopatra's wit and intelligence, Antony became her ally and lover. Skillfully playing on Romans' fear of foreign attack, Octavian rallied support by claiming that Antony planned to make Cleopatra queen of Rome. Octavian then persuaded the residents of Italy and the western provinces to swear a personal oath of loyalty to him, making them all his clients. In 31 B.C.E. Octavian's victory at the naval battle of Actium in northwestern Greece ended the war (Map 5.1). Cleopatra and Antony

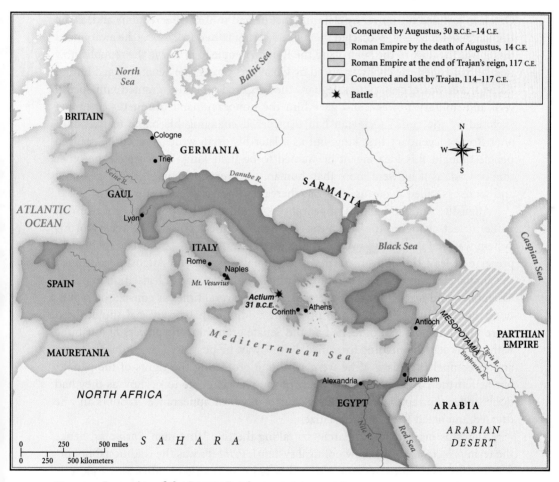

Map 5.1 Expansion of the Roman Empire, 30 B.C.E.–117 C.E.
When Octavian (the future Augustus) captured Egypt in 30 B.C.E. after the suicides of Mark Antony and Cleopatra, he made a significant contribution to the economic strength of Rome because the land of the Nile provided huge amounts of grain and gold. Roman power now encircled the Mediterranean Sea (except for Mauretania, which remained technically under the rule of local kings with Roman approval until c. 44 C.E.). When the emperor Trajan took over the southern part of Mesopotamia in 114–117 C.E., imperial conquest reached its height: Rome's control had never before extended so far east. Hadrian, Trajan's successor, abandoned Mesopotamia, probably because it seemed too far away from Rome to defend. Egypt remained part of the empire until the Arab conquest in 642 C.E.

fled to Egypt, where they both committed suicide in 30 B.C.E., choosing to take their own lives to rob their enemy of celebrity hostages. The general stabbed himself first, bleeding to death in his lover's embrace. The queen then ended her life by letting a poisonous snake, a symbol of Egyptian royal authority, bite her. Octavian's capture of Egypt made him Rome's richest citizen and its unrivaled leader.

Augustus's "Restoration of the Republic," 27 B.C.E.–14 C.E.

Octavian justified his power by claiming that he had restored the republic and, as the Roman people's patron, protected them like a caring father. In 27 B.C.E. he announced that it was the duty of the Senate and the Roman people to preserve the republic now that he had ended the civil war. Awed by Octavian's power, the Senate begged him to do whatever was necessary to safeguard the "restored republic," granted him special civil and military powers, and gave him the honorary name **Augustus**, meaning "favored by the gods." Octavian had considered changing his name to Romulus, after Rome's legendary first king, but as a later historian wrote, "When he realized people thought this idea meant he wanted to be their king, he accepted the other title instead, as if he were more than human; for everything that is most treasured and sacred is called *augustus*." He was thereafter known as Augustus.

Augustus maintained the appearance of traditional republican government while in fact changing the structure of Roman political power. The reality of his system was that it was a monarchy masked as a restored and improved republic. To preserve at least the outward form of traditional government, Augustus continued the annual election of consuls and other officials, the passing of legislation in public assemblies, and respect for the Senate. He served several times as consul, the republic's premier official. So as not to break the tradition that no official should hold more than one post at a time, he had the Senate grant him the powers of a tribune without his actually holding the office. In this way, he possessed the authority to act and to compel citizens as if he were a tribune protecting the rights of the people, but he left the posts open for members of the plebeian elite to occupy, as they had done under the republic. Augustus also kept his own appearance "republican": he dressed and acted like a regular citizen.

Augustus masked his monarchy by taking the title "first man" (*princeps*, hence the term *principate* for his new political system). *Princeps* was the traditional honorary title for the leading senator. Using this as his only title of office was a cleverly calculated move. In the republic, the "first man" had guided Rome based on the respect (**auctoritas**) he had earned; he had no more formal power (*potestas*) than any other leader. By choosing the title *princeps*, Augustus appeared to carry on this valued tradition, but in reality he had taken control of the government. *Princeps* was, in fact, the title of the new kind of ruler that today we call the Roman emperor (from the Latin *imperator,* "commander"). Previously, no one could have exercised the powers of both consul and tribune simultaneously.

Cameo Celebrating Augustus
This cameo, about eight inches by nine inches, was carved early in the Roman Empire. The upper scene probably shows Augustus being crowned—for having saved Roman citizens—by a standing female figure representing the inhabited world. The seated female figure represents Rome and resembles Livia, Augustus's wife, his partner in rule. The man stepping out of the chariot is Tiberius, Livia's son and Augustus's choice to succeed him as princeps. Why do you think Tiberius carries a scepter like that held by Augustus? The lower scene shows defeated enemies subjected to Roman power. How do you think the lower scene relates to the upper scene? (Kunsthistorisches Museum, Wien.)

In 2 B.C.E. Augustus received the symbolic key to his power: the Senate declared him "Father of His Country." He announced that this was the greatest honor Rome could grant. He valued this title because it solidified his image of himself as princeps: a leader governing Romans like a father—stern but caring, requiring obedience and loyalty from his children, but dedicated to taking care of them in return.

The principate brought peace but had a fundamental weakness: the princeps could not automatically pass on his rule to his son. In regular monarchies, the ruler's son inherited his father's position and political legitimacy. Augustus had to create a new process to try to ensure a peaceful succession that would seem legitimate. He therefore said that the Senate would choose his successor, expecting, of course, that it would choose the person he nominated. This new system of succession later resulted in some violent struggles over who should become the next princeps. And since Augustus's successors did not have automatic legitimacy as rulers, they were always quick to suppress any sign of disloyalty or rebellion. Perpetua's refusal to sacrifice, for example, was considered treason and impiety, which was punishable by death, because it disrespected the princeps and angered the gods, thereby threatening the safety of the entire community.

Sources of Power and Legitimacy of the Principate

Augustus and his successors exercised supreme power because they controlled the army and the treasury. Augustus made the military the foundation of his power by turning the republican army—a part-time militia—into a full-time professional force under his command. He made the princeps into the troops' patron by establishing set lengths of service, regular pay, and substantial benefits upon retirement. To cover the added costs, Augustus imposed an inheritance tax on citizens. The rich hated this innovation, but the grateful army obeyed and protected the emperor. Another change Augustus made was to station soldiers—the **praetorian guard**—in Rome itself for the first time. These troops prevented rebellion in the capital and provided an imperial bodyguard, a visible reminder of the emperor's dominance.

To broadcast the political legitimacy he needed, Augustus communicated his image as "Father of His Country"—the patron of everyone in a father's traditional role as protector—with objects from coins to public buildings. As the only mass-produced source of official messages, coins functioned like modern political advertising. The most imposing evidence that Augustus provided of his generosity as a patron came from the mammoth buildings in Rome paid for by the fortune he had inherited from Caesar and then increased in war. The huge Forum of Augustus best illustrates his skill at communicating through bricks and stone (Figure 5.1). Its plaza was centered on a temple to Mars, the Roman god of war. Two-story colonnades stretched out from the temple like wings, sheltering statues of famous Roman heroes as inspirations to future leaders. Augustus's Forum provided a gathering place for religious rituals and ceremonies marking the passage into adulthood of upper-class boys, but it also stressed the themes he wanted to communicate about his new system: peace restored through victory, the foundation of a new age, devotion to the gods who had led Rome to victory, respect for tradition, and his unselfishness in spending money for the community. These messages communicated Augustus's justification for his rule.

Historians debate Augustus's motives for establishing the principate. Was he a cynical tyrant working to destroy the freedoms of the republic? Did he have no choice but to impose a disguised monarchy to reunite a society ripped apart by civil war? Perhaps it is best to see him as a revolutionary bound by tradition. His problem had been the one always facing Roman politicians—how to balance his own personal ambitions, the need for peace, and Rome's tradition of shared rule. Augustus's goals were stability, order, and legitimacy for his system, not political freedom for citizens. His strategy was to employ traditional values to justify changes, as in his reinvention of the meaning of the title "first man." Above all, he extended

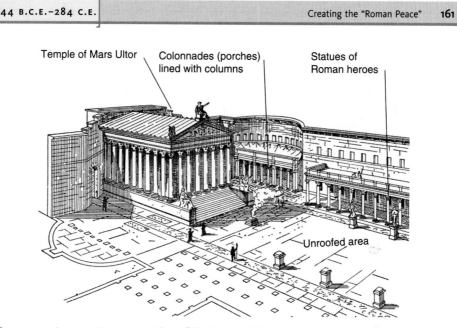

Figure 5.1 Cutaway Reconstruction of the Forum of Augustus
Augustus built this large forum (120 × 90 yards) to commemorate his victory over the assassins of his adoptive father, Julius Caesar. Dedicated in 2 B.C.E., its centerpiece was a marble temple dedicated to the god Mars Ultor ("the Avenger"). Inside the temple he placed statues of Mars, Venus (the divine ancestor of Julius Caesar), and Julius Caesar (as a god), as well as Caesar's sword and works of art. The two curved spaces flanking the temple featured statues of Aeneas and Romulus, Rome's founders. The porches stretching along the open courtyard housed other statues of Roman heroes. The ceremony marking teenage boys' passage into adulthood took place here, where they were surrounded by images of the valorous and glorious men whom they were expected to imitate.

the patron-client system to politics by making the emperor everyone's most important patron, possessing a father's moral authority to guide the lives of all.

Despite frequent illnesses, Augustus ruled until he died in his seventies in 14 C.E. The length of his rule, forty-one years, gave his innovations time to gradually become traditions. In explaining how Augustus managed to change the structure of Roman political power, the famous historian Tacitus observed that by the time Augustus died, "almost no one was still alive who had seen the republic." Augustus transformed republican Rome into imperial Rome by his long life, his military and financial innovations, his care for the capital's poor people, and his manipulation of the traditional vocabulary of politics to disguise his power and proclaim his legitimacy.

Life in Augustan Rome

Augustus's efforts to improve the lives of ordinary people helped make his rule secure. The problems were most serious in the capital city. Archaeology and literature let us sketch a picture of life in Augustan Rome. Although some of the sources refer to times after Augustus and to cities other than the capital, they nevertheless help us understand this period; economic and social conditions were essentially the same in all large cities throughout the early centuries of the empire.

The population of Augustan Rome—probably far over half a million—was vast for the ancient world. No European city would have nearly as many people again until London in the 1700s. The streets were packed: "One man jabs me with his elbow, another whacks me with a pole; my legs are smeared with mud, and from all sides big feet step on me" was the poet Juvenal's description of walking in Rome in the early second century C.E. To ease congestion in the narrow streets, wagon traffic was banned in the daytime. This regulation made nights noisy with the creaking of axles and the shouting of drivers caught in traffic jams.

Most urban residents lived in small apartments in multistory buildings called islands (so named because originally each building had an open strip around it). Outnumbering private homes by more than twenty to one, apartment buildings usually housed shops, bars, and simple restaurants on the first floor. Graffiti— political endorsements, personal insults, advertising, and messages of all kinds— covered many outside walls. The higher the floor, the cheaper were the apartments; the poorest people lived on the top floors in single rooms that they rented by the day. Aqueducts delivered fresh water to public fountains, but because apartments had no plumbing, residents had to lug buckets up the stairs. The wealthy few had piped-in water at ground level. Most tenants lacked bathrooms and had to use public latrines or pots for toilets at home. Some buildings had cesspits, or buckets could be carried down to the streets to be emptied by people who made their living collecting excrement. Lazy tenants flung the foul-smelling contents of these containers out the window.

Officials worked constantly to manage the sixty tons of human waste that Rome's population excreted every day. Augustus's administration improved the city's main sewer, but its untreated contents emptied directly into the Tiber River, which ran through the city. The technology for sanitary disposal of waste simply did not exist. People sometimes left human and animal corpses in the streets, to be gnawed by vultures and dogs until the city's officials had them removed. The poor were not the only people affected by such conditions; a stray mutt once brought a human hand to the table where Vespasian, who would be emperor from 69 to 79 C.E., was eating lunch. Flies buzzing everywhere and a lack of mechanical refrigeration contributed to frequent digestive illnesses; the most popular jewelry of the time was a charm to ward off stomach trouble. Although the wealthy could not eliminate such discomforts, they could make their lives more pleasant with luxuries such as snow rushed from the mountains to ice their drinks and slaves to clean their houses, which were built around courtyards and gardens to let in air and sunshine.

Public baths helped residents keep clean. Because admission fees were low and bath facilities were many, almost everyone could afford to go daily. Baths operated like modern health clubs, as centers for exercising and socializing as well as washing. Bathers progressed through a series of increasingly warm, humid areas until

A Roman City Street

Like Pompeii, the prosperous town of Herculaneum, on the shore of the Bay of Naples, was frozen in time by the massive eruption of the neighboring volcano, Mount Vesuvius, in 79 C.E. A flood of mud from the eruption buried the town and preserved its buildings until they were excavated beginning in the eighteenth century. Typical of a Roman town, it had straight roads paved with large, flat stones and flanked by sidewalks. Balconies jutted from the upper stories of houses, offering residents a shady place to view the lively traffic in the urban streets below. Instead of having yards in front or back, houses often were built around a garden courtyard that was open to the sky. Why do you think urban homes were arranged in this way? (Scala/Art Resource, NY.)

they reached a sauna-like room. They swam naked in hot or cold pools. Men and women bathed apart, either in separate rooms or at different times of the day. Since doctors did not yet understand how infections were transmitted, the untreated pools could spread disease.

City residents faced hazards beyond infectious diseases that Augustus tried to reduce. Since Roman engineers, despite their skill in using concrete, brick, and stone as building materials, lacked the technology to calculate precisely how much weight their constructions could stand, apartment buildings could collapse. Augustus improved public safety by imposing a height limit of seventy feet on new apartment buildings. Fire presented the greatest risk; one of Augustus's most important innovations was to provide Rome with the first public fire department in Western history. He also established the first permanent police force, despite his fondness for stopping to watch the fistfights that often broke out in Rome's crowded streets. There were some downsides of city life the emperor could not change. Tenants routinely threw broken dishes and other trash from their apartment windows, to fall like missiles onto the streets below. "If you are walking to a dinner party in Rome," Juvenal warned, "you would be foolish not to make out your will first. For every open window is a source of potential disaster."

Augustus's most popular support for ordinary people was his guarantee of an adequate food supply. He took on this responsibility as Rome's patron and father, and he spent his personal fortune to pay for imported grain. Distributing grain at public expense to the capital's poor citizens had been a tradition for decades, but Augustus's welfare system expanded to an unprecedented 250,000 primary recipients, plus their families. This statistic suggests that between 600,000 and 700,000 people depended on the emperor for food to survive. Poor Romans usually boiled the grain to make a sticky soup, which they washed down with cheap wine. If they were lucky, they might have some beans, onions, or cheese on the side. The rich, as we learn from an ancient cookbook, ate costlier foods, such as roast pork or shellfish, served with pepper, a salty condiment, or a sweet-and-sour sauce made from honey and vinegar.

Augustus also took on moral responsibility for Roman society. By his time, many wealthy Romans were spending their money on luxuries and costly political careers rather than on raising children. Fearing that the decline in the birthrate would destroy the elite that Rome needed as officials, Augustus passed laws to strengthen marriage and encourage larger families by granting special legal privileges to the parents of three or more children. He made adultery a crime. So seriously did Augustus back these reforms that he exiled his own daughter—his only child—and a granddaughter for sex scandals. His laws had little effect, however, and the old elite families dwindled over the centuries. Recent research suggests that in every generation, up to three-fourths of senatorial-rank families lost their official status (by losing the wealth required for that designation) or died out. Equestrians and men from the provinces who won the ruler's favor took the place of these families in the social hierarchy and in the Senate.

The traditional Roman policy of granting citizenship to liberated slaves helped prevent a decline in the number of citizens. If a slave's descendants became wealthy, they could become members of the social elite. This possibility gave slaves reason to work harder and cooperate with their masters. Conditions of slavery varied widely according to occupation. Slaves in agriculture and manufacturing had harsh lives. Most such workers were men, although women might assist the foremen who managed gangs of rural laborers. The second-century novelist Apuleius wrote this grim description of slaves at work in a flour mill: "Through the holes in their ragged clothes you could see scars from whippings all over their bodies. Some wore only loincloths. Letters had been branded on their foreheads and shackles bound their ankles." Worse than the mills were the mines, where the foremen constantly flogged the miners to keep them digging out the metal ores in dangerous conditions.

Household slaves had an easier physical existence. Most Romans owned slaves to work in their homes, from one or two in modestly well-off families to large numbers in rich houses and, above all, the imperial palace. Domestic slaves were often women, working as nurses, maids, kitchen help, and clothes makers. Some male slaves ran businesses for their masters; to encourage them to work hard, masters allowed them to keep part of the profits to save toward purchasing their freedom someday. Women had less opportunity to earn money. Masters sometimes granted them tips for sexual favors, and female prostitutes (many of whom were slaves) could earn money for themselves. Slaves who managed to earn money would sometimes buy slaves themselves, thereby creating their own hierarchy. A male slave might buy a woman for a mate. They could then have an imitation of a normal family life, though a legal marriage was impossible because they remained their master's property, as did their children. If truly fortunate, slaves could slowly accumulate enough money to buy themselves from their masters or could be freed by their masters' wills. Some inscriptions on tombs testify to masters' affectionate feelings for slaves, but even household servants had to endure violent treatment if their masters were cruel. If they attacked their owners because of brutal treatment, the punishment was death.

Entertainment from the Emperor as Patron

The emperors believed they needed to pay for frequent public entertainment to demonstrate their generosity as patrons caring for their people's needs. They regularly provided mass spectacles featuring hunters killing fierce beasts, wild African animals such as lions mangling condemned criminals, mock naval battles in flooded arenas, gladiatorial combats, and chariot races. Spectators jammed stadiums for these violent shows, seated according to their social rank and gender following an Augustan law: the emperor and senators sat close to the action, while women and the poor sat in the upper tiers. These spectacles communicated a political message claiming legitimacy for the new system of government by showing that the emperor was generous in providing expensive entertainment for his subjects, powerful enough to command life-and-death exhibitions, and dedicated to preserving the social hierarchy.

Gladiatorial combats, which originated under the republic as part of extravagant funerals, became so popular under Augustus that they attracted crowds in the tens of thousands. Gladiators were war captives, criminals, slaves, or free volunteers who underwent long and expensive training to perform in these combats; most were men. Gladiatorial fights were bloody, but only captives and criminals usually fought to the death; professional fighters could have extended careers. To make the fights more exciting, gladiators used a variety of weapons. One favorite bout pitted a

Gladiators Sculpted on a Tomb
This relief sculpture, which adorned a tomb near Rome dating to about 30–10 B.C.E., shows gladiators competing in games held to honor the deceased. Gladiatorial combats originated as part of funeral ceremonies because they portrayed with dramatic energy the violent and inevitable struggle to avoid death. Only the very wealthy could afford to have gladiators perform at their funerals or in spectacles meant to win the people's favor. These gladiators represent a traditional form of fighter called provocator (challenger). A challenger, who fought gladiators only of the same type, used a short sword and a curved shield. He wore a metal belt cinching up a loincloth, forearm and lower-leg guards, a partial chest protector, and a plumed helmet. These men's muscular bodies show the great strength required to be a successful fighter. (Alinari/Art Resource, NY.)

lightly armored fighter, called a net man because he used a net and a trident, against a more heavily armored fish man, so named from the design of his helmet crest. Betting was a great attraction, and spectators could be rowdy. As one Christian Roman complained, "Look at the mob coming to the show—already they're out of their minds! Aggressive, mindless, already in an uproar about their bets! They all share the same suspense, the same madness, the same voice."

Champion gladiators won riches and celebrity but not social respectability. Early in the first century C.E., the senators became alarmed at what they regarded as the disgrace caused by members of the upper class fighting as gladiators. They therefore banned the elite and all freeborn women under age twenty from appearing in gladiatorial shows. Daughters trained by their gladiator fathers had first competed during the republic, and a few women continued to compete until the emperor Septimius Severus (r. 193–211 C.E.) banned them.

Gladiatorial shows, chariot races, and theater productions became an opportunity for ordinary citizens to express their feelings about city life to the emperors, who were expected to attend. On more than one occasion, for example, poorer Romans rioted at shows to protest a shortfall in the free grain supply. In this way, public entertainment served as a two-way form of communication between the ruler and the ruled.

Oratory, Literature, and Portrait Sculpture under the Emperor as Patron

Oratory, literature, and portrait sculpture changed under Augustus to serve the same goal as public entertainment: to express the legitimacy of his transformed system of government. Oratory—the skilled public speaking that was the highest attainment of Roman education—became more restricted. Under the republic, skill in making stinging speeches to criticize political opponents had been such a powerful weapon that it could catapult a "new man" like Cicero, who lacked social and military distinction, to international fame. Under the principate, the emperor's supremacy ruled out freewheeling public speech. Speakers used their skill to praise the emperor as the people's patron at public festivals staged to promote his image as a competent, compassionate, and legitimate ruler.

Education for oratory remained a privilege of wealthy boys. Rome had no free public schools, so the poor had to get basic learning from their parents. Most people had time only for training in practical skills. A character in a satire written at the time of the emperor Nero expressed this narrow attitude toward education: "I didn't study geometry and literary criticism and worthless junk like that. I just learned how to read the letters on signs and how to work out percentages, and I learned weights, measures, and the values of the different kinds of coins."

So much new literature emerged during the rule of Augustus that modern scholars call this period the Golden Age of Latin literature. The emperor himself composed verse and prose and served as the patron of a circle of writers and artists. His favorites were Horace and Virgil. Horace delighted audiences with the rhythms and wit of his short poems on public and private subjects. His poem celebrating Augustus's victory over Antony and Cleopatra at Actium became famous for its opening line, "Now it's time to drink!"

Virgil became the most popular poet of Augustus's time for his epic poem *The Aeneid,* which expresses both praise and subtle criticism of Augustus. Virgil took great pains with his poem, and it remained unfinished at his death. He wanted it burned, but Augustus preserved it. Inspired by Homer's *Iliad* and *Odyssey, The Aeneid* tells the story of the Trojan Aeneas, the most distant ancestor of the Romans. Although the poem describes how the gods supported Rome—in fact, Jupiter is portrayed as promising "imperial rule without limit"—it also describes the painful effort and sorrow that success required. The poem therefore speaks to the complex mix of gain and loss that followed Augustus's transformation of politics and society. Above all, *The Aeneid* provided a moral code for Romans at the time: no matter how tempting the emotional pull of revenge and pride, be merciful to the conquered but destroy the arrogant.

Authors had to be careful not to anger the emperor, their patron. Livy composed a lengthy history of Rome in which he recorded the ruthless actions of Augustus and his supporters. The emperor was unhappy, but he did not punish Livy because his history did explain that success and stability depended on traditional values of loyalty and self-sacrifice. By contrast, the poet Ovid was punished. In his witty poems *Art of Love* and *Love Affairs,* he mocked the emperor's laws on marriage and adultery with tongue-in-cheek tips for conducting secret love affairs and picking up other men's wives at festivals. His *Metamorphoses* (*Transformations*) undermined the idea of hierarchy as natural by telling bizarre stories of supernatural shape changes, with people becoming animals and confusion between the human and the divine. Augustus's anger at Ovid finally boiled over when the poet was rumored to be involved in a sex scandal involving the emperor's granddaughter. In 8 C.E., he exiled the poet to a bleak town on the Black Sea and exiled his grand-daughter as well.

The style of portrait sculpture changed to reflect the emperor's wishes. Augustus used it to project a calm and competent image of himself as "restorer of the repub-lic" and founder of a new age for Rome. When Augustus was growing up, portraits were starkly realistic, portraying the strain of human experience. The sculpture that Augustus ordered displayed a more idealized style, recalling classical Greek portraiture. In famous works of art such as the statue of himself at First Gate or the sculpted frieze on his Altar of Peace, Augustus had himself portrayed as serene and dignified, not careworn and sick as he often was.

REVIEW   How did Augustus bring peace to Rome and transform its political system?

First Gate Statue of Augustus

At six feet eight inches high, this statue stood a foot taller than its subject, Augustus, Rome's first emperor. Found at his wife's country villa at Prima Porta (First Gate), just outside the capital, the statue was probably a copy of a bronze original sculpted about 20 B.C.E., when Augustus was in his early forties. The sculptor showed him as a younger man, using the idealizing techniques of Greek art of the fifth and fourth centuries B.C.E. to emphasize the emperor's dignity. The sculpture is crowded with symbols that express the image of Augustus that he wanted to communicate. His bare feet hint that he was a near-divine hero, and the statue of Cupid, the son of Venus, refers to the Julian family's descent from that goddess. The carving on the breastplate shows a Parthian surrendering to a Roman soldier under the gaze of personified cosmic forces basking in the peace of Augustus's reign. **For more help analyzing this image, see the visual activity for this chapter in the Online Study Guide at** bedfordstmartins.com/huntconcise. (Scala/Art Resource, NY.)

Maintaining the "Roman Peace"

Augustus knew that the biggest threat to his "restored republic" was the kind of violent struggle for power among members of the social elite that had ruined the original republic. His solution was to train an heir from birth to take over as princeps, with the expectation that the Senate would give the new princeps the same powers that he had held. This strategy kept the rule in his family, called the Julio-Claudians, until Nero's death in 68 C.E., and it established the tradition that family dynasties ruled imperial Rome.

Augustus designed the principate to last by making the ruler's goals building loyalty, preventing unrest, financing the army and the administration of a vast territory of diverse provinces, and promoting Roman law and culture as universal standards, while allowing as much local freedom in the provinces as possible. The citizens, in return for their loyalty, expected the emperor to be a generous patron, but the difficulties of long-range communication imposed practical limits on the government's intervention in the lives of the empire's residents, for better or worse.

The Julio-Claudian Emperors, 14–68 C.E.

Augustus believed he needed to make monarchy Rome's permanent government to avoid civil war, but he could expect resistance from the elite if he did not appear to respect the republic's traditions. He therefore enlisted the Senate's cooperation in identifying his successor. He had no biological son, and one after another the young men he adopted died before he did. Finally, in 4 C.E., he adopted someone into the Julian family who would outlive him, his stepson Tiberius (42 B.C.E.–37 C.E.), a member of the Claudian family. Because Tiberius had been an excellent general, the army supported recommending him to the Senate as the next "first man." The senators approved Tiberius in this role after Augustus died in 14 C.E.; thus began the Julio-Claudian dynasty.

Tiberius's bitter personality made him unpopular, but he ruled for twenty-three years (r. 14–37 C.E.) because he had the most important qualification for succeeding as princeps: the army's loyalty. His long reign provided the stable transition period that the principate needed to establish the compromise between the elite and the emperor that made the monarchy workable. On the one hand, the traditional offices of consul, senator, and others continued, filled by the elite; on the other hand, the emperor decided who held office and determined law and policy. In doing this, everyone claimed that the government was still a republic.

Tiberius's reign revealed the problems that an unhappy emperor could create. Tiberius paid a steep personal price for becoming "first man" because, to strengthen their family ties, Augustus had forced him to divorce his beloved wife Vipsania and marry Augustus's daughter, Julia. This marriage was a disaster. Tiberius's bitterness and fear of rivals led him to spend the last decade of his rule away from Rome as a recluse on an island. His withdrawal from governing opened the way for abuses by officials in Rome and kept him from training his successor.

Tiberius named Augustus's great-grandson Gaius (12–41 C.E.), better known as Caligula (r. 37–41 C.E.), to be the next princeps. Although Caligula lacked the personal qualities and training necessary to be a worthy ruler, he still might have been successful because he knew about soldiering. (*Caligula* means "baby boots." Soldiers had given him that nickname as a child because he wore little leather shoes like theirs while growing up in the military camps his father commanded.) Unfortunately for Rome, however, Caligula paid attention only to his personal desires. Ruling through cruelty and violence, he drained the treasury to humor his whims. Suetonius labeled him a "monster." He frequently outraged the elite by fighting mock gladiatorial combats and appearing in public in women's clothing or costumes imitating gods. Two Praetorian Guard commanders murdered him in 41 C.E. to avenge personal insults.

After Caligula's assassination, the Senate debated the possibility of refusing to acknowledge a new "first man" and therefore restoring a true republic. They gave up, however, when Claudius (r. 41–54 C.E.), Augustus's grandnephew and Caligula's uncle, bought the Praetorian Guard's support with money and the soldiers threatened the senators. That Claudius became princeps by threat of force made it clear that the genuine republic would never return because the soldiers would always insist on having an emperor who would promote their interests. Claudius won wider support for his rule by making men from Gaul (France) members of the Senate. This change signaled that elites from provinces outside Italy would be the emperor's partners in governing. In return for keeping their regions peaceful and prosperous, they received offices at Rome. Claudius also changed imperial government by employing freed slaves as top administrators. Because these men owed their positions to the emperor, they could be expected to be loyal.

The last Julio-Claudian emperor was Nero (r. 54–68 C.E.). Only sixteen when he became "first man," Nero loved music and theater, not governing. The spectacular public festivals he sponsored and the cash he distributed to the poor in Rome kept him popular with the masses. A giant fire in 64 C.E. (the incident that led to the legend of Nero "fiddling while Rome burned") made the elite suspect that he had ordered the blaze to clear space for an enormous new palace. Nero outraged the senators by making them attend his singing performances and by bankrupting the treasury to pay for his building project and a trip to sing all over Greece. He raised money by faking charges of treason against senators and equestrians to seize their property. When military commanders in the provinces rebelled against his abuses, he had a servant help him cut his own throat, after wailing, "To die! And such a great performer!"

The Flavian Emperors, 69–96 C.E.

A year of civil war followed in 69 C.E.; four generals warred to become princeps in this "Year of the Four Emperors." Vespasian (r. 69–79 C.E.) won and began the dynasty of the Flavian family. The new emperor took two steps to minimize resistance. First, he had the Senate publicly recognize him as "first man" even though he was not a Julio-Claudian. Second, he encouraged the spread of the imperial cult (worship of the emperor as a living god and sacrifices for the welfare of the emperor's household) in the provinces outside Italy, where most of the empire's population lived. In promoting emperor worship, Vespasian was building on local traditions. In the eastern provinces, the Hellenistic kingdoms had long before established the tradition of worshipping royalty; provincials there had treated Augustus as a living god. The imperial cult communicated the same image of the emperor to people in the provinces as Rome's architecture and sculpture did to people in the city: he was larger than life, deserved loyalty, and provided aid and gifts as a patron. Because emperor worship was already well established in Greece and the ancient Near East, Vespasian concentrated on spreading it in the provinces of Spain, southern France, and North Africa. Italy, however, still had no temples to the living emperor. Traditional Romans looked down on the imperial cult as a provincial tradition. Vespasian, known for his wit, even muttered as he lay dying in 79 C.E., "Oh me! I think I'm becoming a god."

Vespasian's sons Titus (r. 79–81 C.E.) and Domitian (r. 81–96 C.E.) strengthened the principate with hardheaded financial policy, professional administration, and preemptive military campaigns on the frontiers. Titus sent relief to the populations of Pompeii and Herculaneum after a giant volcanic eruption of Mount Vesuvius buried their towns in 79 C.E., and he provided a fifty-thousand-seat stadium for public entertainments by finishing Rome's **Colosseum**, built on arches and outfitted with giant awnings to shade the crowd. This multistory amphitheater was deliberately constructed on the site of the former fishpond in Nero's Golden House to demonstrate the public-spiritedness of the new Flavian dynasty. Domitian balanced the budget and led the army north to hold the line against the Germanic tribes threatening the empire's frontier regions along the Rhine and Danube rivers—an area of conflict for centuries to come.

Domitian handled his success poorly, and his arrogance inspired hatred among the senators, to whom he once sent a letter announcing, "Our lord god, myself, orders you to do this." Enraged by the rebellion of a general in Germany, he executed numerous upper-class citizens as conspirators. Fearing Domitian would execute them, his wife and members of his court murdered him in 96 C.E. As Domitian's murder revealed, the principate had not solved monarchy's enduring weakness: rivalry for rule that was likely to explode into murderous conspiracy and destabilize succession. The danger of civil war always existed, whether generated by ambitious generals or by competition among the emperor's heirs. As Tacitus commented, emperors became like the weather: "We just have to wait for bad ones to pass and hope for good ones to appear."

The Five "Good Emperors" and the Roman Golden Age, 96–180 C.E.

Fortunately for Rome, politically better weather came with the next five emperors— Nerva (r. 96–98 C.E.), Trajan (r. 98–117 C.E.), Hadrian (r. 117–138 C.E.), Antoninus Pius (r. 138–161 C.E.), and Marcus Aurelius (r. 161–180 C.E.). Historians call them the five "good emperors" because they provided peaceful transfers of power for nearly a century. (The first four of them, lacking surviving sons, used adoption to pick capable successors.) The peace and prosperity of this period have led historians to refer to it as Rome's Golden Age. It marked the longest stretch in Roman history without a civil war since the second century B.C.E.

There were foreign wars and a major rebellion to fight during the Golden Age, however. Trajan fought fierce campaigns expanding Roman power northward across the Danube River into Dacia (today Romania) and eastward into Mesopotamia (Map 5.1, page 157). Hadrian earned the hatred of the Senate by executing several senators as alleged conspirators and punished a Jewish revolt by turning Jerusalem into a military colony. Aurelius spent many miserable years at war protecting the Danube region from outside attacks.

The foundations of the Golden Age were the loyalty of the army and the public service of the elites in the provinces. The army remained loyal because the emperors treated it well. To fulfill their obligations as the military's patrons, the emperors supplemented soldiers' regular pay with large bonuses. These financial rewards made a legionary career desirable, and enlistment counted as a privilege restricted to free male citizens. The army, however, also included auxiliary units of noncitizens from the provinces. Serving under Roman officers, they often picked up some Latin and Roman customs, and they improved life in the provinces by constructing public works. Upon discharge, they received Roman citizenship. In this way, the army served as an instrument for spreading a common way of life.

Most provinces needed relatively few garrison troops to keep them peaceful in this period. Even Gaul, which had bitterly resisted the Roman takeover, was now, according to a contemporary witness, "kept in order by 1,200 troops—hardly more soldiers than it has towns." Increasingly, the emperors stationed the legions (units of five thousand to six thousand troops) on the empire's northern and eastern frontiers to defend against potential invaders. During the course of the Golden Age, the emperors evidently concluded that the distance and the difficulty were too great to conquer new territory beyond the frontiers. This decision had an unintended long-term consequence: without the additional income that expansion brought in from plunder, prisoners of war sold into slavery, and additional taxes from conquered peoples, it became increasingly difficult to increase, or even maintain, the pay that kept the army loyal to the emperor.

A loyal army guaranteed the peace that promoted trade and tax revenues in the Golden Age. Long-distance trade for luxury goods such as spices and silk extended as far as India and China. Taxation of agricultural land in the provinces (Italy was exempt) provided the government's principal source of revenue. Most taxes collected in the provinces stayed there to pay for local projects. Most emperors under the early principate attempted to keep taxes low. As Tiberius put it when refusing a request for tax increases from provincial governors, "I want you to shear my sheep, not skin them alive." The imperial administration itself cost relatively little because it was small compared with the size of the population it governed: several hundred top officials governed about fifty million people. Senatorial and equestrian governors with small staffs ran the provinces, which eventually numbered about forty. In Rome, the emperor employed a substantial palace staff, but equestrian officials called prefects managed the city itself.

Voluntary public service by the elites in the provinces was key to the empire's financial health. Local officials called decurions (members of a municipal senate, later called curials) collected taxes due to the central government. They also personally guaranteed that their towns' expenses were covered. If a shortfall occurred in imperial tax collection or in the finances needed to support their towns, these wealthy men would make up the difference from their own pockets.

The status that civic positions brought made the elites willing to serve, despite the potential expense involved. Some received a priesthood in the imperial cult as a reward, an honor open to both men and women. All could hope to catch the emperor's ear for special help for their areas—for example, after an earthquake or flood. The system worked because it sprang from Roman tradition: the local social elites were the patrons of their communities but the clients of the emperor. As long as there were enough rich, public-spirited provincials participating in this system for its nonmonetary rewards, the principate remained financially stable by relying on the republic's tradition of public service.

Law and Population as Sources of Stability

The spread of Roman law and a healthy rate of reproduction in the population were major contributors to the stability of the Golden Age. Romans prided themselves on their ability to order their society through law. As Virgil said, their mission was "to establish law and order within a framework of peace." Even today, the influence of Roman law is still evident in most systems of law in Europe. Roman law was based on the principle of equity, which referred to accomplishing what was "good and fair" even if the letter of the law had to be disregarded. This principle meant, for example, that the intent of parties in a contract outweighed the words of their agreement and that the burden of proof lay with the accuser rather than the accused. The emperor Trajan ruled that no one should be convicted without clear evidence because it was better for a guilty person to go unpunished than for an innocent person to be condemned.

Roman notions of fairness required ranking people in "orders" according to their wealth. The elites in the highest orders made up a tiny portion of the population. Only about one person in fifty thousand had enough money to qualify for the senatorial order, the highest rank, while about one in a thousand belonged to the equestrian order, the next-highest rank. Different purple stripes on clothing identified these orders. The third-highest order consisted of decurions, the local officials in provincial towns.

This idea of ranking came to have important legal consequences under the empire because the emperors believed it promoted social stability. The social distinction between those designated as "better people" and those called "humbler people," which dated back to the republic, became a legal distinction under the principate. The "better people" included senators, equestrians, decurions, and retired army veterans. Everybody else—except slaves, who counted as property, not people—was consigned to the vastly larger group of "humbler people." The latter faced their worst disadvantage in court: the law imposed harsher penalties on them than on "better people" who committed the same crimes. "Humbler people" convicted of capital crimes were regularly executed by being crucified or torn apart by wild animals before a crowd of spectators. "Better people" rarely suffered the death penalty, but if they were condemned to death, they received a quicker and more dignified execution by the sword. "Humbler people" could be tortured in criminal investigations, even if they were citizens; "better people" usually avoided this fate. Romans regarded these differences as fair on the grounds that a person's higher status created a higher level of responsibility for the common good. As one provincial governor expressed it, "Nothing is less equitable than mere equality itself."

Law was crucial for maintaining order, but nothing mattered more to the stability and prosperity of the empire than steady population levels. Keeping up the birthrate was difficult, however, because doctors and midwives had only a few herbal medicines to treat pregnant women and infants. Complications at birth could easily lead to the mother's death because medical practitioners could not stop internal bleeding or cure infections. In addition, although they possessed carefully made instruments for surgery and physical examinations, they were seriously misinformed about pregnancy and reproduction. The upper-class government official Pliny, for example, sent the following report to the grandfather of his third wife, Calpurnia: "You will be very sad to learn that your granddaughter has suffered a miscarriage. She is a young girl and did not realize she was pregnant. As a result she was more active than she should have been and paid a high price." Likewise, gynecologists such as Soranus, who practiced in Rome during the reigns of Trajan and Hadrian, mistakenly recommended the days just after menstruation, when the woman's body was "not congested," as the best time to become pregnant. Soranus, following the common medical treatment of bleeding patients for various ailments, recommended treating exceptionally painful menstruation by drawing blood "from the bend of the arm." Doctors, often freedmen from Greece and other provinces, were considered of low status, unless they served the upper class.

As in earlier times, girls often wed in their early teens to have as many years as possible to bear children; their husbands would typically be around age thirty. Because so many babies died, families had to produce numerous offspring to keep from disappearing. The tombstone of Veturia, a soldier's wife married at age eleven, tells a typical story: "Here I lie, having lived for twenty-seven years. I was married to the same man for sixteen years and bore six children, five of whom died before I did." Richer families usually arranged marriages between spouses who hardly knew each other, although they could grow to love each other in a partnership devoted to family. The emphasis on childbearing in marriage brought many health hazards to women, but to remain single and childless represented social failure. Once children

Midwife's Sign Depicting Childbirth
Childbirth was a dangerous experience for women because of the chance of dying from internal bleeding. This terra-cotta sign from Ostia, the ancient port city of Rome, probably hung outside a midwife's rooms to announce her skill in aiding women in giving birth. It shows a pregnant woman clutching the sides of her chair and supported by another woman while the midwife crouches in front to help deliver the baby. The meaning of the sign was clear to people who were illiterate; a person did not have to be able to read to understand the services that the specialist inside could provide. (Scala/Art Resource, NY.)

were born, they were cared for by their mothers and by servants. Wealthy women routinely hired wet nurses to breast-feed their babies. When Romans wanted to control family size, they relied on female contraception through the use of vaginal sponges or drugs. Like the Greeks, they practiced exposure, more frequently for infant girls than for boys because sons were considered more valuable than daughters as future supporters and protectors of families.

The emperors and some members of the social elite did their best to support reproduction. The emperors aided needy children to encourage larger families, and wealthy people often adopted abandoned or orphaned children in their communities. One North African man gave enough money to support three hundred boys and three hundred girls each year until they grew up. The differing value afforded male and female children was also evident in some of these humanitarian programs, as boys often received more aid than girls.

Romanization in the Provinces

The principate changed the Mediterranean world deeply, but not evenly, by spreading Roman culture in the provinces. Historians call this process **Romanization**. Romanization was a two-way street; it did not mean the imposition of the conquerors' way of life, but rather interactions between the Romans and local peoples that produced new, mixed cultural traditions, from art to language to religion.

Romanization was more evident in some areas of the empire than in others. A wide diversity of peoples lived under Roman rule, speaking different languages, observing different customs, dressing in different styles, and worshipping different gods (Map 5.2). In the remote countryside, especially in the eastern sections of the empire, Romanization had only a modest effect on local customs. Where new cities sprang up, however, Roman influence increased. These communities sprouted up around Roman forts or grew from the settlements of army veterans the emperors had sprinkled throughout the provinces. They became especially influential in western Europe, permanently planting Latin (and the languages that would emerge from it) and Roman law and customs there. Modern cities such as Trier and Cologne in Germany started as Roman towns. As time passed, status gaps between the provinces and Italy lessened. Eventually, emperors came from the provinces; Trajan, from Spain, was the first.

Romanization in the western provinces raised people's standard of living as roads and bridges improved, trade increased, and agriculture flourished under the peaceful conditions provided by the army. Selling supplies to the troops brought new business to farmers and merchants. Greater prosperity under Roman rule made Romanization easier for provincials to accept, and local cultural traditions gradually merged with Roman ways of life.

In the eastern provinces, Romanization had less of a cultural effect. Large cities there, such as Alexandria in Egypt and Antioch in Syria, rivaled Rome in size and splendor (Map 5.1, page 157). In fact, compared with Rome, they boasted more single-family houses, fewer blocks of high-rise apartments, and equally magnificent temples. These cities had been flourishing for centuries and as a result tended to retain their Greek and Near Eastern traditions and languages. The eastern social elites did, however, easily accept the nature of Roman governance: the emperor was their patron, and they were his clients, with the mutual obligations this traditional relationship required. Provincial elites had long been accustomed to this kind of relationship with the ruler because Hellenistic kings had also ruled them in a paternalistic fashion. The non-Roman elites' willing cooperation in the task of governing the provinces was crucial for imperial stability and prosperity.

The continuing vitality of Greek culture and language in prosperous eastern cities supported a flourishing of Roman literature. Romantic adventure novels and satirical sketches were very popular. One of the best-known writers of the period was the essayist and philosopher Plutarch (c. 50–120 C.E.). His moral sense and taste for anecdotes made his works favorite reading well into modern times. The English dramatist William Shakespeare (1564–1616) based several of his plays on Plutarch's *Parallel Lives,* paired biographies of illustrious Greek and Roman men.

Latin literature also thrived in this period. Scholars rank the late first and early second centuries C.E. as its Silver Age, second only to the masterpieces of Augustan

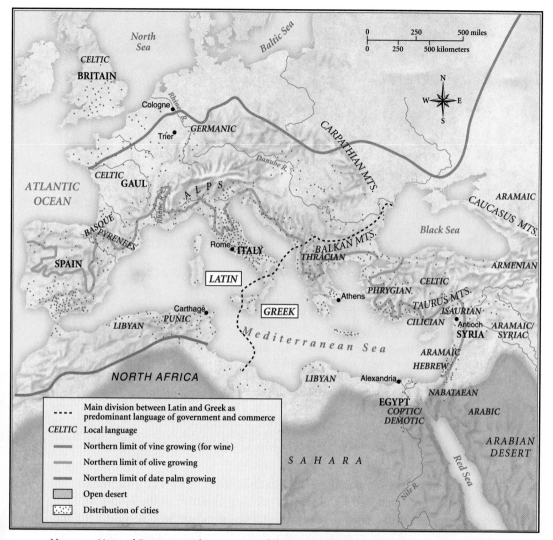

Map 5.2 Natural Features and Languages of the Roman World

The Roman world had great variety in land, languages, and climate. People living there, estimated to have numbered as many as 55 million, spoke dozens of languages, many of which survived until the last years of the empire. The two predominant languages spoken by Roman citizens were Latin in the western part of the empire and Greek in the eastern part. Latin remained the language of law even in the eastern empire. Fields suitable for growing grain were the most valuable land feature because wheat and barley were the basis of the ancient diet. Vineyards and olive groves also were important. Wine was regarded as an essential beverage, and olive oil was the main source of fat for most people and the principal ingredient in soap, perfume, and other products for daily life. **For more help analyzing this map, see the map activity for this chapter in the Online Study Guide at** bedfordstmartins .com/huntconcise**.**

Roman Architecture in North Africa
The Roman town of Thysdrus (today El Djem in Tunisia) built this amphitheater for public entertainment in the early third century C.E. Seating 32,000 spectators (more than the town's total population), it imitated the larger Colosseum in Rome and was the seventh-biggest such building in the empire. Its arched walls soared more than a hundred feet high, and storerooms under the arena floor had three elevators to lift wild animals to the surface. Thysdrus also had a track for chariot racing and a smaller amphitheater. (Erich Lessing/Art Resource, NY.)

literature. The most famous authors wrote with acid wit, verve, and imagination. The historian Tacitus composed his *Annals* as a biting narrative of the Julio-Claudians, laying bare the ruthlessness of Augustus and the personal weaknesses of his successors. The satiric poet Juvenal skewered pretentious Romans and greedy provincials while hilariously describing the problems of being broke in the city. Apuleius intrigued readers with *The Golden Ass,* a sex-filled novel about a man turned into a donkey who regains his body and soul through the power of the Egyptian goddess Isis.

REVIEW   What were the strengths and weaknesses of Roman government and society during the principate after the rule of Augustus?

The Emergence of Christianity

The gradual rise of Christianity to become the leading religion among Romans, a process that took hundreds of years, was the ultimate proof that Romanization was a two-way process of cultural interaction because the new faith first emerged among non-Romans in the eastern part of the empire. The development of Christianity into a new religion separate from Judaism proved the most significant and enduring influence on later history that occurred during the Roman Empire.

Christianity emerged among a splinter group of Jews in Judaea, where, as elsewhere in the empire, Jews were allowed to practice their ancestral religion. The new faith attracted converts slowly; three centuries after the death of Jesus in 30 C.E., Christians remained a small minority. Christianity eventually spread because it had an appeal based on the career of Jesus, a message of salvation, an energetic sense of mission, a democratic openness in its early congregations, and a strong feeling of community.

The Teachings of Jesus

The new religion emerged from the life and teachings of Jesus (c. 4 B.C.E.–30 C.E.; see "The B.C.E./C.E. System for Dates" at the beginning of this book for an explanation of the date given for Jesus's birth). Christianity's background lay in Jewish history. By the time of Jesus's boyhood, some of his fellow Jews in Judaea were agitating for independence from Roman rule, making provincial officials fear rebellion. Jesus's career, therefore, took place in a troubled region. His execution was the standard Roman response to anyone they believed threatened peace and social order. In the two decades after his crucifixion, his devoted followers, particularly Paul of Tarsus, developed a new religion, now called Christianity, that expanded beyond the Jewish community in Palestine.

Christianity offered an answer to a troubling question about divine justice raised by the Jews' long history of defeat and exile: how could a just God allow the wicked to prosper and the righteous to suffer? The question had become prominent in the second century B.C.E., when persecution by the Seleucid king Antiochus IV (r. 175–164 B.C.E.) caused a bloody revolt. This war gave birth to the ideas called apocalypticism (from the Greek meaning "uncovering of the future"). According to this worldview, evil powers, divine and human, controlled the present world. Their rule would soon end, however, when God and his agents revealed their plan to conquer the forces of evil by sending the **Christ** (Greek for "anointed one"; in Hebrew, *Mashiah,* or in English *Messiah*) to win the great battle. A final judgment would follow, bringing eternal punishment for the wicked and eternal reward for the righteous. The apocalypticism that first inspired Jews living in Judaea under Roman rule later motivated Christians and Muslims.

Apocalyptic ideas became controversial around the time of Jesus's birth because most Judaean Jews were angry about Rome's control but disagreed about what their response should be. Some cooperated with their overlords, while others preached rejection of the non-Jewish world and its spiritual corruption. Their local ruler, installed by the Romans, was Herod the Great (r. 37–4 B.C.E.). His Greek style of life broke Jewish law, making him unpopular with his subjects despite his magnificent rebuilding of the holiest Jewish shrine, the great temple in Jerusalem. When a decade of unrest followed Herod's death, Augustus installed a Roman provincial government to oversee the region.

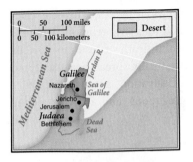

Palestine in the Time of Jesus, 30 C.E.

Jesus began his career as a teacher and healer in his native Galilee, the northern region of Palestine, during the reign of the emperor Tiberius. The books that would later become the Gospels, or the first four books of the Christian New Testament, offer the earliest accounts of his life and teachings; they were composed between about 70 and 90 C.E., decades after Jesus's death. Jesus himself wrote nothing down, and others' accounts of his words and deeds do not always agree on what he said or did. He taught mostly by telling parables, stories with an indirect moral or religious message.

All of the Gospels begin the story of Jesus's career with his baptism by John the Baptist, a prophet who urged people to repent before God's final judgment, which John preached was coming soon. John was executed by the Jewish ruler Herod Antipas, a son of Herod the Great whom the Romans supported; Herod Antipas feared that John's apocalyptic preaching might set off riots. After John's death, Jesus continued his mission by traveling around Judaea's countryside warning people to prepare spiritually for the coming of God's kingdom. Many saw Jesus as the Messiah, but he did not preach immediate revolt against the Romans. Instead, he taught that God's true kingdom was to be sought not on earth but in heaven. He stressed that this kingdom was open to believers regardless of their social status or sinfulness. His emphasis on God's love for humanity and people's responsibility to love one another reflected Jewish religious teachings, as in the first-century scholar Hillel's interpretation of the Hebrew Bible.

An educated Jew who perhaps knew Greek as well as Aramaic, the local language, Jesus realized that he had to reach the urban crowds to make an impact. Therefore, leaving the Galilean villages where he had started, he took his message to the Jewish population of Jerusalem, the region's main city. His miraculous healings and exorcisms and his powerful preaching created a sensation. His popularity attracted the attention of the Jewish authorities, who automatically assumed he aspired to political power. Fearing he might ignite a Jewish revolt, the Roman governor Pontius Pilate ordered his crucifixion, the usual punishment for rebellion, in Jerusalem in 30 C.E.

After Jesus's death, his followers reported that he had appeared to them in person. They proclaimed that God had miraculously raised him from the dead, and they set about convincing other Jews that Jesus was the promised savior and would soon return to judge the world and impose God's kingdom. Jesus's closest disciples, the twelve Apostles (Greek for "messengers"), considered themselves faithful Jews and continued to follow the commandments of Jewish law.

The Career of Paul of Tarsus

The conversion of Paul of Tarsus (c. 10–65 C.E.), a pious Jew of the Diaspora and also a Roman citizen who had previously attacked those who accepted Jesus as the Messiah, was the turning point in the development of Christianity as a new religion appealing to non-Jews. Around three years after Jesus's death, Paul experienced a spiritual vision on the road to Damascus in Syria, which he interpreted as a divine revelation. It inspired him to become a follower of Jesus as the Messiah, or Christ— a Christian, as members of the movement came to be known. According to Paul, Christians believed that Jesus was divine and his crucifixion was the ultimate sacrifice for the sins of humanity. Only by accepting this belief, Paul said, could people expect to win salvation in the world to come.

Seeking to win converts outside Judaea, in about 46 C.E. Paul began to travel to preach to Jews of the Diaspora and to Gentiles (non-Jews) who had adopted some Jewish customs in Syria, Asia Minor, and Greece (Map 5.3). Although Paul stressed the necessity of ethical behavior along traditional Jewish lines, especially

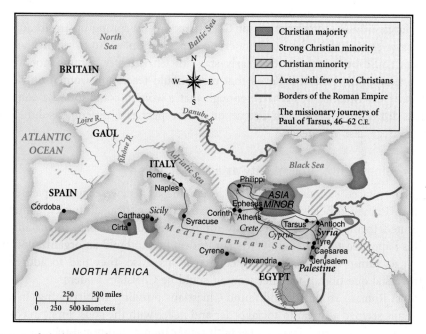

Map 5.3 Christian Populations in the Late Third Century C.E.
Christians remained a minority in the Roman world three hundred years after the crucifixion of Jesus. Certain areas of the empire, however, especially Asia Minor (western Turkey), where Paul of Tarsus had preached, had a concentration of Christians. Most Christians lived in cities and towns, where missionaries had gone to spread their message to crowds of curious listeners. *Paganus*, a Latin word meaning "country person" or "rural villager," came to mean a believer in traditional polytheistic cults— hence the term *pagan*, meaning "non-Christian," often found in modern works on this period.

the rejection of sexual immorality and polytheism, he also taught that converts did not need to obey all of Jewish law. To make conversion easier, Paul did not require men who became Christians to undergo the Jewish initiation rite of circumcision. This view, combined with his teachings that his congregations did not have to observe Jewish dietary restrictions or festivals, created great controversy and led to tensions with Jewish authorities in Jerusalem as well as with the followers of Jesus living there, who still believed that Christians had to follow Jewish law. Roman authorities arrested Paul as a criminal troublemaker; he was executed in about 65 C.E. Hatred of Roman rule in Palestine pushed the Jews to revolt in 66 C.E. When they were defeated in 70 C.E., their temple in Jerusalem was destroyed. This catastrophe meant that the Jewish community lost its religious center, and the separation of Christianity from Judaism begun by Paul gained momentum. In this way Christianity became a separate religion.

Paul's impact on early Christianity can be seen in the number of letters— thirteen—attributed to him in the twenty-seven writings brought together as the New Testament by around 200 C.E. Followers of Jesus came to regard the New Testament as having equal authority with the Hebrew Bible, which they then called the Old Testament. Because teachers such as Paul preached mainly in the cities to reach large crowds, congregations of Christians mostly sprang up in urban areas. Originally these groups had a democratic organization without much hierarchy. Women could be leaders in this early stage of Christianity, though not without controversy; many people believed that men should teach and women only listen. Still, early Christianity was diverse enough that a woman could found a congregation, as did Lydia at Philippi in Greece, or earn respect as a "deacon," as did Phoebe at Cenchreae, also in Greece.

The Development of Christianity as a New Religion

Christianity faced serious obstacles in developing as a new religion separate from Judaism. Roman officials, suspecting Christians of political disloyalty, sometimes persecuted them as traitors, especially for refusing to participate in the imperial cult (as happened to Perpetua). Christian leaders had to build an organization from scratch to administer their growing congregations. Also, they had to address the controversial question of whether women could be Christian leaders.

Most Romans in this period found Christians puzzling and irritating. In short, Christians seemed a threat to social order and peace with the gods. First, in contrast to Jews, Christians proclaimed a new faith rather than a traditional religion handed down from their ancestors. This broke with Roman tradition, in which anything new was seen as dangerous. Next, people feared that tolerating Christians would offend the gods of the official religion; Christians' denial of the old gods and of the emperor's cult seemed sure to provoke natural catastrophes. Christians furthermore aroused contempt because they proclaimed as their divine king a man whom the imperial government had crucified as a criminal. Finally, Christians were accused

Painting of a Sacred Banquet from a Roman Catacomb
Catacombs were the underground chambers Christians used for burials and meetings before their religion was officially recognized. Scenes such as this one seem simultaneously to represent actual meals held to remember the dead, banquets that the blessed dead were thought to have in their heavenly lives, and symbolic gatherings expressing a sense of community and mutual affection among believers. Seven people were usually shown, for reasons still not clear to historians. Women are prominently depicted here in the middle and at either end of the table. The woman at the left is presenting a goblet of wine to the banqueters. As the inscription suggests, she may be a personification of *agape*, the shared love that such sacred banquets commemorated. (© Held Collection/The Bridgeman Art Library.)

of cannibalism and sexual promiscuity because they symbolically ate the body and drank the blood of Jesus during secret communal dinners called Love Feasts, which men and women attended together.

Believing that Christians angered the traditional gods, Romans were quick to blame them for disasters. When a large portion of Rome burned in 64 C.E., Nero punished them as arsonists. As Tacitus wrote, the emperor had innocent Christians "covered with the skins of wild animals and torn to death by dogs, or fastened to crosses and set on fire to provide light at night." The cruelty of their punishment reportedly earned these Christians sympathy from Rome's population. After Nero, the government did not persecute Christians regularly or as a policy because no law specifically banned their religion. Nevertheless, Christians made easy victims for officials hunting for people to blame for crimes or disruptions in public order.

In response to persecution, Christians argued that Romans had nothing to fear from Christianity. They insisted that their faith taught respect for authority and a strict morality. It was not a foreign superstition but the true philosophy that combined the best features of Judaism and Greek thought and was thus a fitting religion for their diverse world. The theologian Tertullian pointed out that although

Christians could not worship the emperors, they did "pray to the true God for their [the emperors'] safety. We pray for a fortunate life for them, a secure rule, . . . a courageous army, a loyal Senate, a virtuous people, a world of peace."

Persecution did not stop Christianity. Tertullian proclaimed, "The blood of the martyrs is the seed of the Church." Christians like Perpetua regarded public trials and executions as an opportunity to become a **martyr** (Greek for "witness") to their faith and thus to strengthen Christians' sense of identity. Their belief that their deaths would lead directly to happiness in heaven allowed them to face painful torture with courage; some even became martyrs on purpose. For example, Ignatius, bishop of Antioch, begged Rome's congregation, which was becoming the most prominent Christian group, not to ask the emperor to show him mercy when he was condemned to die in the Colosseum early in the second century: "Let me be food for the wild animals [in the arena] through whom I can reach God," he pleaded. "I am God's wheat, to be ground up by the teeth of beasts so that I may be found pure bread of Christ." Most Christians tried their best to avoid becoming martyrs, but stories recording the martyrs' courage shaped the identity of this new religion as a faith that gave its believers the spiritual strength to endure great suffering.

The Organization of Hierarchy: Bishops and Women in the New Religion

Many first-century Christians expected that their troubles would end during their lifetimes because Jesus would return to pass judgment on the world and overturn the Roman Empire. When this expectation did not come true, believers began transforming their faith into a religion organized to survive indefinitely, instead of an apocalyptic offshoot of Judaism predicting the immediate end of the world. To make this change, they tried to achieve unity in their beliefs and created a hierarchical organization with bishops as leaders to impose order on congregations.

Unity proved impossible to achieve because early Christians constantly and fiercely disagreed about what they should believe, how they should live, and who had the authority to decide these questions. Some Christians believed they could observe Christ's teachings while keeping their jobs and regular lives. Others insisted it was necessary to withdraw from the everyday world to escape its evil, even abandoning their families and committing themselves to chaste celibacy. Many Christians believed they should not serve in the army because, as soldiers required to worship in the imperial cult, they would betray their faith. Controversy over such questions raged in the numerous congregations that arose in the early empire around the Mediterranean, from Gaul to Africa to the Near East (Map 5.3, page 181).

Although early Christians continued to disagree about doctrine, they realized that their new faith needed an organizational structure if it was to last. They therefore created bishops as religious officials with the authority to specify true doctrine and proper conduct. This was the most important development in organizing a hierarchy intended to preserve Christianity indefinitely. Bishops received their positions through the principle later called **apostolic succession**, which declares that Jesus's Apostles appointed the first bishops as their successors, granting these new officials the powers Jesus had originally given to the Apostles. Those men named as bishops by the Apostles in turn appointed their own successors, and so on. Bishops had the authority to ordain priests with the holy power to administer the sacraments, above all baptism and communion, which believers regarded as necessary for achieving eternal life. Bishops also controlled their congregations' memberships and finances (the money financing early churches came from members' gifts).

The bishops had the authority to define what was true doctrine (orthodoxy) and what was false (heresy), but Christians' disagreements over doctrine were too strong for the bishops to impose unity of belief. In this early stage, the occasional meetings of the bishops of different cities constituted the church's organization. Today it is common to refer to this loose organization as the early Catholic (meaning "universal") church, but even the bishops disagreed among themselves on what beliefs were proper.

A particularly bitter disagreement concerned women's role in the church. In the first congregations, women sometimes held leadership positions. After bishops were established atop the hierarchy, however, women usually were kept in inferior posts. This demotion reflected the view that in Christianity, as in Roman imperial society, women should be subordinate to men. Some congregations took a long time to accept this change, however, and some women still occupied leadership positions during the second and third centuries.

When leadership roles were closed off to them, many women chose not to marry, to demonstrate their devotion to Christ. This commitment to chaste celibacy gave them the power to control their bodies by removing their sexuality from the domination of men. Women choosing this special closeness to God were judged holy and socially superior by other Christians. By rejecting the traditional functions of wife and mother in favor of spiritual excellence, celibate Christian women achieved the independence and authority denied them in the outside world.

Competing Beliefs: Paganism and Philosophy

Most people during the time of the principate were polytheistic (worshipping multiple gods). Today such religious beliefs are labeled *paganism*. That modern term should not be taken to mean that ancient polytheists were immoral. In fact, their beliefs often taught strict moral purity.

Polytheistic worshippers prayed and sacrificed to try to win the favor of all the divinities that could affect human life. These divinities ranged from the traditional gods of the state cults, such as Jupiter and Minerva, to spirits thought to inhabit local groves and springs. International cults such as the Mysteries of Demeter and Persephone at Eleusis outside Athens remained popular. Polytheists never sought a unity of doctrine. They did agree, however, that the old gods favored and protected them and that the imperial cult added to their safety; the success and prosperity of the principate was the proof. Even people who found a more intellectually satisfying understanding of the world in philosophies such as Stoicism respected the traditional cults as symbols of divine protection for Rome. Christianity had to compete with the long and cherished traditions of polytheism to win converts.

The cult of the Egyptian goddess Isis reveals how polytheism could provide believers with a religious experience demanding a moral way of life and arousing strong personal emotions. Isis's cult had already attracted Romans by the time

Mithras Slaying the Bull
Hundreds of shrines to the mysterious god Mithras have been found in the Roman Empire, but the cult remains poorly known because almost no texts exist to explain it. To judge from the many representations in art—such as this wall painting from about 200 C.E., found in the shrine at Marino, south of Rome—the story of Mithras slaying a bull was a central part of the cult's identity. Scholars debate the symbolic meaning of the slaying shown here, in which a snake and a dog lick the bull's blood while a scorpion pinches its testicles. Most agree, however, that Mithras was derived, perhaps as late as the early imperial period, from the ancient Persian divinity Mithra. Only men could be worshippers, and many were soldiers. Earlier scholarly claims of the cult's popularity were exaggerated; its members numbered no more than 1 or 2 percent of the population. Mithraism probably involved complex devotion to astrology, with devotees ranked in grades, each grade protected by a different celestial body. (Scala/Art Resource, NY.)

of Augustus. He tried to suppress it because it was Cleopatra's religion, but Isis's reputation as a kind, compassionate goddess who relieved her followers' suffering made her cult too popular to crush. The Egyptians believed that her tears for starving people caused the Nile to flood every year and bring them good harvests. Her image was that of a loving mother, and in art she is often shown nursing her son. A central doctrine of her cult concerned the death and resurrection of her husband, Osiris. Isis promised her followers a similar hope for life after death.

Isis required her worshippers to behave righteously. Inscriptions put up in public by believers declared the goddess's standards for them by quoting her on her own work for justice: "I broke down the rule of tyrants; I put an end to murders; I caused what is right to be mightier than gold and silver." The main character of Apuleius's novel *The Golden Ass,* whom Isis rescues from his mistaken transformation into a donkey, expresses his intense joy after being spiritually reborn: "O holy and eternal guardian of the human race, who always cherishes mortals and blesses them, you care for the troubles of miserable humans with a sweet mother's love. Neither day nor night, nor any moment of time, ever passes by without your blessings." Other cults also required their believers to lead just lives. Inscriptions from remote villages in Asia Minor, for example, record the confessions of peasants to sexual sins for which their local god had imposed severe penance.

Many upper-class Romans found moral guidance in philosophy. Stoicism was the most popular. Stoics believed in self-discipline above all, and their code of personal ethics left no room for immoral conduct. As the philosopher Seneca explained, "It is easier to prevent harmful emotions from entering the soul than it is to control them once they have entered." Stoicism taught that a creative force combining reason, nature, and divinity directs the universe. Humans share in the essence of this universal force and find happiness and patience by living in harmony with it and always doing their duty. The emperor Marcus Aurelius, in his book *Meditations,* emphasized the Stoic belief that people exist for each other: "Either make them better, or just put up with them," he advised.

Christian and polytheist scholars argued over the merits of Christianity compared to traditional Greek philosophy. The theologian Origen, for example, argued that Christianity, because it was true, was a better guide to correct living than were Greek philosophical ideas. The philosopher Plotinus gave traditional Greek ideas new strength with his books on spiritual philosophy. These ideas, called **Neoplatonism** because their doctrines sprang from Plato's philosophy, influenced many educated Christians as well as polytheists. Neoplatonic religious ideas centered on a human longing to return to the universal Good from which human existence comes. By turning away from the life of the body through the study of philosophy, individual souls could rise to the level of the universal soul, becoming the whole of what as individuals they formed only a potential part. This mystical union with what the Christians would call God could be achieved only through strenuous self-discipline in personal morality as well as intellectual life. Neoplatonism's stress on spiritual purity gave it a powerful appeal

REVIEW   What beliefs and actions separated Christians from pagans?

to educated Christians. Like the cult of Isis or Stoicism, Neoplatonism provided guidance, comfort, and hope through good times or bad.

The Crisis of the Third Century

War, financial shortfalls, and natural disasters combined to create a crisis for the Roman Empire in the third century C.E. Attacks by outsiders on the northern and eastern frontiers forced the emperors to expand the army for defense. The rulers' attempts to find money to pay for these wars fueled inflation and crippled the economy. The public's outrage at these troubles encouraged ambitious generals to seek power by commanding personal armies, once again plunging Rome into civil war in a bloody replay of the destruction of the republic. Earthquakes and epidemics added to the crisis. By the end of the third century C.E., this combination of troubles had shredded the "Roman peace."

Defending the Frontiers

The emperors' supreme duty was to defend the empire. Throughout the principate, they sent military forces to repel invaders from the frontier regions. The most aggressive attackers were Germanic bands that often crossed the Danube and Rhine rivers for raiding. Their constant fighting against Roman troops turned these raiders into powerful armies, and they launched dangerous invasions during the reign of Marcus Aurelius (r. 161–180 C.E.). A major threat also emerged at the empire's eastern edge when a new dynasty, the Sasanids, defeated the Parthian Empire and reenergized the ancient Persian kingdom. By 227, Persia's military power forced the emperors to bring in legions to protect the rich eastern provinces, at the expense of the defense of the northern frontiers. Recognizing the courage of Germanic warriors, the emperors hired them as auxiliary soldiers for the Roman army and settled them on the frontiers as buffers against invasion. By around 200, the army had enrolled perhaps as many as 450,000 legionary and auxiliary troops (the size of the navy remains unknown).

Roman military life was tough. Training constantly, soldiers had to be fit enough to carry forty-pound packs up to twenty miles in five hours, swimming across rivers on the way. The emperors built many permanent forts for garrisons, but an army on the march constructed its own fort every night. Soldiers transported all the materials for a wooden-walled camp everywhere they went. As one ancient commentator noted during the republic, "Infantrymen were little different from loaded pack mules." At one camp in a frontier area, archaeologists found a supply of a million iron nails—ten tons in all. The same fort required seventeen miles of timber for its barracks walls. To outfit a legion with tents required 54,000 calves' hides.

Unlike the republic's wars of conquest, these defensive wars strained imperial finances because they did not bring in much plunder. By the third century C.E., the army had become a source of negative instead of positive cash flow to the treasury, and the economy had not expanded sufficiently to make up the difference. To make matters worse, inflation had driven up prices. A main cause of inflation under the principate may have been, ironically, the long period of peace, which promoted increased demand for the economy's relatively static production of goods and services.

In desperation at their financial problems, some emperors responded to rising prices by debasing imperial coinage in a vain attempt to cut government costs. **Debasement of coinage** meant putting less silver in each coin (there was no paper money) without changing its face value and therefore creating more cash with the same amount of precious metal (see "Taking Measure"). Merchants,

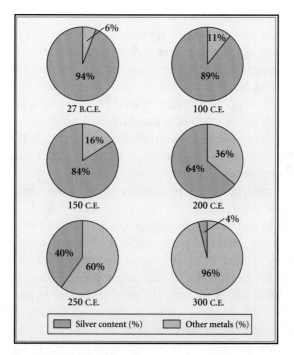

Taking Measure The Falling Value of Roman Imperial Coinage, 27 B.C.E.–300 C.E.
Ancient silver coinage derived its value from its metallic content; the less silver a coin had, the less it was worth. Emperors facing rising government and military expenses but flat or falling revenues tried to cut costs by debasing the coinage—reducing the amount of silver in each coin and increasing the amount of other, cheaper metals. These pie charts reveal the gradual debasement of Roman imperial coinage through the third century C.E., when military expenses apparently skyrocketed. By 300 C.E., coins contained only trace amounts of silver. Merchants and producers had to raise their prices for goods and services when they were being paid with currency that was increasingly less valuable. Thus debasement fueled inflation.

however, raised prices to make up for the reduced value of the debased coins. By 200 C.E., the debased coinage and inflation were ruining the imperial balance sheet and undermining public confidence in the imperial currency. As the soldiers kept demanding that their patrons, the emperors, pay them well, the situation only grew worse. The financial system fell into full collapse in the 250s and 260s.

The Severan Emperors and Financial and Political Catastrophe

Decisions by the emperor Septimius Severus (r. 193–211 C.E.) and his sons drove the imperial government into bankruptcy and instability. The father drained the treasury to satisfy the army, and his sons' murderous rivalry and reckless spending destroyed the government's stability. A soldier's soldier who came from North Africa, Severus became emperor in 193 C.E. after waging a civil war to get rid of the incompetent emperor currently holding power. To restore imperial prestige and acquire money through foreign conquest, Severus fought successful campaigns beyond the frontiers of the provinces, in Mesopotamia and northern Britain.

By this time, the soldiers were angry because inflation had eroded the value of their wages to practically nothing after they bought themselves basic supplies and clothing. They therefore expected the emperors to favor them with gifts of extra money. Severus spent large sums on such gifts, and he also decided to raise the soldiers' pay by one-third. The expanded size of the army made this raise more expensive than the treasury could afford and deepened inflation. The financial consequences of his policy, however, concerned Severus not at all. His deathbed advice to his sons in 211 C.E. was to "stay on good terms with each other, be generous to the soldiers, and pay no attention to anyone else."

Severus's sons undermined the principate's financial and political stability by following only the last two points of his advice. Caracalla (r. 211–217 C.E.) seized the throne for himself by murdering his brother, Geta. Caracalla's violent rule and limitless spending ended the peace and prosperity of the Roman Golden Age. He increased the soldiers' pay by another 40 to 50 percent and spent gigantic sums on building projects to display his glory, including the largest public baths Rome had ever seen, covering blocks and blocks of the city. The need for money to pay his out-of-control expenses put unbearable pressure on the provincial elites responsible for collecting taxes and on the citizens whom they squeezed for ever greater amounts.

In 212 C.E., Caracalla took his most famous step to try to fix the budget crisis: he granted Roman citizenship to almost every man and woman in imperial territory except slaves. His goal was to increase revenues from inheritance taxes and from fees for freeing slaves, which only citizens paid (noncitizens paid other taxes). The greater the number of citizens, he reasoned, the more money (most of it earmarked for the army) the empire would collect. Caracalla, who contemporaries whispered was insane, wrecked the imperial budget, setting in motion the ruinous inflation of the coming decades. Once when his mother criticized him for his excesses, he replied, as he drew his sword, "Never mind, we shall not run out of money as long as I have this."

The empire's financial troubles created political instability. When Macrinus, commander of the Praetorian Guard, murdered Caracalla in 217 C.E. to make himself emperor, Caracalla's female relatives bribed the army to overthrow Macrinus in favor of a young male relative. The restored Severan dynasty did not last long, however, and the assassination of the last Severan emperor in 235 C.E. began a half-century of civil wars that, compounded by natural disasters, destroyed the principate. For the next fifty years, emperors and generals constantly fought to rule. During this period of near anarchy, over two dozen men, often several at a time, held or claimed the throne. Their only qualification was their ability to lead an army and reward the troops for loyalty to their commander instead of to Rome.

The violence and financial distress caused by these civil wars made life miserable in many regions. Battling armies trampled farmers' fields searching for food, making it impossible to keep up normal agricultural production. City council members faced constantly rising demands for tax revenues from every new emperor, and the financial pressure destroyed their commitment to serving their communities. Foreign enemies took advantage of the Roman civil wars, invading from the east and north. Roman fortunes hit bottom in 260 C.E. when Shapur I, king of the Sasanid Empire of Persia, captured the emperor Valerian (r. 253–260 C.E.) while attacking the province of Syria. Imperial territory was in danger of splintering into breakaway regions. Even the tough and competent emperor Aurelian (r. 270–275 C.E.) could do no more to reduce the danger than recover Egypt and Asia Minor from Zenobia, the warrior-queen of Palmyra in Syria. He also had to encircle Rome with a massive wall to ward off surprise attacks by Germanic tribes smashing their way into Italy from the north.

Natural disasters worsened the crisis when strong earthquakes and epidemics struck some of the provinces in the mid-third century C.E. The population declined significantly as food supplies became less dependable, civil war killed soldiers and civilians alike, and infection flared over large regions. The loss of population meant fewer soldiers for the army, whose efficiency as a defense and police force had already declined because of the financial and political chaos. More frontier areas became vulnerable to raids, and roving bands of robbers became increasingly common within the imperial borders. Polytheists explained these horrible times in the traditional way: the state gods were angry. But why? The obvious answer seemed to be the presence of Christians, who denied the existence of the Roman gods and refused to participate in their worship. The emperor Decius (r. 249–251 C.E.) conducted systematic persecutions to eliminate Christians as a way to regain the goodwill of the gods. He justified the violence by calling himself "Restorer of the Cults," proclaiming, "I would rather see a rival to my throne than another bishop of Rome." He ordered all inhabitants of the empire to prove their loyalty to the

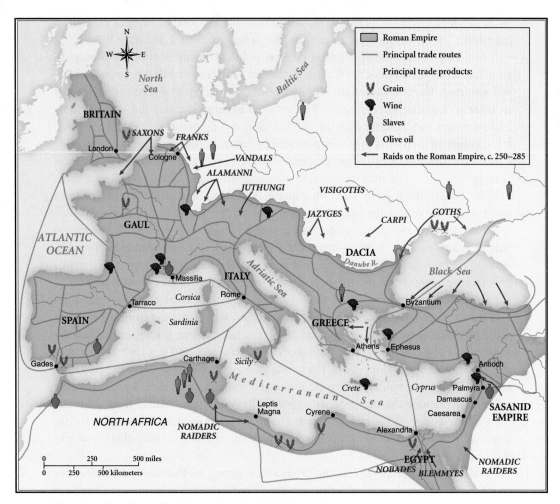

Mapping the West The Roman Empire in Crisis, c. 284 C.E.
By the early 280s C.E., the principate had been torn apart by the fifty years of civil war that had followed the end of the Severan dynasty. Imperial territory remained the same as in the time of Augustus
(Map 5.1, page 157), except for the loss of Dacia during the reign of Aurelian (r. 270–275 C.E.). Attacks
from the north and east had repeatedly penetrated the frontier regions, however. The Sasanid king
Shapur I (r. c. 240–270 C.E.), for example, temporarily held Antioch and captured the emperor Valerian
in 260 C.E. The public humiliation and death in captivity of the elderly imperial ruler indicate the
depths to which Roman fortunes sank in the third century C.E.

state by participating in a sacrifice to its gods. Christians who refused to sacrifice were killed.

These new persecutions did not end the civil war, financial failure, or diseases that had brought on the crisis. By the early 280s C.E., the empire was in danger of fragmenting. Remarkably, in 284 C.E. Diocletian would drag it back to safety in the same way Augustus had begun the principate: by creating a new form of authoritarian leadership.

> **REVIEW** What factors provoked the crisis in Roman government and society in the third century C.E.?

Conclusion

The creation of what we call the Roman Empire demonstrated the continuing and overwhelming importance of tradition as the Romans' guide to life. The new political system that governed the empire, the principate, could only be seen as legitimate if it was proclaimed a restoration of the republic, not a change for the better. Moreover, it also had to make plain the princeps's role in fulfilling the traditional paternalistic obligations of a patron toward his clients. For Romans, "back to the future" was a crucial principle of action.

The "restored republic" turned out to be a success for the majority of people in the empire, who enjoyed relative peace and prosperity for two centuries. It was only the elites that hated and feared the power of the emperor, at least until the Christians became numerous enough to attract unwanted attention from the authorities. Certainly, the diverse peoples of the vast empire did not all get along without prejudice or conflict. The rebellions of the Jews in Judaea provide violent evidence of how unpleasant Roman rule could seem to some. At the same time, it would be wrong to deny that the Roman army and Roman law did bring a stable and prosperous peace to a wider area of the world for a longer time than ever before in history. In the end, the principate failed for reasons that have brought down many governments over time: an inability to deal with the state's bottomless hunger for more revenue, and a failure to develop a system for consistently choosing good leaders and preventing them from abusing their power.

As focused as they were on the value of maintaining traditions, the Romans were also open to learning from cultural interaction with others. They realized that to survive and thrive in a dangerous world, it paid to be innovative in implementing tradition. The most influential innovation of the period, although it was very slow to develop, was the growth of Christianity as a separate religion from

Judaism and a competitor with paganism for the religious identity of the Roman population. Romans, like other ancient peoples, had always been deeply religious, and once they noticed that Christians existed, they took them and their beliefs very seriously. At first the reaction was hostile. How Christianity developed from a new faith that seemed to threaten the traditional "peace of the gods" to the source of most Romans' hope for divine protection and salvation is the central story of Roman history in the period following the principate.

CHAPTER REVIEW QUESTIONS

1. Compare the crisis in the first century B.C.E. that undermined the republic with the crisis in the third century C.E. that undermined the principate.

2. If you had been a first-century C.E. emperor, what would you have done about the Christians and why? What if you had been a third-century C.E. emperor?

For practice quizzes and other study tools, see the Online Study Guide at bedfordstmartins.com/huntconcise.

For primary-source material from this period, see Chapter 6 of *Sources of THE MAKING OF THE WEST*, Third Edition.

TIMELINE

- **c. 33 C.E.** Paul of Tarsus becomes a Christian

27 B.C.E.–14 C.E. Augustus's principate

- **30 C.E.** Jesus of Nazareth crucified in Jerusalem

- **44 B.C.E.** Julius Caesar's assassination reignites civil war

- **8 C.E.** Augustus exiles the poet Ovid

50 B.C.E.	0	50 C.E.	100 C.E.

- **2 B.C.E.** Senate proclaims Augustus "Father of His Country"

- **64 C.E.** Nero blames Christians for great fire in Rome

- **69 C.E.** Civil war in the "Year of the Four Emperors"

- **70 C.E.** Jewish temple in Jerusalem destroyed

Suggested References

Modern scholarly work on the principate reveals how the emperors tried to create political legitimacy and social stability through a combination of military, religious, and artistic policy.

Ando, Clifford. *The Matter of the Gods: Religion and the Roman Empire.* 2008.

Denzey, Nicola. *The Bone Gatherers: The Lost Worlds of Early Christian Women.* 2007.

Futrell, Allison. *Blood in the Arena: The Spectacle of Roman Power.* 1997.

Galinsky, Karl. *Augustan Culture.* 1996.

Goldsworthy, Adrian. *The Complete Roman Army.* 2003.

*Kraemer, Ross Shephard. *Her Share of the Blessings: Women's Religion among Pagans, Jews, and Christians in the Greco-Roman World.* 1992.

MacMullen, Ramsay. *Christianizing the Roman Empire (A.D. 100–400).* 1984.

Roman emperors: http://www.roman-emperors.org/startup.htm

Roth, Roman, and Johannes Keller, eds. "Roman by Integration: Dimensions of Group Identity in Material Culture and Text." Special issue, *Journal of Roman Archaeology.* Suppl. no. 66. 2007.

*Suetonius. *The Twelve Caesars.* Trans. Robert Graves. 2003.

Syme, Ronald. *The Roman Revolution.* 1939; repr. 2002.

*Tacitus. *The Complete Works.* Trans. Alfred John Church and William Jackson Brodribb. 1964.

161–180 C.E. Germanic bands attack northern frontiers during the reign of Marcus Aurelius

250s–260s C.E. Imperial finances collapse from civil war, debased coinage, and inflation

150 C.E.	200 C.E.	250 C.E.	300 C.E.

■ **212 C.E.** Caracalla extends Roman citizenship to almost all free inhabitants of the provinces

■ **284 C.E.** Diocletian becomes emperor

INNOMINE
XPI·VINCAS
SEMPER·

DN·HONORIOSEMP·AVG·

DN·HONORIO·SEMPER·AVG·

PROBVS·FAMVLVS·VC·CONS·OR·D·

PROBVS·FAMVLVS·VC·CONS·ORD·

The Transformation of the Roman Empire

AN EGYPTIAN WOMAN NAMED ISIS wrote a letter to her mother in the third century that archaeologists discovered more than fifteen hundred years later in an excavation near the Nile River. Written in Greek on papyrus, the letter hints at the problems many people experienced during this troubled time.

Emperor Honorius as Christian Victor, c. 406

Both sides of this ivory diptych (folding tablet) depict Honorius, emperor of the western Roman Empire, as a military victor crediting Christ for his success. Petronius Probus presented this gift to the emperor to show his gratitude for being awarded the consulship, the empire's highest honor. On the left, Honorius holds a sign that says, "You will always conquer, in the name of Christ." On the right, he holds a shield and a scepter; a statuette of Victory standing on a globe offers him a victor's wreath. His clothing and armor identify him as a military leader; the inscription above his head proclaims him "Our Master, Always Augustus," while the circle around his head testifies to his special holiness. As this carving shows, Honorius, like other emperors, believed that he had divine backing for his army. In his case, it was not enough: the Goths sacked Rome only four years later. *(Alinari/Art Resource, NY.)*

Every day I pray to the lord Sarapis and his fellow gods to watch over you. I want you to know that I have arrived in Alexandria safely after four days. I send fond greetings to my sister and the children and Elouath and his wife and Dioscorous and her husband and children and Tamalis and her husband and son and Heron and Ammonarion and . . . Sanpat and her children. And if Aion wants to be in the army, let him come. For everybody is in the army.

The letter raises puzzling questions: What were the relationships between Isis and the people she mentions, with their mixture of Greek and Semitic names? Why had she gone to Alexandria? Why did Aion want to become a soldier? Why was "everybody" in the army? The answers, if we knew them, would surely relate to the economic and political crisis that gripped the Roman Empire in the third century. Perhaps financial troubles forced Isis to leave her village to seek work in the city. Perhaps Aion wanted to join the army to earn wages; the emperors were always recruiting more soldiers. Perhaps everybody seemed to be in the army because there was continuous civil war.

Diocletian, emperor beginning in 284, reorganized the government and increased the authority of the emperor. Still, restoring peace and order proved difficult because religious tensions were growing between Christians and followers of traditional polytheistic cults, such as Isis the letter writer, named after the famous Egyptian goddess. Then, unexpectedly, early in the fourth century the emperor Constantine converted to Christianity. By the end of the fourth century, the new faith had become the official religion of Roman government, replacing the traditional gods.

Also at the end of the fourth century, the empire split permanently into western and eastern sections. In the west, non-Roman peoples began migrating into the region, transforming it—and themselves—politically and socially by replacing Roman provincial government with their own new kingdoms. By the fifth century, the weakening of Roman government in western Europe had divided that region into different states, anticipating Europe's modern nations. The provinces of the eastern Roman Empire remained economically vibrant and politically united, becoming (in modern terminology) the **Byzantine Empire** in the sixth century. There, the remaining part of the Roman Empire endured under Christian rule for centuries, until Turkish invaders finally conquered it in 1453.

CHAPTER FOCUS QUESTION   What were the sources of unity and the causes of division in the Roman Empire from the reign of the emperor Diocletian to the emergence of the Byzantine Empire in the sixth century?

Reorganizing the Empire

The emperors Diocletian (r. 284–305) and Constantine (r. 306–337) reorganized the Roman Empire and reinforced the emperor's authority to overcome the troubles that the third-century crisis had created. They differed radically, however, in their treatment of Christians and their attitude toward traditional Roman religion.

The Dominate and Imperial Reorganization

Diocletian ended the third-century crisis by imposing the strongest form of monarchy in Roman history and reorganizing the empire into administrative districts. He was an uneducated military man from outside Italy (Dalmatia, in what is now Croatia), but his exceptional leadership and intelligence propelled him through the ranks until the army made him emperor in 284. Diocletian proclaimed himself *dominus*—"master," what slaves called their owners—to replace Augustus's republican title, *princeps* ("first man"). Roman government from Diocletian onward is therefore called the **dominate** instead of the principate. Senators, consuls, and other traditional republican offices continued to exist, but the emperors held all the power. They reigned as autocrats— true sole rulers—and no longer tried to hide their supremacy, as Augustus had done when he invented the principate. To display their superiority, the emperors of the

Coin Portrait of Emperor Constantine
Constantine had these special, extra-large coins minted to show him as a Christian emperor. The jewels on his helmet and crown, the fancy bridle on his horse, and the scepter indicate his status as ruler, while his armor and shield show his military accomplishments. He proclaims his Christian rule with his scepter's new design—a cross with a globe— and the round badge sticking up from his helmet, which carries the monogram meaning "Christ." He had his soldiers paint this monogram on their shields to win God's favor in battle. (Staatliche Münzsammlung, Munich.)

dominate placed their throne on a raised platform, wore jeweled robes, and surrounded themselves with attendants and ceremony. Constantine wore a diadem—a purple headband sparkling with gems, a symbol of kingship avoided by earlier emperors out of respect for the Roman tradition that the ruler was a citizen, not a monarch. To demonstrate the ruler's superiority, a series of veils now separated palace waiting rooms from the inner space where the emperor listened to people's pleas for help. High-ranking officials received showy titles such as "most perfect" and wore special shoes and belts. The court of the dominate resembled the splendid court of the Great King of Persia a thousand years earlier (see the illustration on page 27). Diocletian, Constantine, and their successors believed that citizens were their subjects. The architecture of the dominate reflected its rulers' all-powerful status. Diocletian's public bath in Rome rivaled earlier emperors' buildings in the capital; its soaring vaults and domes covered a space more than three thousand feet long on each side.

The dominate also used religious language to mark the emperor's special status. The emperors added *et deus* (and God) to *dominus* as their title. Diocletian adopted the title Jovius, claiming Jupiter (Jove), the chief Roman god, as his ancestor. His titles signaled the elevated respect he now demanded from his subjects: he expected to be honored as magnificently as the gods.

The dominate's emperors made law. Relying on a personal staff that isolated them from the outside world, they no longer asked for advice from the elite. Their desire to maintain order led them to impose brutal punishments for crimes. For example, Constantine punished officials who did not keep what he called their "greedy hands" off bribes by having their hands "cut off by the sword"; the guardians of a young girl who allowed a lover to seduce her were punished by having molten lead poured into their mouths. The emperors of the dominate also widened the divide between poor and rich by making punishments even harsher for the large segment of the population legally known as "humbler people." Their laws excused those designated "better people" from most of the harshest penalties for the same crimes.

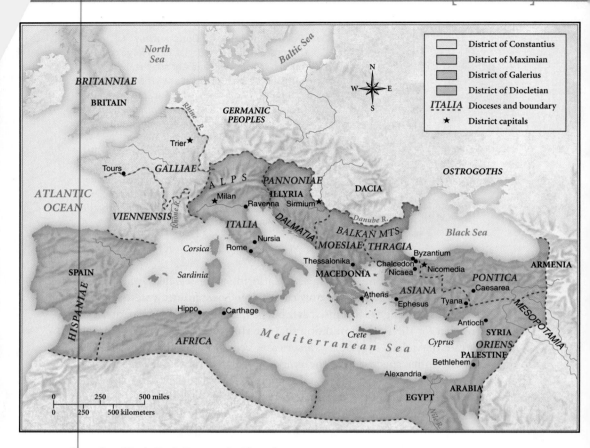

Map 6.1 Diocletian's Reorganization of 293

To try to prevent civil war and increase the emperor's authority, Emperor Diocletian reorganized the Roman Empire into four administrative districts, each governed by its own ruler. He also subdivided the provinces into smaller units and grouped them into twelve dioceses, each overseen by a regional administrator. This map shows the four districts as described in a book written by an imperial official around 360.

Diocletian decided that the empire could not be administered and defended from a single center (that is, Rome). In 293, he therefore divided imperial territory into four administrative districts, two in the west and two in the east (Map 6.1). Having no sons, he appointed three "partners" so that he and they could govern cooperatively in two pairs, each consisting of a senior "Augustus" and a junior "Caesar" as his adopted son and designated successor. Each partner controlled one of the four districts. To prevent disunity, the most senior partner—in this case Diocletian—served as supreme ruler (emperor) and was supposed to receive the loyalty of the others. This **tetrarchy** (rule by four), as modern scholars call it, was Diocletian's attempt to improve defense along the empire's long frontiers and to prevent a civil war over who should become the next emperor.

Diocletian also subdivided the provinces, nearly doubling their number to almost one hundred. He grouped them into twelve dioceses, each under the jurisdiction of a regional governor. To try to keep the governors from becoming powerful enough to threaten the emperors, Diocletian began the process of stripping them of their military authority, restricting them instead to overseeing legal and financial affairs. Generals were put in charge of the defense. Constantine completed this process of separating the provincial leaders' powers.

Although later emperors abandoned the tetrarchy, Diocletian's reorganization of provincial administration into a hierarchy continued. He also ended Rome's thousand years as the empire's capital city. Diocletian lived in Nicomedia, in Asia Minor, and did not even visit Rome until 303, nearly twenty years after he became emperor. He chose four new capitals (Nicomedia, Milan, Trier, and Sirmium; Map 6.1, page 200) for their usefulness as military command posts closer to the frontiers. Italy became just another region in the empire, on an equal footing with the other provinces and subject to the same taxation system, except for the tax-free district of Rome itself—the last trace of the city's former superiority.

Despite Diocletian's reforms, civil war broke out soon after he retired in 305. It took Constantine (r. 306–337), one of the "partners" ruling a region of the empire, almost twenty years to eliminate his rivals. He first proved his ability as a military commander by fighting barbarian tribes who were threatening the northern empire and then led his troops to victory in the civil war. The Roman Senate ultimately hailed him as "the greatest Augustus." His success in war and politics did not extend to his family life: he had one son executed and probably engineered the death of his wife, the empress, for reasons that were kept secret. Near the end of his reign, he named his remaining three sons as joint heirs, ordering them to rule as co-emperors. They failed as bloodily as had the sons of Septimius Severus a century earlier, plunging into war with one another. This civil war informally split the empire on a north-south line along the Balkan peninsula. In 395, the brothers Honorius and Arcadius divided the empire into western and eastern halves, ruling as co-emperors. This division launched the two parts of the empire toward different fates.

The Division of the Empire, c. 395

Each half of the empire had its own capital. Constantinople, near the mouth of the Black Sea, was the eastern capital. This city had been founded a thousand years before by Greeks and was known as Byzantium (today Istanbul, Turkey). Constantine reconstructed the city in 324 and renamed it Constantinople. He chose it for its geography: located on an easily fortified peninsula, it controlled routes for trade and troop movements. To give his "new Rome" the glory of the old capital, Constantine erected a forum, an imperial palace, a hippodrome for chariot races, and huge stat-ues of the traditional gods. The eastern emperors inherited Constantinople as their capital; modern historians, recalling the city's ancient Greek name, use the term *Byzantine Empire* to refer to the eastern section of the original Roman Empire.

Geography determined the site of the western capital as well. The western emperor, Honorius (r. 395–423; see the illustration on page 196), wanted to keep the Alps between his territory and the raiders living to the north. In 404, he made Ravenna, a port on Italy's northeastern coast, the western capital because it was a naval base and an important commercial city. Walls and marshes protected it from attack by land, while its harbor kept it from being starved out in a siege. Although Ravenna never rivaled Constantinople in size or riches, the emperors built spec-tacular churches gleaming with multicolored mosaics there.

Financial Reform and Social Consequences

The empire's financial crisis proved Diocletian's biggest problem. He tried to improve revenues by creating new money, price controls, and a new taxation system. Unfor-tunately, Diocletian miscalculated in establishing values for his new coins and set off a financial panic that bred inflation in many regions. High prices caused people to hoard whatever goods they could buy, and hoarding drove prices even higher. "Hurry and spend all my money you have; buy me any kinds of goods at whatever prices they are available," wrote one official to his servant, fearing yet another decline in the value of the currency.

Diocletian tried to stop inflation by imposing price and wage controls in the worst-hit regions. His Edict on Maximum Prices blamed high prices on profiteers' "unlimited and crazed avarice," banned hoarding, and set limits on the prices that could legally be charged for about a thousand goods and services. The edict soon became ineffective, however, because merchants refused to cooperate, and govern-ment officials were unable to enforce it despite the threat of death or exile as the penalty for violations. In his final years, Diocletian revalued the currency to restore sound money and stable prices, but civil war under Constantine again weakened it. With the currency losing value, the emperors began collecting taxes not only in coin but also in goods. Recent research disputes whether this form of revenue actually replaced taxes paid in coin, as previous scholars believed, or served only as a way to impose higher property taxes, which had to be paid in coin as much as possible. By the end of the fourth century, however, it is clear that the government expected payment in gold and silver and that taxes rose, especially on the local elites. Taxes went mostly to support the army, which required enormous amounts of grain, meat, wine, horses, camels, and mules. The major sources of revenue were a tax on land, assessed according to its productivity, and a head tax on individuals.

The empire was too large for the emperor to enforce consistency in tax rates. In some areas, both men and women from about ages twelve to sixty-five paid the full tax; in others, women paid only one-half the tax assessment, or none at all. Workers in cities probably owed taxes only on their property. They periodically paid "in kind"—laboring without pay on public works projects such as cleaning municipal drains or repairing buildings. Urban businesspeople, from shopkeepers to prostitutes, paid taxes in coin. Members of the senatorial class were exempt from ordinary taxes but had to make other payments when the emperor demanded them.

Since the new tax system could work only if agricultural production remained stable and the government controlled the people liable for the head tax, Diocletian restricted the movement of tenant farmers (*coloni*), who formed the empire's economic base. Coloni had traditionally been free to move to different farms under different landlords. Now tenant farmers were increasingly tied to a particular plot, and their children were required to remain farmers.

The government also restricted workers in other essential occupations. Bakers, for example, could not leave their jobs, and anyone who acquired a baker's property had to assume that occupation. Bakers were essential in producing free bread for Rome's poor, a tradition begun under the republic to prevent food riots. Also, from Constantine's reign on, military service became a lifetime career that sons of soldiers inherited: they had to serve in the army.

The emperors in this period also announced oppressive regulations on the elites in the empire's towns. Almost all men in this class, known as **curials** (or decurions), were obliged sooner or later to serve as unsalaried city council members, who had to use their own funds if necessary to support the community. Their financial responsibilities ranged from maintaining the water supply to feeding troops, but their most expensive duty was covering shortfalls in taxes. The emperors' demands for increased revenue made this a crushing burden, compounding the damage to the curials that the third-century crisis had begun.

The tradition of public service by the elites broke down as wealthy people avoided it to escape financial ruin. To force curials to perform their obligations, the emperors ordered them not to move away from the towns where they had been born; they even had to ask official permission to travel. Forced service on a city council became one of the punishments for a minor crime. These laws made members of the elite try to win exemptions from public service by begging the emperor, bribing high-ranking officials, or taking up occupations that freed them from such obligations (such as being a soldier, an imperial administrator, or a church official). The most desperate people abandoned their homes and property.

The emperors' attempts to stabilize the empire by increasing its revenue also hurt nonelite citizens. The tax rate on land eventually reached one-third of its gross yield. This burden crushed poor farmers. They had to eat most of what they produced just to survive, save enough seed to plant the next crop, and then pay the high tax out of what was left. A bad harvest meant starvation. Conditions became so bad in fifth-century Spain, for example, that peasants openly revolted against imperial control. Financial troubles, especially severe in the west, kept the empire from ever regaining the prosperity of its Golden Age and worsened the friction between government and citizens.

Christianity: From Persecution to Conversion

The official position of Christianity in the Roman Empire changed completely from the reign of Diocletian to that of Constantine. Diocletian believed that Roman government needed to regain the goodwill of the pagan gods by promoting traditional religion and suppressing Christianity. He proclaimed, "The providence of the immortal gods has allowed superior, wise, and upright men in their wisdom to establish good and true principles. It is wrong to oppose these principles or to abandon the ancient religion for some new one."

Blaming Christians for angering the gods, Diocletian in 303 launched the **Great Persecution**. He expelled Christians from his administration, seized their property, tore down their churches, and executed them for refusing to participate in sacrifices. The policy was applied differently in different regions. In the western empire, the violence stopped after about a year; in the east, it continued for a decade. So gruesome were the public executions of martyrs that they aroused the sympathy of some polytheists.

Constantine changed the empire's religious history forever by converting to Christianity. He chose the new faith for the same reason that Diocletian had persecuted it: in the belief that he would receive divine protection for himself and the empire. During the civil war that he had to fight to become emperor after Diocletian resigned, Constantine had a vision in which he was promised the support of the Christian God. His biographer reported that Constantine had also seen a vision of Jesus's cross in the sky surrounded by the words "In this sign you shall be the victor." When Constantine defeated his main rival at the battle of the Milvian Bridge in Rome in 312, he proclaimed that God's miraculous power and goodwill had brought him the victory. He therefore declared himself a Christian emperor. After his conversion, Constantine did not outlaw polytheism or make Christianity the official religion. Instead, he announced religious toleration. The best statement of his new policy survives in the **Edict of Milan** of 313. It proclaimed free choice of religion for everyone and referred to the empire's protection by "the highest divinity"—a general term meant to satisfy both polytheists and Christians.

Constantine wanted to avoid angering polytheists because they still greatly outnumbered Christians, but he did all he could to promote his new religion. These goals called for a careful balancing act. For example, he returned all property seized during the Great Persecution to its Christian owners, but he had the treasury pay back those polytheists who had bought the confiscated property. When he made the Lord's Day a holy occasion each week on which no official business or manufacturing work could be performed, he called it Sunday in honor of two divinities, the Christian God and the pagan sun god. To beautify his new capital, Constantinople, he erected numerous statues of traditional gods around the city. He also respected Roman tradition by holding the office of pontifex maximus (highest priest), a position that all the emperors since Augustus had filled.

REVIEW | What changes did Diocletian and Constantine make to try to restore the peace and prosperity of the empire?

Relief Sculpture of Saturn from North Africa
This pillar shows the god known to the Romans
as Saturn and to the Carthaginians as Ba'al Ham-
mon (one of the gods of the Phoenician founders
of Carthage). This syncretism (identifying gods
as the same even though they carried different
names in different places) was typical of ancient
polytheism and allowed Roman and non-Roman
cults to merge. The smaller figure below the god is
sacrificing a sheep before an altar. The inscription
dates the pillar to 323, a decade after Constantine's
conversion to Christianity. Such objects testifying to
the continuing existence of polytheistic cults remained
common until the end of the fourth century, when the
Christian emperors succeeded in suppressing most public
activities of traditional religion. (© Copyright Martha Cooper/
Peter Arnold, Inc.)

Christianizing the Empire

Constantine's policy of religious toleration began the Christianization of the Roman
Empire. The process was slow and sometimes violent. Not until the end of the fourth
century did the emperors close the traditional gods' temples. Even after the vast majority of people in the empire had become Christians, some polytheists continued to
worship in private. Nevertheless, the transformation from a polytheist empire into a
Christian state was a turning point in global history.

Christianity as the Official Religion

It took a long time for the Christian emperors to make Christianity the official
religion of the empire because polytheists were serious believers. Polytheists and
Christians held some similar beliefs. Both believed spirits and demons had a powerful influence on daily life. Some people combined the religions. For example, a silver
spoon used in the worship of the polytheist forest spirit Faunus has been found

Mosaic of Christ as Sun God
This mosaic comes from a burial chamber in Rome that is now in the Vatican, under the basilica of St. Peter built by Constantine. It perhaps dates to the mid-third century. The depiction of Christ here is similar to a traditional polytheistic representation of the sun god, especially the Greek Apollo: with rays of light shining forth around his head as he rides in a chariot pulled by horses. This symbolism—God is light—reached back to ancient Egypt. Christian artists showed Jesus in this way because he said, "I am the light of the world" (John 8:12). The cloak flaring from Christ's shoulder suggests his movement across the sky. **For more help analyzing this image, see the visual activity for this chapter in the Online Study Guide at** bedfordstmartins.com/huntconcise. (Scala/Art Resource, NY.)

engraved with a fish, a common symbol of Christianity. (The Greek word for "fish," *ichthys,* was thought to be an acronym for the Greek words meaning "Jesus Christ the Son of God, the Savior.")

The differences between polytheists' and Christians' beliefs were much greater than their similarities, however. Above all was the fundamental difference between Christians' belief in one God and polytheists' belief in many gods. Polytheists still participated in festivals and sacrifices to their many gods. Why, they asked, did these joyous occasions not satisfy Christians' desire for contact with divinity? Polytheists also could not understand why Christians believed in a savior who had not established a new kingdom on earth and had been executed as a common criminal. The traditional gods, they insisted, had given a world empire to their worshippers. Moreover, they told Christians, cults such as that of the goddess Isis and philosophies such as Stoicism accepted only the pure of heart as followers. Christianity, by contrast, took in sinners. Why, puzzled polytheists wondered, would any righteous person want to associate with wrongdoers? In short, as one Greek philosopher remarked, Christians had no right to claim that they had the one true religion, for no one had ever discovered a single doctrine providing "the sole path to the liberation of the soul."

The slow pace of religious change revealed how strong polytheism remained in the fourth century, especially among the social elite. In fact, the emperor Julian

(r. 361–363) rebelled against his family's Christianity and tried to impose his philosophical brand of polytheism as Rome's official religion. This rejection of Christianity earned him the name Julian the Apostate (someone who turns against an established faith is called an **apostate**). Deeply religious, he believed in a supreme deity corresponding to the ideas of Greek philosophers: "This divine and completely beautiful universe, from heaven's highest sky to earth's lowest limit, is tied together by the continuous providence of god, has existed forever, and will last forever." Julian's restoration of the traditional gods ended when he died while invading Persia.

The Christian emperors who followed Julian worked to end polytheism. In 382, Gratian (r. 375–383 in the west) removed from the Senate in Rome the Altar of Victory, which Augustus had placed there to remind senators of Rome's success under its ancestral religion. Most important, Gratian stopped public funding for traditional sacrifices. Aurelius Symmachus, a polytheist senator who served as prefect (mayor) of Rome, objected to what he saw as an outrage against Rome's tradition of religious diversity. Protesting the emperors' moves against polytheism, he argued, "We all have our own way of life and our own way of worship. . . . So vast a mystery [as religious truth] cannot be approached by only one path."

Christianity finally replaced traditional polytheism as the state religion in 391, when the emperor Theodosius (r. 379–395 in the east) successfully banned all polytheist sacrifices, even if private individuals paid for the animals. He also made divination (predicting the future) by the inspection of animal entrails punishable as high treason and ordered that all polytheist temples be closed. Many shrines, however, such as the Parthenon in Athens, remained in use for a long time because the empire was too large for the emperors to enforce such laws at the local level. Temples were only gradually converted to churches during the fifth and sixth centuries. Non-Christian schools were not forced to close—the Academy, founded by Plato in Athens in the early fourth century B.C.E., endured for 140 years after Theodosius's reign—but Christians received advantages in government careers. Over time, non-Christians became outsiders in an empire ruled by Christian emperors.

Jews posed a special problem in the opinion of the Christian emperors. Like polytheists, Jews rejected the new official religion. Yet they seemed entitled to special treatment because Jesus had been a Jew and because previous emperors had allowed Jews to practice their religion. Fourth-century and later emperors placed legal restrictions on Jews. For example, they banned Jews from holding government jobs but still required them to take on the financial burdens of curials—without receiving the honor of curial status. By the late sixth century, they increased the pressure on Jews to convert to Christianity by barring them from making wills, receiving inheritances, or testifying in court. Although these developments began the long process that transformed Jews into second-class citizens in later European history, they did not destroy Judaism. Synagogues continued to exist in Palestine, where a few Jews still lived (most had been dispersed throughout the cities of the empire and the lands beyond the eastern border). The study of Jewish law and traditions flourished in this period, leading to the creation of books known as the Palestinian and the Babylonian Talmuds (collections of scholars' interpretations of Jewish law) and the scriptural commentaries of the Midrash (an explanation of the meaning of the Hebrew Bible). These works of religious scholarship provided guidance on how to live according to God's will and greatly influenced later Judaism.

With the emperors being Christians, soldiers could convert to Christianity and still serve in the army. Previously, Christian soldiers had sometimes created disciplinary problems. As one senior infantryman said in 298 at his court-martial for abandoning his duties, "A Christian serving the Lord Christ should not serve the affairs of this world." Once the emperors had become Christians, however, soldiers could justify military duty as supporting Christ.

Christianity's religious and social values helped it grow. It offered believers a strong sense of community in this world as well as the promise of salvation in the next. Wherever they went, Christians could find a warm welcome in the local congregation (Map 6.2). The new religion won converts by performing charitable works—in the tradition of Jews and some polytheist cults—especially in support of the poor, widows, and orphans. By the mid-third century, for example, Rome's congregation was supporting fifteen hundred widows and other poor people. Christianity's emphasis on taking care of others was especially important because people at that time had to depend mostly on friends and relatives for help; state-funded social services were rare.

Women were influential in spreading the new religion. Augustine (354–430), bishop of Hippo in North Africa and perhaps the most influential theologian in Western history, recognized women's contribution to the strengthening of Christianity in a letter he wrote to the unbaptized husband of a baptized woman: "O you men, who fear all the burdens imposed by baptism. The women are far better than you. Chaste and devoted to the faith, it is their presence in large numbers that causes the church to grow." Some women earned high status by giving their property to their congregations or by refusing marriage to dedicate themselves to Christ. Lifelong virgins and widows who chose not to remarry thus joined large donors as especially respected women. These women rejected the traditional social order, in which women were supposed to devote themselves to raising families. But even these holy women were excluded from leadership positions once the church's organization became a hierarchy of bishops matching the male-dominated hierarchy of the Roman world.

Once Christianity was the official religion, bishops became the emperors' partners in local rule, replacing the curials, whose numbers had shrunk drastically from the financial pressures the government had imposed on them but not on bishops. Bishops gained power because they could influence the emperor to direct government funds back to their regions. Regional councils of bishops appointed new bishops and tried to settle disputes over Christian doctrine. Bishops in the largest cities became the most powerful leaders in the church. The main bishop of Carthage, for example, supervised at least one hundred local bishops in the surrounding area. The

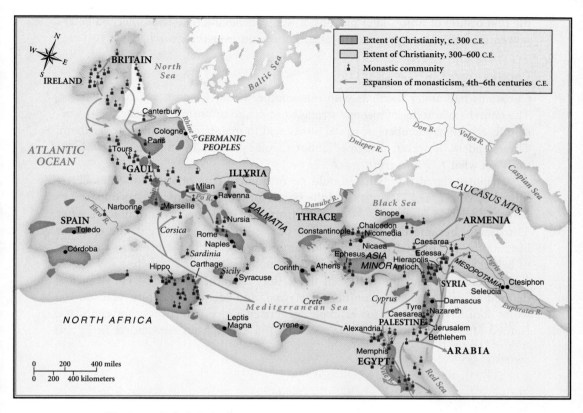

Map 6.2 The Spread of Christianity, 300–600
Christians were still a minority in the population of the Roman Empire in 300, although congregations existed in many cities and towns, especially in the eastern provinces. The emperor Constantine's conversion to Christianity in the early fourth century gave a boost to the new religion. It gained further strength during that century as the Christian emperors provided financial support and eliminated payments for the polytheist cults that had previously made up the state religion. By 600, the preaching of the church's missionaries and the money of the emperors had spread Christianity from one end of the empire to the other.

bishop of Rome became the church's supreme leader in the western empire. The eastern church never agreed that he controlled the entire Christian world, but his dominance in the west won him the title previously applied to many bishops: pope (from *pappas,* Greek for "father"), the name still used for the head of the Roman Catholic church.

The bishops of Rome quoted the New Testament to establish their leadership over other bishops. In the Book of Matthew (16:18–19), Jesus speaks to the Apostle Peter: "You are Peter, and upon this rock I will build my church. . . . I will entrust to you the keys of the kingdom of heaven. Whatever you bind on earth shall be bound in heaven. Whatever you loose on earth shall be loosed in heaven." Because Peter's name means "rock" in Greek and because Peter was believed to have been the first bishop of Rome, later bishops of Rome, believing they had inherited Peter's power, used this passage to justify their command over the church.

Conflict over Christian Beliefs

Christians had angry conflicts with one another about which beliefs were correct. The church's hierarchy of bishops struggled to create uniformity in beliefs and worship to ensure its members' spiritual purity and to maintain its authority over them. These leaders, however, disagreed about theology, too. Christians never achieved unity on what religious truth was.

Disputes flared over what should be orthodoxy (the official doctrines determined by councils of bishops; from the Greek for "correct thinking") as opposed to heresy (deviation from official doctrines; from the Greek for "private choice"). After Christianity became the official religion of the Roman government, the emperor became the top official responsible for enforcing the orthodox creed (a summary of beliefs). He used force against believers whom he regarded as heretics.

Questions about the nature of the Trinity of Father, Son, and Holy Spirit—defined in orthodoxy as a unified, coeternal, and identical divinity—caused the worst conflict. **Arianism**, for example, generated fierce controversy for centuries. Named after its founder, Arius (c. 260–336), a priest from Alexandria in Egypt,

Mosaic of a Family from Edessa in the Middle East

This mosaic, found in a cave tomb, depicts an upper-class family of Edessa in the late Roman imperial period. Edessa was the capital of the small kingdom of Osrhoëne, in northern Mesopotamia. The family's names are given in Syriac, the dialect of Aramaic spoken in their region, and their colorful clothing reflects local traditions. Rome took over the kingdom in 216, and it became famous in Christian history because its king Agbar (r. 179–216) was remembered as the first ruler to convert to Christianity, well before Constantine. By the early fourth century, the story had emerged that after Jesus's death and resurrection, he sent one of his disciples to Edessa, where the disciple painted a picture of Jesus that protected the city from its enemies. The Byzantine emperors proclaimed themselves the heirs of King Agbar and of Jesus's grant to the city of special divine protection. (Photo courtesy Thames & Hudson Ltd., London, from *Vanished Civilizations,* ed. Edward Bacon.)

this set of beliefs taught that Jesus as God's son had not existed eternally. Rather, God the Father had "begot" (created) his son from nothing and given him his special status. Thus Jesus was not coeternal with God and not identical to him in nature. This doctrine implied that the Trinity was divisible and that Christianity's monotheism was not absolute. Arianism found widespread support, perhaps because it eliminated the difficulty of understanding how a son could be as old as his father, and also because ranking the son as inferior to the father corresponded to regular family life. Arius used popular songs to make his views known, and people everywhere argued about the controversy. "When you ask for your change from a shopkeeper," one observer remarked in describing Constantinople, "he lectures you about the Begotten and the Unbegotten. If you ask how much bread costs, the reply is that 'the Father is superior and the Son inferior.'"

Other Christians became so angry about Arius's beliefs about Jesus that Constantine in 325 assembled 220 bishops at the Council of Nicaea to hammer out an agreement. The majority of bishops voted to crack down on Arianism: they banished Arius to the Balkan Mountains and declared that the Father and the Son were "of one substance" and coeternal. Arian's beliefs lived on: Constantine's third son, Constantius II (r. 337–361), favored Arianism, and his missionaries converted many of the barbarian immigrants who later came to live in the empire.

Nestorius, who became bishop of Constantinople in 428, disagreed with the orthodox doctrine of how Jesus's human and divine natures were related to his birth, insisting that his mother, Mary, gave birth to the human that became the temple for the divine. Nestorianism enraged orthodox Christians by rejecting Mary's title as *theotokos* (Greek for "bearer of God"). The bishops of Alexandria and Rome had Nestorius deposed and his doctrines officially rejected at councils held in 430 and 431; they condemned his writings in 435. Nestorian bishops in the eastern empire refused to accept these decisions, however, and they formed a separate church centered in Persia, where for centuries Nestorian Christians flourished under the tolerance of non-Christian rulers. They later became important agents of cross-cultural interaction by establishing communities that still endure in Arabia, India, and China.

The conflict over Donatism illustrates the bitterness of Christian conflicts over beliefs. Following the Great Persecution, in the fourth century a dispute arose in North Africa over whether to readmit to their old congregations those Christians who had cooperated with imperial authorities to avoid persecution. Some North African Christians felt these lapsed members should be forgiven, but the Donatists (followers of the North African priest Donatus) insisted that the church should not be polluted with such "traitors." Most important, Donatists insisted, unfaithful priests and bishops could not administer the sacraments. So angry was the conflict that it even divided Christian families. As one son threatened his mother, "I will join Donatus's followers, and I will drink your blood."

These fiery emotions made it difficult for bishops to enforce orthodoxy as religious truth. The Council of Chalcedon (a town on the outskirts of Constantinople) in 451 was the most important attempt to forge an agreement. Its conclusions on orthodoxy form the basis of what many Christians believe today: Jesus's divine and human natures were mixed within his person but nevertheless remained distinct. Monophysites (a Greek term meaning "single-nature believers") refused to agree, however, arguing that Jesus had only a single, divine nature. They split from the orthodox hierarchy in the sixth century to found independent churches in Egypt (the Coptic church), Ethiopia, Syria, and Armenia.

Augustine had the greatest influence on the doctrines of the western church. Born in North Africa in 354, he fathered a son by a mistress before converting to Christianity under the influence of his mother and Ambrose (c. 339–397), the powerful bishop of Milan. He became bishop of Hippo, but his reputation rests on his writings. By around 500, Augustine and other influential theologians such as Ambrose and Jerome (c. 345–420) had earned the informal title "church fathers" because their views were quoted as authoritative in disputes over orthodoxy. Augustine became the most famous of this group of patristic (from *pater,* Greek for "father") authors.

In his book *City of God,* a "large and difficult work" according to Augustine himself, he rejected the idea that Christianity guaranteed earthly success to Christians. Most important, he said, Christians were not responsible for the barbarian Alaric's sacking of Rome in 410, a disaster that polytheists claimed was the gods' punishment for Romans' abandoning their traditional religion. In addition, Augustine redefined the ideal state as a society of Christians. Not even Plato's doctrines offered a true path to purity, he insisted, because the true struggle for individuals was not between their emotions and reason, but between their desire for earthly pleasures and spiritual purity. The only existence with true meaning was in God's city.

Nevertheless, Augustine wrote, earthly law and government were required because humans were by nature imperfect. Humans lost their original perfection by inheriting a permanently sinful nature after Adam and Eve had disobeyed God in the Garden of Eden. This doctrine of original sin—a subject of theological debate since at least the second century—meant that people suffered from a hereditary moral disease that turned the human will into a corrupting force. Although far inferior to the divine ideal, civil government was necessary to impose moral order on the chaos of human life after the fall from grace in the Garden of Eden. The government therefore had a right to force people to remain united to the church, by violence if necessary.

In *City of God,* Augustine insisted that God's will lay behind the events of history, even if people found his will impossible to understand in detail. He explained that Christians could know with certainty only that God guided history toward an ultimate goal:

> To be truthful, I myself fail to understand why God created mice and frogs, flies and worms. Nevertheless, I recognize that each of these creatures is beautiful in its own way. For when I think about the body and limbs of any

living creature, where do I not find proportion, number, and order showing the unity of concord? Where one discovers proportion, number, and order, one should look for the craftsman.

Next to the nature of Christ, the question of how to understand and control sexual desire presented Christians with the toughest problem in the search for religious truth. Augustine became the most influential source of the belief that sex automatically involved human beings in evil and that they should therefore become ascetics (from the Greek *askesis,* meaning "training"), denying themselves all pleasure. Augustine knew from personal experience how difficult it was to accept this doctrine. In fact, he revealed in his autobiographical work *Confessions* that it took him a long time to pledge to go without sex as part of his conversion to Christianity.

Augustine advocated no sex as the purest choice for Christians because he believed that Adam and Eve's disobedience had forever ruined the original harmony that God had created between human will and human passions. According to Augustine, God punished his disobedient children by making sexual desire a corrupting force that humans could never completely control through will. Although Augustine declared the value of marriage in God's plan, he added that sexual intercourse even between loving spouses carried the sad reminder of humanity's fall from grace. A married couple should "lie down with a certain sadness" to the task of starting a pregnancy, the only acceptable reason for sex. Sexual pleasure could never be a human good.

This doctrine made virginity and avoidance of sex high virtues. In the words of Jerome, they counted as "daily martyrdom." This self-chosen holiness proved especially valuable for women in boosting their status in Christian society. Their sexual abstinence earned them such respect that they could demand privileges usually reserved for men, such as more education in Hebrew and Greek to read the Bible. By the end of the fourth century, sexual purity had become so significant for Christian virtue that congregations began to expect celibate male priests and bishops.

The Beginning of Christian Monasticism

Christian **asceticism** (the denial of pleasure, especially in regard to sex and food) reached its peak in monasticism. The word *monk* (from the Greek *monos,* meaning "single" or "solitary") describes the basis of monasticism: men and women withdrawing from society to live a life of extreme self-denial imitating Jesus's suffering, demonstrating their devotion to God, and praying for divine mercy on the world. The earliest monks lived alone, but soon they formed communities for mutual support in the pursuit of ascetic holiness (Map 6.2, page 209).

Polytheist and Jewish ascetics, motivated by philosophy and religion, had existed before. What made Christian monasticism different were the huge numbers of people it attracted and the high status monks earned. Leaving their families and congregations, they gave up sex, worshipped frequently, wore the roughest clothes, and ate barely enough to survive, aiming to win an inner peace isolated from daily concerns. They reported, however, that they constantly struggled against fantasies of earthly delights, dreaming of plentiful, tasty food more often than of sex.

The earliest Christian ascetics appeared in the late third century in Egypt. Antony (c. 251–356), from a well-to-do family, was among the first. One day, he abruptly abandoned all his property after hearing a sermon based on Jesus's advice to a rich young man to sell his possessions and give the proceeds to the poor (Matt. 19:21). Rejecting his duty to help his sister find a husband, he placed her in a home for unmarried women and spent his life alone in a barren region, demonstrating his excellence by worshipping God.

Monasticism appealed to its followers for many reasons, but above all because it gave ordinary people a way to achieve excellence and recognition. This opportunity seemed all the more valuable after Constantine's conversion and the end of the

Monastery of St. Catherine at Mount Sinai
Jews and Christians regarded this monastery in the desert at the foot of Mount Sinai (on the peninsula between Egypt and Arabia) as holy because Moses had received the Ten Commandments there during the Hebrews' wanderings after their exodus from Egypt. The Byzantine emperor Justinian supported the monastery to promote orthodoxy in a region dominated by Monophysite Christians. The monks at St. Catherine's gained a reputation for exceptional religious devotion: they spent much of their time repeating a simple prayer to Jesus over and over. The monastery obtained its name in the ninth century from a story about angels bringing the body of Catherine of Alexandria there. Catherine was said to have been martyred in the fourth century for refusing to marry the emperor because, in her words, she was the bride of Christ. (Erich Lessing/Art Resource, NY.)

persecutions. Becoming a monk—a living martyrdom—served as the substitute for a martyr's death and imitated the sacrifice of Christ. Individual, or eremetic (hence *hermit*), monks went to great lengths to win fame. In Syria, for example, "holy women" and "holy men" attracted great attention by their feats of endurance. One man lived atop a tall pillar for thirty years in the fifth century, preaching to people gathered below his perch. Egyptian Christians believed that their monks' religious devotion made them living heroes ensuring the annual flooding of the Nile, the duty once linked to the pharaohs' divine power. Exceptionally famous ascetics had even greater influence after death. Their relics—body parts or clothing—became treasured sources of protection and healing. Relics gave believers faith in God's favor by expressing the power of saints (people receiving special honor after their deaths as a reward for their holiness).

In about 323, Pachomius in Upper Egypt organized the first monastic community. In this "coenobitic" (seen-uh-BIT-ick), or "life in common," monasticism, male or female monks formed single-gender settlements to encourage one another along the hard road to holiness. Coenobitic monasticism became the primary form of Christian asceticism. Monasteries were often built close together to divide their labor, with women making clothing, for example, while men farmed.

All monasteries imposed military-style discipline, but they differed in the harshness of their rules and the amount of contact with the outside world. The most isolationist groups arose in the eastern empire, but the followers of Martin of Tours, an ex-soldier of the fourth century famed for his religious deeds, founded communities in the west as harsh as any eastern ones. Basil ("the Great") of Caesarea in Asia Minor started a different tradition in the fourth century: monasteries serving society. He required monks to perform charitable deeds, leading to the foundation of the first hospitals.

A milder, but still strict, code telling monks how to live became the standard in the west from the sixth century on, influencing almost every area of Catholic worship. Called the Benedictine rule after its creator, Benedict (c. 480–553) from Nursia in central Italy, this code prescribed a daily routine of prayers, scriptural readings, and manual labor. The rule divided the day into seven parts, each with a compulsory service of prayers and lessons, collectively called the Divine Office. Unlike harsher codes, Benedict's did not isolate the monks from the outside world or deprive them of sleep, adequate food, or warm clothing. Although his code gave the abbot (the head monk) full authority, it instructed him to listen to what every monk had to say before he decided important matters. The abbot was not allowed to beat the monks severely as punishment for breaking the rules. Communities of women, such as those founded by Basil's sister Macrina and Benedict's sister Scholastica, usually followed the rules of the male monasteries, with an emphasis on the modesty thought necessary for women.

The thousands of Christians who became monks thereafter joined monasteries for social as well as theological reasons. Some had been given as babies to monasteries by parents who could not raise them or were fulfilling religious vows, a practice called oblation. Jerome once gave this advice to a mother about her daughter:

> Let her be brought up in a monastery, let her live among virgins, let her learn to avoid swearing, let her regard lying as a sin against God, let her be ignorant of the world, let her live the angelic life, while in the flesh let her be without the flesh, and let her suppose that all human beings are like herself.

When she reaches adulthood as a virgin, he added, she should avoid the baths so she would not be seen naked or give her body pleasure by dipping in the warm pools. Jerome expressed traditional Roman values favoring males when he promised that God would reward the mother with the birth of sons to compensate for her dedicating her daughter to God. But he also said, "[As monks] we evaluate people's virtue not by their gender but by their character, and judge those to be worthy of the greatest glory who have given up both status and riches."

The monasteries' independence threatened the power of the church's hierarchy. Bishops did not like devoted members of their congregations withdrawing into monasteries, especially because they made donations to their new communities rather than to their local churches. Moreover, monks challenged bishops' authority because holy men and women earned their special status not by having it awarded by the church's leaders but by earning it through their own actions. Bishops and monks did share a spiritual goal—salvation and service to God. While polytheists had enjoyed immediate access to their gods, who were thought to visit the earth constantly, Christians worshipped a God outside this world. Monks bridged the gap between the human and the divine by asking God to be merciful to faithful believers.

REVIEW What were the major disputes among early Christians, and why were they so fierce?

Non-Roman (Barbarian) Kingdoms and the Western Roman Empire

The migrations and attacks of non-Roman peoples ("barbarians," according to Romans) into the western Roman Empire transformed politics, society, and the economy there. Two strong motives drove these diverse groups into Roman territory: to flee the brutal attacks of the Huns (nomads from the steppes of Central Asia) and to benefit from the empire's prosperity. By the 370s, the immigrants' presence had generated great violence in western Europe. As the imperial government's ability to maintain order weakened, these immigrants experienced great changes themselves, transforming from vaguely organized tribes into kingdoms with separate ethnic identities. By the 470s, one of their commanders ruled Italy. That political change has been said to mark the "fall of the Roman Empire." In fact, the lasting effects of the interactions of these non-Roman peoples with the diverse peoples of western Europe and North Africa are better understood as a gradual transformation that made them the heirs of the western Roman Empire and led to the formation of medieval Europe.

Migrations into and Attacks on the Empire

At first, the fourth-century emperors encouraged the migrations of barbarians into the empire. Like the earlier emperors, they recruited these foreign warriors for the Roman army. By the late fourth century, crowds of women and children had followed their men into the empire. The emperors' failure to either absorb the newcomers or expel them led to the fall of the Roman Empire.

Economic weakness from the third-century crisis lessened the emperors' ability to react to the migrations. They had demanded higher taxes during the crisis, forcing landowners to demand higher payments from their tenant farmers (coloni). Many of these tenants responded by illegally running away. Eventually, landowners also had to run away if they could not pay their taxes. This flight left farms deserted: as much as 20 percent of agricultural land lay unfarmed in the most seriously affected areas. The government pressed the farmers who remained to pay even more, but this only made more of them abandon their farms. In the end, the emperors' financial problems meant they could not hire enough soldiers to stop non-Roman peoples from immigrating into the empire.

Non-Roman groups crossed into Roman territory not in carefully planned invasions, but often fleeing for their lives. Fourth-century raids by the Huns drove them from their homelands east of the Rhine and north of the Danube. Mostly small groups of men, women, and children crossed the Roman border as refugees. Their future looked grim because they came with no political or military unity, no clear plan, and not even a shared sense of identity.

Loosely organized in democratic groups and often warring with one another, these diverse bands or tribes originally shared only similar languages and their terror of the Huns. The migrating groups developed different ethnic identities because the Roman government refused to accept them into Roman society. The newcomers therefore created their own kingdoms inside the imperial frontiers. Their desire for security forced them to develop a more tightly structured society to govern their new lands and gave them new identities.

Previously, these peoples had no experience organizing kingdoms. In their homelands, they had lived in small settlements as farmers, herders, and ironworkers. Most bands operated as chiefdoms, whose members could only be persuaded, not forced, to follow the chief. Chiefs maintained their leadership by leading warriors on successful raids to seize cattle and slaves and then giving gifts to their followers. Family life was patriarchal: men headed households and exercised authority over women, children, and slaves. Women earned respect by bearing children, and rich men could have more than one wife and perhaps concubines as well. A clear division of labor made women responsible for agriculture, pottery making, and the production of textiles, while men worked iron and herded cattle. Fighting and raiding were so prized by the men that when a man died, his grave was packed with weapons. Women had some rights of inheritance and could control property; married women received a marriage gift of one-third of their husbands' property.

Households were grouped into clans based on kinship through mothers as well as fathers. The members of a clan were supposed to keep peace among themselves, and violence against another clan member was the worst possible crime. Clans in turn grouped themselves into tribes, multiethnic coalitions that anyone could join. Different tribes identified themselves by their clothing, hairstyles, jewelry, weapons, religious cults, and oral stories.

Assemblies of free male warriors provided the tribes' only political organization. Tribal leaders' functions were mostly religious and military. Tribes tended to be unstable groupings with frequent bloody feuds between clans. Tribal law tried to set limits on the violence permitted in seeking revenge, but laws were oral, not written, and thus open to wide dispute.

Migrations into Roman territory surged when the Huns invaded eastern Europe in the fourth century. Related to the Xiongnu people who had attacked China and Persia, these Turkish-speaking nomads arrived on the Russian plains by 370. They excelled as raiders, launching cavalry attacks far and wide. With elongated skulls (from having been bound between boards in infancy), faces grooved with decorative scars, and arms bristling with tattoos, they terrified their victims. Their skill as horsemen made the Huns legendary. They could shoot their powerful bows while riding at full speed, and they could remain on horseback for days, sleeping atop their horses and packing snacks of raw meat between their thighs and the animal's back.

The eastern emperors in Constantinople bribed the Huns not to attack their territory. The Huns then abandoned their nomadic lifestyle and became landlords, cooperating among themselves to create an empire north of the Danube that forced local farmers to support these new masters. The Huns' most ambitious leader, Attila (r. c. 440–453), extended their domain from the Caspian Sea to the Alps and even farther west. He led attacks into Roman territory as far as Paris and into northern Italy. At Attila's death, the Huns lost their unity and faded from history. By this time, however, the terror that they inspired in the people living in eastern Europe had already started the migrations that transformed the western empire.

The bands that created a new identity as Visigoths after entering imperial territory were the first to experience what became the common pattern of the migrations. Some desperate and poorly organized group would plead with the emperor for protection from the Huns, and the empire would accept them in return for military service. Shredded by constant raids from the Huns, in 376 the Visigoths begged the eastern emperor, Valens (r. 364–378), to let them migrate into the Balkans. They received permission on condition that their warriors enlist in the Roman army to help fight the Huns. When greedy and incompetent Roman officers sent to help the refugee Visigoths instead mistreated them, the immigrants starved; the officials forced them to sell some of their own people into slavery in return for dogs to eat. The hungry Visigoths rebelled. In 378, they attacked and killed Valens in battle at Adrianople in Thrace (Map 6.3). The next eastern emperor, Theodosius I (r. 379–395), had to renegotiate the deal from a position of weakness. His concessions to the Visigoths

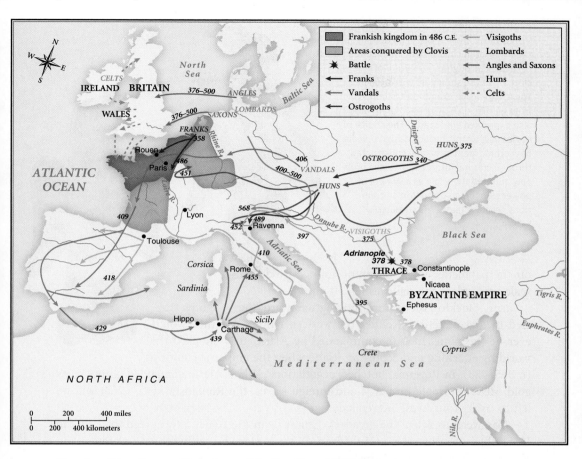

Map 6.3 Migrations and Invasions of the Fourth and Fifth Centuries
The movements of non-Roman peoples (barbarians) into imperial territory transformed the Roman Empire. These migrations began as early as the reign of Domitian (r. 81–96), but in the fourth century, they became a pressing problem for the emperors when the Huns' attacks pushed many multiethnic bands from their homelands in eastern Europe into the empire's northern provinces. Maps cannot really show dynamic processes such as migrations and invasions, and the arrows on this one do not mean that the newcomers came in an unbroken stream. The map does indicate, however, the variety of peoples involved, the wide extent of imperial territory they affected, and the concentration of their effects in the western section of the empire.

established the terms that other bands would seek for themselves and that would create new, self-conscious identities for them: permission to settle permanently inside the imperial borders, freedom to establish a kingdom under their own laws, the title of "federates of the empire" (allies expected to help protect Roman territory), and large annual payments from the emperors.

The eastern emperors soon realized, however, that they could not afford to keep such agreements. They therefore forced the migrating bands westward by cutting

Eagle Brooches (*Fibulae*) from Visigothic Spain
Visigothic women in their kingdom in Spain showed their new ethnic identity by their style of dress, in particular through the tradition of fastening their clothing at the shoulders with brooches. These expensive examples, fashioned from gold inlaid with semiprecious stones, also expressed elite status. The choice of eagles as a Gothic brooch design reveals how ethnic identity can be constructed through cultural interaction: Goths probably adopted the eagle as a symbol of power from Hunnic and Roman traditions. (Photo © The Walters Art Museum, Baltimore.)

off the payments and threatening full-scale war unless the refugees left. With no army blocking them from moving westward, the Visigoths traveled in that direction. Neither the western empire nor they would ever be the same. In 410, commanded by Alaric, they shocked the world by attacking and capturing Rome when the emperor Honorius (r. 395–423), in Ravenna, botched negotiations. When Alaric demanded all the city's gold, silver, movable property, and foreign slaves, the Romans asked, "What will be left to us?" "Your lives," he replied.

Too weak to defeat the invaders, Honorius in 418 reluctantly agreed to settle the Visigoths in southwestern Gaul (France), saving face by calling them federates. The Visigoths then completed their transition from tribal society to new kingdom by doing what no non-Roman group had done before: establishing an ethnic identity and organizing a state. They followed the model of Roman emperors by building mutually beneficial relations with local elites, including Romans. Elite Romans used time-tested ways of flattering their superiors to gain advantages. Sidonius Apollinaris, for example, a noble from Lyon, once purposely lost a backgammon game to the Visigothic king as a way of gaining a favor from the ruler. Honorius tried, without much success, to limit what he saw as barbarian influence on Roman citizens by ordering them not to adopt Visigothic clothing styles.

Historians still debate how the new non-Roman kingdoms financed their governments. The older view is that the newcomers became landowners by forcing Romans to turn over some of their land, slaves, and movable property to them. Recent scholarship argues that Roman taxpayers in the kingdoms did not have to give up land but were instead made directly responsible for paying the expenses of the non-Roman soldiers, who lived mostly in city garrisons. Whatever the arrangements were, the Visigoths found them so profitable that they later expanded into Spain.

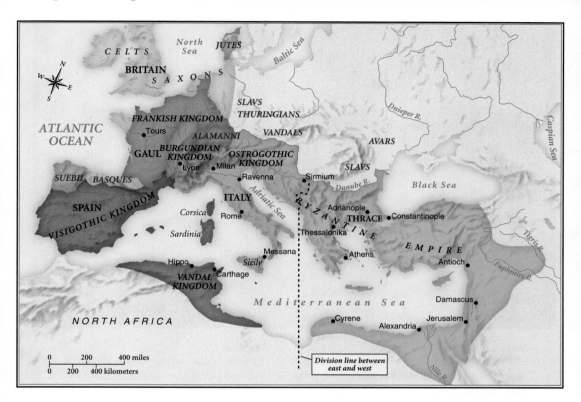

Map 6.4 Peoples and Kingdoms of the Roman World, c. 526
The provinces of the Roman Empire had always been home to a population diverse in language and ethnicity. By the early sixth century, the territory of the western empire had fragmented into diverse political units as well. Italy and most of the former western provinces were kingdoms created and ruled by non-Roman peoples who had moved into former Roman territory over the past several centuries. The eastern empire (the Byzantine Empire) remained under the political control of the emperor in Constantinople. Justinian, who became Byzantine emperor in 527, made it his mission to try to reunite the eastern and western halves of the empire by force. How much do these states correspond to the modern boundaries of states in Europe? **For more help analyzing this map, see the map activity for this chapter in the Online Study Guide at** bedfordstmartins.com/huntconcise.

    The western emperor's deal with the Visigoths motivated other groups to enter Roman territory to create kingdoms and identities (Map 6.4). The process was often violent. In 406, the Vandals, fleeing the Huns, fought their way all through Gaul to the Spanish coast. (The modern word *vandal,* meaning "destroyer of property," preserves their reputation for destruction.) In 429, eighty thousand Vandals crossed to North Africa, where they broke their agreement to become federates and captured the region with fierce attacks. Their new kingdom caused tremendous hardship for local Africans by confiscating property rather than allowing owners to make regular payments to the occupiers. The Vandals further weakened the western emperors by seizing North Africa's tax payments of grain and vegetable oil and disrupting the

Mosaic of Women Exercising
This picture covered a floor in a fourth-century country villa in Sicily that had more than forty rooms decorated with colorful mosaics. The women shown here were perhaps dancers getting in shape for performances, or gymnasts in a show. Members of the Roman elite built such large and expensive houses to try to protect their families from the troubles of the later Roman Empire. Often this strategy failed. Vandal invaders seriously damaged this villa. (Erich Lessing/Art Resource, NY.)

importation of grain to Rome. They also built a navy strong enough to threaten the eastern empire. In 455, the Vandals attacked and plundered Rome, proving the western imperial government was powerless.

Other small groups also managed to break off distant pieces of the weakened western empire. The most significant small band for later history was the Anglo-Saxons. Composed of Angles from what is now Denmark and Saxons from north-western Germany, this group invaded Britain in the 440s after the Roman army had been recalled from the province to defend Italy against the Visigoths. The Anglo-Saxons established their kingdoms by taking territory away from the local Celtic peoples and the remaining Roman inhabitants. Gradually, Anglo-Saxon culture replaced the local traditions of the island's eastern regions; the Celts there lost most of their language, and Christianity survived only in Wales and Ireland.

The Fall of the Roman Empire

The western empire's military weakness led to a change in leadership in 476 that has traditionally, but simplistically, been called the fall of the Roman Empire. In that year a non-Roman commander replaced the Roman emperor in the west, and no Roman would rule there ever again. The idea of a "fall" comes from the best-selling work that made it famous—*The Decline and Fall of the Roman Empire* by the English historian Edward Gibbon (1737–1794). The real story's details, however, reveal the complexity of the political transformation of the western empire under the pressure of non-Roman immigration. The weakness of the imperial army in the west had forced the western emperors to employ non-Roman officers to lead the defense of Italy. By the middle of the fifth century, one general after another decided who would serve as puppet emperor under his control. The last such unfortunate "emperor" was a boy. His father, a former aide to Attila, had rebelled against the emperor and raised his young son to the throne. He gave the child emperor the name Romulus Augustulus, meant to recall both Rome's founder and its first emperor. In 476, after a dispute over pay, soldiers murdered the father and deposed the boy. Pitied as an innocent child, Romulus was given a safe home and a generous pension. The rebels' leader, Odoacer, did not choose another western emperor. Instead, he had the Senate in Rome ask the eastern emperor to recognize his leadership in return for his recognizing the eastern emperor as sole emperor. Odoacer thereafter led Italy supposedly as the eastern emperor's assistant. In truth, he ruled independently.

Theodoric (r. 493–526), a non-Roman general from the eastern empire, overthrew Odoacer and established the Ostrogothic kingdom, which ruled Italy from the capital at Ravenna. He built legitimacy for his new state by preserving traditional Roman institutions, especially the Senate and the office of consul. Theodoric and his Ostrogothic nobles wanted to enjoy the empire's luxury and prestige, not destroy them. For this reason, modern scholars consider it more accurate to speak of the western empire's "transformation" than its "fall" (Map 6.4, page 221), even though the process was often violent.

An Arian Christian, Theodoric followed Constantine's example by announcing a policy of religious toleration: "No one can be forced to believe against his will." Many members of the Roman elite, such as the famous scholars Boethius and Cassiodorus, cooperated with Theodoric to try to establish stable government. Unfortunately, the Ostrogothic emperor executed Boethius, whom he had made a consul but later accused of disloyalty. While in prison, Boethius wrote the *Consolation of Philosophy,* a book that explained divine providence according to the ideas of Stoic and Neoplatonic philosophy, as well as those of Augustine. Boethius's scholarship became vastly influential in medieval Europe.

The Franks were a Germanic people who transformed Roman Gaul into Francia (from which the name *France* comes). They first moved into that region with the permission of the western emperor in the early fourth century. In 507, their king, Clovis (r. 485–511), overthrew the Visigothic king in southern Gaul with support from the eastern emperor. When the emperor named him an honorary Roman consul, Clovis celebrated this ancient honor by having himself crowned with a diadem in the style of the dominate's emperors. He carved out western Europe's largest new kingdom in what is today mostly France. This kingdom grew larger than the neighboring rival kingdoms of the Burgundians and Alamanni in eastern Gaul. Probably persuaded by his Christian wife, Clotilda, to believe that God had helped him defeat the Alamanni, Clovis proclaimed himself an orthodox Christian. To build stability, he forged good relations with Gaul's bishops, who helped him control the people in their regions.

Clovis's dynasty, called Merovingian after the legendary Frankish ancestor Merovech, lasted for another two hundred years, far longer than most other non-Roman royal families in the west. The Merovingian state anticipated the kingdom that emerged later as the forerunner of modern France. The Merovingians survived so long because their new state combined barbarian military might with Roman social and legal traditions.

The Transformation of the Western Empire

The political transformation of the western Roman Empire—the replacement of imperial government by non-Roman kingdoms—created a social transformation as well. Immigrants and Romans combined their traditions to establish new ways of living, above all law codes. Unfortunately, they failed to build a strong economy.

These transformations were meant to continue the empire's glory. The Visigoth king Athaulf (r. 410–415), having married a Roman noblewoman, explained his goals in this way:

> At the start I wanted to erase the Romans' name and turn their land into a Gothic empire, myself doing what Augustus had done. But I have learned that the Goths' freewheeling wildness will never accept the rule of law, and that a state with no law is no state. Thus, I have more wisely chosen another path to glory: reviving the Roman name with Gothic strength. I pray that future generations will remember me as the founder of a Roman restoration.

Roman law greatly influenced the new kings in their efforts to organize new states. The barbarians had never before had written laws. Now that they had transformed themselves into kings ruling Romans as well as their own people, they wanted legal codes to establish justice and order. The Visigothic kings were the first non-Roman leaders to create a written law code. Composed in Latin and dependent on Roman legal tradition, it made the payment of fines and compensation the primary method for resolving disputes.

Clovis also relied on written law in his Merovingian kingdom. His code, published in Latin, supported social order by setting clear penalties for specific crimes. In particular, he established a system of payments intended to defuse feuds between individuals and between clans. This system of penalties included **wergild**, the payment a murderer had to make as compensation for his crime. Most of the money was paid to the victim's kin, but the king received one-third of the amount.

Because law codes correspond to social values, the differing payments offer a glimpse of the relative social value of different categories of people in Clovis's kingdom. The penalty for murdering a woman of childbearing age, a boy under twelve, or a man in the king's service was a massive fine of six hundred gold coins, enough to buy six hundred cattle. The fine for murdering a woman past childbearing age (specified as sixty years), a young girl, or a freeborn man was two hundred gold coins; for murdering ordinary slaves, thirty-five.

The migrations and attacks that transformed the west harmed its already weak economy. The Vandals damaged many towns in Gaul. In the countryside, now outside the control of any central government, wealthy Romans from the social elite built villas on large estates staffed by tenants bound to the land like slaves. The owners of these estates operated them as self-sufficient units by producing all they needed, defending themselves against raids, and refusing to cooperate with imperial officials. The owners shunned membership on city councils and tax collection—the public services that had supplied the lifeblood of Roman administration—although the wealthiest boasted an annual income rivaling that of an entire region in the old western empire. The elite's withdrawal from public service withered Roman provincial government, and the new kingdoms never replaced the traditional services to the population.

A few provincial Romans helped transmit ancient learning to later ages. Cassiodorus, one of the scholars who had worked for Theodoric, founded a monastery on his ancestral estate in Italy in the 550s following his career in imperial administration. He gave the monks the task of copying manuscripts to preserve their contents as old texts disintegrated. His own book *Institutions,* composed to guide his monks, explained the respect for tradition that kept classical traditions alive: in prescribing the works a person of superior education should read, it included ancient secular texts as well as Scripture and Christian literature.

> **REVIEW**   What transformations took place in the Roman Empire from around 370 to the 550s?

The Byzantine (Eastern Roman) Empire

The eastern Roman Empire avoided the transformations that reshaped western Europe. Trade routes and diverse agriculture kept the east richer than the west, and the eastern emperors minimized the effect of the foreign migrations on their territory and blunted the aggression of the Sasanid kingdom in Persia with force, diplomacy, and bribery. By the early sixth century, the empire's eastern half had achieved such power, riches, and ambition that modern historians renamed it the Byzantine Empire; its emperors held power until 1453.

The Byzantine emperors saw themselves as continuing the Roman Empire and guarding its traditions against barbarians. Justinian (r. 527–565), the most famous of the early Byzantine emperors, took this mission so seriously that he bankrupted his treasury with wars to recover the western empire. He tried to impose religious orthodoxy to win God's support for his dream of reunifying the empire. One especially significant contribution of the early Byzantine Empire to later history was preserving classical literature and learning, which nearly disappeared in the west.

Byzantine Society

The Byzantine Empire enjoyed a prosperity that western Europe had lost. Members of the elite imported silk, precious stones, and expensive spices such as pepper from China and India. People of all kinds flocked to the empire's largest cities—Constantinople (the former Byzantium), Damascus, and Alexandria. There, churches with soaring domes testified to the Byzantines' confidence in God's power and favor.

The Byzantine emperors sponsored costly religious festivals and entertainments to rally public support. Rich and poor alike crowded city squares, theaters, and racetracks to enjoy the spectacles. Chariot racing aroused the hottest passions. Constantinople's residents divided themselves into competitive factions, called Blues and Greens after the racing colors of their favorite charioteers, which combined religious and sports rivalries: orthodox Christians became Blues, Monophysites Greens. They clashed as frequently over theological arguments as over race results.

The eastern emperors did everything they could to preserve traditional "Romanness." They feared their empire would become "barbarian," as in the west. They employed foreign mercenaries, but they tried to keep immigrant customs from influencing the empire's residents. They paid special attention to clothing. Eastern emperors banned Constantinople's residents from wearing barbarian-style outfits (especially heavy boots and clothing made from animal fur) instead of traditional Roman clothes (sandals or light shoes and robes). The Byzantines referred to themselves as "Romans" because they saw themselves as the heirs and protectors of Roman traditions. At the same time, they spoke Greek as their native language and used Latin only for government and military communication. (The Latin-speaking western empire referred to them as "Greeks.") Since Byzantine society was deeply multilingual and multiethnic, preserving an unchanging Roman identity was an impossible goal. Travelers around the empire heard countless languages, saw varying styles of dress, and encountered numerous ethnic groups.

For the Byzantines, Romanness included Christianity, but their theological diversity matched their ethnic variety. Bitter controversies over beliefs divided eastern Christians, and emperors joined forces with bishops to impose orthodoxy. They generally opted for words over swords to pressure heretics to accept orthodox theology, but they used violence when persuasion failed. Resorting to such extreme measures against fellow Christians was necessary, they believed, to save lost souls and preserve God's goodwill toward the empire.

In patriarchal Byzantine society, most women followed ancient Mediterranean tradition by focusing their lives on their households and minimizing contact with men outside that circle. Law barred women from many public functions, such as witnessing wills. Subject to the authority of their fathers and husbands, women veiled their heads (though not their faces) to show modesty. Christian theology made divorce more difficult than under Roman law and discouraged remarriage, even for widows. Stiffer legal penalties for sexual offenses also developed. Female prostitution remained legal, but emperors raised the penalties for people forcing girls or slave women to become prostitutes.

As always, women in the imperial family lived by different rules than ordinary women and could directly influence government. Theodora (c. 500–548), wife of the emperor Justinian, became the most influential and talked about of all Byzantine empresses. Using her brains and beauty to overcome her low social status (she was the daughter of a bear trainer and then an actress accused of performing porno-graphic scenes), she married Justinian and advised him in every part of his rule. She helped him make personnel choices for his administration, strongly pushed her religious views in the continuing disputes over Christian doctrine, and rallied her husband's courage in times of crisis. A high-ranking administrator judged her "superior in intelligence to any man."

Byzantine government made the social hierarchy more rigid than ever because it provided services according to people's wealth. It required piles of paperwork and fees for official transactions, from commercial permits to legal complaints. With-out bribery, nothing got done. This arrangement benefited people with status and money: they used their social connections to get a hearing from the right official and used their wealth to pay bribes to get fast action.

The poor could not afford the bribes that government officials expected. Since interest rates were high, they had to take on backbreaking debt to raise the cash to pay officials to help them. This system saved the emperors money: they paid civil servants small salaries because bribes from the public supplemented their incomes. One official, for example, reported that he earned thirty times his annual salary in bribes during his first year in office. To keep unlimited extortion from destroying the system, the emperors published an official list of the maximum bribes that employees could demand. Overall, however, this kind of government generated enormous hostility among poorer subjects.

The Reign of Emperor Justinian, 527–565

Justinian dreamed of reuniting the empire as it had been under Augustus. Born in a small Balkan town, he rose rapidly in imperial service until 527, when he succeeded his uncle as emperor. During his reign, he launched military expeditions to win back western Europe and North Africa from the non-Roman kingdoms. His desire to build imperial glory led him to decorate Constantinople with magnificent and costly buildings. He was also an intellectual with a passion for law and theology. He pushed reforms meant to preserve social order based on hierarchy and maintain divine favor. Justinian's autocratic rule provoked both admiration and fear. The contemporary historian Procopius famously displayed this conflicted response to Justinian. Some of his works praised Justinian's bold initiatives in war and architecture, but Procopius's *Secret History* presented scandalous stories about the alleged cruelty and sexual im-morality of Justinian and his wife, Theodora.

The huge expense of Justinian's plans led to social unrest. His taxes became so heavy and their collection so violent that they provoked a major riot in 532. Known as the Nika Riot, it erupted when the Blue and Green factions united against the em-peror, shouting *"Nika! Nika!"* (Win! Win!). After nine days of violence that left much

Justinian and His Court in Ravenna
This mosaic centered on the Byzantine emperor Justinian (r. 527–565) is opposite Theodora's mosaic in San Vitale Church in Ravenna. Justinian and Theodora had finished building the church, which the Ostrogothic king Theodoric had started, to celebrate their successful campaign to restore Italy to the Roman Empire and retake control of the western capital, Ravenna. The soldiers at left remind viewers of the rulers' aggressive military policy in service of imperial unity. The presence of Maximianus, bishop of Ravenna, standing on Justinian's left and identified by name above his head stresses the theme of cooperation between bishops and emperors in ruling the world. (Scala/Art Resource, NY.)

of the capital in ashes, a panicky Justinian prepared to abandon his throne and flee. Theodora, however, showed the steel in her soul by telling him, "Once born, no one can escape dying, but for one who has held imperial power it would be unbearable to be a fugitive. May I never take off my imperial robes of purple, nor live to see the day when those who meet me will not greet me as their ruler." Shamed, Justinian called out his guard, who crushed the rebellion by slaughtering thirty thousand rioters.

In service to Justinian's plan to reunite the eastern and western empires, his generals defeated the Vandals and Ostrogoths after campaigns that lasted decades. At enormous expense, Justinian's armies reoccupied Italy, the Dalmatian coast, Sicily, Sardinia, Corsica, part of southern Spain, and western North Africa by 562. These successes temporarily restored the old empire's geography: Justinian's territory stretched from the Atlantic to the western edge of Mesopotamia (see "Mapping the West," page 233).

Theodora and Her Court in Ravenna
This mosaic was placed on one wall of the church of San Vitale in Ravenna, facing the matching scene of Theodora's husband, Justinian, and his attendants. Theodora (c. 500–548) wears the jewels, pearls, and rich robes characteristic of Byzantine rulers. She extends in her hands a gem-encrusted bowl, evidently a present to the church. Her gesture imitates the gift giving of the Magi to the baby Jesus, the scene illustrated on the hem of her garment. Like Honorius on page 196, a circle around her head indicates special holiness. (Scala/Art Resource, NY.)

These triumphs carried a tragic price: inflicting horrible damage on Europe and emptying Justinian's treasury. Italy endured the greatest damage, but the east suffered as Justinian demanded still more taxes to finance the western wars and bribe the Sasanids in Mesopotamia not to attack. The tax burden crippled the economy, leading to constant banditry in the countryside. Crowds poured into the capital from rural areas, seeking relief from poverty and robbers.

Natural disasters added to Justinian's troubles. In the 540s, an epidemic killed a third of the empire's inhabitants. A quarter of a million died in Constantinople alone, half the capital's population. This was only the first in a long series of diseases that erased millions of people in the eastern empire over the next two centuries. The loss of so many people created a shortage of army recruits, forced the emperors to hire expensive mercenaries, and left many farms vacant, thus hurting tax revenues.

The pressures on Justinian led him to strengthen his authority by emphasizing his closeness to God and his authority over the people. He had his artists portray the symbols of rule in a Christian context. A gleaming mosaic in his church at San Vitale in Ravenna, for example, displayed a dramatic vision of the emperor's role: Justinian standing at the center of the universe shoulder to shoulder with both the ancient Hebrew leader Abraham and Christ. In legal matters, Justinian proclaimed the emperor the "living law," reviving a Hellenistic royal doctrine.

Justinian's building program in Constantinople expressed his religious devotion and worldly power. Most spectacular of all was his magnificent reconstruction of Constantine's Church of the Holy Wisdom (Hagia Sophia). Its location facing the palace emphasized Justinian's combination of imperial and Christian authority. Creating a new design for churches, his architects erected a huge building on a square plan capped by a dome 107 feet across and soaring 184 feet above the floor. Its interior walls glowed like the sun from the light reflecting off their four acres of gold mosaics. Imported marble of every color added to the sparkling effect. When Justinian first entered his masterpiece, he remarked, "Solomon, I have outdone you," boasting that he had bested the glorious temple the ancient king had built for the Hebrews.

The Soaring Architecture of the Hagia Sophia
Golden mosaics originally reflected a dazzling light from the interior of the Hagia Sophia, the enormous Church of the Holy Wisdom, which the Byzantine emperor Justinian built in the 530s near his palace in Constantinople. A central dome, 184 feet high and supported by four arches resting on massive piers, capped the church's vast interior; the ring of windows at the base of the dome is just visible at the top of the picture. The Hagia Sophia became a mosque after the Turks captured the city in 1453; the large medallions contain religious quotations in Arabic. Now a museum, it continues to host people offering prayers. (© Adam Woolfitt/Corbis.)

Justinian's building up of the emperor's power made Constantinople still more important and reduced the local independence of the empire's other cities. Their councils ceased to govern; imperial officials took over instead. Provincial elites still had to ensure full payment of their areas' taxes, but they lost the compensating reward of deciding local matters. Now the imperial government made all decisions and determined people's social status. Men of property from the provinces who wanted a public career knew they could satisfy their ambitions only by joining the imperial administration.

To strengthen his authority, Justinian had the empire's laws codified to bring uniformity to the inconsistent decisions of earlier emperors. This collection of past decisions, intended to make legal cases go faster and provide class materials for law schools, influenced legal scholars for centuries. Justinian's experts also wrote a textbook for students that proclaimed the principles of a just life: "Live honorably, harm no one else, and give to each his own." This book remained on law school reading lists until modern times.

To win God's goodwill, Justinian enacted reforms to guarantee religious orthodoxy. Harshly enforcing laws against polytheists, he ordered them to be baptized or else lose their lands and official positions. He punished Christians whom he could not convince to accept his version of orthodoxy. In pursuit of sexual purity, his laws made sex between men illegal for the first time in Roman history. Homosexual marriage, apparently not uncommon earlier, had been officially prohibited in the fourth century, but penalties had never before been imposed on men engaging in homosexual activity. Previous emperors had simply taxed male prostitutes. The legal status of homosexual activity between women is unclear; it probably counted as criminal adultery for married women.

Justinian tried to unite orthodox and Monophysite Christians by revising the creed of the Council of Chalcedon, but church leaders in Rome and Constantinople had become too bitterly divided to agree on a unified church. The church's eastern and western divisions were by now launched on the diverging courses that would climax in a formal schism five hundred years later. Perhaps no emperor could have done better, but Justinian's drive for religious orthodoxy only drove Christians farther apart and worked against his dream of a reunited Roman world.

Preserving Classical Literature

The empire's Christianization endangered classical literature because many Christians thought its books were the work of the devil and because, as Christians became authors in great numbers, their works displaced the ancient texts of Greece and Rome as the most important literature of the age. Fortunately for later times, the Byzantine Empire helped preserve a significant fraction of the famous works of the past.

Classical texts survived because educated Christians kept reading ancient Greek and Roman literature. Byzantine scholars valued classical literature because they regarded it as the basis of a high-level education. Many of the classical works available today survived because they served as school texts in the eastern empire. A basic knowledge of famous pre-Christian classics was a requirement for a good career in government service, the goal of most ambitious students. In the words of an imperial decree from the fourth century, "No person shall obtain a post of the first rank unless it shall be shown that he excels in long practice of liberal studies, and that he is so polished in literary matters that words flow from his pen faultlessly."

The use of ancient rhetoric to present Christian theology also helped classical literature survive. When Ambrose, bishop of Milan in the fourth century, composed the first systematic description of Christian ethics for young priests, he imitated the great classical orator Cicero. Theologians employed the dialogue form pioneered by Plato to refute Christian heresies, and polytheist traditions in writing biography influenced the hugely popular Christian literature of saints' lives. Similarly, Christian artists used polytheist traditions to communicate their beliefs in paintings, mosaics, and carved reliefs. Artists showing Christ with a sunburst surrounding his head, for example, took their inspiration from polytheist depictions of the radiant sun as a god (see the illustration on page 206).

A technological innovation also helped preserve classical texts. Previously, scribes had written books on sheets made from thin animal skin or paper made from papyrus, gluing the sheets together and attaching rods at both ends to form scrolls. Readers had to unroll the scrolls to read them. For ease of use, Christians produced their literature in the form of codices, books with bound pages; codices (the plural of *codex*) became the standard form of book production in the Byzantine world. Because codices were less subject to damage from rolling and unrolling and could contain text more efficiently than scrolls, which were inefficient for long works, they aided the preservation of all forms of literature.

Despite the continuing importance of classical Greek and Latin literature in Byzantine education and rhetoric, its survival remained uncertain in a war-torn world governed by Christians. Knowledge of Greek in the transformed west faded so dramatically that almost no one could read the original versions of Homer's *Iliad* and *Odyssey,* the traditional foundations of a polytheist literary education. Latin fared better, and scholars such as Augustine and Jerome knew Rome's ancient literature extremely well. But they also saw its classics as too seductive because the pleasure of reading them could distract Christians from worshipping God. Jerome once had a nightmare of being condemned on Judgment Day for having been a Ciceronian instead of a Christian.

The closing around 530 of Plato's Academy, founded in Athens more than nine hundred years earlier, demonstrated the dangers for classical learning in the Byzantine world. This most famous of classical schools finally shut its doors when many of its scholars moved to Persia to escape restrictions on polytheists and its revenues dwindled because the Athenian elite, its traditional supporters, were increasingly Christianized. The Neoplatonist school at Alexandria, by contrast, continued. Its leader in the late sixth century, John Philoponus, was a Christian. In addition to Christian theology, Philoponus wrote commentaries on Aristotle's works. Some of his ideas anticipated those of Galileo a thousand years later. His work achieved the kind of blending of old and new that was one fruitful possibility of the transformation of the late Roman world—that is, he was a Christian subject of the Byzantine Empire in Egypt, heading a school founded long before by polytheists, studying the works of an ancient Greek philosopher as the inspiration for his innovative scholarship.

The tradition that the present should learn from the past would continue as Western civilization once again remade itself in medieval times.

REVIEW   What role did the emperor Justinian see himself playing in Roman history?

Conclusion

The Roman Empire splintered for reasons that no emperor was strong enough to overcome, once the finances of the state became too small to cover the expenses of defense against barbarian migrations and attacks. The vast size of the empire,

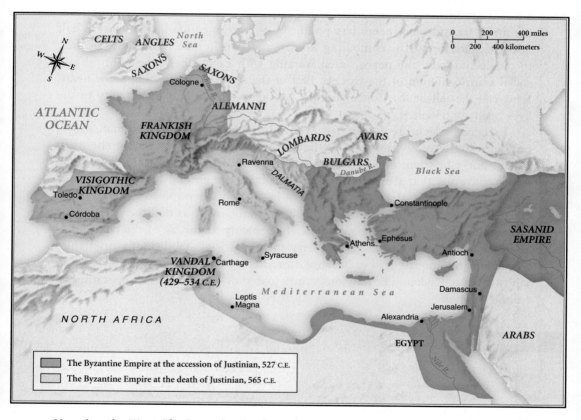

Mapping the West The Byzantine Empire and Western Europe, c. 600
Justinian employed brilliant generals and spent huge sums of money to reconquer Italy, North Africa, and part of Spain to reunite the western and eastern halves of the old Roman Empire. His wars to regain Italy and North Africa eliminated the Ostrogothic and Vandal kingdoms, respectively, but at a huge cost in effort, time (the war in Italy took twenty years), and expense. The resources of the eastern empire were so exhausted that following emperors could not maintain the reunification. By the early seventh century, the Visigoths had taken back all of Spain. Africa, despite serious revolts by local Berber tribes, remained under imperial control until the Arab conquest of the seventh century, but within five years of Justinian's death, the Lombards set up a new kingdom that controlled a large section of Italy. Never again would anyone attempt to reestablish a universal Roman Empire. Compare the political divisions on this map with those on the map at the end of Chapter 5 (page 192) showing Roman territory more than three centuries earlier.

a source of pride to Romans, was a double-edged sword because the length and distance of its frontiers made national defense expensive and difficult, and the traditional Roman desire for glory meant that pulling back voluntarily was not an option. Peoples outside the empire increasingly wanted to immigrate to live inside its territory, so as to share in its relative peace and prosperity.

In building their empire originally, Romans had made it stronger by absorbing outsiders and turning them into productive citizens. The emperors of the late Roman Empire failed to find a way to continue this policy, and the immigrants whom they mistreated or blocked eventually overwhelmed the western empire, so strong was the outsiders' motivation to flee danger in their homelands and find a better life in Roman lands. The barbarians who migrated into the empire from the north transformed themselves politically and changed life in the western half of the empire forever by combining Roman and non-Roman traditions, but they, too, failed to keep the peace, often warring with each other. The political and social transformation of the western half of the Roman Empire that some historians call the fall of the Roman Empire brought violence and uncertainty to the lives of many people.

Religion, which previously had been a force for unity in the Roman world, became a source of division and conflict in the later Roman Empire, both between pagans and Christians and between Christians and Christians. In the past, some scholars argued that Christian beliefs weakened the empire by lessening people's devotion to the state and its defense in favor of devotion to God. In truth, Christian emperors and armies fought just as ferociously as had the polytheistic military of earlier centuries. Moreover, the growing hierarchy of the church cooperated with the political rulers to try to keep social stability. If Christianity weakened the empire, it was because Christians disagreed so sincerely and so violently about what was religious truth that they had trouble cooperating in troubled times.

TIMELINE

- **325** Council of Nicaea
- **324** Constantine refounds Byzantium as Constantinople, the "new Rome"
- **c. 323** Pachomius in Upper Egypt establishes the first monasteries for men and women

- **440s** Anglo-Saxons take over Roman Britain
- **429** Vandals capture Roman North Africa after invading Spain
- **410** Visigoths sack Rome

- **c. 530** Plato's Academy in Athens closes
- **507** Clovis establishes Frankish kingdom in Gaul

 280 C.E.   365 C.E.   450 C.E.   535 C.E.

- **284** Diocletian becomes Roman emperor
- **303** Diocletian begins Great Persecution of Christians
- **312** Constantine wins the battle of the Milvian Bridge in Rome and converts to Christianity

- **391** Theodosius bans polytheist sacrifice and closes the temples of traditional Roman religion
- **395** Roman Empire splits into western and eastern sections

- **451** Council of Chalcedon
- **476** "Fall of the Roman Empire" when the barbarian commander Odoacer deposes the final western emperor, Romulus Augustulus

Whatever the effect of the growth of Christianity on the Roman Empire might have been, its effect on later history is clear and huge. The conversion of Emperor Constantine to Christianity changed the course of the world, a change whose effects dominated the history of the Roman Empire from his time to that of Emperor Justinian, who spared no expense to try to fulfill the eastern empire's self-identified role as the heir to Rome's glory and the guardian of Rome's traditions. But not even Justinian's uncontrolled spending of the Byzantine Empire's money could hold the ancient Roman Empire together. A new European world was on the way, and its birth would be bloody.

CHAPTER REVIEW QUESTIONS

1. What similarities existed between traditional Roman religion and Christianity as the official state religion?

2. Compare the fates of the eastern and western empires after they split apart.

For practice quizzes and other study tools, see the Online Study Guide at bedfordstmartins.com/huntconcise.

For primary-source material from this period, see Chapter 7 of *Sources of THE MAKING OF THE WEST*, Third Edition.

Suggested References

Recent research has deepened our appreciation of the complexity of the religious transformation of the Roman Empire and the emotional depths that the process stirred up for polytheists and Christians.

Brown, Peter. *The Body and Society: Men, Women, and Sexual Renunciation in Early Christianity.* 1988.

Byzantine Empire: http://www.fordham.edu/halsall/byzantium/

*Drew, Katherine Fischer, ed. *The Laws of the Salian Franks.* 1991.

Elsner, Jas. *Imperial Rome and Christian Triumph: The Art of the Roman Empire, A.D. 100–450.* 1998.

*Grubbs, Judith Evans. *Women and Law in the Roman Empire: A Sourcebook on Marriage, Divorce, and Widowhood.* 2002.

Halsall, Guy. *Barbarian Migrations and the Roman West.* 2007.

Heather, Peter. *The Fall of the Roman Empire.* 2005.

*Lee, A. D. *Pagans and Christians in Late Antiquity: A Sourcebook.* 2000.

Little, Lester K., ed. *Plague and the End of Antiquity: The Pandemic of 541–750.* 2006.

MacMullen, Ramsay. *Christianity and Paganism in the Fourth to Eighth Centuries.* 1997.

Odahl, Charles. *Constantine and the Christian Empire.* 2d ed. 2006.

Southern, Pat, and Karen R. Dixon. *The Late Roman Army.* 1996.

7

Islam, Byzantium, and the West

I N THE EIGHTH CENTURY, a Syrian monk named Joshua wrote about the first appearance of Islam in Roman territory: "The Arabs conquered the land of Palestine and the land as far as the great river Euphrates. The Romans fled," he marveled, then continued:

> The first king was a man among them named Muhammad, whom they also called Prophet because he turned them away from cults of all kinds and taught them that there was only one God, creator of the universe. He also instituted laws for them because they were much entangled in the worship of demons.

Dome of the Rock at Jerusalem
Rivaling the great churches of Christendom, the building in Jerusalem called the Dome of the Rock, built in 691, borrowed from late Roman and Byzantine forms even while asserting its Islamic identity. The columns and the capitals atop them, the round arches, the dome, and the mosaics are all from Byzantine models. But the strips of Arabic writing on the dome itself—and in many other parts of the building—assert Islamic doctrine.
(Erich Lessing/Art Resource, NY.)

Joshua was wrong about Muhammad leading the conquest of Palestine—Muhammad died in 632, six years before the fall of Palestine. But he was right to see the Arab movement as a momentous development. In the course of a few decades the Arabs conquered much of the Persian and Roman empires. Joshua was also right to emphasize Muhammad's teachings. It was the fervor of Islam that brought the Arabs out of Arabia and into the regions that hugged the Mediterranean in one direction and led to the Indus River in the other.

In the sixth century, as the western and eastern parts of the Roman Empire went their separate ways, a third power—Arab and Muslim—was taking shape. These three powers have continued in various forms to the present day. The western Roman Empire became today's western Europe. The eastern Roman Empire became Turkey, Greece, and some of eastern Europe, and it played a key role in shaping Russia. The Arab world endures in North Africa and the Middle East.

These diverse cultures share many of the same roots. All were heirs of Hellenistic and Roman traditions. All adhered to monotheism. The western and eastern halves of the Roman Empire had Christianity in common, although they differed at times in interpreting it. Adherents of Islam, the Arab world's religion, believed in the same God as the Jews and Christians. They understood Jesus, however, as God's prophet rather than his son.

The history of the seventh and eighth centuries is a story of adaptation and transformation. Historians consider the changes in this period so remarkable that they speak of the end of one era—antiquity—and the beginning of another—the Middle Ages. They also find the changes in the eastern half of the Roman Empire so important that they use a new term—Byzantium or the Byzantine Empire, from the old Greek name for the city of Constantinople—to describe it.

During the period 600–750, the Islamic, Byzantine, and Western worlds combined elements of their ancient heritage with new values, interests, and conditions. The divergences among them resulted from disparities in geography and climate, material and human resources, skills, beliefs, and local traditions. But these differences should not obscure their fundamental similarities.

CHAPTER FOCUS QUESTION What three cultures took the place of the Roman Empire, and to what extent did each of them both draw on and reject Roman traditions?

Islam: A New Religion and a New Empire

Islam, which means "submission to God" in Arabic, called for all believers to submit to the will of one God. It demanded a revolutionary change from the many warring tribes that populated the Arabian peninsula: unification into one community.

The first to teach Islam was Muhammad, a merchant turned holy man from the Arabian city of Mecca, a major oasis near the Red Sea. Many gods were worshipped in Arabia, but Muhammad recognized only one God, that of the Jews and Christians. He saw himself as God's last prophet, receiving and in turn repeating God's final words to humans. Invited by the city of Medina to come and mediate disputes, Muhammad exercised the powers of both a religious and a secular leader there. This dual role became the model for his successors, known as caliphs. Through a combination of persuasion and force, Muhammad and his coreligionists, the Muslims, converted most of the Arabian peninsula. By the time he died in 632, Islamic conquest and conversion had begun to move northward into Byzantine and Persian territories. In the next generation, the Muslims took over most of Persia and all of Egypt and were on their way across North Africa to Spain. Yet within the regions they conquered with such lightning speed, daily life went on much as before.

The Rise and Development of Islam, c. 610–632

In the seventh century, the Arabian peninsula was populated by both sedentary and nomadic peoples. By far the larger group was sedentary—people who lived in one place. Some were farmers; others lived in oases, where they raised dates (a highly prized food). Some oases were prosperous enough to support merchants and artisans.

The smaller group, the nomads (known as Bedouins), moved from place to place in the desert. They herded goats, sheep, or camels, and they survived largely from the products (leather, milk, and meat) of their animals. Warriors, the Bedouins raided one another for goods and women, valuing their honor highly and prizing bravery and generosity as well. Lacking written literature, they were proud of their oral culture of storytelling and poetry.

Islam began as a religion of the sedentary peoples, but it soon found support and military strength among the nomads. It began in Mecca, a major oasis and commercial center. More important, Mecca was also a religious center, home to a shrine called the Ka'ba, which contained the images of many gods. At the Ka'ba, war and violence among the various tribes that worshipped there were prohibited. The tribe that dominated Mecca, the Quraysh, controlled access to the shrine. The Quraysh taxed the pilgrims who flocked there and sold them food and drink. Visitors, assured of their security, bartered on the sacred grounds, transforming goods seized in raids into commodities of trade.

Mecca was the birthplace of Muhammad (c. 570–632). His early years were unpromising: orphaned at the age of six, he spent two years with his grandfather and then came under the care of his uncle, a leader of the Quraysh tribe. Eventually, Muhammad became a trader. At the age of twenty-five, he married Khadija, a rich widow who had once employed him. They had at least four daughters and lived (to all appearances) happily and comfortably. Yet Muhammad sometimes left home to spend time in a nearby cave in prayer and contemplation, practicing a type of piety similar to that of early Christians.

Arabia in Muhammad's Lifetime

In about 610, on one such retreat, Muhammad heard a voice calling him to worship Allah, the God of the Jews and Christians. (*Allah* means "the God" in Arabic.) He accepted the call as coming from God. Over the next years he received messages that he understood to be divine revelation. Later, when they had been written down and arranged—a process that was completed in the seventh century, after Muhammad's death—these messages became the Qur'an, the holy book of Islam. The Qur'an, which means "recitation," is understood to be God's revelation as told to Muhammad by the angel Gabriel, then recited by Muhammad to others. It starts with the Fatihah, which is frequently also said as an independent prayer beginning as follows:

> In the name of God
> The Compassionate the Caring
> Praise be to God.

Qur'an
More than a "holy book," the Qur'an represents the very words of God. Usually the text appeared on pages wider than they were long, perhaps to differentiate the Qur'an from other books. This particular example dates from the seventh or eighth century. It is written in Kufic script, a formal and majestic form of Arabic that scribes used for the Qur'an until the eleventh century. The round floral decoration on the right-hand page marks a new section of the text. (Copyright Biblioteca Ambrosiana.)

It continues with sections, or suras, of gradually decreasing length. These cover all of human experience and the life to come. For Muslims (literally, "those who submit to Islam") the Qur'an contains the foundations of history, prophecy, and the legal and moral code by which men and women should live.

The Qur'an emphasizes the nuclear family—a man, his wife, and their children—as the basic unit of Muslim society. Islam replaced the identity and protection of the tribe with a new identity: the **ummah**, the community of believers who share both a belief in one God and a set of religious practices.

Stressing individual belief in God and adherence to the Qur'an, Islam has no priests or sacraments, although in time it came to have authoritative religious leaders who interpreted the Qur'an and related texts. The Ka'ba, with its many gods, had attracted numerous tribes from the surrounding area. Muhammad, with his one God, forged an even more universal religion.

The first to convert to Muhammad's faith were his wife, Khadija, and a few friends and members of his immediate family. Muhammad's insistence that the cults of other gods be abandoned in favor of one God brought him into conflict with leading members of the Quraysh, however, whose control over the Ka'ba had given them wealth and prestige. They insulted Muhammad and harassed his adherents.

Disillusioned with the people of Mecca, Muhammad looked elsewhere for groups that would be more receptive to his message. In particular, he expected support from Jews, whose monotheism, in Muhammad's view, prepared them for his own faith. When a few of Muhammad's converts from Medina promised to protect him if he joined them there, he eagerly accepted the invitation, in part because

Medina had a significant Jewish population. In 622, Muhammad immigrated to Medina, an oasis about two hundred miles north of Mecca. This journey, known as the Hijra, proved to be a crucial event for the new movement. At Medina, Muhammad found people ready to listen to his religious message and to regard him as the leader of their community. They expected him to act as a neutral and impartial judge in their interclan disputes. Muhammad's political position in the community set the pattern by which Islamic society would be governed thereafter: rather than simply adding a church to political and cultural life, Muslims made their political and religious institutions inseparable. After Muhammad's death, the year of the Hijra was named the first year of the Islamic calendar; it marks the beginning of the new Islamic era.*

Although successful in Medina, the Muslims felt threatened by the Quraysh in Mecca, who actively opposed the public practice of Islam. For this reason, Muhammad led raids against them. At the battle of Badr in 624, Muhammad and his followers killed forty-nine of the Meccan enemy, took numerous prisoners, and confiscated rich booty. In this way, traditional Bedouin plundering was grafted onto the Muslim duty of jihad.**

The battle of Badr was a great triumph for Muhammad, who was now able to consolidate his position at Medina, gaining new adherents and silencing doubters. The Jews at Medina had not converted to Islam as Muhammad had expected, however. Suspecting them of supporting his enemies, he expelled two Jewish tribes from Medina and executed the male members of another. Although Muslims had originally prayed in the direction of Jerusalem, the center of Jewish worship, Muhammad now had them turn in the direction of Mecca.

At the same time, Muhammad instituted new practices to define Islam as a unique religion. Among these were the *zakat,* a tax on possessions to be used for alms; the fast of Ramadan, which takes place during the ninth month of the Islamic year, the month in which the battle of Badr was fought; the *hajj,* an annual pilgrimage to Mecca that each Muslim is to try to accomplish at least once in his or her lifetime; and the *salat,* formal worship at least three times a day (later increased to five), which might include the *shahadah,* or profession of faith: "There is no god but God, and Muhammad is his Messenger." Detailed regulations for these practices, sometimes called the five pillars of Islam, were worked out in the eighth and early ninth centuries.

Meanwhile, the fierce rivalry between Mecca's tribes and Medina's Muslims began to spill over into the rest of the Arabian peninsula as both sides strove to win converts. Muhammad sent troops to subdue Arabs north and south. In 630, he

---

*Thus 1 A.H. (1 *anno Hegirae,* "year of the Hijra") on the Muslim calendar is equivalent to 622 C.E. on the Christian calendar.

**Jihad* means "striving" and is used in particular in the context of striving against unbelievers. In that sense, it is often translated as "holy war." But it can also mean striving against one's own worst impulses.

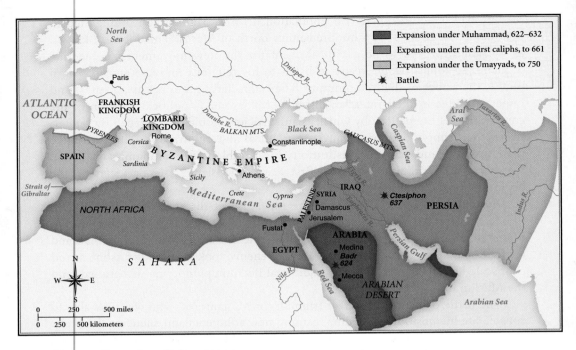

Map 7.1 Expansion of Islam, to 750

In little more than a century, Islamic armies conquered a vast region that included numerous different peoples, cultures, climates, and living conditions. Under the Umayyads, these disparate territories were administered by one ruler from his capital at Damascus. The uniting force was the religion of Islam itself, which gathered all believers into one community, the *ummah*.

entered Mecca with ten thousand men and took over the city, assuring the Quraysh of leniency and offering alliances with tribal leaders. By this time, the prestige of Islam was enough to convince tribes elsewhere to convert. Through a combination of force, conversion, and negotiation, Muhammad was able to unite many, though by no means all, Arabic-speaking tribes under his leadership by the time of his death two years later (Map 7.1).

Muhammad transformed Arab society. As Muhammad's converts "submitted" to Islam, they formed not a tribe but rather a community bound together by the worship of God. Women were accepted into this community, and their status was enhanced. Islam prohibited infanticide, the practice of killing unwanted babies, which had long been used largely against female infants. Men were allowed to have up to four wives at one time, but they were obliged to treat them equally. Wives received dowries and had certain inheritance rights. At first, Muslim women joined men during the salat. Beginning in the eighth century, however, women began to pray apart from men. Like Judaism and Christianity, Islam retained the practices of the patriarchal society in which it arose; women's participation in community life was limited.

Even though Islamic society was a new sort of community, in many ways it functioned as a tribe, or rather a "supertribe," obligated to fight common enemies, share plunder, and resolve peacefully any internal disputes. Muslims participated in group rituals, such as the salat and public recitations. The Qur'an was soon publicly sung by professional reciters, much as the old tribal poetry had been. Most significant for the eventual spread of Islam, Muslim men were warriors, and their armies reaped profits at the point of the sword. But this warfare differed from intertribal fighting; it was the "striving" (jihad) of people who were carrying out the injunction of God against unbelievers. "Strive, O Prophet," says the Qur'an, "against the unbelievers and the hypocrites, and deal with them firmly. Their final abode is Hell: And what a wretched destination!"

Muhammad's Successors, 632–750

Following his death, Muhammad's successors, the caliphs, conquered much of the Roman and Persian worlds. To the west, the Muslims attacked Byzantine territory in Syria with ease and moved into Egypt in the 640s (Map 7.1, page 242). To the east, they invaded the **Sasanid Empire**, defeating the Persians at the gates of their capital, Ctesiphon, in 637. All of Persia was in Muslim hands by 661. During the last half of the seventh century and the beginning of the eighth, Islamic rule extended from Spain to India. How were such conquests possible, especially in so short a time? First, Islamic forces came up against weakened empires. The Byzantine and Sasanid states were exhausted from fighting each other. The cities of the Middle East that had been taken by the Persians and retaken by the Byzantines were depopulated, their few survivors burdened with heavy taxes. Second, the Muslims were welcomed into both Byzantine and Sasanid territories by discontented groups. Many Monophysite Christians in Syria and Egypt, for example, had suffered persecution by the Byzantines and were glad to have new, Islamic overlords.

These were the external reasons for Islamic success. There were also internal reasons. Arabs had long been used to intertribal warfare; now, under the banner of jihad, Muslims exercised their skills as warriors not against one another but rather against unbelievers. Fully armed, on horseback, and employing camels in convoys, they seemed almost a force of nature. Where they conquered, the Muslims built garrison cities, from which soldiers requisitioned taxes and goods. Sometimes whole Arab tribes, including women and children, were imported to settle conquered territory, as happened in parts of Syria. In other regions, a small Muslim settlement, such as the one at Fustat in Egypt, sufficed to gather the spoils of conquest.

These successes hid tensions that developed within the Muslim leadership. Muhammad's death in 632 marked a crisis in the government of the new Islamic state, as different groups sought to promote their own successors. The first caliphs came not from the traditional tribal elite but from a new inner circle of men close to Muhammad and participants in the Hijra. The first two caliphs ruled without serious opposition, but the third, Uthman (r. 644–656), a member of the Umayyad

Arab Coin

The Arabs learned coinage and minting from the Persians and Byzantines whom they conquered. Although one branch of Islam barred depicting the human form, others were less condemning. Thus the Umayyads saw nothing wrong with imitating traditional coinage. The ruler depicted on this silver coin is wearing a headdress that echoes the one worn by the Sasanid ruler depicted on page 248. But the name of this type of coin, *dirham*, was not Persian but Greek, from *drachma*. The Umayyad fiscal system retained the old Roman land tax and was administered by Syrians, who had served Byzantine rulers in the same capacity. (© Copyright, The Trustees of the British Museum.)

family and one of Muhammad's sons-in-law, aroused discontent among other clan members of the inner circle. They supported Uthman's rival, Ali, the husband of Muhammad's daughter Fatimah. When discontented soldiers murdered Uthman, civil war broke out between the Umayyads and Ali's faction. It ended in 661 when Ali was killed by one of his former supporters. The caliphate remained in Umayyad hands from 661 to 750.

Nevertheless, the *Shi'at Ali* (the faction of Ali) did not fade away. Ali's memory lived on among Shi'ite Muslims, who saw in him a symbol of justice and righteousness. For them, Ali's death was the martyrdom of the only true successor to Muhammad. They remained faithful to his dynasty, shunning the caliphs of the other Muslims (Sunni Muslims, as they were later called, from *Sunna,* the practices of Muhammad). The Shi'ites awaited the arrival of the true leader, the imam, who in their view could come only from the house of Ali. The Sunni-Shi'ite split remains a religious and political fact today.

Under the **Umayyad caliphate**, the Muslim world became a state, with its capital at Damascus. Borrowing from the institutions of the civilizations they had conquered, the Muslims issued coins and hired former Byzantine and Persian officials. They made Arabic a tool of centralization, imposing it as the official language on regions not previously united linguistically. Even so, the Islamic world was startlingly multiethnic. It included Arabs, Syrians, Egyptians, Iraqis, and other peoples. It was also multireligious, since Muslims tolerated other "people of the book" (meaning the Bible)—Jews and Christians of every sort. For many of these non-Muslims, the Muslim conquests brought a period of new settlement, urbanism, and literary and artistic flowering.

Peace and Prosperity in Islamic Lands

Ironically, the Islamic warriors brought peace. While the conquerors stayed within their fortified cities or built magnificent hunting lodges in the deserts of Syria, the conquered went back to work, to study, to play, and—in the case of Christians and

Jews, who were considered "protected subjects"—to worship as they pleased in return for the payment of a special tax. At Damascus, local artists and craftspeople worked on the lavish decorations for a mosque using Roman motifs. At Jerusalem, the shrine called the Dome of the Rock used Christian building models for its octagonal form and its interior arches (see the illustration on page 236).

During the seventh and eighth centuries, Muslim scholars wrote down the hitherto largely oral Arabic literature. They determined the definitive form for the Qur'an and compiled pious narratives about Muhammad, called hadith literature. Scribes wrote these works in exquisite calligraphy, handwriting that was also an art form. A literate class, composed mainly of the old Persian and Syrian elite who had now converted to Islam, created new forms of prose writing in Arabic. Employed as civil servants, they composed official documents for their new rulers. They also wrote essays on topics ranging from hunting to ruling. Umayyad poetry explored new worlds of thought and feeling. Patronized by the caliphs, who found in written poetry an important source of propaganda and a buttress for their power, the poets also reached a wider audience that delighted in their clever use of words, their satire, and their invocations of courage, piety, and sometimes erotic love:

> I spent the night as her bed-companion, each enamored of the other,
> And I made her laugh and cry, and stripped her of her clothes.
> I played with her and she vanquished me;
> I made her happy and I angered her.
> That was a night we spent, in my sleep, playing and joyful,
> But the caller to prayer woke me up.

Such poetry scandalized conservative Muslims, brought up on the sober tenets of the Qur'an. But this love poetry was a by-product of the new urban civilization of the Umayyad period, where wealth, cultural mix, and the confidence born of conquest inspired diverse and experimental literary forms. By the time the Umayyad caliphate ended in 750, Islamic civilization was multiethnic, urban, and sophisticated, a true heir of Roman and Persian traditions.

REVIEW How and why did the Muslims conquer so many lands in the relatively short period from 632 to 750?

Byzantium: A Christian Empire under Siege

While Islam was incorporating bits of Rome into its new empire, the Byzantines imagined that they were the continuators of Rome. Emperor Justinian (r. 527–565; (see page 227) had tried to re-create the old Roman Empire by conquest. On the surface he had succeeded. His empire once again included Italy, North Africa, and the Balkans. Vestiges of old Roman society persisted: an educated elite maintained its prestige, town governments continued to function, and old myths and legends were retold in poetry and depicted on silver plates and chests. By 600, however, the eastern empire had begun to undergo a transformation as striking as the one that had earlier remade the western empire. Historians call this reorganized empire the Byzantine Empire, or Byzantium.

From the last third of the sixth century, Byzantium was almost constantly at war, and its territory shrank drastically. Cultural and political change came as well. Cities—except for a few such as Constantinople—decayed, and the countryside became the focus of government and military administration. Following these shifts, the old elite largely disappeared, and classical learning gave way to new forms of education, mainly religious in content. The traditional styles of urban life, dependent on public gathering places and community spirit, faded away.

Wars on the Frontiers, c. 570–750

From about 570 to 750, the Byzantine Empire waged war against invaders on all fronts. Its first major challenge came from the east, from the Sasanid Empire of Persia. Its second came from new groups—Lombards, Slavs, Avars, Bulgars, and Muslims—who pushed into the empire. In the wake of these onslaughts, Byzantium was transformed.

The Persian challenge was the most predictable. Since the third century, the Sasanid kings and Roman emperors had fought sporadically but never with decisive effect on either side. In the middle of the sixth century, however, the Sasanids chose to concentrate their activities on the western half of their empire, Mesopotamia (today Iraq), nearer the Byzantine border (Map 7.2). Reforming the army, which previously had depended on nobles who could provide their own weapons, the Sasanid kings began to pay and arm new warriors drawn from the lower nobility. With the army more fully their own, the kings tried to re-create the Persian Empire of Darius and Xerxes (see page 48). Under Chosroes II (r. 591–628), the Persians invaded the Byzantine Empire in 603. By 613, they had taken Damascus; by 619, they dominated Egypt. In response, the Byzantine emperor Heraclius (r. 610–641) reorganized his army and by 627 had regained the lost territory. The chief outcome of these confrontations was the exhaustion of both sides.

The Byzantines could ill afford this weakness. From every side, new groups were pushing into their empire. The Lombards, a Germanic people, arrived in northern Italy in 568 and by 572 were masters of the Po valley and some inland regions in Italy's south, leaving the Byzantines only Bari, Calabria, and Sicily, as well as Rome and a narrow swath of land through Italy's middle called the Exarchate of Ravenna.

The Byzantines were equally weak in the face of the Slavs, Bulgars, and Avars just beyond the Danube River. The Slavs conducted lightning raids on the Balkan countryside (part of Byzantium at the time). Joined by the Avars—nomadic pastoralists and warriors—they attacked Byzantine cities as well. The Bulgars, entering what is now Bulgaria in the 670s, defeated the Byzantine army and in 681 forced the emperor to recognize the state they had carved out of formerly Byzantine territory. This Bulgar state crippled Byzantine influence in the Balkans and helped

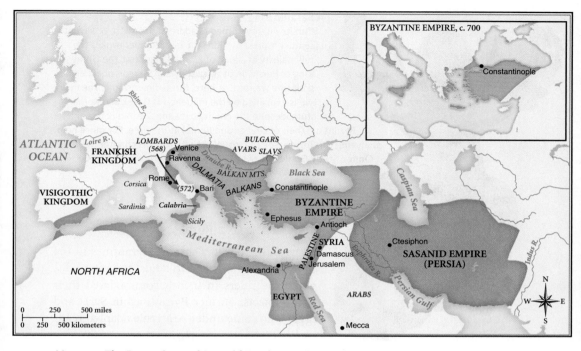

Map 7.2 The Byzantine and Sasanid Empires, c. 600
Justinian hoped to re-create the old Roman Empire, but just a century after his death, Italy was largely conquered by the Lombards. Meanwhile, the Byzantine Empire had to contend with the Sasanid Empire to its east. In 600, these two major powers faced each other uneasily. Three years later, the Sasanid king invaded Byzantine territory. The resulting wars, which lasted until 627, exhausted both empires and left them open to invasion by the Arabs. By 700, the Byzantine Empire was quite small. Compare the inset map here with Map 7.1 (page 242). Where had the Muslims made significant conquests of Byzantine territory?

isolate Byzantium from western Europe. Avar and Slavic control of the Balkans effectively cut off trade and travel between Constantinople and the cities of the Dalmatian coast, and the Bulgar state threw a political barrier across the Danube River. Perhaps as a result of this physical separation, Byzantine historians ceased to be interested in the West, and eastern scholars no longer bothered to learn Latin. The two halves of the Roman Empire, once united, communicated very little in the seventh century.

While fighting these groups on their northern frontier, the Byzantines at the same time had to contend with the Arabs, whose military prowess was creating a new empire and spreading the new religion of Islam. In the hundred years between 630 and 730, Muslim armies succeeded in conquering much of the Byzantine Empire, at times attacking the walls of Constantinople itself. No wonder the patriarch of Jerusalem, chief bishop of the entire Levant, saw in the Arab onslaught the impending end of the world. "Behold," he said, "the Abomination of Desolation, spoken of by the Prophet Daniel, that stands in the Holy Place."

A Sasanid King

With its mighty horned headdress, this sixth- or seventh-century representation of a Sasanid ruler evokes the full majesty of a king of kings. A glance at The Great King of Persia on page 27 shows that traditional Persian sculpture was not, as here, three-dimensional. The new style is explained by the influence of Greek and Roman sculpture, despite the enmity between Sasanid Persia and Byzantium (heir of Greece and Rome) at the time. **For more help analyzing this image, see the visual activity for this chapter in the Online Study Guide at** bedfordstmartins.com/huntconcise**.** (Réunion des Musées Nationaux/Art Resource, NY.)

From an Urban to a Rural Way of Life

As Byzantine borders shrank, Byzantines in the conquered regions had to adjust to new rulers, while the rulers in turn accommodated their new subjects. Former Byzantines in Syria and Egypt who came under Arab rule adapted readily to their conquerors, paying them a special tax but practicing their Christian and Jewish religions in peace. In the cities, they continued practicing their professions in government, scholarship, and business; in the countryside, they stayed on their land and continued to farm. The Balkans experienced greater changes when Slavs and Bulgars came to dominate the peninsula: most cities disappeared, and local populations fled as the newcomers installed themselves on the land. Soon, however, the newcomers recognized the Byzantine emperor's authority, and they began to flirt with Christianity.

Some of the most radical transformations in seventh- and eighth-century Byzantine life occurred not in the conquered territories but in the shrunken empire itself. Under the ceaseless barrage of invaders, many towns, formerly bustling centers of trade and the imperial bureaucracy, vanished or became unrecognizable. The public activities of marketplaces, theaters, and town squares gave way to the private pursuits of table and hearth. Public baths, where people had once gossiped, made deals, and talked politics and philosophy, disappeared in most Byzantine towns—with the significant exception of Constantinople. Warfare reduced some cities to rubble, and when they were rebuilt, the limited resources available went to construct thick defensive walls and solid churches instead of large open marketplaces and baths. Markets moved to overcrowded streets that looked much like the open-air bazaars of the modern Middle East. People under siege sought

The Byzantine Empire, c. 700

protection at home or in churches and avoided public activities. In the Byzantine city of Ephesus, for example, citizens who built the new walls in the seventh century enclosed not the old public edifices but rather their homes and churches (Map 7.3).

Despite the general urban decay, Constantinople and a few other urban centers retained some of their old vitality. The manufacture and trade of fine silk textiles continued. Even though Byzantium's economic life became increasingly rural and barter based in the seventh and eighth centuries, the skills, knowledge, and institutions of urban workers remained. Centuries of devastating wars, however, prevented full use of these resources until after 750.

The social world of this shrunken Byzantium was small and local. Unlike Europe, where a rich and powerful elite dominated the agricultural economy, the Byzantine Empire of the seventh century was principally a realm of free and semi-free peasant farmers. They grew food, herded cattle, and tended vineyards on small plots of land. Farmers interacted mostly with members of their families or with monks at local monasteries; two or three neighbors were enough to ratify a land transfer. As Byzantine cities declined, the class of town councilors (curials), the elite who for centuries had mediated between the emperor and the people, disappeared. Now, on those occasions when farmers came into contact with the state—to

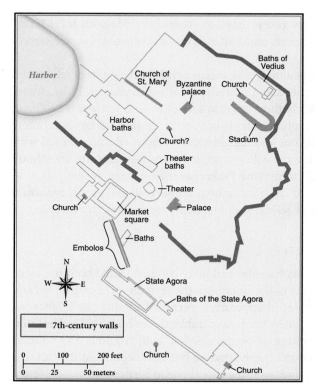

Map 7.3 Diagram of the City of Ephesus
Before the seventh century, Ephesus sprawled around its harbor. Nearest the harbor were baths and churches, including by 500 the bishop's church of St. Mary. To the south was the Embolos—a long, marble-paved avenue adorned with fountains, statues, and arcades and bordered by well-appointed homes. The earthquakes, plague, and invasions of the seventh century changed much. A seventh-century wall embraced the area around the harbor. The Embolos was neglected, and even within the narrow precinct protected by the new wall, baths were allowed to go to ruin, while people made their homes amid the debris. After the Arabs invaded, the bishop moved out of the city altogether.

pay taxes, for example—they felt the impact of the emperor or his representatives directly. There were no local protectors any longer.

Emperors, drawing on the still vigorous Roman legal tradition, promoted local, domestic life with imperial legislation. New laws strengthened the nuclear family by narrowing the grounds for divorce and setting new punishments for marital infidelity. Husbands and wives who committed adultery were whipped and fined, and their noses were slit. Abortion was prohibited, and new protections were set in place against incest with children. Mothers were given equal power with fathers over their offspring; if widowed, they became the legal guardians of their minor children and controlled the household property.

The shift from an urban-centered society to a rural way of life not only changed Byzantine social life and the economy but also affected the empire's military and cultural institutions. The Byzantine navy fought successfully at sea with its powerful weapon of "Greek fire," a mixture of crude oil and resin that was heated and projected via a tube over the water, where it burned and engulfed enemy ships. Determined to win wars on land as well, the imperial government tightened its control over the military by wresting power from other elite families and encouraging the formation of a middle class of farmer-soldiers.

In the seventh century, an emperor, possibly Heraclius, divided the empire into military districts called *themes* and put all civil as well as military matters in each district into the hands of one general. Landless men were lured to join the army with the promise of land and low taxes; they fought side by side with local farmers, who provided their own weapons and horses. The new organization effectively countered frontier attacks.

The disappearance of the old cultural elite meant a shift in the focus of education. Whereas the upper classes had cultivated the study of the pagan classics, hiring tutors or sending their children (primarily their sons) to school to read the works of Greek poets and philosophers, eighth-century parents of every class showed far more interest in giving their children, both sons and daughters, a religious education. Even with the decay of urban centers, cities and villages often retained an elementary school. There teachers used the Book of Psalms (the Psalter) as their primer. Secular, classical learning remained decidedly out of favor throughout the seventh and eighth centuries. Dogmatic writings, biographies of saints, and devotional works took center stage.

Religion, Politics, and Iconoclasm

The importance placed on religious learning and piety complemented both the autocratic imperial ideal and the powers of the bishops in the seventh century. Bishops and their clergy formed a rich and powerful upper class, even in declining cities. Since the spiritual and secular realms were considered inseparable, the bishops wielded political power in their cities, while Byzantine emperors ruled as both religious and political figures. In theory, empire and church were separate but interdependent. In fact, the emperor exercised considerable power over the church: he influenced the appointment of the chief religious official, the patriarch of Constantinople; he called church councils to determine dogma; and he regularly used bishops as local governors.

Bishops functioned as state administrators in their cities. They served as judges and tax collectors. They distributed food in times of famine or siege, provisioned troops, and set up military fortifications. As part of their charitable work, they cared for the sick and the needy. Theoretically, monasteries were under their control. In fact, however, monasteries were enormously powerful institutions that often defied the authority of bishops and even emperors. Because monks commanded immense prestige as the holiest of God's faithful, they could influence the many issues of church doctrine that shook the Byzantine church. Icons, which the monks supported, became the flash point of these controversies.

Icons are images of holy people—Christ, his mother (Mary), and the saints. To Byzantine Christians, icons were far more than mere representations; they were believed to possess holy power that directly affected people's daily lives as well as their chances for salvation. Many seventh-century Byzantines made icons the focus of their religious devotion. To them, the images were like the incarnation of divinity. Icons turned spirit into material substance by manifesting in physical form the holy person they depicted. Many Byzantines, especially monks, considered icons a necessary part of Christian piety.

Other Byzantines, however, detested icons. This was especially true of soldiers on the frontiers.

Icon of St. Peter
In this icon, produced by a Byzantine artist in the first half of the seventh century, the head and shoulders of St. Peter are nearly life-size. Seeing this image is like encountering the saint himself. In his right hand Peter holds the keys of the Kingdom of Heaven; with his left hand, he supports a staff topped by a cross. Above Peter are three medallions: Christ is in the center, flanked by the Virgin Mary and St. John. The golden halos unite the figures both artistically and religiously. (The Art Archive/Kharbine-Tapabor/Boistesselin.)

Shocked by Arab triumphs, they became convinced that the cause of their misfortunes was the biblical injunction against graven (carved) images. When they compared their defeats to Muslim successes, they could not help but notice that Islam prohibited all visual representations of the divine. To these soldiers and others who shared their view, icons revived pagan idolatry and dishonored Christian divinity. As iconoclastic (anti-icon, or, literally, "icon-breaking") feeling grew, some churchmen became outspoken in their opposition to icons.

Byzantine emperors shared these religious objections, and they also had important political reasons for opposing icons. In fact, the issue of icons became a test of their authority. Icons represented intermediaries between worshippers and God; they undermined the emperor's exclusive place in the divine and temporal order. In addition, the emphasis on icons in monastic communities made monks potential threats to imperial power. The emperors hoped to use this issue to break the power of the monasteries. Above all, though, the emperors opposed icons because the army did, and they needed the support of their troops.

After Emperor Leo III ("the Isaurian"; r. 717–741) defeated the Arabs besieging Constantinople in 718, he turned his attention to consolidating his political position. In 726, officers of the imperial court tore down the great golden icon of Christ at the gateway of the palace and replaced it with a cross. This event marked the beginning of the period of **iconoclasm**. Soon afterward, Leo ordered all icons destroyed, a ban that remained in effect, despite much opposition, until 787. A modified ban would be revived in 815 and last until 843. Thereafter, icons again became an important part of Byzantine Christianity.

Iconoclasm had an enormous impact on daily life. At home, where people had their own portable icons, it forced changes in private worship: the devout had to destroy their icons or venerate them in secret. The ban on icons led to ferocious attacks on monasteries: splendid collections of holy images were destroyed; vast properties were confiscated; and monks, who were staunch defenders of icons, were ordered to leave their monasteries, give up their vocations, and marry. In this way iconoclasm destroyed communities that might otherwise have served as centers of resistance to imperial power. Reorganized and reoriented, Byzantium was ready to confront the Arabs with vigor.

REVIEW | What stresses did the Byzantine Empire endure in the seventh and eighth centuries, and how was iconoclasm a response to those stresses?

Western Europe: A Medley of Kingdoms

In contrast to Byzantium, where an emperor still ruled as the successor to Augustus and Constantine, drawing on an unbroken chain of Roman legal and administrative traditions, political power in the West was more diffuse. With the end of Roman imperial government in the western half of the empire, the region was divided into a number of kingdoms: Spain, Italy, England, and Gaul. The primary foundations of power and stability in all of these kingdoms were kinship networks, church patronage, royal courts, and wealth derived from land and plunder. Kings were important, to be sure; but in some places churchmen and rich magnates were even more powerful than royalty. As a focus of religious piety, icons were less important than the power of the saints as exercised through their relics—their bodies and body parts, even clothes and dust from their tombs. These relics represented and wielded the divine forces of God. Although the patterns of daily life and the procedures of government in western Europe remained recognizably Roman, they were also in the process of change, borrowing from and adapting to local traditions.

Frankish Kingdoms with Roman Roots

The most important kingdoms in post-Roman Europe were Frankish. During the sixth century, the Franks had established themselves as dominant in Gaul, and by the seventh century the limits of their kingdoms roughly approximated the eastern borders of present-day France, Belgium, Switzerland, and Luxembourg (Map 7.4). Moreover, their kings, the Merovingians (c. 485–751), had conquered many of the

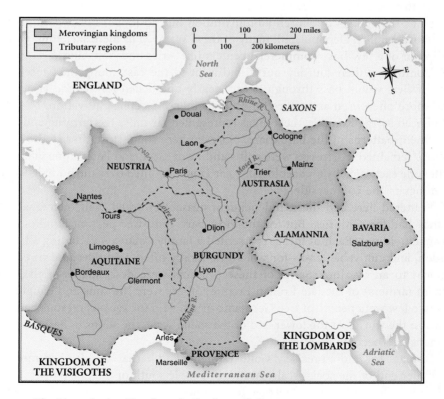

Map 7.4 The Merovingian Kingdoms in the Seventh Century
By the seventh century, there were three powerful Merovingian kingdoms: Neustria, Austrasia, and Burgundy. The important cities of Aquitaine were assigned to one or another of these major kingdoms, while Aquitaine as a whole was assigned to a duke or other governor. Kings did not establish capital cities; they did not even stay in one place. Rather, they continually traveled throughout their kingdoms, making their power felt in person.

peoples beyond the Rhine, foreshadowing the contours of modern Germany. These northern and eastern regions were little Romanized, but the inhabitants of the rest of the Frankish kingdoms lived with bits and pieces of the ancient Roman Empire at their front doors.

Travel was difficult in this world of decaying roads and few amenities. Yet there were many travelers, such as pilgrims on their way to Rome or other shrines and traders transporting commodities and slaves—precious human cargo captured on the borders of the Christian world and sold to wealthy aristocrats, mainly in the Islamic world. Seventh-century travelers in western Europe relied mainly on river routes, for land travel was very slow, and even large groups of people on the roads were vulnerable to attacks by robbers. Such travelers passed through a very diverse landscape. Pilgrims returning north from a trip to Rome might take the Rhône River, passing Roman amphitheaters, farmland neatly and squarely laid out by Roman land surveyors, and great stone palaces and villas along the way. Although these sights would seem quite classical, if the travelers were observant, they would notice the absence of thriving cities. By the seventh century, Roman cities still served as the centers of church administration but no longer boasted commercial or cultural vitality. Depopulated, many of them survived as mere skeletons, with the exception of a few busy commercial centers like Arles and Marseille.

Continuing their journey north and a bit to the east, along the Mosel River, the travelers would pass through dense, nearly untouched forests and agricultural land more often used as pasture for animals than for cereal cultivation. Not much influenced by the Romans, these areas represented far more the farming and village settlement patterns of the barbarians. Yet even here some structures of the Roman Empire remained. Fortresses were still standing at Trier, and large stone villas, such as the one excavated by archaeologists near Douai, loomed over the humble wooden dwellings of the countryside.

Scattered here and there, independent peasants worked their own small plots as they had for centuries. But for the most part, semi-free peasant families settled on smallholdings. Each of these represented a family's manse—including a house, a garden, and cultivable land—for which the family often paid dues and owed labor services to an overlord. Some of these peasants were descendants of the coloni (tenant farmers) of the late Roman Empire; others were the sons and daughters of slaves; a few were people of free Germanic origin who for various reasons had come down in the world. At the lower end of the social scale, the status of barbarians and Romans had become identical.

Romans (or, more precisely, Gallo-Romans) and barbarians also had merged at the upper end of the social scale. Although people south of the Loire River continued to be called Romans and people to the north were called Franks, their cultures were strikingly similar: they shared languages, settlement patterns, and religious sensibilities. Many dialects—both Germanic and Latin-based—were spoken in the western kingdoms in the seventh century. But a man like Gregory, bishop of Tours

Stadium and Amphitheater at Arles
In what is today the south of France, the ruins of an amphitheater built by the Romans still dwarf the surrounding buildings of the modern city of Arles. This huge stadium was even more striking in the seventh century, when the city was impoverished and depopulated. Plague, war, and the dislocation of Roman trade networks forced most people to abandon the cities and live on the land. Only the bishop and his clergy—and individuals who could make a living servicing them—stayed in the cities. At Arles there were monasteries as well, and some of them were thriving. In the mid-sixth century, one of the female convents there housed perhaps two hundred nuns. (Bridgeman-Giraudon/Art Resource, NY.)

(r. 573–c. 594), could expect all of his readers to understand his rough Latin prose: "Though my speech is rude," he wrote,

> I have been unable to be silent as to the struggles between the wicked and the upright; and I have been especially encouraged because, to my surprise, it has often been said by men of our day, that few understand the learned words of the rhetorician but many the rude language of the common people.

Thus Gregory began his *Histories,* a valuable source of information about the Merovingian period. He was trying to evoke the sympathies of his readers, a traditional Roman rhetorical device, but he also expected that his "rude" Latin—the

Reliquary

Relics—saints' precious bodies, body parts, and often simply materials that came into contact with both—were housed in equally precious containers. This reliquary, made of cloisonné enamel (bits of enamel framed by metal), garnets, glass gems, and a cameo, is in the shape of a sarcophagus. On the back is the inscription "Theuderic the priest had this made in honor of Saint Maurice." Theuderic must have given the reliquary to the monastery of Saint-Maurice d'Agaune (today in Switzerland), which was renowned for its long and elaborate liturgy (its daily schedule of prayer) in the late seventh century. (Photo courtesy Thames and Hudson Ltd., London, from *The Dark Ages*, ed. David Talbot Rice.)

plain Latin of everyday speech—would be understood and welcomed by the general public.

Whereas Gallo-Roman aristocrats of the fourth and fifth centuries had lived in isolated villas with their wives, children, slaves, and servants, aristocrats of the seventh century lived in small villages surrounded by the huts of peasants, shepherds, and artisans. These villages, constructed mostly from wood or baked clay, were generally built near a waterway or forest or around a church for protection.

The cities shrank. At Tours, Gregory and his household and clerics still lived in the old Roman city center. But Tours's main focus was now outside the city walls, in a cemetery where a church had been built. The population of the surrounding countryside was pulled to this church as if to a magnet, for it housed the remains of the most important and venerated person in the locale: St. Martin, a fourth-century soldier turned monk. Martin was long dead, but his relics—his bones, teeth, hair, and clothes—could be found in the cemetery outside Tours, where he had served as bishop. In succeeding centuries, he remained a supernatural force for the entire region: a protector, healer, and avenger through whom God manifested divine power. In Gregory's view, for example, Martin's relics (or rather God *through* Martin's relics) had prevented armies from plundering local peasants. Martin was not the only one thought to have great supernatural power; all of God's saints were considered miracle workers.

In the classical world, the dead had been banished from the presence of the living; in the early medieval world, the holy dead held the place of highest esteem. There were no formal procedures for proclaiming saints, but influential community leaders, including local bishops, "recognized" holiness. When, for example, miracles were observed at the site of the supposed tomb of the martyr Benignus in Dijon, the common people went there to ask for help. But only after the martyr himself appeared to the local bishop in a vision, thus dispelling doubts about the occupant of the tomb, was Benignus recognized as a saint. Women as well as men might be considered saints: "[Our Savior] gave us as models [of sanctity] not only men, who fight [against sinfulness] as they should, but also women, who exert themselves in the struggle with success," wrote Gregory as a preface to his story of the nun Monegund, who lived with a few other ascetic women and whose miracles included curing tumors and helping paralyzed limbs move again.

Economic Activity in a Peasant Society

As a bishop, Gregory was aware of some of the sophisticated forms of economic activity in seventh- and eighth-century Europe, such as long-distance trade. Yet most people lived on the edge of survival. Studies of Alpine peat bogs show that from the fifth to the mid-eighth centuries, glaciers advanced and the average temperature in Europe dropped. This climate change spelled shortages in crops. Chronicles, histories, and saints' lives also describe crop shortages, famines, and diseases as a normal part of life. For the year 591 alone, Gregory reported that

> a terrible epidemic killed off the people in Tours and in Nantes. . . . In the town of Limoges a number of people were consumed by fire from heaven for having profaned the Lord's day [Sunday] by transacting business. . . . There was a terrible drought which destroyed all the green pasture. As a result there were great losses of flocks and herds.

An underlying reason for these calamities was the weakness of the agricultural economy. The dry, light soil of the Mediterranean region was easy to till, and wooden implements were no liability there. But in the north of Europe, where the soil was heavy, wet, and difficult to turn, the limitations of wooden implements meant a meager food supply. At the same time, agricultural work was not equitably or efficiently allocated and managed. A leisure class of landowning

Early Medieval Accounting
In the seventh century, grain production was marginal at best. To make sure that it got its share of the crops, at least one enterprising landlord, the monastery of St. Martin at Tours, kept a kind of ledger. This extremely unusual parchment sheet, dating from the second half of the seventh century, lists the amount of grain and wood owed to the monastery by its tenants. (Bibliothèque nationale de France.)

warriors and churchmen lived off the work of peasant men, who tilled the fields, and peasant women, who gardened, brewed, baked, and wove cloth.

Occasionally surpluses developed, either from peaceful agriculture or plunder in warfare, and these were traded, though rarely in an impersonal, commercial manner. Most economic transactions of the seventh and eighth centuries were part of a **gift economy**, a system of give-and-take: booty was taken, tribute was demanded, harvests were hoarded, and coins were minted, all to be redistributed to friends, followers, and dependents. Kings and other rich and powerful men and women amassed gold, silver, ornaments, and jewelry in their treasuries and grain in their storehouses to mark their power, add to their prestige, and demonstrate their generosity. Those benefiting from this bounty included religious people and institutions: monks and nuns in their monasteries, priests and bishops in their churches.

We still have a partial gift economy today. On holidays, for example, goods change hands for social purposes: to consecrate a holy event, to express love and friendship, to show off wealth and status. In the Merovingian world, the gift economy was the dynamic behind most of the occasions when goods and money changed hands.

However, some economic activity in the seventh century was purely commercial and impersonal. In the north of Europe, a thriving North Sea trade was beginning. Older trade networks still tied the West, which supplied slaves and raw materials such as furs and honey, to the East, which provided luxuries and manufactured goods such as silk and papyrus. Trade was a way for the Byzantine, Islamic, and western European descendants of the Roman Empire to keep in tenuous contact with one another. Seventh- and eighth-century sources speak of Byzantines, Syrians, and Jews as the chief intermediaries, many of them living in the still thriving port cities of the Mediterranean. Gregory of Tours associated Jews with commerce, complaining that they sold things "at a higher price than they were worth."

Contrary to Gregory's view, Jews were not involved only, or even primarily, in trade but were almost entirely integrated into every aspect of secular life in many regions of Europe. They used Hebrew in worship, but otherwise they spoke the same languages as Christians and used Latin in their legal documents. Their children were often given the same names as Christians (and, in turn, Christians often took Old Testament biblical names); they dressed like everyone else; they engaged in the same occupations. Many Jews planted and tended vineyards, in part because of the importance of wine in synagogue services, in part because the surplus could easily be sold. Some Jews were rich landowners, with slaves and dependent peasants working for them; others were independent peasants of modest means. Some Jews lived in towns with a small Jewish quarter, where their homes and synagogues were located. Most Jews, however, like their Christian neighbors, lived on the land. Only much later, in the tenth century, would their status change as they were driven from the countryside.

Women were also more fully integrated into society in Merovingian Gaul than they had been in the ancient world. Like Islamic women, those in the West received dowries and could inherit property. They also could be entrepreneurs; documents reveal at least one enterprising peasant woman who sold wine at Tours to earn additional money.

The Powerful in Merovingian Society

Monarchs and aristocrats were the powerful people in Merovingian society. Aristocrats included monks and bishops as well as laypeople. Holding power through hereditary wealth, status, and political influence, they lived off their estates—often scattered throughout Gaul—and the peasants who tilled the soil for them.

Along with administering their estates, many male aristocrats of the period spent their time honing their skills as warriors. Being a great warrior in Merovingian society, as in the otherwise very different world of the Bedouins, meant more than just fighting; it also meant perfecting the virtues necessary for leading armed men. Aristocrats affirmed their skills and comradeship in the hunt, proved their worth in the regular taking of booty, and rewarded their followers afterward at generous banquets. At these feasts, following the dictates of the gift economy, great lords combined fellowship with the redistribution of wealth as they gave abundantly to their followers.

Merovingian aristocrats also valued bedtime. The bed—and procreation—was the focus of marriage. Important both to the survival of aristocratic families and to the transmission of their property and power, marriage was an expensive institution. There was more than one form of marriage. In the most formal, the man gave a generous dowry of clothes, livestock, and land to his bride. After the marriage was consummated, he gave her a "morning gift" of furniture. Very wealthy men also might support one or more concubines, who enjoyed a less formal type of marriage, receiving a morning gift but no dowry. In this period, churchmen had many ideas about the value of marriages, but in practice they had little to do with the matter: people were married in their homes, not in a church.

Some sixth-century aristocrats still patterned their lives on those of the Romans, teaching their children Latin poetry and writing to one another in phrases borrowed from the classical poet Virgil. But already in the seventh century their spoken language, much like Gregory's, had become very different from ancient literary Latin. Some still learned Latin, but they cultivated it mainly to read the Psalms. Just as in Byzantium, a religious culture that emphasized Christian piety over the classics was developing in Europe.

The arrival on the continent of the Irish monk St. Columbanus (d. 615) in about 590 energized this heightened emphasis on religion. St. Columbanus's brand of monasticism, which stressed exile, devotion, and discipline, found much favor among the Merovingian elite. The monasteries that St. Columbanus established in both Gaul and Italy attracted local recruits from the aristocracy, some of them grown men and women. Others were young children, given to the monastery by their parents. This practice, called oblation, was not only accepted but often considered essential for the spiritual well-being of both the children and their families.

Bishops ranked among the most powerful men in Merovingian society. Gregory, for example, considered himself the protector of "his citizens" at Tours. When representatives of the king came to collect taxes, Gregory stopped them in their tracks, warning them that St. Martin would punish anyone who tried to tax his people. "That very day," Gregory reported, "the man who had produced the tax rolls caught a fever and died."

Like other aristocrats, many bishops were married. Church councils demanded celibacy, however, and as the overseers of priests, bishops were expected to be moral supervisors and refrain from sexual relations with their wives. Since bishops were ordinarily appointed late in life, long after they had raised a family, this restriction did not threaten the ideal of a procreative marriage.

Because unions bound together extended families rather than simply husbands and wives, noble parents determined whom their daughters were to marry. Women had some control over their lives, however. If they were widowed without children, they were allowed to sell, give away, exchange, or rent out their dowry estates as they wished. Moreover, men could give their female relatives property outright in written testaments. Fathers so often wanted to share their property with their daughters that an enterprising author created a formula for scribes to follow when drawing up such wills. It began:

> For a long time an ungodly custom has been observed among us that forbids sisters to share with their brothers the paternal land. I reject this impious law: I make you, my beloved daughter, an equal and legitimate heir in all my patrimony [inheritance].

Because of such bequests, dowries, and other gifts, many aristocratic women were very rich. Childless widows frequently gave grand and generous gifts from their vast possessions to the church. But a woman need not have been a widow to control enormous wealth. In 632, for example, the nun Burgundofara, who had never married, drew up a will giving to her monastery the land, slaves, vineyards, pastures, and forests she had received from her two brothers and her father. In the same will, she gave other properties near Paris to her brothers and a sister.

Though legally under the authority of her husband, a Merovingian woman often found ways to assert control over her life and her husband's life as well. Tetradia, wife of Count Eulalius, left her husband, taking all his gold and silver, because "he was in the habit of sleeping with the women-servants in his household . . . [and] neglected his wife. . . . As a result of his excesses, he ran into serious debt, and to meet this he stole his wife's jewelry and money." In a court of law, Tetradia was sentenced to repay Eulalius four times the amount she had taken from him, but she was allowed to keep and live on her own property.

Other women were able to exercise behind-the-scenes control through their sons. Artemia, for example, used the prophecy that her son Nicetius would become a bishop to prevent her husband from taking the bishopric himself. After Nicetius became a bishop (fulfilling the prophecy), he remained at home with his mother well into his thirties, working alongside the servants and teaching the younger children to read the Psalms.

Some Merovingian women exercised direct power. Some were abbesses, leaders of female monasteries and, sometimes, "double monasteries," which had separate facilities for men and women. These could be very substantial centers of population.

The convent at Laon, for example, had three hundred nuns in the seventh century. Because women lived in populous convents or were monopolized by rich men able to support several wives or mistresses at one time, unattached aristocratic women were scarce in society and therefore valuable.

Atop this aristocracy of men and women were the Merovingian kings, rulers of the Frankish kingdoms from about 485 to 751. The **Merovingian dynasty** owed its longevity to good political sense: it had allied itself with local lay aristocrats and ecclesiastical (church) authorities. The kings relied on these men to bolster their power, which was largely based on their tribal war leadership and access to the lion's share of plunder, as well as on their takeover of public lands and some of the legal framework of Roman administration. The kings' courts functioned as schools for the sons of the aristocracy, tightening the bonds between royal and aristocratic families. When kings sent officials—counts and dukes—to rule in their names in various regions of their kingdoms, these regional governors worked with and married into the aristocratic families who had long controlled local affairs.

Both aristocrats and kings had good reason to want a powerful royal authority. The king acted as arbitrator and intermediary for the competing interests of the aristocrats while taking advantage of local opportunities to appoint favorites and gain prestige by giving out land and privileges to supporters and religious institutions. Gregory of Tours's history of the sixth century is filled with stories of bitter battles between Merovingian kings, as royal brothers fought continuously over territories, wives, and revenues. Yet what seemed like royal weakness and violent chaos to the bishop was in fact one way the kings contained local aristocratic tensions, preventing them from spinning out of royal control. By the beginning of the seventh century, three relatively stable kingdoms had emerged: Austrasia to the northeast; Neustria to the west, with its capital city at Paris; and Burgundy, incorporating the southeast (Map 7.4, page 253). These divisions were so useful to local aristocrats and to the Merovingian dynasty alike that even when royal power was united in the hands of one king, Clothar II (r. 584–629), he made his son the independent king of Austrasia.

As the power of the Merovingian kings increased in the seventh century, so did the might of their chief court official, the mayor of the palace. In the following century, allied with the Austrasian aristocracy, one mayoral family would displace the Merovingian dynasty and establish a new royal line, the Carolingians.

Christianity and Classical Culture in the British Isles

The Merovingian kingdoms exemplify some of the ways in which Roman and non-Roman traditions combined; the British Isles show others. Ireland had never been part of the Roman Empire, but it was converted to Christianity early on, as were Roman Britain and parts of Scotland. Invasions by various Celtic and Germanic groups—particularly the Anglo-Saxons, who gave their name to England, "the land of the Angles"—redrew the religious boundaries. Ireland, largely free of invaders, remained Christian, as did Scotland, also relatively untouched by invaders. England, which emerged from the invasions as a mosaic of about a dozen kingdoms ruled by separate Anglo-Saxon kings, became largely pagan.

Christianity was introduced to Anglo-Saxon England from two directions. In the north, Irish monks brought their own brand of Christianity. Converted in the fifth century by St. Patrick and other missionaries, the Irish had rapidly evolved a church organization that corresponded to its rural clan organization. Abbots and abbesses, generally from powerful dynasties, headed monastic *familiae,* communities composed of blood relatives, servants, and slaves, as well as monks or nuns. Bishops were often under the authority of abbots, and monasteries rather than cities were the centers of population settlement in Ireland. Irish missionaries to England were monks, and they set up monasteries modeled on those at home.

In the south of England, Christianity came by way of missionaries sent by Pope Gregory the Great (r. 590–604) in 597. The missionaries, under the leadership of Augustine (not the same Augustine as the bishop of Hippo), intended to convert the king and people of Kent, the southernmost kingdom, and then work their way north. But Augustine and his party brought with them Roman practices that were at odds with those of Irish Christianity, stressing ties to the pope and the organization of the church under bishops rather than abbots. Using the Roman model, they divided England into dioceses, territorial units each headed by a bishop. At the insistence of the pope, England also got two archbishops—one at Canterbury, the other at York—to oversee the bishops. Augustine

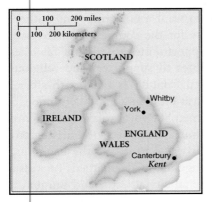

The British Isles

became archbishop of Canterbury. Because he was a monk, he set up a monastery right next to his cathedral, and it became a unique characteristic of the English church to have a community of monks attached to the bishop's church.

A major bone of contention between the Roman and Irish churches involved the calculation of the date of Easter, celebrated by Christians as the day on which Christ rose from the dead. The Roman church insisted that Easter fall on the first Sunday following the first full moon after the spring equinox. The Irish had a different method of determining Easter's date, and therefore they celebrated it on a different day. As everyone agreed that believers could not be saved unless they observed Christ's resurrection properly and on the right day, the conflict over dates was bitter. It was resolved by Oswy, king of Northumbria, who organized a meeting of churchmen, the Synod of Whitby, in 664. Convinced by the synod that Rome spoke with the voice of St. Peter, who was said in the New Testament to hold the keys to the kingdom of heaven, Oswy chose the Roman date. His decision paved the way for the triumph of the Roman brand of Christianity in England.

St. Peter was not the only reason the Anglo-Saxons favored Rome. To many English churchmen, Rome had great prestige because it was a treasure trove of knowledge, piety, and holy objects. Benedict Biscop (c. 630–690), the founder of two important English monasteries, made many difficult trips to Rome, bringing back relics, liturgical vestments, and even a cantor to teach his monks the proper melodies. Above all, he went to Rome to get books. At his monasteries in the north of England, he built up a grand library. In Anglo-Saxon England, as in Scotland and Ireland, all of which lacked a strong classical tradition from Roman times, a book was considered a precious object, to be decorated as finely as a garnet-studded brooch.

The Anglo-Saxons and Irish Celts had a thriving oral culture but extremely limited uses for writing. Books became valuable only when these societies converted to Christianity. Just as Islamic reliance on the Qur'an made possible a literary culture under the Umayyads, so Christian dependence on the Bible, liturgy, and ideas of the church fathers helped make England and Ireland centers of literature and learning in the seventh and eighth centuries. Archbishop Theodore (r. 669–690), who had studied at Constantinople and was one of the most learned men of his day, founded a school at Canterbury where students mined Latin, and even some Greek, manuscripts to comment on biblical texts. Men like Benedict Biscop soon sponsored other centers of learning, using texts from the classical past. Although women did not establish famous schools, many abbesses ruled over monasteries that stressed Christian learning. Here as elsewhere, Latin writings, even pagan texts, were studied diligently, in part because Latin was so foreign a language that mastering it required systematic and formal study. One of Benedict Biscop's pupils was Bede

Page from the Lindisfarne Gospels
This page from a lavishly illuminated manuscript was probably produced in the first third of the eighth century. For the monks at Lindisfarne, England, and elsewhere in the British Isles, books were precious objects, to be decorated much like pieces of jewelry. To introduce each of the four Gospels of the New Testament, the artist—who was also the scribe—produced three elaborate pages: the first was a "portrait" of the evangelist, the second a decorative "carpet" page, and the third the beginning of the text itself. The page depicted here is the beginning of the Gospel according to St. Matthew, which opens with the words "Liber generationis" ("The book of the generation [of Jesus]"). Note how elaborately the first letter, *L*, is treated and how the decoration gradually recedes, so that the last line, though still very embellished, is quite plain in comparison with the others. In this way, the layout of the book led the reader slowly and reverently into the Gospel itself. (© The British Library Board. Cotton Nero D.1.V, f.27.)

(673–735), an Anglo-Saxon monk and a historian of extraordinary breadth. Bede in turn taught a new generation of monks, many of whom became advisers to eighth- and ninth-century rulers.

Much of the vigorous pagan Anglo-Saxon oral tradition was adapted to Christian culture. In contrast to other European regions, where Latin was the primary written language in the seventh and eighth centuries, England made use of the vernacular—the language normally spoken by the people. Written Anglo-Saxon (or Old English) was used in every aspect of English life, from government to entertainment.

Unity in Spain, Division in Italy

In contrast to the British Isles, southern Gaul, Spain, and Italy had long been part of the Roman Empire and preserved many of its traditions. Nevertheless, as new peoples settled and fought over them, their histories diverged dramatically. When the Merovingian king Clovis defeated the Visigoths in 507, their vast kingdom, which had sprawled across southern Gaul and into Spain, was dismembered. By midcentury, the Franks came into possession of most of the Visigothic kingdom in southern Gaul.

In Spain the Visigothic king Leovigild (r. 569–586) established territorial control by military might. But no ruler could hope to maintain power there without the support of the Hispano-Roman population, which included both the great landowners and the leading bishops. Their backing was unthinkable while the Visigoths remained Arian Christians, but in 587 Leovigild's son Reccared (r. 586–601) took the necessary step, converting to Catholic Christianity. Two years later, at the Third Council of Toledo, most of the Arian bishops followed their king by announcing their conversion to Catholicism.

Thereafter, the bishops and kings of Spain cooperated to a degree unprecedented in other regions. The king gave the churchmen free rein to set up their own hierarchy (with the bishop of Toledo at the top) and to meet regularly at synods to regulate and reform the church. The bishops in turn supported their Visigothic king, who ruled as a minister of the Christian people. Rebellion against him was considered the same as rebellion against Christ. The Spanish bishops reinforced this idea by anointing the king, daubing him with holy oil in a ritual that paralleled the ordination of priests and demonstrated divine favor.

While the bishops adopted the king's cause as their own, their lay counterparts, the great landowners, helped supply the king with troops, allowing him to maintain internal order and repel his external enemies. Ironically, it was precisely the centralization and unification of the Visigothic kingdom that proved to be its undoing. When the Arabs arrived in 711, they needed only to kill the king, defeat his army, and capture Toledo to deal it a crushing blow.

By contrast, in Italy the Lombard king constantly faced a hostile papacy in the center of the peninsula and virtually independent dukes in the south. Theoretically

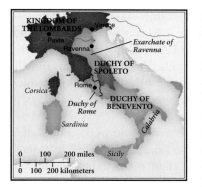

Lombard Italy, Early Eighth Century

royal officers, the dukes of Benevento and Spoleto in fact ruled on their own behalf. Although many Lombards were Catholics, others, including important kings and dukes, were Arians. The official religion varied with the ruler in power. Rather than signal a major political event, the conversion of the Lombards to the Catholic form of Christianity occurred gradually, ending only around the mid-seventh century. Partly as a result of this slow development, the Lombard kings, unlike the Visigoths, Franks, or even the Anglo-Saxons, never enlisted the wholehearted support of any particular group of churchmen.

Lacking a strong and united church to back them up, Lombard kings still had strengths. Chief among these were the traditions of leadership associated with the royal dynasty, the kings' military might, and their control over large estates and surviving Roman institutions in northern Italy. Although the Italian peninsula had been devastated by the wars between the Ostrogoths and the Byzantine Empire, the Lombard kings took advantage of the urban organization of Italian society and economy, assigning dukes to city bases and setting up a royal capital at Pavia. Recalling emperors like Constantine and Justinian, the kings built churches, monasteries, and other places of worship in the royal capital. They maintained city walls, issued laws, and minted coins. Revenues from tolls, sales taxes, port duties, and court fines filled their coffers, though their inability to revive the Roman land tax was a major weakness. The greatest challenge for the Lombard kings came from sharing the peninsula with Rome. As soon as the kings began to make serious headway into southern Italy against the duchies of Spoleto and Benevento, the pope began to fear for his own position.

In fact, the pope's position in Italy had long been uncertain. On the one hand, believing he was the successor of St. Peter and head of the church, he wielded real secular power. Pope Gregory the Great in many ways laid the foundations for the papacy's later spiritual and temporal triumphs. During his tenure, the pope became the greatest landowner in Italy; he organized the defenses of Rome and paid for its army; he heard court cases, made treaties, and provided welfare services. The missionary expedition he sent to England was only a small part of his involvement in the rest of Europe. A prolific author of spiritual works and biblical commentaries, Gregory summarized and simplified the ideas of church fathers like St. Augustine of Hippo, making them accessible to a wider audience. His practical handbook for the clergy, *Pastoral Rule*, was matched by practical reforms within the church: in Italy, for example, he tried to impose regular elections of bishops and to enforce clerical celibacy. On the other hand, even this pope was not independent. He was under the rule of the emperor, who lived in Constantinople.

Within a century, however, the situation changed as imperial authority began to unravel in Rome. In 691, Emperor Justinian II (r. 685–695) convened a council that determined 102 rules for the church. He sent them to Rome for papal endorsement. Most of the rules were unobjectionable, but Pope Sergius I (r. 687–701) was unwilling to agree to them as a whole because they permitted priestly marriage (which the Roman church did not want to allow) and prohibited fasting on Saturdays in Lent (which the Roman church required).

Outraged by Sergius's refusal, Justinian tried to arrest the pope, but Italian armies (theoretically under the emperor) came to the pontiff's aid, and Justinian's arresting officer hid under the pope's bed. The incident reveals that some local forces were already willing to rally to the side of the pope against the emperor. By now Constantinople's influence and authority over Rome was weak at best. Sheer distance, as well as diminishing imperial power in Italy, meant that the popes were in effect the leaders of the parts of Italy not controlled by the Lombards.

The gap between Byzantium and the papacy widened even more in the early eighth century when Emperor Leo III tried to increase the taxes on papal property to pay for his wars against the Arab invaders. The pope responded by leading a general tax revolt. Meanwhile, Leo's fierce policy of iconoclasm collided with the pope's tolerance of images. In the West, Christian piety hardly focused on icons, but the pope was not willing to allow sacred images and icons to be destroyed. He argued that holy images could and should be venerated, though not worshipped.

The pope's difficulties with the emperor were matched by increasing friction between the pope and the Lombards. The Lombard kings had gradually managed to bring under their control the duchies of Spoleto and Benevento, as well as part of the Exarchate of Ravenna. By the mid-eighth century, the popes feared that Rome would fall to the Lombards, and Pope Zachary (r. 741–752) looked northward for friends. He created an ally by sanctioning the deposition of the last Merovingian king and his replacement by the first Carolingian king, Pippin III ("the Short"; r. 751–768). In 753, Zachary's successor, Pope Stephen II (r. 752–757), called on Pippin to march to Italy with an army to fight the Lombards. Thus, events at Rome had a major impact on the history not only of Italy but of the Frankish kingdoms as well.

REVIEW | What were the similarities and differences among the kingdoms that emerged in western Europe, and how did their histories combine and diverge?

Conclusion

The Islamic world, Byzantium, and western Europe built on the legacies of Rome. Although Muslims were the newcomers to the Roman world, their religion, Islam, was influenced by Jewish and Christian monotheism, both with roots in Roman culture. Once the Muslim Arabs embarked on military conquests, they became the heirs of Rome in other ways: preserving Byzantine cities, hiring Syrian civil servants, and adopting Mediterranean artistic styles. Drawing on

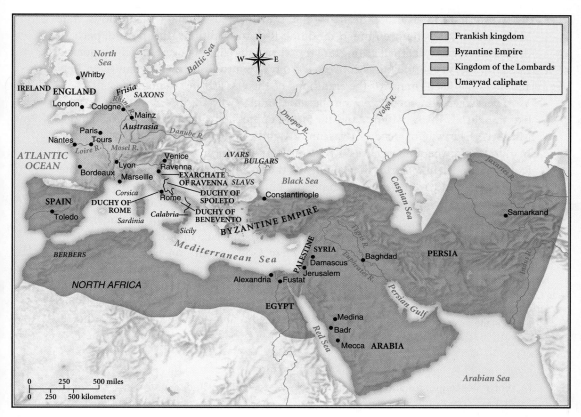

Mapping the West Europe and the Mediterranean, c. 750
The major political event of the period 600–750 was the emergence of Islam and the creation of an Islamic state that reached from Spain to the Indus River. The Byzantine Empire, once a great power, was dwarfed—and half swallowed up—by its Islamic neighbor. To the west were fledgling barbarian kingdoms, mere trifles on the world stage. The next centuries, however, would prove their resourcefulness and durability. **For more help analyzing this map, see the map activity for this chapter in the Online Study Guide at** bedfordstmartins.com/huntconcise**.**

Roman and Persian traditions, the Umayyad dynasty created a powerful Islamic state, with a culture that generally tolerated a wide variety of economic, religious, and social institutions, so long as the conquered peoples paid taxes to their Muslim overlords.

Byzantium directly inherited the central political institutions of Rome: its emperor still called himself the Roman emperor; its cities, laws, and religion—Christianity— were Roman. However, the changes of the seventh and eighth centuries—contraction of territory, urban decline, disappearance of the old elite, and a ban on icons— whittled away at this Roman character. By 750, Byzantium was less Roman than it was a new, resilient political and cultural entity, a Christian state on the borders of the new Muslim empire.

Western Europe also inherited—and transformed—Roman institutions. The Merovingian kings built on much-modified Roman traditions. In England, parts of the Roman legacy—Latin learning and the Christian religion—were largely imported. In Spain, the Visigothic kings converted from Arian to Roman Christianity. In Italy and at Rome itself, many of the traditions of the classical past endured.

Everywhere, the social hierarchy became simpler, with the loss of "middle" groups, like the curials in Byzantium, and the near-suppression of tribal affiliations among Muslims. Everywhere, religion was more tightly tied to politics than ever before. In Byzantium, the emperor was a religious force, presiding over the destruction of icons. In the Islamic world, the caliph was the successor to Muhammad, a religious and political leader. In western Europe, the kings allied with churchmen in order to rule. Despite their many differences, all of these leaders had a common understanding of their place in a divine scheme: they were God's agents on earth, ruling over God's people. In the next century they would consolidate their power. Little did they know that soon thereafter local elites would be able to assert greater authority than ever before.

CHAPTER REVIEW QUESTIONS

1. What were the similarities and the differences in political organization in the Islamic, Byzantine, and western European worlds in the seventh century?
2. Compare and contrast the role of religion in Islamic, Byzantine, and western European societies in the seventh century.

For practice quizzes and other study tools, see the Online Study Guide at bedfordstmartins.com/huntconcise.

For primary-source material from this period, see Chapter 8 of *Sources of THE MAKING OF THE WEST*, Third Edition.

TIMELINE

■ **664** Synod of Whitby; Oswy, the king of Northumbria (England) opts for Roman Christianity

661–750 Umayyad caliphate

■ **661** Death of Ali; origin of the Sunni-Shi'ite split

630–730 Period of Islamic conquests

■ **622** Muhammad's Hijra to Medina and beginning of Islamic calendar

610–641 Reign of Emperor Heraclius

| 570 | 660 | 750 | 840 |

c. 570–632 Life of Muhammad, the Prophet of Islam

■ **c. 590** Columbanus, an Irish monk, arrives on the European continent

590–604 Papacy of Gregory the Great

■ **597** Sent by Pope Gregory the Great, Augustine arrives in England to convert the Anglo-Saxons

■ **718** Major Arab attack on Constantinople repulsed

726–843 Period of iconoclasm in Byzantium

Suggested References

Taken together, early Islam is well covered by Berkey (for religion) and Kennedy (for politics). Ousterhout and Brubaker's book covers a crucial period in Byzantine history. Smith provides an excellent synthesis of developments in the West.

Berkey, Jonathan P. *The Formation of Islam: Religion and Society in the Near East, 600–1800.* 2003.

*Byzantium sourcebook: http://www.fordham.edu/halsall/sbook1c.html

Christie, Neil. *From Constantine to Charlemagne: An Archeology of Italy, AD 300–800.* 2006.

Connor, Carolyn L. *Women of Byzantium.* 2004.

*Gregory of Tours. *The History of the Franks.* Trans. Lewis Thorpe. 1976.

Heinzelmann, Martin. *Gregory of Tours: History and Society in the Sixth Century.* 2001.

Hen, Yitzhak. *Roman Barbarians: The Royal Court and Culture in the Early Medieval West.* 2007.

*Islamic History Sourcebook: http://www.fordham.edu/halsall/islam/islamsbook.html

Kennedy, Hugh. *The Prophet and the Age of the Caliphates: The Islamic Near East from the Sixth to the Eleventh Century.* 2d ed. 2004.

Ousterhout, Robert, and Leslie Brubaker, eds. *The Sacred Image East and West.* 1995.

Smith, Julia M. H. *Europe after Rome: A New Cultural History, 500–1000.* 2005.

Wickham, Chris. *Framing the Early Middle Ages: Europe and the Mediterranean, 400–800.* 2005.

8

Emperors, Caliphs, and Local Lords

N 841, A FIFTEEN-YEAR-OLD BOY named William went to serve at the court of Charles the Bald, king of the Franks. William's father was Bernard, an extremely powerful noble. His mother was Dhuoda, a well-educated, pious, and able woman who administered the family's estates in the south of France while her husband occupied himself in court politics and royal administration. In 841, however, politics had become dangerous. King Charles was fighting with his brothers over his portion of the empire forged by his grandfather Charlemagne, and Bernard held a precarious position at the young king's court. In fact, William was sent to Charles's court as a kind of hostage, to ensure Bernard's loyalty. Anxious about her son, Dhuoda wrote a handbook of advice for him. There she told him where his loyalties ought to lie:

Carolingian Mother

This depiction of a nursing mother is a detail from a full-page illustration of the biblical story of the Creation and Fall in a Carolingian Bible manuscript made in the ninth century. The mother is Eve, cast out of the Garden of Eden and suckling her firstborn, Cain. Christian mothers had an important model in Mary, the mother of Jesus, and Eve's dignified placement within a bower of garlands may reflect this association. (© *The British Library Board. Add. 10546 f.5v det.*)

In the human understanding of things, royal and imperial appearance and power seem preeminent in the world, and the custom of men is to account those men's actions and their names ahead of all others. . . . But despite all this . . . I caution you to render first to him whose son you are special, faithful, steadfast loyalty as long as you shall live.

William heeded his mother's words, with tragic results: when Bernard ran afoul of Charles and was executed, William died in a failed attempt to avenge his father.

Dhuoda's handbook reveals the volatile political atmosphere of the mid-ninth century, and her advice to her son points to one of its causes: a crisis of loyalty.

Loyalty to emperors, caliphs, and kings—all of whom were symbols of unity cutting across regional and family ties—competed with allegiances to local authorities;

271

those, in turn, vied with family loyalties. Everywhere—in the Islamic world, Byzantium, and the West—the period 750–1050 would see first the rise of powerful central rulers and then their fall, as power fragmented and became more regional.

At Byzantium, military triumphs brought the emperors enormous prestige. A renaissance of culture and art took place at Constantinople. Even so, newly powerful families soon began to dominate the Byzantine countryside. In the Islamic world, a dynastic revolution in 750 ousted the Umayyads from the caliphate and replaced them with a new family, the **Abbasids**. Yet Abbasid power, too, began to ebb as regional Islamic rulers came to the fore. In the West, Charlemagne—a Frankish king from a new dynasty, the Carolingians—forged an empire that embraced most of Europe. But this new state, like the others, turned out to be fragile, disintegrating within a generation of Charlemagne's death. In the West, even more than in the Byzantine and Islamic worlds, power fell into the hands of local strongmen.

All along the fringes of these realms, new political entities began to develop, conditioned by the religion and culture of their more dominant neighbors. Russia grew up in the shadow of Byzantium, as did Bulgaria and Serbia. The West was more crucial for the development of central Europe. By the year 1050, the contours of modern Europe and the Middle East were dimly visible.

CHAPTER FOCUS QUESTION What forces led to the dissolution—or weakening—of centralized governments in the period 750–1050, and what institutions took their place?

Byzantium's Renewed Strength and Influence

Between 750 and 850, Byzantium beat back Muslim attacks in Asia Minor and began to rebuild. After 850 it went on the offensive. Military victories brought new wealth and power to the imperial court, and the emperors supported a vast program of literary and artistic revival—the Macedonian renaissance—at Constantinople. But while the emperor dominated at the capital, a new landowning elite began to control the countryside. On its northern front, Byzantium helped create new Slavic realms.

Imperial Power

While the *themes,* with their territorial military organization, took care of attacks on Byzantine territory, new mobile armies made up of the best troops the emperor could muster moved aggressively outward beginning around 850. By 1025, the empire extended from the Danube in the north to the Euphrates in the south (Map 8.1). The Byzantines had not controlled so much territory since their wars with the Sasanid Persians four hundred years earlier.

Military victories gave new prestige to the army and the imperial court. The emperors drew revenues from vast and growing imperial estates. They could demand services and money from the population at will—requiring citizens to build bridges and roads, to offer lodging to the imperial retinue, and to pay taxes in cash. The emperors used their wealth to create a lavish court culture, surrounding themselves

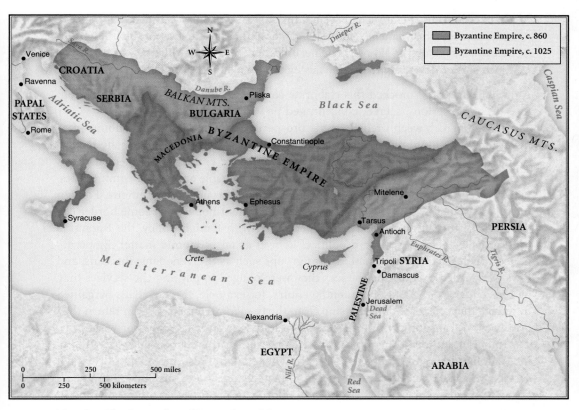

Map 8.1 The Expansion of Byzantium, 860–1025
In 860, the Byzantine Empire was still only a fraction of its former size. To the west, it had lost most of Italy. To the east, it held only part of Asia Minor. On its northern flank, the Bulgarians had set up an independent state. By 1025, however, the empire had ballooned, its western half embracing all of the Balkans, its eastern arm extending around the Black Sea, and its southeastern fringe reaching nearly to Tripoli. The year 1025 marked the Byzantine Empire's greatest size after the rise of Islam. **For more help analyzing this map, see the map activity for this chapter in the Online Study Guide at** bedfordstmartins.com/huntconcise.

with servants, slaves, family members, and civil servants. Eunuchs (castrated men who could not pose a threat to the imperial line) were entrusted with some of the highest posts in government. From their powerful position, the emperors negotiated with other rulers, exchanging ambassadors and receiving and entertaining diplomats with elaborate ceremonies. One such diplomat, Liutprand, bishop of the northern Italian city of Cremona, reported on his audience with Emperor Constantine VII ("Porphyrogenitos"; r. 913–959):

> Leaning upon the shoulders of two eunuchs I was brought into the emperor's presence. At my approach [mechanical] lions began to roar and birds to cry out, each according to its kind. . . . After I had three times made obeisance to the emperor with my face upon the ground, I lifted my head, and behold! the

man whom just before I had seen sitting on a moderately elevated seat had now changed his raiment [clothes] and was sitting on the level of the ceiling. How it was done I could not imagine, unless perhaps he was lifted up by some such sort of device as we use for raising the timbers of a wine press.

Although Liutprand mocked this elaborate court ceremonial, it had a real function: to express the serious, sacred, concentrated power of imperial majesty.

The emperor's wealth relied on the prosperity of an agricultural economy organized for trade. Byzantine commerce depended on a careful balance of state regulation and individual enterprise. The emperor controlled craft and commercial guilds to ensure imperial revenues and a stable supply of valuable and useful commodities, while entrepreneurs organized most of the fairs held throughout the empire. Foreign merchants traded within the empire, either at Constantinople or in some border cities. Because this international trade intertwined with foreign policy, the Byzantine government considered trade a political as well as an economic matter. Emperors issued privileges to certain "nations" (as groups such as the Venetians, Russians, and Jews were called), regulating the fees they were obliged to pay and the services they had to render. At the end of the tenth century, for example, the Venetians bargained to reduce their customs dues per ship from thirty *solidi* (coins) to two; in return they promised to transport Byzantine soldiers to Italy whenever the emperor wished.

Imperial authority was not absolute, however. In the countryside, particularly in Anatolia, powerful families—often army generals but also members of the civil service and the church—bought and dominated huge tracts of land. Many peasants became dependents of these great landlords, tilling the soil without owning it. Although the new magnates were a potential counterweight to imperial power, they ordinarily believed that their interests coincided with the emperor's. They were glad to profit from imperial victories and the expansion of Byzantine territory.

The Macedonian Renaissance, c. 870–c. 1025

Flush with victory and recalling Byzantium's past glory, the emperors revived classical intellectual pursuits. Basil I (r. 867–886), who came from Macedonia, founded the imperial dynasty that presided over the so-called Macedonian renaissance (c. 870–c. 1025). The *renaissance** (French for "rebirth") was made possible by an intellectual elite—families which, even in the anxious years of the eighth century, had persisted in studying the classics despite the trend toward a simple religious education.

Now, with the empire slowly regaining its military eminence and with icons permanently restored in 843, the scholarly elite thrived again. Byzantine artists produced new works, and emperors and other members of the new court society, liberated from the sober taboos of iconoclasm, sponsored sumptuous artistic

---

*The word *renaissance* is commonly used in connection with a revival of classical art, languages, and culture in Italy during the period c. 1350–1500. However, it is also used for any artistic, intellectual, or cultural flowering nourished by classical traditions. It has both meanings in this book.

The Crowning of Emperor Constantine Porphyrogenitos
This ivory relief was carved at Constantinople in the middle of the tenth century. The artist wanted to emphasize hierarchy and symbolism, not nature. Christ is shown crowning Constantine Porphyrogenitos (r. 913–959). What message do you suppose the artist wanted to telegraph by placing Christ higher than the emperor and by having the emperor slightly incline his head to receive the crown? **For more help analyzing this image, see the visual activity for this chapter in the Online Study Guide at** bedfordstmartins.com/huntconcise**.** (Hirmer Fotoarchiv, Munich, Germany.)

productions. Emperor Constantine Porphyrogenitos wrote books about geography and history and financed the work of other scholars and artists. He even supervised the details of his craftspeople's products, insisting on exacting standards. "Who could enumerate how many artisans the Porphyrogenitos corrected? He corrected the stonemasons, the carpenters, the goldsmiths, the silversmiths, and the blacksmiths," wrote a historian supported by the same emperor's patronage.

The emperors were joined by other members of the imperial court, who also sponsored writers, philosophers, and historians. Scholars wrote summaries of classical literature, encyclopedias of ancient knowledge, and commentaries on classical authors. Others copied religious and theological manuscripts, such as sermons, liturgical texts, Bibles, and Psalters. They hoped to revive the intellectual and artistic achievements at the height of imperial Roman rule. But the Macedonian renaissance could not possibly succeed in this endeavor; too much had changed since the time of Justinian. Nevertheless, the renaissance permanently integrated classical forms into Byzantine political and religious life.

The Macedonian Renaissance
This manuscript illumination, made at Constantinople in the mid-ninth century, combines Christian and classical elements in a harmonious composition. David, author of the Psalms, sits in the center. Like the classical Orpheus, he plays music that attracts and tames the beasts. In the right-hand corner, a figure labeled "Bethlehem" is modeled on a lounging river or mountain god. Compare this image with The Crowning of Emperor Constantine Porphyrogenitos on page 275 and describe, using these two objects, the various styles and subject matters of the Macedonian renaissance. (Bibliothèque nationale de France.)

In Byzantium's Shadow: Bulgaria, Serbia, Russia

The shape of what was to become modern eastern Europe was created during the period 850–950. By 800, Slavic settlements dotted the area from the Danube River down to Greece and from the Black Sea to Croatia. The ruler of the Bulgarians, called the *khagan,* ruled over the largest realm, northwest of Constantinople.

The Balkans, c. 850–950

Under Khagan Krum (r. c. 803–814) and his son, Bulgarian rule stretched west to the Tisza River in modern Hungary. At about the same time as Krum's triumphant expansion, however, the Byzantine Empire began its own campaigns to conquer, convert, and control these Slavic regions, today known as the Balkans.

The Byzantine offensive to the north and west began under Emperor Nicephorus I (r. 802–811), who waged war against the Slavs of Greece in the Peloponnese, set up a new Christian diocese there, organized it as a new military theme, and forcibly resettled Christians in the area to counteract Slavic paganism. The Byzantines followed this pattern of conquest as they pushed northward. By 900, Byzantium ruled all of Greece.

Still under Nicephorus, the Byzantines launched a massive attack against the Bulgarians, took the chief city of Pliska, plundered it, burned it to the ground, and then marched against Krum's encampment in the Balkan Mountains. Krum took advantage of his position, however. He attacked the imperial troops, killed Nicephorus, and brought home the emperor's skull in triumph. Cleaned out and lined with silver, the skull served as the victorious Krum's drinking goblet. In 816, the two sides agreed to a peace that lasted for thirty years. But hostility remained, and intermittent skirmishes between the Bulgarians and Byzantines gave way to longer wars throughout the tenth century. Emperor Basil II (r. 963–1025) led the Byzantines in a slow, methodical conquest (1001–1018). Aptly called "the Bulgar-Slayer," Basil brought the entire region under Byzantine control and forced its ruler to accept the Byzantine form of Christianity. Around the same time, the Serbs, encouraged by Byzantium to oppose the Bulgarians, began to form the political community that would become Serbia.

Religion played an important role in the Byzantine conquest of the Balkans. In 863, the brothers Cyril and Methodius were sent as Christian missionaries from Byzantium to the Slavs. Well educated in both classical and religious texts, they spoke one Slavic dialect fluently and devised an alphabet for the Slavic language (which, until then, existed only orally) based on Greek forms. It was the ancestor of the Cyrillic alphabet used in Bulgaria, Serbia, and Russia today.

The region that would eventually become Russia lay outside the sphere of direct Byzantine rule in the ninth and tenth centuries. However, like Serbia and Bulgaria, it came under increasingly strong Byzantine cultural and religious influence. Vikings— Scandinavian adventurers who ranged over vast stretches of ninth-century Europe seeking trade, booty, and land—had penetrated Russia from the north and imposed their rule over the Slavs inhabiting the broad river valleys connecting the Baltic Sea with the Black Sea and thence with Constantinople. Like the Bulgars in Bulgaria, the Scandinavian Vikings gradually blended into the larger Slavic population. At the end of the ninth century, a chief named Oleg established control over most of the tribes in southwestern Russia and forced peoples farther away to pay him tribute. The tribal association that he created formed the nucleus of Kievan Russia, named for Kiev, the city that became the commercial center of the region and today is the capital of Ukraine.

The relationship between Kievan Russia and Byzantium began with war, developed through trade agreements, and was eventually sustained by religion. Around 905, Oleg launched a military expedition to Constantinople, forcing the Byzantines to pay a large fee and open their doors to Russian traders in exchange for peace. At the time, only a few Christians and Jews—and probably some Muslims—lived in Russia alongside a mainly pagan population. The Russians' conversion to Christianity was spearheaded by Vladimir (r. c. 980–1015), the grand prince of Kiev and all of Russia. Under the influence of the Byzantine emperor Basil II, Vladimir agreed to adopt the Byzantine form of Christianity. He took a variant of the name Basil in honor of the emperor and married the emperor's sister Anna; then he reportedly had all the people of his state baptized in the Dnieper River.

Vladimir's conversion represented a wider pattern. Slavic realms such as Moravia, Serbia, and Bulgaria adopted the Byzantine form of Christianity. Meanwhile, the rulers and peoples of Poland, Hungary, Denmark, and Norway were converted under the auspices of the Roman church. This development reinforced the emerging split between orthodox Byzantine Christianity in the eastern half of the former Roman Empire and Roman Catholicism in the west. Russia's conversion to the Byzantine form of Christianity was especially significant. Russia was geographically as close to the Islamic world as to the Christian; it could conceivably have become an Islamic land. By converting to Byzantine Christianity, Russia made itself the heir to Byzantium and its church, customs, art, and political ideology. Adopting Christianity linked Russia to the Christian world, but choosing Byzantine rather than Roman Christianity served to isolate Russia later from western Europe.

Wishing to counteract such isolation, Russian rulers at times sought to cement relations with central and western Europe, which were tied to Catholic Rome. Prince Iaroslav the Wise (r. 1019–1054) forged such links through his own marriage and the marriages of his sons and daughters to rulers and princely families in France, Hungary, and Scandinavia. Iaroslav encouraged intellectual and artistic developments to connect Russian culture to the classical past. But after his death, civil wars broke out, shredding what unity Russia had known. Massive invasions by outsiders, particularly from the east, further weakened Kievan rulers, who were eventually displaced by princes from northern Russia. At the crossroads of East and West, Russia could meet and adopt a great variety of traditions, but its situation also opened it to unremitting military pressures.

REVIEW | Where and how did the Byzantine Empire expand during the period 750–1050?

The Caliphate and Its Fragmentation

A new dynasty of caliphs—the Abbasids—first brought unity and then, in their decline, fragmentation to the Islamic world. Caliphs continued to rule in name only, while regional rulers took over the real business of governing Islamic lands. Local traditions based on religious and political differences played an increasingly important role in people's lives. Yet even in the eleventh century, the Islamic world had a clear sense of its own unity, based on language, commerce, and intellectual achievements that crossed regional boundaries.

The Abbasid Caliphate, 750–c. 950

In 750, a civil war ousted the Umayyads and raised the Abbasids to the caliphate. The Abbasids found support in an uneasy coalition of Shi'ites (the faction loyal to Ali's memory) and non-Arabs who had been excluded from Umayyad government and now demanded a place in political life. The new regime signaled a revolution. The center of the Islamic state shifted from Damascus, with its roots in the Roman tradition, to Baghdad, a new capital city built by the Abbasids right next to Ctesiphon, which had been the Sasanid capital. Here the Abbasid caliphs followed Persian courtly models. They controlled a centralized government served by a staff of civil servants, and they appointed regional governors to carry out their policies at the local level.

From Baghdad, the Abbasid caliph Harun al-Rashid (r. 786–809) ruled over a flourishing empire. His contemporary Frankish ruler, Charlemagne, was impressed with the elephant Harun sent him as a gift, along with monkeys, spices, and medicines. But these items were mainstays of everyday commerce in Harun's Iraq. A mid-ninth-century list of imports listed "tigers, panthers, elephants, panther skins, rubies, white sandal[wood], ebony, and coconuts" from India as well as "silk, chinaware, paper, ink, peacocks, racing horses, saddles, felts, [and] cinnamon" from China.

The Abbasid dynasty began to decline after Harun's death. Obliged to support a huge army and an increasingly complex civil service, the Abbasids found their tax base inadequate. They needed to collect revenues from their provinces, such as Syria and Egypt, but the governors of those regions often refused to send the revenues. After Harun's caliphate, ex-soldiers, seeking better salaries, recognized different caliphs and fought for power in savage civil wars. The caliphs tried to bypass the regular army, made up largely of free Muslim foot soldiers, by turning to Turkish slaves—Mamluks—bought and armed to serve as mounted cavalry. But the caliphate's dwindling revenues could not sustain a loyal or powerful military force. In the tenth century the caliphs became figureheads only, as independent rulers established themselves in the various Islamic regions. For military support, many of these new rulers turned to independent military commanders who led Mamluk troops. Well paid to maintain their mounts and arms, many Mamluks gained renown and, after being freed by their masters, high positions at the courts of regional rulers. In the thirteenth century, some of them became rulers themselves.

Regional Diversity

A faraway caliph could not command sufficient allegiance from local leaders once he demanded more in taxes than he gave back in favors. The forces of fragmentation were strong in the Islamic world: it was, after all, based on the conquest of many diverse regions, each with its own deeply rooted traditions and culture. The Islamic religion, with its Sunni-Shi'ite split, also became

Fatimid Tableware
The elites under the Fatimid rulers cultivated a luxurious lifestyle that included dining on porcelain tableware, which was glazed and fired several times to produce an iridescent effect. Trade contacts with China inspired the Islamic world to mimic Chinese pottery. (© 2011 by Benaki Museum, Athens.)

a source of polarization. Western Europeans knew almost nothing about Muslims and ordinarily called them all Saracens (from the Latin for "Arabs") without distinction. But, in fact, as today, Muslims were of different ethnicities, practiced different customs, and identified with different regions. With the fragmentation of political and religious unity, each of the tenth- and early-eleventh-century Islamic states built on local traditions under local rulers (Map 8.2).

The most important and successful of these states was formed by the Fatimids, a group of Shi'ites who took their name from Fatimah, Muhammad's daughter and the wife of Ali. Allying with the Berbers in North Africa, the Fatimids established themselves in 909 as rulers in the region now called Tunisia. The Fatimid Ubayd Allah claimed to be not only the true imam (descendant of Ali) but also the *mahdi,* the "divinely guided" messiah, come to bring justice on earth. In 969, the Fatimids declared themselves rulers of Egypt, and eventually they controlled parts of North Africa, Arabia, and even Syria. Their dynasty lasted for about two hundred years.

While the Shi'ites dominated Egypt, Sunni Muslims ruled al-Andalus, the Islamic central and southern heart of Spain. Unlike the other independent Islamic states forged during the ninth and tenth centuries, the Spanish emirate of Córdoba (so called because its ruler took the secular title *emir,* "commander," and fixed his capital at Córdoba) was created near the start of the Abbasid caliphate, in 756. During the Abbasid revolution, Abd al-Rahman—a member of the Umayyad family—fled

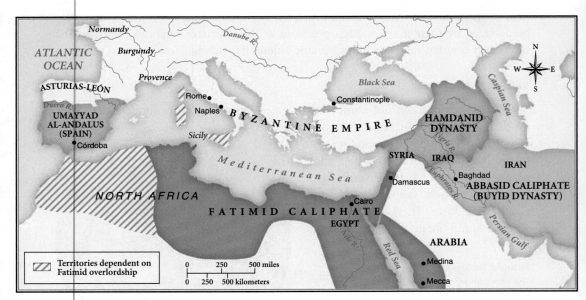

Map 8.2 Islamic States, c. 1000
A glance back at Map 7.1 (page 242) will quickly demonstrate the fragmentation of the once united Islamic caliphate. In 750, one caliph ruled territory stretching from Spain to India. In 1000, there was more than one caliphate—claimed by the Umayyads in Spain, the Fatimids based in Egypt, and the Abbasids in Iran—as well as several other ruling dynasties.

to North Africa, gathered an army, invaded Spain, and was declared emir after only one battle. He and his Umayyad successors ruled a broad range of peoples, including many Jews and Christians. After the initial Islamic conquest of Spain, the Christians there adopted so much of the new language and so many of the customs that Muslims called them Mozarabs, or "would-be Arabs." They were free to worship and live according to their own laws. Some Mozarabs were content with their status; others converted to Islam; still others intermarried with Muslims.

Abd al-Rahman III (r. 912–961) took the title of caliph, and the caliphate of Córdoba that he created lasted from 929 to 1031. Under Abd al-Rahman's rule, members of all religious groups in al-Andalus were given not only freedom of worship but also equal opportunity to rise in the civil service. The caliph also initiated important diplomatic contacts with Byzantine and European rulers, ignoring the weak and tiny Christian kingdoms squeezed into northern Spain. Yet under later caliphs, al-Andalus experienced the same political fragmentation that was occurring everywhere else. The caliphate of Córdoba broke up in 1031, and rulers of small, independent regions, called *taifas,* took power.

Although the regions of the Islamic world were culturally and politically diverse, they maintained a measure of unity through trade networks and language. Their principal bond was Arabic, the language of the Qur'an. At once poetic and sacred, Arabic was also the language of commerce and government from Baghdad to Córdoba. Moreover, despite political differences, borders were open: an artisan could move from Córdoba to Cairo; a landowner in North Africa might very well own property in al-Andalus; a young man from North Africa would think nothing of going to Iran to find a wife; a young girl purchased as a slave in Mecca might become part of a prince's harem in Baghdad. With few barriers to commerce (though every city and town had its own customs dues), traders regularly dealt in various, often exotic, goods.

Although the primary reason for these open borders was Islam itself, the openness extended to non-Muslims as well. The commercial activities of the Tustari brothers, Jewish merchants from southern Iran, were typical in the Arabic-speaking world. By 1026, the Tustaris had established a flourishing business in Egypt. Although they did not have "branch offices," informal contacts with friends and family allowed them to import fine textiles from Iran to sell in Egypt and to export Egyptian fabrics to sell in Iran.

The sophisticated Islamic society of the tenth and eleventh centuries supported networks even more vast than those of the Tustaris. Muslim merchants traded tin from England; salt and gold from Timbuktu in west-central Africa; amber, gold, and copper from Russia; and slaves from every region.

The Islamic Renaissance, c. 790–c. 1050

The dissolution of the caliphate into separate political entities multiplied the centers of learning and intellectual productivity. Unlike the Macedonian renaissance of Byzantium, which was concentrated in Constantinople, the Islamic renaissance occurred throughout the Islamic world. It was particularly dazzling in capital cities such as Córdoba, where tenth-century rulers presided over a brilliant court culture, patronizing scholars, poets, and artists. The library at Córdoba contained the largest collection of books in Europe at that time.

Elsewhere, as early as the eighth century, the Abbasid caliphs endowed research libraries and set up centers for translation. Scholars explored the writings of the ancients, including the classics of Persia, India, and Greece. Some read, translated, and commented on the works of ancient philosophers. Others worked on astronomy. Still others wrote on mathematics. Al-Khwarizmi (d. 850) wrote a book on algebra (the word itself is from the Arab *al-jabr*) and another on the Indian method of calculation, using the numbers 1, 2, and 3. He introduced the number zero, essential for differentiating 1 from 10, for example. When these numerals started to be used in western Europe in the twelfth century, they were called Arabic, as they are still known today.

The newly independent Islamic rulers supported science as well as mathematics. For example, Ibn Sina (980–1037), known in the West as Avicenna, wrote books on

A Dancing Constellation
The study of sciences such as medicine, physics, and astronomy flourished in the tenth and eleventh centuries in the cosmopolitan Islamic world. This whimsical depiction of Andromeda C, a constellation in the Northern Hemisphere, illustrates the *Book of Images of the Fixed Stars,* an astronomical treatise written around 965 by al-Sufi at the request of his pupil, the ruler of Iran. Al-Sufi drew from classical treatises, particularly the *Almagest* by Ptolemy. This copy of his book, probably made by his son in 1009, also drew on classical models for its illustrations. But instead of Greek clothing, Andromeda wears the pantaloons and skirt of an Islamic dancer. (Bodleian Library, University of Oxford; MS Marsh 144 page 167.)

logic, the natural sciences, and physics. His *Canon of Medicine* systematized earlier treatises and reconciled them with his own experience as a physician. Active in the centers of power, he served as vizier (prime minister) to various rulers.

Long before there were universities in the West, the Islamic world had important institutions of higher learning. Rich Muslims, generally of the ruling elite, demonstrated their piety and charity by establishing schools. Each school, or **madrasa**, was located within or attached to a mosque. Sometimes visiting scholars held passionate public debates at these schools. More regularly, professors conducted classes throughout the day on the interpretation of the Qur'an and other literary or legal texts. Students, all male, attended the classes that suited their achievement levels and interests. Most students paid a fee for learning, but there were also students who received scholarships.

At Byzantium and in the West, scholars were obliged to write on expensive parchment (made from animal skins); only the elite could afford their books. In the Islamic world, however, merchants, scholars, doctors, and others wrote on paper, which was inexpensive. The Islamic renaissance affected not just the very rich but a large and literate middle class.

REVIEW   What forces led to the fragmentation of the Islamic world in the tenth and eleventh centuries, and what factors nevertheless gave it a measure of unity?

The Creation and Division of a New European Empire

Just as in the Byzantine and Islamic worlds, so too in the West, the period 750–1050 began with the formation of a strong empire, ruled by one man. By the mid-ninth century, however, this empire began to fragment, as local rulers took power into their own hands. In 751 a new dynasty, the Carolingians, came to rule in a now united Frankish kingdom just one year after the Abbasids gained the caliphate in Iraq. Charlemagne, the most powerful of these Carolingian monarchs, conquered new territory, took the title of emperor, and presided over a revival of Christian classical culture known as the Carolingian renaissance. He ruled at the local level through counts and other military men. Nevertheless, the unity of the Carolingian Empire—based largely on conquest, a measure of prosperity, and personal allegiance to Charlemagne—was shaky. Its weaknesses were exacerbated by attacks from Viking, Muslim, and Magyar invaders. Charlemagne's successors divided his empire among themselves and saw it divided further as local leaders took defense—and rule—into their own hands.

The Rise of the Carolingians

The Carolingians were among many aristocratic families on the rise during the Merovingian period. Like the others, they were important landowners, but unlike the others, they gained exceptional power by monopolizing the position of "palace mayor"—a sort of prime minister—under the Merovingian kings. Charles Martel, palace mayor from 714 to 741, gave the name **Carolingian** (from *Carolus*, Latin for "Charles") to the dynasty. Renowned for defeating an invading army of Muslims from al-Andalus near Poitiers in 732, he also contended vigorously against other aristocrats who were carving out independent lordships for themselves. Charles and his family turned aristocratic factions against one another, rewarded followers, crushed enemies, and dominated whole regions by supporting monasteries that served as focal points for both religious piety and land donations.

The Carolingians also allied themselves with the Roman papacy and its adherents. They supported missionaries like the Anglo-Saxon Boniface (680–754), who went to areas on the fringes of the Carolingian realm as the pope's ambassador. To reform the local forms of Christianity that these regions had long ago adopted, Boniface set up a hierarchical church organization and founded monasteries dedicated to the Benedictine rule. His newly appointed bishops were loyal to Rome and the Carolingians. Charles Martel's son Pippin III (d. 768) turned to the pope even more directly. When he deposed the Merovingian king in 751, taking over the kingship himself, Pippin petitioned Pope Zachary to legitimize the act. The pope agreed. The Carolingians returned the favor a few years later when the pope asked for their help in defense against the hostile Lombards. That papal request signaled a major shift. Before 754, the papacy had been part of the Byzantine Empire; after that date, it turned to Europe for protection. Pippin launched a successful campaign against the Lombard king that ended in 756 with the so-called Donation of Pippin, a peace accord between the Lombards and the pope. The treaty gave back to the pope cities that had been taken by the Lombard king. The new arrangement recognized what the papacy had long ago created: a territorial "republic of St. Peter" ruled by the pope, not by the Byzantine emperor. Henceforth the fate of Italy would be tied largely to the policies of the pope and the Frankish kings to the north, not to the emperors of the East.

Partnership with the Roman church gave the Carolingian dynasty a Christian aura, expressed in symbolic form by anointment. Bishops rubbed holy oil on the foreheads and shoulders of Carolingian kings during their coronation ceremonies, imitating the Old Testament kings who had been anointed by God.

Charlemagne and His Kingdom, 768–814

The most famous Carolingian king was Charles (r. 768–814), called "the Great" (*le Magne* in Old French) by his contemporaries—thus Charlemagne. Epic poems portrayed Charlemagne as a just, brave, wise, and warlike king. Einhard, Charlemagne's courtier and younger contemporary, portrayed his ruler as the model of a Roman emperor. Some scholars at his court described him as another David, the anointed Old Testament king. Modern historians are less dazzled than his contemporaries were, noting that he was complex, contradictory, and sometimes brutal. He loved listening to readings from St. Augustine's *City of God* and supported major scholarly enterprises, yet he never learned to write. He was devout, building a beautiful chapel at his major residence at Aachen, yet he rejected the advice of churchmen when they told him to convert pagans rather than force baptism on them. He waged many successful wars, yet he thereby destroyed the buffer states surrounding the Frankish kingdoms, unleashing a new round of invasions even before his death. Behind these contradictions, however, lay a unifying vision. Charlemagne dreamed of an empire that would unite the military and intellectual traditions of the Roman and Germanic worlds with the legacy of Christianity. This vision lay at the core of his political activity, his building programs, and his support of scholarship and education.

During the early years of his reign, Charlemagne conquered lands in all directions (Map 8.3). He invaded Italy, seizing the crown of the Lombard kings and annexing northern Italy in 774. He then moved northward and began a long and difficult war against the Saxons, concluded only after more than thirty years of fighting. He forcibly annexed Saxon territory and converted the Saxon people to

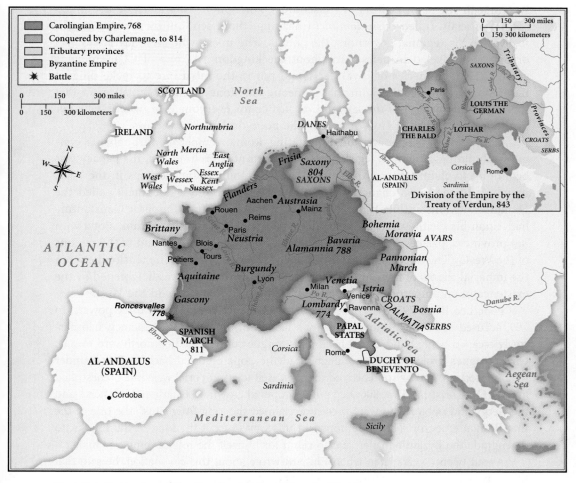

Map 8.3 Expansion of the Carolingian Empire under Charlemagne
The conquests of Charlemagne temporarily united almost all of western Europe under one ruler. Although this great empire broke apart (the inset shows the divisions of the Treaty of Verdun), the legacy of that unity remained, even serving as one of the inspirations behind today's European Union.

Christianity through mass baptisms at the point of the sword. To the southeast, Charlemagne waged a campaign against the Avars, the people who had fought the Byzantines almost two centuries before. To the southwest, Charlemagne led an expedition to Spain, setting up a march, or military buffer region, between al-Andalus and his own realm. By the 790s, Charlemagne's kingdom stretched eastward across Germany, southeast to what is today Austria, and south to Spain and Italy.

Such power in the West was unheard of since the time of the Roman Empire. Charlemagne began to act according to the old Roman imperial model. He sponsored building programs to symbolize his authority, standardized weights and measures, and became a patron of intellectual and artistic efforts. He built a capital city at Aachen, complete with a church patterned on one built by Emperor Justinian at Ravenna in the sixth century. To discourage corruption, Charlemagne appointed special officials, called *missi dominici* (meaning "those sent out by the lord king"), to oversee his regional governors, the counts. The missi, who were lay aristocrats or bishops, traveled in pairs throughout the kingdom. As one of Charlemagne's capitularies (summaries of royal decisions) put it, the missi "are to make diligent inquiry wherever people claim that someone has done them an injustice, so that the missi fully carry out the law and do justice for everyone everywhere, whether in the holy churches of God or among the poor, orphans, or widows."

While Charlemagne was busy imitating Roman emperors through his conquests, building programs, legislation, and efforts at church reform, the papacy was beginning to claim imperial power for itself. At some point, perhaps in the 760s, members of the papal chancery, or writing office, created a document called the Donation of Constantine. It declared that the fourth-century Emperor Constantine had, upon his death, given the pope his crown, cloak, and military rank along with "all provinces, palaces, and districts of the city of Rome and Italy and of the regions of the West." (The document was much later proved a forgery.) The tension between the imperial claims of the Carolingians and those of the pope was heightened by the existence of an emperor at Constantinople who also had rights in the West.

Pope Leo III (r. 795–816) upset the delicate balance among these three powers. In 799, accused of adultery and perjury by a faction of the Roman aristocracy, Leo narrowly escaped being blinded and having his tongue cut out. He fled northward to seek Charlemagne's protection. Charlemagne had the pope escorted back to Rome under royal protection, and he soon arrived there himself to an imperial welcome orchestrated by Leo. On Christmas Day, 800, Leo put an imperial crown on Charlemagne's head, and the clergy and nobles who were present acclaimed the king "Augustus," the title of the first Roman emperor. The pope hoped in this way to exalt the king of the Franks, to downgrade the Byzantine ruler, and to claim for himself the role of "emperor maker."

About twenty years later, when Einhard wrote about this coronation, he said that the imperial title at first so displeased Charlemagne "that he stated that, if he had known in advance of the pope's plan, he would not have entered the church that day." In fact, Charlemagne did not use any title but king for more than a year afterward. But it is unlikely that he was completely surprised by the imperial title; his advisers certainly had been thinking about claiming it. He might have hesitated adopting it because he feared the reaction of the Byzantines, as Einhard went on to suggest, or he might have objected to the papal role in his crowning rather than to the crown itself. When Charlemagne finally did call himself emperor, after establishing a peace with the Byzantines, he used a long and revealing title: "Charles, the most serene Augustus, crowned by God, great and peaceful Emperor who governs the Roman Empire and who is, by the mercy of God, king of the Franks and the Lombards." According to this title, Charlemagne was not the Roman emperor crowned by the pope but rather God's emperor, who governed the Roman Empire along with his many other duties.

The Carolingian Renaissance, c. 790–c. 900

Charlemagne inaugurated—and his successors continued to support—a revival of learning designed to enhance the glory of the kings, educate their officials, reform the liturgy, and purify the faith. Like the renaissances of the Byzantine and Islamic worlds, the Carolingian renaissance resuscitated the learning of the past. Scholars studied Roman imperial writers such as Suetonius and Virgil; they read and commented on the works of the church fathers; and they worked to establish complete and accurate texts of everything they read and prized.

The English scholar Alcuin (c. 732–804), a member of the circle of scholars whom Charlemagne recruited to form a center of study, brought with him the traditions of Anglo-Saxon scholarship that had been developed by men such as Benedict Biscop and Bede. Invited to Aachen, Alcuin became Charlemagne's chief adviser, writing letters on the king's behalf, counseling him on royal policy, and tutoring the king's household, including the women and girls. Charlemagne's sister and daughter, for example, often asked Alcuin to explain passages from the Gospel to them. Charlemagne entrusted Alcuin with the task of preparing an improved edition of the Vulgate, the Latin Bible read in all church services.

The Carolingian renaissance depended on an elite staff of scholars such as Alcuin, yet its educational program had a broader impact. In one of his capitularies, Charlemagne ordered that the cathedrals and monasteries of his kingdom teach reading and writing to all who were able to learn. Some churchmen expressed the hope that schools for children (perhaps they were thinking of girls as well as boys) would be established even in small villages and hamlets. Although this dream was never realized, it shows that even before the Islamic world was organizing the madrasa system of schools, the Carolingians were thinking about the importance of religious education for more than a small elite.

Art, like scholarship, served Carolingian political and religious goals. Carolingian artists turned to models from Byzantium (perhaps some refugees from Byzantine iconoclasm joined them) and Italy to illustrate Gospels, Psalters, scientific treatises, and literary manuscripts.

The ambitious Carolingian program endured, even after the Carolingian dynasty had faded to a memory. The work of locating, understanding, and transmitting models of the past continued in a number of monastic schools. In the twelfth century, scholars would build on the foundations laid by the Carolingian renaissance. The very print of this textbook depends on one achievement of the period: modern letter fonts are based on the clear and beautiful letter forms, called Caroline minuscule, invented in the ninth century to standardize manuscript handwriting and make it more readable.

Charlemagne's Successors, 814–911

Charlemagne's son Louis the Pious (r. 814–840) was also crowned emperor, and he took his role as guarantor of the Christian empire even more seriously than his father did. He brought the monastic reformer Benedict of Aniane to court and issued a capitulary in 817 imposing a uniform way of life, based on the Benedictine rule, on all the monasteries of the empire. This moment marked the effective adoption of the Benedictine rule as the monastic standard in the West. Louis also regularized the practices of his notaries, who issued his documents and privileges, and he continued to use missi to administer justice throughout the realm.

In a new development of the coronation ritual, Louis's first wife, Ermengard, was crowned empress by the pope in 816. In 817, their firstborn son, Lothar, was given the title emperor and made co-ruler with his father. Their other sons, Pippin and Louis (later called Louis the German), were made subkings under imperial rule. Louis the Pious hoped in this way to ensure the unity of the empire while satisfying the claims of his and Ermengard's three sons. But Louis's plans were thwarted by events.

Ermengard died, and Louis married Judith, reputed to be the most beautiful woman in the kingdom. In 823, Judith and Louis had a son, Charles (later known as Charles the Bald, to whose court Dhuoda's son William was sent). The three sons of Ermengard, bitter over the birth of another royal heir, rebelled against their father and fought one another for more than a decade. Finally, after Louis the Pious's death in 840, the **Treaty of Verdun** (843) divided the empire among the three remaining brothers (Pippin had died in 838) in an arrangement that would roughly define the future political contours of western Europe (see the inset for Map 8.3, page 285). The western third, bequeathed to Charles the Bald, would eventually become France. The eastern third, handed to Louis the German, would become Germany. The "Middle Kingdom," which was given to Lothar along with the imperial title, had a different fate: parts of it were absorbed by France and Germany, and the rest eventually formed the modern states of the Netherlands, Belgium, Luxembourg, Switzerland, and Italy.

In 843, the European-wide empire of Charlemagne dissolved. Forged by conquest, it had been supported by a small group of privileged aristocrats with lands and offices stretching across the entire realm. Their loyalty—based on shared values, real friendship, expectations of gain, and formal ties of vassalage—was crucial to the success of the Carolingians. The empire had also been supported by an ideal, shared by educated laymen and churchmen alike, of conquest and Christian belief working together to bring good order to the earthly state. But powerful forces operated against the Carolingian Empire. Once the empire's borders were fixed and conquests ceased, the aristocrats could no longer hope for new lands and offices. They put down roots in

King David, Carolingian Style
In this sumptuously illustrated Bible made for King Charles the Bald, David plays the harp and dances on a cloud. Above and below him are his musicians with their instruments. Compare this view of David with the Byzantine image on page 276. (Bibliothèque nationale de France.)

particular regions and began to gather their own followers. Powerful local traditions such as different languages also undermined imperial unity. Finally, as Dhuoda revealed, some people disagreed with the imperial ideal. By asking her son to put his father before the emperor, she demonstrated her belief in the primacy of the family and the intimate and personal ties that bound it together. Dhuoda's ideal represented a new sensibility that saw real value in the breaking apart of Charlemagne's empire into smaller, more intimate local units.

Land and Power

The Carolingian economy, based on trade and agriculture, contributed to both the rise and the dissolution of the Carolingian Empire. At the outset, the empire's wealth came from land and plunder. After the booty from war ceased to pour in, the Carolingians still had access to money and goods. To the north, in Viking trading stations such as Haithabu (today Hedeby, in northern Germany), archaeologists have found Carolingian glass and pots alongside Islamic coins and cloth, evidence that the Carolingian economy intermingled with that of the Abbasid caliphate. Silver from the Islamic world probably came north up the Volga River through Russia to the Baltic Sea. There the coins were melted down, and the silver was traded to the Carolingians in return for wine, jugs, glasses, and other manufactured goods. The Carolingians turned the silver into coins of their own, to be used throughout the empire for small-scale local trade. The weakening of the Abbasid caliphate in the mid-ninth century disrupted this far-flung trade network and contributed to the weakening of the Carolingians at about the same time.

Land provided the most important source of Carolingian wealth and power. Like the landholders of the late Roman Empire and the Merovingian period, Carolingian aristocrats held many estates, scattered throughout the Frankish kingdom. But in the Carolingian period these estates were reorganized, and their productivity was carefully calculated. Modern historians often call these estates **manors**.

A typical manor was Villeneuve Saint-Georges, which belonged to the monastery of Saint-Germain-des-Prés (today in Paris) in the ninth century. Villeneuve consisted of arable fields, vineyards, meadows where animals could roam, and woodlands, all scattered about the countryside rather than connected in a compact unit. The land was not tilled by slave gangs, as had been the custom on the great estates of the Roman Empire, but rather by peasant families, each one settled on its own manse, which consisted of a house, a garden, and small sections of the arable land. The peasants farmed the land that belonged to them and also worked the demesne, the very large manse of the lord (in the case of Villeneuve, the lord was the abbey of Saint-Germain). These peasant farms marked a major social and economic development. Whereas agricultural slaves had worked in gangs on their owner's estates and had not been allowed to marry and have children, the peasants on Villeneuve and on other Carolingian estates normally lived with their families and could not be displaced from their manses. In this sense, the peasant household of the Carolingian period was the precursor of the modern nuclear family.

Peasants at Villeneuve practiced the most progressive sort of plowing, known as the three-field system, in which they farmed two-thirds of the arable land at one time. They planted one-third with winter wheat and one-third with summer crops, leaving the remaining third fallow, to restore its fertility. The crops sown and the fallow field were then rotated so that land use was repeated only every three years. This method of organizing the land produced larger yields (because two-thirds of the land was cultivated each year) than the still prevalent two-field system, in which only half of the arable land was cultivated one year, while the other half lay fallow.

All the peasants at Villeneuve were dependents of the monastery and owed dues and services to Saint-Germain. The peasants' obligations varied enormously. One family, for example, owed four silver coins, wine, wood, three hens, and fifteen eggs every year, and the men had to plow the fields of the demesne. Another family owed the intensive labor of working the vineyards. One woman was required to weave cloth and feed the chickens. Peasant women spent much time at the lord's house in the *gynaeceum*—the women's workshop, where they made and dyed cloth and sewed garments—or in the kitchens as cooks. Peasant men spent most of their time in the fields.

Manors organized on the model of Villeneuve were profitable. Like other lords, the Carolingians benefited from their extensive estates. Nevertheless, farming was still too primitive to return great surpluses. Further, as the lands belonging to the king were divided up in the wake of the partitioning of the empire and new invasions, Carolingian dependence on manors scattered throughout the kingdom proved to be a source of weakness.

Viking, Muslim, and Magyar Invasions, c. 790–955

Carolingian kings and counts confronted new groups—Vikings, Muslims, and Magyars—along their borders (Map 8.4). As royal sons fought one another and as counts and other powerful men sought to carve out their own principalities, some

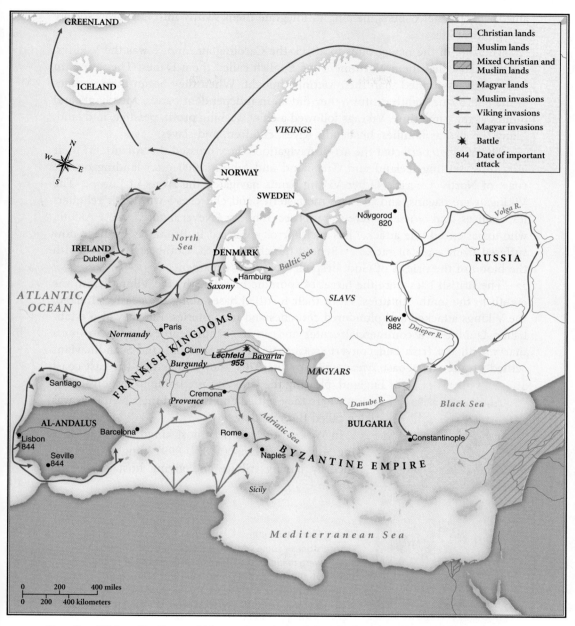

Map 8.4 Viking, Muslim, and Magyar Invasions of the Ninth and Tenth Centuries

Bristling with multicolored arrows, this map suggests that western Europe was continually and thoroughly pillaged by invaders for almost two centuries. That impression is only partially true; it must be offset by several factors. First, not all the invaders came at once. The Viking raids were about over when the Magyar attacks began. Second, the invaders were not entirely unwelcome. The Magyars were for a time enlisted as mercenaries by the king of Italy, and some Muslims were allied to local lords in Provence. Third, the invasions, though widespread, were local in effect. Note, for example, that the Viking raids were largely limited to rivers and coastal areas.

allied with the newcomers, helping to integrate them swiftly into European society and political life.

The first of the new groups to attack the Carolingian Empire was the Vikings. The Franks called them Northmen; the English called them Danes. They were, in fact, much less united than their victims thought. When they began their voyages at the end of the eighth century, they did so in independent bands. Merchants and pirates at the same time, Vikings followed a chief, seeking profit, prestige, and land. Many traveled as families: husbands, wives, children, and slaves.

The Vikings perfected the art of navigation. They crossed the Atlantic in their longships, settling Iceland and Greenland and (about 1000 C.E.) landing on the coast of North America. Other Viking bands navigated the rivers of Europe. The Vikings were pagans, and to them monasteries and churches—with their reliquaries, chalices, and crosses—were storehouses of booty. "Never before," wrote Alcuin, who experienced one attack, "has such terror appeared in Britain as we have now suffered from a pagan race. . . . Behold the church of St. Cuthbert spattered with the blood of the priests of God, despoiled of all its ornaments."

The British Isles were the target of sporadic invasions by the Vikings from the eighth to the tenth centuries. From their fortified bases along the coast of Ireland, the Vikings attacked and plundered churches and monasteries. But they also established Dublin as a commercial center and, in the tenth century, began to intermarry with the Irish and convert to Christianity. In Scotland, the Scandinavians settled on the west coast. Meanwhile, by the 870s, they had settled the east coast of England, plowing the land and preparing to live on it. The region where they settled and imposed their own laws was later called the Danelaw.

In Wessex, the southernmost kingdom of England, King Alfred the Great (r. 871–899) bought time and peace by paying tribute and giving hostages to the

Viking Picture Stone

Picture stones—some very elaborate, others with simple incisions—were made on the island of Gotland, today part of Sweden, from the fifth to the twelfth centuries. This one, dating from the eighth or ninth century, has four interrelated scenes. The bottom scene is a battle between people defending a farm and archers outside. The woman in the enclosure above is either Gudrun mourning her brother Gunnar, who was thrown into a snake pit, or Sigyn, the faithful wife of the god Loke, catching in a bowl the venom that a snake pours down on her chained husband. The ship in the next scene is the ship of death that takes heroes to heaven. At the very top is heaven (Valhalla), where heroes hunt and feast for all eternity. (Photo: Raymond Hejdstrom.)

Danes. Such tribute, later called Danegeld, was collected as a tax that eventually became the basis of a relatively lucrative taxation system in England. Then in 878, Alfred led an army that, as his biographer put it, "gained the victory through God's will. He destroyed the Vikings with great slaughter and pursued those who fled . . . hacking them down." Thereafter, the pressures of invasion eased as Alfred reorganized his army, set up strongholds, and deployed new warships.

On the continent of Europe, the invaders set up trading posts and settled where they had originally raided. Beginning about 850, their attacks became well-organized expeditions for regional control. At the end of the ninth century, one contingent settled in the region of France that soon took the name Normandy, land of the Northmen. The new inhabitants converted to Christianity during the tenth century. Rollo, the Viking leader in Normandy, accepted Christianity in 911 when the Frankish king Charles the Simple (or Straightforward) formally ceded Normandy to him.

Normandy was not the only new Christian state created in the north during the tenth and eleventh centuries. Scandinavia itself was transformed with the creation of the powerful kingdom of Denmark. There had been kings in Scandinavia before the tenth century, but they had been weak, their power challenged by nearby chieftains. The Vikings had been led by these chieftains, each competing for booty to win prestige, land, and power back home. During the course of their raids, they and their followers came into contact with new cultures and learned from them. Meanwhile, the Carolingians and the English supported missionaries in Scandinavia. By the middle of the tenth century, the Danish kings and their people had become Christian. Following the model of the Christian kings to their south, the Danish kings built up an effective monarchy, with a royal mint and local agents who depended on them. By about 1000, the Danes had extended their control to parts of Sweden, Norway, and even England.

Far from Denmark, Muslims took advantage of Byzantium's early weakness. The dynasty that preceded the Fatimids in Egypt developed a navy that, over the ninth and tenth centuries, gradually conquered Sicily, which had been under Byzantine rule. By the middle of the tenth century, independent Islamic princes ruled all of Sicily. Around the same time, other raiders from North Africa set up bases on other Mediterranean islands, while pirates from al-Andalus built a stronghold in Provence (in southern France). Liutprand of Cremona was horrified:

> [Muslim pirates from al-Andalus], disembarking under cover of night, entered the manor house unobserved and murdered—O grievous tale!—the Christian inhabitants. They then took the place as their own . . . [fortified it and] started stealthy raids on all the neighboring country. . . . Meanwhile the people of Provence close by, swayed by envy and mutual jealousy, began to cut one another's throats, plunder each other's substance, and do every sort of conceivable mischief. . . . [Furthermore, they called upon the Muslims] and in company with them proceeded to crush their neighbors.

In this way the Muslims, though outsiders, were drawn into local Provençal disputes. They were ousted only in 972, when they caused a scandal by capturing the holiest man of his era, Abbot Maieul of Cluny. Outraged, the count of Provence launched a successful attack against their hideout.

The last of the invaders were the Magyars. Nomadic people from the Urals (today northeastern Russia) who spoke a language unrelated to any other in Europe (except Finnish), the Magyars made their first appearance in the West around 899 in the Danube basin. Until then, the region had been predominantly Slavic, but the Magyars drove a wedge between the Slavs near the Frankish kingdom and those bordering on Byzantium. The Bulgarians, Serbs, and Russians, as we have seen, were driven into the Byzantine orbit, while the Slavs nearer the Frankish kingdom came under the influence of Germany.

From their bases in present-day Hungary, the Magyars raided far to the west, attacking Germany, Italy, and even southern Gaul frequently between 899 and 955. Then in 955, the German king Otto I defeated a marauding party of Magyars at the battle of Lechfeld. Otto's victory, his subsequent military reorganization of his eastern frontiers, and the cessation of Magyar raids around this time made Otto a great hero to his contemporaries. Historians today, however, think the containment of the Magyars had more to do with their internal transformation from nomads to farmers than with their military defeat.

The Viking, Muslim, and Magyar invasions were the final onslaught western Europe experienced from outsiders. In some ways they were a continuation of the invasions that had rocked the Roman Empire in the fourth and fifth centuries. Loosely organized in war bands, the new groups entered western Europe looking for wealth but stayed on to become absorbed in the region's post-invasion society.

> **REVIEW**   What were the strengths and weaknesses of the Carolingian institutions of government, warfare, and education?

After the Carolingians: The Emergence of Local Rule

The Carolingian Empire was too diverse to remain united. Although Latin was the language of official documents and most literary and ecclesiastical texts, few people spoke it; instead they used a wide variety of different languages and dialects. The king demanded loyalty from everyone, but most people knew only his representative, the local count. As the empire ceased to expand and was instead attacked by outsiders, the counts and other powerful regional rulers stopped looking to the king for new lands and offices and began to develop and exploit what they already had. They became powerful lords, commanding warriors and peasants, building castles, setting up markets, collecting revenues, and keeping the peace. A new warrior class of lords and **vassals** came to dominate post-Carolingian society.

Not all of Europe, however, came under the control of rural leaders. In northern and central Italy, where cities had never lost their importance, urban elites ruled over the surrounding countryside. Everywhere, kings retained a certain amount of power; in some places, such as Germany and England, they were extremely effective. Central European monarchies formed under the influence of Germany.* Nevertheless, throughout this period, it was local allegiances that mattered most to the societies of Europe.

Public Power and Private Relationships

Both kings and less powerful men commanded others by ensuring their personal loyalty. In the ninth century, the Carolingian kings had their *fideles,* "faithful men." Among these were the counts. In addition to a share in the revenues of their administrative district, the county, each count received benefices, later also called fiefs, which were temporary grants of land given in return for service. These short-term arrangements often became permanent when a count's son inherited the job and the fiefs of his father. By the end of the ninth century, fiefs could often be passed on to heirs.

In the wake of the invasions, more and more warriors were drawn into similar networks of dependency, but not with the king: they became the faithful men—the vassals—of local lords. From the Latin word for "fief" comes the word *feudal,* and some historians use the term *feudalism* to describe the social and economic system created by the relationship among vassals, lords, and fiefs.**

Medieval people often said that their society consisted of three groups: those who prayed, those who fought, and those who worked. Members of all these groups were involved in a hierarchy of dependency and linked by personal bonds, but the upper classes—the prayers (monks) and the fighters (knights)—were free. Their brand of dependency was prestigious, whether they were vassals, lords, or both. In fact, a typical warrior was lord of several vassals even while serving as the vassal of another lord. Monasteries normally had vassals to fight for them, and their abbots in turn were likely to be vassals of a king or other powerful lord.

Vassalage grew up as an alternative to public power and at the same time as a way to strengthen what little public power there was. Given the impoverished economic conditions of western Europe, its primitive methods of communication, and its lack of unifying traditions, kings relied on vassals who were personally loyal to them to muster troops, collect taxes, and administer justice. When in the ninth century the Carolingian Empire broke up politically and power fell into the hands of local lords, those lords, too, needed "faithful men" to protect them and carry

---

*Terms such as *Germany, France,* and *Italy* are used here for the sake of convenience. They refer to regions, not to the nation-states that would eventually become associated with those names.

**Many historians regard *feudalism* as a problematic term. Does it mean "anarchy"? Some historians have used it that way. Does it mean "a hierarchical scheme of lords and knights"? This is another common definition. And there are others as well. This imprecision has led some historians to drop the word altogether. Moreover, feudalism implies that one way of life dominated the Middle Ages, when in fact there were numerous social, political, and economic arrangements. For these reasons, *feudalism* rarely appears in *The Making of the West.*

out their orders. And vassals needed lords. At the low end of the social scale, poor vassals depended on their lords to feed, clothe, house, and arm them. They hoped that they would be rewarded for their service with a fief of their own, with which they could support themselves and a family. At the upper end of the social scale, vassals looked to lords to enrich them further.

Many upper-class laywomen participated in the society of fighters and prayers as wives and mothers of vassals and lords. A few women were themselves vassals, and some were lords (or, rather, ladies, the female counterpart). Other women entered convents and became members of the social group that prayed. Through its abbess, or a man standing in for her, a convent often had vassals as well. Many elite women engaged in property transactions, whether alone, with other family members, or as part of a group, such as a convent. (See "Taking Measure.")

Becoming a vassal involved both ritual gestures and verbal promises. In a ceremony witnessed by others, the vassal-to-be knelt and, placing his hands between the hands of his lord, said, "I promise to be your man." This act, known as homage, was followed by the promise of **fealty**—fidelity, trust, and service—which the vassal swore with his hand on a saint's relics or on a Bible. In many regions, the vassal and the lord kissed one another. In an age when many people could not read, a public ceremony such as this represented a visual and verbal contract. Vassalage bound the lord and vassal to one another with reciprocal obligations, usually military. Knights, as the premier fighters of the day, were the most desirable vassals.

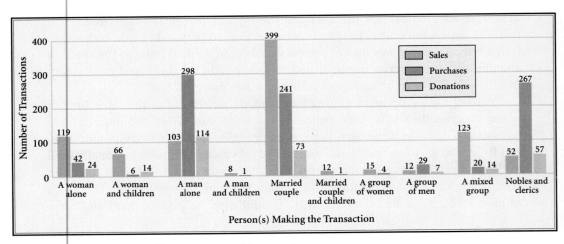

Taking Measure Sellers, Buyers, and Donors, 800–1000
How did ladies get their wealth, and what did they do with it? Two counties in northeastern Spain, Osona and Manresa, are particularly rich in documentation for the period 880–1000. We have 2,121 charters (legal documents) attesting to sales, purchases, and donations of land from this period. As the graph shows, few women purchased property, which suggests that they gained their land mainly through inheritance. As for what they did with it, by themselves they were more likely to sell property than men who were alone; as part of a married couple, they were often involved in sales. They were less likely than men to make donations, many of which went to churches or monasteries.

At the bottom of the social scale were those who worked—the peasants. In the Carolingian period, many peasants were free; they did not live on a manor, or if they did, they owed very little to its lord. But as power fell into the hands of local rulers, fewer and fewer peasants remained free. Rather, they were made dependent on lords, not as vassals but as **serfs**. Serfdom was a dependency separate from and completely unlike that of a vassal. Serfdom was not voluntary but inherited. No serf did homage or fealty to his lord; no serf kissed his lord as an equal. Vassals served their lords as warriors. Serfs worked as laborers on the land of their lord and paid him taxes and dues. Peasants constituted the majority of the population, but unlike knights, who were celebrated in song, they were barely noticed by the upper classes—except as a source of revenue. By the year 1000, though there were still some free peasants, many were serfs and therefore subject to a lord. Most important, they belonged to the land: when a lord sold a field to someone else, the serfs who cultivated that field got a new lord. They could not be sold apart from their land, but they were also not free to leave it.

New methods of cultivation and a slightly warmer climate helped transform the rural landscape, making it more productive and thus able to support a larger population. With a growing number of men and women to work the land, however, the lower classes now had more mouths to feed and faced the hardship of food shortages. Landlords began reorganizing their estates to run more efficiently. In the tenth century, the three-field system became more prevalent; heavy plows that could turn the heavy northern soils came into wider use; and horses (more effective than oxen) were harnessed to pull the plows. The result was surplus food and a better standard of living for nearly everyone.

In search of greater profits, some lords lightened the dues and services of peasants temporarily, giving them a chance to open up new lands by draining marshes and cutting down forests. Some landlords converted dues and labor services into money payments, a boon for both lords and peasants. Rather than receiving hens and eggs they might not need, lords now received money to spend on what they wanted. Peasants benefited as well because their taxes were fixed despite inflation. Thus, as the prices of their hens and eggs went up, they could sell them, reaping a profit in spite of the dues they owed their lords.

By the year 1000, many peasants lived in populous rural settlements, true villages. Surrounded by arable land, meadows, woods, and wasteland, villages developed a sense of community. Boundaries—sometimes real fortifications, sometimes simple markers—told nonresidents to keep out and to find shelter in huts located outside the village limits.

The church often formed the focal point of local activity. There people met, received the sacraments, drew up contracts, and buried their dead. Religious feasts and festivals joined the rituals of farming to mark the seasons. The church dominated the village in another way: men and women owed it a tax called a **tithe** (equivalent to one-tenth of their crops or income, paid in money or in kind), which was first instituted on a regular basis by the Carolingians.

Village peasants developed a sense of common purpose based on their interdependence, as they shared oxen or horses for the teams that pulled their village's plow or turned to village craftsmen to fix their wheels or shoe their horses. A sense of solidarity sometimes encouraged peasants to band together to ask for privileges as a group. Near Verona, in northern Italy, for example, twenty-five men living around the castle of Nogara in 920 joined together to ask their lord, the abbot of Nonantola, to allow them to lease plots of land, houses, and pasturage in return for a small yearly rent and the promise to defend the castle. The abbot granted their request.

Village solidarity could be compromised, however, by conflicting loyalties and obligations. A peasant in one village might very well have one piece of land connected with a certain manor and another bit of land on a different estate, and he or she might owe several lords different kinds of dues. Even peasants of one village working for one lord might owe him varied services and taxes for different pieces of land.

Obligations differed even more strikingly across the regions of Europe. The principal distinction was between free peasants—such as small landowners in Saxony and other parts of Germany, who had no lords—and serfs, who were especially common in France and England. In Italy, peasants ranged from small independent landowners to leaseholders (like the tenants at Nogara); most were both, owning a parcel in one place and leasing another nearby.

As the power of kings began to weaken, the system of peasant obligations became part of a larger system of local rule. When landlords consolidated their power over their manors, they collected not only dues and services but also fees for the use of their flour mills, bakehouses, and breweries. Some built castles—fortified strongholds—and imposed the even wider powers of the **ban**: the right to collect taxes, hear court cases, levy fines, and muster men for defense.

In France, for example, as the king's power waned, political control fell into the hands of counts and other princes. By the year 1000, castles had become the key to their power. In the south of France, power was so fragmented that each man who controlled a castle—a **castellan**—was a virtual ruler, although often with a very limited reach. In northwestern France, territorial princes, basing their rule on the control of many castles, dominated much broader regions. For example, Fulk Nera, count of Anjou (r. 987–1040), built more than thirteen castles and captured others from rival counts. By the end of his life, he controlled a region extending from Blois to Nantes along the Loire valley.

Castellans extended their authority by subjecting everyone near their castles to their bans. Peasants, whether they worked on a castellan's estates or not, had to pay him a variety of dues for his "protection" and judicial rights over them. Castellans also established links with wealthy landholders in the region, tempting or coercing them to become vassals. Lay castellans often supported local monasteries and controlled the appointment of local priests. But churchmen themselves sometimes held the position of territorial lord; a good example is the archbishop of Milan in the eleventh century.

The development of nearly independent local political units, dominated by a castle and controlled by a military elite, marks an important turning point in western Europe. Although this development did not occur everywhere simultaneously (and in some places it hardly occurred at all), the social, political, and cultural life of Europe was now dominated by landowners who saw themselves as military men and regional leaders.

Warriors and Warfare

Not all warriors were alike. At the top of this elite group were the kings, counts, and dukes. Below them, but on the rise, were the castellans; and still farther down the social scale were knights.

Nevertheless, they all shared a common lifestyle. High astride their horses, wearing shirts of chain mail and helmets of flat metal plates riveted together, knights and those above them marked a military revolution—a shift from a reliance on foot soldiers to a focus on cavalry. The war season started in May, when the grasses were high enough for horses to forage. Horseshoes allowed armies to move faster than ever before and to negotiate rough terrain previously unsuitable for battle. Stirrups, probably invented by Asiatic nomadic tribes, allowed the mounted warrior to hold his seat. This made it possible for knights to thrust at the enemy with heavy lances; the light javelin of ancient warfare was abandoned.

Lords and their vassals often lived together. In the lord's great hall they ate, enjoyed listening to music, songs, and stories, and bedded down for the night. They went out hunting together and went off to the battlefield as a group as well. More powerful vassals—counts, for example—lived on their own fiefs and hardly ever saw their lord (probably the king), except when doing homage and fealty—once during their lifetimes—or

Two Cities Besieged
In about 900, the monks of the monastery of St. Gall, in what is today Switzerland, produced a Psalter with numerous illuminations. The illustration for Psalm 59, which tells of King David's victories, used four pages. This page was the fourth. On the top level, David's army besieges a fortified city from two directions. On the right are foot soldiers, one of whom holds a burning torch to set the city afire. On the left are horsemen—led by their standard-bearer—with lances and bows and arrows. Within the city, four soldiers protect themselves with shields, while four other men seem to be cowering behind the city. In the bottom register, a different city burns fiercely (note the towers on fire). This city lacks defenders; the people within it are unarmed. Although this illumination purports to show David's victories, in fact it nicely represents the equipment and strategies of ninth-century warfare.
(Stiftsbibliothek St. Gallen, Switzerland.)

serving him in battle, for perhaps forty days a year. They themselves were lords of knightly vassals who were not married and who lived, ate, and hunted with them.

No matter how old they might be, unmarried knights who lived with their lords were called youths by their contemporaries. Such perpetual bachelors were something new, the result of a profound transformation in the organization of families and inheritance. Before the eleventh century, noble families recognized all their children as heirs and divided their estates accordingly. In the mid-ninth century, for example, one count and his wife willed their large estates, scattered from Belgium to Italy, to their four sons and three daughters. (True, they gave the boys far more than the girls, and the oldest boy far more than the others.)

By around the year 1000, French nobles, adapting to diminished opportunities for land and office and wary of fragmenting the estates they had, changed both the conception of the family and the way property passed to the next generation. Recognizing the overriding claims of one son, often the eldest, they handed down their entire inheritance to him. (In cases where the heir is indeed the eldest son, this system of inheritance is called primogeniture.) The heir, in turn, traced his lineage only through the male line, backward through his father and forward through his own eldest son. Such patrilineal families left many younger sons without an inheritance and therefore without the prospect of marrying and founding families. Instead, younger sons lived at the courts of the great as "youths," or they joined the church as clerics or monks. The development of territorial rule and patrilineal families went hand in hand, as fathers passed down to one son not only manors but titles, castles, and the authority of the ban.

Patrilineal inheritance tended to bypass daughters and so tended to work against the interests of aristocratic women. In families without sons, however, widows and daughters did inherit property. Wives often acted as lords of estates when their husbands were at war. Moreover, all aristocratic women played an important role in this warrior society, whether in the monastery (where they prayed for the souls of their families) or through their marriages (where they helped forge alliances between their own and their husbands' families).

Highly militarized, post-Carolingian society was almost constantly at war. Warfare benefited territorial rulers in the short term, but in the long run their revenues suffered, as armies plundered the countryside and sacked walled cities. Bishops, who were themselves from the class of lords and warriors, worried about the dangers to church property. Peasants cried out against wars that destroyed their crops or forced them to join regional infantries. Monks and religious thinkers were appalled at violence that was not in the service of an anointed king. By the end of the tenth century, all classes clamored for peace.

Sentiments against local violence came together in a movement called the **Peace of God**, which began in the south of France and by 1050 had spread over a wide region. Meetings of bishops, counts, and lords, and often crowds of lower-class men and women, set forth the provisions of this peace. "No man in the counties or bishoprics shall seize a horse, colt, ox, cow, ass, or the burdens which it carries. . . . No one shall seize a peasant, man or woman," ran the decree of one council held in 990. Anyone who violated this peace was to be excommunicated: cut off from the community of the faithful, denied the services of the church and the hope of salvation.

The peace proclaimed at local councils like this limited some violence but did not address the problem of conflict between armed men. A second set of agreements, the Truce of God, soon supplemented the Peace of God. The truce prohibited fighting between warriors at certain times: on Sunday because it was the Lord's Day, on Saturday because it was a reminder of Holy Saturday, on Friday because it symbolized Good Friday, and on Thursday because it stood for Holy Thursday. Enforcement of the truce fell to the local knights and nobles, who swore over saints' relics to uphold it and to fight anyone who broke it.

The Peace of God and Truce of God were only two of the ways in which men and women contained and defused violent confrontations in the tenth and eleventh centuries. At times, lords and their vassals mediated wars and feuds in assemblies called *placita*. In other instances, monks or laymen tried to find solutions to disputes that would leave the honor of both parties intact. Rather than try to establish guilt or innocence, winners or losers, these methods of adjudication often resulted in compromises on both sides.

Political Communities in Italy, England, and France

The political systems that emerged in the wake of the breakup of the Carolingian Empire were as varied as the regions of Europe. In Italy, cities were the centers of power, still reflecting, though feebly, the political organization of ancient Rome. In England, strong kings came to the fore. In France, as we have seen, great lords dominated the countryside; there the king was relatively weak.

Whereas in France great landlords built their castles in the countryside, in northern and central Italy they often constructed their family seats within the walls of cities. Churches, often as many as fifty or sixty, also were built within city walls, the proud work of rich laypeople or bishops. From their perches within the cities, the great landholders of Italy, both lay and religious, dominated the countryside. Italian cities also functioned as important marketplaces. Peasants sold their surplus goods there; artisans and merchants lived within the walls; foreign traders offered their wares there. These members of the lower classes were supported by the noble rich, who in Italy even more than elsewhere depended on cash to satisfy their desires. In the course of the ninth and tenth centuries, both servile and free tenants became renters who paid in currency.

Social and political life in Italy favored a familial organization somewhat different from the patrilineal families of France. To prevent the partitioning of their properties among heirs, families organized themselves by formal contract into *consorteria,* in which all male members shared the profits of the family's inheritance and all women were excluded. The consorterial family was like a blood-related corporation, a social unit on which early Italian businesses and banks would later be modeled.

Whereas Italy was urban, England was rural. In the face of the Viking invasions in England, King Alfred of Wessex (r. 871–899) developed new mechanisms of royal government, instituting reforms that his successors continued. He fortified settlements throughout Wessex and divided the army into two parts. The duty of one was to defend the fortifications (or *burhs*); the other operated as a mobile unit. Alfred also started a navy. These military innovations cost money, and the assessments fell on peasants' holdings.

Alfred sought to strengthen his kingdom's religious integrity as well as its regional fortifications. In the ninth century, people interpreted invasions as God's punishment for their sins. Alfred began a program of religious reform and renewal by bringing scholars to his court to write and to educate others. Above all, Alfred wanted to translate key religious works from Latin into Anglo-Saxon. He was determined to "turn into the language that we can all understand certain books which are the most necessary for all men to know." Alfred and scholars under his guidance translated works by church fathers such as Gregory the Great and St. Augustine. Even the Psalms, until now sung only in Hebrew, Greek, and Latin, were rendered into Anglo-Saxon. In most of ninth- and tenth-century Europe, Latin remained the language of scholarship and writing, separate from the language people spoke. In England, however, the vernacular—the common spoken language—was also a literary language. With Alfred's work giving it greater legitimacy, Anglo-Saxon came to be used alongside Latin for both literature and royal administration.

Alfred's reforms strengthened not only defense, education, and religion but also royal power. He consolidated his control over Wessex and fought the Danish kings, who by the mid-870s had taken Northumbria, northeastern Mercia, and East Anglia. Eventually, as he fought the Danes who were pushing south and west, he was recognized as king of all the English not under Danish rule. He issued a law code, the first by an English king since 695. Unlike earlier codes, drawn up for each separate kingdom of England, Alfred's laws were drawn from and intended for all the English kingdoms. In this way, Alfred became the first king of all the English.

Alfred's successors rolled back Danish rule in England. "Then the Norsemen departed in their nailed ships, bloodstained survivors of spears," wrote one poet about a battle the Vikings lost in 937. But many Vikings remained. Converted to Christianity, their great men joined Anglo-Saxons

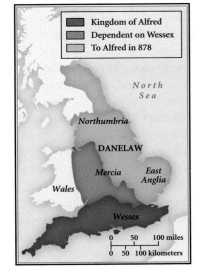

England in the Age of King Alfred, 871–899

in attending the English king at court. As peace returned, new administrative subdivisions—shires (counties) and hundreds (districts)—were established throughout England for judicial and taxation purposes. The powerful men of the kingdom swore fealty to the king, promising to be enemies of his enemies, friends of his friends. England was united and organized to support a strong ruler.

Alfred's grandson Edgar (r. c. 959–975) commanded all the possibilities early medieval kingship offered. He was the sworn lord of all the great men of the kingdom. He controlled appointments to the English church and sponsored monastic reform. In 973, following the continental fashion, he was anointed. The fortifications of the kingdom were in his hands, as was the army, and he took responsibility for keeping the peace by proclaiming certain crimes—arson and theft—to be under his special jurisdiction and mobilizing the machinery of the shire and the hundred to find and punish thieves.

Despite its apparent centralization, England was not a unified state in the modern sense, and the king's control was often weak. Many royal officials were great landowners who (as on the continent) worked for the king because doing so was in their best interest. When it was not, they allied with different claimants to the throne. This political fragility may have helped the Danish king Cnut (or Canute) to conquer England. As king of England from 1017 to 1035, Cnut reinforced the already strong connections between England and Scandinavia while keeping intact much of the administrative, ecclesiastical, and military apparatus already established in England by the Anglo-Saxons (Map 8.4, page 291). By Cnut's time Scandinavian traditions had largely merged with those of the rest of Europe, and the Vikings were no longer an alien culture.

French kings had a harder time than the English coping with the invasions because their realm was much larger. They had no chance to build up their defenses slowly from one powerful base. During most of the tenth century, Carolingian kings alternated on the throne with kings from another family. As the Carolingian dynasty waned, the most powerful men of the kingdom—dukes, counts, and important bishops—at last came together to elect as king Hugh Capet (r. 987–996), a lord of considerable prestige yet relatively little power. His election marked the end of Carolingian rule and the beginning of the new **Capetian dynasty**, which would hand down the royal title from father to son until the fourteenth century.

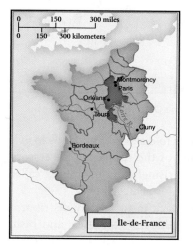

The Kingdom of the Franks under Hugh Capet, 987–996

In the eleventh century, the reach of the Capetian kings was limited by territorial lordships in the vicinity. The king's scattered but substantial estates lay in the north of France, in the region around Paris—the Île-de-France (literally, "island of France"). His castles and his vassals were there. Independent castellans, however, controlled areas nearby. In the sense that he was a neighbor of castellans and not much more powerful militarily than they, the king of the Franks—who would only later take the territorial title "king of France"—was just another local strongman. Yet the Capetian kings enjoyed considerable prestige. They were anointed with holy oil, and they represented the idea of unity inherited from Charlemagne. Most of the counts, at least in the north of France, became their vassals. They did not promise to obey the king, but they did vow not to try to kill or depose him.

Emperors and Kings in Central and Eastern Europe

In contrast with the development of territorial lordships in France, Germany's fragmentation hardly began before it was reversed. Five duchies (regions ruled by dukes) emerged in Germany in the late Carolingian period, each much larger than the counties and castellanies of France. With the death in 911 of the last Carolingian king in Germany, Louis the Child, the dukes elected one of themselves as king over all. Then, as the Magyar invasions increased, the dukes gave the royal title to the powerful duke of Saxony, Henry I (r. 919–936), who proceeded to set up fortifications and reorganize his army, crowning his efforts with a major defeat of a Magyar army in 933. Otto I (r. 936–973), the son of Henry I, was an even greater military hero. His defeat of the Magyar forces in 955 gave him prestige and helped solidify his dynasty. In 951, he marched into Italy and took the Lombard crown. Against the Slavs, with whom the Germans shared a border, Otto set up marches (military buffers) from which he could make expeditions and hold off counterattacks. After the pope crowned him emperor in 962, he claimed the Middle Kingdom carved out by the Treaty of Verdun and cast himself as the agent of Roman imperial renewal.

The Ottonian Empire, 936–1002

Otto's victories brought tribute, plunder, plum positions to disburse, and lands to give away, ensuring him a following among the great men of the realm. His successors, Otto II (r. 961–983), Otto III (r. 983–1002)—not surprisingly, the dynasty is called the "Ottonian"—and Henry II (r. 1002–1024), built on his achievements.

Granted power by the magnates, the kings gave back in turn: they distributed lands and appointed their aristocratic supporters to duchies, counties, and bishoprics. Always, however, their decisions were tempered by hereditary claims and plenty of lobbying by influential men at court and at the great assemblies that met with the king to hammer out policies. The role of kings in appointing bishops and archbishops was particularly important because bishoprics, unlike counties and duchies, could not be inherited. Otto I created new eastern bishoprics, endowing them with extensive lands and subjecting the local peasantry to their overlordship.

Otto III Receiving Gifts
This triumphal image is from a book of Gospels made for Otto III (r. 983–1002). The crowned women on the left are personifications of the four parts of Otto's empire: Sclavinia (the Slavic lands), Germania (Germany), Gallia (Gaul), and Roma (Rome). Each holds a gift in tribute and homage to the emperor, who sits on a throne holding the symbols of his power (an orb and scepter). He is flanked by representatives of the church (on his right) and the army (on his left). Why do you suppose the artist separated the image of the emperor from that of the women? What does the body language of the women tell you about the relations that Otto wanted to portray between himself and the parts of his empire? Can you relate this manuscript, which was made in 997–1000, to Otto's conquest over the Slavs in 997? (Bayerische Staatsbibliothek, Munich.)

In some areas of Germany, bishops gained the power of the ban: they collected revenues, took over the rights of justice, and called men to arms. Answering to the king and furnishing him with troops, the bishops became royal officials while also carrying out their pastoral and religious duties. German kings claimed the right to select bishops (usually with the consent of the cathedral clergy) and to "invest" them by participating in the ceremony that installed them in office. Bishops and archbishops joined the king at court: many had been schooled there in their youth, while in their more mature years, they taught new young clergy as well as princes and noblewomen.

Like all the strong rulers of the day, whether in Europe or in the Byzantine and Islamic worlds, the Ottonians presided over a renaissance of learning. For example, the tutor of Otto III was Gerbert (later Pope Sylvester II), the best-educated man of his time. Gerbert knew how to calculate with Arabic numerals. He spent "large sums of money to pay copyists and to acquire [books]," as he put it. He studied the classics as models of rhetoric and argument, and he reveled in logic and debate. Not only did churchmen and kings support Ottonian scholarship, but to an unprecedented extent noblewomen in Germany also acquired an education and participated in the intellectual revival. Aristocratic women spent much of their wealth on learning. Living at home with their kinsfolk and servants or in convents that provided them with comfortable private apartments, noblewomen studied and wrote books. They also supported other artists and scholars.

The German kings' policies played a crucial role in the political communities on Germany's eastern border. Hand in hand with the papacy, the Ottonians fostered the emergence of Christian monarchies aligned with the Roman church in the regions that today constitute the Czech and Slovak republics, Poland, and Hungary. The Czechs, who lived in the region of Bohemia, converted under the rule of Václav (r. 920–929), who thereby gained recognition in Germany as the duke of Bohemia. He and his successors did not become kings, remaining politically within the German sphere. Václav's murder by his younger brother made him a martyr and the patron saint of Bohemia, a symbol around which later movements for independence rallied.

The Poles gained a greater measure of independence than the Czechs. In 966, Mieszko I (r. 963–992), the leader of the Slavic tribe known as the Polanians, accepted baptism to head off the attacks that the Germans were already mounting against pagan Slavic peoples along the Baltic coast and east of the Elbe River. Busily engaged in bringing the other Slavic tribes of Poland under his control, he skillfully shifted his alliances with various German princes to suit his needs. In 991, Mieszko placed his realm under the protection of the pope, establishing a tradition of Polish loyalty to the Roman church. Mieszko's son Boleslaw the Brave (r. 992–1025) greatly extended Poland's boundaries, at one time or another ruling from the Bohemian border to Kiev. In 1000, he gained a royal crown with papal blessing.

Hungary's case was similar to that of Poland. The Magyars settled in the region known today as Hungary. They became landowners, using the native Slavs to till the soil. At the end of the tenth century, the Magyar ruler Stephen I (r. 997–1038) accepted Christianity. In return, German knights and monks helped him consolidate his power and convert his people. According to legend, the crown placed on Stephen's head in 1000 or 1001, like Boleslaw's crown, was sent to him by the pope. To this day, the crown of St. Stephen remains the most hallowed symbol of Hungarian nationhood.

Symbols of rulership such as crowns, consecrated by Christian priests and accorded a prestige almost akin to saints' relics, were among the most vital institutions of royal rule in central Europe. The economic basis for the power of central European rulers gradually shifted from slave raids to agriculture. This change encouraged a proliferation of regional centers of power that challenged monarchical rule. From the eleventh century onward, all the medieval Slavic states would face a constant problem of internal division.

REVIEW After the dissolution of the Carolingian Empire, what political systems developed in western, northern, eastern, and central Europe, and how did these systems differ from one another?

Conclusion

In 800, the model of the Roman Empire was still powerful: whether in Europe, at Byzantium, or in the Islamic world, political systems were centralized, monarchical, and imperial. Byzantine emperors writing their learned books, Abbasid caliphs holding court in their resplendent new palace at Baghdad, and Carolingian emperors issuing their directives for reform to the missi dominici all mimicked the Roman

Mapping the West Europe and the Mediterranean, c. 1050
"The Empire" here refers to the area ruled by the Ottonian emperors. But the clear borders and distinct colors of the "states" on this map distort an essential truth: none of them had centralized governments that controlled whole territories, as in modern states. Instead, there were numerous regional rulers within each, and there were numerous overlapping claims of jurisdiction. The next centuries would show both the weaknesses and the surprising strengths of this fragmentation.

emperors. Yet these rulers confronted tensions and regional pressures that tended to decentralize political power. Byzantium felt this fragmentation least, yet even there the emergence of a new elite led to decentralization and the emperor's loss of control over the countryside. In the Islamic world, economic crisis, religious tension, and the ambitions of powerful local rulers decisively weakened the caliphate and opened the way to separate successor states. In western Europe, powerful independent landowners strove with greater or lesser success (depending on the region) to establish themselves as effective rulers. By 1050, the states that would become those of modern Europe began to form.

Local conditions determined political and economic organizations. Between 900 and 1000, for example, French society was transformed by the development of territorial lordships, patrilineal families, and ties of vassalage. These factors figured less prominently in Germany, where a central monarchy remained, buttressed by churchmen and conquests to the east. We shall see in the next chapter, however, how fragile this centralization was to be.

CHAPTER REVIEW QUESTIONS

1. How were the Byzantine, Islamic, and European economies similar? How did they differ? How did these economies interact?
2. Compare the effects of the barbarian invasions into the Roman Empire with the effects of the Viking, Muslim, and Magyar invasions into the Carolingian Empire.

For practice quizzes and other study tools, see the Online Study Guide at bedfordstmartins.com/huntconcise.

For primary-source material from this period, see Chapter 9 of *Sources of THE MAKING OF THE WEST,* Third Edition.

TIMELINE

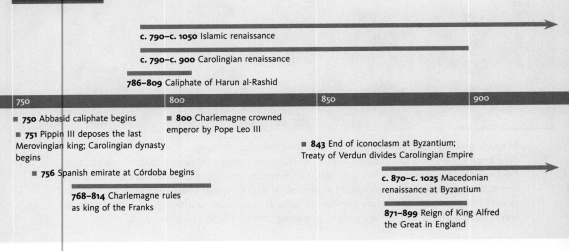

c. 790–c. 1050 Islamic renaissance

c. 790–c. 900 Carolingian renaissance

786–809 Caliphate of Harun al-Rashid

750	800	850	900

■ **750** Abbasid caliphate begins

■ **751** Pippin III deposes the last Merovingian king; Carolingian dynasty begins

■ **756** Spanish emirate at Córdoba begins

768–814 Charlemagne rules as king of the Franks

■ **800** Charlemagne crowned emperor by Pope Leo III

■ **843** End of iconoclasm at Byzantium; Treaty of Verdun divides Carolingian Empire

c. **870–c. 1025** Macedonian renaissance at Byzantium

871–899 Reign of King Alfred the Great in England

Suggested References

Excellent recent biographies allow for interesting comparisons of rulers: Becher's *Charlemagne*, Cooperson's *al-Ma'mun* (an important Abbasid caliph), and Nelson's *Charles the Bald*. Many primary sources for the Carolingian period are translated by Paul Dutton. Political disintegration used to be seen as a bad thing, but recent historians, such as Duby and Head and Landes, value the diversity and local developments that it permitted.

Becher, Matthias. *Charlemagne*. 2003.

Byzantine art: http://historylink101.com/lessons/art_history_lessons/ma/byzantine_art.htm

Cooperson, Michael. *Al-Ma'mun*. 2005.

Duby, Georges. *The Early Growth of the European Economy: Warriors and Peasants from the Seventh to the Twelfth Century*. Trans. H. B. Clark. 1974.

*Dutton, Paul Edward. *Carolingian Civilization: A Reader*. 2d ed. 2004.

Franklin, Simon, and Jonathan Shepard. *The Emergence of Rus, 750–1200*. 1996.

Garland, Lynda. *Byzantine Empresses: Women and Power in Byzantium, A.D. 527–1204*. 1999.

Head, Thomas, and Richard Landes, eds. *The Peace of God: Social Violence and Religious Response in France around the Year 1000*. 1992.

McCormick, Michael. *Origins of the European Economy: Communications and Commerce, A.D. 300–900*. 2001.

Moore, R. I. *The First European Revolution, c. 970–1215*. 2000.

Nelson, Janet. *Charles the Bald*. 1987.

*Psellus, Michael. *Fourteen Byzantine Rulers: The Chronographia*. Trans. E. R. A. Sewter. 1966.

955 Otto I defeats Magyars   **c. 1000** Beginning of age of the castellans in France

| 950 | 1000 | 1050 | 1100 |

963–1025 Reign of Byzantine emperor Basil II ("the Bulgar-Slayer")

969–1171 Fatimid dynasty in Egypt

The Flowering of the Middle Ages

I N THE MIDDLE OF THE TWELFTH CENTURY, a sculptor was hired to add friezes depicting scenes from the Old and New Testaments to the facade of the grand new hilltop cathedral at Lincoln, England. He portrayed in striking fashion the deaths of the poor man Lazarus and the rich man Dives. Their fates could not have been more different. While Lazarus was carried to heaven by two angels, a contented-looking devil poked Dives and two other rich men straight into the mouth of hell—headfirst.

Dives and Lazarus
At the time this sculpted depiction of the rich man Dives (bottom) and the poor man Lazarus (top) was made, the town of Lincoln was expanding both within and outside its Roman walls. Within the walls were the precincts of the fishmongers, the grain sellers, and the poultry merchants. Outside the walls were the bakers, the soapmakers, and the salt sellers. The town was highly attuned to moneymaking—both its pleasures and its dangers. *(Conway Library, Courtauld Institute of Art, London.)*

The sculptor's work reflected a widespread change in attitudes toward money. In the Carolingian and post-Carolingian period, wealth was considered, in general, a very good thing. Rich kings were praised for their generosity, sumptuous manuscripts were highly prized, and splendid churches like Charlemagne's chapel at Aachen were widely admired. This view changed over the course of the eleventh century. A new money economy, burgeoning cities, and the growth of a well-heeled merchant and trading class led many observers to condemn wealth and to emphasize its corrupting influence. Even participants in the new economy shared this perspective: Lincoln's new cathedral was built right next to a marketplace, and its twelfth-century bishops—who were themselves rich men—wanted to warn moneymaking parishioners about the perils of wealth.

The most salient feature of the period 1050–1200 was increasing wealth. Cities, trade, and agricultural production swelled. The resulting worldliness met with a wide variety of responses. Some people tried to flee the new commercial society; others tried to reform it; and still others embraced, enjoyed, or tried to

understand it. Within one century, the development of a profit economy transformed western European communities. Many villages and fortifications became
cities where traders, merchants, and artisans conducted business. Although most
people still lived in less populated, rural areas, their lives were touched in many
ways by the new cash economy. Economic concerns drove changes within the
church, where a movement for reform gathered steam. Money helped redefine the
role of the clergy, while popes, kings, and princes came to exercise new forms of
power. At the same time, city dwellers began to demand their own governments.
Monks, nuns, and clerics reformulated the nature of their communities, seeking
newly intense spiritual lives. All of these developments inspired (and in turn were
inspired by) new ideas, new forms of scholarship, and new methods of inquiry.
The rapid pace of religious, political, and economic change was matched by new
developments in thought, learning, and artistic expression.

CHAPTER FOCUS QUESTION   How important
was the new commercial economy to church
reform, centralizing monarchies, and new forms
of scholarship and piety?

The Commercial Revolution

As the population of Europe expanded in the eleventh century, cities, long-distance
trade networks, local markets, and new business arrangements meshed to create a
profit-based economy. With improvements in agriculture and more land in cultivation, the great estates of the eleventh century produced surpluses that helped feed,
and therefore made possible, a new urban population. The result was the **commercial
revolution** of the Middle Ages. It produced the institutions that would be the direct
ancestors of modern business and commerce.

Centers of Commerce and Commercial Life

New commercial centers developed around castles and monasteries and within the
walls of ancient towns. Great lords in the countryside—including monasteries—were
eager to take advantage of the profits generated by their estates. In the late tenth
century, they had reorganized their lands for greater productivity, encouraged their
peasants to cultivate new land, and converted services and dues to money payments.
Now with ready cash, they not only fostered the development of fairs—temporary
markets where they and their peasants could sell their surpluses and buy other
goods—but also encouraged traders and craftspeople to settle down near them. The
lords gained at each step: their purchases brought them an enhanced lifestyle and
greater prestige, while they charged merchants tolls and sales taxes, which yielded
even greater profits from trade. Sometimes markets formed just outside the walls
of older cities; these gradually merged into new and enlarged urban communities
as town walls were built around them to protect the inhabitants. At other times

informal country markets came to be housed in permanent structures. Along the Rhine and in other river valleys, cities sprang up to service the merchants who traversed the route between Italy and the north (Map 9.1).

By the mid-twelfth century rural life was increasingly organized for the marketplace in many regions of western Europe. This opened up opportunities for both peasants and lords, but it also burdened some with unwelcome obligations. Great lords hired trained, literate agents to administer their estates, calculate profits and

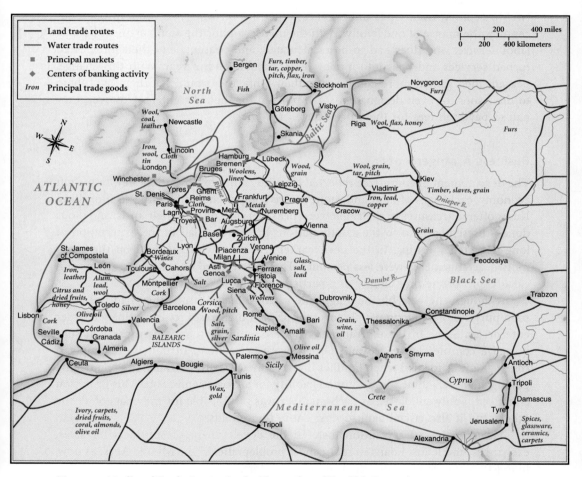

Map 9.1 Medieval Trade Routes in the Eleventh and Twelfth Centuries
In the medieval world, bulk goods from the north (furs, fish, and wood) were traded for luxury goods from the south (ivory, spices, olive oil, and ceramics). Already regions were beginning to specialize. England, for example, supplied raw wool, and Flanders (Ypres, Ghent) specialized in turning that wool into cloth and shipping it to the fairs of Champagne (whose capital was Troyes) or Germany. Italian cities channeled goods from the Muslim and Byzantine worlds northward and exported European goods southward and eastward.

losses, and make marketing decisions. Some offered special privileges to peasants who would do the backbreaking work of plowing marginal land. In Flanders, where land was regularly inundated by seawater, the great monasteries sponsored drainage projects, and newly dug canals linking the cities to the agricultural regions let boats ply the waters to nearly every nook and cranny of the region.

The new initiatives supported an increasing population. On old estates the rise in population strained the manse organization that had developed in Carolingian Europe, where each household was settled on the land that supported it. In the twelfth century, twenty peasant families might live on what had been, in the tenth century, the manse of one family. With the manse supporting so many more people, labor services and dues had to be recalculated, and peasants and their lords often turned services and dues into money rents, payable once a year. With this change, peasant men gained more control over their plots: they could sell them, will them to their sons, or even designate a small portion for their daughters. However, they had to pay high fees for these privileges.

Business Arrangements

The development of commerce reflected changing attitudes toward money. In the gift economy, exchanges of land and money were components of ongoing relationships. Kings offered treasures to their followers, peasants gave dues to their lords, and pious donors presented land to the saintly patrons of churches, all in the expectation of long-term relationships. In the new market economy, which thrived on the profit motive, arrangements were less personal. They often relied on written contracts and calculations of the profitability of a particular business venture.

Although the new business agreements took many forms, they had the common purpose of bringing people together to pool their resources and finance larger enterprises. Some of these arrangements were temporary, such as those that supported a commercial sea voyage. Others were permanent. In Italy, for example, a *compagnia* was formed when families invested their wealth in trade. The compagnia gave its members joint and unlimited liability for all losses and debts. This provision enhanced family solidarity, as each member was responsible for the debts of all the others; but it also risked bankrupting entire households.

The commercial revolution fostered the development of contracts for sales, exchanges, and loans. Loans were the most problematic. In the Middle Ages, as now, interest payments were the chief inducement for an investor to supply money. To circumvent the church's ban on usury (profiting from loans), interest was often disguised in contracts as a penalty for "late payment." The new willingness to finance business enterprises with loans signaled a changed attitude toward credit: risk was acceptable if it brought profit.

Contracts and partnerships were just two of the ways in which money resources were pooled to make large-scale productive enterprises and new industries possible. In fact, light industry began in the eleventh century. One of the earliest products to benefit from new industrial technologies was cloth. Water mills powered machines such as flails to clean and thicken cloth and presses to extract oil from fibers. Machines were also used to exploit raw materials more efficiently: new deep-mining technology provided Europeans with hitherto untapped sources of metals. At the same time, forging techniques improved, and iron was for the first time regularly used for agricultural tools and plows. This in turn made for better farming, and better farming fed the commercial revolution. Metals were also used for weapons, armor, and coins.

Whether fashioned by machines or handworkers, products relied on the expertise of artisans able to finish the cloth, mint the coins, and forge the weapons. To regulate and protect their products and trades, craftspeople and others involved in commerce formed **guilds**—local social, religious, and economic associations whose members plied the same trades. By the late twelfth century, guilds had become corporations defined by statutes and rules. They controlled their membership and determined dues, working hours, wages, and standards for materials and products. Producing wool cloth involved numerous guilds—shearers, weavers, fullers (people who beat the cloth to make it bulkier), and dyers. These guilds generally worked under the supervision of the merchant guild that imported the raw wool. Some guilds were more prestigious than others; in Florence, for example, professional guilds of notaries and judges ranked above craft guilds.

Within each guild of artisans or merchants existed another kind of hierarchy. Apprentices were at the bottom, journeymen and (less often) journeywomen (journey being a term for workers paid by the day) in the middle, and masters at the top. Apprentices were boys and occasionally girls placed under the tutelage of a master for a number of years to learn a trade. Once trained, the apprentice became a simple day laborer working for a wage. Journeywomen earned far less than journeymen and were active in fewer trades. Even the men's careers were precarious; only a few of them would become masters—the ones who dominated the offices and policies of the guild, hired the day laborers, and recruited and educated the apprentices.

Rural labor was not organized into guilds. But here, too, work was transformed by the commercial revolution. The most important change was in the work that women did. Formerly occupied with grinding grain, women gradually found

Comb for Wool
This stout wooden comb, which was used in the first half of the eleventh century to remove the tangles in raw wool, had two sets of teeth. (Collection Musée dauphinois [inv.90.14.81], Grenoble—France.)

this task taken over by water- and animal-powered mills. Instead, women turned to spinning, producing the wool threads that were then used by male weavers operating heavy looms in the towns.

Self-Government for the Towns

Guilds were one way townspeople expressed their mutual concerns and harnessed their collective energies. Movements for self-government were another. Townspeople banded together for protection and freedom.

Both to themselves and to outsiders, townspeople seemed different. Tradespeople, artisans, ship captains, innkeepers, and money changers did not fit into the old categories of medieval types—those who pray, those who fight, and those who work. Just knowing they were different gave townspeople a sense of solidarity with one another. But practical reasons also contributed to their feeling of common purpose: they lived in close quarters with one another, and they shared a mutual interest in reliable coinage, laws to facilitate commerce, freedom from servile dues and services, and independence to buy and sell as the market dictated. Already in the early twelfth century, the king of England granted to the citizens of Newcastle-upon-Tyne the privilege that any unfree peasant who lived there unclaimed by his lord for a year and a day would thereafter be a free person. To townspeople, freedom meant having their own officials and law courts. They petitioned the political powers that ruled them—bishops, kings, counts, castellans—for the right to govern themselves. Often they formed **communes**, sworn associations of townspeople that generally cut across the boundaries of rich and poor, merchants and craftspeople, clergy and laity.

Collective movements for urban self-government emerged especially in Italy, France, and Germany. Italian cities were centers of regional political power even before the commercial revolution. Castellans constructed their fortifications in the cities, and bishops ruled the countryside from behind city walls. The commercial revolution swelled Italian cities with tradespeople, whose interest in self-government was often fueled by religious as well as economic concerns. At Milan in the second half of the eleventh century, popular discontent with the archbishop, who effectively ruled the city, led to numerous armed clashes. In 1097, the Milanese succeeded in transferring political power from the archbishop and his clergy to a government of leading men of the city who called themselves consuls. The title recalled the government of the ancient Roman republic, affirming the consuls' status as representatives of the people. Like the archbishops' power before, the consuls' rule extended beyond the town walls into the *contado,* the outlying countryside.

Outside Italy, movements for city independence took place within the framework of larger kingdoms or principalities. Such movements were sometimes violent, as at Milan, but at other times they were peaceful. For example, William Clito, who claimed the county of Flanders (today in Belgium), willingly granted the citizens of Saint-Omer the rights they asked for in 1127 in return for their support of his claims. He recognized them as legally free, gave them the right to mint coins, allowed them their own laws and courts, and lifted certain tolls and taxes.

REVIEW   What new professions and institutions arose as a result of the commercial revolution?

Church Reform and Its Aftermath

The commercial revolution affected the church. Bishops ruled over many cities. Kings appointed many bishops. Local lords installed priests in their parish churches. Churchmen gave gifts and money to these secular powers for their offices. Now, with the commercial revolution sensitizing them to the crasser uses of money, some people took offense at this mingling of sacred and secular. The impulse to "free the church from the world" was as old as the origins of monasticism, but beginning in the tenth century and more insistently in the eleventh, reformers demanded that the church as a whole remodel itself and become free of secular entanglements.

This freedom was from the start as much a matter of power as of religion. Most people had long believed that their ruler—whether king, duke, count, or castellan—reigned by the grace of God and had the right to control the churches in his territory. But by the second half of the eleventh century, more and more people saw a great deal wrong with secular power over the church. They looked to the papacy to lead the movement of church reform. The most important moment came in 1075, when Pope Gregory VII called on King Henry IV, who claimed rulership in both Germany and Italy, to end his appointment of churchmen. This demand brought about a major civil war in Germany and a great upheaval in the distribution of power everywhere. By the early 1100s, a reformed church, with the pope at its head, had become institutionalized, penetrating into areas of life never before touched by churchmen. Church reform began as a way to free the church from the world, but in the end the church was equally involved in the new world it had helped to create.

Beginnings of the Reform Movement

The idea of freeing the church from the world began in the tenth century with no particular program and only a vague idea of what it might mean. At the Benedictine monastery of Cluny, for example, which was founded in 910, there was no organized program of reform. Nevertheless, the founders of the monastery, the duke and duchess of Aquitaine, wanted to "free" it from the world. They achieved this goal by endowing the monastery with property but then giving it and its worldly possessions to St. Peter and St. Paul. In this way, they put control of the monastery into the hands of the two most powerful heavenly saints. They designated the pope, as the successor of St. Peter, to be the monastery's worldly protector if anyone should bother or threaten it. The whole notion of "freedom" at this point was very vague. But Cluny's prestige was great because of its status as St. Peter's property and because of the elaborate round of prayers that its monks carried out with scrupulous devotion.

The Cluniac monks fulfilled the role of "those who pray" in a way that dazzled their contemporaries. Through their prayers they seemed to guarantee the salvation of all Christians. Rulers, bishops, rich landowners, and even serfs (if they could) gave Cluny donations of land, joining their contributions to the land of St. Peter. Powerful men and women called on the Cluniac monks to reform new monasteries along the Cluniac model.

The abbots of Cluny came to see themselves as reformers of the world as well. They believed in clerical celibacy, preaching against the prevailing norm that let parish priests and even bishops marry. They also thought that the laity could be reformed, become more virtuous, and cease their oppression of the poor. In the eleventh century, the Cluniacs began to link their program of internal monastic and external worldly reform to the papacy. They asked the popes to help them when Cluniac lands were encroached upon by bishops and laypeople at the same time as the papacy itself was becoming interested in reform.

Around the time when the Cluniacs were joining their fate to that of the popes, a small group of clerics and monks in Germany began calling for systematic reform within the church. They buttressed their arguments with new interpretations of canon law—the laws decreed over the centuries at church councils and by bishops and popes. They concentrated on two breaches of those laws: clerical marriage and **simony** (buying church offices).

Emperor Henry III (r. 1039–1056) supported the reformers. Taking seriously his position as the anointed of God, Henry felt responsible for the well-being of the church in his empire. He denounced simony and personally refused to accept money or gifts when he appointed bishops to their posts. When in 1046 three men, each representing a different faction of the Roman aristocracy, claimed to be pope, Henry, as ruler of Rome, traveled to Italy to settle the matter. The Synod of Sutri (1046), over which he presided, deposed all three popes and elected another. In 1049, Henry appointed Leo IX (r. 1049–1054) to the papacy.

This appointment marked an unanticipated turning point for the emperor when Leo set out to reform the church under papal, rather than imperial, control. He traveled to France and Germany, holding councils to condemn simoniac bishops (bishops guilty of simony). He sponsored the creation of a canon law textbook, the *Collection in 74 Titles,* which emphasized the pope's power. To the papal court, Leo brought the most zealous reformers of his day: Humbert of Silva Candida, Peter Damian, and Hildebrand (later Pope Gregory VII).

At first, Leo's claims to new power over the church hierarchy were ignored by clergy and secular rulers alike. But Leo insisted, and gradually his view prevailed. He maintained it in the Byzantine world as well. In 1054, Leo sent Humbert of Silva Candida to Constantinople on a diplomatic mission to argue for the new, lofty claims of the pope. Furious at the contemptuous way he was treated by the patriarch, Humbert excommunicated him and soon afterward condemned the entire Greek Orthodox Church. In retaliation, the patriarch and his bishops excommunicated Humbert and his party, threatening them with eternal damnation. Clashes between the two churches had occurred before and had been patched up, but this one, called the **Great Schism** (1054), proved insurmountable.* Thereafter, the Roman Catholic and Greek Orthodox churches were largely separate.

Later popes continued Leo's program to expand papal power. When military adventurers from Normandy began carving out states for themselves in southern Italy, the popes in nearby Rome felt threatened. After waging unsuccessful war against the interlopers, the papacy made the best of a bad situation by granting the Normans Sicily and parts of southern Italy as a fief, turning its former enemies into vassals. Similarly, the papacy participated in wars in Spain, where it supported Christians against the dominant Muslims. The political fragmentation of al-Andalus into small, weak taifas (independent, Muslim-ruled principalities) made it seem fair game to the Christians to the north. Slowly the idea of the *reconquista*, the Christian reconquest of Spain, took shape, fed by religious fervor as well as worldly ambition.

Gregorian Reform and the Investiture Conflict, 1073–1085

The papal reform movement is above all associated with Pope Gregory VII (r. 1073–1085) and is therefore often called the **Gregorian reform**. Gregory began as a lowly Roman cleric, Hildebrand, with the job of administering the papal estates and rose slowly in the hierarchy. A passionate advocate of papal primacy (the theory that the pope was head of the church), he was not afraid to clash with Emperor Henry IV (r. 1056–1106) over leadership of the church. In his view, the emperor was just a layman who had no right to meddle in church affairs—an astonishing thought at the time, given the religious and spiritual roles associated with rulers.

Henry IV had been brought up in the traditions of his father, Henry III, a pious church reformer who considered it part of his duty to appoint bishops and even popes to ensure the well-being of both church and state. Henry IV believed that he and his bishops—who were, at the same time, his most valuable supporters and administrators—were the rightful leaders of the church. He had no intention of allowing the pope to become head of the church.

The great confrontation between Gregory and Henry began over the appointment of the archbishop of Milan. Gregory disputed Henry's right to "invest" the archbishop (put him into office). In the investiture ritual, the emperor or his representative symbolically gave the church and the land that went with it to the priest, bishop, or archbishop chosen for the job. When, in 1075, Henry invested his own candidate as archbishop of Milan, Gregory called on Henry to "give more respectful attention to the master of the Church"; he meant St. Peter and his living

---

*The mutual excommunications led to a permanent breach between the churches that largely remained in effect until 1965, when Pope Paul VI and Patriarch Athenagoras I made a joint declaration regretting "the offensive words" and sentences of excommunication on both sides, deploring "the effective rupture of ecclesiastical communion," and expressing the hope that the "differences between the Roman Catholic Church and the Orthodox Church" would be overcome in time.

representative, Gregory himself. In reply, Henry and the German bishops called on Gregory to resign from the papacy. This was the beginning of what historians delicately call the **Investiture Conflict** or Investiture Controversy. In fact, it was a war. In February 1076, Gregory called a synod that both excommunicated Henry and suspended him from office, authorizing anyone in Henry's kingdom to rebel against him. The German princes (as German aristocrats were called) saw an opportunity to increase their power; they threatened to elect another king.

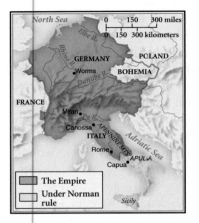

The World of the Investiture Conflict, c. 1075–1122

His fortunes low, Henry traveled to intercept Gregory, who was journeying northward to join the rebellious princes. In early 1077, the king and pope met at Canossa, high in central Italy's Apennine Mountains. Gregory was inside a fortress there; Henry stood outside as a penitent—barefoot in the cold and snow. The gesture was an astute move by Henry because no priest could refuse absolution to a penitent; Gregory had to lift the excommunication and receive Henry back into the church. But Gregory had the advantage of making the king humble himself before the majesty of the pope.

Although Henry was technically back in the fold, nothing of substance had been resolved, and civil war began. The princes elected an antiking (a king chosen illegally), and Henry and his supporters elected an antipope. From 1077 to 1122, papal and imperial armies waged intermittent war. Long after the original antagonists, Gregory and Henry, had died, the Concordat of Worms (1122) ended the fighting with a compromise that relied on a conceptual distinction between two parts of the investiture ceremony—the spiritual (in which a man received the symbols of his clerical office) and the secular (in which he received the symbols of the material goods that would allow him to function). Under the terms of the Concordat of Worms, in the first part of the ceremony, a churchman would give the bishop the ring and staff (symbols of church office). In the second part, the emperor or his representative would touch the bishop with a scepter, a symbolic gesture that stood for the land and other possessions that went with his office. Elections of bishops in Germany would take place "in the presence of the emperor"—that is, under his influence. In Italy, the pope would have a comparable role.

Superficially, nothing much had changed; secular rulers would continue to have a part in choosing and investing churchmen. In fact, however, almost no one any longer claimed that the king was head of the church. Just as the new investiture ceremony broke the ritual into spiritual and secular parts, so too it implied a new notion of kingship that separated it from priesthood. The Investiture Conflict did not produce the modern distinction between church and state—that would develop only very slowly—but it set the wheels in motion.

The most important changes brought about by the Investiture Conflict were on the ground: the political landscape in both Italy and Germany was irrevocably transformed. In Germany, the princes consolidated their lands and their positions at the expense of royal power. They gradually became virtual monarchs within their own principalities; the emperor, though retaining his title, eventually became a figurehead. In Italy, the emperor lost power to the cities.

The Italian communes were formed in the crucible of the war between the pope and the emperor. In fierce communal struggles, city factions, motivated in part by local grievances but often claiming to fight on behalf of the papal or the imperial cause, created their own governing bodies, as in Milan. In the course of the twelfth century, northern Italian cities became used to self-government.

The Sweep of Reform

Church reform involved much more than the clash of popes, emperors, and their supporters. It penetrated deeply into the daily lives of ordinary Christians, in part through the church's new emphasis on the sacraments—the regular means (according to the Catholic church) by which God's heavenly grace infused mundane existence. Eleventh-century church reformers began the process—which continued into the thirteenth century—of emphasizing the importance of the sacraments and the special nature of the priest, whose chief role was to administer them.

In the sacrament of marriage, for example, the effective involvement of the church in the wedding of a man and woman came only after the Gregorian reform. Not until the twelfth century did people regularly come to be married by a priest, and only then did churchmen assume jurisdiction over marital disputes, not simply in cases involving royalty but also in those of lesser aristocrats. At the same time, churchmen began to stress the sanctity of marriage. Hugh of St. Victor argued that marriage was the union of a man and woman who loved one another.

The reformers also proclaimed the special importance of the sacrament of the Mass, holy communion through the body and blood of Christ. Gregory VII called the Mass "the greatest thing in the Christian religion." No layman, no matter how powerful, and no woman of any sort could perform anything equal to it, for the Mass was the key to salvation.

The new emphasis on the difference between the priest (who could celebrate Mass) and the laity (who could not) led to vigorous enforcement of an old element of church discipline: the celibacy of priests. The demand for a celibate clergy had far-reaching significance for the history of the church. It distanced western clerics even farther from their eastern Orthodox counterparts (whose priests did not practice celibacy), exacerbating the Great Schism of 1054. It also broke with traditional local practice, for clerical marriage was customary in many places in Europe. Gregorian reformers exhorted every cleric in higher orders, from the humble parish priest to the exalted bishop, to refrain from marriage or to abandon his wife. In 1123 the pope proclaimed all clerical marriages invalid.

The rule about clerical marriages was only one in a veritable explosion of canon law. Canon law had begun simply as rules determined at church councils or papal declarations. Attempts to gather together and organize these laws had been made before the eleventh century. But the proliferation of rules during that century, along with the desire of Gregorians to clarify church law as they saw it, made a systematic collection even more necessary. This was supplied in about 1140 by the *Concordance of Discordant Canons,* also known as the *Decretum,* a landmark work by Gratian, a monk who taught law at Bologna in northern Italy. Gratian gathered thousands of passages from the decrees of popes and councils with the intention of showing their harmony. If he found any "discord," he strove to show how they applied to different situations. A bit later a different legal scholar revised and expanded the *Decretum,* adding Roman law to the mix. Meanwhile, the papacy itself was gradually developing its own court of law to hear cases and rule on petitions.

Before the Gregorian reform the papacy had been relatively powerless and much loved; afterward, it was very powerful and often resented. A satire written about 1100, in the style of the Gospels, made bitter fun of the costs of bringing cases to the papal court:

> There came to the court a certain wealthy clerk, fat and thick, and gross, who in the sedition [rebellion] had committed murder. He first gave to the dispenser, second to the treasurer, third to the cardinals. But they thought among themselves that they should receive more. The Lord Pope, hearing that his cardinals had received many gifts, was sick, nigh unto death. But the rich man sent to him a couch of gold and silver and immediately he was made whole.

With his law courts, bureaucracy, and financial apparatus, the pope had become a monarch.

Early Crusades and Crusader States

Asserting itself as head of the Christian church and leader of its reform movement, the papacy sometimes supported and proclaimed holy wars to advance the cause of Christianity. The most important of these were the crusades. Combinations of war and pilgrimage—the popular practice of making a pious voyage to a sacred shrine to petition for help or cure—the early crusades sent armed European Christians into battle against Muslims in the Holy Land, the place where Christ had lived and died.

The crusaders established several tiny states in the Levant, holding on to them precariously until 1291. Although the crusades ultimately "failed," in the sense that the crusaders did not succeed in permanently retaining the Holy Land for Christendom, they were a pivotal episode in Western civilization. They marked the first stage of European overseas expansion—what later would become imperialism.

The First Crusade (1096–1099) began with the entry of the Seljuk Turks into Asia Minor (Map 9.2). In the 1050s, taking advantage of the political fragmentation of the Muslim world, the Seljuks, converts to Sunni Islam, captured Baghdad, subjugated the caliphate, and began to threaten Byzantium. The difficulties the Byzantine emperor Romanus IV had in pulling together an army to attack the Turks in 1071 reveal how weak his position had become. Unable to muster Byzantine troops, Romanus had to rely on a mercenary army made up of Normans, Franks, Slavs, and even Turks. In 1071, this motley force met the Seljuks at Manzikert, in what is today eastern Turkey. The battle was a disaster for Romanus: the Seljuks routed his army and captured him. Manzikert marked the end of Byzantine domination in the region. The Turks, gradually settling in Asia Minor, extended their control across the Byzantine Empire and beyond, all the way to Jerusalem, which had been under Muslim control since the seventh century.

In 1095, the Byzantine emperor Alexius I appealed for help to Pope Urban II (r. 1088–1099), hoping to get new mercenary troops for a fresh offensive. Urban II

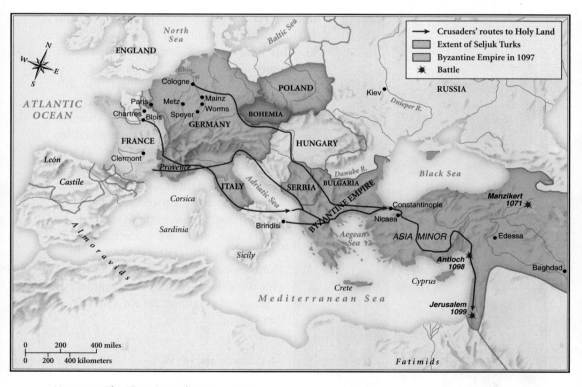

Map 9.2 The First Crusade, 1096–1099
The First Crusade was a major military undertaking that required organization, movement over both land and sea, and enormous resources. Four main groups were responsible for the conquest of Jerusalem. One group began at Cologne, in northern Germany; another group started from Blois, in France; a third originated to the west of Provence; and a fourth launched ships from Brindisi, at the heel of Italy. All joined up at Constantinople, where their leaders negotiated with Alexius I for help and supplies in return for a pledge of vassalage to the emperor. **For more help analyzing this map, see the map activity for this chapter in the Online Study Guide at** bedfordstmartins.com/huntconcise.

chose to interpret the request in his own way. That year, at the Council of Clermont (in France), Urban moved outside the church and addressed an already excited throng:

> Oh, race of Franks, race from across the mountains, race beloved and chosen by God. . . . Let hatred depart from among you, let your quarrels end, let wars cease, and let all dissensions and controversies slumber. Enter upon the road to the Holy Sepulcher; wrest that land from the wicked race, and subject it to yourselves.

The crowd reportedly responded with one voice: "God wills it." Urban's call gave the papacy a new position of leadership, one that complemented in a military arena the place the popes had gained in the church hierarchy.

Men and women, rich and poor, young and old, heeded Urban's call. They abandoned their homes and braved the rough journey to the Holy Land to fight for their God. They also went because they wanted land and booty. Some knights joined the expedition because they were obligated to follow their lord. Although women were discouraged from going on the crusade, some crusaders were accompanied by their wives. Other women went as servants. Children, old men, and women, not able to fight, made the cords for siege engines—giant machines used to hurl stones at enemy fortifications. As more crusades were undertaken during the twelfth century, the transport and supply of these armies became a lucrative business for the commercial classes of maritime Italian cities such as Venice.

A Crusader and His Wife
How do we know that the man on the left is a crusader? On his shirt is a cross, the sign worn by all men going on the crusades. In his right hand is a pilgrim's staff, a useful reminder that the crusades were sometimes considered less a matter of war than of penance and piety. What does the embrace of the crusader's wife imply about marital love in the twelfth century?
(© Musée Lorrain, Nancy/Photo: P. Mignot.)

The main objective of the First Crusade—to take the Holy Land from the Muslims and subject it to Christian rule—was accomplished largely because of Muslim disunity. After nearly a year of ineffectual attacks, the crusaders took Antioch on June 28, 1098. The following year, on July 15, 1099, they seized Jerusalem. By 1109 they had carved out several tiny states in the Holy Land.

Because the crusader states were created by conquest, they were treated as lordships. The rulers granted fiefs to their own vassals, and some of these men in turn gave portions of their holdings as fiefs to some of their own vassals. Since most Europeans went home after the First Crusade, the rulers who remained learned to coexist with the indigenous population, which included Muslims, Jews, and Greek Orthodox Christians. They encouraged a lively trade at their ports, which received merchants from Italy, Byzantium, and Islamic cities. The main concern of these rulers, however, was military. They set up castles and recruited knights from Europe. So organized for war was this society that it produced a new and militant kind of monasticism: the Knights Templar, who vowed themselves to poverty and chastity.

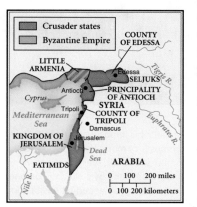

The Crusader States, 1109

But rather than withdraw into the cloister, the Templars, whose name came from their living quarters in the area of the former Jewish temple at Jerusalem, devoted themselves to warfare. Their first mission—to protect the pilgrimage routes from Palestine to Jerusalem—soon diversified. They manned the town garrisons of the crusader states and transported money from Europe to the Holy Land. In this way the Templars became enormously wealthy, with branch "banks" in major cities across Europe.

The presence of the Templars did not prevent the Seljuks from taking the city of Edessa in 1144. The event marked the slow but steady shrinking of the crusader states. New crusades were called, but none was successful. The Second Crusade (1147–1149) came to a disastrous end. After besieging the walls of Damascus for only four days, the crusaders, whose leaders could not keep the peace among themselves, gave up and went home. Soon the Muslims took all of Syria, and under the leadership of Saladin (1138–1193), they took Jerusalem in 1187. This in turn led to the call for the Third Crusade (1189–1192). Led by the greatest rulers of Europe—Emperor Frederick I, Philip II of France, Leopold of Austria, and Richard I of England—the Third Crusade nevertheless accomplished little, and the crusader states were reduced to a few tiny outposts.

Jews as Strangers

The same militant piety that inspired the crusades was turned against Jews. Sentiment against Jews grew over time. Once the Roman Empire became Christian, Jews

Krak-des-Chevaliers
The Hospitallers, a religious military order much like the Templars, built this imposing castle in 1142 on the site of a Muslim fortification in Syria. A large community of perhaps fifty monk-knights and their hired mercenaries lived there. To the northeast (in back of the complex seen here) was a fortified village that served the needs of the castle. Peasants raised grain, which was ground by a windmill on one wall of the castle. For water, there were reservoirs to catch the rain, wells, and an aqueduct (visible on the right). Twelve toilets connected to a common drain. The monks worshipped in a chapel within the inner walls. The outer walls, built of masonry, completely enclosed the inner buildings, making Krak one of the most important places for refuge and defense in the crusader states. (Maynard Owen Williams/ National Geographic Image Collection.)

were prohibited by Roman law from owning Christian slaves or marrying Christian women. Church laws added to these restrictions. Socially isolated and branded as outcasts, Jews served as scapegoats who helped define the larger society as orthodox. But only at the end of the eleventh century did severe persecution begin.

Forced out of the countryside during the eleventh century by castellans and other regional rulers, most Jews ended up in the cities as craftsmen or merchants. But they were not allowed into guilds, and many were therefore pushed into the one profession that Christians could not practice, moneylending. Jews thus provided capital for the developing commercial society, whose Christian members were prohibited from charging interest by the Bible's restrictions against usury.

Many Jews lived in the flourishing commercial region of the Rhineland. Under Henry IV, Jews in Speyer and elsewhere in the Empire received protection from the local bishop (an imperial appointee) in return for paying a tax. Within these cities, the Jews lived in their own neighborhoods, in tightly knit communities focused on their synagogues. Synagogues served not only as houses of worship but also as schools and community centers. Jews also participated in the life of the larger Christian community. Archbishop Anno of Cologne dealt with Jewish moneylenders, and other Jews in Cologne were allowed to trade their wares at the fairs there.

Among the earliest anti-Jewish attacks were those directed against these Rhineland Jews. Some of the crusaders of the First Crusade declared it ridiculous to attack Muslims when other infidels lived in their own backyards. "That's doing our work backward," they said, as they moved into the Rhineland to force conversions or to kill. Some Jews found refuge with bishops or in the houses of Christian friends, but in many cities—Metz, Speyer, Worms, Mainz, and Cologne—they were massacred.

In the course of the twelfth century, Jews were attacked elsewhere as well. European rulers claimed Jews as their serfs and Jewish property as their own. King Henry II of England (r. 1154–1189) imposed new and arbitrary taxes on the Jewish community. In France, persecuting Jews and confiscating their property benefited both the treasury and the authoritative image of the king. Early in the reign of the French king Philip II, known as Philip Augustus (r. 1180–1223), royal agents surprised Jews at Sabbath worship in their synagogues and seized their goods, demanding that they redeem their own property for a large sum of money. Shortly thereafter, Philip canceled 80 percent of all debts owed to Jews; the remaining 20 percent was to be paid directly to the king. About a year later, in 1182, Philip expelled the Jews from the Île-de-France. When he allowed them to return in 1198, he permitted them to be only moneylenders or money changers, taxed and monitored by royal officials.

Limiting Jews to moneylending in an increasingly commercial economy and then persecuting them served the interests of lords in debt to Jewish creditors. For example, in 1190, local nobles orchestrated a brutal attack on the Jews of York, England. Their purpose was to rid themselves of their debts and of the Jews to whom they owed money. Churchmen, too, used credit in a money economy but resented the fiscal obligations it imposed. With their drive to create centralized territorial states and their desire to make their authority known

The Jew as Other
Medieval artists often portrayed people not as individuals but rather as "types" that could be identified by physical markers. In the second half of the twelfth century, Jews were increasingly portrayed as looking different from Christians. This illustration shows clerics borrowing money from a Jew. What physical features do all the clerics have in common? (Be sure to look at the clothes as well as the hairstyles.) What distinguishes the layman (standing behind the Jew) from the clerics? The Jew is identified by his pointed hat. In fact, however, Jews did not regularly wear this type of hat until they were forced to do so in some regions of Europe in the late thirteenth century. (Bayerische Staatsbibliothek, Munich.)

and felt, powerful rulers of Europe—churchmen and laymen alike—exploited and coerced Jews while drawing upon and encouraging widespread anti-Jewish feeling. Although Jews must have looked exactly like Christians in reality, Jews now became clearly identified in sculpture and in drawings by markers such as conical hats and, increasingly, demeaning features.

Attacks against Jews were inspired by more than resentment against Jewish money and the desire for power and control. They also grew out of the codification of Christian religious doctrine and Christians' anxiety about their own institutions. For example, in the twelfth century, church leaders promulgated a newly rigorous definition of the Eucharist, declaring that when the bread and wine were blessed by the priest during Mass, they became the true body and blood of Christ. For some believers this meant that Christ, wounded and bleeding, lay on the altar. Miracle tales sometimes reported that the elements of the Eucharist bled. Reflecting Christian anxieties about the presence of real flesh on the altar, sensational stories—originating in clerical circles but soon widely circulated—told of Jews who secretly sacrificed Christian children in a morbid revisiting of the crucifixion of Jesus. This charge, called "blood libel" by historians, led to massacres of Jews in cities in England, France, Spain, and Germany. Jews had no rituals involving blood sacrifice at all, but they were convenient and vulnerable scapegoats for Christian guilt and anxiety.

REVIEW What were the causes and consequences of the Gregorian reform?

The Revival of Monarchies

Attacks on Jews reveal the ugly side of a wider development: kings and other rulers were enhancing and consolidating their power. They created new and revived old ideologies to justify their power; they hired officials to work for them; and they found vassals and churchmen to support them. The money that flowed into their treasuries from the new urban economy increased their effectiveness.

Byzantium in Its Prime

The First Crusade was an unanticipated result of a monarchical revival at Byzantium. In 1081, ten years after the disastrous battle at Manzikert, the energetic soldier Alexius Comnenus (r. 1081–1118) seized the imperial throne. He faced considerable unrest in Constantinople, whose populace suffered from a combination of high taxes and rising living costs. In addition, the Byzantine Empire was under attack on every side—by Normans in southern Italy, Seljuk Turks in Asia Minor, and new groups in the Balkans. But Alexius managed to turn actual and potential enemies against one another.

When Alexius asked Pope Urban II to supply him with some western troops to fight his enemies, he was shocked and disappointed to learn that crusaders rather than mercenaries were on the way. But Alexius had to make the best of what he could get. For his army, he could no longer rely on the *theme* system. He had to use mercenaries and to call on the great magnates of his realm to join him with their own troops. In return for their services he gave these nobles *pronoia* grants, lifetime possession of large imperial estates and their dependent peasants. Beyond his military needs, the emperor found support in the patriarch and Byzantine clergy, for emperor and church depended on each other to suppress heresy and foster orthodoxy. The emperors of the Comnenian dynasty (1081–1185) thus gained a measure of increased imperial power, but at the price of important concessions to the nobility.

In the eleventh and twelfth centuries, Constantinople remained a rich, sophisticated, and highly cultured city. Sculptors and other artists strove to depict ideals of human beauty and elegance. Churches built during the period were decorated with elaborate depictions of the cosmos. Significant innovations occurred in Byzantine scholarship and literature. The Neoplatonic tradition of late antiquity had always influenced Byzantine religious and philosophical thought, but now scholars renewed their interest in the wellsprings of classical Greek philosophy, particularly Plato and Aristotle. The revival of these writings in eleventh- and twelfth-century Byzantium would have profound consequences for both eastern and western European civilization in the centuries to come as ancient Greek thought gradually penetrated scholarly circles.

Norman and Angevin England

In Europe, the twelfth-century kings of England were the most powerful monarchs before 1200 because they ruled their whole kingdom by right of conquest. When the Anglo-Saxon king Edward the Confessor (r. 1042–1066) died childless in 1066, the duke of Normandy, William (1027–1087), claimed the throne of England. Gathering a force recruited from many parts of France, he launched an invasion. His armies clashed with those of another claimant to the throne, Harold, at Hastings on October 14, 1066. In one of history's rare decisive battles, William won and took over the realm.

Some people in England gladly supported William, considering his victory a verdict from God and hoping to be granted a place in the new order themselves. But William, known to posterity by the epithet "the Conqueror," wanted to

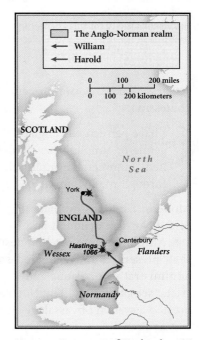

Norman Conquest of England, 1066

replace, not assimilate, the Anglo-Saxons. In the course of William's reign, families from continental Europe almost totally supplanted the English aristocracy. And although the English peasantry remained—now with new lords—the peasants were

Bayeux "Tapestry"
This famous "tapestry" is misnamed; it is really an embroidery, 231 feet long and 20 inches wide, created to tell the story of William's conquest of England from his point of view. In this detail, Norman archers are lined up at the bottom. Above them, Norman knights on horseback attack English foot soldiers wielding long battle-axes. Who seems to be winning? **For more help analyzing this image, see the visual activity for this chapter in the Online Study Guide at** bedfordstmartins.com/huntconcise. (Tapisserie de Bayeux. By special permission of the City of Bayeux, France.)

severely shaken. A twelfth-century historian claimed to record William's deathbed confession:

> I have persecuted [England's] native inhabitants beyond all reason. Whether gentle or simple, I have cruelly oppressed them; many I unjustly disinherited; innumerable multitudes, especially in the county of York, perished through me by famine or the sword.

Modern historians estimate that one out of five people in England died as a result of the Norman conquest and its immediate aftermath.

Although the Normans destroyed a generation of English men and women, they preserved and extended some Anglo-Saxon institutions, retaining the old administrative divisions and legal system of shires (counties) and hundreds (districts; see page 302). The Normans also drew from continental institutions. They created a system of vassalage culminating in the king and buttressed by his castles, just as French kings were trying to do at about the same time (see page 334). But because all of England was the king's by conquest, he could treat it as his booty. William kept about 20 percent of the land for himself and divided the rest, distributing it in large but scattered fiefs to a relatively small number of his barons and family members, lay and ecclesiastical, as well as to some lesser men, such as personal servants and soldiers. In turn, these men and their vassals owed the king military service along with certain dues, such as reliefs (money paid upon inheriting a fief) and aids (payments made on important occasions).

Those were the revenues expected from the nobles, but the king of England commanded the peasantry as well. In 1086, twenty years after his conquest, William ordered a survey and census of England, popularly called Domesday because, like the records of people judged at doomsday, it provided facts that could not be appealed. It was the most extensive inventory of land, livestock, taxes, and population that had yet been compiled in Europe.

The Norman conquest tied England to the languages, politics, institutions, and culture of France and Flanders. Modern English is an amalgam of Anglo-Saxon and Norman French. English commerce was linked to the wool industry in Flanders. St. Anselm (1033–1109), the archbishop of Canterbury (England), was born in Italy and was the abbot of a monastery in Normandy before crossing the English Channel. The barons of England retained their estates in Normandy and elsewhere, and the kings of England often spent more time on the continent than they did on the island. When William's son Henry I (r. 1100–1135) died without male heirs, civil war erupted: the throne of England was fought over by two French counts.

The eventual outcome of that civil war (1139–1153) was the accession to the English throne of Henry II (r. 1154–1189),* Henry I's grandson. He was not only count of Anjou (his father was Count Geoffrey of Anjou) but also, by an astute marriage to Eleanor of Aquitaine in 1152, duke of Aquitaine. His father, who had conquered Normandy, had named Henry duke there, and Henry also exercised hegemony over Poitou and Brittany. Although technically a vassal of the king of France (as a result of his continental lands), Henry in effect ruled a territory that stretched from England to the south of France (Map 9.3).

Henry's marriage to Eleanor brought him both a huge duchy and a feisty queen, who bore him the sons he needed to maintain his dynasty. Before her marriage to Henry, Eleanor had been married to King Louis VII of France. Louis had the marriage annulled because she bore him only daughters. Nevertheless, as queen of France, Eleanor enjoyed an important position. She disputed with St. Bernard, the most renowned churchman of the day, and she accompanied her husband on the Second Crusade, bringing more troops than he did. She determined to separate from Louis even before he considered leaving her. Married to Henry, she had much less power. After plotting unsuccessfully against Henry with one of their sons, she spent most of her time, until her husband's death in 1189, confined under guard at Winchester Castle.

As king of England, Henry immediately set to work to undo the damage to the monarchy caused by the civil war, during which the English barons and high churchmen had gained new privileges and powers, building private castles

---

*Henry II is known as the first Angevin (from *Anjou*) king of England because by inheritance, he was count of Anjou. But the dynasty he began also has another name. His father, Count Geoffrey of Anjou, was nicknamed *Plantagenet,* from *genet,* a shrub that he liked, and historians sometimes use that name to refer to the entire dynasty. Thus Henry II was the first Plantagenet as well as the first Angevin king of England.

Map 9.3 Europe in the Age of Henry II and Frederick Barbarossa, 1150–1190
The second half of the twelfth century was dominated by two men, King Henry II and Emperor Frederick Barbarossa. Of the two, Frederick seemed to control more land, but this was deceptive. Although he was emperor, he had great difficulty ruling the territory that was theoretically part of his empire. Frederick's base was in central Germany, and even there he had to contend with powerful vassals. Henry II's territory was more compact but also more surely under his control.

as symbols of their strength. Henry destroyed or confiscated the new castles and regained crown lands. Then he proceeded to extend monarchical power, above all by imposing royal justice.

Henry's judicial reforms built on an already well-developed English system. The Anglo-Saxon kings had established royal district courts and appointed sheriffs to police the shires, call up men to fight, and haul criminals into court. The Norman kings retained these courts, which all the free men of the shires were summoned to attend. To these institutions, Henry II added a system of judicial visitations called eyres (from the Latin *iter*, "journey"). Under this system, royal justices made regular trips to every locality in England. Henry declared that some crimes, such as murder, arson, and rape, were so heinous as to violate the "king's peace," no matter where they were committed. The king required local representatives of the knightly class to meet during each eyre and either give the sheriff the names of those suspected of committing crimes in the vicinity or arrest the suspects and hand them over to the royal justices. During the eyres, the justices also heard cases between individuals, today called civil cases. Free men and women (that is, people of the knightly class or above) could bring their disputes over matters such as inheritance, dowries, and property claims to the king's justices. Earlier courts had generally relied on duels between litigants to determine verdicts. Henry's new system offered a different option—an inquest under royal supervision.

The new system was praised for its efficiency, speed, and effectiveness by the king's supporters. They might have added that the king also quickly gained a large treasury. The exchequer, as the financial bureau of England was called, recorded all the fines paid for judgments and the sums collected for writs. The amounts, entered on parchment sewn together and stored as rolls, became the Receipt Rolls and Pipe Rolls, the first of many such records of the English monarchy and an indication that writing had become a mechanism for institutionalizing royal power in England.

The stiffest opposition to Henry's extension of royal courts came from

Hanging Thieves
The development of common law in England meant mobilizing royal agents to bring charges and arrest people throughout the land. In 1124, the royal justice Ralph Basset hanged forty-four thieves. It could not have been very shocking in that context to see, in this miniature from around 1130, eight thieves hanged for breaking into the shrine of St. Edmund. Under Henry II, all cases of murder, arson, and rape were considered crimes against the king himself. The result was not just the enhancement of the king's power but also new definitions of crime, more thorough policing, and more systematic punishments. Even so, hanging was probably no more frequent than it had been before. (Pierpont Morgan Library/Art Resource, NY.)

the church, where a separate system of trial and punishment had long been available to the clergy and to others who enjoyed church protection. The punishments that these courts meted out were generally quite mild. Jealous of their prerogatives, churchmen refused to submit to the jurisdiction of Henry's courts, and the ensuing contest between Henry and his archbishop, Thomas Becket (1118–1170), became the greatest battle between church and state in the twelfth century. Their conflict over jurisdiction simmered for six years, until Henry's henchmen murdered Thomas, unintentionally transforming him into a martyr. Although Henry's role in the murder remained ambiguous, he had to do public penance for the deed largely because of the general outcry. In the end, both church courts and royal courts expanded to address the concerns of an increasingly litigious society.

Praising the King of France

The twelfth-century kings of France were much less obviously powerful than their English and Byzantine counterparts. Yet they, too, took part in the monarchical revival. Louis VI ("the Fat"; r. 1108–1137), so heavy that he had to be hoisted onto his horse with a crane, was a tireless defender of royal power. We know a good deal about him because his contemporary and close associate, Suger (1081–1152), abbot of Saint-Denis, wrote Louis's biography. When Louis set himself the task of consolidating his rule in the Île-de-France, Suger portrayed the king as a righteous hero. He thought of the king as the head of a political hierarchy in which Louis had rights over the French nobles because they were his vassals or when they broke the peace.

Suger also believed that Louis had a religious role: to protect the church and the poor. He viewed Louis as another Charlemagne, a ruler for all society, not merely an overlord of the nobility. Louis waged war to keep God's peace. To be sure, the Gregorian reform had made its mark: Suger did not claim Louis was head of the church. Nevertheless, he emphasized the royal dignity and its importance to the papacy. When a pope happened to arrive in France, Louis, not yet king, and his father, Philip I (r. 1052–1108), bowed low, but (recalled Suger) "the pope lifted them up and made them sit before him like devout sons of the apostles. In the manner of a wise man acting wisely, he conferred with them privately on the present condition of the church." Here the pope was shown needing royal advice.

When Louis VI died in 1137, Suger's notion of the might and right of the king of France reflected reality in an extremely small area. Nevertheless, Louis laid the groundwork for the gradual extension of royal power in France. As the lord of vassals, the king could call upon his men to aid him in times of war (though the great ones sometimes disregarded his wishes and chose not to help). As a king and landlord, he could obtain many dues and taxes. Officials enforced his royal laws and collected taxes. With money and land, Louis could dispense the favors and give the gifts that added to his prestige and his power. Louis VI and Suger together created the territorial core and royal ideal of the future French monarchy. Louis's grandson Philip Augustus would build on this foundation, greatly expanding the territory of the French monarchy in the thirteenth century.

Remaking the Empire

The Investiture Conflict and the civil war it generated (1075–1122) strengthened the German princes and weakened the emperors. For decades, the princes enjoyed near independence, building castles on their properties and establishing control over whole territories. To ensure that the emperors who succeeded Henry V (r. 1106–1125) would be weak, the princes supported only rulers who agreed to give them new lands and powers. A ruler's success depended on his ability to juggle the many conflicting interests of his own royal and imperial offices, his family, and the German princes. He also had to contend with the increasing influence of the papacy and the Italian communes, which were forging alliances with one another and with the German princes, preventing the consolidation of power under a strong German monarch during the first half of the twelfth century.

Weakness at the top, however, meant constant warfare among princely factions. Eventually the German princes became exhausted by conflict and in 1152 elected Frederick I ("Barbarossa"; r. 1152–1190) as the first Hohenstaufen king of Germany. He was an impressive man with a striking red-blond beard (hence *Barbarossa,* or "red-beard") and a firm sense of his position. Frederick affirmed royal rights even when he handed out duchies and allowed others to name bishops, because in return for these political powers he required the princes to concede formally and publicly that they held their rights and territories from him as their lord. By making them his vassals—though with nearly royal rights within their principalities—Frederick defined the princes' relationship to the German king: they were powerful yet personally subordinate to him. In this way, Frederick hoped to save the monarchy and to coordinate royal and princely rule, thus ending Germany's chronic civil wars. Frederick used the lord-vassal relationship to give himself a free hand to rule while placating the princes.

Since the Investiture Conflict, the emperor had ruled Italy in name only. The communes of the northern cities guarded their liberties jealously, and the pope considered Italy his own sphere of influence. Frederick's territorial base north of Italy (in Swabia) and his designs on northern Italy threatened those interests (Map 9.3, page 332). Some historians have criticized Frederick for "entangling" himself in Italy, but Frederick's title was *emperor,* a position that demanded he intervene there. To fault him for not concentrating on Germany is to blame him for lacking modern wisdom, which knows from hindsight that European polities developed into nation-states, such as France, Germany, and Italy. There was nothing inevitable about the development of nation-states, however, and Frederick should not be condemned for failing to see into the future. In addition, control of Italy made sense even for Frederick's effectiveness in Germany. His base in

Swabia together with northern Italy would give him a compact and central territory. Moreover, the flourishing commercial cities of Italy would make him rich. Taxes on agricultural production there alone yielded thirty thousand silver talents annually, an incredible sum.

By alternately negotiating with and fighting against the great cities of northern Italy, especially Milan, Frederick achieved military control there in 1158. No longer able to make Italian bishops royal governors, as German kings had done earlier—the Investiture Conflict had effectively ended that practice—Frederick insisted that the communes be governed by magistrates from outside the communes who were appointed (or at least authorized) by him. Here is where Frederick made his mistake: the heavy hand of these officials, many of them from Germany, created enormous resentment. By 1167, most of the cities of northern Italy had joined with Pope Alexander III (r. 1159–1181) to form the Lombard League against Frederick. Defeated at the battle of Legnano (near Milan) in 1176, Frederick made peace with Alexander and withdrew most of his forces from Italy. The battle marked the triumph of the city over the crown in Italy, which would not have a centralized government until the nineteenth century; Italy's political history would instead be that of its various regions and their dominant cities.

The Courtly Culture of Europe

With the consolidation of territory, wealth, and power in the second half of the twelfth century, kings, barons, princes, and their wives and daughters created a newly opulent court culture. For the first time on the European continent, poems and songs were written in the vernacular, the spoken language, rather than in Latin. They celebrated the lives of the nobility and were meant to be read aloud or sung as entertainment. Already at the beginning of the twelfth century, Duke William IX of Aquitaine (1071–1126), the grandfather of Eleanor of Aquitaine, had written lyric poems in Occitan, the vernacular spoken in southern France. Perhaps influenced by love poetry in Arabic and Hebrew from al-Andalus, his own poetry in turn provided a model for poetic forms that gained great popularity. The final four-line stanza of one such poem demonstrates the composer's skill with words:

Per aquesta fri e tremble,	For this one I shiver and tremble,
quar de tan bon' amor l'am;	I love her with such a good love;
qu'anc no cug qu'en nasques	I do not think the like of her was
semble	ever born
en semblan de gran linh n'Adam.	in the long line of Lord Adam.

The rhyme scheme of this poem appears to be simple—*tremble* rhymes with *semble*, *l'am* with *n'Adam*. But the poem has five earlier verses, each six lines long and all containing the -*am*, -*am* rhyme in the fourth and sixth lines, while every other line within each verse rhymes as well. The whole scheme is dazzlingly complex.

William was followed by other troubadours—lyric poets who wrote in Occitan (Figure 9.1). Whether male or female, their subject was love. The Contessa de Dia (flourished c. 1160) wrote about her unrequited love for a man:

> So bitter do I feel toward him
> whom I love more than anything.
> With him my mercy and fine manners [*cortesia*] are in vain.

The key to troubadour verse was the notion of *cortesia* (courtesy), which referred to the refinement of people living at court and to their struggle to achieve an ideal of virtue.

Historians and literary critics used to use the term *courtly love* to emphasize one of the themes of courtly literature: the poet expresses overwhelming love for a beautiful married noblewoman who is far above him in status and utterly unattainable. But this was only one of many aspects of love that the troubadours sang about. Some boasted of sexual conquests; others played with the notion of equality between lovers; still others preached that love was the source of virtue. The overall theme of this literature was not courtly love but the power of women. No wonder Eleanor of Aquitaine and other aristocratic women patronized the troubadours: they enjoyed the image that the poetry gave them of themselves. Nor was that image a delusion.

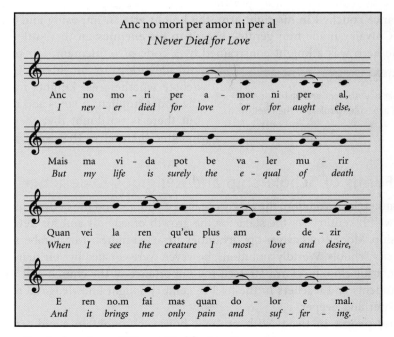

Figure 9.1 Troubadour Song: "I Never Died for Love"
This music is the first part of a song that the troubadour poet Peire Vidal wrote sometime between 1175 and 1205. It has been adapted here for the treble clef. There is no time signature, but the music may easily be played by calculating one beat for each note, except for the two-note slurs, which fit into one beat together.

There were many powerful female lords in southern France. They owned property, had vassals, led battles, decided disputes, and entered into and broke political alliances as their advantage dictated. Both men and women appreciated troubadour poetry, which recognized and praised women's power even as it eroticized it.

From southern France the lyric love song spread to Italy, northern France, England, and Germany—regions where Occitan was a foreign language. Similar poetry appeared in other vernacular languages: the *minnesingers* (literally, "love singers") sang in German; the *trouvères* sang in the Old French of northern France. Some poets wrote much longer works—long heroic poems focused on war (later called epics) or equally long romantic poems about love (later called romances). Romances, often inspired by the legend of King Arthur, reached the zenith of their popularity during the late twelfth and early thirteenth centuries. A good example is *Lancelot* by Chrétien de Troyes (c. 1150–1190). The hero, in love with Queen Guinevere, the wife of his lord, King Arthur, will do anything for her. When she sees him, the greatest knight in Christendom, fighting in a tournament, she tests his love for her by asking him to do his "worst." The poor knight is then obliged to lose all his battles until she changes her mind.

Lancelot was the perfect chivalric knight. The word *chivalry* derives from the French word *cheval* (horse); the fact that the knight was a horseman marked him as a warrior of the most prestigious sort. Perched high on his mount, his heavy lance couched in his right arm, the knight was an imposing and menacing figure. Chivalry made him gentle—except to his enemies on the battlefield. The chivalric hero was a knight constrained by a code of refinement, fair play, piety, and devotion to an ideal. Historians debate whether real knights lived up to the codes implicit in epics and romances, but there is no doubt that they liked to imagine themselves that way.

REVIEW What new sources and institutions of power became available to rulers in the twelfth century?

New Forms of Scholarship and Religious Experience

The commercial revolution, the newly organized church, and the revived monarchies of the twelfth century set the stage for the growth of schools and for new forms of scholarship. Money and career opportunities attracted unheard-of numbers of young men to city schools. Worldly ambitions, however, were equaled by spiritual ones. The movement for church reform stressed the importance of the church and its beliefs. Many students and teachers in the twelfth century sought knowledge to make their faith clearer and deeper.

Other people in the twelfth century, however, sought to avoid schools and commerce. Some found refuge in the measured ceremonies and artistic splendor of Benedictine monasteries such as Cluny. Others considered these vast monastic complexes to be ostentatious and worldly. Rejecting the opulence of cities and the splendor of well-endowed monasteries alike, some pursued a monastic life of poverty, while others, like St. Francis, rejected even the shelter of the cloister.

Schools, Scholars, and the New Learning

Schools had been connected to monasteries and cathedrals since the Carolingian period. They served to train new recruits to become either monks or priests. Some were better endowed with books and masters (teachers) than others; a few developed a reputation for a certain theological approach or specialized in a certain branch of learning, such as literature, medicine, or law. By the end of the eleventh century, the best schools were generally in the larger cities: Reims, Paris, Bologna, Montpellier. Eager students flocked to them. Teachers at cathedral schools found themselves forced to find larger halls to accommodate the crush of students. Other teachers simply declared themselves "masters" and set up shop by renting a room. If they could prove their mettle in the classroom, they had no trouble finding paying students.

Because schools had hitherto been the training ground for clergymen, all students not only were male but also were considered clerics, whether or not they had been ordained. Many students went from school to school, sampling the offerings of different teachers. They could take to the roads because the consolidation of castellanies, counties, and kingdoms made violence against travelers less frequent. Urban centers soon responded to the needs of transients with markets, taverns, and lodgings. Using Latin, Europe's common language, students could drift from, say, Italy to Spain, Germany, England, and France, wherever a noted master had settled. Along with crusaders, pilgrims, and merchants, students made the roads of Europe very crowded indeed.

What the students sought above all was knowledge of the seven liberal arts. Grammar, rhetoric, and logic (or dialectic) belonged to the

A Teacher and His Students
This miniature, which illustrates the hierarchical relationship between students and teachers in the twelfth century, appears in a late-twelfth-century manuscript of a commentary written by Gilbert (d. 1154), bishop of Poitiers. Although some considered Gilbert's ideas in this commentary to be heretical, he escaped condemnation. The artist asserts Gilbert's orthodoxy by depicting him with a halo, in the full dress of a bishop, speaking from his throne. Below Gilbert are three of his disciples, also with halos. The artist's positive view of Gilbert is echoed by modern historians, who recognize Gilbert as a pioneer in his approach to scriptural commentary. (Bibliothèque municipale de Valenciennes.)

"beginning" arts, the so-called trivium. Logic, involving the technical analysis of texts as well as the application and manipulation of mental constructs, was a transitional subject leading to the second, higher part of the liberal arts, the quadrivium. This comprised four areas of study that we might call theoretical math and science: arithmetic, geometry, music (theory rather than practice), and astronomy. Of all these subjects, logic excited the most intense interest. Medieval students and masters were convinced that logic clarified every issue, even questions about the nature of God. With logic, they thought, one could prove that what one believed on faith was in fact true. At the end of the twelfth century, some Western scholars took advantage of Islamic achievements. At Islamic centers in Spain and Sicily the Greek texts of Aristotle, with their sophisticated logic, had already been translated into Arabic and closely commented on. Now Christian scholars translated the Arabic texts into Latin, making Aristotle and other ancient writers their own.

After studying the liberal arts, some students went on to study medicine, theology, or law. At Bologna, for example, students studied Lombard, Roman, and canon law. Men skilled in canon law served popes and bishops; popes, kings, princes, and communes all found that Roman law, which claimed the emperor as its source, justified their claims to power. The University of Paris, established at the very end of the twelfth century, concentrated on theology. Montpellier, in the south of France, was noted for its medical education. With books expensive and hard to find, lectures were the chief method of communication. These were centered on important texts: the teacher read an excerpt aloud, delivered his commentary on it, and disputed any contrary commentaries that rival teachers might have proposed. Students committed the lectures to memory.

Universities functioned as guilds, with the teachers in the role of masters and the students in the position of apprentices (except at Bologna, where the students, usually older men experienced in administration, had their own guild). Like guilds, they set prices (in this case, fees), determined standards (in this case, the knowledge that had to be learned), and regulated discipline. Given generous privileges by both popes and kings, who valued the services of scholars, universities were sometimes at odds with townspeople. It is common to speak of "town against gown"—the "gown" referring to the garb worn by the students and masters (and imitated by the American graduation gown). Students could be rowdy and worse; townspeople resented a self-governing body of transients in their midst. Yet pub owners, innkeepers, food purveyors, and landlords benefited from the patronage of students and masters, and generally town-gown relations were good.

The remarkable renewal of scholarship in the twelfth century had an unexpected benefit: we know a great deal about the men—and a few of the women—involved in it because they wrote so much, often about themselves. Three important figures typify the scholars of the period: Abelard and Heloise, who embraced the new learning wholeheartedly and retired to monasteries only when forced to do so, and Hildegard of Bingen, who spent most of her life happily in a cloister yet wrote knowingly about the world.

Peter Abelard (1079–1142) was one of the twelfth century's greatest thinkers. Turning his back on a career as a warrior and lord, he studied in Paris and soon began to write influential works on ethics, logic, and theology. Around 1120 he prepared a textbook for his students, the *Sic et Non* (*Yes and No*), unusual because it presented opposing positions on various subjects without reconciling them. Abelard challenged his students to make sense of the conflicts and resolve the contradictions themselves.

Abelard's fame as a teacher was such that a Parisian cleric named Fulbert gave him room and board and engaged him as tutor for Heloise (c. 1100–c. 1163/1164), Fulbert's niece. Brought up under her uncle's guardianship, Heloise had been sent as a young girl to a convent school, where she received a thorough education in Latin and Christian literature. Her uncle hoped to continue her education at home by hiring Abelard. Abelard, however, became her secret lover as well as her tutor. "Our desires left no stage of love-making untried," wrote Abelard in his *Historia calamitatum* (*Story of My Calamities*), his autobiographical account. When Heloise became pregnant, Abelard insisted they marry. They did so clandestinely, informing only a very few, such as Fulbert, for the new emphasis on clerical celibacy meant that Abelard's professional success and prestige would have been compromised if news of his marriage were made public. After they were married, Heloise and Abelard rarely saw one another. Suspecting that Abelard had abandoned his niece, Fulbert plotted a cruel punishment: he paid a servant to castrate Abelard. Soon after, husband and wife entered separate monasteries.

For Heloise, separation from Abelard was a lasting misfortune. For Abelard, however, the loss of Heloise and even his castration were not the worst disasters of his life. The cruelest blow came later, and it was directed at his intellect. He wrote a book that applied "human and logical reasons" (as he put it) to the Trinity. The book was condemned at the Council of Soissons in 1121, and he was forced to throw it into the flames, page by page. Bitterly weeping at the injustice, Abelard lamented, "This open violence had come upon me only because of the purity of my intentions and love of our Faith which had compelled me to write." Abelard had written the treatise on the Trinity for his students, maintaining that "words were useless if the intelligence could not follow them, [and] that nothing could be believed unless it was first understood." For Abelard, logic was the key to knowledge, and knowledge the key to faith.

Unlike Abelard and Heloise, Hildegard of Bingen (1098–1179) did not attend the city schools or learn under one of their scholars. Placed in a German convent at age eight, she received her schooling there and took vows as a nun. In 1136, she was elected abbess of the convent. Shortly thereafter, very abruptly, she began to write and to preach. She was probably the only woman authorized by the church to preach in her day.

Writing and preaching were the sudden external manifestations of an inner life that had been extraordinary from the beginning. Even as a child, Hildegard had experienced visions—of invisible things, of the future, and (always) of a special kind of light. These visions were intermingled with pain and sickness. Only in her forties did Hildegard interpret her sickness and her visions as gifts from God. In her *Scivias*

(*Know the Ways of the Lord*, 1151), Hildegard described some of her visions and explained their meaning. She interpreted them as containing nothing less than the full story of creation and redemption, a **summa** (compendium) of church doctrine.

Benedictine Monks and Artistic Splendor

Hildegard's contentment within the confines of her cloister was characteristic of many Benedictine monks and nuns. Known as black monks and nuns because they dyed their robes black, the Benedictines reached the height of their popularity in the eleventh century. Monasteries often housed hundreds of monks; convents for nuns were usually less populated. Cluny was one of the largest monasteries, with some four hundred brothers in the mid-eleventh century.

The chief occupation of the monks, as befitted (in their view) citizens of heaven, was prayer. The black monks and nuns devoted themselves to singing psalms and other prayers specified in the Benedictine rule, adding to them still more psalms. The rule called for chanting the entire Psalter—150 psalms—over the course of a week, but some monks, like those at Cluny, chanted that number in a day. Such prayer was neither private nor silent. Black monks had to know not only the words but also the music that went with their prayers. This was plainchant, also known as Gregorian chant, which consisted of melodies, each sung in unison, without

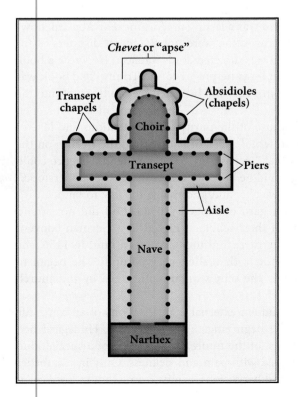

Figure 9.2 Floor Plan of a Romanesque Church

As churchgoers entered a Romanesque church, they passed through the narthex, an anteroom decorated with sculptured depictions of important scenes from the Bible. Walking through the portal of the narthex, they entered the church's nave, at the east end of which—just after the crossing of the transept and in front of the choir—was the altar, the focus of the Mass. Walking down the nave, they passed tall, massive piers leading up to the vault (roof) of the nave. Each of these piers was decorated with sculpture, and the walls were brightly painted. Romanesque churches were both lively and colorful (because of their decoration) and solemn and somber (because of their heavy stones and massive scale).

accompaniment. Although plainchant was rhythmically free, lacking a regular beat, its melodies ranged from extremely simple to highly ornate and embellished. By the twelfth century, a large repertoire of melodies had grown up—at first through oral composition and transmission and then in written notation, which was invented in the ninth century.

The **Romanesque** church—so called because its round arches and other architectural elements reminded modern art historians of Roman buildings—was the place in which black monks spent most of the day chanting the psalms. Built of stone, it might be small or large, but it was always decorated with inventive sculpture and/or wall paintings. The various parts of the church—the chapels in the *chevet,* or "apse" (at the east end of the building), for example—were treated as discrete units, retaining the forms of cubes, cones, and cylinders (Figure 9.2).

In such a setting, gilded reliquaries and altars made of silver, precious gems, and pearls were the fitting accoutrements of worship. Prayer, liturgy, and music in this way complemented the gift economy: richly clad in vestments of the finest materials, intoning the liturgy in the most splendid of churches, monks and priests offered up the gift of prayer to God; in return they begged for the gift of salvation of their souls and the souls of all the faithful.

New Monastic Orders of Poverty

Not everyone agreed that such opulence pleased God. At the end of the eleventh century, the new commercial economy and the profit motive that fueled it led many to reject wealth and to embrace poverty as a key element of religious life. The Carthusian order founded by Bruno of Cologne was one such group. Settling far from any city, each

Painted Vault
This fresco of Christ as ruler of the universe, his hand raised in a gesture of blessing, is one of many paintings in the Romanesque church of San Isidore de León, built in northwest Spain in the eleventh century. Surrounding Christ are the symbols of the four evangelists: the ox for Luke, the lion for Mark, the eagle for John, and the man for Matthew. (The Art Archive.)

monk took a vow of silence and lived as a hermit in his own small hut. Occasionally the monks gathered for prayer in a common prayer room, or oratory. When not engaged in prayer or meditation, the Carthusians copied manuscripts. They considered this task part of their religious vocation, a way to preach God's word with their hands rather than their mouths. The Carthusian order grew slowly. Each monastery was limited to only twelve monks, the number of Christ's Apostles.

The Cistercians, by contrast, expanded rapidly. Rejecting even the luxury of dyeing their robes, they left them the original color of wool—hence their nickname, white monks. The Cistercian order began as a single monastery, Cîteaux (in Latin, Cistercium) in France, founded in 1098. It grew rapidly under the leadership of St. Bernard (c. 1090–1153), abbot of the important Cistercian monastery Clairvaux. Despite the Cistercian order's official repudiation of female houses, many convents followed its lead and adopted its customs. Women were as eager as men to live the life of simplicity and poverty that they believed the Apostles had enjoyed and endured.

Although the Cistercians held up the Benedictine rule as the foundation of their customs, they elaborated a style of life all their own, largely governed by the goal of simplicity. Cistercian churches, though built of stone, were initially unlike the great Romanesque churches of the Benedictines. They were remarkably standardized; the church and the rest of the buildings of one Cistercian monastery were almost exactly like those of the others (Figure 9.3). The churches were small, made of smoothly hewn, undecorated stone. Wall paintings and sculpture were prohibited. Illuminated by the pure white light that came through clear glass windows, Cistercian houses were luminous, cool, and serene.

There were two sorts of white monks: *conversi,* or "lay brothers," toiled in the fields; choir monks dedicated themselves to private prayer and contemplation and to monastic administration. By the end of the twelfth century, the Cistercians had a closely monitored network of houses, and each year the Cistercian abbots met to hammer out legislation for all of them. The abbot of the motherhouse (or founding house) visited the daughter houses annually to make sure the legislation was being followed. Each house, whether mother or daughter, had large and highly organized farms and grazing lands called granges. Cistercian monks spent much of their time managing their estates and flocks, both of which were yielding handsome profits by the end of the twelfth century. Clearly part of the agricultural and commercial revolutions of the Middle Ages, the Cistercian order made managerial expertise a part of the monastic life.

At the same time, the Cistercians elaborated a spirituality of intense personal emotion. As Bernard said:

Often enough when we approach the altar to pray our hearts are dry and lukewarm. But if we persevere, there comes an unexpected infusion of grace, our breast expands as it were, and our interior is filled with an overflowing love.

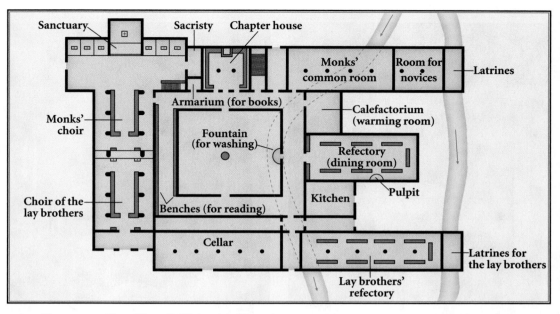

Figure 9.3 Floor Plan of a Cistercian Monastery
Cistercian monasteries seldom deviated much from this standard plan, which perfectly suited their double lifestyle: one half for the lay brothers, who worked in the fields; the other half for the monks, who spent their days praying. This plan shows the first floor. Above were dormitories: the lay brothers slept above their cellar and refectory; the monks slept above their chapter house (where the rule of St. Benedict was read to them), common room, and room for novices. No one had a private bedroom, just as the rule prescribed.

The Cistercians emphasized not only human emotion but also Christ's and Mary's humanity. While pilgrims continued to stream to the tombs and reliquaries of saints, the Cistercians dedicated all their churches to the Virgin Mary (for whom they had no relics) because for them she signified the model of a loving mother. Indeed, the Cistercians regularly used maternal imagery (as Bernard's description invoking the metaphor of a flowing breast illustrates) to describe the nurturing care provided to humans by Jesus himself. The Cistercians' God was approachable, human, protective, even mothering.

Similar views of God were held by many who were not members of the Cistercian order. Their spirituality signaled wider changes. For example, around 1099, St. Anselm wrote a theological treatise titled *Why God Became Man,* in which he argued that since man had sinned, only a sinless man could redeem him. St. Anselm's work represented a new theological focus on the redemptive power of human charity, including that of Jesus as a human being.

Religious Fervor and Dissent

Christ's humanity became the focus of men and women of every age and every walk of life. They made Christ's childhood, agony, death, and presence in the Eucharist—the bread and wine that became the body and blood of Christ in the

Saint-Savin-sur-Gartempe

The nave of the church of Saint-Savin was built between 1095 and 1115. Its barrel (or tunnel) vault is typical of Romanesque churches, as is its sense of liveliness, variety, and color. The columns, decorated with striped or wavy patterns, are topped by carved capitals, each one different from the next. The entire vault is covered with frescoes painted in shades of brown, ocher, and yellow depicting scenes from the Old Testament. What were the purposes of such decorations? (Bridgeman-Giraudon/Art Resource, NY.)

Eberbech

Compare the nave of Eberbech, a Cistercian church built between 1170 and 1186, with the nave of Saint-Savin. What at Saint-Savin appears full of variety and color is here subdued by order and calm. There are no wall paintings in a Cistercian church, no variegated columns—nothing that might distract the worshipper. Yet a close look reveals subtle points of interest. How has the architect played with angles, planes, and light in the vaulting? Are the walls utterly smooth? What decorative elements can you see on the massive piers between the arches? (akg-images/ Stefan Drechsel.)

Mass—the most important experiences of their own lives. They punctuated their daily routines with scriptural reading, fasting, and charity. New religious groups sprouted in the towns and cities. Some of this intense religiosity developed into official, orthodox movements within the church; other religious movements so threatened established doctrine that church leaders declared them heretical.

St. Francis (c. 1182–1226) founded the most famous orthodox religious movement of the day—the Franciscans. Francis was a child of the commercial revolution. Expected to follow his well-to-do father in the cloth trade at Assisi in Italy, Francis experienced doubts, dreams, and illnesses, which spurred him to religious self-examination. In time, he renounced his family's wealth, dramatically marking the decision by casting off all his clothes and standing naked before his father, a crowd of spectators, and the bishop of Assisi. Francis then put on a simple robe and went about preaching penance to anyone who would listen. Adopting the life of a mendicant (one who begs for his livelihood), he accepted no money (only hospitality), walked without shoes, wore only one coarse tunic, and refused to be cloistered. Intending to follow the model of Christ, he received, as his biographers put it, a miraculous gift of grace: the stigmata, bleeding sores corresponding to the wounds Christ suffered on the cross.

By all accounts Francis was a spellbinding speaker, and he attracted many followers. Recognized as a religious order by the pope, the Brothers of St. Francis (or **friars**, from the Latin term for "brothers") spent their time preaching, ministering to lepers, and doing manual labor. Eventually they dispersed, setting up fraternal groups throughout Italy and then in France, Spain, the Holy Land, Germany, and England. Unlike the Carthusians and Cistercians, who had rejected cities, the friars sought town life, preaching to urban crowds and begging for their daily bread. St. Francis converted both men and women. In 1212, a young noblewoman named Clare formed the nucleus of a community of pious women, which became the Order of the Sisters of St. Francis. At first the women worked alongside the friars, but the church disapproved of their activities in the world, and soon Franciscan sisters were confined to cloisters under the Benedictine rule.

Clare was one of many women who sought a new kind of religious expression. In northern Europe at the end of the twelfth century, laywomen who lived together in informal pious communities were called Beguines. Without permanent vows or an established rule, the Beguines chose to be celibate (though they were free to leave and marry) and often made their living by weaving cloth or working with the sick and old. Although their daily occupations were ordinary, the Beguines' private, internal lives were often emotional and ecstatic, infused with the combined imagery of love and religion so pervasive in both monasteries and courts.

More hardheaded was St. Dominic (1170–1221), founder of the Dominicans, an order of friars patterned very closely on the Franciscans. Like Francis, Dominic and his followers rejected material riches and instead went about on foot, preaching and begging. Their initial audience was not the men and women of the Italian cities, however, but rather the people of southern France, where new doctrines that contradicted those officially accepted by the church—and therefore labeled "heretical"—had become very popular.

Dominic and his friars were responding to an unprecedented explosion of heresies, part of the ferment of ideas and experiments in social life that were characteristic of medieval city growth. Among the most visible of the heretics were the dualists, who saw the world torn between two great forces—one good, the other evil. Dualism became a prominent ingredient in religious life in Italy and the Rhineland by the end of the twelfth century. Another center of dualism was Languedoc, an area of southern France; there the dualists were called Albigensians, a name derived from the Languedoc town of Albi.

Described collectively as Cathars, or "Pure Ones," the Albigensians, like other dualists, believed that the devil had created the material world. Therefore they renounced the world, rejecting wealth, sex, and meat. Their repudiation of sex reflected some of the attitudes of eleventh-century church reformers (whose orthodoxy, however, was never in doubt), and their rejection of wealth echoed the same concerns that moved the Cistercians to worship in plain churches and St. Francis to embrace poverty. In many ways the dualists simply took these attitudes to an extreme. But unlike orthodox reformers, they also challenged the efficacy and value of the church hierarchy. Cathars considered themselves followers of Christ's original message, but the church called them heretics.

The church also condemned other, nondualist groups as heretical, not on doctrinal grounds but because these groups allowed their lay members to preach, challenging the authority of the church hierarchy. In Lyon (in southeastern France) in the 1170s, for example, a rich merchant named Waldo decided to take literally the Gospel message "If you wish to be perfect, then go and sell everything you have, and give to the poor" (Matt. 19:21). The same message had inspired countless monks and would worry the church far less several decades later, when St. Francis established his new order. But when Waldo went into the street and gave away his belongings, announcing, "I am not really insane, as you think," he scandalized not only the bystanders but the church as well. Refusing to retire to a monastery, Waldo and his followers, men and women called Waldensians, lived in poverty and went about preaching, quoting the Gospel in the vernacular so that everyone would understand. But the papacy rebuffed Waldo's bid to preach freely, and the Waldensians— denounced, excommunicated, and expelled from Lyon—wandered to Languedoc, Italy, northern Spain, and the Mosel valley (in Germany).

REVIEW | How did the money economy affect religious life?

Conclusion

The commercial revolution and the building boom it spurred profoundly changed the look of Europe. Thriving cities of merchants and artisans brought trade, new wealth, and new institutions to the West. Mutual and fraternal organizations like the commune, the compagnia, and the guilds expressed and reinforced the solidarity and economic interests of city dwellers.

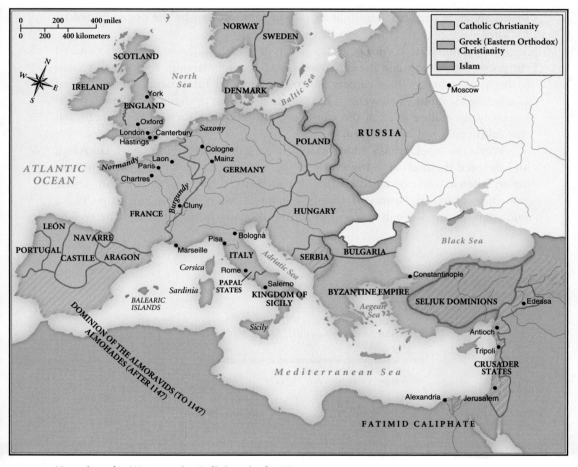

Mapping the West Major Religions in the West, c. 1200
The broad washes of color on this map tell a striking story: by 1150, there were three major religions, each corresponding to a broad region. To the west, north of the Mediterranean Sea, Catholic Christianity held sway; to the east, the Greek Orthodox church was ascendant; all along the southern Mediterranean, Islam triumphed. Only a few places defied this logic: one was the crusader states, a tiny outpost of Catholics who ruled over a largely Muslim population. What this map does not show are the details: Jewish communities in many cities, lively varieties of Islamic beliefs within the Muslim world, communities of Coptic Christians in Egypt, and scattered groups of heretics in Catholic lands.

Political centralization accompanied economic growth, as kings and popes exerted their authority and tested its limits. The Gregorian reform pitted the emperor against the pope, and two separate political hierarchies emerged: the secular and the ecclesiastical. The two might cooperate, as Suger and Louis VI showed in their mutual respect, admiration, and dependence. But they might also clash, as Becket did with Henry II. Secular and religious leaders developed new and largely separate systems of administration, reflecting the new distinctions that separated clergy from laity. Although in some ways growing apart, the two groups never worked together so closely as in the crusades, military pilgrimages inspired by the pope and led by lay lords.

The commercial economy, political stability, and ecclesiastical needs fostered the growth of schools and the achievements of new scholarship. Young men sought learning to enhance their careers and bring personal fulfillment; women gained excellent educations in convents. Logic fascinated some students because it seemed to clarify the nature of both the world and God. Others, such as St. Bernard, felt that faith could not be analyzed.

While the black monks added to their hours of worship, built lavish churches, and devoted themselves to the music of the plainchant, the white monks insisted on an intense, interior spiritual life in a monastery shorn of decoration. Other reformers, such as Bruno of Cologne, sought isolation and hardship. These reformers rejected urban society yet unintentionally reflected it: the Cistercians

TIMELINE

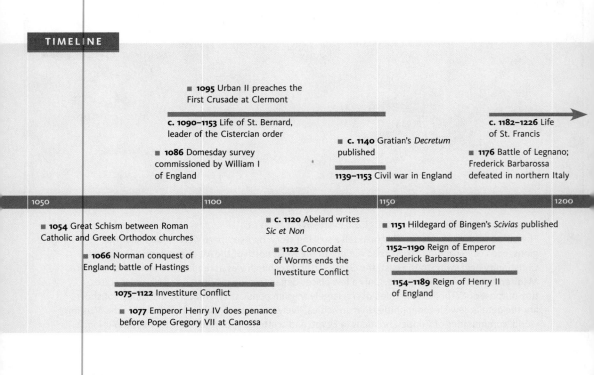

■ **1095** Urban II preaches the First Crusade at Clermont

c. 1090–1153 Life of St. Bernard, leader of the Cistercian order

■ **1086** Domesday survey commissioned by William I of England

■ **c. 1140** Gratian's *Decretum* published

1139–1153 Civil war in England

c. 1182–1226 Life of St. Francis

■ **1176** Battle of Legnano; Frederick Barbarossa defeated in northern Italy

| 1050 | 1100 | 1150 | 1200 |

■ **1054** Great Schism between Roman Catholic and Greek Orthodox churches

■ **1066** Norman conquest of England; battle of Hastings

1075–1122 Investiture Conflict

■ **1077** Emperor Henry IV does penance before Pope Gregory VII at Canossa

■ **c. 1120** Abelard writes *Sic et Non*

■ **1122** Concordat of Worms ends the Investiture Conflict

■ **1151** Hildegard of Bingen's *Scivias* published

1152–1190 Reign of Emperor Frederick Barbarossa

1154–1189 Reign of Henry II of England

were as anxious as any tradesman about the success of their granges, and the Carthusians were dedicated to their books. With the Franciscans and Dominicans, as well as heretical groups such as the Cathars, laypeople were drawn to participate actively in a deeply felt imitation of Christ's life and sufferings. Yet this new piety, paired with new power, contributed to the persecution of Jews and the periodic call for crusades against Muslims.

CHAPTER REVIEW QUESTIONS

1. What were the similarities and differences between the powers wielded by the Carolingian kings and those wielded by twelfth-century rulers?

2. Contrast the purposes and the institutions of the gift economy discussed in Chapter 7 with those of the new profit economy.

For practice quizzes and other study tools, see the Online Study Guide at bedfordstmartins.com/huntconcise.

For primary-source material from this period, see Chapters 10 and 11 of *Sources of THE MAKING OF THE WEST*, Third Edition.

Suggested References

All aspects of the Gregorian reform are treated in the succinct book by Miller. The crusades, always a popular topic, have two new historians in Asbridge and Tyerman. Little's book on the commercial economy and religious movements is a classic.

Asbridge, Thomas. *The First Crusade: A New History*. 2004.

Bartlett, Robert. *England under the Norman and Angevin Kings, 1075–1225*. 2000.

Boynton, Susan. *Shaping a Monastic Identity: Liturgy and History at the Imperial Abbey of Farfa, 1000–1125*. 2006.

Clanchy, Michael. *Abelard: A Medieval Life*. 1997.

Hildegard of Bingen: http://www.healingchants.com/hvb_links.html

Hudson, John. *The Formation of the English Common Law: Law and Society in England from the Norman Conquest to Magna Carta*. 1996.

Little, Lester K. *Religious Poverty and the Profit Economy in Medieval Europe*. 1978.

*Lopez, Robert S., and Irving W. Raymond, eds. *Medieval Trade in the Mediterranean World*. 1955.

Miller, Maureen C. *Power and the Holy in the Ages of the Investiture Conflict*. 2005.

Thomas, Hugh M. *The Norman Conquest: England after William the Conqueror*. 2008.

Tyerman, Christopher. *God's War: A New History of the Crusades*. 2006.

Wheeler, Bonnie, and John Carmi Parsons, ed. *Eleanor of Aquitaine: Lord and Lady*. 2003.

The Medieval Search for Order

I N THE SECOND HALF of the thirteenth century, a wealthy patron asked a Parisian workshop specializing in manuscript illuminations to decorate Aristotle's *On the Length and Shortness of Life*. Most Parisian illuminators knew very well how to illustrate the Bible, liturgical books, and the writings of the church fathers. But Aristotle was a Greek who had lived before the time of Christ, and he was skeptical about the possibility of an afterlife. His treatise on the length of life ended with death. The artists in the workshop ignored this fact, however, and illustrated Aristotle's work as if he had believed in the immortal soul. As shown in the illustration opposite, the workshop artists decorated an initial (the first letter of a word) in the book with a depiction of the Christian Mass for the dead, a rite that is performed for the eternal salvation of the soul. In this way, they subtly but surely made Aristotle part of the orderly system of Christian belief and practice.

Christianizing Aristotle
This illumination was created for a thirteenth-century Latin translation of Aristotle's *On the Length and Shortness of Life*. Although Aristotle did not believe in the eternity of the soul, the artists nevertheless placed a depiction of the Christian Mass for the dead in one of the book's initials, in this way revealing their conviction that the ancient teachings of Aristotle and Christian practice worked together.
(© Biblioteca Apostolica Vaticana [Vatican] Vat. Lat. 2071, f. 297.)

In Europe during the period 1200–1340, people at all levels, from workshop artists to kings and popes, expected to find order and unity in a world they believed was created by God. Sometimes their search for order led to compromise and adaptation, as in the case of the artists illustrating Aristotle's work. As medieval thinkers, writers, musicians, and artists reconciled faith with reason, they discovered the commonalities in the sacred and secular realms. Because of this, historians sometimes speak of the "medieval synthesis."

The quest for order also led to new institutions of power and control. Kings insisted on ruling whole territories and everyone within them. Although the often competing needs of kings and their subjects led to the development of representative

353

political institutions, rulers used these institutions to increase their control over their realms. Church laws were promulgated to regulate the lives of both clergy and laity. Throughout the period, the church sought to stamp out heresy, which led to the **Inquisition** and the persecution of whole communities of dissidents. In addition, as the conquests of the Mongols—invaders of China as well as the West—opened up new trade routes, more crusades were launched to bring everyone into the Christian fold.

Conflict also arose between church and state. In the mid-thirteenth century, the pope sought to destroy the emperor and very nearly did so. At the end of the century, the French and English kings sought to diminish the pope's power and succeeded quite well. Thus the end result of the desire for order was in many cases not unity, harmony, and synthesis, but rather discord.

CHAPTER FOCUS QUESTION   In what areas of life did thirteenth-century Europeans try to impose order, and how successful were these attempts?

War, Conquest, and Settlement

In the thirteenth and early fourteenth centuries, Europeans aggressively moved outward in nearly all directions. While some warriors pushed north and east on the Baltic coast, others attacked Constantinople, and still others pursued the reconquista of Spain. In the south of France and in Sicily, crusaders with the pope's blessing waged war against people whom the church declared to be heretics, including a Christian king. Far beyond Europe's eastern fringes, merchants like Marco Polo traveled to and settled in lands ruled by the Mongols.

The Northern Crusades

Long before the twelfth century, the peoples living along the Baltic coast—partly pagan, mostly Slavic- or Baltic-speaking—had learned to glean a living and a profit from the inhospitable soil and climate. Through fishing and trading, they supplied the rest of Europe and Russia with slaves, furs, amber, wax, and dried fish. Like the Vikings, they combined commercial competition with outright raiding. The Danes and the Saxons (that is, the Germans in Saxony) both benefited and suffered from their presence.

When St. Bernard began to preach the Second Crusade in Germany, he discovered that the Germans were eager to attack unbelievers—the ones right next door to them! St. Bernard pressed the pope to add these northern heathens to the list of those against whom holy war should be launched, and he urged their conversion or extermination. Thus began the Northern Crusades, which continued intermittently until the early fifteenth century.

The king of Denmark and the duke of Saxony launched the first phase of the Northern Crusades. Their initial attacks were uncoordinated; in some instances they even fought each other. Then, in key raids in the 1160s and 1170s, the two leaders worked together briefly to bring much of the region west of the Oder River under their control. They took some land outright—the Saxon duke apportioned conquered territory to his followers, for example—but more often the Slavic princes surrendered and had their territories reinstated once they became vassals of the Christian rulers.

In 1198, Pope Innocent III (r. 1198–1216) declared a crusade against the Livs, even farther to the north and east. A military order—the Order of Sword Brothers, later supplanted by the Teutonic Knights—was set up to lead crusading armies, and a bishopric, the see of Riga, was established at the mouth of the Dvina River. The native populations were obliged to submit, whether by material inducements (the crusaders helped the Livs raid the Estonians, for example) or by sheer force. Repeatedly they agreed to a truce and baptism, and just as repeatedly they rebelled. In some areas, the crusaders resorted to scorched-earth tactics. By 1300, they had secured Livonia, Prussia, Estonia, and Finland. Only Lithuania managed to resist conquest and conversion (Map 10.1).

Though less well known than the crusades to the Holy Land, the Northern Crusades had far more lasting effects: they settled the Baltic region with German-speaking lords and peasants, and they forged a permanent relationship between the very north of Europe and its neighbors to the south and west. With the Baltic dotted with churches and monasteries and its peoples dipped into baptismal waters, the region would gradually adopt the institutions of western medieval society—cities, guilds, universities, castles, and manors.

The Capture of Constantinople

Four years after calling the crusade against the Livs, Pope Innocent III declared the Fourth Crusade (1202–1204) to the Holy Land. He hoped to reverse the failures of the Second and Third Crusades, but attitudes and circumstances beyond his control took over the new enterprise. Prejudice, religious zeal, and opportunism had become characteristic of western European dealings with the Byzantine Greeks. These attitudes help explain what happened from 1202 to 1204. The crusading army turned out to be far smaller than had been expected. Its leaders could not pay the Venetians, who had fitted out a large fleet of ships in anticipation of carrying multitudes of warriors across the Mediterranean to Jerusalem. The Venetians seized the opportunity to exact a different form of payment by convincing the crusade's leaders to attack Zara, a Christian city that was Venice's competitor in the Adriatic (Map 10.1, page 356). The Venetians then set their sights on Constantinople, hoping to control it and gain a commercial monopoly there. They persuaded the crusaders to join them on behalf of Alexius, a member of the ousted imperial family. Alexius claimed the Byzantine throne and promised the crusaders that he would reunite the eastern and western churches and fund the expedition to the Holy Land. Most of the crusaders convinced themselves that the cause was noble. "Never," wrote a contemporary, "was so great an enterprise undertaken by any people since the creation of the world."

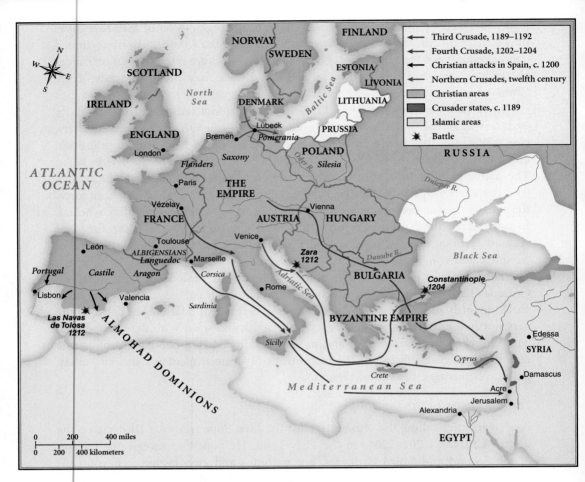

Map 10.1 Crusades and Anti-Heretic Campaigns, 1150–1204
Europeans aggressively expanded their territory during the second half of the twelfth century. To the north, German knights pushed into the lands bordering the Baltic Sea; to the south, Spanish warriors moved into the remaining strip of al-Andalus; to the east, new crusades were undertaken to shore up the tiny European outpost in the Holy Land. Although most of these aggressive activities had the establishment of Christianity as at least one motive, the conquest of Constantinople in 1204 had no such justification. It grew in part out of general European hostility toward Byzantium but mainly out of Venice's commercial ambitions.

The siege of Constantinople lasted nearly a year. Finally, on April 12, 1204, the city fell to the crusaders. Their deal with Alexius had broken down, and the crusaders brutally sacked Constantinople, killing residents and plundering treasure and relics. When one crusader discovered a cache of relics, a chronicler recalled, "he plunged both hands in and, girding up his loins, he filled the folds of his gown with the holy booty of the Church." The loss of that "holy booty" was, for the Byzantines, a great tragedy. The bishop of Ephesus wrote:

And so the streets, squares, houses of two and three stories, sacred places, nunneries, houses for nuns and monks, sacred churches, even the Great Church of God and the imperial palace, were filled with men of the enemy, all of them maddened by war and murderous in spirit. . . . [T]hey tore children from their mothers and mothers from their children, and they defiled the virgins in the holy chapels, fearing neither God's anger nor man's vengeance.

But to the Europeans, it was the Byzantines' just deserts.

Pope Innocent condemned the looting of Constantinople, but he also took advantage of it, ordering the crusaders to stay there for a year to consolidate their gains. The crusade leaders chose one among themselves, Baldwin of Flanders, to be Byzantine emperor, and he, the other princes, and the Venetians parceled out the Byzantine Empire. This new Latin Empire of Constantinople lasted until 1261, when the Byzantines recaptured the city and some of its outlying territory. No longer a strong state after 1204, Byzantium was always overshadowed and hemmed in by the military might of the Muslims and Europeans.

Popes continued to call crusades to the Holy Land until the mid-fifteenth century, but the Fourth Crusade marked the last major mobilization of men and leaders. Working against these expeditions were new values that placed a premium on the *interior* pilgrimage of the soul and celebrated rulers who stayed home to care for their people. The crusades to the Holy Land served as an outlet for religious fervor, ambition, prejudice, and aggression, but they had very little lasting positive effect. They managed to stimulate the European economy slightly, and they inspired a vast literature of songs and chronicles. Such achievements must be weighed against the lives lost on both sides and the religious polarization and prejudices that the crusades fed upon and fortified. The bitterest fruit of the crusades was the destruction of Byzantium. The Latin conquest of Constantinople in 1204 irrevocably weakened the one buffer state standing between Europe and Islam.

The Spanish Reconquista Advances

By 1200, Christian Spain had achieved the political configuration that would last for centuries: to the east was the kingdom of Aragon, to the west was Portugal, and in between was Castile, which in 1230 merged with León (Map 10.2). The leaders of these kingdoms competed for territory and power. Above all, they sought an advantage against the Muslims, who still ruled a strip of southern Spain. The reconquista, which had begun against the Muslim taifas (small, independent Muslim states) continued in full force, aided by Muslim disunity. The taifas not only were in competition with one another but also were beset from the south by the Almoravids and, after 1147, the Almohades, Muslims from North Africa. Claiming religious purity, these Berber groups declared their own holy war against al-Andalus. These simultaneous threats caused alliances within Spain to be based on political as well

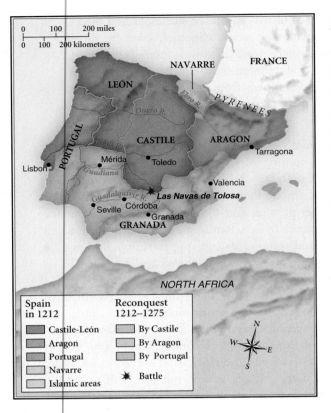

Map 10.2 The Reconquista Triumphs, 1212–1275

A major turning point in the reconquista was the battle of Las Navas de Tolosa (1212). This marked not only the defeat of the Muslims but also the triumph of Castile, which had originally been a tributary of León. In the course of the twelfth century, Castile became a power in its own right; in 1230, León and Castile merged into one kingdom. During the thirteenth century, Castile-León (and, to a lesser extent, Portugal and Aragon) conquered most of the rest of the Iberian peninsula, leaving only Granada under Islamic rule.

as religious considerations. The Muslim ruler of Valencia, for example, declared himself a vassal of the king of Castile and bitterly opposed the Berber expansion.

The crusading ideal, however, held no room for such subtleties. During the 1140s, armies under the command of the Christian kings of Portugal, Castile, and Aragon scored resounding victories against Muslim cities. Enlisting the aid of crusaders on their way to the Holy Land in 1147, the king of Portugal promised land, plunder, and protection to all who would help him attack Muslim-controlled Lisbon. His efforts succeeded, and Lisbon's Muslim inhabitants fled or were slain, its Mozarabic bishop (the bishop of the Christians living under Muslim rule) was killed, and a crusader from England was set up as bishop. In the 1170s, the Almohades conquered the Muslim south and advanced toward the cities taken by the Christians, but their exertions had no lasting effect. In 1212, a crusading army of Spaniards led by the kings of Aragon and Castile defeated the Almohades decisively at Las Navas de Tolosa. "On their side 100,000 armed men or more fell in the battle," the king of Castile wrote afterward, "but of the army of the Lord . . . incredible though it may be, unless it be a miracle, hardly 25 or 30 Christians of our whole army fell. O what happiness! O what thanksgiving!" The turning point in the reconquista had been reached (Map 10.2). The Almohades continued to lose strength, and Christian armies marched from victory to victory. Mérida fell in 1230, Córdoba in 1236, and Seville in 1248. By 1275, all that remained of Muslim-controlled Spain was a thin wedge of territory around Granada.

Reconquista

In the north of Spain, Christians adopted the figure of St. James, considered the Apostle to Spain, as the supernatural leader of their armies against the Muslims to the south. On this tympanum (the space within the archway over a door) from the cathedral of St. James (Santiago) at Compostela, James is shown as a knight on horseback, holding a flag and a sword. He was known as "the Moor-Slayer," or slayer of Muslims. (Institut Amatller de Arte Hispanico. Arxiu Mas.)

Putting Down the Heretics in Their Midst

In the thirteenth century, church and secular powers combined not only to conquer pagans and Muslims on the borders of Europe but also to stamp out heresy in their midst. The papacy declared crusades against the dualist Albigensians of southern France and even against a reigning emperor, Frederick II.

The Dominican efforts against the Cathar Albigensians (see page 348) were not effective enough to wipe out the movement. In 1208, the murder of a papal legate (an official representative of the pope) in southern France prompted Pope Innocent III to demand that princes from the north of France take up the sword, invade Languedoc, seize the land from the heretics, and populate it with orthodox Christians. This Albigensian Crusade (1209–1229) marked the first time the pope offered warriors fighting an enemy in Christian Europe all the spiritual and temporal benefits of a crusade to the Holy Land. Innocent suspended the crusaders' monetary debts and promised that their sins would be forgiven after forty days' service.

Like all crusades, the Albigensian Crusade had political as well as religious dimensions. It pitted southern French princes with Cathar connections against northern French leaders eager to demonstrate their piety and win new possessions. After twenty years of fighting, leadership of the crusade was taken over in 1229 by

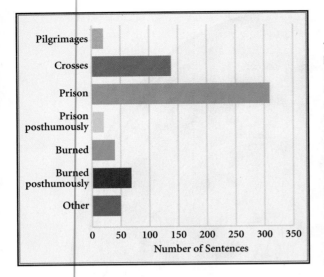

Pilgrimages
Crosses
Prison
Prison posthumously
Burned
Burned posthumously
Other

0   50   100   150   200   250   300   350
Number of Sentences

Taking Measure Sentences Imposed by an Inquisitor, 1308–1323
How harsh was the Inquisition? Did its agents regularly burn people alive? How frequently did they imprison people or order them to wear crosses on their clothing? The register of offenses and punishments kept by Bernard Gui, an inquisitor in Languedoc from 1308 to 1323, shows that only a relatively small number of people were burned alive. Of the 633 punishments handed down by Gui's tribunal, nearly half of the guilty were sentenced to prison, usually for life. Those listed as having been burned or sent to prison posthumously died before their sentences could be carried out.

the Capetian kings of France. Southern resistance was broken, and Languedoc was brought under the French crown.

Meanwhile, the papacy set up the Inquisition in southern France to discover undetected heretics. The Inquisition was a legal proceeding. First the inquisitors typically called the people of a district to a "preaching," where they gave a sermon and promised clemency to those who confessed their heresy promptly. Then, at a general inquest, they questioned each man and woman who seemed to know something about heresy: "Have you ever seen any heretics . . . ? Have you heard them preach? Attended any of their ceremonies? Adored heretics?" The judges assigned relatively lenient penalties to those who were not aware that they held heretical beliefs and to heretics who quickly recanted. But others were punished, even if they recanted. (See "Taking Measure.") Anyone who died while still a heretic could not be buried in consecrated ground—cemeteries specially blessed and set apart for believers. Raymond VII, count of Toulouse, saw the body of his father, who died excommunicated, rot in its coffin as the pope denied all requests for a Christian burial. Houses where heretics had resided or even simply entered were burned, and the sites were turned into garbage dumps. Children of heretics could not inherit any property or become priests, even if they adopted orthodox views.

In the thirteenth century, for the first time, long-term imprisonment became a tool to repress heresy, even if the heretic confessed:

> We, friars of the Order of Preachers . . . deputed as inquisitors of heretical depravity in the city and diocese of Toulouse by apostolic authority: . . . It is our will, because they [certain named men and women] have rashly transgressed against God and holy church in the ways aforesaid [by seeing heretics, adoring them, hearing their preaching, and believing them to be good],

that they be thrust into perpetual prison to do condign [appropriate] penance, and we command them to remain there in perpetuity. . . . However, we grant permission to Raymond Sabbatier to remain with his father, who is an invalid and who, it is reported, is a Catholic and a poor man, as long as his father shall live.

Raymond's privilege was quite unusual.

The inquisitors also used imprisonment to force people to recant, to give the names of other heretics, or to admit a plot. One heretic, for example, confessed to participating in a wicked (and imaginary) meeting of lepers who planned to poison all the wells. As the quest for religious order and conformity spawned wild fantasies of deviance, the inquisitors pinned their paranoia on real people.

The Inquisition created a new group—penitent heretics—who lived on the margins of Christian society. Forced to wear huge yellow fabric crosses sewn on the front and back of their shirts, they were publicly disgraced. Moreover, every Sunday and every feast day penitent heretics had to attend church twice; and during religious processions these men and women were required to join with the clergy and the faithful, carrying large branches in their hands as a sign of their penance.

One "heretic" was an emperor: Frederick II (r. 1212–1250). Innocent III—the pope who called the Fourth Crusade, the crusade against the Livs, and the Albigensian Crusade—had given the imperial crown to Frederick, but his successors regretted this bitterly. Like his grandfather Frederick Barbarossa, Frederick II, who was king of Sicily as well as Germany, sought to control Italy. This policy was intolerable to the papacy, which had its own ambitions on the peninsula.

Frederick was an amazing ruler: his contemporaries called him *stupor mundi*, "wonder of the world." Heir to two cultures, Sicilian on his mother's side and German on his father's, he cut a worldly and sophisticated figure. In Sicily, he moved easily within a diverse culture of Jews, Muslims, and Christians. There he could play the role of all-powerful ruler. In Germany, where Christian princes—often churchmen with military retinues—were acutely aware of their rights and privileges, he was less at home.

Frederick had a three-pronged imperial strategy. First, to ensure that opponents in Germany would not hound him, he granted the princes important concessions, finalized in 1232. These privileges allowed the German princes to turn their principalities into virtually independent states. Second, Frederick revamped the government of Sicily to give himself more control and yield greater profits. His *Constitutions of Melfi* (1231), an eclectic body of laws, called for nearly all court cases to be heard by royal justices, regularized commercial privileges, and set up a system of taxation. Third, Frederick sought to enter Italy through Lombardy, as his grandfather had done (Map 10.3).

The papacy followed Frederick's every move, excommunicating him a number of times. The most serious of these condemnations came in 1245, when the pope and other churchmen, assembled at the Council of Lyon, excommunicated and

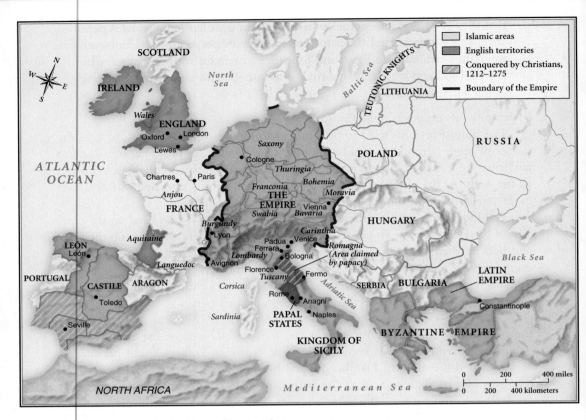

Map 10.3 Europe in the Time of Frederick II, r. 1212–1250
King of Sicily and Germany and emperor as well, Frederick ruled over territory that encircled—and threatened—the papacy. Excommunicated several times, Frederick spent much of his career fighting the pope's forces. In the process, he conceded so much power to the German princes that the emperor thenceforth had little power in Germany. Meanwhile, rulers of smaller states, such as England, France, and Castile-León, were increasing their power and authority. **For more help analyzing this map, see the map activity for this chapter in the Online Study Guide at** bedfordstmartins.com/huntconcise.

deposed Frederick, absolving his vassals and subjects of their fealty to him and forbidding anyone to support him. "He has deservedly become suspect of heresy," the council intoned, explaining that "he has despised and continues to despise the keys of the church [the symbol of St. Peter and thus of the pope], causing the sacred rites to be celebrated or rather . . . to be profaned. . . . Besides, he is joined in odious friendship with the Saracens [Muslims]." By 1248, papal legates were preaching a crusade against Frederick and all his followers. Two years later, Frederick died.

The fact that Frederick's vision of the Empire failed is of less long-term importance than the way it failed. His concessions to the German princes meant that Germany would remain divided under numerous regional princes until the nineteenth century. Between 1254 and 1273, the princes kept the German throne empty. Splintered into factions, they elected two different foreigners, who spent their time fighting each other. In one of history's strange twists, it was during this low point of the German monarchy that the term *Holy Roman Empire* was coined.

In 1273, the princes at last united and elected a German, Rudolf (r. 1273–1291), whose family, the Habsburgs, was new to imperial power. Rudolf used the imperial title to help him gain Austria for his dynasty, but he did not try to fulfill the meaning of the imperial title in Italy. For the first time, the word *emperor* was freed from its association with Italy and Rome. For the Habsburgs, the title Holy Roman Emperor was prestigious but otherwise meaningless. In 1356 the reigning emperor published the Golden Bull,* which named the seven German princes who henceforth were to be the electors of the emperor. They included three churchmen (the archbishop of Mainz was one) and four laymen (including the duke of Saxony). The office of "king of the Romans," as the emperor was called, was completely divorced from papal power, and Germany was henceforth to be ruled by the princes.

Italy at the End of the Thirteenth Century

As for Italy, Frederick's failure meant that the cities of northern Italy would continue their independent course, while the papacy ensured that Frederick's heirs would not continue to rule in Sicily. The popes called on other rulers to take over the island—first Henry III of England and then Charles of Anjou. Forces loyal to Frederick's family turned to the king of Aragon (Spain). That move left two enduring claimants to Sicily's crown—the royal family of Aragon and the house of Anjou—and it spawned a long war impoverishing the region.

In the struggle between pope and emperor, the pope had clearly won. The moment marked a high point in the political power of the medieval papacy. Nevertheless, some agreed with Frederick II's view that by tampering with secular matters the popes had demeaned and sullied their office: "These men who feign holiness," Frederick had sneered, are "drunk with the pleasures of the world." Scattered throughout Germany were people who believed that Frederick was a divine scourge sent to overpower a materialistic papacy. The papacy won the war against Frederick, but at a cost. Even the saintly king of France criticized the popes for doing "new and unheard of things." By making its war against Frederick part of its crusade against heresy, the papacy came under attack for using religion as a political tool.

---

*Official documents issued by emperors and popes are called *bulls* because they were often authenticated by a *bulla,* or seal. This document was called the Golden Bull because of its golden seal.

The Mongol Takeover

Europeans were not the only warring society in the thirteenth century. To the east, the Mongols (sometimes called Tatars or Tartars) created an aggressive army under the leadership of Chingiz (or Genghis) Khan and his sons. In part, economic necessity impelled them out of Mongolia: climatic change had reduced the grasslands that sustained their animals and their nomadic way of life. But they were also inspired by Chingiz's hope of conquering the world. In the 1230s, the Mongols began concerted attacks on Europe—in Russia, Poland, and Hungary—where weak native princes were no match for the Mongols' formidable armies and tactics. Only the death of their Great Khan, Chingiz's son Ogodei (1186–1241)—styled the khagan, or "khan of khans"—and disputes over his succession prevented a concentrated assault on Germany. In the 1250s, the Mongols took Iran, Iraq, and Syria.

The Mongols' sophisticated and devastating military tactics contributed to their overwhelming success. Organizing their campaigns at meetings held far in advance of a planned attack, they devised two- and three-flank operations. The invasion of Hungary, for example, was two-pronged: one division of the Mongol army arrived from Russia, while the other moved through Poland and Germany. Many Hungarians perished in the assault as the Mongols, fighting mainly on horseback and wielding heavy lances and powerful bows whose arrows traveled far and penetrated deeply, crushed the Hungarian force of mixed infantry and cavalry (Map 10.4). Although the Mongols were beaten off, everyone expected them to attack again. In desperation, King Béla IV of Hungary appealed to the pope: "Most of the kingdom of Hungary has been reduced to a desert by the scourge of the Tartars [Mongols], and it is surrounded like a sheepfold by different infidel peoples." Luckily for Béla, the second attack never came. But Hungary was now a frontier not between two versions of Christianity (eastern and Roman Catholic), but between the east and the west.

Russia was a different story. There the Mongols established long-term control. At Vladimir, in the north, they broke through the walls of the city and burned the people huddled for protection in the cathedral. In 1240, they captured Kiev and made the mouth of the Volga River the seat of their power. The Mongols dominated Russia's principalities for about two hundred years.

The Mongol Empire in Russia, later called the **Golden Horde** (*golden* probably from the color of their leader's tent; *horde* from a Turkic word meaning "court"), adopted much of the native government apparatus. The Mongols standardized the collection of taxes and the recruitment of troops by basing them on a population census, and they allowed Russian princes to continue ruling as long as they paid homage and tribute to the khan. Although the Mongols of the Golden Horde converted to Islam, they exempted the Russian church from taxes in return for prayers for their leaders.

The Mongols changed the political configuration of Europe and Asia. Willing to deal with Westerners, they welcomed European missionaries and traders. The

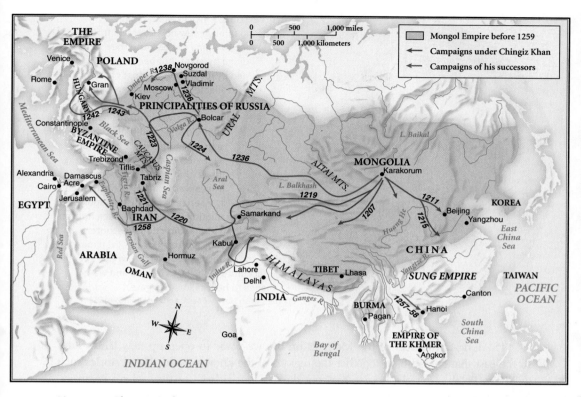

Map 10.4 The Mongol Invasions, to 1259
The Mongols were the first people to tie the eastern world to the west. Their conquest of China, which took place at about the same time as their invasions of Russia and Iran, opened up trade relations across regions formerly separated by language, religion, and political regimes.

most famous of these travelers was Marco Polo (1254–1324), son of a merchant family from Venice. Marco's father and uncle had already been to China once, and Marco joined them on their second expedition. He stayed in China for nearly two years, but others stayed even longer. In fact, evidence suggests that an entire community of Venetian traders lived in the city of Yangzhou in the mid-fourteenth century.

Merchants paved the way for missionaries. Friars (preachers to the cities of Europe) became missionaries to new continents as well. In 1289, the pope made the Franciscan John of Monte Corvino his envoy to China. Preaching in India along the way, John arrived in China four or five years after setting out, converting one local ruler and building a church. A few years later, now at Beijing, he boasted that he had converted six thousand people, constructed two churches, and translated the New Testament and the Psalter into the native language.

Pietro Vesconte's World Map, c. 1320
The Polo family knew how to travel from Venice to China not because they were guided by maps, but because they were led by local escorts. Most of the maps available in their day were symbolic rather than accurate. Pietro Vesconte's world map is partly in that old style, but it also shows a growing interest in precision. Note, for example, the "rhumb lines" that crisscross the map. These were carefully constructed as a series of equidistant spokes radiating from a point, each indicating a wind direction. Vesconte was copying "portolan charts," the most scientific maps of his day, which gave accurate indications of land and water shapes to help sailors navigate.
(© The British Library Board. Add. 27376 ff.187v-188.)

The long-term effect of the Mongols on the west was to open up new land routes to the east that helped bind together the regions of the known world. Travel stories such as Marco Polo's inspired others to seek out the fabulous riches—textiles, ginger, ceramics, copper—of China and other places in the east. In a sense, the Mongols initiated the search for exotic goods and missionary opportunities that culminated in the European "discovery" of a new world, the Americas.

REVIEW   Where and how did the desire for order and uniformity lead to aggressive military action during the period 1200–1340?

Politics of Order and Control

In the thirteenth century, Europeans for the first time spoke of their rulers not as kings of peoples (for example, king of the Franks) but as kings of territories (for example, king of France). This new designation reflected an important new element in medieval rulership. However strong earlier rulers had been, their political power had been personal, depending on ties of kinship, friendship, and vassalage. Now their power was territorial, touching all who lived within the borders of their states. This new conception, reinforced by renewed interest in Roman legal concepts and supplemented by old-fashioned personal networks, served as a foundation for strong, central rule—most strikingly in western Europe but in central and eastern Europe as well.

France: From Acorn to Oak

Even with the achievements of Louis VI, the French monarchy remained weak, a realm surrounded by powerful neighbors. This changed under Philip Augustus

(r. 1180–1223), whose acquisitive policies toward Jews (see page 327) were matched by his territorial ambitions. When Philip first came to the throne, the royal domain,

The Consolidation of France under Philip Augustus, r. 1180–1223

the Île-de-France, was sandwiched between territory controlled by the counts of Flanders, Champagne, and Anjou. By far the most powerful ruler on the European continent was King Henry II of England, who was both count of Anjou and duke of Normandy. He also held the duchy of Aquitaine through his wife while exercising hegemony over Poitou and Brittany.

Henry and the counts of Flanders and Champagne vied to control the young king of France. Philip, however, quickly learned to play them off against one another. Contemporaries were astounded when Philip successfully gained territory to the north and west. Most important, he gained Normandy and nearby counties from Henry II's son King John in 1204. Then he made good on his claim at the decisive battle of Bouvines in 1214.

Pivotal forces led to the extension of the French king's power and the territorial integrity of France. The Second Crusade (1147–1149) had brought together many French lords as vassals of the king and united them against a common foe. The language they spoke was becoming increasingly uniform and "French." This in itself did not create a larger French kingdom, however. That came about through royal strategy. Rather than give his new territories out as fiefs, Philip determined to govern them himself.* In Normandy, in particular, he demanded that the aristocrats become his vassals, and he sent his officials to collect taxes and hear cases. Philip also instituted a new kind of French administration, based on writing. Before his day, most French royal arrangements were committed to memory rather than to parchment. If decrees were written at all, they were saved by the recipient, not by the government. For example, when a monastery wanted a confirmation of its privileges from the king, its own scribes wrote the document for its archives to preserve the monastery against possible future challenges. The king did keep some documents, which generally followed him in his travels like personal possessions. But in 1194, in a battle with the king of England, Philip lost his meager cache of documents along with much treasure when he had to abandon his baggage train. After 1194, the king had all his decrees written down, and he established permanent repositories in which to keep them.

---

*Philip was particularly successful in imposing royal control in Normandy. Later French kings gave most of the other territories to collateral members of the royal family.

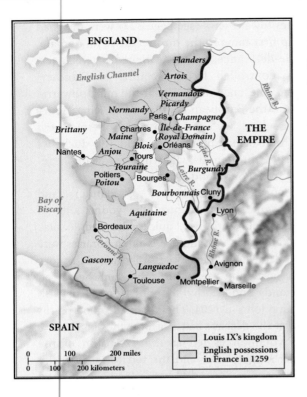

Map 10.5 France under Louis IX, r. 1226–1270
Louis IX did not expand his kingdom as dramatically as his grandfather Philip Augustus had done. He was greatly admired nevertheless, for he was seen by contemporaries as a model of Christian charity, piety, and justice. After his death, Louis IX was recognized as a saint and thus posthumously enhanced the prestige of the French monarchy.

To do the daily work of government, Philip relied on members of the lesser nobility—knights and clerics, many of whom were "masters" educated in the city schools of France. They served as officers of his court; as *prévôts* (provosts), who oversaw the king's estates and collected his taxes; and as *baillis* (bailiffs; called seneschals in the south), who supervised the provosts and functioned as regional judges, presiding over courts that met monthly and making the king's power felt locally as never before.

Under Philip's grandson Louis IX (r. 1226–1270), the Capetian monarchy reached the height of its prestige if not its power. Louis was revered not because he was a military leader, but because he was an administrator, judge, and "just father" of his people. On warm summer days, he would sit under a tree in the woods near his castle at Vincennes, on the outskirts of Paris, hearing disputes and dispensing justice personally. He used his administrators to impose royal law and justice throughout his kingdom. Over the city of Paris he appointed a salaried officer who could be supervised and fired if necessary. During his reign, the influence of the parlement of Paris, the royal court of justice, increased significantly. Originally a changeable and movable body, part of the king's personal entourage when he dealt with litigation, it was now permanently housed in Paris and staffed by professional judges who heard cases and recorded their decisions. Unlike his grandfather Philip, Louis did not try to expand his territory. He inherited a large kingdom that included Poitou and Languedoc (gained during the Albigensian Crusade)(Map 10.5), and he was content. Although the king of England attacked him continually to try to regain territory lost under Philip, Louis remained unprovoked. Rather than prolong the fighting, he conceded a bit and made peace. At the same time, Louis was a zealous crusader. He took seriously the need to defend the Holy Land when most of his contemporaries were weary of the idea.

Louis was respectful of the church and the pope; he accepted limits on his authority in relation to the church and never claimed power over spiritual matters. Nevertheless, Louis vigorously maintained the dignity of the king and his rights. He expected royal and ecclesiastical power to work in harmony, and he refused to let the church dictate how he should use his temporal authority. When French bishops wanted royal officers to support the church's sentences of excommunication, Louis declared that he would authorize his officials to do so only if he were given full knowledge of each case so that he could judge them for himself. Louis's biographer described the scene that followed:

> After consulting together the prelates informed the king that they would not give him such knowledge, since this was solely a matter for the ecclesiastical court. The king replied that he in his turn would not give them knowledge of such matters as fell within his jurisdiction, nor order his officers to compel all excommunicated persons to obtain absolution. . . . "For if I did so," he added, "I should be acting contrary to God's laws and the principles of justice."

As a result, royal and ecclesiastical power would work side by side, neither subservient to the other.

It is easy for historians to fault Louis for his policies toward Jews. His hatred of them was well known. He did not exactly advocate violence against them, but he sometimes subjected them to arrest, canceling the debts that Christians owed to them (but collecting part of those debts into the royal treasury) and confiscating their belongings. In 1253, he ordered Jews to live "by the labor of their hands" or leave France. He meant that they should no longer lend money, in effect taking away their only means of support. Louis's contemporaries did not criticize him for his policies; if anything, his hatred of Jews enhanced his reputation.

In fact, many of Louis's contemporaries considered him a saint, praising his care for the poor and sick, the pains and penances he inflicted on himself, and his regular participation in church services. In 1297, Pope Boniface VIII canonized him as St. Louis. The result was enormous prestige for the French monarchy. This prestige, joined with the renown of Paris as the center of scholarship and the repute of French courts as the epitome of chivalry, made France the cultural model of Europe.

England: Crisis and Consolidation

What the French king gained the English king lost. Henry II had been very strong, and his son Richard I (r. 1189–1199) was called "the Lion-Hearted" for his boldness. Under these men, the English monarchy was powerful and rich. Its power derived largely from its judicial and administrative apparatus. Its wealth came from court fees, income from numerous royal estates both in England and on the continent, taxes from cities, and customary feudal dues (called aids) collected from barons and knights. These aids were extraordinary taxes, demanded (traditionally) by the king on occasions such as the knighting of his eldest son and the marriage of his eldest daughter. Enriched by the commercial economy of the late twelfth century, the English kings encouraged their knights and barons not to serve them personally in battle but instead to pay the king a tax called scutage in lieu of service. The monarchs preferred to hire mercenaries both as troops to fight external enemies and as policemen to enforce the king's will at home.

But Richard died young, and his brother and heir, John (r. 1199–1216), lost badly to Philip Augustus. John was widely disliked by his contemporaries, who accused him of asserting his will in a high-handed way. But to understand John, it is necessary to appreciate how desperate he was to keep his continental possessions. After he lost his northern French territories to Philip, John did everything he could to add to the crown revenues so he could pay for an army to fight the French. He forced his vassals to pay ever-increasing scutages and extorted money in the form of new feudal aids. He compelled the widows of his vassals to marry men of his choosing or pay him a hefty fee if they refused. John's heavy investment in this war effort, however, could not prevent the defeat of his army at the battle of Bouvines in 1214, and this defeat caused discontented English barons to rebel openly against the king. At Runnymede in June 1215, John was forced to agree to the charter of baronial liberties that has come to be called Magna Carta, "Great Charter."

The English barons intended Magna Carta (so named to distinguish it from a smaller charter issued around the same time concerning the royal forests) to be a conservative document defining the "customary" obligations and rights of the nobility and forbidding the king to break from these customs without consulting his barons. "No widow shall be forced to marry so long as she wishes to live without a husband," it declared, continuing:

> No scutage or aid shall be imposed in our kingdom unless by common counsel of our kingdom, except for [the customary purposes:] ransoming our person, for making our eldest son a knight, and for once marrying our eldest daughter.

In its most famous clause, Magna Carta provided that

> no free man shall be arrested or imprisoned or disseised [deprived of his property] or outlawed or exiled or in any way victimized, neither will we attack him or send anyone to attack him, except by the lawful judgment of his peers or by the law of the land.

Thus Magna Carta established that all free men in the land had certain customs and rights in common and that the king had to uphold those customs and rights. In this way, it documented the subordination of the king to custom, implying that the king was not above the law. Magna Carta shows that the growth of royal power was matched by the self-confidence of the English barons, certain of their rights and eager to articulate them.

When it was drawn up, Magna Carta applied only to a small elite—the "free men" of the realm. It did not promise a jury trial by peers to everyone, nor did it secure the rights of Englishmen in general. But in the course of time, the definition of *free men* expanded to include all the king's subjects, and the rights guaranteed by Magna Carta came to be understood as applying to all.

Papal Monarchy

As the kings of France and England were gaining newly precise roles, so too were the popes. Innocent III was the most powerful, respected, and prestigious of the medieval popes. The first pope to have a university training, Innocent had studied theology at Paris and law at Bologna. From theology, he learned to tease new meaning out of the pope's position: he thought of himself as ruling in the place of Christ the King. In his view, secular kings and emperors existed to help the pope. From law, Innocent gained his conception of the pope as lawmaker and of law as an instrument of moral reformation.

Utilizing the traditional method of declaring church law, Innocent convened and presided over a council in 1215 at the pope's Lateran Palace in Rome. Known as the Fourth Lateran Council, it aimed to reform not only the clergy but also the laity. Innocent and the other assembled churchmen hoped to create a well-ordered society united under the authority of the church.

For laymen and laywomen, perhaps the most important canons of the Fourth Lateran Council concerned the sacraments, the rites the church believed Jesus had instituted to confer sanctifying grace. One canon required Christians to attend Mass and confess their sins to a priest at least once a year. At the same time, the council explained with new precision the transformation of bread and wine (the Eucharist) in the Mass. In the twelfth century, a newly rigorous understanding of this transformation had already been publicized, according to which Christ's body and blood were truly contained in the sacrament that looked like bread and wine on the altar.

The Fourth Lateran Council not only declared this to be dogma (authoritative teaching) but also explained it by using a technical term coined by twelfth-century scholars. The bread and wine were *transubstantiated:* although the Eucharist continued to *look* like bread and wine, with its consecration during the Mass the bread became the actual flesh and the wine the real blood of Christ. The council's emphasis on this potent event strengthened the role of the priesthood, for only a priest could celebrate this mystery (that is, transform the bread and wine into Christ's body and blood) through which God's grace was transmitted to the faithful.

Innocent III wanted the council to condemn Christian men who had intercourse with Jewish women and then claimed "ignorance" as their excuse. But the council went even further, requiring all Jews to advertise their religion by some outward sign: "We decree that [Jews] of either sex in every Christian province at all times shall be distinguished from other people by the character of their dress in public." Like all church rules, this canon took effect only when local rulers enforced it. In many instances, they did so with zeal, not so much because they were eager to humiliate Jews but rather because they could make money selling exemptions to Jews who were willing to pay to avoid the requirements. Nonetheless, sooner or later Jews almost everywhere had to wear a badge as a sign of their second-class status. In southern France and in a few places in Spain, Jews were supposed to wear round badges. In England, the city of Salisbury demanded that they wear special clothing. In Vienna, they were told to put on pointed hats (see the illustration on page 327).

The Fourth Lateran Council's longest decree blasted heretics: "Those condemned as heretics shall be handed over to the secular authorities for punishment." If the secular authority did not "purge his or her land of heretical filth," the heretic was to be excommunicated. If he had vassals, they were to be released from their oaths of fealty, and the heretic's land was to be taken over by orthodox Christians. Rulers heeded these demands. Already some had taken up arms against heretics in the Albigensian Crusade (1209–1229). The Fourth Lateran Council was also responsible for setting up the Inquisition.

The council's mission to regulate and Christianize lay behavior was carried forward by Dominican and Franciscan friars. Both orders focused on travel, preaching, and poverty—vocations that brought them into cities and towns. Soon their members dominated the fledgling city universities and were sending into the community friar-preachers trained by them. Townspeople flocked to such preachers because they wanted to know how the Christian message applied to their daily lives. They were concerned, for example, about the ethics of moneymaking, sex in marriage, and family life. In turn, the preachers represented the front line of the church. They

Friars and Usurers
How did the friars treat money? As this illustration shows, they fled it. In fact, the founder of the Franciscans, St. Francis, refused to touch money. At first, the friars begged for food and shelter. Even when their numbers grew and they began forming communities and living in monasteries, they insisted on personal poverty while ministering to city dwellers. In this illumination from about 1250, a Franciscan (in light-colored robes) and a Dominican (in black) reject offers from two usurers, whose profession they are thus shown to condemn. Other friars, however, including Thomas Aquinas, worked out justifications for some of the urban moneymaking professions. (Bibliothèque nationale de France.) **For more help analyzing this image, see the visual activity for this chapter in the Online Study Guide at** bedfordstmartins.com/huntconcise.

A Lady and Her Loving Falcon
This sumptuous velvet and silk pouch, made by an embroideress in about 1320, shows a lady in the position of falconer. The falcon, a bird ordinarily used as an aid in hunting, is here depicted as the lady's lover. He is flying toward her to place a crown of greenery on her head while she touches him tenderly on the shoulder. In her other hand she holds the leash with which she trained him. (© Musée de Tissus, Lyon.)

met the laity on their own turf and taught them to bend their activities to church teachings. Many members of the lay community became "tertiaries" of the orders, adopting lives of simplicity, prayer, and works of charity yet continuing to live in the world, raising families and tending to the tasks of daily life. Even kings became tertiaries.

The third orders were not the only outlets for lay piety. In particular, women throughout Europe found a great variety of religious refuges. As in previous centuries, powerful families founded nunneries, especially within urban areas. These were primarily for the daughters of the wealthy. Ordinary women found different modes of religious expression. Some were attracted by the quiet life and rapturous mysticism of the Beguines; others found comfort in the life of charity and service of women's mendicant orders, such as those connected to the Franciscans; and still others lived happily as wives and mothers, punctuating their domestic duties with religious devotions. Elisabeth of Hungary, who married a German prince at the age of fourteen, raised three children. At the same time, she devoted her life to fasting, prayer, and service to the poor.

Of course, many women were not as devout as Elisabeth. In the countryside, they cooked their porridge, brewed their ale, and raised their children. They attended church regularly, but only on major feast days or for "churching"—the ritual of purification after a pregnancy. In the cities, women who scratched out a meager living sometimes made pilgrimages to relic shrines to seek divine help or cures. Religion was part of these women's lives but did not dominate them.

The church's attempt to define and control the Eucharist had some unintended consequences for a number of women who made religion the focus of their lives. The new emphasis on the transformed bread and wine induced these pious women to eat nothing but the Eucharist. One such woman, Angela of Foligno, reported that the consecrated bread swelled in her mouth, tasting sweeter than any other food. In the minds of these holy women, Christ's crucifixion was the literal sacrifice of his body, to be eaten by sinful men and women as the way to redeem themselves. Renouncing all other food became part of a life of service to others, as many of these devout women gave the food they refused to eat to the poor. Even if not engaged in community service, holy women felt that their suffering itself was a work of charity, helping to release souls from purgatory, the place where (the church taught) souls were cleansed of their sins.

The Kings Triumph

The Fourth Lateran Council was the high-water mark of the medieval papacy. However, the growing prestige and actual jurisdiction of secular rulers changed the balance of power between church and state in the course of the thirteenth century. At the end of that century, when the pope clashed with the kings of France and England, the kings were the clear winners, and the papacy lost both prestige and power.

The clash began over taxing the clergy. The French king Philip IV (r. 1285–1314), known as Philip the Fair, and the English king Edward I (r. 1272–1307) financed their wars (mainly against one another) by taxing the clergy along with everyone else. The new principle of national sovereignty that they were claiming led them to assert jurisdiction over all people, even churchmen, who lived within their borders. For the pope, however, the principle at stake was his role as head of the clergy. In response to clerical taxation, Boniface VIII (r. 1294–1303) declared that only the pope could authorize such taxes. Threatening to excommunicate kings who taxed prelates without papal permission, he called upon clerics to disobey any such royal orders.

Edward and Philip reacted swiftly. Taking advantage of the important role that English courts played in protecting the peace, Edward declared that all clerics who refused to pay their taxes would be considered outlaws—literally, "outside the law." Clergymen who were robbed, for example, would have no appeal against their attackers; if accused of crimes, they would have no defense in court. Relying on a different strategy, Philip forbade the exportation of precious metals, money, or jewels, effectively sealing the French borders. Immediately the English clergy cried out for legal protection, while the papacy itself clamored for the revenues it had long enjoyed from French pilgrims, litigants, and travelers. Boniface was forced to back down, conceding in 1297 that kings had the right to tax the clergy of their kingdoms in emergencies.

But the crisis was not over. In 1301, Philip the Fair tested his jurisdiction in southern France by arresting the bishop of Pamiers on a charge of treason for slandering the king by comparing him with an owl, "the handsomest of birds which is worth absolutely nothing." Imprisoning a bishop violated the principle, maintained both by the pope and by French law, that a clergyman was not subject to lay justice. Boniface reacted angrily, and Philip seized the opportunity to ridicule and humiliate the pope, orchestrating a public relations campaign against him. Boniface's reply, a bull titled *Unam Sanctam* (1302), intensified the situation by declaring bluntly "that it is altogether necessary to salvation for every human creature to be subject to the Roman Pontiff." At meetings of the king's inner circle, Philip's agents declared Boniface a false pope, accusing him of sexual perversion, various crimes, and heresy. In 1303, royal agents, acting under Philip's orders, invaded Boniface's palace at Anagni (southeast of Rome) to capture the pope, bring him to France, and try him. Fearing for the pope's life, however, the people of Anagni joined forces and drove the French agents out of town. Boniface died shortly thereafter, but the king had made his power felt. The next two popes pardoned Philip and his agents for their actions.

Just as Frederick II's defeat showed the weakness of the Empire, so Boniface's humiliation showed the limits of the papacy. The two powers that claimed "universal" authority had little weight in the face of the new, limited, but tightly controlled national states. After 1303, popes continued to criticize kings, but their words had less and less impact. In the face of powerful medieval states such as France, Spain, and England—supported by vast revenues, judicial apparatuses, representative institutions, and even the loyalty of churchmen—the papacy could make little headway. The delicate balance between church and state, a hallmark of the years of Louis IX, broke down by the end of the thirteenth century.

In 1309, forced from Rome by civil strife, the papacy settled at Avignon, a city technically in the Holy Roman Empire but very close to, and influenced by, France (Map 10.5, page 368). Here the popes remained until 1378. Italians called the

Boniface VIII
The sculptor who depicted Pope Boniface VIII made him young, majestic, authoritative, sober, and calm. Yet Boniface could not have been very calm, for his authority was challenged at every turn. (Scala/Art Resource, NY.)

period from 1309 to 1378 the Babylonian captivity, likening the popes' absence from Rome to the ancient Israelites' exile to Babylon (2 Kings 25:11). The Avignon popes, many of them French, established a sober and efficient organization that took in regular revenues and gave the papacy more say than ever before in the appointment of churchmen. They would, however, slowly abandon the idea of leading all of Christendom and would tacitly recognize the growing power of the secular states to regulate their internal affairs.

Power Shifts in the Italian Communes

During the thirteenth century, the Italian communes continued to extend their control over the surrounding countryside as independent city-states. While generally presenting a united front to outsiders, factions within the communes fought for control and its spoils. In the early thirteenth century, these factions represented noble families. In the course of the century, however, newer groups, generally though not exclusively from the non-noble classes, attempted to seize the reins of government in the communes. The *popolo* (people), as such groups were called, incorporated members of city associations such as craft and merchant guilds, parishes, and the commune itself. In fact, the popolo was a kind of alternative commune, a sworn association in each city that dedicated itself to upholding the interests of its members. Armed and militant, the popolo demanded a share in city government, particularly to gain a voice in matters of taxation. In 1222 at Piacenza, for example (see "Mapping the West," page 389), the popolo won half the government offices; a year later, they and the nobles worked out a plan to share the election of their city's *podestà*, or "chief executive." Such power sharing often resulted from the popolo's struggle for rights. In some cities, however, nobles overcame and dissolved the popolo, while in others the popolo virtually excluded the nobles from government. Constantly confronting one another—quarreling, feuding, and compromising—these factions turned Italian cities into centers of civil discord.

Weakened by this constant friction, the communes were tempting prey for great regional nobles who, allying with one or another faction, established themselves as *signori* (singular *signore*, "lord") of the cities, keeping the peace at the price of repression. In these circumstances, the commune gave way to the *signoria* (a state ruled by a signore), and one family began to dominate the government. The communes ceased to exist, and many Italian cities fell under the control of despots. The fate of Piacenza was typical. First dominated by nobles, its commune had granted the popolo a voice by 1225. By midcentury, however, the signore's power had eclipsed that of both the nobles and the popolo.

New-Style Associations amid the Monarchies

Although the thirteenth century was the age of newly strong signori or monarchs, there were some exceptions. Under the leadership of Lübeck, the cities of northern Germany trading between the Baltic and North seas banded together to form the

Hanseatic League (or Hanse). It was one fruit of the Northern Crusades; even the Teutonic Knights were members. Merchants in these cities dominated the northern grain trade, and their control over this commodity gave them power. They were able to declare embargoes against enemies and monopolies for themselves. Throughout the thirteenth and fourteenth centuries, the Hanseatic League dominated the Baltic region.

Similarly independent were the self-governing peasant and town communes in the high Alpine valleys that became the united Swiss Confederation. In 1291, the peasants of Uri, Schwyz, and Unterwalden swore a perpetual alliance against their oppressive Habsburg overlord. After defeating a Habsburg army in 1315, these free peasants took the name "Confederates" and developed a new alliance that would become Switzerland. In the process, the Swiss enshrined their freedom in the legend of William Tell, their national hero, who was forced by a Habsburg official to prove his archery skills by shooting an apple placed on the head of his own son. This act so outraged the citizens that they rose up against Habsburg rule. By 1353, the important cantons of Lucerne, Zurich, and Bern had joined the confederation. It continued to acquire new members into the sixteenth century, defeating armies sent by different princes to undermine its liberties.

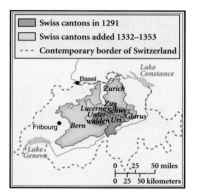

Growth of the Swiss Confederation, to 1353

Legend:
- Swiss cantons in 1291
- Swiss cantons added 1332–1353
- Contemporary border of Switzerland

The Birth of Representative Institutions

Monarchies found it useful to embrace groups beyond the narrow elite of the aristocracy. One of the ways in which Philip the Fair orchestrated his public relations campaign against Pope Boniface was to convene representatives of the clergy, nobles, and townspeople to explain, justify, and propagandize his position. This new assembly, which met at Paris in 1302, was the ancestor of the Estates General, which would meet sporadically for centuries thereafter—for the last time in 1789, at the beginning of the French Revolution. (In France, the various orders—clergy, nobles, and commoners—were called estates.) After Philip's agents declared Boniface a false pope, the king sent his commissioners to the various provinces of France to convene local meetings to repeat his charges against Boniface and gain support. Clergy, local nobles, townspeople, and even villagers attending these meetings almost unanimously denounced the pope.

As in France, representative institutions elsewhere began as political tools with which rulers hoped to broaden their support. All across Europe—from Spain to Poland, from England to Hungary—rulers summoned parliaments. These assemblies grew out of the ad hoc advisory sessions kings customarily held with their nobles and clergy, men who informally represented the two most powerful classes, or "orders," of medieval society. Although these bodies differed from place to place, the impulse behind their creation was similar. They began (as in France) as assemblies where kings celebrated their royal power and prestige and where the "orders" simply assented to royal policy. In the thirteenth century, the advisory sessions became solemn, formal meetings of representatives of the "orders" to the kings' chief councils—the precursors of parliamentary sessions. Eventually these bodies became organs through which people not ordinarily at court could articulate their wishes.

One of the earliest such representative institutions was created in Castile-León (part of present-day Spain). Sometimes the king of Castile-León called together only the clergy and nobles, but other times he sent for representatives of the towns, especially when he wanted the help of town militias. As townsmen gradually began to participate regularly in advisory sessions called *cortes,* kings came to depend on them and their support. In turn, commoners became more fully integrated into the work of royal government. Because of their wealth, they were crucial to this work. Enriched by plunder from the reconquista, the villages of Castile-León had become major commercial centers, dominating the countryside. Town leaders— called *caballeros villanos,* or "city horsemen," because they were rich enough to fight on horseback—monopolized municipal offices. In 1188, when King Alfonso IX (r. 1188–1230) summoned townsmen to the cortes, the city caballeros served as their representatives, agreeing to Alfonso's plea for military and financial support and for help in consolidating his rule. Once convened at court, these wealthy townsmen joined bishops and noblemen in formally counseling the king and assenting to royal decisions. Beginning with Alfonso X (r. 1252–1284), Castilian monarchs regularly called on the cortes to participate in major political and military decisions and to assent to new taxes to finance them.

The English Parliament* also developed as a tool of royal government. In this case, however, the king's control was complicated by the power of the barons, manifested, for example, in Magna Carta. In the twelfth century, King Henry II had consulted prelates and barons at Great Councils, using these parliaments as his tool to ratify and gain support for his policies. Although Magna Carta had nothing to do with such councils, the barons thought the document gave them an important and permanent role in royal government as the king's advisers and a solid guarantee of their customary rights and privileges. When Henry III (r. 1216–1272) was crowned at the age of nine, he was king in name only for the first sixteen years of his reign. During that period, England was governed by a council consisting of a few barons, professional administrators, and a papal legate. Though not quite "government by Parliament," this council set a precedent for baronial participation in government.

---

*Although *parliament* and *parlement* are very similar words, both deriving from the French word *parler* (to speak), the institutions they named were very different. The Parlement of France was a law court, whereas the English Parliament, though beginning as a court to redress grievances, had by 1327 become above all a representative institution. The major French representative assembly, later called the Estates General, first convened at the beginning of the fourteenth century.

An English parliament that included commoners came into being in the midst of war and as a result of political weakness. Henry so alienated nobles and commoners alike by his wars, debts, choice of advisers, and demands for money that the barons threatened to rebel. At a meeting at Oxford in 1258, they forced Henry to dismiss his foreign advisers; to rule with the advice of a Council of Fifteen, chosen jointly by the barons and the king; and to limit the terms of his chief officers. However, this new government was also torn apart by disputes among the barons, and civil war erupted in 1264. At the battle of Lewes in the same year, the leader of the baronial opposition, Simon de Montfort (c. 1208–1265), routed the king's forces, captured the king, and became England's de facto ruler. Because only a minority of the barons followed Simon, he sought new support by convening a parliament in 1265. He summoned not only the earls, barons, and churchmen who backed him but also representatives from the towns—the "commons"—and he appealed for their help. Thus, for the first time, the English commons were given a voice in government. Simon's brief rule ended that very year, and Henry's son Edward I became a rallying point for royalists (backers of the king). Edward's constant need for new revenues led him to call regular sessions of Parliament. Without meaning to do so, he solidified its role as a regular institution of royal government in England. Thus, in England, representative government emerged out of the interplay between royal initiatives and baronial revolts.

> **REVIEW**   Compare the administrative tools of the papal monarchy with those of secular monarchies in France, England, and Spain.

The Medieval Synthesis

Just as the church wanted to regulate worldly life in accordance with God's plan for salvation, so contemporary thinkers, writers, musicians, and artists sought to harmonize the secular with the sacred realms. Scholars wrote treatises that reconciled faith with reason, poets and musicians sang of the links between heaven and earth, and artists expressed the same ideas in stone and sculpture and on parchment. In the face of many contradictions, all of these groups were largely successful in communicating an orderly image of the world.

Scholasticism: Harmonizing Faith and Reason

Scholasticism was the culmination of the method of logical inquiry and exposition pioneered by masters like Peter Abelard (see page 341). In the thirteenth century, the method was used to summarize and reconcile all knowledge. Many of the thirteenth-century scholastics (those who practiced scholasticism) were members of the Dominican and Franciscan orders and taught in the universities. On the whole, they were confident that knowledge obtained through the senses and reason was compatible with knowledge known through faith and revelation. One of their goals was to demonstrate this harmony. The scholastic summa (plural summae), or summary of knowledge, was a systematic exposition of the answer to every possible question about human morality, the physical world, society, belief, action, and theology.

The method of the summa borrowed much of the vocabulary and many of the rules of logic outlined by Aristotle. Even though Aristotle was a pagan, scholastics considered his coherent and rational body of thought the most perfect that human reason alone could devise. Because they had the benefit of Christ's revelations, scholastics considered themselves able to take Aristotle's philosophy one step further and reconcile human reason with Christian faith. Confident in their method and conclusions, scholastics embraced the world and its issues.

Some scholastics considered questions about the natural world. Albertus Magnus (c. 1200–1280) was a major theologian who also contributed to the fields of biology, botany, astronomy, and physics. His reconsideration of Aristotle's views on motion led the way to distinctions that helped scientists in the sixteenth and seventeenth centuries arrive at the modern notion of inertia.

One of Albertus's students was St. Thomas Aquinas (c. 1225–1274), perhaps the most famous scholastic. Huge of build and renowned for his composure in debate, Thomas came from a noble Italian family that had hoped to see him become a powerful bishop rather than a poor university professor. When he was about eighteen years old, he defied his family's wishes and joined the Dominicans. Soon he was studying at Cologne with Albertus. At thirty-two he became a master at the University of Paris. Like many other scholastics, Thomas considered Aristotle "the Philosopher," the authoritative voice of human reason, which he sought to reconcile with divine revelation in a universal and harmonious scheme. In 1273, he finished his monumental *Summa Theologiae* (sometimes called *Summa Theologica*), intended to cover all important topics, human and divine. Thomas divided these topics into questions, exploring each one thoroughly and systematically, and concluding each question with a decisive position and a refutation of opposing views.

Many of Thomas's questions spoke to the keenest concerns of his day. He asked, for example, whether it was lawful to sell something for more than it was worth. Thomas arranged his argument systematically, quoting first authorities that seemed to declare every sort of selling practice, even deceptive ones, to be lawful. This was the *sic* (or "yes") position. Then he quoted an authority that opposed selling something for more than it was worth. This was the *non*. Following that, he gave his own argument, prefaced by the words "I answer that." Unlike Abelard, whose method left differences unresolved, Thomas wanted to harmonize the two points of view, so he pointed out that price and worth depended on the circumstances of the buyer and seller, and he concluded that charging more than a seller had originally paid could be legitimate at times.

For townspeople engaged in commerce and worried about biblical prohibitions on moneymaking, Thomas's ideas about selling practices addressed burning questions. Hoping to go to heaven as well as reap the profits of their business ventures, laypeople listened eagerly to preachers who delivered their sermons in the vernacular but who based their ideas on the Latin summae of Thomas and other scholastics. Thomas's conclusions aided townspeople in justifying their worldly activities. In his own day, Thomas Aquinas was a controversial figure, and his ideas, emphasizing reason, were by no means universally accepted. In Thomas's view, God, nature, and reason were in harmony, so Aristotle's arguments could be used to explore both the human and the divine orders.

The work of the thirteenth-century scholastics to unite the secular with the sacred continued for another generation after Thomas. Yet at the beginning of the fourteenth century, fissures began to appear. In the summae of John Duns Scotus (c. 1266–1308), for example, the world and God were less compatible. John, whose name "Duns Scotus" betrays his Scottish origin, was a Franciscan who taught at both Oxford and Paris. For John, human reason could know truth only through the "special illumination of the uncreated light"—that is, by divine illumination. This was a Neoplatonic idea that had long inspired medieval thinkers. But unlike his predecessors, John believed that this illumination came not as a matter of course but only when God chose to intervene. John and others sometimes experienced God as willful rather than reasonable. Human reason could not soar to God; God's will alone determined whether a person could know him. In this way, John separated the divine and secular realms.

Like John, William of Ockham (c. 1285–1349), an English Franciscan who was one of the most eminent theologians of his age, rejected any confident synthesis of Christian doctrine and Aristotelian philosophy. Ockham believed that universal concepts had no reality in nature but instead existed only as mere representations, names in the mind—a philosophy that came to be called nominalism. Perceiving and analyzing such concepts as "man" or "papal infallibility" offered no assurance that the concepts expressed truth. Observation and human reason were limited as means to understanding the universe and knowing God. Ockham's insistence that the simplest explanation was the best came to be known as "Ockham's razor." Where human reason left off, God's covenant with his faithful took over.

New Syntheses in Writing and Music

Thirteenth-century writers and musicians, as confident in their powers as any king or scholastic, presented complicated ideas and feelings as harmonious and unified syntheses. Writers explored the relations between this world and the next; musicians found ways to bridge sacred and secular forms of music.

Dante Alighieri (1265–1321), perhaps the greatest vernacular poet of the Middle Ages, harmonized the scholastic universe with the mysteries of faith and the poetry of love. Born in Florence in a time of political turmoil, Dante incorporated the heroes and villains of his day into his most famous poem, the *Commedia*, written between 1313 and 1321. Later known as the *Divine Comedy*, Dante's poem describes the poet taking an imaginary journey from Hell to Purgatory and finally to Paradise. The poem is an allegory in which every person and object must be understood at more than one level. At the most literal level, the poem is about Dante's travels. At a deeper level, it is about the soul's search for meaning and enlightenment and its ultimate discovery of God in the light of divine love. Just as Thomas Aquinas thought that Aristotle's logic could lead to important truths, so Dante used the pagan poet Virgil as his guide through Hell and Purgatory. And just as Thomas believed that faith went beyond reason to even higher truths, so Dante found a new guide representing earthly love to lead him through most of Paradise. This guide was Beatrice, a Florentine girl with whom Dante had fallen in love as a boy and whom he never forgot. But only the Virgin Mary, representing faith and divine love, could bring Dante to the culmination of his journey—a blinding and inexpressibly awesome vision of God:

> What I then saw is more than tongue can say.
> Our human speech is dark before the vision.
> The ravished memory swoons and falls away.

Dante's poem electrified a wide audience. By elevating one dialect of Italian—the language that ordinary Florentines used in their everyday lives—to a language of exquisite poetry, Dante was able to communicate the scholastics' harmonious and optimistic vision of the universe in an even more exciting and accessible way. So influential was his work that it is no exaggeration to say that modern Italian is based on Dante's Florentine dialect.

Other writers of the period used different methods to express the harmony of heaven and earth. The anonymous author of *Quest of the Holy Grail* (c. 1225), for example, wrote about the adventures of the knights of King Arthur's Round Table to convey the doctrine of transubstantiation and the wonder of the vision of God. In *The Romance of the Rose,* begun by one author (Guillaume de Lorris, a poet in the romantic tradition) and finished by another (Jean de Meun, a poet in the scholastic tradition), a lover seeks the rose, his true love. In the long dream that the poem describes, the narrator's search for the rose is thwarted by personifications of love, shame, reason, abstinence, and so on. They present him with arguments for and against love, not incidentally commenting on people of the poets' own day. In the end, sexual love is made part of the divine scheme—and the lover plucks the rose.

Musicians, like poets, developed new forms that bridged sacred and secular subjects in the thirteenth and fourteenth centuries. This connection appears in the most distinctive musical form of the thirteenth century, the motet (from the French *mot,* meaning "word"). The motet is an example of **polyphony**, music that consists of two or more melodies performed simultaneously. Before about 1215, most polyphony was sacred; purely secular polyphony was not common before the fourteenth century. The motet, a unique merging of the sacred and the secular, evidently originated in Paris, the center of scholastic culture as well.

The typical thirteenth-century motet has three melody lines (or "voices"). The lowest, usually from a liturgical chant melody, has no words and may have been played on an instrument rather than sung. The remaining melodies have different texts, either Latin or French (or one of each), which are sung simultaneously. Latin texts are usually sacred, whereas French ones are secular, dealing with themes such as love and springtime. In one example, the top voice chirps in quick rhythm about a lady's charms ("Fair maiden, lovely and comely; pretty maiden, courteous and pleasing, delicious one"); the middle voice slowly and mournfully laments the "malady" of love; and the lowest voice sings a liturgical melody. The motet thus weaves the sacred (the chant melody in the lowest voice) and the secular (the French texts in the upper voices) into a sophisticated tapestry of music.

Like the scholastic summae, motets were written by and for a clerical elite. Yet they incorporated the music of ordinary people, such as the calls of street vendors and the boisterous songs of students. In turn, they touched the lives of everyone, for polyphony influenced every form of music, from the Mass to popular songs that entertained and diverted laypeople and churchmen alike.

Complementing the motet's complexity was a new notation for rhythm. Until the thirteenth century, musical notation could indicate pitch but had no way to denote the duration of the notes. In that century, music theorists developed increasingly precise methods to indicate rhythm. Franco of Cologne, for example, in his *Art of Measurable Song* (c. 1280), used different shapes to mark the number of beats each note should be held. His system became the basis of modern musical notation. Because each note could now be allotted a specific duration, written music could express new and complicated rhythms. The music of the thirteenth century reflected both the melding of the secular and the sacred and the possibilities for greater order and control.

The Order of High Gothic

Just as polyphonic music united the sacred with the secular, so **Gothic** architecture, sculpture, and painting expressed the order and harmony of the universe. The term *Gothic* was originally used to belittle medieval art and architecture, but it now refers with admiration to a particular style used in the twelfth to fifteenth centuries. Its chief characteristic is the use of pointed arches, which began as architectural motifs but were soon adopted in every art form. Gothic churches appealed to the senses the way that scholastic argument appealed to human reason: both were designed to lead people to knowledge that touched the divine. Being in a Gothic church was a foretaste of heaven.

Gothic architecture began around 1135, with the project of Abbot Suger, the close associate of King Louis the Fat (see page 334), to remodel portions of the church of Saint-Denis. Suger's rebuilding of Saint-Denis was part of the fruitful melding of royal and ecclesiastical interests and ideals in the north of France. At the west end of his church, the point where the faithful entered, Suger decorated the portals with figures of Old Testament kings, queens, and patriarchs, signaling the links between the present king and his illustrious predecessors. Within the church, Suger rebuilt the *chevet*, or apse, using pointed arches and stained glass to let in light, which he believed would transport the worshipper from the "slime of earth" to the "purity of Heaven." Suger thought that the Father of lights, God himself, "illuminated" the minds of the beholders via the light that filtered through the stained-glass windows. Soon the style that Suger pioneered was taken up across northern France and then, in the 1250s, as French culture gained enormous prestige under Louis IX, all across

French Gothic: Sainte-Chapelle
Gothic architecture opened up the walls of the church to windows, as may be seen at Sainte-Chapelle, the private chapel of the French king Louis IX (St. Louis) in Paris. Consecrated in 1248, it was built to house Christ's crown of thorns and other relics of the Passion. This photo shows the interior of the upper chapel looking east. Filled with "stained" glass—the colors were added to the ingredients of the glass before they were heated, melted, and blown—the windows glow like jewels. Moreover, each has a story to tell: the life of Christ, major events from the Old Testament, the lives of saints. Compare the use of windows, walls, vault, and piers here with that of the Romanesque church Saint-Savin on page 346.
(Bridgeman-Giraudon/Art Resource, NY.)

Europe. Gothic was an urban architecture, reflecting—in its towering heights, jewel-like windows, and bright ornaments—the aspirations, pride, and confidence of rich and powerful merchants, artisans, and bishops. A Gothic church, usually a cathedral (the bishop's principal church), was the focal point of a city.

Building Gothic cathedrals was a community project, enlisting the labor and support of an entire urban center. New cathedrals required a small army of quarrymen, builders, carpenters, and glass cutters. Bishops, papal legates, and clerics planned and helped pay for these grand churches, but townspeople also generously financed them and filled them to attend Mass and visit relics. Guilds raised money to pay for stained-glass windows that depicted and celebrated their own patron saints. In turn, towns made money when pilgrims came to visit relics, and sightseers arrived to marvel at their great churches. At Chartres, near Paris, for example, which had the relic of the Virgin's tunic, crowds thronged the streets, the poor buying small lead figures of the Virgin, the rich purchasing wearable replicas of her tunic. Churches were centers of commercial activity. In their basements, wine merchants plied their trade, while other vendors sold goods outside.

The technologies that made Gothic churches possible were all known before the twelfth century. But Suger's church showed how they could be brought together to achieve a particularly dazzling effect. Gothic techniques included ribbed vaulting, which gave a sense of precision and order; pointed arches, which produced a feeling of soaring height; and flying buttresses, which took the weight of the vault off the walls (Figure 10.1). The buttresses permitted much of the wall to be cut away and the open spaces to be filled with glass.

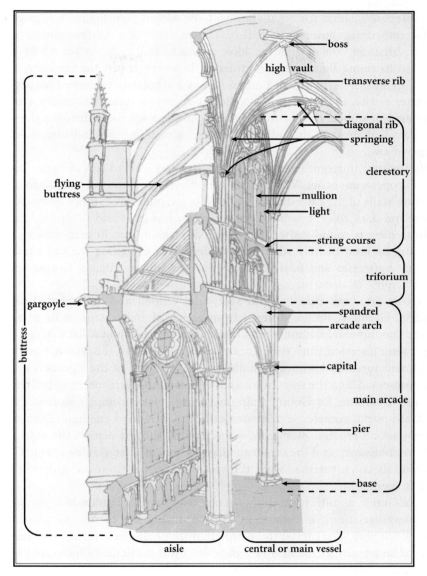

Figure 10.1 Elements of a Gothic Cathedral
Bristling on the outside with stone flying buttresses, the Gothic cathedral was lofty and serene on the inside. The buttresses, which held the weight of the vault, allowed Gothic architects to pierce the walls with windows running the full length of the church. Within, thick piers anchored on sturdy bases became thin columns as they mounted over the triforium and clerestory (windows), blossoming into ribs at the top. Whether plain or ornate, the ribs gave definition and drew attention to the high, pointed vault.

Romanesque church exteriors, with their massive walls and clearly articulated parts, prepare visitors for what they will see within (see Figure 9.2, page 342). Gothic cathedrals, however, surprise. The exterior of a Gothic church has an opaque, bristling, and forbidding look owing to the dark surface of its stained glass and its flying buttresses. The interior, however, is just the opposite. It is all soaring lightness, harmony, and order. Just as a scholastic presented his argument with utter clarity, so the interior of a Gothic church revealed its structure through its skeleton of ribbed vaults and piers. And just as a scholastic bridged the earthly and celestial realms, so the cathedral elicited a response beyond reason, evoking a sense of awe.

By the mid-thirteenth century, Gothic architecture had spread from France to other European countries. Yet the style varied by region, most dramatically in Italy. The outer walls of the cathedral at Orvieto, for example, are built of alternate bricks of light and dark color, providing texture instead of glass and light; the vault over the large nave is round rather than pointed, recalling the Roman aqueducts that could still be seen in Italy when the builders were designing the cathedral. With no flying buttresses and relatively little portal sculpture, Italian Gothic churches convey a spirit of austerity.

Gothic art, both painting and sculpture, echoed and decorated the Gothic cathedral. Gothic sculpture differed from earlier church sculpture in its naturalism and monumentality. Romanesque sculpture played upon a flat surface; Gothic figures were liberated from their background. Sculpted in the round, they turned, moved, and interacted with one another. The positions of the figures, the people they represented, and the ways in which they interacted were meant to be "read" like a scholastic summa, for Gothic sculpture often depicted complex stories or scenes. The south portal complex of Chartres cathedral is a good example. Each massive doorway tells a separate story through sculpture: the left depicts the martyrs, the right the confessors, and the center the Last Judgment. Like Dante's *Divine Comedy,* these portals taken together show the soul's pilgrimage from the suffering of this world to eternal life.

Like Gothic architecture, Gothic sculpture began in France and was adopted, with many variations, elsewhere in Europe during the thirteenth century. The German sculptor who carved the tympanum (the half-circle form) over the south portal of Strasbourg's cathedral (see page 387) was particularly interested in emotional expression. As the Virgin Mary dies, the figures around her bend and gesture, showing their grief with their hands and faces.

By the early fourteenth century, the expressive sculptures so prominent in architecture were reflected in painting as well. This new style is evident in the work of Giotto (1266–1337), a Florentine artist who helped change the emphasis of painting, which had been predominantly symbolic, decorative, and intellectual. For example, Giotto filled the walls of a private chapel at Padua with paintings depicting scenes of Christ's life. Here he experimented with the illusion of depth. Giotto's figures, appearing weighty

German Gothic: Strasbourg
The Virgin Mary is mourned in this tympanum over the portal of the Strasbourg cathedral's south transept (the arm that crosses the church from north to south). Here, in German Gothic, the emphasis is on emotion and expressivity. Notice the depiction of Mary, with her bedclothes agitated and her body contorted. Why do you suppose Christ stands in the center of the tympanum, as if he is one of the mourners? What is he holding in the crook of his arm? (Hint: The souls of the dead are often shown as miniature people.) (Foto Marburg/Art Resource, NY.)

and voluminous, express a range of emotions as they seem to move across interior and exterior spaces (see page 388). In bringing sculptural realism to a flat surface, Giotto stressed three-dimensionality, illusional space, and human emotion. By melding earthly sensibilities with religious themes, Giotto found yet another way to bring together the natural and divine realms.

> **REVIEW**   How did artists, architects, musicians, and scholastics try to link this world with the divine?

Conclusion

In the thirteenth and early fourteenth centuries, western Europeans sought order through control. They aggressively expanded outward, from the Baltic to Gibraltar. They sacked Constantinople in 1204 and proclaimed their own emperor. They treated the Mongol hegemony in the east as an opportunity for trade and missionary work.

Powerful territorial kings and princes created new bureaucratic institutions. They hired staffs to handle their accounts, record acts, collect taxes, issue writs, and preside over courts. Flourishing cities, a growing money economy, and trade

Giotto, *Birth of the Virgin*
Giotto's depiction of the Virgin Mary's birth pays attention to the homey details of a thirteenth-century Florentine aristocratic household. The baby is bathed and swaddled by maidservants in the bottom tier, while above she is handed to her mother, St. Anne, who reaches out eagerly for the child. (The Art Archive/Scrovegni Chapel, Padua/Dagli Orti [A].)

and manufacturing (see Chapter 9) provided the finances necessary to support the personnel now used by medieval governments. The universities became the training grounds for the new administrators as well as for urban preachers.

Both the church and the state became more assertive. The Fourth Lateran Council was an attempt to regulate intimate aspects of the lives of all, even laypeople and non-Christians. The conflict between Boniface and Philip showed how the French king could galvanize his subjects—even his clergy—on behalf of the interests of the state. In England, where John agreed to Magna Carta, it was the barons who helped forge a notion of government that transcended the king. By contrast, the artists and architects of the time sought to bring together two separate entities—the worldly and the divine.

New power, new piety, and new exclusivity arose in a society both more confident and less tolerant. Crusaders fought against an increasing variety of foes, not only in the Holy Land but also in Spain, in southern France, and on Europe's northern frontiers. With heretics voicing criticism and maintaining their beliefs, the

Mapping the West Europe, c. 1340
The Empire, now called the Holy Roman Empire, still dominated the map of Europe in 1340, but the emperor himself had little power. Each principality—often each city—was ruled separately and independently. To the east, the Ottoman Turks were just beginning to make themselves felt. In the course of the next century, they would disrupt the Mongol hegemony and become a great power.

church, led by the papacy, defined orthodoxy and declared dissenters its enemies. Jews, who had once been fairly well integrated into the Christian community, were treated ambivalently, alternately used and abused. The Baltic peoples became targets for new evangelical and armed zeal; the Greeks became the butt of envy, hostility, and finally enmity. Confident and aggressive, the leaders of Christian Europe in the thirteenth and early fourteenth centuries attempted to impose their rule, legislate morality, and create a unified worldview impregnable to attack. But the drive for order would soon be challenged by economic and political crises and epidemic disease.

CHAPTER REVIEW QUESTIONS
1. Why was Innocent III more successful than Boniface VIII in carrying out his objectives?
2. Compare the origins and outcomes of the challenges faced by Boniface VIII with those confronted by Gregory VII in the eleventh century.

For practice quizzes and other study tools, see the Online Study Guide at bedfordstmartins.com/huntconcise.

For primary-source material from this period, see Chapters 11 and 12 of *Sources of* THE MAKING OF THE WEST, Third Edition.

Suggested References

Bartlett takes up the physical expansion of Europe, while Dante and Thomas Aquinas demonstrate its intellectual range. Bynum deftly ties together religious, theological, and gender issues. The politics of the period always had religious implications, and religious movements always had political ramifications, as Jordan and Moore show in different ways.

Bartlett, Robert. *The Making of Europe: Conquest, Colonization, and Cultural Change, 950–1350.* 1993.

Bergreen, Laurence. *Marco Polo: From Venice to Xanadu.* 2007.

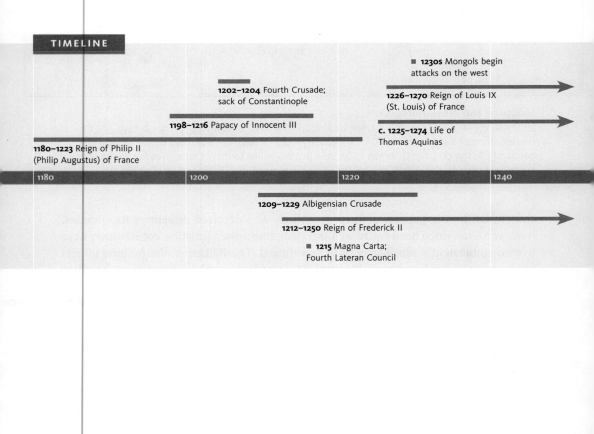

TIMELINE

1230s Mongols begin attacks on the west

1202–1204 Fourth Crusade; sack of Constantinople

1226–1270 Reign of Louis IX (St. Louis) of France

1198–1216 Papacy of Innocent III

c. 1225–1274 Life of Thomas Aquinas

1180–1223 Reign of Philip II (Philip Augustus) of France

| 1180 | 1200 | 1220 | 1240 |

1209–1229 Albigensian Crusade

1212–1250 Reign of Frederick II

1215 Magna Carta; Fourth Lateran Council

Burnham, Louisa A. *So Great a Light, So Great a Smoke: The Beguin Heretics of Languedoc.* 2008.

Bynum, Caroline Walker. *Holy Feast and Holy Fast: The Religious Significance of Food to Medieval Women.* 1987.

*Dante. *The Divine Comedy.* Many editions; recommended are translations by Mark Musa, John Ciardi, and Robert Pinsky.

Jones, Philip J. *The Italian City-State: From Commune to Signoria.* 1997.

Jordan, William Chester. *The French Monarchy and the Jews: From Philip Augustus to the Last Capetians.* 1989.

Moore, R. I. *The Formation of a Persecuting Society: Power and Deviance in Western Europe, 950–1250.* 2d ed. 2007.

O'Callaghan, Joseph F. *The Cortes of Castile-León, 1188–1350.* 1989.

Rubin, Miri. *Corpus Christi: The Eucharist in Late Medieval Culture.* 1991.

*Thomas Aquinas, *Summa Theologiae* (English translation): http://www.newadvent.org/summa/

Tolan, John Victor. *Sons of Ishmael: Muslims through European Eyes in the Middle Ages.* 2008.

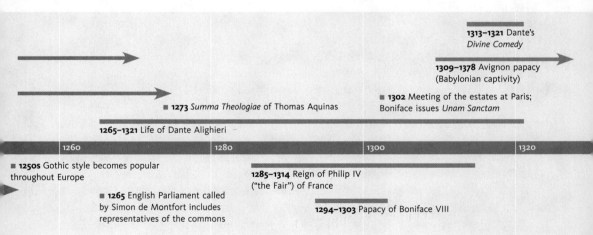

1313–1321 Dante's *Divine Comedy*

1309–1378 Avignon papacy (Babylonian captivity)

1302 Meeting of the estates at Paris; Boniface issues *Unam Sanctam*

1273 *Summa Theologiae* of Thomas Aquinas

1265–1321 Life of Dante Alighieri

| 1260 | 1280 | 1300 | 1320 |

1250s Gothic style becomes popular throughout Europe

1285–1314 Reign of Philip IV ("the Fair") of France

1265 English Parliament called by Simon de Montfort includes representatives of the commons

1294–1303 Papacy of Boniface VIII

Crisis and Renaissance

N 1453, THE OTTOMAN TURKS turned their cannons on Constantinople and blasted the city's walls. The fall of Constantinople, which spelled the end of the Byzantine Empire, was an enormous shock to Europeans. Some, like the pope, called for a crusade against the Ottomans. Others, like the writer Lauro Quirini, sneered, calling the Turks "a barbaric, uncultivated race, without established customs, or laws, [who live] a careless, vagrant, arbitrary life."

But the Ottomans didn't consider themselves uncultivated or arbitrary. In fact, they shared many of the values and tastes of the Europeans who were so hostile to them. Sultan Mehmed II employed European architects to construct his new palace, the Topkapi Saray, in the city that was once called Constantinople and was now normally called Istanbul. He also commissioned the Venetian Gentile Bellini to paint his portrait. In this, he was no different from the most fashionable European rulers of the day.

Portrait of Mehmed II
The Ottoman ruler Mehmed II (r. 1451–1481) saw himself as a Renaissance patron of the arts, and he called upon the most famous artists and architects of the day to work for him. The painter of this portrait, Gentile Bellini, was from a well-known family of artists in Venice and served at Mehmed's court in 1479–1480. The revival of portraiture, so characteristic of Renaissance tastes, was as important to the Turkish sultans as to European rulers. (*Erich Lessing/Art Resource, NY.*)

Mehmed's actions and interests sum up the three main features of the period 1340–1500: a crisis in the global order, as the Ottomans created a new and long-lived state; political consolidation; and the artistic and cultural movement known as the Renaissance.

During this period a series of crises struck Europe. The disease known as the **Black Death** tore at the fabric of communities and families, though survivors and their children reaped the benefits of higher wages and better living standards. The **Hundred Years' War**, fought between France and England from 1337 to 1453, brought untold misery to the French countryside. Following their conquest of Constantinople, the Ottoman Turks penetrated far into the Balkans. And a crisis in the church, called the **Great Schism**, pitted pope against pope and divided Europe into separate camps.

These crises were met and overcome in large measure through the policies of newly consolidated states. New political entities such as Poland-Lithuania and Muscovy rose to prominence. France and England became centralized monarchies. Italy's political mosaic began to coalesce into five territorial states. And the Iberian kingdoms of Portugal and Spain expanded European domination to Africa, Asia, and the Americas.

Meeting the needs of men and women in crisis while often catering to the wishes of newly rich and powerful rulers, the Renaissance—a word that means "rebirth" and refers to the revival of classical culture—gave Europe new styles of living, ruling, and thinking. A new vocabulary drawn from classical literature, as well as astonishing new forms of art and music based on ancient precedents, were used both to confront and to mask the crises of the day.

CHAPTER FOCUS QUESTION   What were the roles of the newly consolidated states of Europe in both the crises of the period and the Renaissance?

Crisis: Disease, War, and Schism

The crises began in the mid-fourteenth century. The Black Death decimated the population; the Hundred Years' War buffeted France, England, and the Low Countries; and the Ottoman Turks began their conquest of formerly Byzantine territory. Soon two and then three rival popes divided the church. In the wake of these crises, many ordinary folk sought solace in new forms of piety, some of them heretical.

Economic Contraction and the Black Death

Bad weather and overpopulation contributed to a series of famines at the beginning of the fourteenth century. Population growth meant that peasants had to divide their plots into ever smaller parcels or farm marginal land. Their income and the quality of their diet eroded. In the great urban centers, where thousands depended on steady employment and cheap bread, a bad harvest, always followed by sharply rising food prices, meant hunger and eventual famine.

A cooling of the European climate also contributed to the crisis in the food supply. Europe entered a colder period, with a succession of severe winters beginning in 1315. Crop failures were widespread. In many cities of northwestern Europe, the price of bread tripled, and thousands starved to death. The Great Famine (1315–1322) left many people hungry, sick, and weak.

At midcentury, a terrible disease, later called the Black Death (1346–c. 1350), hit Europe. Possibly bubonic plague, possibly another as yet unidentified disease, the Black Death attacked the region between the Black and Caspian seas in 1346 (Map 11.1). In 1347, many members of the Genoese colony in Caffa, in the Crimea, fell to the disease, which then traveled westward, to Byzantium, the Middle East, the North African coast, and Europe. By January 1348, the Black Death had infected southern Italy and France. Soon it spread to all of Italy, the Balkans, and most of

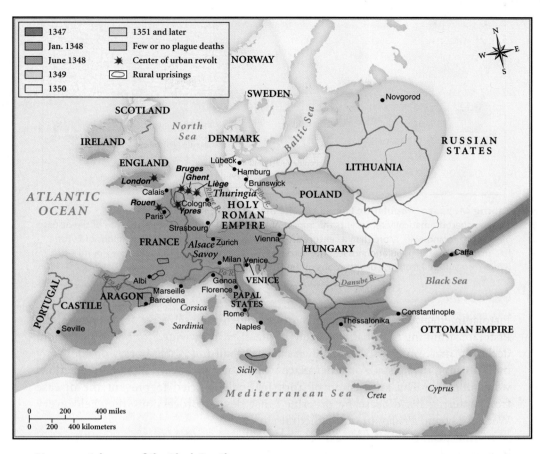

Map 11.1 Advance of the Black Death
The gradual but deadly spread of the Black Death followed the roads and waterways of Europe. **For more help analyzing this map, see the map activity for this chapter in the Online Study Guide at** bedfordstmartins.com/huntconcise.

France. The disease then crept northward to Germany, England, and Scandinavia, reaching the Russian city of Novgorod around 1350.

Nothing like this had struck Europe before. Inhabitants of cities, where crowding and filth increased the chances of contagion, died in massive numbers. Florence lost almost two-thirds of its population of ninety thousand; Siena, like most cities visited by the disease, lost half its people. Rural areas suffered fewer deaths, but regional differences were pronounced. (See "Taking Measure," page 396.) Further outbreaks of the disease, though not called the Black Death, occurred in Europe in 1361, 1368–1369, 1371, 1375, 1390, and 1405. They continued, with longer dormant intervals, into the eighteenth century.

In some places, responses to the Black Death were immediate and practical. At the Italian city of Pistoia in 1348, for example, the government decreed that no citizen could go to nearby Pisa or Lucca, nor could people from those cities enter

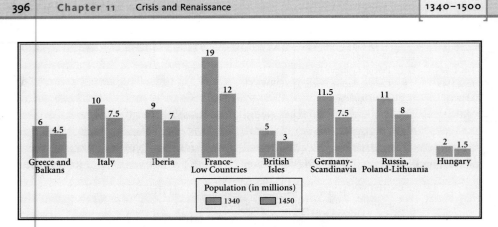

Taking Measure Population Losses and the Black Death, 1340–1450
This bar chart dramatically represents the impact of the Black Death and the recurrence of the disease between 1340 and 1450. More than a century after the Black Death, none of these regions of Europe had made up for the population losses. The hardest-hit areas were France and the Low Countries, which also suffered from the devastations of the Hundred Years' War.

Pistoia; in effect, Pistoia established a quarantine. In the same set of ordinances, the Pistoians, thinking that "bad air" brought the disease, provided for better sanitation, declaring that "butchers and retailers of meat shall not stable horses or allow any mud or dung in the shop or other place where they sell meat." Elsewhere reactions were religious. The archbishop of York in England tried to prevent the disease from entering his diocese by ordering "that devout processions [be] held every Wednesday and Friday in our cathedral church."

Some people took more extreme measures. Lamenting their sins—which they believed had brought on the Black Death and other calamities—and attempting to placate God, groups of men and women wandered from city to city with whips in their hands. Entering a church, they took off their shirts or blouses, lay down one by one on the church floor, and, according to the chronicler Henry of Hervordia (d. 1370),

> one of them would strike the first with a whip, saying, "May God grant you remission [forgiveness] of all your sins. Arise." And he would get up, and do the same to the second, and all the others in turn did the same. When they were all on their feet, and arranged two by two in procession, two of them in the middle of the column would begin singing a hymn in a high voice, with a sweet melody.

Churchmen did not approve of the flagellants, as these people were called, because they took on the preaching and penance that was supposed to be done by the clergy. Nevertheless, the flagellants aroused popular sympathy wherever they went. The religious enthusiasm they inspired often culminated in violence against Jews, as rumors circulated that Jews were responsible for the Black Death. Old charges that Jews were plotting to "wipe out all the Christians with poison and had poisoned wells and springs everywhere," as one Franciscan friar put it, revived. In Germany especially thousands of Jews were slaughtered. Many fled to Poland, which was less affected by the Black Death and where the authorities welcomed Jews as productive taxpayers. In western and central Europe, however, the persecutions impoverished Jews.

Preoccupation with death led to the popularity of a theme called the Dance of Death as a subject of art, literature, and performance. It featured a procession of people of every age, sex, and rank making their way to the grave. Preachers and poets talked and wrote on the theme. Yet at the same time the Black Death helped inspire this bleak view of the world, it brought new opportunities for those who survived its murderous path. With a smaller population to feed, less land was needed for farming. Marginal land that had been cultivated was returned to pasture, meadow, or forest. Landlords diversified their products. Wheat had been the favored crop before the Black Death, but barley—the key ingredient in beer—turned out to be more profitable afterward. Animal products continued to fetch a high price, and some landlords switched from farming to animal husbandry.

These changes in agriculture meant a better standard of living. The peasants and urban workers who survived the Black Death were able to negotiate better working conditions or higher wages from their landlords or employers. With more money to spend, people could afford a better and more varied diet that included beer and meat. Even commoners could now afford finery, a fact that threatened to erase the lines between the nobles and everyone else. Many Italian cities passed laws to prohibit ostentatious dress among every class of citizens. These laws were generally ineffective, however, as families continued to announce their rank and prestige by wearing lavish clothes.

Each attack of the disease brought with it, a few years later, a slight jump in the birthrate. It is unlikely that women became more fertile. Rather, the cause of the increased birthrate was more subtle: with good employment opportunities, couples married at younger ages and with greater frequency than they had previously. "After the end of the epidemic," one chronicler wrote, "the men and women who stayed alive did everything to get married."

The Black Death also had an effect on patterns of education. The survivors' children needed schooling, but the disease spared neither the students nor the professors of the old universities. As the disease ebbed, new local colleges and universities were built, partly to train a new generation for the priesthood and partly to satisfy local donors—many of them rulers—who, riding on a sea of wealth left behind by the dead, wanted to be known as patrons of education. Thus, in 1348, in the midst of the Black Death, Holy Roman Emperor Charles IV chartered a university at Prague. The king of Poland founded Cracow University, and a Habsburg duke created the University of Vienna. Rather than travel to Paris or Bologna, young men living east of the Rhine River now tended to study closer to home.

The Hundred Years' War, 1337–1453

In France, the misery wrought by disease was compounded by the devastation of war. Since the Norman invasion of England in the eleventh century (see page 329), the king of England had held land on the continent. The French kings continually

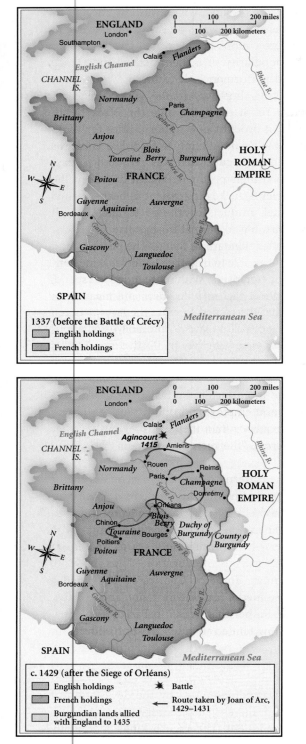

chipped away at it, however, and by the beginning of the fourteenth century England retained only the area around Bordeaux, called Guyenne. In 1337, after a series of challenges and skirmishes, King Philip VI of France declared Guyenne to be his; King Edward III of England in turn declared himself king of France. The Hundred Years' War had begun.

The war had four phases (Map 11.2). The first three saw the progressive weakening of French power, the strengthening of England, and the creation of a new kingdom, Burgundy, which for a crucial time allied itself with England. The fourth phase, which began when King Henry V (r. 1413–1422) of England invaded France and achieved a great victory at the battle of Agincourt in 1415, ended in a complete reversal and the ousting of the English from the continent for good.

That reversal was largely begun by a woman, Joan of Arc (1412–1431). The sixteen-year-old arrived at the court of the dauphin (the uncrowned king of France) wearing armor, riding a horse, and leading a small army. Full of charisma and confidence at a desperate hour, Joan convinced the dauphin that she had been sent by God. She was allowed to fight (and win) a battle at Orléans in 1429. At her urging and under her leadership, the dauphin traveled deep into enemy territory to be anointed and crowned King Charles VII at the cathedral in Reims, following the tradition of French monarchs. Despite Joan's victory at Orléans and the anointing of Charles, the French allowed her to be captured and turned over to the English in 1431. Tried as a witch, she was burned at the stake. But her bad luck was matched by French good fortune. The duke of Burgundy recognized Charles VII as king of France, and Charles entered Paris in 1437. Skirmish by skirmish, the English were driven from French soil.

The Hundred Years' War drew other countries into its vortex. Mercenaries for both sides came from Germany, Switzerland, and the Netherlands; the best crossbowmen came from Genoa. The textile workers of Flanders rose up against their French-leaning count when the war cut off their supply of raw wool. In 1369, the marriage of the heiress of Flanders and the duke of Burgundy created a powerful new state, the duchy of Burgundy, which allied itself with England until 1435. Then, riding the wave of French victories, it switched sides. The dukes of Burgundy created a glittering court, a center of art and culture, but their state was short-lived. Clashing with the Swiss Confederation, the duchy of Burgundy began to fall apart in 1474.

The French chronicler Jean Froissart, writing around 1400, considered the Hundred Years' War to be a chivalric adventure. But even Froissart had to admit that the armies were made up mainly of mercenaries rather than knights. These men, who fought for pay and plunder, cared nothing about the king for whom they were

Map 11.2 The Hundred Years' War, 1337–1453
During the Hundred Years' War, English kings, aided by the new state of Burgundy, contested the French monarchy for the domination of France. For many decades, the English seemed to be winning, but the French prevailed in the end.

Joan of Arc, c. 1430
Painted in the style of the French-Flemish school, this manuscript illustration contrasts the metallic hardness of Joan's armor and sword with the soft, fluttering banner depicting God and two angels. With her right hand upturned and clasping a sword, and her left turned down to support the banner, Joan strikes a perfect pose as a messenger of God, similar to the angels depicted above. **For more help analyzing this image, see the visual activity for this chapter in the Online Study Guide at** bedfordstmartins.com/huntconcise**. (© akg-images, London.)

supposed to be fighting. They formed "Free Companies" and during lulls in the war lived off the French countryside, terrorizing the peasants and exacting "protection" money.

Some of the soldiers recruited by both sides, both mercenaries and nonmercenaries, were archers. The French archers tended to use crossbows, whose heavy, deadly arrows were released by a mechanism that even a townsman could master. The English employed longbows, which could shoot five arrows for every one launched with a crossbow. Gunpowder was introduced during this war, and cannons were forged. Handguns also were beginning to be used, their effect about equal to that of crossbows.

The Spoils of War
This illustration from Jean Froissart's *Chronicles* depicts soldiers pillaging a conquered city. During the Hundred Years' War, looting became the main source of income for mercenary troops and contributed to the general misery of late-medieval society. Food, furniture, and even everyday household items were taken. (Bibliothèque nationale de France.)

By the end of the war, chivalry was only a dream (though one that continued to inspire soldiers even up to the First World War). Heavy artillery and foot soldiers, tightly massed together in formations of many thousands of men, were the face of the new military. The army was becoming more professional and centralized. In the 1440s the French king created a permanent army of mounted soldiers, paying them wages and subjecting them to regular inspection.

The outbreak of the Hundred Years' War led to popular revolts. Although the Flemish count supported France, the townspeople, dependent on England for the raw wool they wove into cloth, revolted in 1338. The count fled to France, but discord among and within the towns allowed his successor to return in 1348. Revolts continued to flare up thereafter, but the new count allowed the towns a measure of self-government, maintained some distance from French influence, and managed on the whole to keep the peace. Later, as we have seen, Flanders became part of the duchy of Burgundy, an ally of England.

In France, the Parisians chafed against the high taxes they were forced to pay to finance the war. When the English captured the French king John at the battle of Poitiers in 1356, Étienne Marcel, provost of the Paris merchants, and other disillusioned members of the estates of France (the representatives of the clergy, nobility, and commons) met in Paris to discuss political reform, the incompetence of the French army, and taxes. Under Marcel's leadership, the Parisians took control of the city. In response, the royal army blockaded Paris and cut off its food supply. Later that year, Marcel was assassinated, and the Parisian revolt came to an end.

In that same year, 1358, the French peasants, weary of the Free Companies that were ravaging the countryside and disgusted by the military incompetence of the nobility, rose up in protest. Their revolt, derisively called the Jacquerie (from the word *jacque,* or "peasant"), was quickly put down by the nobility.

Similar revolts took place in England. Wat Tyler's Rebellion started as an uprising in much of southern and central England after royal agents tried to collect a poll tax (a tax on each household) to finance the Hundred Years' War. Refusing to pay and refusing to be arrested, the commons (peasants and small householders) rose up in rebellion in 1381. They massed in various groups and marched to London to see the king, whom they professed to support. There they made a radical demand: an end to serfdom. Although the rebellion was put down and its leaders executed, the death knell of serfdom in England had been sounded, as the peasants returned home to bargain with their lords for better terms.

Finally, the Hundred Years' War started a period of financial hard times. During the war, the English king Edward III borrowed heavily from the largest Italian banking houses, the Bardi and Peruzzi of Florence. With many of their assets tied up in loans to the English monarchy, the Italian bankers had no choice but to extend more credit, hoping to recover their initial investments. In the early 1340s, however, Edward defaulted, and the once illustrious houses went bankrupt. Meanwhile, diminished production and trade eventually caused turmoil in northern Europe and a crisis for financiers in the Low Countries. Bruges, the financial center of northwestern Europe, saw its power fade during the fifteenth century when several of its money changers went bankrupt.

The Ottoman Conquests

The rise of the Ottoman Turks, a new Islamic group, was the most astonishing development of the late thirteenth century, when they began a holy war against Byzantium. Under Osman I (r. 1280–1324), who gave the dynasty its name, and his successors, the Ottomans became a formidable force in Anatolia and the Balkans, where political disunity opened the door for their advances (Map 11.3). By the end of the fourteenth century, they had reduced the Byzantine Empire to the city of Constantinople, Thessalonika, and a narrow strip of land in modern-day Greece. Farther to the west, the Ottomans defeated a joint Hungarian-Serbian army at the Maritsa River (1364), alerting Europe for the first time to the threat of an Islamic

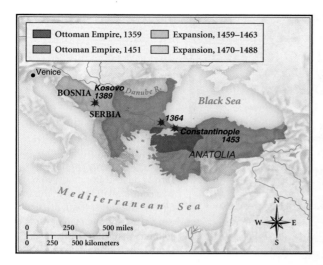

Ottoman Empire, 1359   Expansion, 1459–1463
Ottoman Empire, 1451   Expansion, 1470–1488

Venice
BOSNIA Kosovo *Danube R.*
1389
SERBIA
Black Sea
1364
Constantinople
1453
ANATOLIA
Mediterranean Sea

0   250   500 miles
0   250   500 kilometers

Map 11.3 Ottoman Expansion in the Fourteenth and Fifteenth Centuries
The Balkans were the major theater of expansion for the Ottoman Empire. The Byzantine Empire was reduced to the city of Constantinople and surrounded by the Ottomans before its final fall in 1453.

invasion. Pope Urban V called vainly for a crusade. In the Balkans, the Ottomans skillfully exploited Christian disunity, playing local interests against one another. An Ottoman army, allied with the Bulgarians and some Serbian princes, won the battle of Kosovo (1389), destroying the last organized Christian resistance south of the Danube. (Even today the battle remains a rallying cry for Serbian nationalists.) The Ottomans secured control of southeastern Europe after 1396, when they crushed a crusading army summoned by Pope Boniface IX.

After Mehmed II (r. 1451–1481) ascended the Ottoman throne, he laid siege to Constantinople in 1453. The Byzantine capital, a city of 100,000, could muster only six thousand defenders (including a small contingent of Genoese) against an Ottoman force estimated at between 200,000 and 400,000 men. The city's walls were no match for fifteenth-century cannons. The last Byzantine emperor, Constantine XI ("Palaeologos"), died in battle, some sixty thousand residents were carried off into slavery, and the city was sacked. Mehmed entered Constantinople in triumph and rendered thanks to God in Justinian's Church of the Holy Wisdom (Hagia Sophia), which he turned into a mosque.

Mehmed wanted to be the new ruler of the Roman Empire—a Muslim Roman Empire. We have seen that he turned to the west for his artistic commissions, such as his Topkapi palace and his portrait. The Ottoman sultan employed Christian slave children raised as Muslims to be his Janissaries, the backbone of the Ottoman army. At the sultan's court, Christian women were prominent in the harem, and as a consequence many Ottoman princes had Greek or Serbian mothers. Christian princes and converts to Islam served in the emerging Ottoman administration. In conquered areas, existing religious and social structures remained intact when local people accepted Ottoman overlordship and paid taxes. Only in areas of persistent resistance did the Ottomans drive out or massacre the inhabitants, settling Turkish tribes in their place. A distinctive pattern of Balkan history was therefore established

The Siege of Constantinople, 1453
Bertrandon de la Broquiere wrote his *Overseas Voyage* in the 1430s for the duke of Burgundy, who was contemplating a new crusade against the Turks. "I will discuss the means and the men necessary to break their power and defeat them in battle and gain their territory," he wrote, adding, "I don't think it would be very hard to break and defeat them, given their lack of arms." Within two decades, however, the Turks had taken Constantinople. When an artist was commissioned around 1455 to illustrate Bertrandon's work, he or she chose to show the siege. In this picture, you can see the tents of the Turkish captains, their cannons and cannonballs just behind them, and, across the water, the city of Constantinople with its doomed defenders. (Bibliothèque Nationale, Paris/The Bridgeman Art Library.)

at the beginning of the Ottoman conquest: extremely diverse ethnic and religious communities were woven together into the fabric of an efficient central state.

The Great Schism, 1378–1417

Even as war and disease threatened Europeans' material and physical well-being, a crisis in the church, precipitated by a scandal in the papacy, tore at their spiritual life. The move of the papacy from Rome to Avignon in 1309 (see page 375) had caused an outcry, especially among Italians, distraught by the election of French popes and anxious to see the papacy return to Rome. Some critics, such as Marsilius of Padua, were disillusioned with the institution of the papacy itself. Marsilius, a physician and lawyer by training, argued in *The Defender of the Peace* (1324) that the source of all power lay within the people: "The law-making power or the first and real effective source of law is the people or the body of citizens or the prevailing part of the people according to its election or its will expressed in general convention by vote." Applied to the papacy, Marsilius's argument meant that Christians themselves formed the church and that the pope should be elected by a general council representing all Christians.

When Pope Gregory XI (r. 1370–1378) left Avignon to return to Rome in 1377, the scandal of the Avignon papacy seemed to be over. But Rome itself presented a problem. Glad to have the papacy back, the Romans were determined never to lose it again. When the cardinals—many of whom came from Spain, Italy, and France—met to elect Gregory's successor, the Roman popolo, who controlled the city, demanded that they choose a Roman: "A Roman! A Roman! A Roman or at least an Italian! Or else we'll kill them all." Expecting to gain an important place in papal government, the cardinals chose an Italian, who took the name Urban VI. But Urban had no intention of kowtowing to the cardinals. Instead, he exalted the power of the pope and began to reduce the cardinals' wealth and privileges. The cardinals from France decided that they had made a big mistake. Many left Rome for a meeting at Anagni, where they claimed that Urban's election had been irregular and called on him to resign. When he refused, they elected a Frenchman as pope. He took the name Clement VII and soon moved his papal court back to Avignon, but not before he and Urban had excommunicated each other. The Great Schism (1378–1417) had begun.

All of Europe was drawn into the dispute. The king of France supported Clement; the king of England favored Urban. Some European states—Burgundy, Scotland, and Castile, for example—lined up on the side of France. Others—the Holy Roman Empire, Poland, and Hungary—supported Urban. Portugal switched sides four times, depending on which alliance offered it the most advantages. Each pope declared that those who followed the other were to be deprived of the rights of church membership; in effect, everyone in Europe was excommunicated by one or the other of the popes.

Contrary to the ideas of Marsilius, church law said that only a pope could summon a general council of the church—a sort of parliament of high churchmen. But given the state of confusion in Christendom, many intellectuals argued that the crisis justified calling a general council to represent the body of the faithful, even against the wishes of an unwilling pope—or popes. They spearheaded the conciliar movement—a movement to have the cardinals or the Holy Roman Emperor call a council.

In 1408, long after Urban and Clement had passed away, the conciliar movement succeeded when cardinals from both sides met and declared their resolve "to pursue the union of the Church . . . by way of abdication of both papal contenders." With support from both England and France, the cardinals called for a council to be held at Pisa in 1409. Both popes refused to attend, and the council deposed them, electing a third pope, Alexander V. The "deposed" popes refused to budge, even though most of the European powers abandoned them. Alexander's successor, John XXIII, turned to the emperor to arrange for another council.

The Council of Constance (1414–1418) met to resolve the papal crisis and to institute church reforms. The delegates deposed John XXIII and accepted the resignation of the pope at Rome. After long negotiations with rulers still supporting the Avignon pope, all allegiance to him was withdrawn, and he was deposed. The council then elected Martin V, who was recognized as pope by every important ruler of Europe. The Great Schism had come to an end.

New Forms of Piety and Heresy

The Great Schism, along with the miseries of disease and war, caused enormous anxiety among ordinary Christians. Worried about the salvation of their souls, pious men and women eagerly sought new forms of religious solace. The plenary indulgence—full forgiveness of sins, which had been originally offered to crusaders who died while fighting for the cause—was now offered to those who made a pilgrimage to Rome or one of the other designated holy places during declared Holy Years. Sins could be wiped away through confession and contrition, but some guilt remained that could be removed only through good deeds or in purgatory. As the idea of purgatory—the place where sins were fully purged—took full form, new indulgences were offered for good works to reduce the time there. Thus, for example, the duchess of Brittany was granted a hundred days off her purgatorial punishments when she allowed the Feast of Corpus Christi to be preached in her chapel. Lesser folk might obtain indulgences in more modest ways.

Both clergy and laity became more interested than ever in the education of young people as a way to deepen their faith and spiritual life. The Brethren of the Common Life—laypeople, mainly in the Low Countries, who devoted themselves to pious works—set up a model school at Deventer, and humanists in Italy emphasized primary school education. Priests were expected to teach the faithful the basics of the Christian religion.

Home was also a place for devotion. Portable images of Mary, the mother of God, and of the life and passion of Christ proliferated. They were meant to be contemplated by ordinary Christians at convenient moments throughout the day. People purchased or commissioned copies of Books of Hours, which contained prayers to be said on the appropriate day at the hours indicated in the Benedictine rule. Books of Hours included calendars, sometimes splendidly illustrated with depictions of the seasons and labors of the year. Other illustrations reminded readers of the life and suffering of Christ.

On the streets of towns, priests marched in dignified processions, carrying the sanctified bread of the Mass—the very body of Christ—in tall, splendid containers called monstrances, which trumpeted the importance and dignity of the Eucharistic wafer. Like images of the Lord's life and crucifixion, the monstrance emphasized Christ's body. Christ's blood was perhaps even more important. It was considered "wonderful blood," the blood that had brought people's redemption. The image of a bleeding, crucified Christ was seen repeatedly in depictions of the day. Viewers were meant to think about Christ's pain and feel it themselves, mentally participating in his death on the cross. Flagellants, as we have seen, literally drew their own blood.

Religious anxieties, intellectual dissent, and social unrest combined to create new heretical movements in England and Bohemia. In England the Lollards (a derisive name given to them by their opponents, from the Middle Dutch *lollaerd*, or "mumbler") were inspired by the Oxford scholar John Wycliffe (c. 1330–1384), who had come to believe that the true church was the community of believers rather than the clerical hierarchy. Wycliffe criticized monasticism, excommunication, and the Mass. He wanted people to read the Bible in the vernacular rather than in Latin, arguing that true believers, not corrupt priests, formed the church.

Wycliffe's followers included scholars and members of the gentry (lesser nobles), as well as artisans and other humbler folk. His supporters translated the Bible into English and produced many sermons to publicize his views. They influenced the priest John Ball, one of the leaders of Wat Tyler's Rebellion. Ball rallied the crowds with the chant "When Adam dug and Eve spun / Who then was the gentleman?" From questioning the church hierarchy, some Lollards advanced to challenging social inequality of every sort. After Wycliffe's death, the Lollards were persecuted in England. Groups of them remained underground, only to reemerge with the coming of the Reformation (see Chapter 12).

The Bohemian Hussites—named after one of their leaders, Jan Hus (1372?–1415)—had greater success. Their central demand—that the faithful receive not just the bread (the body) but also the wine (the blood) at Mass—brought together several passionately held desires and beliefs. The blood of Christ was particularly important to the devout, and the Hussite call to allow the laity to drink the wine from the chalice reflected this focus on its redemptive power. Furthermore, the call for communion in both bread and wine signified a desire for equality. Bohemia was an exceptionally divided country, with an urban German-speaking elite, including merchants, artisans, bishops, and scholars, and a Czech-speaking nobility and peasantry that was beginning to seek better opportunities. (Hus himself was a Czech of peasant stock who became a professor at the University of Prague.) When priests celebrated Mass, they had the privilege of drinking the wine. The Hussites, who were largely Czech laity, wanted the same privilege and, with it, recognition of their dignity and worth.

Condemned by the church as a heretic, Hus was protected by the Bohemian nobility until he was lured to the Council of Constance by the Holy Roman Emperor Sigismund "to justify himself before all men." Though promised safe conduct, Hus was arrested when he arrived at the council. After refusing to recant his views, he was declared a heretic and burned at the stake.

Hus's death caused an uproar, and his movement became a full-scale national revolt of Czechs against Germans. Sigismund called crusades against the Hussites, but all of his expeditions were soundly defeated. Radical groups of Hussites organized several new communities in southern Bohemia at Mount Tabor, named after the New Testament spot where the transfiguration of Christ was thought to have taken place (Matt. 7:1–8). Here the radicals attempted to live according to the example of the first Apostles. They recognized no secular lord, gave women some political rights, and created a simple liturgy in the Czech language. Negotiations with Sigismund and his successor led by 1450 to the Hussites' tentative incorporation into the Bohemian political system and the right to receive communion in "both kinds" (wine and bread). The Hussites made Bohemia intensely aware of its Czech, rather than its German, identity.

The Hussite Revolution, 1415–1436

REVIEW | What crises did Europeans confront in the fourteenth and fifteenth centuries, and how did they handle them?

The New Map of Europe

As both a symptom and a result of these crises, political consolidation was taking place all across Europe in the period 1340–1500. As we have seen, the Ottoman Empire joined European powers in the Balkans. Eastern Europe took shape when the capital of the Holy Roman Empire moved to Prague and the duke of Lithuania married the queen of Poland, uniting those two states. In western Europe, the union of Aragon and Castile via the marriage of their respective rulers created Spain. In England and France, consolidation meant the strengthening of the central monarchies. The few states that organized and maintained themselves as republics—Switzerland, Venice, and Florence—were run by elites. Nowhere was the consolidation of the period clearer than in Italy. In 1340 it was dotted with numerous small city-states. By 1500 it was dominated by five major powers: Milan, Venice, and Florence in the north, the papacy in the middle, and the kingdom of Naples in the south.

New States in Eastern Europe

In the eastern half of the Holy Roman Empire, Bohemia gained new status as the seat of the Luxembourg imperial dynasty (Emperor Sigismund was its last representative). This development bred a religious and political crisis when the Hussites clashed with Sigismund. The chief beneficiary of the violence was the nobility, both Catholic and Hussite, but they quarreled among themselves, especially about who should be king. No Joan of Arc appeared to declare the national will, and most of Europe considered Bohemia a heretic state.

Farther north, it was the cities rather than the landed nobility that held power. Allied cities, such as the Hanseatic League (see page 376), were common. By the fourteenth century, the Hanseatic League linked the Baltic coast with Russia, Norway, the British Isles, France, and even (via imperial cities like Augsburg and Nuremberg) the cities of Italy. When threatened by rival powers in Denmark and Norway in 1367–1370, the league waged war and won the peace. In the fifteenth century it confronted new rivals and began a long and slow decline.

To the east of the Hanseatic cities, two new monarchies took shape in northeastern Europe: Poland and Lithuania. Poland had begun to form in the tenth century. Powerful nobles soon dominated it, and Mongol invasions devastated the land. But recovery was under way by 1300. Unlike almost every other part of Europe, Poland expanded demographically and economically during the fourteenth century. Jews migrated there to escape persecution in western Europe, and both Jewish and German settlers helped build thriving towns like Cracow. Monarchical consolidation began thereafter.

On Poland's eastern flank was Lithuania, the only major holdout from Christianity in eastern Europe. As it expanded into southern Russia, however, its grand dukes flirted with both the Roman Catholic and Orthodox churches. In 1386, Grand Duke Jogailo (c. 1351–1434), taking advantage of a hiatus in the Polish ruling dynasty, united both states when he married Queen Jadwiga of Poland, received a Catholic baptism, and was elected by the Polish nobility as King Wladyslaw II ("Jagiello"). As part of the negotiations prior to these events, he promised to convert Lithuania, and after his coronation he sent churchmen there to begin the long, slow process. The union of Poland and Lithuania lasted, with some interruptions, until 1772 (Map 11.4, page 410).

Powerful States in Western Europe

Four powerful states dominated western Europe during the fifteenth century. The kingdom of Spain and the duchy of Burgundy were created by marriage; the newly powerful kingdoms of France and England were forged in the crucible of war. By the end of the century, however, Burgundy had disappeared, leaving three exceptionally powerful monarchies.

Decades of violence on the Iberian peninsula ended when Isabella of Castile and Ferdinand of Aragon married in 1469 and restored law and order in the decades that followed. Castile was the powerhouse, with Aragon its lesser neighbor and Navarre a pawn between the two. When the king and queen joined forces, they ruled together over their separate dominions, allowing each to retain its traditional laws and privileges. The union of

Unification of Spain, Late Fifteenth Century

Map 11.4 Eastern Europe in the Fifteenth Century
Crucial to the new political developments of the fifteenth century was the rise of Muscovy and Poland-Lithuania.

Castile and Aragon was the first step toward a united Spain and a centralized monarchy there.

Relying on a lucrative taxation system, pliant meetings of the cortes (the representative institution that voted taxes), and an ideology that glorified the monarchy, Ferdinand and Isabella consolidated their power. They had an extensive bureaucracy to handle financial matters and a well-staffed writing office. They sent their own officials to rule over towns that had previously been self-governing, and they established regional courts of law.

Once Ferdinand and Isabella established their rule over Castile and Aragon, they sought to impose religious uniformity and purity. First they began systematically persecuting the *conversos* (converts)—Jews who had converted to Christianity in the aftermath of vicious attacks on Jews at Seville, Córdoba, Toledo, and other Spanish towns in 1391. During the first half of the fifteenth century they and their descendants (still called conversos, even though their children had been born and baptized in the Christian faith) took advantage of the opportunities open to educated Christians, in many instances rising to high positions in both the church and the state and marrying into "Old Christian" families. The conversos' success bred resentment, and their commitment to Christianity was questioned as well.

Local massacres of conversos began even before Isabella and Ferdinand married. In 1467, for example, two conversos in Toledo were hanged "as traitors and captains of the heretical conversos." The terms "traitors" and "heretical" are telling: because conversos were technically no longer Jews, their persecution was justified by branding them as heretics who undermined the monarchy. In 1478, Ferdinand and Isabella set up the Inquisition in Spain to continue, on behalf of the crown, what the towns had started. Treating the conversos as heretics, the inquisitors imposed harsh sentences, expelling or burning most of them. That was not enough (in the view of the monarchs) to purify the land. In 1492, Ferdinand and Isabella decreed that all Jews in Spain must convert or leave the country. Some did convert, but the experiences of the former conversos soured most on the prospect, and many Jews—perhaps 150,000—left Spain, scattering around the Mediterranean.

Meanwhile, Ferdinand and Isabella determined to defeat Granada, the last Muslim stronghold in Spain. Disunity within Granada's ruling family allowed the conquest to proceed, and in January 1492—just a few months before they expelled the Jews—Ferdinand and Isabella made their triumphal entry into the Alhambra, the former residence of the Muslim king of Granada. Although they initially promised freedom of religion to the Muslims who chose to remain, the royal couple also provided a fleet of boats to evacuate those who chose exile. In 1502, they demanded that all Muslims adopt Christianity or leave the kingdom.

United with less tumult, the duchy of Burgundy—created when the duke of Burgundy and heiress of Flanders married in 1369—was nevertheless disunited linguistically and geographically. Its success and expansion in the fifteenth century were the result of military might and careful statecraft. Soon, however, Burgundy fell to the militias of its neighbors. The chief importance of the duchy of Burgundy was its support of the arts; the dukes were great patrons of Renaissance culture.

By contrast, France, one of Burgundy's neighbors, became more powerful in the years before 1500. It made a quick recovery from the Hundred Years' War and expanded under Louis XI (r. 1461–1483). Soon after most of Burgundy fell to him, Louis also inherited much of southern France. After he inherited claims to the duchy of Milan and the kingdom of Naples, he was ready to invade Italy. By the end of the century, France had doubled its territory, assuming boundaries close to its modern ones, and was looking to expand even further.

To strengthen royal power at home, Louis promoted industry and commerce, imposed permanent salt and land taxes, maintained western Europe's first standing army (created by his predecessor), and suspended the meetings of the estates, which included the clergy, the nobility, and representatives from the major towns of France. The French kings had already increased their power with important concessions from the papacy. In addition, the Pragmatic Sanction of Bourges (1438) had asserted the superiority of a general church council over the pope. Claiming special sacredness because of their anointment, the kings established what would come to be known as Gallicanism (after Gaul, the ancient Roman name for France), in which the French king would effectively control ecclesiastical revenues and the appointment of French bishops.

The experience of England was only slightly less fortunate. The Hundred Years' War led to intermittent civil wars that came to be called the Wars of the Roses (1460s–1485). They ended with the victory of Henry Tudor, who took the title of Henry VII (r. 1485–1509). Though long, the Wars of the Roses caused relatively little damage; the battles were generally short, and, in the words of one chronicler, "neither the country, nor the people nor the houses, were wasted, destroyed or demolished, but the calamities and misfortunes of the war fell only upon the soldiers, and especially on the nobility."

As a result, the English economy continued to grow during the fifteenth century. The cloth industry expanded considerably, and the English used much of the raw wool they had been exporting to the Low Countries to manufacture goods at home. London merchants, taking a vigorous role in trade, also assumed greater political prominence, not only in governing London but also as bankers to kings and members of Parliament. In the countryside the landed classes—the nobility, the gentry (the lesser nobility), and the yeomanry (free farmers)—benefited from rising farm and land-rent income as the population increased slowly but steadily. The Tudor monarchs took advantage of the general prosperity to bolster both their treasury and their power.

It did not matter whether a state was run by a monarch or a small elite; consolidation was the watchword. Switzerland, Venice, and Florence were republics that prided themselves on traditions of self-rule. At the same time, however, they were in every case dominated by elites—or even by one family.

In the late thirteenth century, Swiss cantons had formed an alliance that eventually became the Swiss Confederation (see page 377). Though not united by a comprehensive constitution, the Swiss Confederation was nevertheless an effective political force. Wealthy merchants and tradesmen dominated the cities of the confederation, and in the fifteenth century they managed to supplant the landed nobility. At the same time, the power of the rural communes gave some ordinary folk political importance. No king, duke, or count ever became head of the confederation. In its fiercely independent stance against the Holy Roman Empire, it became a symbol of republican freedom. Yet it was also dominated by the wealthy. Poor Swiss foot soldiers made their living by hiring themselves out as mercenaries, fueling the wars of kings in the rest of Europe.

Similarly, Venice proudly proclaimed itself a republic but was ruled by a small elite. Built on a lagoon, Venice by 1400 ruled an extensive empire. Its merchant ships plied the waters stretching from the Black Sea to the Mediterranean and out to the Atlantic Ocean, and it had an excellent navy. Now, for the first time, it turned its attention inland, looking to conquer the cities of northern Italy. In the early fifteenth century, Venice took over Brescia, Verona, Padua, Belluno, and many other cities, eventually coming up against the equally powerful city-state of Milan to its west. Between 1450 and 1454, two coalitions—one led by Milan, the other by Venice—fought for territorial control of the eastern half of northern Italy. Financial exhaustion and fear of an invasion by France or the Ottoman Turks led to the Peace of Lodi in 1454. With that peace, it was clear that Italy was no longer a collection of small cities and their contados (the surrounding countryside) but a country of large, territorial city-states.

It is no accident that the Peace of Lodi was signed one year after the Ottoman conquest of Constantinople; Venice wanted to redirect its might against the Turks. But the Venetians also knew that peace was good for business; they traded with the Ottomans, and the two powers influenced each other's art and culture. Gentile Bellini's portrait of Mehmed is a good example of the importance of Venetian artists at the Ottoman court.

Venice was never ruled by a signore (lord). Far from being a hereditary monarch, the doge—the leading magistrate at Venice—was elected by the Great Council. But that council itself was dominated by the most important families. It is unclear why the lower classes at Venice did not rebel and demand their own political power, as happened in so many other Italian cities. The answer may be that Venice's foundation on water demanded so much central planning, citywide effort to maintain buildings and services, and the dedication of public funds to provide the population with necessities that it fostered a greater sense of community than could be found elsewhere.

Florence, like Venice, was also a republic. Unlike Venice, it came to be ruled by one family. Also unlike Venice, its society and political life were turbulent, as social classes and political factions competed for power. The most important of these civil uprisings was the Ciompi Revolt of 1378. Named after the wool workers (ciompi), laborers so lowly they had not been allowed to form a guild, the revolt led to the creation of a guild, along with a new distribution of power in the city. By 1382, however, the upper classes were once again monopolizing the government, and now with even less sympathy for the commoners.

By 1434, the Medici family had become the dominant power in Florence. The patriarch of this family, Cosimo de' Medici (1389–1464), founded his political power on the wealth of the Medici bank, which handled papal finances and had numerous branch offices in Italian and northern European cities. Backed by this money, Cosimo took over Florentine politics. He determined which men could take public office, and he established new committees made up of men loyal to him to govern the city. He kept the old forms of the Florentine constitution intact, governing behind the scenes not by force but through a broad consensus among the ruling elite.

Cosimo's grandson Lorenzo the Magnificent (1449–1492), who assumed power in 1467, bolstered the regime's legitimacy with his patronage of the humanities and arts. He himself was a poet and avid collector of antiquities. He intended to build a grand library made of marble at his palace but died before it was completed. More successful was his sculpture garden, which he filled with ancient works. Serving on various Florentine committees in charge of building, renovating, and adorning the churches of the city, Lorenzo employed important artists and architects to work on his own palaces as well. He probably encouraged the young Michelangelo; he certainly patronized the poet Angelo Poliziano, whose verses inspired Botticelli's *Birth of Venus* (see the illustration on page 421). No wonder writers and poets sang his praises.

But the Medici family also had enemies. In 1478, Lorenzo narrowly escaped an assassination attempt, and his successor was driven out of Florence in 1494. The Medici returned to power in 1512, only to be driven out again in 1527. In 1530, the republic fell for good as the Medici once again took power, this time declaring themselves dukes of Florence.

The Tools of Power

Whether monarchies, duchies, or republics, the newly consolidated states of the fifteenth century exercised their power more thoroughly than ever before. Sometimes they reached into the intimate lives of their subjects or citizens.

A good example of the ways in which governments peeked into people's lives—and picked their pockets—is the Florentine *catasto*. This was an inventory of households within the city and its outlying territory made for the purposes of taxation in 1427. The Domesday survey conducted in England in 1086 had been the most complete census of its day. But the catasto bested Domesday in thoroughness and inquisitiveness. It inquired about names, types of houses, and animals. It asked people to identify their trades, and their answers reveal the levels of Florentine society, ranging from agricultural laborers with no land of their own to soldiers, cooks, grave diggers, scribes, merchants, doctors, wine dealers, innkeepers, and tanners. The catasto inquired about private and public investments, real estate holdings, and taxable assets. Finally, it turned to the sex of the head of the family, his or her age and marital status, and the number of mouths to feed in the household. An identification number was assigned to each household.

The catasto shows that in 1427 Florence and its outlying regions had a population of more than 260,000. Although the city itself had only thirty-eight thousand inhabitants (about 15 percent of the total population), it held 67 percent of the wealth. Some 60 percent of Florentine households belonged to the "little people"— artisans and small merchants. The "fat people" (*popolo grosso,* what we would call the upper middle class) made up 30 percent of the urban population and included wealthy merchants, leading artisans, notaries, doctors, and other professionals. At the bottom of the hierarchy were slaves and servants, largely women from the surrounding countryside employed in domestic service. At the top, a tiny elite of wealthy patricians, bankers, and wool merchants controlled the state and owned more than one-quarter of its wealth. This was the group that produced the Medici family.

Most Florentine households consisted of at least six people, not all of whom were members of the family. Wealthier families had more children, while childless couples existed almost exclusively among the poor. The rich gave their infants to wet nurses to breast-feed, while the poor often left their children to public charity. Florence was rightly proud of its orphanage: it both provided for the city's poorer children and was built in the newest and finest Renaissance style.

> **REVIEW**   What were the chief political entities in the year 1500, and how did they come to be so powerful?

New Forms of Thought and Expression: The Renaissance

Whether monarchies, principalities, or republics, states throughout Europe used their new power and money to foster Renaissance writers, artists, and musicians. Most textbooks divide the period 1340–1500 into two chapters, one covering the crises and the other the Renaissance. But this is misleading; both phenomena happened at the same time. In many ways, the Renaissance was a response to the crises. It revived elements of the classical past—the Greek philosophers before Aristotle, Hellenistic artists, and Roman rhetoricians—in order to deal with contemporary issues. Humanists modeled their writing on the Latin of Cicero, architects looked back to ancient notions of public space, artists adopted classical forms, and musicians used classical texts. Yet they were very much involved in the movements of their own day.

Renaissance Humanism

Humanism was a literary and linguistic movement—an attempt to revive classical Latin (and later Greek), as well as the values and sensibilities that came with the language. It began among men and women living in the Italian city-states, where many saw parallels between their urban, independent lives and the experiences of the city-states of the ancient world. Humanism was a way to confront the crises—and praise the advances—of the fourteenth through sixteenth centuries. Humanists wrote poetry, history, moral philosophy, and grammar books, all patterned on classical models.

A good example of the aim of humanists is provided by three delegates to the Council of Constance—Cincius Romanus, Poggius Bracciolinus, and Bartholomaeus Politianus. One day they decided to take time off from the council for a "rescue mission." Cincius described the escapade to one of his Latin teachers back in Italy:

> In Germany there are many monasteries with libraries full of Latin books. This aroused the hope in me that some of the works of Cicero, Varro, Livy, and other great men of learning, which seem to have completely vanished, might come to light if a careful search were instituted. A few days ago, [we] went by agreement to the town of St. Gall. As soon as we went into the library [of the monastery there], we found *Jason's Argonauticon,* written by C. Valerius Flaccus in verse that is both splendid and dignified and not far removed from poetic majesty. Then we found some discussion in prose of a number of Cicero's orations.

Cicero, Varro, Livy, and Valerius Flaccus were pagan Latin writers. Even though Cincius and his friends were working for Pope John XXIII, they loved the writings of the ancients, whose Latin was, in their view, "splendid and dignified," unlike the Latin that was used in their own time, which they found debased and faulty. They saw themselves as the resuscitators of ancient language, literature, and culture. Cincius continued:

> When we carefully inspected the nearby tower of the church of St. Gall in which countless books were kept like captives and the library neglected and infested with dust, worms, soot, and all the things associated with the destruction of books, we all burst into tears. . . . Truly if this library could speak for itself, it would cry loudly: ". . . Snatch me from this prison. . . ." There were in that monastery an abbot and monks totally devoid of any knowledge of literature. What barbarous hostility to the Latin tongue! What damned dregs of humanity!

The monks were barbarians, and Cincius and his companions were heroic raiders swooping in to liberate the captive books.

That Cincius was employed by the pope yet considered the monks of St. Gall barbarians was no oddity. Most humanists combined sincere Christian piety with their new appreciation of the pagan past. Besides, they needed to work in order to live, and they took employment where they found it. Some humanists worked for the church, others were civil servants, and still others were notaries. A few were rich men who had a taste for literary subjects.

The first humanist, most historians agree, was Francis Petrarch (1304–1374). He was born in Arezzo, a town about fifty miles southeast of Florence. As a boy, he moved around a lot (his father was exiled from Florence), ending up in the region of Avignon, where he received his earliest schooling and fell in love with classical literature. After a brief flirtation with legal studies at the behest of his father, Petrarch gave up law and devoted himself to writing poetry, in both Italian and Latin. When writing in Italian, he drew on the traditions of the troubadours, dedicating poems of longing to an unattainable and idealized woman named Laura. When writing in Latin, he was much influenced by classical poetry.

On the one hand, a boyhood in Avignon made Petrarch sensitive to the failings of the church: he was the writer who coined the phrase "Babylonian captivity." On the other hand, he took minor religious orders there, which afforded him a modest living. Struggling between what he considered a life of dissipation (he fathered two children out of wedlock) and a religious vocation, he resolved the conflict at last in his book *On the Solitary Life,* in which he claimed that the solitude needed for reading the classics was akin to the solitude practiced by those who devoted themselves to God. For Petrarch, humanism was a vocation, a calling.

Less famous, but for that reason perhaps more representative of humanists in general, was Lauro Quirini (1420–1475?), the man who (as we saw at the start of this chapter) considered the Turks to be barbarians. Educated at the University of

Padua, Quirini eventually got a law degree there. He wrote numerous letters and essays, corresponding with other humanists on topics such as the nature of the state and the character of true nobility. He spent the last half of his life in Crete, where he traded various commodities—alum, cloth, wine, Greek books. Believing that the Ottomans had destroyed the libraries of Constantinople, he wrote to Pope Nicholas V, "The language and literature of the Greeks, invented, augmented, and perfected over so long a period with such labor and industry, will certainly perish." But the fact that he himself participated in the lively trade of Greek books proved his prediction wrong.

If Quirini represents the ordinary humanist, Giovanni Pico della Mirandola (1463–1494) was perhaps the most flamboyant. Born near Ferrara of a noble family, Pico received a humanist education at home before going on to Bologna to study law and to Padua to study philosophy. Soon he was picking up Hebrew, Aramaic, and Arabic. A convinced eclectic, he thought that Jewish mystical writings supported Christian Scriptures, and in 1486 he proposed that he publicly defend at Rome nine hundred theses drawn from diverse sources. The church found some of the theses heretical, however, and banned the whole affair. But Pico's *Oration on the Dignity of Man,* which he intended to deliver before his defense, summed up the humanist view of humanity: the creative individual, armed only with his (or her) "desires and judgment," could choose to become a boor or an angel. Humanity's potential was unlimited.

Christine de Pisan (c. 1365–c. 1430) exemplifies a humanist who chose to fashion herself into a writer and courtier. Born in Venice and educated in France, Christine de Pisan was married and then widowed young. Forced to support herself, her mother, and her three young children, she began to write poems inspired by classical models, depending on rich patrons to admire her work and pay her to write more. Many members of the upper nobility supported her, including Duke Philip the Bold of Burgundy, Queen Isabelle of Bavaria, and the English earl of Salisbury. But this cast of characters did not mean she sided with the English during the Hundred Years' War. On the contrary, she lamented the violence on all sides, and Joan of Arc's early victories inspired her to write a hymn to "the Maid":

> We've never heard
> About a marvel quite so great,
> For all the heroes who have lived
> In history can't measure up
> In bravery against the Maid.

Even more political was the humanist Niccolò Machiavelli (1469–1527), whose small handbook *The Prince* (1513) argued that the state was an artifice of human creation to be conquered, shaped, and administered by princes according to the principles of power politics. Was it better for a ruler to be loved or feared by his subjects? Machiavelli answered coldly: "It may be answered that one should wish to be both, but, because it is difficult to unite them in one person, it is much safer to be feared than loved." Today the word *Machiavellian* means "coldly calculating": the end justifies the means.

Some historians deny Machiavelli the status of a humanist. But when he wrote in *The Prince* about his study of the ancients, he was identifying himself with the humanist movement. His contemporaries certainly considered him one, appointing him (in 1498) chancellor of Florence, a position normally held by humanists.

Through their activities as educators, writers, and civil servants, professional humanists gave new vigor to the humanist curriculum of grammar, rhetoric, poetry, history, and moral philosophy. By the end of the fifteenth century, the Renaissance was a European-wide phenomenon, and the humanist agenda—a good command of classical Latin, with perhaps some knowledge of Greek—had come to be one of the requirements of an educated person.

The invention of the printing press in the 1440s by a German goldsmith named Johannes Gutenberg made the world of letters more accessible to a literate audience. The key to Gutenberg's innovation was movable type—reusable metal letters, numbers, and various other characters. The typesetter arranged the characters by hand, page by page, to create a printable text. The surface of the type was inked, and sheets of paper pressed against the type picked up an impression of the text. Numerous copies could be made with only a small amount of human labor. This was a revolutionary departure from the old practice of copying by hand, making possible the mass production of identical books and pamphlets.

The printing press depended on paper production. The art of papermaking came to Europe from the Islamic world (which had borrowed it from China). By the fourteenth century, paper mills were operating in Italy, producing paper that was more fragile but much cheaper than parchment or vellum, the animal skins that Europeans had previously used for writing. To produce paper, old rags were soaked in a chemical solution, beaten by mallets into a pulp, washed with water, treated, and dried in sheets—a method that still produces good-quality paper today.

After the 1440s, printing spread rapidly from Germany to other European countries. The German cities of Cologne, Strasbourg, Nuremberg, and Augsburg all had major presses. In 1467, two German printers established the first press in Rome and produced twelve thousand volumes in five years, a feat that previously would have required a thousand scribes working full-time. By 1480, many Italian cities had established their own presses. In the 1490s, the German city of Frankfurt am Main became an international meeting place for printers and booksellers. The Frankfurt Book Fair, where printers from different nations exhibited their newest titles, represented a major international cultural event and remains an unbroken tradition to this day.

The invention of mechanical printing gave rise to a communications revolution as significant as the widespread use of the personal computer today. The multiplication of standardized texts altered the thinking habits of Europeans by freeing individuals from having to memorize everything they learned; it made possible the relatively speedy and inexpensive dissemination of knowledge; and it created a wider community of scholars, no longer dependent on personal patronage or church sponsorship for texts. Printing facilitated the free expression and exchange of ideas, and its disruptive potential did not go unnoticed by political and ecclesiastical authorities. Emperors and bishops in Germany, the homeland of the printing industry, moved quickly to issue censorship regulations.

The Prestige of Renaissance Art

The lure of the classical past was as strong in the arts as in literature. Architects and artists admired ancient Athens and Rome and drew on their traditions. At the same time, they modified classical models, combining them with medieval forms. Working for patrons—churchmen, secular rulers, rich patrons, or republican governments— Renaissance artists used both past and present to express the patriotism, religious piety, and prestige of their benefactors.

The change was clear even on the streets of the cities. Medieval cities had grown without planning: streets turned back on themselves; churches sat cheek by jowl with private houses. In the Renaissance, however, the whole city was reimagined as a place of order and harmony. The Florentine architect Leon Battista Alberti (1404–1472) proposed that each building in a city be proportioned to fit harmoniously with all the others and that city spaces allow for all necessary public activities: there should be market squares, play areas, and grounds for military exercises. In Renaissance cities, the agora and forum (the public spaces of the classical world) appeared once again, but in a new guise, as the piazza (a plaza or open square). Architects carved out spaces around their new buildings, and they built graceful covered walkways (porticos) of columns and arches. The artist Pietro Perugino (1445–1523) depicted Christ giving the keys of the kingdom of heaven to the Apostle Peter in an idealized city piazza, at the center of which was a perfectly proportioned church.

The same principles applied to the architecture of the Renaissance court. At Urbino, Duke Federico, a great patron of humanists and artists, commissioned a new palace. The architect, probably Luciano Laurana, designed its courtyard as a public space, a sort of piazza within a palace. A city had both public and private spaces; similarly, public rooms at the ducal palace gave way to a modest space for the duke's private quarters: a bedroom, a bathroom, a chapel, and, most important, his study, filled with books.

The Gothic cathedral of the Middle Ages was a cluster of graceful spikes and soaring arches. Renaissance architects appreciated its vigor and energy, but they tamed it with regular geometrical forms inspired by classical buildings. Classical forms were applied to previously built structures as well as new ones. Florence's Santa Maria Novella, for example, had been a typical Gothic church when it was first built. But when Alberti, the man who believed in public spaces and harmonious buildings, was commissioned to replace its facade, he drew on Roman temple forms.

Powerful groups within the cities, whether guilds, communes, or princely families, sponsored the new art. In 1400, the Florentines held a competition for new bronze doors for their baptistery. The entry of Lorenzo Ghiberti (1378?–1455) depicted the sacrifice of Isaac, the Old Testament story in which God tests Abraham's

Pietro Perugino, *Christ Giving the Keys to St. Peter*
This fresco on one of the side walls of the Sistine Chapel in the papal palace at Rome (now the Vatican) depicts the transfer of power in Christ's church. Inspired by the architecture of the ancient world, Perugino set the action in a large piazza flanked by Roman triumphal arches. (© Vatican Museums and Galleries, Vatican City, Italy/The Bridgeman Art Library.)

faith by ordering him to sacrifice his son. Cast in one piece, a major technological feat at the time, it shows a young, nude Isaac modeled on a classical sculpture. At the same time, Ghiberti drew on medieval models for his depiction of Abraham. In this way, he gracefully melded old and new elements—and won the contest.

In addition to using the forms of classical art, Renaissance artists also mined the ancient world for new subjects. Venus, the Roman goddess of love and beauty, had numerous stories attached to her name. At first glance, *The Birth of Venus* (page 421) by Sandro Botticelli (c. 1445–1510) seems simply an illustration of the tale of Venus's rise from the sea. In fact, however, Botticelli's work is much more complicated, drawing on the ideas of Marsilio Ficino (1433–1499) and the poetry of Angelo Poliziano (1454–1494). According to Ficino, Venus was "humanitas"—the essence of the humanities. For Poliziano, she was

> fair Venus, mother of the cupids.
> Zephyr bathes the meadow with dew
> spreading a thousand lovely fragrances:
> wherever he flies he clothes the countryside
> in roses, lilies, violets, and other flowers.

In Botticelli's painting, Zephyr, one of the winds, blows, while Venus receives a fine robe embroidered with leaves and flowers.

Sandro Botticelli, *The Birth of Venus*
Venus had been depicted in art before Botticelli's painting, but he was the first artist since antiquity to portray her in the nude. (© Galleria degli Uffizi, Florence, Italy/Giraudon/The Bridgeman Art Library.)

The Sacrifice of Isaac and *The Birth of Venus* show some of the ways in which Renaissance artists used ancient models. Other artists perfected perspective—the illusion of three-dimensional space—to a degree that even classical antiquity had not anticipated. The development of the laws of perspective accompanied the introduction of long-range weaponry, such as cannons. In fact, some artists who excelled in using perspective, such as Leonardo da Vinci (1452–1519), were military engineers as well. In Leonardo's painting *The Annunciation* (page 422), sight lines meeting at a point on the horizon open wide precisely where the angel kneels and Mary responds in surprise.

Ghiberti, Botticelli, and Leonardo were all Italian artists. While they were creating their works, a northern Renaissance was taking place as well. At the court of France during the Hundred Years' War, kings commissioned portraits of themselves—sometimes unflattering ones—just as Roman leaders had once commissioned their own busts. Soon it was the fashion for everyone who could afford it to have his or her portrait made, as naturalistically as possible. Compare the image of Joan of Arc on page 400 with the painting of the Virgin Mary and Chancellor Nicolas Rolin completed by the Dutch artist Jan van Eyck around 1433 (see page 423). The artist who depicted Joan wanted to show a young woman dressed

Leonardo da Vinci, *The Annunciation*
Working with a traditional Christian theme (the moment when the angel Gabriel announced to the Virgin Mary that she would give birth to Christ), Leonardo produced a work of great originality, drawing the viewer's eye from a vanishing point in the distance to the subject of the painting. The ability to subordinate the background to the foreground was a great contribution of Renaissance perspective. (Scala/Ministero per i Beni e le Attività Culturali/Art Resource, NY.)

in armor—any young woman. The image was meant to be symbolic. By contrast, van Eyck and his patron wanted to show a particular person, Nicolas Rolin. The very wrinkles of Rolin's neck proclaim his individuality. Though shown in a pious pose, Rolin is the key figure in the picture; the Virgin and baby Jesus sit a bit to the back and in the shadows. Meanwhile, the grand view of a city spreads out behind them, underscoring Rolin's stature in the community. Van Eyck was a master of perspective, and he used it here to emphasize Rolin's gravity and importance. Rolin was indeed an eminent man: he worked for the duke of Burgundy and was the founder of a hospital at Beaune and a religious order of nurses to serve it. Van Eyck conveyed his prominence in this portrait.

The Music of the Courts

Patrons of the new arts also used music to add glamour and glory to their courts and reputations. Renaissance rulers spent as much as 6 percent of their annual revenue to support musicians and composers. The Avignon papacy, in its own way one such court, was a major sponsor of sacred music. Whether secular or religious, music was appreciated for its ability to express the innermost feelings of the individual.

Every proper court had its own musicians. Some served as chaplains, writing music for the ruler's private chapel—the place where his court and household heard Mass. When Josquin Desprez (1440–1521) served as the duke of Ferrara's chaplain,

Jan van Eyck, *The Virgin of Chancellor Rolin*
Van Eyck portrays the Virgin and Chancellor Rolin as if they were contemporaries sharing a nice chat. Only the angel, who is placing a crown on the Virgin's head, suggests that something out of the ordinary is happening. (Erich Lessing/Art Resource, NY.)

he wrote a Mass that used the musical equivalents of the letters of the duke's name (the Italian version of *do re mi*) as its theme. Isabella d'Este (1474–1539), the daughter of the duke, employed her own musicians—singers, woodwind and string players, percussionists, and keyboard players—while her husband, the duke of Mantua, had his own band. When her brother sent her poems to copy, she had her favorite musician set them to music. This was one of the ways in which humanists and musicians worked together: the poems that interested composers and rulers alike were of the newest sort, patterned on classical forms. Isabella particularly favored Petrarch's poems.

The church, too, was a major sponsor of music. Every feast required music, and the papal schism inadvertently encouraged more musical production than usual, as rival popes tried to best one another in the realm of pageantry and sound. Churches needed choirs, and many composers got their start as choirboys. But that job could last well into adulthood. In the fourteenth century, the men who sang in the choir at Reims, for example, received a yearly stipend and an extra fee every time the choir sang the Mass and the liturgical offices of the day.

When the composer Johannes Ockeghem, chaplain for three French kings, died in 1497, his fellow musicians vied in expressing their grief in song. Josquin Desprez was among them, and his composition illustrates how the addition of classical elements to very traditional musical forms enhanced music's emotive power. Josquin's work combines personal grief with religious liturgy and the feelings expressed in classical elegies. The piece uses five voices. Inspired by classical mythology, four of the voices sing in the vernacular French about the "nymphs of the wood" coming together to mourn. But the fifth voice intones the words of the liturgy: "Requiescat in pace" (May he rest in peace). At the very moment in the song when the four vernacular voices lament Ockeghem's burial in the dark ground, the liturgical voice sings of the heavenly light. The contrast makes the song more moving. By drawing on the classical past, Renaissance musicians found new ways in which to express emotion.

REVIEW How and why did Renaissance humanists, artists, and musicians revive classical traditions?

On the Threshold of Global History

Only in the fifteenth century did Europe become a major player in world history. Before the maritime explorations of Portugal and Spain, Europe had remained at the periphery of world events. Fourteenth-century Mongols had been more interested in conquering China and Persia—lands with sophisticated cultures—than in invading Europe; Persian historians of the early fifteenth century dismissed Europeans as "barbaric Franks"; and China's Ming dynasty rulers, who sent maritime expeditions to Southeast Asia and East Africa around 1400, seemed unaware of Europeans, even though Marco Polo and other Italian merchants had appeared at the court of the preceding Mongol Yuan dynasty.

In the fifteenth century, Portuguese and Spanish vessels, followed a century later by English, French, and Dutch ships, sailed across the Atlantic, Indian, and Pacific oceans, bringing with them people, merchandise, crops, and diseases in a global exchange that would shape the modern world. For the first time, the people of the Americas were brought into contact with a larger historical force that threatened to destroy not only their culture but also their existence. European exploitation and conquest defined this historical era of transition from the medieval to the modern world, as Europeans left the Baltic and the Mediterranean for wider oceans.

The Divided Mediterranean

In the second half of the fifteenth century, the Mediterranean Sea, which had dominated medieval maritime trade, began to lose its preeminence to the Atlantic Ocean. To win control over the Mediterranean, the Ottomans embarked on an ambitious naval program to transform their empire into a major maritime power. War and piracy disrupted the flow of Christian trade: the Venetians mobilized all their resources to fight off Turkish advances, and the Genoese largely abandoned the eastern Mediterranean for trade opportunities presented by the Atlantic.

Mediterranean trade used ships made with relatively backward naval technology. The most common ship, the galley—a flat-bottomed vessel propelled mainly by oarsmen with the help of a sail—dated from the time of ancient Rome. Most galleys could not withstand open-ocean voyages, although Florentine and Genoese galleys did make long journeys to Flanders and England, hugging the coast for protection. The galley's dependence on human labor was a more serious handicap. Because prisoners of war and convicted criminals toiled as oarsmen on both Christian and Muslim ships, victory in war or the enforcement of criminal penalties was crucial to a state's ability to float large numbers of galleys. Slaves, too, sometimes provided the necessary labor.

Portuguese Confrontations

The exploration of the Atlantic began with the Portuguese (Map 11.5). By 1415, they had captured Ceuta on the Moroccan coast, establishing a foothold in Africa. Thereafter, Portuguese voyages sailed farther down the West African coast. By midcentury, a chain of Portuguese forts reached Guinea, protecting the trade in gold and slaves. At home, the royal house of Portugal financed the fleets, with crucial roles played by Prince Peter, regent between 1440 and 1448; his more famous younger brother Prince Henry the Navigator; and King John II. As a governor of the noble crusading Order of Christ, Henry financed many voyages out of the order's revenues. Private monies also helped, as leading Lisbon merchants participated in financing the gold and slave trades off the Guinea coast.

In 1455, Pope Nicholas V authorized Portuguese overseas expansion, praising King John II's crusading spirit and granting him and his successors a monopoly on trade with inhabitants of the newly "discovered" regions. In 1487–1488, Bartholomeu Dias took advantage of the prevailing winds in the South Atlantic to reach the Cape of Good Hope. A mere ten years later (1497–1499), under the captainship of Vasco da Gama, a Portuguese fleet rounded the cape and reached Calicut, India, center of the spice trade. By 1517, a chain of Portuguese forts dotted the Indian Ocean. In 1519, Ferdinand Magellan, a Portuguese sailor in Spanish service, led the first expedition to circumnavigate the globe.

In many ways a continuation of the struggle against the Muslims on the Iberian peninsula, Portugal's maritime voyages displayed that country's mixed motives of piety, glory, and greed. The sailors dreamed of finding gold mines in West Africa and a mysterious Christian kingdom established by a mythical "Prester John." They hoped to reach the spice-producing lands of South and Southeast Asia by sea and to bypass the Ottoman Turks, who controlled the traditional land routes between Europe and Asia.

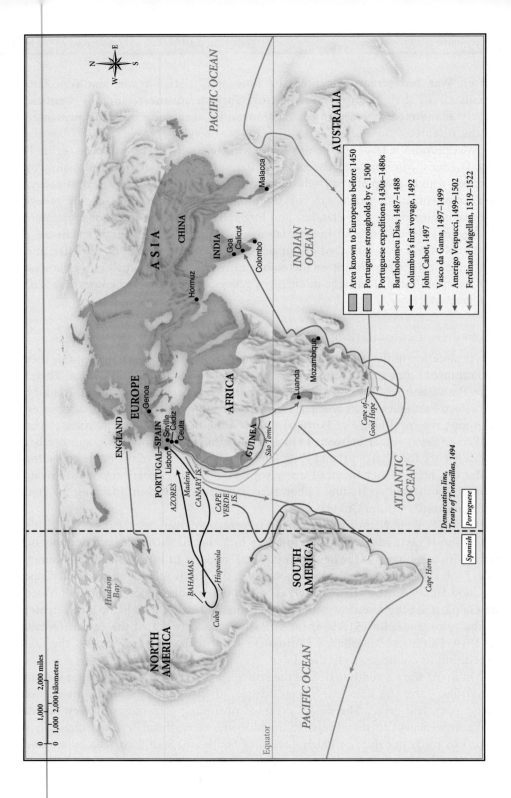

PACIFIC OCEAN

AUSTRALIA

Malacca

ASIA

CHINA

INDIA
Goa
Calicut
Colombo

Hormuz

INDIAN
OCEAN

EUROPE
Genoa

AFRICA

Mozambique

ENGLAND

Luanda

PORTUGAL–SPAIN
Lisbon • Seville
Cadiz
Ceuta

GUINEA

São Tomé

Cape of
Good Hope

AZORES
Madeira
CANARY IS.

ATLANTIC
OCEAN

CAPE
VERDE
IS.

Demarcation line,
Treaty of Tordesillas, 1494

Spanish | Portuguese

BAHAMAS
Hispaniola

Cuba

NORTH
AMERICA

Hudson
Bay

SOUTH
AMERICA

Cape Horn

PACIFIC OCEAN

Equator

0   1,000   2,000 miles
0   1,000 2,000 kilometers

Area known to Europeans before 1450
Portuguese strongholds by c. 1500
Portuguese expeditions 1430s–1480s
Bartholomeu Dias, 1487–1488
Columbus's first voyage, 1492
John Cabot, 1497
Vasco da Gama, 1497–1499
Amerigo Vespucci, 1499–1502
Ferdinand Magellan, 1519–1522

N
W   E
S

The new voyages depended for their success on several technological break-throughs. The lateen (triangular) sail permitted ships to tack against headwinds. Light caravels and heavy galleons, however different in size, were alike in using more than one mast and sail, harnessing wind—rather than human—power to move them. Better charts, maps, and instruments made long-distance voyages less risky.

After the voyages of Christopher Columbus, Portugal's interests clashed with those of Spain. Mediated by Pope Alexander VI, the 1494 Treaty of Tordesillas reconciled Portugal and Spain by dividing the Atlantic world between the two royal houses. A demarcation 370 leagues west of the Cape Verde Islands divided the Atlantic Ocean, reserving for Portugal the western coast of Africa and the route to India and giving Spain the oceans and lands to the west. Unwittingly, this agreement also allowed Portugal to claim Brazil in 1500, which Pedro Álvares Cabral (1467–1520) accidentally "discovered" on his voyage to India.

The Voyages of Columbus

Historians agree that Christopher Columbus (1451–1506) was born of Genoese parents; beyond that, we have little accurate information about this man who brought together the history of Europe and the Americas. In 1476, he arrived in Portugal, apparently a survivor in a naval battle between a Franco-Portuguese and a Genoese fleet. In 1479, he married a Portuguese noblewoman. He spent the next few years mostly in Portuguese service, gaining valuable experience in regular voyages down the west coast of Africa. In 1485, after the death of his wife, Columbus settled in Spain.

Fifteenth-century Europeans already knew that Asia lay beyond the vast Atlantic Ocean, and *The Travels of Marco Polo,* written more than a century earlier, still exerted a powerful hold on European images of the East. Columbus read it many times, along with other travel books, and proposed to sail west across the Atlantic to reach the lands of the khan, unaware that the Mongol Empire had already collapsed in eastern Asia. Vastly underestimating the distances, he dreamed of finding a new route to the East's gold and spices and partook of the larger European vision that had inspired the Portuguese voyages. (His critics had a much more accurate idea of the globe's size and of the difficulty of the venture. No one believed that the

Map 11.5 Early Voyages of World Exploration
At the end of the fifteenth century, Europeans began moving aggressively across the globe. Beginning with initial forays along the African coast, their voyages soon widened out to transatlantic crossings and, by 1522, the circumnavigation of the world. The web of arrows on this map suggests an earth bound together by many threads, and this is partly true, for never again would the two halves of the globe be isolated. At the same time, the threads pulled in one direction only—toward the Europeans. Africa was exploited for gold and slaves, while the discovery of precious metals fueled the explorations and settlements of Central and South America.

world was flat!) After the Portuguese and French monarchs rejected his proposal, Columbus found royal patronage with the recently proclaimed Catholic monarchs Isabella of Castile and Ferdinand of Aragon. In August 1492, equipped with a modest fleet of three ships and about ninety men, Columbus set sail across the Atlantic. His contract stipulated that he would claim Castilian sovereignty over any new land and inhabitants and share any profits with the crown.

Reaching what we know today as the Bahamas on October 12, Columbus mistook the islands to be part of the East Indies, not far from Japan and "the lands of the Great Khan." As the Castilians explored the Caribbean islands, they encountered communities of peaceful Indians, the Arawaks, who were awed by the Europeans' military technology, not to mention their appearance. Exchanging gifts of beads and broken glass for Arawak gold—an exchange that convinced Columbus of the trusting nature of the Indians—the crew established peaceful relationships with many communities. Yet despite many positive entries in the ship's log referring to Columbus's personal goodwill toward the Indians, the Europeans' objectives were clear: find gold, subjugate the Indians, and propagate Christianity.

Excited by the prospect of easy riches, many flocked to join Columbus's second voyage. When Columbus departed Cádiz in September 1493, he commanded seventeen ships that carried between twelve hundred and fifteen hundred men, many believing all they had to do was "load the gold into the ships." Failing to find the imaginary gold mines and spices, however, the colonial enterprise quickly switched its focus to finding slaves. Columbus and his crew first enslaved the Caribs, enemies of the Arawaks; in 1494, Columbus proposed a regular slave trade based in Hispaniola. The Spaniards exported enslaved Indians to Spain, and slave traders sold them in Seville. Soon the Spaniards began importing sugarcane from the Portuguese island of Madeira and forced large numbers of Indians to work on plantations to produce more sugar for export to Europe. Columbus himself was edged out of this new enterprise. When the Spanish monarchs realized the vast potential for material gain that lay in their new dominions, they asserted direct royal authority by sending officials and priests to the Americas, which were later named after the Italian Amerigo Vespucci, who led a voyage across the Atlantic in 1499–1502.

Columbus's place in history embodies the fundamental transformations of his age. A Genoese in the service of Portuguese and Spanish employers, Columbus's career illustrates the changing balance between the Mediterranean and the Atlantic. His voyages of 1492–1493 would eventually draw a triangle of exchange among Europe, the Americas, and Africa, an exchange gigantic in its historical impact and its human cost.

A New Era in Slavery

During the Middle Ages and Renaissance, female slaves served as domestic servants in wealthy Mediterranean homes, and male slaves toiled in the galleys of Ottoman and Christian fleets. Some were captured in war or by piracy; others, Africans, were

Dürer's Engraving of Katharina, an African Woman
Like other artists in early-sixteenth-century Europe, Albrecht Dürer would have seen in person Africans who were living in Portugal and Spain as students, servants, and slaves. (Foto Marburg/Art Resource, NY.)

sold by African and Bedouin traders to Christian buyers. In western Asia, impoverished parents sometimes sold their children into servitude. Many people in the Balkans became slaves when their land was devastated by Ottoman invasions. Slaves were Greek, Slav, European, African, and Turk.

The Portuguese maritime voyages changed this picture. From the fifteenth century on, Africans increasingly filled the ranks of slaves. Exploiting warfare in West Africa, the Portuguese traded in gold and "pieces," as African slaves were called, a practice condemned at home by some conscientious clergy. Critical voices, however, could not deny the enormous profits the slave trade brought to Portugal. Most slaves toiled on the sugar plantations of the Portuguese Atlantic islands and in Brazil. A fortunate few labored as domestic servants in Portugal, where African freedmen and slaves, some 35,000 in the early sixteenth century, constituted almost 3 percent of the population, a much higher percentage than in other European countries. In the Americas, slavery would flourish as an institution of exploitation.

Europeans in a New World

In 1500, on the eve of European invasion, the native peoples of the Americas were divided into many sedentary and nomadic societies. Among the settled peoples, the largest political and social organizations were in the Mexican and Peruvian highlands. The Aztecs and Incas ruled over subjugated Indian populations in their respective empires. With an elaborate religious culture and a rigid social and political hierarchy, the Aztecs and Incas based their civilizations in large urban capitals.

The Spanish explorers organized their expeditions to the mainland from a base in the Caribbean. Two prominent leaders, Hernán Cortés (1485–1547) and Francisco Pizarro (c. 1475–1541), gathered men and arms and set off in search of gold. Catholic priests accompanied the fortune hunters to bring Christianity to allegedly uncivilized peoples and thus to justify brutal conquests. His small band swollen by peoples who had been subjugated by the Aztecs, Cortés captured the Aztec capital, Tenochtitlán, in 1519. To the south, Pizarro conquered the Andean highlands, exploiting a civil war between rival Incan kings. By the mid-sixteenth century, the Spanish Empire stretched unbroken from Mexico to Chile.

Not to be outdone by the Spaniards, other European powers joined the scramble for gold in the New World. In 1500, a Portuguese fleet led by Pedro Álvares Cabral landed in Brazil, but Portugal did not begin colonizing there until 1532, when it established a permanent fort on the coast. In North America, the French went in search of a "northwest passage" to China. By 1504, French fishermen had appeared in Newfoundland. Thirty years later, Jacques Cartier led three voyages that explored the St. Lawrence River as far as Montreal. An early attempt in 1541 to settle Canada failed because of the harsh winter and Indian hostility, and John Cabot's 1497 voyage to find a northern route to Asia also failed. More permanent settlements in Canada and the present-day United States would succeed only in the seventeenth century.

REVIEW Which European countries led the way in maritime expansion, and what were their motives?

Conclusion

Confronted by disease, economic contraction, war, popular uprisings, and a disgraced papacy, Europe's ruling classes grasped the reins of power ever more tightly, creating more centralized and institutionalized states. Muscovy and Poland-Lithuania formed in the east, while western European kings, dukes, and even republics consolidated their rule.

Surrounding themselves with artists, musicians, and humanists, these new-style rulers supported the Renaissance—an attempt to resuscitate the classical past for the purposes of the present. The Renaissance, which emphasized human potential and achievement, was one of Europe's most brilliant periods of artistic activity, one that glorified both God and humanity. Inspired by ancient models, Renaissance humanists

Mapping the West **Renaissance Europe, c. 1500**
By 1500, the shape of early modern Europe was largely set. It would remain stable until the eighteenth century, except for the disappearance of an independent Hungarian kingdom, which was conquered by the Ottomans in 1529.

revived classical literary style, Renaissance architects planned cities as well as buildings, Renaissance artists demonstrated a new appreciation for the human body and the illusion of depth, and Renaissance musicians invented new forms of polyphony. The Renaissance began mainly in the city-states of Italy, but it spread throughout much of Europe. At the courts of great kings and dukes, even the Ottoman sultan, Renaissance music, art, and literature served as a way to celebrate the grandeur of rulers who controlled more of the apparatuses of government—armies, artillery, courts, and taxes—than ever before.

Political consolidation fueled intense competition among the European powers for more land, money, and glory. Rulers paid explorers to expand their frontiers, first to Africa and then across the Atlantic Ocean to the Americas, ushering in the first period of global history. Few at the time would have guessed that Europe would soon enter yet another period of turmoil, one brought about not by demographic and economic collapse but by a profound crisis of conscience that the brilliance of Renaissance civilization had tended to obscure.

CHAPTER REVIEW QUESTIONS
1. How did Renaissance states differ from medieval monarchies?
2. How did the Ottomans' impact on Europe differ from the Mongols'?

For practice quizzes and other study tools, see the Online Study Guide at bedfordstmartins.com/huntconcise.

For primary-source material from this period, see Chapters 13 and 14 of *Sources of THE MAKING OF THE WEST,* Third Edition.

TIMELINE

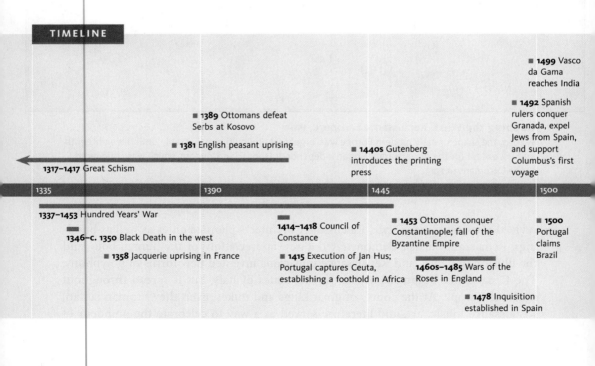

- **1499** Vasco da Gama reaches India

- **1492** Spanish rulers conquer Granada, expel Jews from Spain, and support Columbus's first voyage

- **1389** Ottomans defeat Serbs at Kosovo

- **1381** English peasant uprising

- **1440s** Gutenberg introduces the printing press

1317–1417 Great Schism

| 1335 | 1390 | 1445 | 1500 |

1337–1453 Hundred Years' War

- **1453** Ottomans conquer Constantinople; fall of the Byzantine Empire

- **1500** Portugal claims Brazil

1346–c. 1350 Black Death in the west

1414–1418 Council of Constance

- **1358** Jacquerie uprising in France

- **1415** Execution of Jan Hus; Portugal captures Ceuta, establishing a foothold in Africa

1460s–1485 Wars of the Roses in England

- **1478** Inquisition established in Spain

Suggested References

The old view of historians associated the Renaissance primarily with Florence, but now the Renaissance is seen as a European movement (Kirkpatrick, Knecht) and even part of Ottoman culture (Jardine and Brotton). Similarly, the traditional view of "Europe discovering the world" has been replaced by a more nuanced and complex discussion (Abulafia) that includes non-European views and uses Asian, African, and Mesoamerican sources.

Aberth, John. *From the Brink of the Apocalypse: Confronting Famine, War, Plague, and Death in the Later Middle Ages.* 2001.

Abulafia, David, ed. *The Discovery of Mankind: Atlantic Encounters in the Age of Columbus.* 2008.

Bisaha, Nancy. *Creating East and West: Renaissance Humanists and the Ottoman Turks.* 2004.

*Froissart, Jean. *Chronicles.* Trans. Geoffrey Brereton. 1968.

*Horrox, Rosemary, ed. and trans. *The Black Death.* 1994.

Jardine, Lisa, and Jerry Brotton. *Global Interests: Renaissance Art between East and West.* 2000.

Jordan, William Chester. *The Great Famine: Northern Europe in the Early Fourteenth Century.* 1996.

Kirkpatrick, Robin. *The European Renaissance, 1400–1600.* 2002.

Knecht, R. J. *The French Renaissance Court, 1483–1589.* 2008.

Plague and public health in Renaissance Europe: http://jefferson.village.virginia.edu/osheim/intro.html

Renaissance art in Italy: http://witcombe.sbc.edu/ARTHrenaissanceitaly.html

Russell-Wood, A. J. R. *A World on the Move: The Portuguese in Africa, Asia, and America, 1415–1808.* 1992.

Thomas, Hugh. *Rivers of Gold: The Rise of the Spanish Empire, from Columbus to Magellan.* 2003.

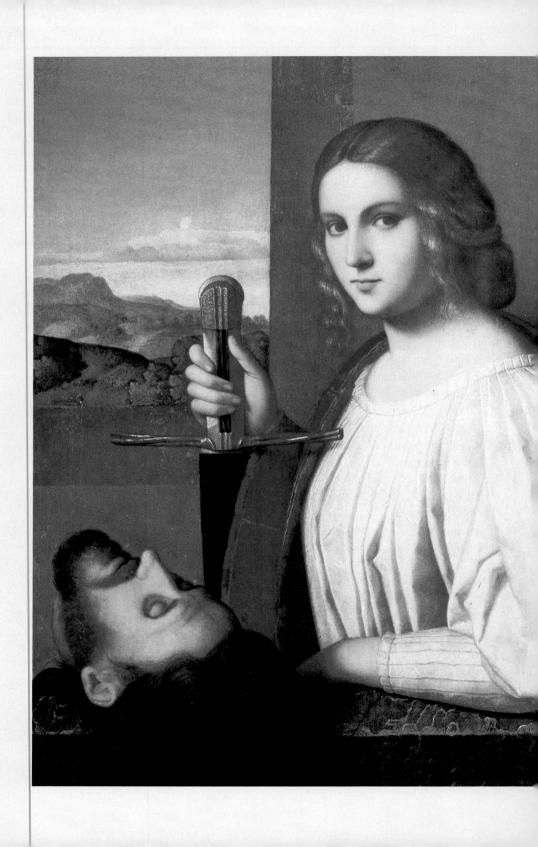

Struggles over Beliefs

HILLE FEIKEN LEFT THE NORTHERN GERMAN CITY of Münster on June 16, 1534, elegantly dressed, bedecked with jewels, and determined to kill. Münster, which religious radicals had declared a holy city, lay under siege by armies loyal to the local Catholic bishop—her intended victim. Hille crossed enemy lines and tried to persuade the commander of the besieging troops to take her to the bishop, promising to reveal a secret means of recapturing the city. When a defector from her camp recognized Hille and betrayed her, she was beheaded.

Hille Feiken belonged to the religious group known as **Anabaptists**, who wanted to form a holy community separate from the rest of society. Anabaptists organized in response to the Protestant Reformation, which was set in motion by the German friar Martin Luther in 1517 and quickly became a sweeping movement to uproot church abuses and restore early Christian teachings. Supporters of Luther were called **Protestants**, those who protested. Inspired by Luther and then by other reformers, ordinary men and women across much of Europe attempted to remake their heaven and earth. Their stories intertwined with bloody struggles among princes for domination in Europe, an age-old conflict now complicated by the clash of rival faiths.

Vincenzo Catena, *Judith*
The Book of Judith tells the story of a beautiful young Israelite who presents herself to Holofernes, the general of an army besieging Jerusalem. His guard lowered by wine and Judith's charms, Holofernes falls victim to Judith, who assassinates him and cuts off his head, thus frightening off the enemy and saving her people. In this painting from the 1520s, the Venetian artist Vincenzo Catena conveys Judith's strength, beauty, and commitment to her task—one that Hille Feiken sought to reenact so that she might free her own besieged city of Münster. *(akg-images/Cameraphoto.)*

Struggles over religious beliefs frequently erupted into armed confrontation, culminating in the Thirty Years' War of 1618–1648, which devastated the lands of central Europe. The orgy of mutual destruction in this war left no winners in the religious struggle, and the cynical manipulation of religious issues by both Catholic and Protestant leaders showed that political interests eventually outweighed those of religion. The extreme violence of religious conflict pushed rulers and political thinkers to seek other, non-religious grounds for governmental authority. Few would argue for genuine toleration of religious differences, but many began to insist that the interests of states had to take priority over the desire for religious conformity.

Although particularly dramatic and deadly, the church-state crisis was only one of a series of upheavals that shaped this era. After decades of rapid economic and population growth in the sixteenth century, a major economic downturn led to food shortages, famine, and disease in the first half of the seventeenth century. An upheaval in worldviews was also in the making, catalyzed by increasing knowledge of the new worlds discovered overseas and in the heavens. The development of new scientific methods of research would ultimately reshape Western attitudes toward religion and state power, as Europeans desperately sought alternatives to wars over religious beliefs.

CHAPTER FOCUS QUESTION   Why did struggles over religious beliefs in the sixteenth and seventeenth centuries provoke such violence?

The Protestant Reformation

Since the mid-fifteenth century, many clerics had tried to reform the church from within, criticizing clerical abuses and calling for moral renewal, but their efforts came up against the church's inertia and resistance. At the beginning of the sixteenth century, widespread popular piety and anticlericalism existed side by side, fomenting a volatile mixture of need and resentment. A young German friar, tormented by his own religious doubts, was to become the spokesman for a generation. From its origins as a theological dispute, Martin Luther's reform movement sparked explosive protests. By the time he died in 1546, half of western Europe had renounced allegiance to the Roman Catholic church. Christian unity fractured, opening the way not only to widespread turmoil but also to a host of new attitudes about the nature of religious and political authority.

Popular Piety and Christian Humanism

Numerous signs pointed to an intense spiritual anxiety among the laity. New shrines sprang up, reports of miracles multiplied, and prayer books sold briskly. Critics complained that the church gave external behavior more weight than spiritual intentions. In receiving the sacrament of penance—one of the central pillars of the Roman church—sinners were expected to examine their consciences, sincerely confess their sins to a priest, and receive forgiveness. In practice, however, some priests abused their authority by demanding sexual or monetary favors in return for forgiveness. Priests also sold **indulgences**, which according to doctrine could alleviate suffering in purgatory after death. The faithful were supposed to earn indulgences by performing certain religious tasks—going on pilgrimage, attending Mass, doing holy works. The sale of indulgences as a substitution for performing good works suggested that the church was more interested in making money than in saving souls.

Dissatisfaction with the official church prompted some Christian intellectuals to link their scholarship to the cause of social reform and to dream of ideal societies based on peace and morality. The Dutch scholar Desiderius Erasmus (c. 1466–1536) and the English lawyer Thomas More (1478–1535) stood out as representatives of these Christian humanists, who, unlike Italian humanists, placed their primary emphasis on Christian piety. Each established close links to the powerful. Erasmus was on intimate terms with kings and popes, and his fame spread across Europe. More became lord chancellor to England's king Henry VIII.

Erasmus advocated a simple piety devoid of greed and the lust for power, but he also promoted the new humanist learning. To this end he devoted years to translating a new Latin edition of the New Testament from the original Greek. He argued ironically in *The Praise of Folly* (1509) that the wise appeared foolish, because modesty, humility, and poverty had few adherents in this world. Although Erasmus mocked the clergy's corruption and Christian princes' bloody ambitions, he emphasized the role of education in reforming individuals and through them society as a whole. Even ordinary table manners drew his attention. In the *Colloquies* (1523), a compilation of Latin dialogues intended as language-learning exercises, he advised his cultivated readers not to pick their noses at meals and not to speak while stuffing their mouths. Challenged by angry younger men and radical ideas once the Reformation took hold, Erasmus chose Christian unity over reform and schism. He died in the Swiss city of Basel, isolated from the Protestant community and condemned by many in the Catholic church, who found his writings too critical of the church's authority.

Erasmus's good friend Thomas More, to whom *The Praise of Folly* was dedicated,* met with even greater suffering for his beliefs. He would later pay with his life for upholding conscience over political expediency. Inspired by the recent voyages of discovery, More's best-known work, *Utopia* (1516), describes an imaginary ideal place that offered a stark contrast to his own society. Because utopians enjoyed public schools, communal kitchens, hospitals, and nurseries, they had no need for money. Greed and private property disappeared in this world. Dedicated to the pursuit of knowledge and natural religion, Utopia knew neither crime nor war (*Utopia* means both "no place" and "best place" in Greek). Despite a few oddities—voluntary slavery, for instance, and strictly controlled travel—Utopia seemed a paradise compared with the increasing violence in a Europe divided by religion.

Martin Luther and the German Nation

Like Erasmus and More, Martin Luther (1483–1546) pursued a life of scholarship, but a personal crisis of faith led him to break with the Roman church and establish a competing one. The son of a miner, Luther abandoned his studies in the law to enter the Augustinian order. The choice of a monastic life did not resolve Luther's doubts about his own salvation. Appalled at his own sense of sinfulness and the weakness of human nature, he lived in terror of God's justice despite frequent confessions and penance.

---

*The Latin title *Encomium Moriae* (*The Praise of Folly*) was a pun on More's name and the Latin word meaning "folly."

A pilgrimage to Rome only deepened his unease with the institutional church. Sent to study theology by a sympathetic superior, Luther gradually came to new insights through his study of Scripture. He later described his breakthrough experience:

> At last, by the mercy of God, meditating day and night, I gave heed to the context of the words [in Romans 1:17], namely, "In [the Gospel] the righteousness of God is revealed, as it is written, 'He who through faith is righteous shall live.'" There I began to understand that the righteousness of God is that by which the righteous live by a gift of God, namely by faith.

Luther soon came into conflict with the church authorities. In 1516, the new archbishop ordered the sale of indulgences to help cover the cost of constructing St. Peter's Basilica in Rome and also to defray his expenses in pursuing his election. Such blatant profiteering outraged many, including Luther, who now served as professor of theology at the University of Wittenberg. In 1517, Luther composed ninety-five theses—propositions for an academic debate—that questioned indulgence peddling and the purchase of church offices. Once they became public, the theses unleashed a torrent of pent-up resentment and frustration among the laypeople. This apparently ordinary academic dispute soon engulfed the Holy Roman Empire in conflict.

As Luther developed his ideas more fully, rupture became inevitable. In 1520, he published three treatises that laid out his theological position, attacked the papacy in Rome as the embodiment of the Antichrist, and called upon the German princes to reform the church themselves. Luther insisted that faith alone, not good works or penance, could save sinners from damnation. Faith came from the believer's personal relationship with God, which he or she cultivated through individual study of Scripture. Ordinary laypeople thus made up "the priesthood of all believers," who had no need of a professional caste of clerics to show them the way to salvation. The attack on the church's authority could not have been more dramatic.

Luther Triumphs over His Catholic Opponents
This 1521 woodcut by Matthias Gnidias shows Martin Luther, Bible in hand, standing above his Catholic opponent, the Franciscan friar Thomas Murner, who is depicted here as the biblical monster Leviathan. The monster breathes "ignis, fumus, & sulphur"—fire, smoke, and sulfur. The vertical Latin caption declares that the Lord will visit the earth with his sword and kill the monster. Both Protestants and Catholics used woodcuts and illustrations extensively as propaganda to appeal to the vast majority of people who were illiterate.

From Rome's perspective, the "Luther Affair," as church officials called it, was essentially a matter of clerical discipline. Rome ordered Luther to obey his superiors and keep quiet. But the church establishment had seriously misjudged the extent of Luther's influence. Luther's ideas, published in numerous German and Latin editions, spread rapidly throughout the Holy Roman Empire, unleashing forces that Luther himself could not control. Social, nationalist, and religious protests fused into an explosive mass very similar to the Czech revolution that Jan Hus had inspired a century earlier. Like Hus, Luther appeared before an emperor: in 1521, he defended his faith before Charles V (r. 1520–1558), the newly elected Holy Roman Emperor, who at the age of nineteen was the ruler of the Low Countries, Spain, Spain's Italian and New World dominions, and the Austrian Habsburg lands. At the Imperial Diet of Worms, the formal assembly presided over by this powerful ruler, Luther shocked Germans by declaring his admiration for the Czech heretic. But unlike Hus, Luther did not suffer martyrdom because he enjoyed the protection of his local lord, the elector of Saxony (one of the seven German princes entitled to elect the Holy Roman Emperor). Luther also had the support of many literate townspeople who were eager to read the Scriptures for themselves.

What began as an urban movement turned into a war in the countryside in 1525. The church was the largest landowner in the Holy Roman Empire: about one-seventh of the empire's territory consisted of ecclesiastical principalities in which bishops and abbots exercised both secular and churchly power. Peasants had to pay taxes to both the church and their lords. In the spring of 1525, many peasants in southern and central Germany rose in rebellion, sometimes inspired by wandering preachers. Urban workers and artisans joined the peasant bands, plundering monasteries, refusing to pay church taxes, and demanding village autonomy, the abolition of serfdom, and the right to appoint their own pastors. In Thuringia, the rebels were led by an ex-priest, Thomas Müntzer (1468?–1525), who promised to chastise the wicked and thus clear the way for the Last Judgment.

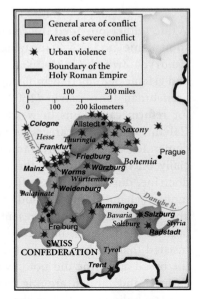

The uprising of 1525, known as the Peasants' War, split the reform movement. In Thuringia, Catholics and reformers joined hands to kill Müntzer and crush his supporters. All over the empire, princes rallied their troops to defeat the peasants and hunt down their leaders. By the end of 1525, more than 100,000 rebels had been killed and others maimed, imprisoned, or exiled.

The Peasants' War, 1525

Luther had tried to mediate, criticizing the princes for their brutality toward the peasants but also warning the rebels against mixing religion and social protest.

The Progress of the Reformation

1517	Martin Luther disseminates ninety-five theses attacking the sale of indulgences and other church practices
1520	Reformer Huldrych Zwingli breaks with Rome
1525	Radical reformer Thomas Müntzer killed in the Peasants' War
1529	Lutheran German princes protest the condemnation of religious reform by Charles V; genesis of the term *Protestants*
1534	English Parliament establishes King Henry VIII as head of the Anglican church, severing ties to Rome
1534–1535	Anabaptists control the city of Münster, Germany, in a failed experiment to create a holy community
1541	John Calvin and his followers take control in Geneva, making that city the center of Calvinist reforms

Luther believed that rulers were ordained by God and thus must be obeyed even if they were tyrants. The kingdom of God belonged not to this world but to the next. When the rebels ignored his appeal to stop, Luther called on the princes to destroy "the devil's work" and slaughter the rebels. Fundamentally conservative in its political philosophy, the Lutheran church would henceforth depend on established political authority for its protection.

Emerging as the champions of an orderly religious reform, many German princes eventually confronted Emperor Charles V, who supported Rome. In 1529, Charles declared the Roman Catholic faith the empire's only legitimate religion. Proclaiming their allegiance to the reform cause, the Lutheran German princes protested and thus came to be called Protestants.

Huldrych Zwingli and John Calvin

While Luther provided the religious leadership for northern Germany, the south soon came under the influence of reformers based in Switzerland. In 1520, Huldrych Zwingli (1484–1531), the son of a Swiss village leader, broke with Rome and established his reform headquarters in German-speaking Zurich. In 1541, the Frenchman John Calvin (1509–1564) made French-speaking Geneva his center for reform campaigns in western Europe (Map 12.1). Like Luther, Zwingli and Calvin began their careers as priests, but in contrast to their predecessor, they demanded an even more radical break with the Roman Catholic church, especially on the question of the sacrament of communion. According to Catholic doctrine, during the Mass officiated by a priest the bread and wine of holy communion changed into the body and blood of Christ. Luther believed that the body and blood were actually present in the bread and wine, but only because of the faith of the believer, not because a priest officiated. Zwingli pushed further and insisted that the bread and wine simply symbolized Christ's union with believers; the bread and wine did not change in substance. Calvin took a position between Zwingli and Luther, arguing that the sacrament of communion was more than just symbolic but insisting that it was entirely in God's power, dependent neither on the priest nor on the individual's faith. All efforts to mediate between these positions failed.

Map 12.1 The Spread of Protestantism in the Sixteenth Century

The Protestant Reformation divided northern and southern Europe. From its heartland in the Holy Roman Empire, the Reformation spread to Scandinavia, England, and Scotland and made considerable inroads into the Low Countries, France, eastern Europe, the Swiss Confederation, and even parts of northern Italy. While the Mediterranean countries remained loyal to Rome, religious divisions characterized the landscape of Europe from the British Isles in the west to Poland in the east.

In Zurich, Zwingli tolerated no dissent. When laypeople secretly set up their own new sect, called Anabaptists, Zwingli immediately attacked them. The Anabaptists believed that only adults had the free will to truly understand and accept baptism and therefore had to be rebaptized (*anabaptism* means "rebaptism"). How could a baby knowingly choose Christ? Rebaptism symbolized the Anabaptists' determination to withdraw from a social order corrupted, as they saw it, by power and evil. They therefore rejected the authority of courts and magistrates and refused to bear arms or swear oaths of allegiance. When persuasion failed to convince them, Zwingli urged Zurich magistrates to impose the death sentence.

Anabaptism spread quickly from Zurich to many cities in southern Germany, despite the Holy Roman Empire's general condemnation of the movement in 1529. In 1534, one incendiary Anabaptist group, believing that the end of the world was imminent, seized control of the northwestern German town of Münster. Proclaiming themselves a community of saints and imitating the ancient Israelites, they were initially governed by twelve elders and later by Jan of Leiden, a Dutch Anabaptist tailor who claimed to be the prophesied leader—a second "King David."

The Münster Anabaptists abolished private property and dissolved traditional marriages, allowing men, like Old Testament patriarchs, to have multiple wives, to the chagrin of many women. In 1535, Münster fell to a combined Protestant and Catholic army. Many Anabaptists died in battle or, like Hille Feiken, were executed. The remnants of the Anabaptist movement survived under the determined pacifist leadership of the Dutch reformer Menno Simons (1496–1561), whose followers were eventually named Mennonites.

As a young priest, Calvin had believed it might be possible to reform the Roman Catholic church from within, but gradually he came to share Luther and Zwingli's conviction that only fundamental change could restore the true religion. While Calvin moved toward the Protestant position, his homeland of France experienced increasing turmoil over religion. On Sunday, October 18, 1534, in the so-called Affair of the Placards, Parisians found church doors posted with broadsheets denouncing the Catholic Mass. The government arrested hundreds of French Protestants and executed scores of them, precipitating the flight into exile of many others, including Calvin.

Calvin did not intend to settle in Geneva, but when he stopped there, a local reformer threatened him with God's curse if he did not stay and help organize reform in the city. After intense conflict between the supporters of reform, many of whom were French refugees, and the opposition, led by the traditional elite families, the Calvinists triumphed in 1541. Geneva soon followed the precepts laid out in Calvin's great work, *The Institutes of the Christian Religion,* first published in 1536. Calvin followed the other Protestant reformers in insisting that God is almighty and humans cannot earn their salvation by good works, and then he went a step further, arguing that no Christian can be certain of salvation. With his doctrine of **predestination**, Calvin asserted that God had foreordained every man, woman, and child to salvation or damnation—even before the creation of the world. Only God knew who was among the "elect."

In practice, however, Calvinist doctrine demanded rigorous discipline: the knowledge that a small group of "elect" would be saved should guide the actions of the godly in an uncertain world. Fusing church and society into what followers named the Reformed church, Geneva became a single theocratic community, in which dissent was not tolerated. The Genevan magistrates arrested the Spanish physician Michael Servetus when he passed through in 1553 because he had published books attacking Calvin and questioning the doctrine of the Trinity, the belief shared by virtually all Christians that God exists in three persons—the Father, Son (Christ), and Holy Spirit. Servetus was executed at Calvin's insistence. Geneva quickly became the new center of the Reformation, sending out pastors trained for mission work and exporting books that taught Calvinist doctrines. The Calvinist movement spread to France, the Netherlands, England, Scotland, the German states, Poland, Hungary, and eventually New England, becoming the established form of the Reformation in many of these countries (Map 12.1, page 441).

Protestantism in England

Until 1527, England's king Henry VIII (r. 1509–1547) firmly opposed the Reformation, even receiving the title "Defender of the Faith" from Pope Leo X for a treatise Henry wrote against Luther. Henry's family problems changed his mind. Henry had married Catherine of Aragon (d. 1536), the daughter of Ferdinand and Isabella of Spain and the aunt of Charles V, and the marriage had produced a daughter, Princess Mary (known as Mary Tudor). Henry wanted a male heir to consolidate the rule of his Tudor dynasty, and he had fallen in love with Anne Boleyn, a lady-in-waiting at court and a strong supporter of the Reformation. In 1527, Henry asked the reigning pope, Clement VII, to declare his eighteen-year marriage to Catherine invalid on the grounds that she was the widow of his older brother, Arthur. Arthur and Catherine's marriage, which apparently was never consummated, had been annulled by Pope Julius II. When Henry failed to secure a papal dispensation for his divorce, he chose two Protestants as his new loyal servants: Thomas Cromwell (1485–1540) as chancellor and Thomas Cranmer (1489–1556) as archbishop of Canterbury. Under their leadership the English Parliament declared Henry's marriage to Catherine invalid, allowing him to marry Anne Boleyn; passed the Act of Supremacy of 1534, establishing Henry as the head of the Anglican church (the Church of England); and began confiscating the properties of the Catholic monasteries. Henry thus doubled his revenues.

By 1536, Henry had grown tired of Anne Boleyn, who had given birth to the future Queen Elizabeth I but had produced no sons. The king, who would go on to marry four other wives but father only one son, Edward (by his third wife, Jane Seymour), had Anne beheaded on the charge of adultery, an act that he defined as treason. Thomas More, once Henry's chancellor, had been executed in 1535 for treason—in his case, for refusing to recognize Henry as "the only supreme head on earth of the Church of England"—and Cromwell suffered the same fate in 1540 when he lost favor. After Henry's death in 1547, the Anglican church, nominally

Elizabeth Regina.

2. PARALIPOM. 6.
Domine Deus Israel, non est similis tui Deus in cælo & in ter-
ra, qui pacta custodis & misericordiam cum seruis tuis, qui
ambulant coram te in toto corde suo.

Queen Elizabeth I of England
The Anglican (Church of England) Prayer Book of 1569 included a hand-colored print of Queen Elizabeth saying her prayers. As queen, Elizabeth was also the official head of the Church of England (the scepter or sword at her feet symbolizes her power). She named bishops and made final decisions about every aspect of church governance. **For more help analyzing this image, see the visual activity for this chapter in the Online Study Guide at** bedfordstmartins.com/huntconcise. (HIP/Art Resource, NY.)

Protestant, still retained much traditional Catholic doctrine and ritual. But the principle of royal supremacy in religious matters would remain a lasting feature of Henry's reforms.

When Henry's Protestant son, Edward VI (r. 1547–1553), died at age sixteen, his half sister Mary Tudor (r. 1553–1558) succeeded him, and the Catholic Mass was spontaneously restored in most places without bloodshed. Mary intended to reestablish Catholicism and the authority of Rome, but she lost popularity when she ordered some three hundred Protestants burned at the stake as heretics, including Cranmer. Hundreds more fled. In 1554 she married the Catholic king of Spain, Philip II, which prompted a brief and unsuccessful rebellion. When Mary died in 1558, Anne Boleyn's daughter, Elizabeth, came to the throne and the Anglican cause again gained momentum. As Elizabeth I (r. 1558–1603) moved to solidify her personal power and the authority of the Anglican church, she had to squash uprisings by Catholics in the north and at least two serious plots against her life. She also had to hold off Calvinist **Puritans**, who pushed for more reform, and Spain's Philip II, who first wanted to be her husband and then, failing that, planned to invade her country to restore Catholicism.

The Puritans were strict Calvinists who opposed all vestiges of Catholic ritual in the Church of England. After Elizabeth became queen, many Puritans returned from exile abroad, but Elizabeth resisted their demands for drastic changes in Anglican ritual and governance. She had assumed control as "supreme governor" of the Church of England, and she therefore appointed all bishops. The Church of England's Thirty-nine

Articles of Religion, issued in 1563, incorporated elements of Catholic ritual along with Calvinist doctrines. Puritan ministers angrily denounced the Church of England's "popish attire . . . and a thousand more abominations." Puritans tried to undercut the bishops' authority by placing control of church administration in the hands of the local congregation. Elizabeth rejected this Calvinist "presbyterianism." The Puritans nonetheless steadily gained influence. Known for their emphasis on strict moral lives, the Puritans tried to close the theaters and Sunday fairs and insisted that every father "make his house a little church" by teaching the children to read the Bible. The precise nature of church government would remain a subject of contention for generations to come.

Elizabeth made the most of her limited means and consolidated the country's position as a Protestant power. In her early years, she held out the prospect of marriage to many political suitors but never married. She cajoled Parliament with references to her female weaknesses, but she showed steely-eyed determination in protecting the monarchy's interests. Her chosen successor, James I (r. 1603–1625), came to the throne as king of Scotland, England, and Ireland. Elizabeth left James secure in a kingdom of growing stature in world politics.

Reshaping Society through Religion

For all their differences over doctrine and church organization, the Protestant reformers shared a desire to instill greater discipline in Christian worship and in social behavior. As a consequence, they advocated changes in education and marriage to create a God-fearing, pious, and orderly Christian society. Some of these efforts grew out of developments that stretched back to the Middle Ages, but others, such as an emphasis on literacy, appeared first in Protestant Europe.

Prior to the Reformation, the Latin Vulgate was the only Bible authorized by the church; as a result, priests interpreted the Bible for their parishioners. In 1522, Martin Luther translated Erasmus's Greek New Testament into German because he believed that everyone should read the Bible for him- or herself. Within twelve years, printers published more than 200,000 copies of it, an immense number for the time. In 1534, Luther completed a German translation of the Old Testament. Inspired by Luther's example during a visit to Wittenberg, the Englishman William Tyndale (1495–1536) translated the Bible into English. After he had his translation printed in Germany and the Low Countries, Tyndale smuggled copies into England in 1526, while England was still Catholic.

Although the vernacular Bible was a prized possession in many Protestant households, Bible reading did not become widespread until the 1600s. To educate children in the new religious principles and replace the late medieval church schools, the Protestant reformers set up state school systems. Luther urged the German princes to use the proceeds of confiscated church properties to establish primary schools in every parish for boys and girls ages six to twelve. The Protestant churches also developed a secondary system of higher schools for boys, called gymnasia (from the Greek *gymnasion*), in which the study of Greek and Latin classics and religious instruction prepared future pastors, scholars, and officials for university study.

Like the reforms of education, Protestant efforts to reshape marriage reflected their concern to discipline individual behavior and institute an orderly Christian society. Protestant magistrates established marital courts, passed new marriage laws, closed brothels, and inflicted harsher punishments for sexual deviance. Under canon law, the Catholic church recognized any promise made between two consenting adults (with the legal age of twelve for females, fourteen for males) as a valid marriage. In rural areas and among the urban poor, most couples simply lived together as common-law husband and wife, and some couples never even registered with the church. Protestant governments declared a marriage illegitimate if the partners failed to register their marriage with a local official and a pastor. They usually also required parental consent, thus giving parents immense power in regulating marriage and the transmission of family property.

Taught to become obedient spouses and affectionate companions in Christ, women approached this new sexual regime with ambivalence. The new laws stipulated that women could seek divorce for desertion, impotence, and flagrant abuse, although in practice the marital courts encouraged reconciliation. These improvements came at a price, however: Protestant women were expected to be obedient wives, helpful companions, and loving mothers, but they could no longer join the convent and pursue their own religious paths outside the family. Luther's wife, Katharina von Bora, typified the new ideal Protestant woman. A former nun, she accepted her prescribed role in a patriarchal household: once married, Katharina ran the couple's household, feeding their children, relatives, and student boarders. Although she deferred to Luther—she addressed him as "Herr Doktor"—she nonetheless defended a woman's right as an equal in marriage. Other Protestant

The Disciplined Home
Proper table manners reflected discipline and morality in the godly household, an ideal of the religious reformers of the sixteenth century. The householder, the father-patriarch, leads his wife and children in prayer before a meal. The orderly behavior parallels the comfort (oven, smoked-glass windows, chandeliers, timbered ceiling, and cabinets) of a well-off patrician family. (Staatsbibliothek Bamberg, Germany.)

women spoke out even more decisively. Katharina Zell, wife of the Strasbourg reformer Matthew Zell, wrote hymns, fed the sick and imprisoned, and denounced the intolerance of the new Protestant clergy. Rebuking one for his persecution of dissenters, she wrote, "You young fellows tread on the graves of the first fathers of this church in Strasbourg and punish all who disagree with you, but faith cannot be forced." She also insisted that women should have a voice in religious affairs.

Catholic Renewal and Missionary Zeal

Reacting to the waves of Protestant challenge, the Catholic church mobilized for defense in a movement that is called by some the Counter-Reformation and by others Catholic Reform. Pope Paul III (r. 1534–1549) convened a general church council to codify church doctrine, and he personally approved the founding of new religious orders to undertake aggressive missionary efforts. The Council of Trent (Map 12.1, page 441) met intermittently between 1545 and 1563, when it concluded its work. Its decisions shaped the essential character of Catholicism until the 1960s. Emphatically rejecting the major Protestant positions, the council reasserted the supremacy of clerical authority over the laity and reaffirmed that the bread and wine of communion actually become Christ's body and blood. It required that all weddings take place in churches and be registered by the parish clergy and explicitly refused to allow divorce. All hopes of reconciliation between Protestants and Catholics faded.

Most important of the new Catholic religious orders was the Society of Jesus. Its founder was Ignatius of Loyola (1491–1556), a Spanish nobleman and charismatic former military officer, who abandoned his quest for military glory in favor of serving the church. Ignatius soon attracted other young men to his side, and in 1540 the pope recognized his small band of Jesuits. Over time, the Jesuits founded hundreds of colleges in Spain, Portugal, France, Italy, the German states, Hungary, Bohemia, and Poland. Among their alumni would be princes, philosophers, lawyers, churchmen, and officials—the elite of Catholic Europe. In 1544 the pope recognized a new order for women, the Company of Saint Ursula, known as the Ursulines, who devoted themselves to the education of girls. Together these new religious orders restored the confidence of the faithful in the dedication and power of the Catholic church.

Catholic missionaries set sail throughout the globe to bring Roman Catholicism to Africans, Asians, and native Americans. They saw their effort as proof of the truth of Roman Catholicism and the success of their missions as a sign of divine favor, both particularly important in the face of Protestant challenge. To ensure rapid Christianization, European missionaries focused initially on winning over local elites. A number of young African nobles went to Portugal to be trained in theology. Catholic missionaries preached the Gospel to Confucian scholar-officials in China and to the samurai (the warrior aristocracy) in Japan. Measured in numbers alone, the Catholic missionary enterprise seemed highly successful: by the second half of the sixteenth century, vast multitudes of native Americans had become

The Portuguese in Japan
In this sixteenth-century Japanese black-lacquer screen painting of Portuguese missionaries, the Jesuits are dressed in black and the Franciscans in brown. At the lower left corner is a Portuguese nobleman depicted with exaggerated "Western" features. The Japanese considered themselves lighter in skin color than the Portuguese, whom they classified as "barbarians." In turn, the Portuguese classified Japanese (and Chinese) as "whites." The perception of ethnic differences in the sixteenth century depended less on skin color than on clothing, eating habits, and other cultural signals. Color classifications were unstable and changed over time. By the late seventeenth century, Europeans no longer regarded Asians as "white." (The Granger Collection, NY.)

Christians at least in name, and thirty years after Francis Xavier's 1549 landing in Japan, the Jesuits could claim over 100,000 Japanese converts.

After an initial period of relatively little racial discrimination, the Catholic church in the Americas and Africa adopted strict rules based on color. For example, the first Mexican Ecclesiastical Provincial Council in 1555 declared that holy orders were not to be conferred on Indians, mestizos (people of mixed European-Indian parentage), or mulattoes (people of mixed European-African heritage), groups deemed "inherently unworthy of the sacerdotal [priestly] office." Europeans reinforced their sense of racial superiority with their perception of the "treachery" that native Americans and Africans exhibited whenever they resisted domination. Frustrated in his efforts to convert Brazilian Indians, a Jesuit missionary wrote to his superior in Rome in 1563 that "for this kind of people it is better to be preaching with the sword and rod of iron." The Dominican Bartolomé de Las Casas (1474–1566) criticized the treatment of the Indians in Spanish America, yet even he argued that Africans should be imported in order to relieve the indigenous peoples, who were being worked to death.

> **REVIEW** In what ways did Luther, Zwingli, and Calvin challenge the Roman Catholic church?

State Power and Religious Conflict, 1500–1618

Even as religious disputes heightened the potential for conflict within Europe, the European powers continued to fight their traditional dynastic wars and still faced the military threat posed by the Muslim Ottoman Turks in the east. But these wars did not long deflect attention from increasing divisions within European countries. Rulers viewed religious divisions as a dangerous challenge to the unity of their realms and the stability of their regimes; a subject could very well swear greater allegiance to God than to his lord. Yet rulers often proved powerless to stem the rising tide of religious strife. Lutheranism flourished in the northern German states and Scandinavia; Calvinism spread from its headquarters in the Swiss city of Geneva all the way to England and Poland-Lithuania. The rapid expansion of Lutheranism and Calvinism created deadly political conflicts between Protestants and Catholics.

Wars among the Habsburgs, Valois, and Ottomans

While the Reformation was taking hold in the German states, the Catholic powers of Spain and France fought each other for the domination of Europe (Map 12.2). French claims over Italian territories sparked conflict in 1494, but the ensuing Italian Wars soon involved most Christian monarchs and the Muslim Ottoman sultan as well. Despite some spectacular and bloody turns of fortune, no one power ultimately emerged victorious. In 1525, the troops of the Habsburg emperor Charles V crushed the French army at Pavia, Italy, and captured the French king Francis I (r. 1515–1547). Charles treated Francis as an honored guest but held him in Spain until he agreed to renounce his claims to Italy. Furious at this humiliation, Francis repudiated the agreement the moment he returned to France, reigniting the conflict. In 1527, Charles's troops invaded and then pillaged Rome to punish the pope for allying with the French. Among the imperial troops were German Protestant mercenaries, who pillaged Catholic churches. The sack of Rome shocked the Catholic church hierarchy and helped turn it toward renewal.

Charles could not crush the French in one swift blow because he also had to counter the Muslim Ottomans in Hungary and along the Mediterranean coast. The Ottoman Empire reached its height of power under Sultan Suleiman I ("the

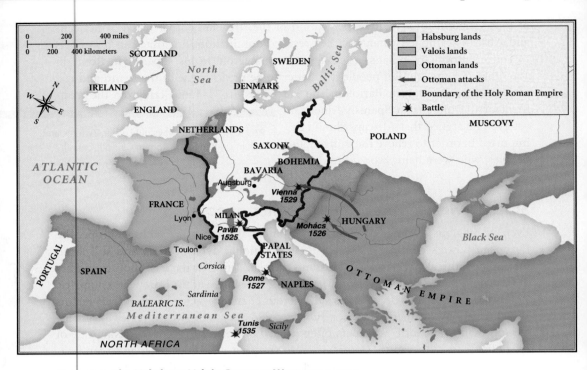

Map 12.2 The Habsburg-Valois-Ottoman Wars, 1494–1559
As the dominant European power, the Habsburg dynasty fought on two fronts: a religious war against the Islamic Ottoman Empire and a political war against the French Valois, who challenged Habsburg hegemony. The Mediterranean, the Balkans, and the Low Countries all became theaters of war.

Magnificent"; r. 1520–1566). In 1526, a Turkish force destroyed the Hungarian army at Mohács. Three years later, the Ottoman army laid siege to Vienna; though unsuccessful, the siege shocked Christian Europe. In 1535, Charles V tried to capture Tunis, the lair of North African pirates under Ottoman rule. Desperate to overcome Charles's superior forces in Europe, Francis I eagerly forged an alliance with the Turkish sultan. The Turkish fleet besieged Nice, on the southern coast of France, to help the French wrest it from imperial occupiers. Francis even ordered all inhabitants of nearby Toulon to vacate their town so that he could turn it into a Muslim colony for eight months, complete with a mosque and slave market. The Franco-Turkish alliance, however brief, showed that the age-old idea of a Christian crusade against Islam had to make way for a new political strategy that considered religion as but one factor in power politics.

In 1559, the French king finally acknowledged defeat and signed the peace treaty of Cateau-Cambrésis. By then, years of conflict had drained the treasuries of all the monarchs. Fueled by warfare, armies grew in size, firepower became ever more deadly, and costs soared. For example, heavier artillery pieces meant that the rectangular walls of medieval cities had to be transformed into fortresses with

The Siege of Vienna, 1529
This illustration from an Ottoman manuscript of 1588 depicts the Turkish siege of Vienna (the siege guns can be seen in the center of the picture). Sultan Suleiman I ("the Magnificent") led an army of more than 100,000 men against Vienna, the capital of the Austrian Habsburg lands. Several attacks on the city failed, and the Ottomans withdrew in October 1529. They maintained control over Hungary, but the logistics of moving so many men and horses kept them from advancing any farther west into Europe. (The Art Archive/Topkapi Museum, Istanbul/Dagli Orti.)

jutting forts and gun emplacements. Charles V boasted the largest army in Europe—but he could not make ends meet with the proceeds from taxation, the sale of offices, and even outright confiscation. Charles and his French opponents both relied on private bankers for funds to make ends meet. Bankers, like the Fugger family of the southern German imperial city of Augsburg, charged as much as 14 to 18 percent interest on their loans and amassed huge fortunes.

French Wars of Religion

During the 1540s and 1550s, one-third of the French nobles converted to Calvinism, usually influenced by noblewomen who protected pastors, provided money and advice, and helped found schools and establish relief for the poor. As many as twelve hundred Reformed churches were established, especially in southern and western France. The Catholic Valois monarchy tried to maintain a balance of power between Catholics and Calvinists. Francis I and his successor, Henry II (r. 1547–1559), both succeeded to a degree. But when Henry was accidentally killed during a jousting tournament, the weakened monarchy could no longer hold together the fragile realm. Henry was succeeded first by his fifteen-year-old son, Francis II, who died in 1560, and then by his ten-year-old son, Charles IX (r. 1560–1574).

Catherine de Médicis (1519–1589), the Italian wife of Henry II, acted as regent for her young son. She first urged limited toleration for the Calvinists—called **Huguenots** in

France—in an attempt to maintain political stability, but she could not prevent the eruption of civil war between Catholics and Huguenots in 1562. Although a Catholic herself, Catherine desperately tried to play the Catholic and Huguenot factions off against each other so that neither would dominate. To this end, she arranged the marriage of her daughter Marguerite to Henry of Navarre, head of the Bourbon family, which had converted to Calvinism. Just four days after the wedding in August 1572, assassins tried but failed to kill one of the Huguenot nobles allied with the Bourbons, Gaspard de Coligny. Panicked at the thought of Huguenot revenge and perhaps herself implicated in the botched plot, Catherine convinced her son to order the killing of leading Huguenots. On St. Bartholomew's Day, August 24, a bloodbath began, fueled by years of growing animosity between Catholics and Protestants. In three days, Catholic mobs murdered three thousand Huguenots in Paris. Thousands more died in the provinces over the next six weeks. The pope joyfully ordered the church bells rung throughout Catholic Europe; Spain's Philip II wrote Catherine that it was "the best and most cheerful news which at present could come to me." Protestants and Catholics alike now saw the conflict as an international struggle for survival that required aid to coreligionists in other countries. In this way, the French Wars of Religion paved the way for wider international conflicts over religion in the future.

Protestant Churches in France, 1562

The religious division in France grew even more dangerous when Charles IX died and his brother Henry III (r. 1574–1589) became king. Like his brothers before him, Henry III failed to produce an heir. Next in line to succeed the throne was none other than the Calvinist Bourbon leader Henry of Navarre. Because Henry III saw an even greater threat to his authority in a newly formed Catholic League, which had requested Spain's help in rooting out Protestantism in France, he took action against the league. In 1588, he summoned two prominent league leaders to a meeting and had his men kill them. A few months later a fanatical monk stabbed Henry III to death, and Henry of Navarre became Henry IV (r. 1589–1610), despite Spain's attempt to block his way with military intervention.

The new king soon concluded that to establish control over the war-weary country, he had to place the interests of the French state ahead of his Protestant faith. In 1593, Henry IV publicly embraced Catholicism, reputedly explaining his conversion with the phrase "Paris is worth a Mass." In 1598, he made peace with Spain and issued the Edict of Nantes, in which he granted the Huguenots a large measure of religious toleration. The approximately 1.25 million Huguenots became a legally protected minority within an officially Catholic kingdom of some 20 million people. Protestants were free to worship in specified towns and were allowed their own troops, fortresses, and even courts. Few believed in religious toleration, but Henry IV followed the advice of those neutral Catholics and Calvinists called **politiques** who urged him to give priority to the development of a durable state. Although their opponents hated them for their compromising spirit, the politiques believed that religious disputes could be resolved only in the peace provided by strong government.

The Edict of Nantes ended the French Wars of Religion, but Henry still needed to reestablish monarchical authority. He used court festivities and royal processions to rally subjects around him, and he developed a new class of royal officials to counterbalance the fractious nobility. In exchange for an annual payment, officials who had purchased their offices could pass them on to heirs or sell them to someone else. By buying offices that eventually ennobled their holders, rich middle-class merchants and lawyers could become part of a new social elite known as the nobility of the robe (named after the robes that magistrates wore, much like those judges wear today). New income raised by the increased sale of offices reduced the state debt and helped Henry build the base for a strong monarchy. His efforts did not, however, prevent his own assassination in 1610 after nineteen unsuccessful attempts.

Challenges to Habsburg Power

Charles V proved more successful at fending off the Turks and subduing the French than he did at resolving growing religious conflicts inside his empire. After the Imperial Diet of Regensburg in 1541 failed to patch up the theological differences between Protestants and Catholics, Charles secured papal support for a war against the Schmalkaldic League, a powerful alliance of Lutheran princes and cities. Charles's army occupied the German imperial cities in the south, restoring Catholic patricians and suppressing the Reformation wherever they triumphed. In 1547, Charles defeated the Schmalkaldic League armies at Mühlberg and captured the leading Lutheran princes. Jubilant, he proclaimed the Interim, which restored Catholics' right to worship in Protestant lands while still permitting Lutherans to celebrate their own services. Riots broke out in many cities as resistance to the Interim spread. Charles's victory proved short-lived, for after one of his former allies, Duke Maurice of Saxony, joined the other side, the princes revived the war in 1552 and chased a surprised, unprepared, and practically bankrupt emperor back to Italy.

Forced to negotiate, Charles V agreed to the Peace of Augsburg in 1555. The settlement recognized the Lutheran church in the empire; accepted the secularization of church lands but kept the remaining ecclesiastical territories (mainly the bishoprics) for Catholics; and, most important, established the principle that all princes, whether Catholic or Lutheran, enjoyed the sole right to determine the religion of their lands and subjects. Significantly, the agreement excluded Calvinist, Anabaptist, and other dissenting groups from the settlement. The Peace of Augsburg preserved a fragile peace in central Europe until 1618, but the exclusion of Calvinists planted the seeds of future conflict.

Exhausted by constant war and depressed by the disunity in Christian Europe, Charles V resigned his many thrones in 1555 and 1556, leaving his Netherlandish-Burgundian and Spanish dominions to his son, Philip II, and his Austrian lands to his brother, Ferdinand, who was also elected Holy Roman Emperor to succeed Charles. Retiring to a monastery in southern Spain, the once powerful Christian monarch spent his last years quietly seeking salvation. Although Philip II of Spain (r. 1556–1598) ruled over fewer territories than his father, his inheritance still left him the most powerful ruler in Europe (Map 12.3). In addition to the western Habsburg lands in

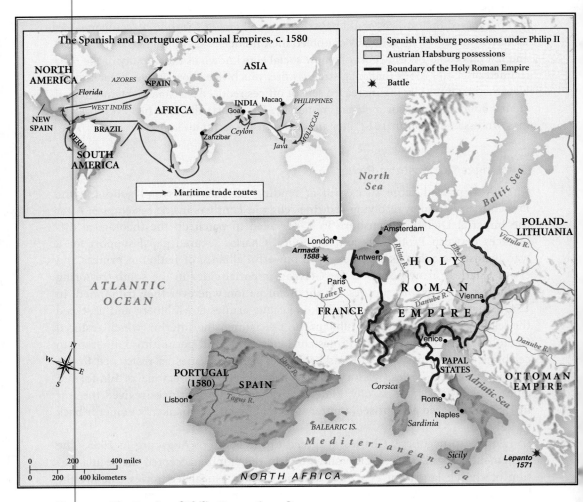

Map 12.3 The Empire of Philip II, r. 1556–1598
The Spanish king Philip II drew revenues from a truly worldwide empire. In 1580, he was the richest European ruler, but the demands of governing such far-flung territories eventually drained many of his resources. **For more help analyzing this map, see the map activity for this chapter in the Online Study Guide at** bedfordstmartins.com/huntconcise.

Spain and the Netherlands, he had inherited all the Spanish colonies recently settled in the New World of the Americas. In 1580, when the king of Portugal died without a direct heir, Philip took over this neighboring realm with its rich empire in Africa, India, and the Americas. Gold and silver funneled from the colonies supported his campaigns against the Ottoman Turks and French and English Protestants.

A deeply devout Catholic, Philip II came to the Spanish throne at age twenty-eight, determined to restore Catholic unity in Europe and lead the Christian defense against the Muslims. In 1571, Philip joined with Venice and the papacy to defeat the Turks in a great sea battle off the Greek coast at Lepanto. But Philip could not rest on his laurels. Between 1568 and 1570, the Moriscos—Muslim converts to Christianity who remained secretly faithful to Islam—had revolted in the south of Spain, killing ninety priests and fifteen hundred Christians. The victory at Lepanto destroyed any prospect that the Turks might come to their aid, yet Philip nonetheless forced fifty thousand Moriscos to leave their villages and resettle in other regions. In 1609, his successor, Philip III, ordered their expulsion, and by 1614 some 300,000 Moriscos had been forced to relocate to North Africa.

The Calvinists of the Netherlands were less easily intimidated than the Moriscos: they were far from Spain and accustomed to being left alone. In 1566, Calvinists in the Netherlands attacked Catholic churches, smashing stained-glass windows and statues of the Virgin

Philip II of Spain
The king of Spain is shown here (kneeling in black) with his allies at the battle of Lepanto, the doge of Venice on his left and Pope Pius V on his right. El Greco painted this canvas, sometimes called *The Dream of Philip II*, in 1578 or 1579. The painting is typically mannerist in the way it crowds figures into every available space, uses larger-than-life or elongated bodies, and creates new and often bizarre visual effects. What can we conclude about Philip II's character from the way he is depicted here? (© National Gallery, London/Art Resource, NY.)

Mary. Philip sent an army, which executed more than eleven hundred people during the next six years. When resistance revived, the Spanish responded with more force, culminating in November 1576, when Philip's armies sacked Antwerp, then Europe's wealthiest commercial city. In eleven days of horror known as the Spanish Fury, the Spanish soldiers slaughtered seven thousand people. Shocked into response, the ten Catholic southern provinces joined with the seven Protestant northern provinces and expelled the Spaniards. In 1579, however, the Catholic southern provinces returned to the Spanish fold. Despite the assassination in 1584 of William of Orange, the leader of the anti-Spanish forces, Spanish troops never regained control in the north.

Spain would not formally recognize Dutch independence until 1648, but by the end of the sixteenth century the Dutch Republic was a self-governing state sheltering a variety of religious groups. The princes of Orange (whose name came from family lands near the city of Orange, in southern France) resembled a ruling family in the Dutch Republic, but their powers paled next to those of local interests. Urban merchant and professional families known as regents controlled the towns and provinces. Each province (Holland was the most populous of the seven provinces) governed itself and sent delegates to the one common institution, the States General. Well situated for maritime commerce, the Dutch Republic developed a thriving economy based on shipping and shipbuilding. By 1670, the Dutch commercial fleet was larger than the English, French, Spanish, Portuguese, and Austrian fleets combined.

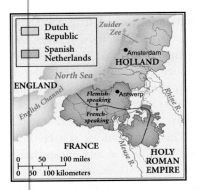

The Netherlands during the Revolt, c. 1580

The Dutch Republic tolerated more religious diversity than the other European states. One-third of the Dutch population remained Catholic, and the secular authorities allowed Catholics to worship as they chose in private. Because Protestant sects could generally count on toleration from local regents, they remained peaceful. The Dutch Republic also had a relatively large Jewish population because many Jews had settled there after being driven out of Spain and Portugal. From 1597, Jews could worship openly in their synagogues. This openness to various religions helped make the Dutch Republic one of Europe's chief intellectual and scientific centers in the seventeenth and eighteenth centuries.

The brief marriage of Philip II to Mary Tudor (Mary I of England) did not produce an heir, but it gave him reason to resist England's return to Protestantism. When Mary died, Elizabeth rejected Philip's proposal of marriage and eventually provided funds and troops to the Dutch rebels. Philip bided his time as long as Elizabeth remained unmarried and her Catholic cousin Mary Stuart—better known as Mary, Queen of Scots—stood next in line to inherit the English throne. In 1567,

Scottish Calvinists forced Mary to abdicate the throne of Scotland in favor of her year-old son, James (eventually James I of England), who was then raised as a Protestant. The Scottish Calvinists feared Mary's connections to Catholic France; her mother was French and devoutly Catholic, and Mary had earlier been married to France's Francis II (who died in 1560). After her abdication, Mary spent nearly twenty years under house arrest in England, fomenting plots against Elizabeth. In 1587, when Mary's letter offering her succession rights to Philip was discovered, Elizabeth overcame her reluctance to execute a fellow monarch and ordered Mary's beheading.

In response, Pope Sixtus V decided to subsidize a Catholic crusade under Philip's leadership against the heretical queen. At the end of May 1588, Philip II sent his armada (Spanish for "fleet") of 130 ships from Lisbon toward the English Channel. The English scattered the Spanish Armada by sending blazing fireships into its midst. A great gale then forced the Spanish to flee around Scotland. By the time the Armada limped home in September, half the ships had been lost and thousands of sailors were dead or starving. Protestants throughout Europe rejoiced. A Spanish monk lamented, "Almost the whole of Spain went into mourning." When Philip II died in 1598, his great empire was beginning to lose its luster. The costs of fighting the French, the Dutch, and the English had mounted, and an overburdened peasantry could no longer pay the taxes required to meet rising expenses. In his novel *Don Quixote* (1605), the Spanish writer Miguel de Cervantes (who had himself been wounded at Lepanto and been held captive in Algiers, then served as a royal tax collector) captured the sadness of Spain's loss of grandeur. His hero, a minor nobleman, reads so many romances and books of chivalry that he loses his wits and wanders the countryside hoping to re-create the heroic deeds of times past.

> **REVIEW** How did the power of states depend on unity in religion?

The Thirty Years' War and the Balance of Power, 1618–1648

In 1618, a new series of violent conflicts between Catholics and Protestants erupted in the Holy Roman Empire. The final and most deadly of the wars of religion, the Thirty Years' War eventually drew in most of the European states. By the end of the war in 1648, many central European lands lay in ruins and many rulers were bankrupt. Reformation and Counter-Reformation had shattered the Christian humanist dream of peace and unity. The Thirty Years' War brought the preceding religious conflicts to a head and by its very violence effectively removed religion from future European disputes. Although religion still divided people *within* various states, after 1648 religion no longer provided the rationale for wars *between* European states. Out of the carnage would emerge centralized and powerful states that made increasing demands on ordinary people.

Origins and Course of the War

The fighting that devastated central Europe had its origins in religious, political, and ethnic divisions within the Holy Roman Empire. The Austrian Habsburg emperor and four of the seven electors who chose him were Catholic; the other three electors were Protestants. The Peace of Augsburg of 1555 was supposed to maintain the balance between Catholics and Lutherans, but it had no mechanism for resolving conflicts. Tensions rose as the Jesuits won many Lutheran cities back to Catholicism and as Calvinism, unrecognized under the agreement, made inroads into Lutheran areas. By 1613, two of the three Protestant electors had become Calvinists. When the Catholic Habsburg heir Archduke Ferdinand was crowned king of Bohemia in 1617, he began to curtail the religious freedom previously granted to Protestants. Protestants wanted to build new churches; Ferdinand wanted to stop them. Tensions boiled over when two Catholic deputy governors tried to dissolve the meetings of Protestants.

On May 23, 1618, a crowd of angry Protestants surged up the stairs of the royal castle in Prague, trapped the two Catholic deputies, dragged them screaming for mercy to the windows, and hurled them to the pavement below. Because they landed in a dung heap, the deputies survived. Although no one died, this "defenestration" (from the French for "window," *la fenêtre*) of Prague touched off a new cycle of conflict. The Czechs, the largest ethnic group in Bohemia, established a Protestant assembly to spearhead resistance. A year later, when Ferdinand was elected emperor (as Ferdinand II, r. 1619–1637), the rebellious Bohemians deposed him and chose in his place the young Calvinist Frederick V of the Palatinate (r. 1616–1623). A quick series of clashes ended in 1620 when the imperial armies defeated the

The Horrors of the Thirty Years' War
The French artist Jacques Callot produced this etching of the Thirty Years' War as part of a series called The Miseries and Misfortunes of War (1633). It shows the rape, torture, and pillaging inflicted by soldiers on noncombatants they found in their path. (The Granger Collection, NY.)

outmanned Czechs at the battle of White Mountain, near Prague (Map 12.4). Like the martyrdom of the religious reformer Jan Hus in 1415, White Mountain became an enduring symbol of the Czechs' desire for self-determination. They would not gain their independence until 1918.

White Mountain did not end the war. Private mercenary armies (armies for hire) began to form during the fighting, and the emperor had virtually no control over them. In 1625, a Czech Protestant, Albrecht von Wallenstein (1583–1634), offered to raise an army for the Catholic emperor and soon had in his employ 125,000 soldiers, who occupied and plundered much of Protestant Germany with the emperor's approval. In response, the Lutheran king of Denmark, Christian IV (r. 1596–1648), invaded to protect the Protestants and to extend his own influence.

Map 12.4 The Thirty Years' War and the Peace of Westphalia, 1648
The Thirty Years' War involved many of the major continental European powers. The arrows marking invasion routes show that most of the fighting took place in central Europe, in the lands of the Holy Roman Empire. The German states and Bohemia sustained the greatest damage during the fighting. None of the combatants emerged unscathed because even ultimate winners such as Sweden and France depleted their resources of men and money.

Wallenstein's forces defeated him. Emboldened by his general's victories, Ferdinand issued the Edict of Restitution in 1629, which outlawed Calvinism in the empire and reclaimed Catholic church properties confiscated by the Lutherans.

With Protestant interests in serious jeopardy, Gustavus Adolphus (r. 1611–1632) of Sweden marched into Germany in 1630. A Lutheran by religion, he also hoped to gain control over trade in northern Europe, where he had already ejected the Poles from present-day Latvia and Estonia. Poland and Lithuania had joined in a commonwealth (common state) in 1569, and many Polish and Lithuanian nobles converted to Lutheranism or Calvinism, but this did not ensure common cause with Sweden. Gustavus's highly trained army of some 100,000 soldiers made Sweden, with a population of only one million, the supreme power of northern Europe, even more powerful than Russia, which had barely recovered from the "Time of Troubles" that had followed on the rule of Tsar Ivan IV (r. 1533–1584). Known as "Ivan the Terrible" because of his rages, during one of which he killed his son and heir, Ivan had initiated Russian expansion eastward into Siberia, but his moves westward had run up against the Poles and the Swedes.

Although Gustavus had religious motives for intervening in German affairs, events soon showed that power politics trumped religious interests. The Catholic French government under the leadership of Louis XIII (r. 1610–1643) and his chief minister, Cardinal Richelieu (1585–1642), offered to subsidize Gustavus—and the Lutheran ruler accepted. The French hoped to counter Spanish involvement in the war and win influence and perhaps territory in the Holy Roman Empire. Gustavus defeated the imperial army and occupied the Catholic parts of southern Germany before he was killed at the battle of Lützen in 1632 (Map 12.4, page 459). Once again the tide turned, but this time it swept Wallenstein with it. Because Wallenstein was rumored to be negotiating with Protestant powers, Ferdinand dismissed his general and had his henchmen assassinate Wallenstein.

France openly joined the fray in 1635 by declaring war on Spain and soon after forged an alliance with the Calvinist Dutch to aid them in their struggle for independence from Spain. The two Catholic powers, France and Spain, pummeled each other. The Swedes kept up their pressure in Germany, the Dutch attacked the Spanish fleet, and a series of internal revolts shook the cash-strapped Spanish crown. In 1640, peasants in the rich northeastern province of Catalonia rebelled, overrunning Barcelona and killing the viceroy; the Catalans resented government confiscation of their crops and demands that they house and feed soldiers on their way to the French frontier. The Portuguese revolted in 1640 and proclaimed independence. In 1643, the Spanish suffered their first major defeat at French hands. Although the Spanish were forced to concede independence to Portugal (part of Spain only since 1580), they eventually suppressed the Catalan revolt.

France, too, faced exhaustion after years of rising taxes and recurrent revolts. In 1642, Richelieu died. Louis XIII followed him a few months later and was succeeded by his five-year-old son, Louis XIV. With the queen mother, Anne of Austria, serving as regent and depending on the Italian cardinal Mazarin for advice, French politics once again moved into a period of instability, rumor, and crisis. All sides were ready for peace.

Effects of Constant Fighting

When peace negotiations began in the 1640s, they did not come a moment too soon for the ordinary people of Europe. Some towns faced up to ten or eleven prolonged sieges during the fighting. In 1648, as negotiations dragged on, a Swedish army sacked the rich cultural capital of Prague, plundered its churches and castles, and effectively eliminated it as a center of culture and learning. Even worse suffering took place in the countryside. Peasants fled their villages, which were often burned down. War and intermittent outbreaks of plague cost some German towns one-third or more of their population. One-third of the inhabitants of Bohemia also perished.

Soldiers did not fare all that much better. Governments increasingly short of funds often failed to pay the troops, and frequent mutinies, looting, and pillaging resulted. Armies attracted all sorts of displaced people desperately in need of provisions. In the last year of the Thirty Years' War, the Imperial-Bavarian Army had 40,000 men entitled to draw rations—and more than 100,000 wives, prostitutes, servants, children, maids, and other camp followers forced to scrounge for their own food. The bureaucracies of early-seventeenth-century Europe simply could not cope with such demands: armies and their hangers-on had to live off the countryside.

Peace of Westphalia, 1648

The comprehensive settlement finally provided by the Peace of Westphalia—named after the German province where negotiations took place—would serve as a model for resolving conflict among warring European states. For the first time, a diplomatic congress addressed international disputes, and the signatories to the treaties guaranteed the resulting settlement. A method still in use, the congress was the first to bring all parties together, rather than two or three at a time.

France and Sweden gained most from the Peace of Westphalia. Although France and Spain continued fighting until 1659, France replaced Spain as the prevailing power on the European continent and acquired parts of Alsace, a region on its eastern border that would remain a source of conflict between French and German rulers well into the twentieth century. Baltic conflicts would not be resolved until 1661, but Sweden took several northern territories from the Holy Roman Empire (Map 12.4, page 459).

The Habsburgs lost the most. The Spanish Habsburgs recognized Dutch independence after eighty years of war. The Swiss Confederation and the German princes demanded autonomy from the Austrian Habsburg rulers of the Holy Roman Empire. Each German prince gained the right to establish Lutheranism, Catholicism, or Calvinism in his state, a right denied to Calvinist rulers by the earlier Peace of Augsburg. The independence ceded to German princes sustained political divisions that would remain until the nineteenth century. After losing considerable territory in the west, the Austrian Habsburgs turned eastward to concentrate on restoring Catholicism to Bohemia and wresting Hungary from the Turks.

The Peace of Westphalia permanently settled the distributions of the main religions in the Holy Roman Empire: Lutheranism would dominate in the north, Calvinism in the area of the Rhine River, and Catholicism in the south (see "Mapping the West," page 477). In the future, warfare between European states would be undertaken for reasons of national security, commercial ambition, or dynastic pride rather than to enforce religious uniformity. As the politiques of the late sixteenth century had hoped, state interests now outweighed motivations of faith in political affairs.

Growth of State Authority

Warfare increased the reach of states: as the size of armies increased, governments needed more men, more money, and more supervisory officials. Most armies in the 1550s had fewer than 50,000 men, but Gustavus Adolphus had 100,000 men under arms in 1631. In France, the rate of land tax paid by peasants doubled in the eight years after France joined the Thirty Years' War. In addition to raising taxes, governments deliberately depreciated the value of the currency, which often resulted in inflation and soaring prices; sold new offices; and manipulated the embryonic stock and bond markets. When all else failed, they declared bankruptcy. The Spanish government, for example, did so three times in the first half of the seventeenth century.

As the demand for soldiers and for the money to supply them rose, the number of state employees multiplied, paperwork proliferated, and appointment to office began to depend on university education in the law. Monarchs relied on advisers who began to take on the role of modern prime ministers. As the French king Louis XIII's chief minister, Richelieu arranged support for the Lutheran Gustavus even though Richelieu was a cardinal of the Catholic church. His priority was **raison d'état** (reason of state)—that is, the state's interest above all else. Richelieu silenced Protestants within France because they had become too independent, and he crushed noble and popular resistance to Louis's policies. He set up intendants—delegates from the king's council dispatched to the provinces—to oversee police, army, and financial affairs. Richelieu and his intendants still had to contend with the thousands of officials who had bought their offices and therefore owned them as personal property.

To justify the growth of state authority and the expansion of government bureaucracies, rulers carefully cultivated their royal images. James I of England explicitly argued that he ruled by divine right and was accountable only to God: "Kings are not only God's lieutenant on earth, but even by God himself they are called gods." Words rarely sufficed to make the point, however, and rulers used displays at court to overawe their subjects. Already in the 1530s, the French court of Francis I had numbered sixteen hundred people, including officials, guards, cooks, physicians, librarians, musicians, dwarfs, and animal trainers. When the court changed residence, which it did frequently, no fewer than eighteen thousand horses were required to transport the people, furniture, and documents—not to mention the dogs and falcons for the royal hunt. Hunting and mock battles honed the military skills of the male courtiers. Francis once staged a mock combat at court involving twelve hundred "warriors," and he led a party to lay siege to a model town during which several players were accidentally killed.

Just as soldiers had to learn new drills for combat, courtiers had to learn to follow precise rituals. In his influential treatise *The Courtier* (1528), the Italian diplomat Baldassare Castiglione (1478–1529) depicted the ideal courtier as a gentleman who spoke in a refined language and carried himself with nobility and dignity in the service of his prince and his lady. Spain's king Philip IV (r. 1621–1665) translated this notion of courtesy into detailed regulations that set the wages, duties, and ceremonial functions of every courtier. State funerals, public festivities, and court displays, like the acquisition of art and the building of sumptuous palaces, served to underline the power and glory of the ruler.

> **REVIEW** Why did a war fought over religious disputes result in stronger states?

From Growth to Recession

The Protestant Reformation started in a period of economic growth, but by the time of the Thirty Years' War recession had set in. In the sixteenth century, despite religious and political turbulence, population grew, doubling in Spain and increasing 70 percent in England. The supply of precious metals swelled, too. Spanish gold imports from the American colonies peaked in the 1550s, silver in the 1590s (see "Taking Measure"). The flood of gold and silver fueled an astounding inflation in food prices in western Europe—400 percent in the sixteenth century. When recession

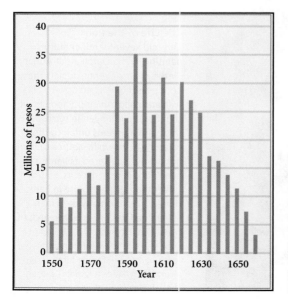

Taking Measure The Rise and Fall of Silver Imports to Spain, 1550–1660 Gold and silver from the New World enabled the king of Spain to pursue aggressive policies in Europe and around the world. At what point did silver imports, shown here, reach their highest level? Was the fall in silver imports precipitous or gradual? What can we conclude about the resources available to the Spanish king?

struck after 1600, all the economic indicators slumped: silver imports declined; textile production collapsed; agricultural prices dropped. Overall, Europe's population may actually have declined, from 85 million in 1550 to 80 million in 1650.

Causes and Consequences of Economic Crisis

Historians have long disagreed about the causes of the early-seventeenth-century recession. Some cite the inability of agriculture to support a growing population by the end of the sixteenth century. Others blame the Thirty Years' War, the states' demands for more taxes, the irregularities in money supply resulting from rudimentary banking practices, or the waste caused by middle-class expenditures in the desire to emulate the nobility. To this list of causes, recent researchers have added climate change. Global cooling translated into advancing glaciers, falling temperatures, and great storms, like the one that blocked the escape of the Spanish Armada. Bad harvests, food shortages, and famine followed in short order.

Economic crisis dramatically altered the rural landscape. As prices began to stagnate and population growth slowed, farmers converted grain-growing land to pasture or vineyards. In some places, peasants abandoned their villages and left

The Life of the Poor
This mid-seventeenth-century painting by the Dutch artist Adriaen Pietersz van de Venne depicts the poor peasant weighed down by his wife and child. An empty food bowl signifies their hunger. In retrospect, this painting seems unfair to the wife: she is shown in clothes that are not nearly as tattered as her husband's and is portrayed as a burden rather than as a helpmate in hard times. In reality, many poor men abandoned their homes in search of work, leaving their wives behind to cope with hungry children and what remained of the family farm. (Allen Memorial Art Museum, Oberlin College, Mrs. F. F. Prentiss Fund, 1960.)

land to waste, as had happened during the plague epidemic of the late fourteenth century. The only country that emerged relatively unscathed from this downturn was the Dutch Republic, principally because it had long excelled in agricultural innovation. Inhabiting Europe's most densely populated area, the Dutch developed systems of field drainage, crop rotation, and animal husbandry that provided high yields of grain for both people and animals. After the Dutch, the English fared best; unlike the Spanish, the English never depended on New World gold and silver, and unlike most continental European countries, England escaped the direct impact of the Thirty Years' War.

When grain harvests fell short, peasants immediately suffered because outside of England and the Dutch Republic, grain had replaced more expensive meat as the essential staple of most Europeans' diets. Peasants lived on bread, soup with a little fat or oil, peas or lentils, garden vegetables in season, and only occasionally a piece of meat or fish. Usually the adverse years differed from place to place, but from 1594 to 1597 most of Europe suffered from shortages that triggered revolts from Ireland to Muscovy. To head off social disorder, the English government drew up a new Poor Law in 1597 that required each community to support its poor. Many other governments also increased relief efforts.

Most people, however, did not respond to their dismal circumstances by rebelling or mounting insurrections. They simply left their huts and hovels and took to the road in search of food and charity. Overwhelmed officials recorded pitiful tales of suffering. Women and children died while waiting in line for food at convents or churches. Husbands left their wives and families to search for better conditions in other parishes or even other countries. Those left behind might be reduced to eating chestnuts, roots, bark, and grass. In eastern France in 1637, a witness reported, "The roads were paved with people. . . . Finally it came to cannibalism." Eventually compassion gave way to fear as these hungry vagabonds, who sometimes banded together to beg for bread, became more aggressive, occasionally threatening to burn a barn if they were not given food.

Successive bad harvests led to malnutrition, which weakened people and made them more susceptible to such epidemic diseases as the plague, typhoid fever, typhus, dysentery, smallpox, and influenza. Disease did not spare the rich, although many epidemics hit the poor hardest. The plague was feared most: in one year it could kill up to half a town or village's population, and it struck with no discernible pattern. Nearly 5 percent of France's population died in the plague epidemic of 1628–1632.

Economic crisis heightened the contrast between prosperity and poverty. In England, the Dutch Republic, northern France, and northwestern Germany, the peasantry was disappearing: improvements gave some peasants the means to become farmers who rented substantial holdings, produced for the market, and in good times enjoyed relative comfort and higher status. Those who could not afford to plant new crops such as buckwheat or to use techniques that ensured higher yields became simple laborers with little or no land of their own. One-half to four-fifths of the peasants in Europe did not have enough land to support a family.

They descended deeper into debt during difficult times and often lost their land to wealthier farmers or to city officials intent on developing rural estates.

Families reacted almost immediately to economic crisis. During bad harvests, they postponed marriages and had fewer children. When hard times passed, more people married and had more children. But even in the best of times, one-fifth to one-quarter of all children died in their first year, and half died before age twenty. Ten percent of women died in childbirth, and even in the richest homes childbirth often occasioned an atmosphere of panic. It might be assumed that families would have more children to compensate for high death rates, but from around 1600 to 1800, families in all ranks of society started to limit the number of children. Because methods of contraception were not widely known, they did this for the most part by marrying later; the average age at marriage during the seventeenth century rose from the early twenties to the late twenties. The average family had about four children. Poorer families seem to have had fewer children, wealthier ones more. Peasant couples, especially in eastern and southeastern Europe, had more children than urban couples because cultivation still required intensive manual labor.

The consequences of late marriage were profound. Young men and women were expected to put off marriage (and sexual intercourse) until their mid- to late twenties—if they were among the lucky 50 percent who lived that long and not among the 10 percent who never married. Because both the Reformation and the Counter-Reformation stressed sexual fidelity and abstinence before marriage, the number of births out of wedlock was relatively small (2 to 5 percent of births); premarital intercourse was generally tolerated only after a couple had announced their engagement.

The Economic Balance of Power

Just as the recession produced winners and losers among ordinary people, it also created winners and losers among the competing states of Europe. The seventeenth-century downturn ended the dominance of Mediterranean economies, which had endured since the time of the Greeks and Romans, and ushered in the new powers of northwestern Europe with their growing Atlantic economies. With expanding populations and geographical positions that promoted Atlantic trade, England and the Dutch Republic vied with France to become the leading mercantile powers. Northern Italian industries were eclipsed; Spanish commerce with the New World dropped. Amsterdam replaced Seville, Venice, Genoa, and Antwerp as the center of European trade and commerce. The plague also had differing effects. Whereas central Europe and the Mediterranean countries took generations to recover from its ravages, northwestern Europe quickly replaced its lost population, no doubt because this area's people had suffered less from the effects of the Thirty Years' War and from the malnutrition related to the economic crisis.

All but the remnants of serfdom had disappeared in western Europe, but in eastern Europe nobles reinforced their dominance over peasants, and the burden of serfdom increased. The price rise of the sixteenth century had prompted Polish and eastern German nobles to expand their holdings and step up their production of grain for western markets. Although noble landlords lost income in the economic downturn of the first half of the seventeenth century, their peasants gained nothing. Those who were already dependent became serfs—completely tied to the land. In Muscovy, the complete enserfment of the peasantry would eventually be recognized in the Code of Laws in 1649. Although enserfment produced short-term profits for landlords, in the long run it retarded economic development in eastern Europe and kept most of the population in a stranglehold of illiteracy and hardship.

Competition for colonies overseas intensified because many European states, including Sweden and Denmark, hoped it would tip the balance of power in their favor. According to the doctrine of mercantilism, governments should sponsor policies to increase national wealth and make sure new sources of wealth did not fall into the hands of their competitors. To this end, rulers chartered private joint-stock companies to enrich investors by importing fish, furs, tobacco, and precious metals, if they could be found, and to develop new markets for European products. Because Spain and Portugal had divided among themselves the rich spoils of South America, other prospective colonizers had to carve niches in seemingly less hospitable places, especially North America and the Caribbean. Eventually the English, French, and Dutch would dominate commerce with these colonies (Map 14.1, page 524).

What began as a competition for national wealth between trading companies soon evolved, sometimes by accident, into permanent colonies with whole new communities. Originally, the warm climate of Virginia made it an attractive destination for the Pilgrims, a small English sect that, unlike the Puritans, attempted to separate from the Church of England. But the *Mayflower,* which sailed for Virginia with Pilgrim emigrants, landed far to the north in Massachusetts, where in 1620 the settlers founded New Plymouth Colony. As the religious situation for English Puritans worsened, wealthier people became willing to emigrate, and in 1629 a prominent group of Puritans incorporated themselves as the Massachusetts Bay Company. They founded a virtually self-governing colony headquartered in Boston.

Colonization gradually spread. Migrating settlers, including dissident Puritans, soon founded new settlements in Connecticut and Rhode Island. Catholic refugees from England established a much smaller colony in Maryland. By the 1640s, the English North American colonies had more than fifty thousand people—not including the Indians, whose numbers had been decimated by epidemics and wars—and the foundations of representative government in locally chosen colonial assemblies.

By contrast, French Canada had only about three thousand European inhabitants by 1640. Because the French government refused to let Protestants emigrate from France and establish a foothold in the New World, it denied itself a ready population for the settling of permanent colonies abroad. Both England and France turned their attention to the Caribbean in the 1620s and 1630s when they occupied the islands of the West Indies after driving off the native Caribs. These islands would prove ideal for a plantation economy of tobacco and sugarcane.

REVIEW What were the consequences of economic recession in the early 1600s?

A Clash of Worldviews

The countries that moved ahead economically in this period—England, the Dutch Republic, and to some extent France—turned out to be the most receptive to new secular worldviews. Although secularization did not entail a loss of religious faith, it did prompt a search for nonreligious explanations for political authority and natural phenomena. During the late sixteenth and early seventeenth centuries, art, political theory, and science all began to break some of their bonds with religion. A "scientific revolution" was in the making. Yet traditional attitudes such as belief in magic and witchcraft did not disappear. People of all classes accepted supernatural explanations for natural phenomena, a view only gradually and partially undermined by new ideas.

The Arts in an Age of Religious Conflict

A new form of artistic expression—professional theater—developed to express secular values in this age of conflict over religious beliefs. In previous centuries, traveling companies made their living by playing at major religious festivals. In London, Seville, and Madrid, the first professional acting companies performed before paying audiences in the 1570s. A huge outpouring of playwriting followed. The Spanish playwright Lope de Vega (1562–1635) alone wrote more than fifteen hundred plays. Between 1580 and 1640, three hundred English playwrights produced works for a hundred different acting companies. Theaters did a banner business despite Puritan opposition in England and Catholic objections in Spain. Shopkeepers, apprentices, lawyers, and court nobles crowded into open-air theaters to see everything from bawdy farces to profound tragedies.

The most enduring and influential playwright of the time was the Englishman William Shakespeare (1564–1616), son of a glovemaker, who wrote three dozen plays and acted in one of the chief troupes. Shakespeare never referred to religious disputes in his plays and did not set the action in contemporary England. Yet his works clearly reflected the political concerns of his age: the nature of power and the crisis of authority. Three of his greatest tragedies—*Hamlet* (1601), *King Lear* (1605), and *Macbeth* (1606)—show the uncertainty and even chaos that result when power is misappropriated or misused. In each play, family relationships are linked to questions about the legitimacy of government, just as they were for Elizabeth I herself. Hamlet's mother marries the man who murdered his royal father and usurped the crown; Macbeth's wife persuades him to murder the king and seize the throne. Like many real-life people, Shakespeare's tragic characters found little peace in the turmoil of their times.

Although many rulers commissioned paintings on secular subjects for their own uses, religion still played an important role in painting, especially in Catholic Europe. The popes competed with secular rulers to hire the most talented painters and sculptors. Pope Julius II, for example, engaged the Florentine Michelangelo Buonarroti (1475–1564) to paint the walls and ceiling of the Sistine Chapel and to prepare a tomb and sculpture for himself. Michelangelo's talents served to glorify a papacy under siege, just as other artists burnished the images of secular rulers.

In the late sixteenth century, the artistic style known as **mannerism** departed abruptly from the Renaissance perspective of painters like Michelangelo. An almost theatrical style, mannerism allowed painters to distort perspective to convey a message or emphasize a theme. The most famous mannerist painter, El Greco, created new and often strange visual effects. The religious intensity of his pictures shows that faith still motivated many artists, as it did much political conflict.

The most important new style was the **baroque**, which featured exaggerated lighting, intense emotions, release from restraint, and even a kind of artistic sensationalism. *Baroque* was not used as a label by people living at the time; in the eighteenth century, art critics coined the word to mean shockingly bizarre, confused, and extravagant, and until the late nineteenth century, art historians and collectors largely disdained the baroque style. Closely tied to the Counter-Reformation, this style melodramatically reaffirmed the emotional depths of the Catholic faith and glorified both church and monarchy. The first great baroque painter was Peter Paul Rubens (1577–1640). Born in the Spanish Netherlands and trained in Italy, Rubens painted vivid, exuberant pictures on religious themes. The style spread from Rome to other Italian states and then into central Europe, Spain, and the Spanish Netherlands. The Spanish built baroque churches in their American colonies as part of their massive conversion campaign. The great Dutch Protestant painters of the next generation, such as Rembrandt van Rijn (1606–1669),

sometimes used biblical subjects, but their pictures were more realistic and focused on everyday scenes. Many of them suggested the Protestant concern for an inner life and personal faith rather than the public expression of religiosity.

Differences in musical style also reflected religious divisions. The new Protestant churches developed their own distinct music, which differentiated their worship from the Catholic Mass. Unlike

Baroque Painting
The baroque painter Peter Paul Rubens used monumental canvases like this one from the Antwerp cathedral to celebrate the Catholic religion. Known as *The Elevation of the Cross*, this painting from 1610 to 1611 shows one of the most important moments in the story of the crucifixion of Jesus. (© Onze Lieve Vrouwkerk, Antwerp Cathedral, Belgium/The Bridgeman Art Library.)

Catholic services, for which professional musicians sang in Latin, Protestant services invited the entire congregation to sing, thereby encouraging participation. Martin Luther, an accomplished lute player, composed many hymns in German, including "Ein' feste Burg" ("A Mighty Fortress"). Protestants sang hymns before going into battle, and Protestant martyrs sang before their executions.

A new secular musical form, the opera, grew up parallel to the baroque style in the visual arts. First influential in the Italian states, opera combined music, drama, dance, and scenery in a grand sensual display, often with themes chosen to please the ruler and the aristocracy. Like Shakespeare, opera composers often turned to familiar stories their audiences would recognize and readily follow. One of the most innovative composers of opera was Claudio Monteverdi (1567–1643), whose work contributed to the development of both opera and the orchestra. His earliest operatic production, *Orfeo* (1607), was the first to require an orchestra of about forty instruments and to include instrumental as well as vocal sections.

The Natural Laws of Politics

In reaction to the wars over religious beliefs, jurists and scholars not only began to defend the primacy of state interests over those of religious conformity but also insisted on secular explanations for politics. Machiavelli had pointed in this direction with his prescriptions for Renaissance princes in the early sixteenth century, but the intellectual movement gathered steam in the aftermath of the religious violence unleashed by the Reformation. Religious toleration could not take hold until government could be organized on some principle other than one king, one faith. The French politiques Michel de Montaigne and Jean Bodin and the Dutch jurist Hugo Grotius started the search for those principles.

Michel de Montaigne (1533–1592) was a French magistrate who resigned his office in the midst of the wars of religion to write about the need for tolerance and open-mindedness. Although himself a Catholic, Montaigne painted on the beams of his study the words "All that is certain is that nothing is certain." In short and pointed essays filled with personal reflection, he revived the ancient doctrine of skepticism, which held that total certainty is never attainable—a doctrine, like toleration of religious differences, that was repugnant to Protestants and Catholics alike, both of whom were certain that their religion was the right one. Montaigne also questioned the common European habit of calling newly discovered peoples in the New World barbarous and savage: "Everyone gives the title of barbarism to everything that is not in use in his own country."

The French Catholic lawyer Jean Bodin (1530–1596) sought systematic secular answers to the problem of disorder in *The Six Books of the Republic* (1576). Comparing the different forms of government throughout history, he identified three basic types of sovereignty: monarchy, aristocracy, and democracy. Only strong monarchical power offered hope for maintaining order, he insisted. Bodin rejected any doctrine of the right to resist tyrannical authority: "I denied that it was the function of a good man or of a good citizen to offer violence to his prince for any reason, however great a tyrant he might be" (and, it might be added, whatever his ideas on religion). Bodin's ideas helped lay the foundation for absolutism, the idea that the monarch should be the sole and uncontested source of power. Nonetheless, the very discussion of types of governments in the abstract implied that they might be subject to choice rather than simply being God given, as most rulers maintained.

During the Dutch revolt against Spain, the jurist Hugo Grotius (1583–1645) gave new meaning to the notion of "natural law"—laws of nature that give legitimacy to government and stand above the actions of any particular ruler or religious group. Grotius argued that natural law stood beyond the reach of either secular or divine authority; it would be valid even if God did not exist. By this account, natural law—not Scripture, religious authority, or tradition—should govern politics. Such ideas got Grotius into trouble with both Catholics and Protestants. When the Dutch Protestant government arrested him, his wife helped him escape from prison by hiding him in a chest of books. Grotius was one of the first to argue that international conventions should govern the treatment of prisoners of war and the making of peace treaties.

At the same time that Grotius expanded the principles of natural law, many jurists worked on codifying the huge amount of legislation and jurisprudence devoted to legal forms of torture. Most states and the courts of the Catholic church used torture when the crime was serious and the evidence seemed to point to a particular defendant but no definitive proof had been established. The judges ordered torture—hanging the accused by the hands with a rope thrown over a beam, pressing the legs in a leg screw, or just tying the hands very tightly—to extract a confession, which had to be given with a medical expert and notary present and had to be repeated without torture. Children, pregnant women, the elderly, aristocrats, kings, and even professors were exempt.

Grotius's conception of natural law directly challenged the use of torture. To be in accord with natural law, Grotius argued, governments had to defend natural rights, which he defined as life, body, freedom, and honor. Grotius's ideas would influence John Locke and the American revolutionaries of the eighteenth century. Although Grotius did not encourage rebellion in the name of natural law or rights, he did hope that someday all governments would adhere to these principles and stop killing their own and one another's subjects in the name of religion. Natural law and natural rights would play an important role in the founding of constitutional governments from the 1640s forward and in the establishment of various charters of human rights in our own time.

The Scientific Revolution

Although the Catholic and Protestant churches encouraged the study of science and many prominent scientists were themselves clerics, the search for a secular, scientific method of determining the laws of nature eventually challenged the traditional accounts of natural phenomena. A revolution in astronomy undermined the view of the second-century Greek astronomer Ptolemy, endorsed by the Catholic church, which held that the sun revolved around the earth. Remarkable advances took place in medicine, too, which laid the foundations for modern anatomy and pharmacology. Conflicts between the new science and religion followed almost immediately, but toward the end of the seventeenth century Isaac Newton provided a new mathematical explanation for movement both on earth and in the heavens. It made the **scientific method** the new standard of truth.

The traditional account derived from Ptolemy put the earth at the center of the cosmos. Above the earth were fixed the moon, the stars, and the planets in concentric crystalline spheres; beyond these fixed spheres dwelt God and the angels. The sun revolved around the earth, the heavens were perfect and unchanging, and the earth was "corrupted." In 1543, the Polish clergyman Nicolaus Copernicus (1473–1543) attacked the Ptolemaic account in his treatise *On the Revolution of the Celestial Spheres*. He argued that it was mathematically simpler to calculate orbits if the earth and planets revolved around the sun, a view known as **heliocentrism** (a sun-centered universe).

Copernicus's views began to attract widespread attention in the early seventeenth century, when astronomers systematically collected evidence that undermined the Ptolemaic view. A leader among them was the Danish astronomer Tycho Brahe (1546–1601), whose observations of a new star in 1572 and a comet in 1577 called into question the Aristotelian view that the universe was unchanging. Brahe still rejected heliocentrism, but the assistant he employed when he moved to Prague in 1599, Johannes Kepler (1571–1630), was converted to the Copernican view. Kepler continued Brahe's collection of planetary observations and used the evidence to develop his three laws of planetary motion, published between 1609 and 1619. Kepler's laws provided mathematical backing for heliocentrism and directly challenged the claim long held, even by Copernicus, that planetary motion was circular. Kepler's first law stated that the orbits of the planets were ellipses, with the sun always at one focus of the ellipse.

The Italian Galileo Galilei (1564–1642) provided more evidence to support the heliocentric view and also challenged the doctrine that the heavens were perfect and unchanging. In 1609, he developed an improved telescope and then observed the earth's moon, four satellites of Jupiter, the phases of Venus (a cycle of changing physical appearances like that of the moon), and sunspots. The moon, the planets, and the sun were no more perfect than the earth, he insisted, and the shadows he could see on the moon could only be the product of hills and valleys like those on earth. Because he recognized the utility of the new science for everyday projects and hoped to appeal to a lay audience of merchants and aristocrats, Galileo was the first scientist to publish his studies in the vernacular (Italian) rather than in Latin.

Since his discoveries challenged the Bible as well as the commonsensical view that the sun rose and set while the earth stood still, Galileo's work alarmed the Catholic church. In 1616, the church forbade Galileo to teach that the earth moved and in 1633 accused him of not obeying the earlier order. Forced to appear before the Inquisition, he agreed to publicly recant his assertion that the earth moved to save himself from torture and death. Afterward he lived under house arrest and could publish his work only in the Dutch Republic, which had become a haven for scientists and thinkers who challenged conventional ideas.

Startling breakthroughs took place in medicine, too. Until the mid-sixteenth century, medical knowledge in Europe had been based on the writings of the second-century Greek physician Galen, a contemporary of Ptolemy. In the same year that Copernicus challenged the traditions of astronomy (1543), the Flemish scientist Andreas Vesalius (1514–1564) did the same for anatomy. He published a new illustrated anatomical text, *On the Construction of the Human Body,* that revised Galen's work by drawing on public dissections in the medical faculties of European universities. Theophrastus Bombastus von Hohenheim, better known as Paracelsus (1493–1541), went even further than Vesalius. He burned Galen's text at the University of Basel, where he was a professor of medicine. Paracelsus experimented with new drugs, performed operations (at the time most academic physicians taught medical theory, not practice), and pursued his interests in magic, alchemy, and astrology. He helped establish the modern science of pharmacology.

The Englishman William Harvey (1578–1657) also used dissection to examine the circulation of blood within the body, demonstrating how the heart worked as a pump. The heart and its valves were "a piece of machinery," Harvey claimed. They obeyed mechanical laws just as the planets and earth revolved around the sun in a mechanical universe. Nature could be understood by experiment and rational deduction, not by following traditional authorities.

In the 1630s, the European intellectual elite began to accept the new scientific views. Ancient learning, the churches and their theologians, and even cherished popular beliefs seemed to be undermined by a new standard of truth—the scientific method, which was based on systematic experiments and rational deduction. Two men were chiefly responsible for spreading the prestige of the scientific method, the English politician Sir Francis Bacon (1561–1626) and the French mathematician and philosopher René Descartes (1596–1650). Respectively, they represented the two essential processes of the scientific method: (1) inductive reasoning through observation and experimental research and (2) deductive reasoning from self-evident principles.

In *The Advancement of Learning* (1605), Bacon attacked reliance on ancient writers and optimistically predicted that the scientific method would lead to social progress. The minds of the medieval scholars, he said, had been "shut up in the cells of a few authors (chiefly Aristotle, their dictator) as their persons were shut up in the cells of monasteries and colleges." Knowledge, in Bacon's view, must be empirically based—that is, gained by observation and experiment. Claiming that God had called the Catholic church "to account for their degenerate manners and ceremonies," Bacon looked to the Protestant English state, which he served as lord chancellor, for leadership on the road to scientific advancement.

Although Descartes agreed with Bacon's denunciation of traditional learning, he saw that the attack on tradition might only replace the dogmatism of the churches with the skepticism of Montaigne—that nothing at all was certain. A Catholic who served in the Thirty Years' War, Descartes insisted that human reason could not only unravel the secrets of nature but also prove the existence of God. He aimed to establish the new science on more secure philosophical foundations, those of mathematics and logic. Not coincidentally, Descartes invented analytic geometry. In his *Discourse on Method* (1637), he argued that mathematical and mechanical principles provided the key to understanding all of nature, including the actions of people and states. All prior assumptions must be repudiated in favor of one elementary principle: "I think, therefore I am." Everything else could—and should—be doubted, but even doubt showed the certain existence of someone thinking. Begin with the simple and go on to the complex, he asserted, and believe only those ideas that present themselves "clearly and distinctly." Although Descartes hoped to secure the authority of both church and state, his reliance on human reason alone irritated authorities, and his books were banned in many places. He moved to the Dutch Republic to work in peace. Scientific research, like economic growth, became centered in the northern, Protestant countries, where it was less constrained by church control.

Building on the work of Copernicus, Kepler, and Galileo, the English scientist Isaac Newton (1642–1727) finally synthesized astronomy and physics with his **law of universal gravitation**, further enhancing the prestige of the new science. Yet Newton also aimed to reconcile faith and science. By proving that the physical universe followed rational principles, Newton argued, scientists could prove the existence of God and so liberate humans from doubt and the fear of chaos. Newton applied mathematical principles to formulate three physical laws: (1) in the absence of external force, an object in motion continues in a straight line; (2) the rate of change in the motion of an object is a result of the forces acting on it; and (3) the action and reaction between two objects are equal and opposite. The basis of Newtonian physics thus required understanding mass, inertia, force, velocity, and acceleration—all key concepts in modern science.

Extending these principles to the entire universe in his masterwork, *Principia Mathematica* (1687), Newton united celestial and terrestrial mechanics— astronomy and physics—with his law of universal gravitation. This law holds that every body in the universe exerts over every other body an attractive force directly proportional to the product of their masses and inversely proportional to the square of the distance between them. The law of gravitation explained Kepler's elliptical planetary orbits just as it accounted for the motion of ordinary objects on earth. Once set in motion, the universe operated like clockwork, with no need for God's continuing intervention. Gravity, though a mysterious force, could be expressed mathematically. Not all scientists accepted Newton's theories immediately, but within a couple of generations his work was preeminent, partly because of experimental verification. His breakthroughs remained the basis for all physics until the advent of relativity theory and quantum mechanics in the early twentieth century.

Magic and Witchcraft

Despite the new emphasis on clear reasoning, observation, and independence from past authorities, science had not yet become entirely separate from magic. Paracelsus and Newton studied alchemy alongside other scientific pursuits; magic and science were still closely linked. In a world in which most people believed in astrology, magical healing, prophecy, and ghosts, it is hardly surprising that many of Europe's learned people also firmly believed in witchcraft, the exercise of magical powers gained by a pact with the devil. The same Jean Bodin who argued against religious fanaticism insisted on death for witches—and for those magistrates who would not prosecute them. In France alone, 345 books and pamphlets on witchcraft appeared between 1550 and 1650. Trials of witches peaked in Europe between 1560 and 1640, the very time of the celebrated breakthroughs of the new science. Montaigne was one of the few to speak out against executing accused witches. "It is taking one's conjectures rather seriously to roast someone alive for them," he wrote in 1580.

Belief in witches was not new in the sixteenth century. Witches had long been thought capable of almost anything: passing through walls, flying through the air, destroying crops, and causing personal catastrophes from miscarriage to demonic possession. What was new was the official persecution, justified by the notion that witches were agents of Satan whom the righteous must oppose. In a time of economic crisis, plague, warfare, and the clash of religious differences, witchcraft trials provided an outlet for social stress and anxiety, legitimated by state power. At the same time, the trials seem to have been part of the religious reform movement itself. Denunciation and persecution of witches coincided with the spread of reform, both Protestant and Catholic. The trials concentrated especially in the German lands of the Holy Roman Empire, the boiling cauldron of the Thirty Years' War.

The victims of the persecution were overwhelmingly female: women accounted for 80 percent of the accused witches in about 100,000 trials in Europe and North

Giving a Child to Satan
This woodcut from Francesco Maria Guazzo's *Compendium Maleficarum* of 1608 shows witches giving a child to the devil. Many believed that witches made a pact with the devil to carry out his evil deeds. (The Art Archive/Dagli Orti [A].)

America during the sixteenth and seventeenth centuries. About one-third were sentenced to death. Before 1400, when witchcraft trials were rare, nearly one-half of those accused had been men. Two Catholic clergymen compiled a guide for detecting witches, the *Malleus Maleficarum* (Hammer of Witches), which was published in 1486 and reissued countless times in the sixteenth and seventeenth centuries. Official descriptions of witchcraft oozed lurid details of sexual orgies, incest, homosexuality, and cannibalism, in which women acted as the devil's sexual slaves. Social factors help explain the prominence of women among the accused. The poorest and most socially marginal people in most communities were elderly spinsters and widows. Because they were thought likely to hanker after revenge on those more fortunate, they were singled out as witches.

Witchcraft trials declined when scientific thinking about causes and effects raised questions about the evidence used in court: how could judges or jurors be certain that someone was a witch? The tide turned everywhere at about the same time, as physicians, lawyers, judges, and even clergy came to suspect that accusations were based on popular superstition and peasant untrustworthiness. In 1682, a French royal decree treated witchcraft as fraud and imposture, meaning that the law did not recognize anyone as a witch. In 1693, the jurors who had convicted twenty witches in Salem, Massachusetts, recanted, claiming, "We justly fear that we were sadly deluded and mistaken." The Salem jurors had not stopped believing in witches; they had simply lost confidence in their ability to identify them. When physicians and judges had believed in witches and persecuted them officially, with torture, witches had gone to their deaths in record numbers. But when the same groups distanced themselves from popular beliefs, the trials and the executions stopped.

REVIEW   How could belief in witchcraft and the rising prestige of the scientific method coexist?

Conclusion

The witchcraft persecutions reflected the traumas of these times of religious war and economic decline. Marauding armies combined with economic depression, disease, and the threat of starvation to shatter the lives of many ordinary Europeans, while religious conflicts shaped the destinies of every European power in this period. These conflicts began with the Protestant Reformation, which dispelled forever the Christian humanist dream of peace and unity, and came to a head from 1618 to 1648 in the Thirty Years' War, which cut a path of destruction through central Europe and involved most of the European powers. Shocked by the effects of religious violence, European rulers agreed to a peace that effectively removed disputes between Catholics and Protestants from the international arena.

The growing separation of political motives from religious ones did not mean that violence or conflict had ended, however. Struggles for religious uniformity within states would continue, though on a smaller scale. Bigger armies required more state involvement, and almost everywhere rulers emerged from these decades

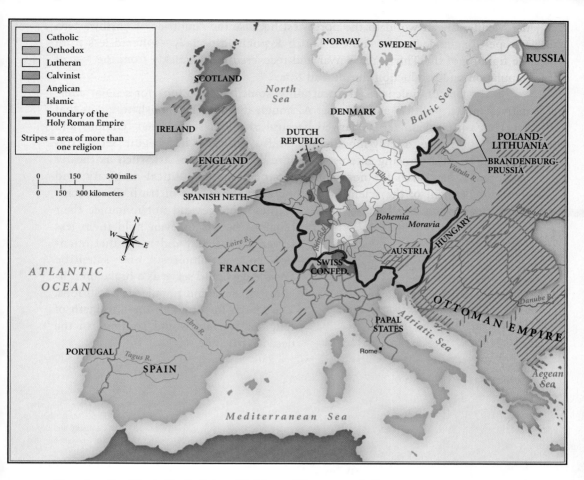

Mapping the West The Religious Divisions of Europe, c. 1648
The Peace of Westphalia recognized major religious divisions within Europe that have endured for the most part to the present day. Catholicism dominated in southern Europe, Lutheranism had its stronghold in northern Europe, and Calvinism flourished along the Rhine River. In southeastern Europe, the Islamic Ottoman Turks accommodated the Greek Orthodox Christians under their rule but bitterly fought the Catholic Austrian Habsburgs for control of Hungary.

of conflict with expanded powers. The growth of state power directly changed the lives of ordinary people: more men went into the armies, and most families paid higher taxes. The constant extension of state power is one of the defining themes of modern history; religious warfare gave it a jump start.

For all their increased power, rulers could not control economic, social, or intellectual trends, much as they often tried. The economic downturn of the seventeenth century produced unexpected consequences for European states even while it made life miserable for many ordinary people. Economic power and vibrancy shifted from the Mediterranean world to the northwest because the countries of northwestern Europe—England, France, and the Dutch Republic especially—suffered less from the fighting of the Thirty Years' War and recovered more quickly from the loss of population and production during bad times.

In the face of violence and uncertainty, some began to look for secular alternatives in art, politics, and science. Although it would be foolish to claim that everyone's mental universe changed because of the clash between religious and secular worldviews, a truly monumental shift in attitudes had begun. Secularization combined a growing interest in nonreligious forms of art, such as theater and opera; the search for nonreligious foundations of political authority; and the establishment of the scientific method as the standard of truth. Proponents of these changes did not renounce their religious beliefs or even hold them less fervently, but they did insist that attention to state interests and scientific knowledge could serve as a brake on religious violence and popular superstitions. The search for order in the aftermath of religious warfare would continue in the decades to come.

CHAPTER REVIEW QUESTIONS
1. How did the balance of power in Europe shift between 1500 and 1648? What were the main reasons for the shift?
2. Relate the new developments in the arts and sciences to the political and economic changes in this period of crisis.

TIMELINE

- **1629** English Puritans set up the Massachusetts Bay Company and begin to colonize New England
- **1618** Thirty Years' War begins
- **1555** Peace of Augsburg
- **1598** Edict of Nantes ends French Wars of Religion
- **1545–1563** Council of Trent

1500   1550   1600   1650

- **1517** Martin Luther criticizes the sale of indulgences and other church practices, igniting the Reformation
- **1571** Battle of Lepanto marks victory of the West over Ottomans at sea
- **1633** Galileo Galilei forced to recant his support of heliocentrism
- **1534** Henry VIII declared head of the Anglican church
- **1572** St. Bartholomew's Day Massacre (August 24)
- **1588** Defeat of the Spanish Armada by England
- **1648** Peace of Westphalia ends the Thirty Years' War

For practice quizzes and other study tools, see the Online Study Guide at
bedfordstmartins.com/huntconcise.

For primary-source material from this period, see Chapters 14 and 15 of
Sources of THE MAKING OF THE WEST, Third Edition.

Suggested References

Religion, warfare, science, witchcraft, and the travails of everyday life have all been
the subject of groundbreaking research, yet the personalities of individual rulers still
make for great stories, too.

Benedict, Philip. *Christ's Churches Purely Reformed: A Social History of Calvinism.* 2002.

Bonney, Richard. *The Thirty Years' War.* 2002.

Braudel, Fernand. *The Mediterranean and the Mediterranean World in the Age of Philip the Second.* Trans. Siân Reynolds. 2 vols. 1972, 1973.

Briggs, Robin. *Witches and Neighbors: The Social and Cultural Context of European Witchcraft.* 1996.

*Diefendorf, Barbara B. *The Saint Bartholomew's Day Massacre: A Brief History with Documents.* 2009.

Erasmus: The Praise of Folly and Other Writings. Trans. Robert M. Adams. 1989.

Galileo Project: http://galileo.rice.edu

Hsia, R. Po-chia. *The World of the Catholic Renewal.* 1997.

Jacob, James. *The Scientific Revolution.* 1998.

Luther's life and thought: http://www.luther.de/en

Lynn, John A. *Women, Armies, and Warfare in Early Modern Europe.* 2008.

Patterson, Benton Rain. *With the Heart of a King: Elizabeth I of England, Philip II of Spain, and the Fight for a Nation's Soul and Crown.* 2007.

State Building and the Search for Order

URING A WEEK IN MAY 1664, King Louis XIV of France organized a series of entertainments for his court at Versailles, where he had recently begun the construction of a magnificent new palace. More than six hundred members of his court attended the series of spectacles called "The Delights of the Enchanted Island." The carefully orchestrated activities opened with an elaborate parade of the king and his courtiers, accompanied by an eighteen-foot-high float in the form of a chariot dedicated to Apollo, the Greek god of the sun and Louis's personally chosen emblem. During the week, the king's favorite artists presented works prepared especially for the occasion, including ballets, plays, and musical concerts. Equestrian tournaments, visits to the king's personal collection of wild animals and birds, and a huge fireworks display captivated the audience. Every detail of the festivities appeared in an official program published the same year.

Louis XIV and His Bodyguards
One of Louis XIV's court painters, Adam Frans van der Meulen, depicted the king arriving at the Palace of Versailles, still under construction (the painting dates from 1669). None of the gardens, pools, or statues had yet been installed. Louis is the only figure facing the viewer, and his dress is much more colorful than that of anyone else in the painting. *(Réunion des Musées Nationaux/Art Resource, NY.)*

Louis XIV spared no expense in promoting his image, especially to those most dangerous to him, the leading nobles of the kingdom. Other rulers either followed his example or explicitly rejected it, but they could not afford to ignore it. All governments faced the daunting task of rebuilding authority after the wars over religion and the economic recession of the early seventeenth century. As part of his campaign to emphasize his majesty, Louis encouraged leading nobles to dispense huge sums to entertain him and his court. He always spent even more in order to show that he was richer and more powerful than any noble or than any other monarch.

Louis XIV's model of state building was known as **absolutism**, a system of government in which the ruler claimed sole and uncontestable power. Although absolutism exerted great influence, especially in central and eastern Europe, it faced competition from **constitutionalism**, a system in which the ruler had to share power with parliaments made up of elected representatives. Constitutionalism led to weakness in Poland-Lithuania, but it provided a strong foundation for state power in England, the English North American colonies, and the Dutch Republic. Constitutionalism triumphed in England, however, only after one king had been executed as a traitor and another had been deposed.

Whether absolutist or constitutionalist, states faced similar challenges to state building in the mid-seventeenth century. Competition in the international arena required resources, and all states raised taxes, provoking popular protests and even rebellions. The wars over religion that had culminated in the Thirty Years' War (1618–1648) left many economies in dire straits, and, even more significant, they created a need for new explanations of political authority. Monarchs still relied on religion to justify their divine right to rule, but they increasingly sought secular defenses of their powers, too. Absolutism and constitutionalism were the two main responses to the threat of disorder and breakdown left as a legacy of the wars over religion.

The search for order took place not only at the level of states and rulers but also in intellectual, cultural, and social life. Thomas Hobbes and John Locke famously sought to ground political authority in a **social contract**. Artists looked for ways of glorifying power and expressing order and symmetry in their work. As states consolidated their power, elites endeavored to distinguish themselves more clearly from the lower orders. The upper classes emulated the manners developed at court and tried in every way to distance themselves from anything viewed as vulgar or lower-class. Officials, clergy, and laypeople all worked to reform the poor, now seen as a major source of disorder.

CHAPTER FOCUS QUESTION   What were the chief differences between absolutism and constitutionalism?

Louis XIV: Model of Absolutism

The French king Louis XIV (r. 1643–1715) personified the absolutist ruler who in theory shared his power with no one. Louis personally made all important state decisions and left no room for dissent. In 1651, he reputedly told the Paris high court of justice, *"L'état, c'est moi"* (I am the state), emphasizing that state authority rested in him personally. Louis cleverly manipulated the affections and ambitions of his courtiers, chose as his ministers middle-class men who owed everything to him, built up Europe's largest army, and snuffed out every hint of religious or political opposition. Yet the absoluteness of his power should not be exaggerated. Like all other rulers of his time, Louis depended on the cooperation of many others: local officials who enforced his decrees, peasants and artisans who joined his armies and paid his taxes, creditors who loaned crucial funds, and nobles who joined court festivities organized to glorify the king rather than stay at home and cause trouble.

The Fronde, 1648–1653

Louis XIV built on a long French tradition of increasing centralization of state authority, but before he could extend it, he had to weather a series of revolts known as the **Fronde**. Derived from the French word for a child's slingshot, the term was used by critics to signify that the revolts were mere child's play. In fact, they posed an unprecedented threat to the French crown. Louis was only five when he came to the throne in 1643 upon the death of his father, Louis XIII. Louis XIV's mother, Anne of Austria, and her Italian-born adviser and rumored lover, Cardinal Mazarin (1602–1661), ruled in the young monarch's name. To meet the financial pressure of fighting the Thirty Years' War and then even after the peace to keep up a draining war against Spain, Mazarin sold new offices, raised taxes, and forced creditors to extend loans to the government. In 1648, a coalition of his opponents presented him with a charter of demands that, if granted, would have given the **parlements** (high courts) a form of constitutional power with the right to approve

The Fronde, 1648–1653

new taxes. Mazarin responded by arresting the coalition's leaders. He soon faced a series of revolts that at one time or another involved nearly every social group in France and lasted until 1653.

Faced with barricades in the streets of Paris, Anne took Louis and fled the city. As civil war threatened, Mazarin and Anne agreed to compromise with the parlements. The nobles then tried to reassert their own claims to power by raising private armies. The middle and lower classes chafed at the constant tax increases and in some places organized revolts. Conflicts erupted throughout the kingdom, and rampaging soldiers devastated rural areas and disrupted commerce. Neither the nobles nor the judges of the parlements really wanted to overthrow the king; they simply wanted a greater share in power. But Louis XIV never forgot the humiliation and uncertainty that marred his childhood. Years later he recalled an incident in which a band of Parisians had invaded his bedchamber to determine whether he had fled the city, and he declared the event an affront not only to himself but also to the state. His own policies as ruler would be designed to prevent the repetition of any such revolts.

Court Culture as an Element of Absolutism

When Cardinal Mazarin died in 1661, Louis XIV decided to rule without a first minister. He described the dangers of his situation in memoirs he wrote later for his son's instruction: "Everywhere was disorder. My Court as a whole was still very far removed from the sentiments in which I trust you will find it." Typically quarrelsome, the French nobles had long exercised local authority by maintaining their own fighting forces, meting out justice on their estates, arranging jobs for underlings, and resolving their own conflicts through dueling.

Louis set out to domesticate the warrior-nobles by replacing violence with court ritual. Using a systematic policy of bestowing pensions, offices, honors, gifts, and the threat of disfavor or punishment, he made himself the center of French power and culture. The aristocracy soon vied for his favor, attended the ballets and theatricals he put on, and learned the rules of etiquette he supervised. Great nobles competed for the honor of holding his shirt when he dressed, foreign ambassadors squabbled for places near him, and royal mistresses basked in the glow of his personal favor. Louis de Rouvroy, duke of Saint-Simon (1675–1755), complained, "There was nothing he [Louis XIV] liked so much as flattery . . . the coarser and clumsier it was, the more he relished it." Madame de Lafayette described the effects on court life in her novel *The Princess of Cleves* (1678): "The Court gravitated around ambition. Nobody was tranquil or indifferent—everybody was busily trying to better his or her position by pleasing, by helping, or by hindering somebody else."

Louis XIV used every form of art—mock battles, theatrical performances, paintings, sculpture, poetry, medals, histories, even the ritual of his dinner—to enhance his personal prestige. Calling himself "the Sun King," Louis adorned his palace with statues of Apollo and emulated the style of the ancient Roman emperors. The king's officials treated the arts as a branch of government. Louis's ministers set up royal academies of dance, painting, architecture, and music and took control of the Académie Française (French Academy), which to this day decides on correct usage of the French language. A royal furniture workshop at the Gobelins tapestry works on the outskirts of Paris turned out the delicate and ornate pieces whose style bore the king's name. Louis's government also regulated the number and locations of theaters and closely censored all forms of publication.

Music and theater enjoyed special prominence. Louis commissioned operas to celebrate royal marriages, baptisms, and military victories. The king himself danced in ballets if a role seemed especially important. Playwrights presented their new plays directly to the court. Pierre Corneille and Jean-Baptiste Racine wrote tragedies set in Greece or Rome that celebrated the new aristocratic virtues that Louis aimed to inculcate: a reverence for order and self-control.

Louis glorified his image through massive public works projects as well. Military facilities, such as veterans' hospitals and fortified towns on the frontiers, represented his military might. Urban improvements, such as the reconstruction of the Louvre palace in Paris, proved his wealth. But his most ambitious project was the construction of a new palace at Versailles, twelve miles from the turbulent capital. Building began in the 1660s, and by 1685, the frenzied effort engaged 36,000 workers, not including the thousands of troops who diverted a local river to supply water for pools and fountains. Even the gardens reflected the spirit of Louis XIV's rule: their geometrical

The Palace of Versailles
This painting by Jean-Baptiste Martin from the late seventeenth century gives a good view of one section of the palace and especially the geometrically arranged gardens. (Réunion des Musées Nationaux/ Art Resource, NY.)

arrangements and clear lines showed that art and design could tame nature and that order and control defined the exercise of power. Versailles symbolized Louis's success in reining in the nobility and dominating Europe. Other monarchs eagerly mimicked French fashion and often conducted their business in French.

By the time Louis actually moved from the Louvre to Versailles in 1682, he had reigned as monarch for thirty-nine years. Fifteen thousand people crowded into the palace's apartments, including all the highest military officers, the ministers of state, and the separate households of each member of the royal family. After the death of his queen in 1683, Louis secretly married his mistress, Françoise d'Aubigné, marquise de Maintenon, and conducted most state affairs from her apartments at the palace. De Maintenon's opponents at court complained that she controlled all the appointments, but her efforts focused on her own projects, including her favorite: the founding in 1686 of a royal school for girls from impoverished noble families. She also inspired one of Louis XIV's most fateful decisions—to root out any alternatives to Roman Catholicism.

Enforcing Religious Conformity

Louis believed that he ruled by divine right. As Bishop Jacques-Benigne Bossuet (1627–1704) explained, "We have seen that kings take the place of God." Louis believed it was his duty as God's lieutenant to bring his subjects to the one true religion. He first focused on the Jansenists, Catholics whose doctrines and practices resembled some aspects of Protestantism. Following the posthumous publication of the book *Augustinus* (1640) by the Flemish theologian Cornelius Jansen (1585–1638), the Jansenists stressed the need for God's grace in achieving salvation. They emphasized the importance of original sin and insisted on an austere religious practice. Prominent among the Jansenists was Blaise Pascal (1623–1662), a mathematician of genius, who wrote his *Provincial Letters* (1656–1657) to defend Jansenism against charges of heresy. Many judges in the parlements likewise endorsed Jansenist doctrines.

Some questioned Louis's understanding of the finer points of Catholic doctrine. According to his German-born sister-in-law, Louis himself "has never read anything about religion, nor the Bible either, and just goes along believing whatever he is told." Louis rejected any teaching that gave priority to considerations of individual conscience over the demands of the official church hierarchy. He insisted on obedience to authority. Therefore, in 1660 he began enforcing various papal bulls (decrees) against Jansenism and closed down Jansenist theological centers. Jansenists were forced underground for the rest of his reign.

After many years of escalating pressure on the Calvinist Huguenots, Louis revoked the Edict of Nantes in 1685 and eliminated all of the Calvinists' rights. Louis considered the edict (1598), by which his grandfather Henry IV granted the Protestants religious freedom and a degree of political independence, a temporary measure, and he fervently hoped to reconvert the Huguenots to Catholicism. He closed their churches and schools, purged all Calvinists from official positions, and forced Calvinist ministers into exile even while refusing to let ordinary Protestants leave. Nonetheless, at least 150,000 Huguenots refused to submit and fled to England, Brandenburg-Prussia, or the Dutch Republic. Refugee Calvinists soon wrote essays and books denouncing Louis XIV's absolutism. Protestant European countries were shocked by this crackdown on religious dissent and would cite it when they went to war against Louis.

Extending State Authority at Home and Abroad

Louis XIV could not have enforced his religious policies without the services of a nationwide **bureaucracy**. The word *bureaucracy*—a network of state officials carrying out orders according to a regular and routine line of authority—comes from *bureau,* the French word for "desk," which came to mean "office," in the sense of both a physical space and a position of authority. Louis extended the bureaucratic forms his predecessors had developed, especially the use of intendants, officials who held their positions directly from the king rather than owning their offices. Louis handpicked them to represent his will against entrenched local interests such as the parlements, provincial estates, and noble governors. The intendants reduced local powers over finances and insisted on more efficient tax collection. Despite the doubling of taxes in Louis's reign, the local rebellions that had so beset the crown from the 1620s to the 1640s subsided in the face of these better-organized state forces.

Louis's success in consolidating his authority depended on hard work, an eye for detail, and an ear to the ground. In his memoirs he explained his priorities:

> to be well-informed on an infinite number of matters about which we are supposed to know nothing; to elicit from our subjects what they hide from us with the greatest care; to discover the most remote opinions of our courtiers and the most hidden interests of those who come to us with quite contrary professions [claims].

To gather all this information, Louis relied on a series of talented ministers, usually of modest origins, who gained fame, fortune, and even noble status by serving the king. Most important among them was Jean-Baptiste Colbert (1619–1683), the son of a wool merchant turned royal official. Colbert had managed Mazarin's personal finances and worked his way up under Louis XIV to become controller general, the head of royal finances, public works, and the navy.

Colbert followed the policy of **mercantilism**, which held that governments must intervene to increase national wealth by whatever means possible. Such government intervention inevitably increased the role and eventually the number of bureaucrats needed. Under Colbert, the French government established overseas trading companies, granted manufacturing monopolies, and standardized production methods for textiles, paper, and soap. A government inspection system regulated the quality of finished goods and compelled all craftsmen to organize into guilds, in which masters could supervise the work of the journeymen and apprentices. To protect French production, Colbert rescinded many internal customs fees while enacting high tariffs on foreign imports. To compete more effectively with England and the Dutch Republic, Colbert also subsidized shipbuilding, a policy that dramatically expanded the number of seaworthy vessels. Such mercantilist measures aimed to ensure France's prominence in world markets and to provide the resources needed to fight wars against its increasingly long list of enemies. Although later economists questioned the value of this state intervention in the economy, nearly every government in Europe embraced mercantilism.

Colbert's mercantilist projects extended to Canada, where in 1663 he took control of the trading company that had founded New France. He transplanted several thousand peasants from western France to the present-day province of Quebec, which France had claimed since 1608, and he sent fifteen hundred soldiers to fend off the Iroquois, who regularly raided French fur-trading convoys. Shows of French military force, including the burning of Indian villages and winter food supplies, forced the Iroquois to make peace, and from 1666 to 1680 French traders moved westward with minimal interference. In 1672, the fur trader Louis Jolliet and Jesuit missionary Jacques Marquette reached the upper Mississippi River and traveled downstream as far as Arkansas. In 1684, the French explorer Sieur de La Salle ventured all the way down to the Gulf of Mexico, claiming a vast territory for Louis XIV and calling it Louisiana after him. Louis and Colbert encouraged colonial settlement as part of their rivalry with the English and Dutch in the New World.

Colonial settlement occupied only a small portion of Louis XIV's attention, however, for his main foreign policy goal was to extend French power in Europe. In pursuing this purpose, he inevitably came up against the Spanish and Austrian Habsburgs, whose lands encircled his. To expand French power, Louis needed the biggest possible army. The ministry of war centralized the organization of French troops. Barracks built in major towns received supplies from a central distribution system. The state began to provide uniforms for the soldiers and to offer veterans some hospital care. A militia draft instituted in 1688 supplemented the army in times of war and enrolled 100,000 men. Louis's wartime army could field a force as large as that of all his enemies combined.

Louis gained new enemies as he tried to expand the territory under his rule. In 1667–1668, in the first of his major wars after assuming personal direction of French affairs, Louis defeated the Spanish armies but had to make peace when England, Sweden, and the Dutch Republic joined the war. In the Treaty of Aix-la-Chapelle in 1668, he gained control of towns on the border of the Spanish Netherlands (Map 13.1). Pamphlets sponsored by the Habsburgs accused Louis of aiming for "universal monarchy," or domination of Europe.

In 1672, Louis XIV opened hostilities against the Dutch because they stood in the way of his acquisition of more territory in the Spanish Netherlands. He declared war again on Spain in 1673. By now the Dutch had allied themselves with their former Spanish masters to hold off the French. Louis also marched his troops into territories of the Holy Roman Empire, provoking many of the German princes to join with the emperor, the Spanish, and the Dutch in an alliance against Louis, now denounced as a "Christian Turk" for his imperialist ambitions. But the French armies more than held their own. Faced with bloody yet inconclusive results on the battlefield, the parties agreed to the Treaty of Nijmegen of 1678–1679, which ceded several Flemish towns and Franche-Comté to Louis (Map 13.1, page 489). These territorial additions were costly: French government deficits soared, and increases in taxes touched off the most serious antitax revolt of Louis's reign in 1675.

Louis had no intention of standing still. Heartened by the Habsburgs' seeming weakness, he pushed eastward, seizing the city of Strasbourg in 1681 and invading the province of Lorraine in 1684. Lorraine would remain a subject of contention between France and its neighbors for nearly three centuries. In 1688, Louis attacked some of the small German cities of the Holy Roman Empire and was soon involved in a long war against a coalition made up of England, Spain, Sweden, the Dutch Republic, the Austrian emperor, and various German princes. Between 1689 and 1697, the coalition fought Louis to a stalemate. When hostilities ended in the Treaty of Rijswijk in 1697, Louis returned many of his conquests made since 1678, with

Map 13.1 Louis XIV's Acquisitions, 1668–1697
Every ruler in Europe hoped to extend his or her territorial control, and war was often the result. Louis XIV steadily encroached on the Spanish Netherlands to the north and the lands of the Holy Roman Empire to the east. Although coalitions of European powers reined in Louis's grander ambitions, he incorporated many neighboring territories into the French crown.

the exception of Strasbourg (Map 13.1). Louis never lost his taste for war, but his enemies learned how to set limits on his ambitions.

Louis was the last French ruler before Napoleon to accompany his troops to the battlefield. In later generations, as the military became more professional, French rulers left the fighting to their generals. Although Louis had managed to suppress the private armies of his noble courtiers, he constantly promoted his own military prowess in order to keep his noble officers under his sway. He had miniature battle scenes painted on his high heels and commissioned tapestries showing his military processions into cities, even those he did not take by force. He seized every occasion to assert his supremacy, insisting that other fleets salute his ships first.

War required money and men, which Louis obtained by expanding state control over finances, conscription into the army, and military supply. Thus absolutism and warfare fed each other, as the bureaucracy created new ways to raise and maintain an army and the army's success in war justified the expansion of state power. But constant warfare also eroded the state's resources. Further administrative and legal reform, the elimination of the buying and selling of offices, and the lowering of taxes—all were made impossible by the need for more money.

The playwright Corneille wrote, no doubt optimistically, "The people are very happy when they die for their kings." What is certain is that the wars touched many peasant and urban families. The people who lived on the routes leading to the battlefields had to house and feed soldiers; only nobles were exempt from this requirement. Everyone, moreover, paid the higher taxes that were necessary to support the army. By the end of Louis's reign, one in six Frenchmen had served in the military.

REVIEW   How "absolute" was the power of Louis XIV?

Absolutism in Central and Eastern Europe

Central and eastern European rulers saw in Louis XIV a powerful model of absolutist state building. Yet they did not blindly emulate the Sun King, in part because they confronted conditions peculiar to their regions. The ruler of Brandenburg-Prussia had to rebuild lands ravaged by the Thirty Years' War and unite far-flung territories. The Austrian Habsburgs needed to govern a mosaic of ethnic and religious groups while fighting off the Ottoman Turks. The Russian tsars wanted to extend their power over a large but relatively impoverished empire. The great exception to absolutism in eastern Europe was Poland-Lithuania, where a long crisis virtually destroyed central authority and sucked much of eastern Europe into its turbulent wake.

Brandenburg-Prussia and Sweden: Militaristic Absolutism

Brandenburg-Prussia began as a puny state on the Elbe River, but it would have a remarkable future. In the nineteenth century, it would unify the disparate German states into modern-day Germany. The ruler of Brandenburg was an elector, one of the seven German princes entitled to select the Holy Roman Emperor. Since the sixteenth century, the ruler of Brandenburg had also controlled the duchy of East Prussia; after 1618, the state was called Brandenburg-Prussia. Despite meager resources, Frederick William of Hohenzollern, the Great Elector of Brandenburg-Prussia (r. 1640–1688), succeeded in welding his scattered lands into an absolutist state.

Pressured first by the necessities of fighting the Thirty Years' War and then by the demands of reconstruction, Frederick William determined to force his territories' estates (representative institutions) to grant him a dependable income. The Great Elector struck a deal with the Junkers (nobles) of each land: in exchange for allowing him to collect higher taxes to support his growing army, he gave them complete control over the peasants. The tactic worked. By the end of his reign the estates met only on ceremonial occasions.

State	Soldiers	Population	Ratio of soldiers/ total population
France	300,000	20 million	1:66
Russia	220,000	14 million	1:64
Austria	100,000	8 million	1:80
Sweden	40,000	1 million	1:25
Brandenburg-Prussia	30,000	2 million	1:66
England	24,000	5 million	1:210

*Figures for the end of the seventeenth century, ranging from 1688 for Prussia to 1710 for France

Taking Measure The Seventeenth-Century Army
The figures in this chart are only approximate, but they tell an important story. What conclusions can we draw about the relative weight of the military in the different European states? Why would England's army have been so much smaller than the other states'? Is the absolute or the relative size of the military the more important indicator?

Supplied with a steady income, Frederick William could devote his attention to military and bureaucratic consolidation. Over forty years he expanded his army from eight thousand to thirty thousand men (see "Taking Measure"). The army mirrored the rigid domination of nobles over peasants that characterized Brandenburg-Prussian society: peasants filled the ranks, and Junkers became officers. Nobles also took positions as bureaucratic officials, but military needs always had priority. The Great Elector named special war commissars to take charge not only of military affairs but also of tax collection. To hasten military dispatches, he also established one of Europe's first state postal systems.

As a Calvinist ruler, Frederick William disdained the ostentation of the French court, even while following the absolutist model of centralizing state power. He boldly rebuffed Louis XIV by welcoming twenty thousand French Huguenot refugees after Louis's revocation of the Edict of Nantes. In pursuing policies that promoted state power, Frederick William adroitly switched sides in Louis's wars and would stop at almost nothing to crush resistance at home. In 1701, his son Frederick I (r. 1688–1713) persuaded Holy Roman Emperor Leopold I to grant him the title "king in Prussia." Prussia had arrived as an important power (Map 13.2).

Across the Baltic, Sweden also stood out as an example of absolutist consolidation. In the Thirty Years' War, King Gustavus Adolphus's superb generalship and highly trained army had made Sweden the supreme power of northern Europe. The huge but sparsely populated state included not only most of present-day Sweden but also Finland, Estonia, half of Latvia, and much of the Baltic coastline of modern Poland

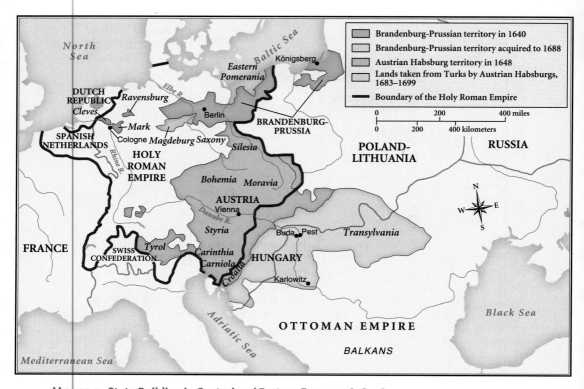

Map 13.2 State Building in Central and Eastern Europe, 1648–1699
The Austrian Habsburgs had long contested the Ottoman Turks for dominance of eastern Europe, and by 1699 they had pushed the Turks out of Hungary. In central Europe, the Austrian Habsburgs confronted the growing power of Brandenburg-Prussia, which had emerged from relative obscurity after the Thirty Years' War to begin an aggressive program of expanding its military and its territorial base. As emperor of the Holy Roman Empire, the Austrian Habsburg ruler governed a huge expanse of territory, but the emperor's control was in fact only partial because of guarantees of local autonomy.

and Germany. The Baltic, in short, was a Swedish lake. After Gustavus Adolphus died, his daughter Queen Christina (r. 1632–1654) conceded much authority to the estates. Absorbed by religion and philosophy, Christina eventually abdicated and converted to Catholicism. Her successors temporarily made Sweden an absolute monarchy.

Absolutism in Sweden (as in neighboring Denmark-Norway) took the form of the estates standing aside while the king led the army on lucrative foreign campaigns. The aristocracy went along because it staffed the bureaucracy and reaped war profits. Though intrigued by French culture, Sweden also gleamed with national pride. In 1668, the nobility demanded the introduction of a distinctive national costume: should Swedes, they asked, "who are so glorious and renowned a nation . . . let ourselves be led by the nose by a parcel of French dancing-masters"? Sweden spent the forty years after 1654 continuously warring with its neighbors. By the 1690s, war expenses began to outrun the small Swedish population's ability to pay, threatening the continuation of absolutism.

An Uneasy Balance: Austrian Habsburgs and Ottoman Turks

Holy Roman Emperor Leopold I (r. 1658–1705) ruled over a variety of territories of different ethnicities, languages, and religions, yet in ways similar to his French and Prussian counterparts, he gradually consolidated his power. Like all the Holy Roman emperors since 1438, Leopold was an Austrian Habsburg. He was simultaneously duke of Upper and Lower Silesia, count of Tyrol, archduke of Upper and Lower Austria, king of Bohemia, king of Hungary and Croatia, and ruler of Styria and Moravia (Map 13.2, page 492). Some of these territories were provinces in the Holy Roman Empire; others were simply ruled from Vienna as Habsburg family holdings.

Leopold needed to build up his armies and state authority in order to defend the Holy Roman Empire's international position, which had been weakened by the Thirty Years' War, and to push back the Ottoman Turks, who steadily encroached from the southeast. The emperor and his closest officials took control over recruiting, provisioning, and strategic planning and worked to replace the mercenaries hired during the Thirty Years' War with a permanent standing army that promoted professional discipline. To pay for the army and to staff his growing bureaucracy, Leopold had to gain the support of local aristocrats and chip away at the powers of the provincial institutions. Intent on replacing Bohemian nobles who had supported the 1618 revolt against Austrian authority, the Habsburgs promoted a new nobility made up of Czechs, Germans, Italians, Spaniards, and even Irish, who used German as their common tongue, professed Catholicism, and loyally served the Austrian dynasty. Bohemia became a virtual Austrian colony. "You have utterly destroyed our home, our ancient kingdom," lamented a Czech Jesuit in 1670, addressing Leopold. "Of smiling towns you have made straggling villages." Austrian censors prohibited publication of this protest for over a century.

In addition to holding Louis XIV in check on his western frontiers, Leopold confronted the ever-present challenge of the Ottoman Turks to his east. In 1683, the Turks once again pushed all the way to the gates of Vienna and laid siege to the Austrian capital. After reaching this high-water mark, however, Turkish power ebbed. With the help of Polish cavalry, the Austrians finally broke the siege and turned the tide in a major counteroffensive. By the Treaty of Karlowitz of 1699, the Ottoman Turks surrendered almost all of Hungary to the Austrians (Map 13.2, page 492).

Hungary's "liberation" from the Turks came at a high price. The fighting laid waste vast stretches of Hungary's central plain, and the population may have declined as much as 65 percent since 1600. To repopulate the land, the Austrians settled large communities of foreigners: Romanians, Croats, Serbs, and Germans. Magyar (Hungarian) speakers became a minority, and the seeds were sown for the poisonous nationality conflicts that would take place in nineteenth- and twentieth-century Hungary, Romania, and Yugoslavia.

The Siege of Vienna, 1683
This detail from a painting by Franz Geffels shows the camp of the Ottoman Turks. The Turkish armies surrounded Vienna on July 14, 1683. Jan Sobieski led an army of Poles that joined with Austrian and German forces to beat back the Turks on September 12. (© The Art Archive/Corbis.)

Once the Turks had been beaten back, Austrian rule over Hungary tightened. In 1687, the Habsburg dynasty's hereditary right to the Hungarian crown was acknowledged by the Hungarian diet, a parliament revived by Leopold in 1681 to gain the support of Hungarian nobles. The diet was dominated by nobles who had amassed huge holdings in the liberated territories. They formed the core of a pro-Habsburg Hungarian aristocracy that would buttress the dynasty until it fell in 1918. As the Turks retreated from Hungary, Leopold systematically rebuilt churches, monasteries, roadside shrines, and monuments in the flamboyant Austrian baroque style.

The Ottoman Turks also pursued state consolidation, but in a very different fashion from the Europeans. The Ottoman state extended its authority through a combination of settlement and military control. Hundreds of thousands of Turkish families moved with Turkish soldiers into the Balkan peninsula in the 1400s and 1500s. As locals converted to Islam, administration passed gradually into their hands. In the Ottoman homeland of Anatolia, the sultans, the Ottoman rulers, were often challenged by mutinous army officers. Despite frequent palace coups and assassinations, the Ottoman state survived by hiring restive peasants as mercenaries and by playing bureaucratic elites off one another. This constantly shifting social and political system explains how the coup-ridden Ottoman state could appear "weak" in Western eyes and still pose a massive military threat on Europe's southeastern borders. In the end, the Ottoman state lasted much longer than Louis XIV's absolute monarchy.

Russia: Foundations of Bureaucratic Absolutism

Seventeenth-century Russia seemed a world apart from the Europe of Louis XIV. Straddling Europe and Asia, it stretched across Siberia to the Pacific Ocean. Western visitors either sneered or shuddered at the "barbarism" of Russian life, and Russians reciprocated by nursing deep suspicions of everything foreign. But under the surface, Russia was evolving along paths much like the rest of absolutist Europe; the tsars increased their power by surmounting internal disorder and coming to an accommodation with noble landlords.

When Tsar Alexei (r. 1645–1676) tried to extend state authority by imposing new administrative structures and taxes in 1648, Moscow and other cities erupted in bloody rioting. The government immediately doused the fire. In 1649, Alexei convoked the Assembly of the Land (consisting of noble delegates from the provinces) to consult on a sweeping law code to organize Russian society in a strict social hierarchy that would last for nearly two centuries. The code of 1649 assigned all subjects to a hereditary class according to their current occupation or state needs. Slaves and free peasants were merged into a serf class. As serfs they could not change occupations or move; they were tightly tied to the soil and to their noble masters. To prevent tax evasion, the code also forbade townspeople to move from the community where they resided. Nobles owed absolute obedience to the tsar and were required to serve in the army, but in return no other group could own estates worked by serfs. Serfs became the chattel of their lords, who could sell them like horses or land. Their conditions of life differed little from those of the slaves on the plantations in the Americas.

Some peasants resisted enserfment. In 1667, Stenka Razin led a huge rebellion in southern Russia that promised liberation from "the traitors and bloodsuckers of the peasant communes"—the great noble landowners, local governors, and Moscow courtiers. Razin was a Cossack, the name given to bandit gangs consisting of runaway serfs and poor nobles in southern Russia and Ukraine. Captured four years later by the tsar's army, Razin was dismembered, his head and limbs publicly displayed and his body thrown to the dogs. Thousands of his followers also suffered grisly deaths, but his memory lived on in folk songs and legends. Landlords successfully petitioned for the abolition of the statute of limitations on runaway serfs and for harsh penalties against those who harbored runaways. The increase in Russian state authority went hand in hand with the enforcement of serfdom.

To extend his power and emulate his western rivals, Tsar Alexei wanted a bigger army, exclusive control over state policy, and a greater say in religious matters. The size of the army increased dramatically from 35,000 in the 1630s to 220,000 by the end of the century (see "Taking Measure," page 491). The Assembly of the Land, once an important source of noble consultation, never met again after 1653. In 1666, the Russian Orthodox church reaffirmed the tsar's role as God's direct representative on earth and took action against a religious group called the Old Believers, who rejected church efforts to bring Russian worship in line with Byzantine tradition. Whole communities of Old Believers starved or burned themselves to death rather than submit. Religious schism opened a gulf between the Russian people and the crown.

Stenka Razin in Captivity
After leading a revolt of thousands of serfs, peasants, and members of non-Russian tribes of the middle and lower Volga region, Razin was captured by Russian forces and led off to Moscow, where he was executed in 1671. He has been the subject of songs, legends, and poems ever since. (RIA Novosti.)

The tsar's emulation of western rivals extended to culture, too. Alexei set up the first Western-style theater in the Kremlin, and his daughter Sophia translated French plays. Nobles and ordinary citizens commissioned portraits of themselves instead of buying only religious icons. The most adventurous nobles began to wear German-style clothing. A long struggle over Western influence had begun.

Poland-Lithuania Overwhelmed

Unlike the other eastern European powers, Poland-Lithuania did not follow the absolutist model. Decades of war weakened the monarchy and made the great nobles into practically autonomous warlords. They used the parliament and demands for constitutionalism to stymie monarchical power. The result was a precipitous slide into political disarray and weakness.

In 1648, Ukrainian Cossack warriors revolted against the king of Poland-Lithuania, inaugurating two decades of tumult known as the Deluge. In 1654, the Cossacks offered Ukraine to Russian rule, provoking a Russo-Polish war that ended in 1667 when the tsar annexed eastern Ukraine and Kiev. Sweden, Brandenburg-Prussia, and Transylvania sent armies to seize territory, too. As much as a third of the Polish population eventually perished in the fighting. The once prosperous Jewish and Protestant minorities suffered great losses: some 56,000 Jews were killed by either the Cossacks, Polish peasants, or Russian troops. One rabbi wrote, "We were slaughtered each day, in a more agonizing way than cattle: they are butchered quickly, while we were being executed slowly." Surviving Jews moved from towns to shtetls (Jewish villages), where they could survive only by petty trading, moneylending, tax gathering, and tavern leasing—activities that fanned peasant anti-Semitism. Desperate for protection amid the war, most Protestants backed the violently anti-Catholic Swedes, and the victorious Catholic majority branded them as traitors, forcing some Protestants to seek refuge as far away as the Dutch Republic and England. In Poland-Lithuania, once an outpost of religious toleration, it came to be assumed that a good Pole was a Catholic.

The commonwealth revived briefly when Jan Sobieski (r. 1674–1696) was elected king. He gained a reputation throughout Europe when he led 25,000 Polish cavalrymen into battle in the siege of Vienna in 1683. His cavalry helped rout the Turks and turned the tide against the Ottomans. Married to a politically shrewd French princess, Sobieski openly admired Louis XIV's France. Despite his efforts to rebuild the monarchy, he could not halt Poland-Lithuania's decline into powerlessness.

Elsewhere the ravages of war had created opportunities for kings to increase their power, but in Poland-Lithuania the great nobles gained all the advantage. They dominated the Sejm (parliament), and to maintain an equilibrium among themselves, they each wielded an absolute veto power. This "free veto" constitutional system soon deadlocked parliamentary government. The monarchy lost its room to maneuver, and with it much of its remaining power. An appalled Croat visitor in 1658 commented, "Among the Poles there is no order in the state. . . . Everybody who is stronger thinks to have the right to oppress the weaker, just as the wolves and bears are free to capture and kill cattle. . . . Such abominable depravity is called by the Poles 'aristocratic freedom.'" The Polish version of constitutionalism fatally weakened the state and made it prey to its neighbors.

REVIEW   Why did absolutism succeed everywhere in eastern Europe except Poland-Lithuania?

Constitutionalism in England

In the second half of the seventeenth century, western and eastern Europe began to move in different directions. In general, the farther east one traveled, the more absolutist the style of government (with the exception of Poland-Lithuania) and the greater the gulf between landlord and peasant. In eastern Europe, nobles lorded over their serfs but owed almost slavish obedience in turn to their rulers. In western Europe, even in absolutist France, serfdom had almost entirely disappeared, and nobles and rulers alike faced greater challenges to their control. The greatest challenges of all would come in England.

This outcome might seem surprising, for the English monarchs enjoyed many advantages compared with their continental rivals: they needed less money for their armies because they had stayed out of the Thirty Years' War, and their island kingdom was in theory easier to rule because they governed a relatively homogeneous population only one-fourth the size of France's with few regional institutions to block the ruler's will. Yet the English rulers failed in their efforts to install absolutist policies. The English revolutions of 1642–1660 and 1688–1689 overturned two kings, confirmed the constitutional powers of an elected parliament, and laid the foundation for the idea that government must guarantee certain rights under the law.

England Turned Upside Down, 1642–1660

Disputes about the right to levy taxes and the nature of authority in the Church of England had long troubled the relationship between the English crown and Parliament. For over a hundred years, wealthy English landowners had been accustomed to participating in government through Parliament and expected to be consulted on royal policy. Although England had no one constitutional document, customary procedures and a variety of laws, judicial decisions, charters, and petitions granted by the king regulated relations between king and Parliament. When Charles I tried to assert his authority over Parliament, a civil war broke out. It set in motion an unpredictable chain of events, which included an extraordinary ferment of religious and political ideas. Some historians view the English civil war of 1642–1646 as the last great war of religion because it pitted Puritans against those trying to push the Anglican church toward Catholicism, but it should be considered the first modern revolution because it gave birth to democratic political and religious movements.

Charles I (r. 1625–1649) inherited the problems that had been left by his father, James I, and James's predecessor, Elizabeth I. Elizabeth had defended the crown's right to regulate religion, but neither she nor James definitively reined in the Puritans. In addition, James antagonized Parliament by selling monopolies and titles to raise money and by relying increasingly on the advice of his favorite courtier, George Villiers, rumored to be his lover. Charles consequently faced an increasingly aggressive Parliament when he inherited the throne. In 1628, Parliament forced Charles to agree to the Petition of Right, by which he promised not to levy taxes without its consent. Charles hoped to avoid further interference with his plans by simply refusing to call Parliament into session between 1629 and 1640.

Religious tensions brought conflicts over the king's authority to a head. The Puritans had long agitated for the removal of any vestiges of Catholicism, but Charles, married to a French Catholic, moved in the opposite direction. With Charles's encouragement, the archbishop of Canterbury, William Laud (1573–1645), imposed increasingly elaborate ceremonies on the Anglican church. Angered by these moves toward "popery," the Puritans poured forth vituperative pamphlets and sermons. In response Laud hauled them before the feared Court of Star Chamber, a special court consisting of handpicked members of the king's council. The Court of Star Chamber came to stand for royal tyranny and religious persecution because it rode roughshod over the regular judicial process and imposed its own penalties. The court ordered harsh sentences for Laud's Puritan critics; they were whipped, pilloried, and branded and even had their ears cut off and their noses split. When Laud tried to apply his policies to Scotland, however, they backfired completely. The stubborn Presbyterian Scots rioted against the imposition of bishops and a prayer book modeled on the Anglican Book of Common Prayer. In 1640 the Scots invaded the north of England and defeated Charles's army. To raise money, Charles called Parliament into session and unwittingly opened the door to a constitutional and religious crisis.

Reformers in the House of Commons (the lower house of Parliament) seized the opportunity to undo what they saw as the growing royal tyranny of the 1630s. Parliament removed Laud from office, ordered the execution of an unpopular royal commander, abolished the Court of Star Chamber, repealed recently levied taxes, and provided for a parliamentary assembly at least once every three years, thus establishing a constitutional check on royal authority. Moderate reformers expected to stop there and resisted Puritan pressure to abolish bishops and eliminate the Anglican prayer book. But their hand was forced in January 1642, when Charles and his soldiers invaded Parliament and tried unsuccessfully to arrest those leaders who had moved to curb his power. Faced with mounting opposition within London, Charles withdrew from the city and prepared to fight.

The ensuing civil war between king and Parliament lasted four years (1642–1646) and divided the country. The king's army of royalists, known as Cavaliers, enjoyed the most support in northern and western England. The parliamentary forces, called Roundheads because they cut their hair short, had their stronghold in the southeast, including London. Although Puritans dominated on the parliamentary side, they were divided about the proper form of church government: the Presbyterians wanted a Calvinist church with some central authority, whereas the Independents favored entirely autonomous congregations free from other church government (hence the term *congregationalism,* often associated with the Independents). Putting aside their differences for the sake of military victory, the Puritans united under an obscure member of the House of Commons, the country gentleman Oliver Cromwell (1599–1658). Cromwell was one of the generals of the New Model Army, so called because it was a disciplined national force rather than a hodgepodge of local militias. The New Model Army defeated the Cavaliers at the battle of Naseby in 1645. Charles fled to Scotland but was turned over by the Scots in 1647.

England during the Civil War, 1642–1646

Although the civil war between king and Parliament had ended in victory for Parliament, divisions within the Puritan ranks now came to the fore: the Presbyterians dominated Parliament, but the Independents controlled the army. The disputes between elites drew lower-class groups into the debate. When Parliament tried to disband the New Model Army in 1647, disgruntled soldiers protested. Called Levellers because of their insistence on leveling social differences, the soldiers took on their officers in a series of debates about the nature of political authority. The Levellers demanded that Parliament meet annually, that members be paid so as to allow common people to participate, and that all male heads of households be allowed to vote. Their ideal of political participation excluded servants, the propertyless, and women but offered access to artisans, shopkeepers, and modest farmers. Cromwell and other army leaders rejected the Levellers' demands as threatening to property owners. Cromwell insisted, "You have no other way to deal with these men but to break them in pieces. . . . If you do not break them they will break you."

Just as political differences between Presbyterians and Independents helped spark new political movements, so too did their conflicts over church organization foster the emergence of new religious doctrines. The new sects had in common only their emphasis on the "inner light" of individual religious inspiration and a disdain for hierarchical authority. Their emphasis on equality before God and greater participation in church governance appealed to the middle and lower classes. The Baptists, for example, insisted on adult baptism because they believed that Christians should choose their own church and that every child should not automatically become a member of the Church of England. Quaker men pointedly refused to take off their hats as a sign of respect to men in authority. Manifesting their religious experience by trembling, or "quaking," the Quakers believed that anyone, man or woman, inspired by a direct experience of God could preach.

Parliamentary leaders feared that the new sects would overturn the whole social hierarchy. Rumors abounded, for example, of naked Quakers running through the streets waiting for a "sign." Some sects did advocate sweeping change. Diggers promoted rural communism—collective ownership of all property. Seekers and Ranters questioned just about everything. A few men advocated free love. In keeping with their notions of equality and individual inspiration, many of the new sects provided opportunities for women to become preachers and prophets. Women also presented petitions, participated prominently in street demonstrations, distributed tracts, and occasionally even dressed as men, wearing swords and joining armies. The outspoken women in new sects like the Quakers underscored the threat of a social order turned upside down. These developments convinced the political elite that tolerating the new sects would lead to skepticism, anarchy, and debauchery.

At the heart of the continuing political struggle was the question of what to do with the king, who tried to negotiate with the Presbyterians in Parliament. In late 1648, Independents in the army purged the Presbyterians from Parliament, leaving a "rump" of about seventy members. This Rump Parliament then created a high court to try Charles I. The court found him guilty of attempting to establish "an unlimited and tyrannical power" and pronounced a death sentence. On January 30, 1649, Charles was beheaded before an enormous crowd, which reportedly groaned as one when the axe fell. Although many had objected to Charles's autocratic rule, few had wanted him killed. For royalists, Charles immediately became a martyr, and reports of miracles, such as the curing of blindness by the touch of a handkerchief soaked in his blood, soon circulated. In 1650, the dead king's son Charles (the future Charles II) allied with Scottish royalists, but Cromwell's forces routed them. Charles escaped to France.

Printed in the year Year, of the Hang-mans down-fall, 1649.

Execution of Charles I
This print of the execution of the English king Charles I on January 30, 1649, appeared on the first page of the fictitious confessions of his executioner, Richard Brandon, who supposedly claimed to feel pains in his own neck from the moment he cut off Charles's head. (© British Library, London, UK/The Bridgeman Art Library.)

The Rump Parliament abolished the monarchy and the House of Lords (the upper house of Parliament). It set up a republic with Cromwell as head of the Council of State. Cromwell did not tolerate dissent from his policies. He saw the hand of God in events and himself as God's agent. When plans for mutiny within the army were discovered, Cromwell had the perpetrators executed. Although Cromwell allowed the various Puritan sects to worship rather freely and permitted Jews with needed skills to return to England for the first time since the thirteenth century, Catholics could not worship publicly, nor could Anglicans use the Book of Common Prayer. The elites, many of whom were still Anglicans, were troubled by Cromwell's religious policies but pleased to see some social order reestablished.

The new regime aimed to extend state power just as Charles I had before. Cromwell laid the foundation for a Great Britain made up of England, Wales, Ireland, and Scotland by reconquering Scotland and subduing Ireland. Anti-English rebels in Ireland had seized the occasion of troubles between king and Parliament to revolt in 1641. When Cromwell's position was secured in 1649, he went to Ireland with a large force and easily defeated the rebels, massacring whole garrisons and their priests. He encouraged expropriating the lands of the Irish "barbarous wretches," and Scottish immigrants resettled the northern county of Ulster. This seventeenth-century English conquest left a legacy of bitterness that the Irish even today call "the curse of Cromwell." In 1651, Parliament turned its attention overseas, putting mercantilist ideas into practice in the first Navigation Act, which allowed imports only if they were carried on English ships or came directly from the producers of goods. The Navigation Act was aimed at the Dutch, who dominated world trade; Cromwell tried to carry the policy further by waging naval war on the Dutch from 1652 to 1654.

At home, however, Cromwell faced growing resistance. His wars required a budget twice the size of Charles I's, and his increases in property taxes and customs duties alienated landowners and merchants. In 1653, when the Rump Parliament considered disbanding the army, Cromwell abolished Parliament in a military coup and made himself Lord Protector. His regime came to be known as the Protectorate. Cromwell silenced his critics by banning newspapers and using networks of spies and mail readers to keep tabs on his enemies. Cromwell's death in 1658 revived the prospect of civil war and political chaos. In 1660, a newly elected, staunchly Anglican Parliament invited Charles II, the son of the executed king, to return from exile. The period between the regicide of Charles I and the restoration of Charles II came to be known as the Interregnum (literally, "between reigns").

The Restoration and the "Glorious Revolution" of 1688

The traditional monarchical form of government was reinstated in 1660, restoring the king to full partnership with Parliament. Charles II (r. 1660–1685) promised to extend religious toleration, especially to Catholics, with whom he sympathized. Yet in the first years of his reign more than a thousand Puritan ministers lost their positions, and after 1664, attending a service other than one conforming with the Anglican prayer book was illegal. Natural disasters also marred the early years of the restoration of the monarchy. The plague stalked London's rat-infested streets in May 1665 and claimed more than thirty thousand victims by September. Then in 1666, the Great Fire swept the city, causing cataclysmic destruction. The crown now had a city as well as a monarchy to rebuild.

The restoration of monarchy made some in Parliament fear that the English government would come to resemble French absolutism. This fear was not unfounded. In 1670, Charles II made a secret agreement, soon leaked, with Louis XIV in which he promised to announce his conversion to Catholicism in exchange for money for a war against the Dutch. Charles never proclaimed himself a Catholic, but in his Declaration of Indulgence (1673) he did suspend all laws against Catholics and Protestant dissenters. Parliament refused to continue funding the Dutch war unless Charles rescinded his Declaration of Indulgence. Asserting its authority further, Parliament passed the Test Act in 1673, requiring all government officials to profess allegiance to the Church of England and in effect disavow Catholic doctrine. Then in 1678, Parliament precipitated the so-called Exclusion Crisis by explicitly denying the throne to a Roman Catholic. This action was aimed at the king's brother and heir, James, an open convert to Catholicism. Charles refused to allow it to become law.

The dynastic crisis over the succession of a Catholic gave rise to two distinct factions in Parliament: the Tories, who supported a strong, hereditary monarchy

Great Fire of London, 1666

This painting shows the three-day fire at its height. The writer John Evelyn described the scene in his diary: "All the sky was of a fiery aspect, like the top of a burning oven, and the light seen above 40 miles round about for many nights. God grant mine eyes may never behold the like, who now saw above 10,000 houses all in one flame; the noise and cracking and thunder of people, the fall of towers, houses, and churches, was like an hideous storm." Everyone in London at the time felt overwhelmed by the catastrophe, and many attributed it to God's punishment for the upheavals of the 1640s and 1650s. (Museum of London.)

and the restored ceremony of the Anglican church, and the Whigs, who advocated parliamentary supremacy and toleration for Protestant dissenters such as Presbyterians. The Tories favored James's succession despite his Catholicism, whereas the Whigs opposed a Catholic monarch. The loose moral atmosphere of Charles's court also offended some Whigs, who complained tongue in cheek that Charles was father of his country in much too literal a fashion (he had fathered more than one child by his mistresses but had produced no legitimate heir).

Upon Charles's death, James succeeded to the throne as James II (r. 1685–1688). James pursued pro-Catholic and absolutist policies even more aggressively than his brother. When a male heir—who would take precedence over James's two adult Protestant daughters and be reared a Catholic—was born, Tories and Whigs banded together. They invited the Dutch ruler William, prince of Orange and the husband of James's older daughter, Mary, to invade England. James fled to France, Parliament declared that he had abdicated, and hardly any blood was shed. Parliament offered the throne jointly to William (r. 1689–1702) and Mary (r. 1689–1694) on the condition that they accept a bill of rights guaranteeing Parliament's full partnership in a constitutional government.

In the Bill of Rights (1689), William and Mary agreed not to raise a standing army or to levy taxes without Parliament's consent. They also agreed to call meetings of Parliament at least every three years, to guarantee free elections to parliamentary seats, and to abide by Parliament's decisions and not suspend duly passed laws. The agreement gave England's constitutional government a written, legal basis by formally recognizing Parliament as a self-contained, independent body that shared power with the rulers. Victorious supporters of the coup declared it the **Glorious Revolution**. Constitutionalism had triumphed over absolutism in England.

The propertied classes who controlled Parliament prevented any resurgence of the popular turmoil of the 1640s. The Toleration Act of 1689 granted all Protestants freedom of worship, though non-Anglicans were still excluded from the universities; Catholics got no rights but were often left alone to worship privately. When the Catholics in Ireland rose to defend James II, William and Mary's troops brutally suppressed them. With the Whigs in power and the Tories in opposition, wealthy landowners now controlled political life throughout the realm. Differences between the factions had become minor; the Tories simply enjoyed less access to the king's patronage.

> **REVIEW** | What differences over religion and politics caused the conflict between king and Parliament in England?

Other Outposts of Constitutionalism

When William and Mary came to the throne in England in 1689, the Dutch and English put aside the rivalries that had brought them to war against each other in 1652–1654, 1665–1667, and 1672–1674. Under William, the Dutch Republic and England together led the coalition that blocked Louis XIV's efforts to dominate continental Europe. The two states had much in common: oriented toward commerce, especially overseas, they were the successful exceptions to absolutism in Europe. Also among the few outposts of constitutionalism in the seventeenth century were the English North American colonies, which developed representative government while the English were preoccupied with their revolutions at home. Constitutionalism was not the only factor shaping this Atlantic world; as constitutionalism developed in the colonies, so too did the enslavement of black Africans as a new labor force.

The Dutch Republic

When the Dutch Republic gained formal independence from Spain in 1648, it had already established a decentralized, constitutional state. Rich merchants called regents effectively controlled the internal affairs of each province and through the Estates General (an assembly made up of deputies from each province) named the *stadholder,* the executive officer responsible for defense and for representing the state at all ceremonial occasions. They almost always chose one of the princes of the house of Orange, but the prince of Orange resembled a president more than a king.

The decentralized state encouraged and protected trade, and the Dutch Republic soon became Europe's financial capital. The Bank of Amsterdam offered interest rates less than half those available in England and France. Praised for their industriousness, thrift, and cleanliness—and maligned as greedy, dull "butterboxes"—the Dutch dominated overseas commerce with their shipping (Map 13.3). They imported products from all over the world: spices, tea, and silk from Asia; sugar and tobacco from

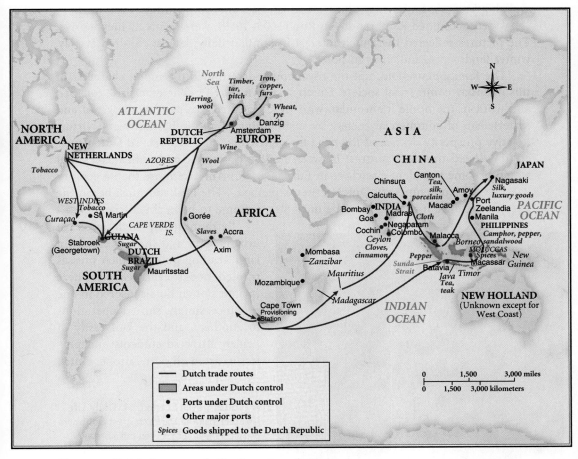

Map 13.3 Dutch Commerce in the Seventeenth Century
Even before gaining formal independence from Spain in 1648, the Dutch had begun to compete with the Spanish and Portuguese all over the world. In 1602, a group of merchants established the Dutch East India Company, which soon offered investors an annual rate of return of 35 percent on the trade in spices with countries located on the Indian Ocean. Global commerce gave the Dutch the highest standard of living in Europe and soon attracted the envy of the French and English. **For more help analyzing this map, see the map activity for this chapter in the Online Study Guide at** bedfordstmartins.com/huntconcise.

the Americas; wool from England and Spain; timber and furs from Scandinavia; grain from eastern Europe. A widely reprinted history of Amsterdam that appeared in 1662 described the city as "risen through the hand of God to the peak of prosperity and greatness. . . . The whole world stands amazed at its riches."

The Dutch rapidly became the most prosperous and best-educated people in Europe. Middle-class people supported the visual arts, especially painting, to an unprecedented degree. In the town of Delft, with a population of thirty thousand, for example, two-thirds of the households owned paintings. Whereas in other countries, kings, nobles, and churches bought art, Dutch buyers were merchants, artisans, and shopkeepers. Engravings, illustrated histories, and oil paintings, even those of the widely acclaimed Rembrandt van Rijn (1606–1669), were relatively inexpensive. The pictures reflected the Dutch interest in familiar daily details: children at play, winter landscapes, and ships in port.

The family household, not the royal court, determined the moral character of this intensely commercial society. Dutch society fostered public enterprise for men and work in the home for women, who were expected to filter out the greed and materialism of commercial society by maintaining domestic harmony and virtue. Relative prosperity decreased the need for married women to work, so Dutch society developed the clear contrast between middle-class male and female roles that would become prevalent elsewhere in Europe and in America more than a century later. As one contemporary Dutch writer explained, "The husband must be on the street to practice his trade; the wife must stay at home to be in the kitchen."

Extraordinarily high levels of urbanization and literacy created a large reading public. Dutch presses printed books censored elsewhere (printers or authors censored in one province simply shifted operations to another), and the University of Leiden attracted students and professors from all over Europe. Dutch

A Typical Dutch Scene from Daily Life
Jan Steen painted *The Baker Arent Oostwaard and His Wife* in 1658. Steen ran a brewery and tavern in addition to painting, and he was known for his interest in the details of daily life. Dutch artists popularized this kind of "genre" painting, which showed ordinary people at work and play. **For more help analyzing this image, see the visual activity for this chapter in the Online Study Guide at** bedfordstmartins.com/ huntconcise. (Rijksmuseum, Amsterdam.)

tolerance extended to the works of Benedict Spinoza (1633–1677), a Jewish philosopher and biblical scholar who was expelled by his synagogue for alleged atheism but was left alone by the Dutch authorities. Spinoza strove to reconcile religion with science and mathematics, but his work scandalized many Christians and Jews because he seemed to equate God and nature. Like nature, Spinoza's God followed unchangeable laws and could not be influenced by human actions, prayers, or faith.

Dutch learning, painting, and commerce all enjoyed wide renown in the seventeenth century, but this luster proved hard to maintain. The Dutch lived in a world of international rivalries in which strong central authority gave their enemies an advantage. Though inconclusive, the naval wars with England drained the state's revenues. Even more dangerous were the land wars with France, which continued into the eighteenth century. The Dutch survived these challenges but increasingly depended on alliances with other powers, such as England. By the end of the seventeenth century, the regent elite had become more exclusive, more preoccupied with ostentation, less tolerant of deviations from strict Calvinism, and more concerned with imitating French styles than with encouraging their own.

Freedom and Slavery in the New World

The French and English also increasingly overshadowed the Dutch in the New World colonies. While the Dutch concentrated on shipping, including the slave trade, the French and English established settler colonies that would eventually provide fabulous revenues to the home countries. Many European governments encouraged private companies to vie for their share of the slave trade, and slavery began to take clear institutional form in the New World in this period. While whites found in the colonies greater political and religious freedom than in Europe, they subjected black Africans to the most degrading forms of bondage.

After the Spanish and Portuguese had shown that African slaves could be transported and forced to labor in South and Central America, the English and French endeavored to set up similar labor systems in their new Caribbean island colonies. White planters with large tracts of land bought African slaves to work fields of sugarcane, and as they gradually built up their holdings, the planters displaced most of the original white settlers, who moved to mainland North American colonies. After 1661, when Barbados instituted a slave code that stripped all Africans of rights under English law, slavery became codified as an inherited status that applied only to blacks. The result was a society of extremes: the very wealthy whites—about 7 percent of the population in Barbados—and the enslaved, powerless black majority. The English brought little of their religious or constitutional practices to the Caribbean. Other Caribbean colonies followed a similar pattern of development. Louis XIV promulgated a "black code" in 1685 to regulate the legal status of slaves in the French colonies. Although one of his aims was to prevent non-Catholics from owning slaves in the French colonies, the code had much the same effect as the English codes on the slaves themselves: they had virtually no legal rights.

The highest church and government authorities in Catholic and Protestant countries alike condoned the gradually expanding slave trade. The governments of England, France, Spain, Portugal, the Dutch Republic, and Denmark all encouraged private companies to traffic in black Africans. The Dutch West India Company was the most successful of them in this period. In the early 1600s, about 9,000 Africans were exported from Africa to the New World every year; by 1700, this figure had increased to 25,000 annually. Historians advance several different reasons for the increase in the slave trade: some claim that improvements in muskets made European slavers more formidable; others cite the rising price of slaves, which made their sale more attractive to Africans; still others focus on factors internal to Africa, such as the increasing size of African armies and their use of muskets in fighting and capturing other Africans for sale as slaves. Whatever the reason, the way had been prepared for the development of an Atlantic economy based on slavery.

Virtually left to themselves during the upheavals in England, the fledgling English colonies in North America developed representative government on their own. Almost every colony had a governor and a two-house legislature. The colonial legislatures constantly sought to increase their power and resisted the efforts of Charles II and James II to reaffirm royal control. William and Mary reluctantly allowed emerging colonial elites more control over local affairs. The social and political elite among the settlers hoped to impose an English social hierarchy dominated by rich landowners. Ordinary immigrants to the colonies, however, took advantage of plentiful land to carve out their own farms using white servants and, later in some colonies, African slaves.

For native Americans, the expanding European presence meant something else altogether. They faced death through unfamiliar diseases and warfare and the accelerating loss of their homelands. Unlike white settlers, native Americans believed that land was a divine gift provided for their collective use and not subject to individual ownership. As a result, Europeans' claims that they owned exclusive land rights caused frequent skirmishes. In 1675–1676, for instance, three tribes allied under Metacomet (called King Philip by the English) threatened the survival of New England settlers, who savagely repulsed the attacks and sold their captives as slaves. Whites portrayed native Americans as conspiring villains and sneaky heathens, akin to Africans in their savagery.

REVIEW   How could outposts of constitutionalism coexist with slavery?

The Search for Order in Elite and Popular Culture

While freedom and slavery simultaneously took root in the New World, the conflict between absolutist and constitutional forms of government in Europe was giving rise to profound new thinking about the foundations of the political order. Concerns about order were not limited to politics. Poetry, painting, and architecture reflected those preoccupations, too. As European states, both absolutist and constitutional, expanded their powers, elites worked to distinguish themselves from the lower classes. They developed new codes of correct behavior for themselves and tried to teach order and discipline to their social inferiors.

Social Contract Theory: Hobbes and Locke

Two figures stood out prominently in the debates over the foundations of political authority: Thomas Hobbes and John Locke. Their writings helped shape the modern subject of political science. Hobbes justified absolute authority; Locke provided the rationale for constitutionalism. Yet both argued that all authority came not from divine right but from a social contract between citizens.

Thomas Hobbes (1588–1679) was a royalist who sat out the English civil war of the 1640s in France, where he tutored the future king Charles II. Returning to England in 1651, he published his masterpiece, *Leviathan,* in which he argued for unlimited authority in a ruler. Absolute authority could be vested in either a king or a parliament; it had to be absolute, he insisted, in order to overcome the defects of human nature. Believing that people are essentially self-centered and driven by the "right to self-preservation," Hobbes made his case by referring to science, not religion. To Hobbes, human life in a state of nature—that is, any situation without firm authority—was "solitary, poor, nasty, brutish, and short." He believed that the desire for power and natural greed would inevitably lead to unfettered competition. Only the assurance of social order could make people secure enough to act according to law; consequently, giving up personal liberty, he maintained, was the price of collective security. Rulers derived their power, he concluded, from a contract by which people gave up their natural rights to an absolute authority that guaranteed their rights in society.

Hobbes's notion of rule by an absolute authority left no room for political dissent or nonconformity, and it infuriated both royalists and supporters of Parliament. He enraged royalists by arguing that authority came not from divine right but from the social contract between citizens. Parliamentary supporters resisted Hobbes's claim that rulers must possess absolute authority to prevent the greater evil of anarchy; they believed that a constitution should guarantee shared power between king and parliament and protect individual liberties. Like Machiavelli before him, Hobbes became associated with a cynical, pessimistic view of human nature, and future political theorists often began their arguments by refuting Hobbes.

Rejecting both Hobbes and the more traditional royalist defenses of absolute authority, John Locke (1632–1704) used the notion of a social contract to provide a foundation for constitutionalism. Locke experienced political life firsthand as the physician, secretary, and intellectual companion of the earl of Shaftesbury, a leading English Whig. In 1683, Locke fled with Shaftesbury to the Dutch Republic when Charles II clamped down on those conspiring to prevent his Catholic brother from succeeding him. There Locke continued work on his *Two Treatises of Government,* which, when published in 1690, served to justify the Glorious Revolution of 1688. Locke's position was thoroughly anti-absolutist. He denied the divine right of kings and ridiculed the common royalist idea that political power in the state mirrored the father's authority in the family. Like Hobbes, he posited a state of nature that applied to all people. Unlike Hobbes, he thought people were reasonable and the state of nature peaceful.

Locke insisted that government's only purpose was to protect life, liberty, and property, a notion that linked economic and political freedom. Ultimate authority rested in the will of a majority of men who owned property, and government should be limited to its basic purpose of protection. A ruler who failed to uphold his part of the social contract between the ruler and the populace could be justifiably resisted, an idea that would become crucial for the leaders of the American Revolution a century later. For England's landowners, however, Locke helped validate a revolution that consolidated their interests and ensured their privileges in the social hierarchy.

Locke defended his optimistic view of human nature in the immensely influential *Essay concerning Human Understanding* (1690). He denied the existence of any innate ideas and asserted instead that each human is born with a mind that is a tabula rasa (blank slate). Everything humans know, he claimed, comes from sensory experience, not from anything inherent in human nature. Locke's views promoted the belief that "all men are created equal," a belief that challenged absolutist forms of rule and ultimately raised questions about women's roles as well. Not surprisingly, Locke devoted considerable energy to rethinking educational practices; he believed that education crucially shaped the human personality by channeling all sensory experience. Although he himself owned shares in the Royal African Company and justified slavery, Locke's writings were later used by abolitionists in their campaign against slavery.

Freedom and Order in the Arts and Sciences

Hobbes and Locke were not alone in wrestling with the conflicts between desires for greater freedom and the need for reassuring order. The French mathematician Blaise Pascal vividly captured the fear of chaos in his *Pensées* (*Thoughts*) of 1660: "I look on all sides, and I see only darkness everywhere. Nature presents to me nothing which is not a matter of doubt and concern. . . . It is incomprehensible that God should exist, and incomprehensible that He should not exist." Poets, artists, and scientists all tried to make sense of the individual's place within what Pascal called "the eternal silence of these infinite spaces."

The English Puritan poet John Milton (1608–1674) responded to the challenge by giving priority to individual liberty. In 1643, in the midst of the civil war between king and Parliament, he published writings in favor of divorce. When Parliament enacted a censorship law aimed at such literature, Milton countered in 1644 with one of the first defenses of freedom of the press, *Areopagitica* (*Tribunal of Opinion*). Forced into retirement after the restoration of the monarchy, Milton published in 1667 his epic poem *Paradise Lost*. He used Adam and Eve's Fall to meditate on human freedom and the tragedies of rebellion. Although Milton wanted to "justify the ways of God to man," his Satan, the proud angel who challenges God, is so compelling as to be heroic. Individuals must learn the limits of their freedom, Milton seems to say, and yet the

Gian Lorenzo Bernini, *Ecstasy of St. Teresa of Ávila*
This ultimate statement of baroque sculpture captures all the drama and even sensationalism of a mystical religious faith. Bernini based the figures in this piece, created around 1650, on a vision reported by St. Teresa in which she saw an angel: "In his hands I saw a great golden spear, and at the iron tip there appeared to be a point of fire. This he plunged into my heart several times so that it penetrated my entrails. When he pulled it out I felt that he took them with it, and left me utterly consumed by the great love of God." (Scala/Art Resource, NY.)

desire for liberty remains essential to their nature as humans, creating at times a tragic discord.

The dominant artistic styles on the continent, the baroque and the classical, both submerged the individual in a grander design, emphasizing the majesty of authority. The baroque style proved to be especially suitable for public displays of faith and power that overawed individual beholders. The combination of religious and political purposes in baroque art is best exemplified in the architecture and sculpture of Gian Lorenzo Bernini (1598–1680), the papacy's official artist. His architectural masterpiece was the gigantic square facing St. Peter's Basilica in Rome (1656–1671). His use of freestanding colonnades and a huge open space is meant to impress the individual observer with the power of the popes and the Catholic religion.

Bernini sculpted tombs and statues for the popes and private patrons. In 1665, Louis XIV hired Bernini to plan the rebuilding of the Louvre palace in Paris but then rejected his ideas as incompatible with French tastes. Although France was a Catholic country, French painters, sculptors, and architects, like their patron Louis XIV, preferred the standards of **classicism** to those of the baroque. French artists developed classicism to be a national style, distinct from the baroque style that was closely associated with France's enemies, the Austrian and Spanish Habsburgs. As its name suggests, classicism reflected the ideals of the art of antiquity; geometric shapes, order, and harmony of lines took precedence over the sensuous, exuberant, and emotional forms of the baroque. Rather than being overshadowed by the sheer power of emotional display, in classicism the individual could be found at the intersection of converging, symmetrical, straight lines. These influences were apparent in the work

French Classicism
This painting by Nicolas Poussin, *Discovery of Achilles on Skyros* (1649–1650), shows the French interest in classical themes and ideals. In the Greek story, Thetis dresses her son Achilles as a young woman and hides him on the island of Skyros so that he will not have to fight in the Trojan War. When a chest of treasures is offered to the women, Achilles reveals himself (he is the figure on the far right) because he cannot resist the sword. In telling the story, Poussin emphasizes harmony and almost a sedateness of composition, avoiding the exuberance and emotionalism of the baroque style. (Photograph © 2011 Museum of Fine Arts, Boston.)

of the leading French painters of the period, Nicolas Poussin (1594–1665) and Claude Lorrain (1600–1682), both of whom worked in Rome and tried to re-create classical Roman values in their mythological scenes and Roman landscapes.

Art might also serve the interests of science. One of the most skilled illustrators of insects and flowers was Maria Sibylla Merian (1646–1717), a German-born painter-scholar whose engravings were widely celebrated for their brilliant realism and microscopic clarity. Merian sought her own version of freedom by separating from her husband and joining a sect called the Labadists (after its French founder, Jean de Labadie), whose members did not believe in formal marriage ties and established a colony in the northern Dutch province of Friesland. After moving there with her daughters, Merian went with missionaries from the sect to the Dutch colony of Surinam in South America and painted watercolors of the exotic flowers, birds, and insects she found in the jungle around the cocoa and sugarcane plantations. In the seventeenth century, many women became known for their still lifes and especially their paintings of flowers. Paintings by the Dutch artist Rachel Ruysch, for example, fetched higher prices than works by Rembrandt.

Because of their exclusion from most universities, women only rarely participated in the new scientific discoveries. In 1667, nonetheless, the English Royal Society invited Margaret Cavendish—a writer of poems, essays, letters, and philosophical treatises—to attend a meeting to watch the exhibition of experiments. She attacked the use of telescopes and microscopes because she detected in the new experimentalism a mechanistic view of the world that exalted masculine prowess and challenged the Christian belief in free will. She nonetheless urged the formal education of women, complaining that "we are kept like birds in cages to hop up and down in our houses." She insisted, "Many of our Sex may have as much wit, and be capable of Learning as well as men."

Scientists needed freedom to publish their results, as Galileo had discovered, yet they also required support in order to carry out their work. As the scientific revolution of Galileo, Kepler, and Newton steadily gained new adherents, rulers seized upon the potential for enhancing their prestige and glory. Various German princes funded the work of Gottfried Wilhelm Leibniz (1646–1716), one of the inventors, along with Newton, of calculus. A lawyer, diplomat, and scholar who wrote about metaphysics, logic, and history, Leibniz, like Milton, ultimately wanted to explain the ways of God to humans. His most controversial view was that we live in the best of all possible worlds because it was created by a perfect God. Leibniz did not intend to expound a mindless optimism. He thought of God as like a mathematician who aims to solve problems in the simplest and most elegant fashion. Many modern scientific principles, such as the conservation of energy, followed from Leibniz's view. Leibniz also helped establish scientific societies in the German states. Government involvement in science was greatest in France, where it became an arm of mercantilist policy. In 1666, Jean-Baptiste Colbert founded the Royal Academy of Sciences, which supplied fifteen scientists with government stipends.

Women and Manners

Philosophers, poets, and painters all imaginatively explored the place of the individual within a larger whole, but real-life individuals had to learn to navigate their own social worlds. Manners—the learning of individual self-discipline—were essential skills of social navigation, and women usually took the lead in teaching them. Under the tutelage of their mothers and wives, nobles learned to hide all that was crass and to maintain a fine sense of social distinction. In some ways, aristocratic men were expected to act more like women. Just as women had long been expected to please men, now aristocratic men had to please their monarch or patron by displaying proper manners and conversing with elegance and wit. Men as well as women had to master the art of pleasing, which included a facility with foreign languages (especially French), skill in dance, a taste for fine music, and attention to dress.

As part of the evolution of new aristocratic ideals, nobles learned to disdain all that was lowly. The upper classes began to reject popular festivals and fairs in favor of private theaters, where seats were relatively expensive and behavior was formal. Clowns and buffoons now seemed vulgar; the last king of England to keep a court fool was Charles I. The greatest French playwright of the seventeenth century, Molière (the pen name of Jean-Baptiste Poquelin, 1622–1673), wrote sparkling comedies of manners that revealed much about the new aristocratic behavior. Molière's play *The*

Middle-Class Gentleman, first performed at the royal court in 1670, revolves around the yearning of a rich, middle-class Frenchman, Monsieur Jourdain, to learn to act like a *gentilhomme* (meaning both "gentleman" and "nobleman" in French). By making fun of Jourdain's outlandish aspirations, the play seems to have been an attempt to reassure the nobles at court: only true nobles by blood could hope to act like nobles. But the play also shows how the middle classes were learning to emulate the nobility: if one could learn to *act* nobly through self-discipline, could not anyone with some education and money pass himself off as noble?

As Molière's play demonstrates, new attention to manners trickled down from the court to the middle class. A French treatise on manners from 1672 explained:

> If everyone is eating from the same dish, you should take care not to put your hand into it before those of higher rank have done so. . . . Formerly one was permitted . . . to dip one's bread into the sauce, provided only that one had not already bitten it. Nowadays that would be a kind of rusticity. Formerly one was allowed to take from one's mouth what one could not eat and drop it on the floor, provided it was done skillfully. Now that would be very disgusting.

The key words "rusticity" and "disgusting" reveal the association of unacceptable social behavior with the peasantry, dirt, and repulsion. Courtly manners often permeated the upper reaches of society by means of the salon, an informal gathering held regularly in private homes and presided over by a socially eminent woman. In 1661, one French author claimed to have identified 251 Parisian women as hostesses of salons. Although the French government occasionally worried that these gatherings might be seditious, the three main topics of conversation were love, literature, and philosophy. Hostesses often worked hard to encourage the careers of budding authors. Before publishing a manuscript, many authors would read their compositions to a salon gathering. Corneille, Racine, and even Bishop Bossuet sought female approval for their writings.

Women who wrote on their own faced many obstacles. Marie-Madeleine Pioche de la Vergne, known as Madame de Lafayette, wrote several short novels that were published anonymously because it was considered inappropriate for aristocratic women to appear in print. After the publication of *The Princess of Cleves* in 1678, she denied having written it. Hannah Wooley, the English author of many books on domestic conduct, published under the name of her first husband. Women were known for writing wonderful letters, many of which circulated in handwritten form; hardly any appeared in print during the authors' lifetimes. In the 1650s, despite these limitations, French women began to turn out best sellers in a new type of literature, the novel. Their success prompted the philosopher Pierre Bayle to remark in 1697 that "our best French novels for a long time have been written by women."

The new importance of women in the world of manners and letters did not sit well with everyone. Although the French writer François Poulain de la Barre (1647–1723), in a series of works published in the 1670s, used the new science to assert the equality of women's minds, most men resisted the idea. Clergymen, lawyers, scholars, and playwrights attacked women's growing public influence. Women, they complained, were corrupting forces and needed restraint. Women were accused of raising "the banner of prostitution in the salons, in the promenades, and in the streets." Molière wrote plays denouncing women's pretension to judge literary merit. English playwrights derided learned women by creating characters with names such as Lady Knowall, Lady Meanwell, and Mrs. Lovewit. A real-life target of the English playwrights was Aphra Behn (1640–1689), one of the first professional woman authors, who supported herself as a journalist and also wrote plays and poetry. Her short novel *Oroonoko* (1688) tells the story of an African prince mistakenly sold into slavery. The story was so successful that it was adapted by playwrights and performed repeatedly in England and France for the next hundred years. Behn responded to her critics by arguing that there was "no reason why women should not write as well as men."

Reforming Popular Culture

The illiterate peasants who made up most of Europe's population had little or no knowledge of political theory, philosophy, or novels, no matter who authored them. Their culture had three main elements: the skills needed to work at farming or in a trade; popular forms of entertainment such as village fairs and dances; and their religion, which shaped every aspect of life and death. In the seventeenth century the division between elite and popular culture widened as elites insisted on their difference from the lower orders and pushed forward the ongoing effort to instill religious and social discipline in their social inferiors.

Building upon campaigns against popular "paganism" that began during the sixteenth-century Protestant and Catholic reform movements, Protestant and Catholic churches alike pushed hard to change popular religious practices. Puritans in England tried to root out maypole dances, Sunday village fairs, gambling, taverns, and bawdy ballads because they interfered with sober observance of the Sabbath. In Lutheran Norway, pastors denounced a widespread belief in the miracle-working powers of St. Olaf. The word *superstition* previously meant "false religion" (Protestantism was a superstition for Catholics, Catholicism for Protestants). In the seventeenth century, it took on its modern meaning of irrational fears, beliefs, and practices, which anyone educated or refined would avoid. *Superstition* became synonymous with popular or ignorant beliefs.

The Catholic campaign against superstitious practices found a ready ally in Louis XIV. While he reformed the nobles at court through etiquette and manners, Catholic bishops in the French provinces trained parish priests to reform their flocks by using catechisms in local dialects and insisting that parishioners attend Mass. The church faced a formidable challenge. One bishop in France complained in 1671, "Can you believe that there are in this diocese entire villages where no one has even heard of Jesus Christ?" In some places, believers sacrificed animals to the Virgin Mary, prayed to the new moon, and worshipped at the sources of streams as in pre-Christian times.

Like its Protestant counterpart, the Catholic campaign against ignorance and superstition helped extend state power. Clergy, officials, and local police worked together to limit carnival celebrations (festivities before the beginning of Lent that often had a riotous character), to regulate pilgrimages to shrines, and to replace

Corpus Christi Procession in Peru
The Catholic campaign against paganism extended to Spanish possessions in the New World. This painting shows a Catholic procession by Incas that took place in the late 1670s in Cuzco, Peru. The Inca in front is wearing his native dress; he is followed by a float and religious figures carrying traditional Catholic imagery. (Museo del Arzobispo, Cuzco, Peru.)

"indecent" images of saints with more restrained and decorous ones. In Catholicism, the cult of the Virgin Mary and devotions closely connected with Jesus, such as the Holy Sacrament and the Sacred Heart, took precedence over the celebration of more popular saints who seemed to have pagan origins or were credited with unverified miracles. Reformers everywhere tried to limit the number of feast days on the grounds that they encouraged lewd behavior.

The campaign for more disciplined religious practices helped generate a new attitude toward the poor. Poverty previously had been closely linked with charity and virtue in Christianity: it was a Christian duty to give alms to the poor, and Jesus and many of the saints had purposely chosen lives of poverty. In the sixteenth and seventeenth centuries, the upper classes, the church, and the state increasingly regarded the poor as dangerous, deceitful, and lacking in character. "Criminal laziness is the source of all their vices," wrote a Jesuit expert on the poor. The courts had previously expelled beggars from cities; now local leaders, both Catholic and Protestant, tried to reform their character. In the sixteenth century, local and state officials began to levy taxes for more organized poor relief; after the mid-seventeenth century officials began to transform hospitals into houses of confinement for beggars. In Catholic France, upper-class women's religious associations, known as confraternities, set up asylums that confined prostitutes (by arrest if necessary) and rehabilitated them. Confraternities also founded hospices where orphans learned order and respect. Such groups advocated harsh discipline as the cure for poverty.

Although hard times had increased the numbers of poor people and the rates of violent crime as well, the most important changes were attitudinal. The elites wanted to separate the very poor from society either to change them or to keep them from contaminating others. Hospitals became holding pens for society's unwanted

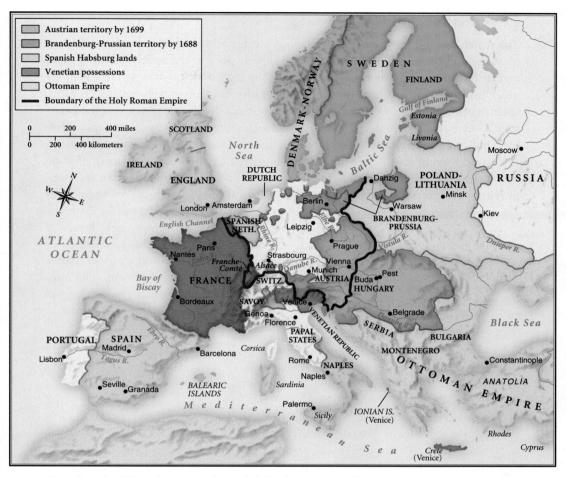

Mapping the West Europe at the End of the Seventeenth Century
Size was not necessarily an advantage in the late 1600s. Poland-Lithuania, a large country on the map, had been fatally weakened by internal conflicts. In the next century it would disappear entirely. While the Ottoman Empire still controlled an extensive territory, outside of Anatolia its rule depended on intermediaries. The Austrian Habsburgs had pushed the Turks out of Hungary and back into the Balkans. The tiny Dutch Republic, meanwhile, had become very rich through international commerce and was the envy of far larger nations.

members, where the poor joined the disabled, the incurably diseased, and the insane. The founding of hospitals demonstrates the connection between these attitudes and state building. In 1676, Louis XIV ordered every French city to establish a hospital, and his government took charge of their finances. Other rulers soon followed the same path.

> **REVIEW**   In what ways did elite and popular culture become more separate during the second half of the seventeenth century?

Conclusion

The search for order in the wake of religious warfare and political upheaval took place on various levels, from the reform of the disorderly poor to the establishment of more regular bureaucratic routines in government. The biggest factor shaping the search for order was the growth of state power. Whether absolutist or constitutionalist in form, seventeenth-century states all aimed to penetrate more deeply into the lives of their subjects. They wanted more men for their armed forces, higher taxes to support their projects, and more control over foreign trade, religious dissent, and society's unwanted.

Some tearing had begun to appear, however, in the seamless fabric of state power. In England, the Dutch Republic, and the English North American colonies, property owners successfully demanded constitutional guarantees of their right to participate in government. In the eighteenth century, moreover, new levels of economic growth and the appearance of new social groups would exert pressures on the European state system. The success of seventeenth-century rulers created the political and economic conditions in which their critics would flourish.

CHAPTER REVIEW QUESTIONS
1. What are the most important differences between absolutism and constitutionalism as political systems?
2. Why was the search for order a major theme in science, politics, and the arts during the second half of the seventeenth century?

For practice quizzes and other study tools, see the Online Study Guide at bedfordstmartins.com/huntconcise.

For primary-source material from this period, see Chapter 16 of *Sources of THE MAKING OF THE WEST,* Third Edition.

TIMELINE

- **1651** Thomas Hobbes publishes *Leviathan*
- **1649** Execution of Charles I of England; new Russian legal code enacted
- **1667** Louis XIV begins the first of many wars that continue throughout his reign

1640 — 1650 — 1660

- **1642–1646** Civil war between King Charles I and Parliament in England
- **1648** Thirty Years' War ends; the Fronde revolt challenges royal authority in France; Ukrainian Cossack warriors rebel against the king of Poland-Lithuania
- **1660** Monarchy restored in England
- **1661** Slave code set up in Barbados

Suggested References

Recent studies have insisted that absolutism could never be entirely absolute because the king depended on collaboration to enforce his policies. Some of the best sources for Louis XIV's reign are the letters written by important noblewomen.

Barkey, Karen. *The Ottoman Route to State Centralization.* 1994.

*Beik, William. *Louis XIV and Absolutism: A Brief Study with Documents.* 2000.

Brook, Timothy. *Vermeer's Hat: The Seventeenth Century and the Dawn of the Global World.* 2008.

Cowart, Georgia. *The Triumph of Pleasure: Louis XIV and the Politics of Spectacle.* 2008.

Cromwell, Oliver: http://www.olivercromwell.org/

Davis, Natalie Zemon. *Women on the Margins: Three Seventeenth-Century Lives.* 1995.

*Forster, Elborg, trans. *A Woman's Life in the Court of the Sun King: Elisabeth Charlotte, Duchesse d'Orléans.* 1984.

France in America (site of the Library of Congress on French colonies in North America): http://international.loc.gov/intldl/fiahtml/fiatheme.html#track1

Hill, Christopher. *The World Turned Upside Down: Radical Ideas during the English Revolution.* 1972.

Kotilaine, Jarmo, and Marshall Poe, eds. *Modernizing Muscovy: Reform and Social Change in Seventeenth-Century Russia.* 2004.

*Pincus, Steven C. A. *England's Glorious Revolution, 1688–1689: A Brief History with Documents.* 2006.

Versailles: http://www.chateauversailles.fr

Wilkinson, Richard. *Louis XIV.* 2007.

■ **1678** Marie-Madeleine Pioche de la Vergne (Madame de Lafayette) anonymously publishes *The Princess of Cleves*

■ **1670** Molière's play *The Middle-Class Gentleman* first performed at the French court

■ **1688** Parliament forces James II to abdicate and invites the daughter of James II, Mary, and her husband, William of Orange, to take the English throne in the "Glorious Revolution"

1670   1680   1690

■ **1683** Austrian Habsburgs break the Turkish siege of Vienna

■ **1690** John Locke publishes *Two Treatises of Government* and *Essay concerning Human Understanding*

■ **1685** Louis XIV revokes toleration for French Protestants granted by the Edict of Nantes

JOHANN SEBASTIAN BACH (1685–1750), composer of mighty organ fugues and church cantatas, was not above amusing his Leipzig audiences, many of them university students. In 1732 he produced a cantata about a young woman in love with coffee. Her old-fashioned father rages that he won't find her a husband unless she gives up the fad. She agrees, secretly vowing to admit no suitor who will not promise in the marriage contract to let her brew coffee whenever she wants. Bach offers this conclusion:

London Coffeehouse
This gouache (a variant on watercolor painting) from about 1725 depicts a scene from a London coffeehouse located in the courtyard of the Royal Exchange (merchants' bank). Middle-class men, wearing wigs, read newspapers, drink coffee, smoke pipes, and discuss the news of the day. The coffeehouse draws them out of their homes into the new public sphere. *(© British Museum, London, England/The Bridgeman Art Library.)*

The cat won't give up its mouse,
Girls stay faithful coffee-sisters
Mother loves her coffee habit,
Grandma sips it gladly too—
Why then shout at the daughters?

Bach's era might well be called the age of coffee. European travelers at the end of the sixteenth century had noticed Middle Eastern people drinking a "black drink," *kavah*. Few Europeans sampled it at first, and the Arab monopoly on its production kept prices high. This changed around 1700 when the Dutch East India Company introduced coffee plants to Java and other Indonesian islands. Coffee production then spread to the French Caribbean, where African slaves provided the plantation labor. In Europe, imported coffee spurred the development of a new kind of meeting place: London's first coffeehouse opened in 1652, and the idea spread quickly to other European cities. Coffeehouses became gathering places for men to drink, read newspapers, and talk politics. Even Isaac Newton had his favorite coffeehouse. As a London newspaper commented in 1737, "There's scarce an Alley in City and Suburbs but has a Coffeehouse in it, which may be called the School of Public Spirit, where every Man over Daily and Weekly Journals, a Mug, or a Dram . . . devotes himself to that glorious one, his Country."

European consumption of coffee, tea, chocolate, and other novelties increased dramatically as European nations forged worldwide economic links. At the center of this new world economy was the **Atlantic system**, which bound together western Europe, Africa, and the Americas. Europeans bought slaves in western Africa, transported and sold them in their colonies in North and South America and the Caribbean, bought commodities such as coffee and sugar produced by the new colonial **plantations**, and then sold the goods in European ports for refining and reshipment. This Atlantic system first took clear shape in the early eighteenth century; it was the hub of European expansion all over the world.

Coffee drinking was one example among many of the new social and cultural patterns that took root between 1690 and 1740. Improvements in agricultural production at home reinforced the effects of trade overseas; Europeans now had more disposable income for "extras," and they spent their money not only in the new coffeehouses and cafés that sprang up all over Europe but also on newspapers, musical concerts, paintings, and novels. A new middle-class public began to make its presence felt in every domain of culture and social life, creating a new public sphere that would ultimately transform the nature of politics on both sides of the Atlantic.

Although the rise of the Atlantic system gave Europe new prominence in the global context, European rulers still focused most of their political, diplomatic, and military energies on their rivalries within Europe. A coalition of countries succeeded in containing French aggression, and a more balanced diplomatic system emerged. In eastern Europe, Prussia and Austria had to contend with the rising power of Russia under Peter the Great. In western Europe, both Spain and the Dutch Republic declined in influence but continued to vie with Britain and France for colonial spoils in the Atlantic. The more evenly matched competition among the great powers encouraged the development of diplomatic skills and drew attention to public health as a way of encouraging population growth.

In the aftermath of Louis XIV's revocation of the Edict of Nantes in 1685, a new intellectual movement known as the **Enlightenment** began to germinate. French Protestant refugees began to publish works critical of absolutism in politics and religion. Increased prosperity, the growth of a middle-class public, and the decline in warfare after Louis XIV's death in 1715 all fostered the development of this new critical spirit. Fed by the popularization of science and the growing interest in travel literature, the Enlightenment encouraged greater skepticism about religious and state authority. Building on the growth of the new public sphere, eventually the movement would question almost every aspect of social and political life in Europe. The Enlightenment began in western Europe in those countries—Britain, France, and the Dutch Republic—most affected by the new Atlantic system. It, too, was a product of the age of coffee.

CHAPTER FOCUS QUESTION   What were the most important consequences of the growth of the Atlantic system?

The Atlantic System and the World Economy

European ships had been circling the globe since the early 1500s, and European colonization had dramatically altered the landscape and populations of the Americas, yet only in the 1700s did Europe draw most of the rest of the world into its economic orbit. Western European trading nations sent ships loaded with goods to buy slaves from local rulers on the western coast of Africa; transported the slaves to the colonies in North and South America and the Caribbean and sold them to the owners of plantations producing coffee, sugar, cotton, and tobacco; and bought the raw commodities produced in the colonies and shipped them back to Europe, where they were refined or processed and then sold to other parts of Europe and the world. This Atlantic system and the growth of international trade helped create a new consumer society.

Slavery and the Atlantic System

Spain and Portugal had dominated Atlantic trade in the sixteenth and seventeenth centuries, but in the eighteenth century European trade in the Atlantic rapidly expanded and became more systematically interconnected (Map 14.1). By 1650, Portugal had already sent 200,000 African slaves to Brazil to work on the new sugar plantations (large tracts of lands farmed by slave labor). Realizing that plantations producing staples for Europeans could bring fabulous wealth, the European powers grew less interested in the dwindling trade in precious metals and more eager to colonize. Large-scale planters of sugar, tobacco, and coffee displaced small farmers who relied on one or two servants. Planters and their plantations won out because slave labor was cheap and therefore able to produce mass quantities of commodities at low prices.

State-chartered private companies from Portugal, Spain, France, Britain, the Dutch Republic, Prussia, and even Denmark exploited the 3,500-mile coastline of West Africa for slaves. Before 1675, most blacks taken from Africa had been sent to Brazil or Spanish America on Portuguese ships, but by 1725 more than 60 percent of African slaves landed in the Caribbean (Figure 14.1), and more and more of them were carried on British or French ships. All in all, 90 percent of the slaves were transported by Portuguese, British, or French ships. After 1700, the plantation economy also began to expand on the North American mainland. The numbers stagger the imagination. More than 11 million Africans were transported to the Americas before the slave trade began to wind down after 1850. Some 1.4 million died during the passage across the ocean. Many traders gained spectacular wealth, but companies did not always make profits. The English Royal African Company, for example, delivered 100,000 slaves to the Caribbean and imported 30,000 tons of sugar to Britain, yet lost money after the few profitable years following its founding in 1672.

The balance of white and black populations in the New World colonies was determined by the staples produced. New England merchants and farmers bought few slaves because they did not own plantations. Blacks—both slave and free—made

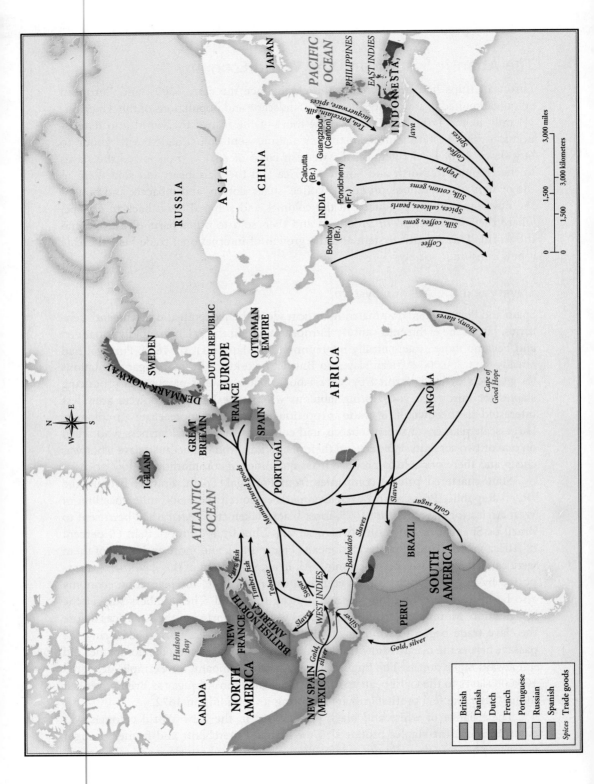

Map 14.1 European Trade Patterns, c. 1740

By 1740, the European powers had colonized much of North and South America and incorporated their American colonies into a worldwide system of commerce centered on the slave trade and plantation production of staple crops. Europeans still sought spices and luxury goods in China and the East Indies, but outside of Java, few Europeans had settled permanently in these areas. How did control over colonies determine dominance in this period? **For more help analyzing this map, see the map activity for this chapter in the Online Study Guide at** bedfordstmartins.com/huntconcise.

up only 3 percent of the population in eighteenth-century New England, compared with 60 percent in South Carolina. On the whole, the British North American colonies contained a higher proportion of African Americans from 1730 to 1765 than at any other time in American history. The imbalance of whites and blacks was even more extreme in the Caribbean. In the early 1700s, the British sugar islands had a population of about 150,000 people, only 30,000 of them Europeans. The remaining 80 percent were African slaves, as most indigenous people died fighting Europeans or the diseases they brought.

Enslaved women and men suffered terribly. Most had been sold to European traders by Africans from the west coast who acquired them through warfare or kidnapping. The vast majority were between fourteen and thirty-five years old. Before they were crammed onto ships for the three-month transatlantic trip, their heads were shaved, they were stripped naked, and some were branded with red-hot irons. Men and women were separated. Men were shackled with leg irons. Sailors and officers raped the women whenever they wished and beat those who refused their

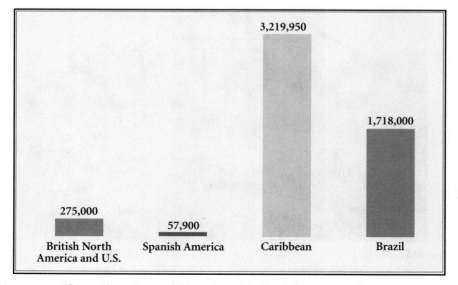

Figure 14.1 African Slaves Imported into American Territories, 1701–1800

During the eighteenth century, planters in the newly established Caribbean colonies imported millions of African slaves to work the new plantations. The vast majority of African slaves transported to the Americas ended up either in the Caribbean or in Brazil.

advances. In the cramped and appalling conditions aboard ship, as many as one-fourth of the slaves died in transit.

Once they landed, slaves were forced into degrading and oppressive conditions. As soon as masters bought slaves, they gave them new names, often only first names, and in some colonies branded them as personal property. Slaves had no social identities of their own; they were expected to learn their master's language and to do any job assigned. Slaves worked fifteen- to seventeen-hour days and were fed only enough to keep them on their feet. Brazilian slaves consumed more calories than the poorest Brazilians do today, but that hardly made them well fed. The death rate among slaves was high, especially in Brazil, where quick shifts in the weather, lack of clothing, and squalid living conditions made them susceptible to a variety of deadly illnesses.

Not surprisingly, despite the threat of torture or death on recapture, slaves sometimes ran away. In Brazil, runaways hid in *quilombos* (hideouts) in the forests or backcountry. When the quilombo of Palmares was discovered and destroyed in 1695, it had thirty thousand fugitives, who had formed their own social organization complete with elected kings and councils of elders. Outright revolt was uncommon,

Caribbean Sugar Mill
This seventeenth-century engraving of a sugar mill, or grinder, makes the work seem much less difficult than it was in practice. Slaves cut the sugarcane and then hauled it from the fields to the mill, where it was crushed. Many slaves lost fingers or hands in the process. The slaves then collected the juice (bottom center) and carried it to the boilers (bottom left and right). The sap was poured into molds and dried. The bricks of raw sugar were then exported to Europe for refining. (The Granger Collection, NY.)

especially before the nineteenth century, but other forms of resistance included stealing food, breaking tools, and feigning illness or stupidity. Slaveholders' fears about conspiracy and revolt lurked beneath the surface of every slave-based society. In 1710, the royal governor of Virginia reminded the colonial legislature of the need for unceasing vigilance: "We are not to Depend on Either Their Stupidity, or that Babel of Languages among 'em; freedom Wears a Cap which Can Without a Tongue, Call Togather all Those who Long to Shake off the fetters of Slavery." Masters defended whipping and other forms of physical punishment as essential to maintaining discipline. Laws called for the castration of a slave who struck a white person.

Plantation owners often left their colonial possessions in the care of agents and collected the revenue to live as wealthy landowners back home, where they built opulent mansions and gained influence in local and national politics. William Beckford, for example, was sent from Jamaica to England to attend school as a young boy. When he inherited sugar plantations and shipping companies from his father and older brother, he moved the headquarters of the family business to London in the 1730s to be close to the government and financial markets. His holdings formed the single most powerful economic interest in Jamaica, but he preferred to live in England, where he could collect art for his many luxurious homes, hold political office (he served as lord mayor of London and in Parliament), and even lend money to the government.

The slave trade permanently altered consumption patterns for ordinary people. Sugar had been prescribed as medicine before the end of the sixteenth century, but the development of plantations in Brazil and the Caribbean made it a standard food item. By 1700, the British sent home fifty million pounds of sugar a year, a figure that doubled by 1730. During the French Revolution of the 1790s, sugar shortages would become a cause for rioting in Paris. Equally pervasive was the spread of tobacco. By the 1720s, Britain imported two hundred shiploads of tobacco from Virginia and Maryland every year, and men of every country and class smoked pipes or took snuff.

The traffic in slaves disturbed many Europeans. As a government memorandum to the Spanish king explained in 1610, "Modern theologians in published books commonly report on, and condemn as unjust, the acts of enslavement which take place in provinces of this Royal Empire." Between 1667 and 1671, the French Dominican monk Father Du Tertre published three volumes in which he denounced the mistreatment of slaves in the French colonies.

In the 1700s, however, slaveholders began to justify their actions by demeaning the mental and spiritual qualities of enslaved Africans. White Europeans and colonists sometimes described black slaves as animal-like, akin to apes. A leading New England Puritan asserted this about black slaves: "Indeed their *Stupidity* is a *Discouragement*. It may seem, unto as little purpose, to *Teach,* as to *wash an Aethiopian* [Ethiopian]." One of the great paradoxes of this time was that talk of liberty and self-evident rights, especially prevalent in Britain and its North American colonies, coexisted with the belief that some people were meant to be slaves. Although Christians believed in principle in a kind of spiritual equality between blacks and whites, the churches often defended or at least did not oppose the inequities of slavery.

World Trade and Settlement

The Atlantic system helped extend European trade relations across the globe. The textiles that British shippers exchanged for slaves on the west coast of Africa, for example, were manufactured in India and exported by the British East India Company, a government-chartered joint-stock company that ended up virtually ruling India. As much as one-quarter of the British exports to Africa in the eighteenth century were actually reexports from India. To expand its trade in the rest of the world, Europeans seized territories and tried to establish permanent settlements. The eighteenth-century extension of European power prepared the way for western global domination in the nineteenth and twentieth centuries.

In contrast to the sparsely inhabited trading outposts in Asia and Africa, the colonies in the Americas bulged with settlers. The British North American colonies, for example, contained about 1.5 million nonnative (that is, white settler and black slave) residents by 1750. While the Spanish competed with the Portuguese for control of South America, the French competed with the British for control of North America. Spanish and British settlers came to blows over the boundary between the British colonies and Florida, which was held by Spain.

Local economies shaped colonial social relations. Men in French trapper communities in Canada, for example, had little in common with the men and women of the plantation societies in Barbados or Brazil. Racial attitudes also differed from place to place. The Spanish and Portuguese tolerated intermarriage with the native populations in both America and Asia. Sexual contact, both inside and outside marriage, fostered greater racial variety in the Spanish and Portuguese colonies than in the French and British territories (though mixed-race people could be found everywhere). By 1800, **mestizos**, children of Spanish men and Indian women, accounted for more than a quarter of the population in the Spanish colonies, and many of them aspired to join the local elite. Greater racial diversity seems not to have improved the treatment of slaves, however, which was probably harshest in Portuguese Brazil.

Where intermarriage between colonizers and natives was common, conversion to Christianity proved most successful. Although the Indians maintained many of their native religious beliefs, the majority of Indians in the Spanish colonies had come to consider themselves Catholics by 1700. Indian carpenters and artisans in the villages produced innumerable altars, retables (painted panels), and sculpted images to adorn their local churches, and individual families put up domestic shrines. Yet the clergy remained overwhelmingly Spanish: the church hierarchy concluded that the Indians' humility and innocence made them unsuitable for the priesthood.

In the early years of American colonization, many more men than women emigrated from Europe. At the end of the seventeenth century, the gender imbalance began to decline but remained substantial. Two and a half times as many men as women were among the immigrants leaving Liverpool, England, between 1697 and 1707, for example. Women who emigrated as indentured servants ran great risks: if they did not die of disease during the voyage, they might end up giving birth to illegitimate children (the fate of at least one in five servant women) or being virtually sold into marriage.

The uncertainties of life in the American colonies provided new opportunities for European women and men willing to live outside the law, however. In the 1500s and 1600s, the English and Dutch governments had routinely authorized pirates to prey on the shipping of their rivals, the Spanish and Portuguese. Then, in the late 1600s, English, French, and Dutch bands made up of deserters and crews from wrecked vessels began to form their own associations of pirates, especially in the Caribbean. Called **buccaneers** from their custom of curing strips of beef, called *boucan* by the native Caribs of the islands, the pirates governed themselves and preyed on everyone's shipping without regard to national origin. After 1700, the colonial governments tried to stamp out piracy. As one English judge argued in 1705, "A pirate is in perpetual war with every individual and every state. . . . They are worse than ravenous beasts."

White settlements in Africa and Asia remained small and almost insignificant, except for their long-term potential. Europeans had little contact with East Africa and almost none with Africa's vast interior. A few Portuguese trading posts in Angola and Dutch farms on the Cape of Good Hope provided the only toeholds for future expansion. In China, the emperors had welcomed Catholic missionaries at court in the seventeenth century, but the priests' credibility diminished as they squabbled among themselves and associated with European merchants, whom the Chinese considered pirates. "The barbarians [Europeans] are like wild beasts," one Chinese official concluded. In 1720, only one thousand Europeans resided in Guangzhou (Canton), the sole place where foreigners could legally trade for spices, tea, and silk (Map 14.1, page 524).

Europeans exercised more influence in India and Java, in the East Indies. Dutch coffee production in Java and nearby islands increased phenomenally in the early 1700s, and many Dutch settled there to oversee production and trade. In India, Dutch, British, French, Portuguese, and Danish companies competed for spices, cotton, and silk. By the 1740s the British and French had become the leading rivals in India, just as they were in North America. Both countries extended their power as India's Muslim rulers lost control to local Hindu princes, rebellious Sikhs, invading Persians, and their own provincial governors. A few thousand Europeans lived in India, though many thousands more soldiers were stationed there to protect them. The staple of trade with India in the early 1700s was calico—lightweight, brightly colored cotton cloth that caught on as a fashion in Europe.

Europeans who visited India were especially struck by what they viewed as exotic religious practices. In a book published in 1696 of his travels to western India, an Anglican minister described fakirs (religious ascetics), "some of whom show their devotion by a shameless appearance, and walking naked." Such writings increased European interest in the outside world, but they also fed a European sense of superiority that helped excuse violent forms of colonial domination.

India Cottons and Trade with the East
This colored cotton cloth (now faded with age) was painted and embroidered in Madras, in southern India, in the late 1600s. The male figure with the mustache may be a European, but the female figures are clearly Asian. Europeans, especially the British, discovered that they could make big profits on the export of Indian cotton cloth to Europe. They also traded Indian cotton in Africa for slaves and sold large quantities in the colonies. (V&A Images/Victoria and Albert Museum, London.)

The Birth of a Consumer Society

Worldwide colonization produced new supplies of goods, from coffee to calico, and population growth in Europe fueled demand for them. Beginning first in Britain, then in France and the Italian states, and finally in eastern Europe, population surged, growing by about 20 percent between 1700 and 1750. The gap between a fast-growing northwestern Europe and a more stagnant southern and central Europe now diminished as regions that had lost population during the seventeenth-century downturn recovered. Cities in particular grew. Between 1600 and 1750, London's population more than tripled, and Paris's more than doubled.

Although contemporaries could not have realized it then, this was the start of the modern "population explosion." It appears that a decline in the death rate, rather than a rise in the birthrate, explains the turnaround. Three main factors contributed to this decline in the death rate: better weather and hence more bountiful harvests, improved agricultural techniques, and the plague's disappearance after 1720.

By the early eighteenth century, the effects of economic expansion and population growth brought about a **consumer revolution**. The British East India Company began to import into Britain huge quantities of calico. British imports of tobacco doubled between 1672 and 1700. At Nantes, the center of the French sugar trade, imports quadrupled between 1698 and 1733. Tea, chocolate, and coffee became virtual necessities. In the 1670s, only a trickle of tea reached London, but by 1720 the East India Company sent 9 million pounds to England—a figure that rose to 37 million pounds by 1750. In 1700, England had two thousand coffeehouses; by 1740, every English country town had at least two. Paris got its first cafés at the end of the seventeenth century; Berlin opened its first coffeehouse in 1714; Bach's Leipzig boasted eight coffeehouses by 1725.

The birth of consumer society did not go unnoticed by eyewitnesses. In the English economic literature of the 1690s, writers began to express a new view of humans as consuming animals with boundless appetites. Such opinions gained a wide audience with the appearance of Bernard Mandeville's poem *Fable of the Bees* (1705), which argued that private vices might have public benefits. Mandeville insisted that pride, self-interest, and the desire for material goods (all Christian vices) in fact promoted economic prosperity: "every part was full of Vice, Yet the whole mass a Paradise." Many authors attacked the new doctrine of consumerism, and the French government banned the poem's publication. But Mandeville had captured the essence of the emerging market for consumption.

> **REVIEW** How is consumerism related to slavery?

New Social and Cultural Patterns

The impact of the Atlantic system and world trade was most apparent in the cities, where people had more money for consumer goods and more opportunities to participate in new public activities. But rural changes also had significant long-term influence, as a revolution in agricultural techniques made it possible to feed more and more people with a smaller agricultural workforce. As population increased, more people moved to the cities, where they found themselves caught up in innovative urban customs such as attending musical concerts and reading novels. Along with a general increase in literacy, these activities helped create a new public sphere ready to respond to new styles and new ideas. Social and cultural changes were not uniform across Europe, however; as usual, people's experiences varied depending on whether they lived in wealth or poverty, in urban or rural areas, or in eastern or western Europe.

The Agricultural Revolution

Although Britain, France, and the Dutch Republic shared the enthusiasm for consumer goods, Britain's domestic market grew most quickly. In Britain, as agricultural output increased 43 percent over the course of the 1700s, the population increased by 70 percent. The British imported grain to feed the growing population, but they also benefited from the development of techniques that together constituted an

agricultural revolution. No new machinery propelled this revolution—just more aggressive attitudes toward investment and management. The Dutch and Flemish had pioneered many of these techniques in the 1600s, but the British took them further.

Four major changes occurred in British agriculture that eventually spread to other countries. First, farmers increased the amount of land under cultivation by draining wetlands and by growing crops on previously uncultivated common lands (acreage maintained by the community for grazing). Second, farmers who could afford to do so consolidated smaller, scattered plots into larger, more efficient units. Third, livestock raising became more closely linked to crop growing, and the yields of each increased. (See "Taking Measure.") For centuries, most farmers had rotated their fields in and out of production to replenish the soil. Now farmers planted carefully chosen fodder crops such as clover and turnips that added nutrients to the soil, thereby eliminating the need to leave a field fallow (unplanted) every two or three years. With more fodder available, farmers could raise more livestock, which in turn produced more manure to fertilize grain fields. Fourth, selective breeding of animals combined with the increase in fodder to improve the quality and size of herds. New crops had only a slight impact. Potatoes, for example, were introduced

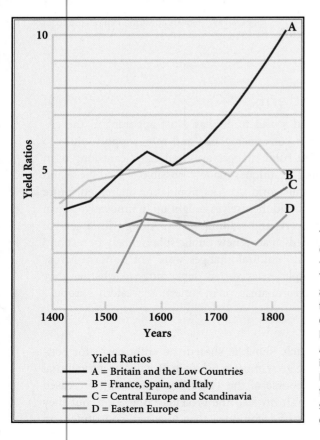

Yield Ratios
- A = Britain and the Low Countries
- B = France, Spain, and Italy
- C = Central Europe and Scandinavia
- D = Eastern Europe

Taking Measure Relationship of Crop Harvested to Seed Used, 1400–1800

The impact and even the timing of the agricultural revolution can be seen in this figure, based on yield ratios (the number of grains produced for each seed planted). Britain, the Dutch Republic, and the Austrian Netherlands all experienced huge increases in crop yields after 1700. Other European regions lagged behind right into the 1800s. What are the economic and social consequences of having a higher crop yield?

to Europe from South America in the 1500s, but because people feared they might cause leprosy, tuberculosis, or fevers, they were not grown in quantity until the late 1700s. By the 1730s and 1740s, agricultural output had increased dramatically, and prices for food had fallen because of these interconnected innovations.

Changes in agricultural practices did not benefit all landowners equally. The biggest British landowners consolidated their holdings in the "enclosure movement." They put pressure on small farmers and villagers to sell their land or give up their common lands. The big landlords then fenced off ("enclosed") their property. Because enclosure eliminated community grazing rights, it frequently sparked a struggle between the big landlords and villagers, and in Britain it normally required an act of Parliament. Such acts became increasingly common in the second half of the eighteenth century, and by the century's end six million acres of common lands had been enclosed and developed. "Improvers" produced more food more efficiently and thus supported a growing population.

Contrary to the fears of contemporaries, small farmers and cottagers (those with little or no property) were not forced off the land all at once. But most villagers could not afford the litigation involved in resisting enclosure, and small landholders consequently had to sell out to landlords or farmers with larger plots. Landlords with large holdings leased their estates to tenant farmers at constantly increasing rents, and tenant farmers in turn employed cottagers as salaried agricultural workers. In this way the English peasantry largely disappeared, replaced by a more hierarchical society of big landlords, enterprising tenant farmers, and poor agricultural laborers.

The new agricultural techniques spread slowly from Britain and the Low Countries (the Dutch Republic and the Austrian Netherlands) to the rest of western Europe. Outside a few pockets in northern France and the western German states, however, subsistence agriculture (producing just enough to get by rather than surpluses for the market) continued to dominate farming in western Europe and Scandinavia. In southwestern Germany, for example, 80 percent of the peasants produced no surplus because their plots were too small. Unlike the populations of the highly urbanized Low Countries (where half the people lived in towns and cities), most Europeans, western and eastern, eked out an existence in the countryside.

In eastern Europe, the condition of peasants worsened in the areas where landlords tried hardest to improve their yields. To produce more for the Baltic grain market, aristocratic landholders in Prussia, Poland, and parts of Russia drained wetlands, cultivated moors, and built dikes. They also forced peasants off lands the peasants worked for themselves, increased compulsory labor services (the critical element in serfdom), and began to manage their estates directly. Some eastern landowners grew fabulously wealthy. The Potocki family in the Polish Ukraine, for example, owned three million acres of land and had 130,000 serfs. In parts of Poland and Russia, the serfs hardly differed from slaves in status, and their "masters" ran their huge estates much like American plantations.

Social Life in the Cities

Because of emigration from the countryside, cities grew in population and consequently exercised more influence on culture and social life. Between 1650 and 1750, cities with at least 10,000 inhabitants increased in population by 44 percent. From the eighteenth century onward, urban growth would be continuous. Along with the general growth of cities, an important south-to-north shift occurred in the pattern of urbanization. Around 1500, half of the people in cities of at least 10,000 residents could be found in the Italian states, Spain, or Portugal; by 1700, the urbanization of northwestern and southern Europe was roughly equal. Eastern Europe, despite the huge cities of Istanbul and Moscow, was still less urban than western Europe. London was by far the most populous European city, with 675,000 inhabitants in 1750; Berlin had 90,000 people, Warsaw only 23,000.

Many landowners kept a residence in town, so the separation between rural and city life was not as extreme as might be imagined, at least not for the very rich. At the top of the ladder in the big cities were the landed nobles. Some of them filled their lives only with conspicuous consumption of fine food, extravagant clothing, coaches, books, and opera; others held key political, administrative, or judicial offices. However they spent their time, these rich families employed thousands of artisans, shopkeepers, and domestic servants. Many English peers (the highest-ranking nobles) had thirty or forty servants at each of their homes.

The middle classes of officials, merchants, professionals, and landowners occupied the next rung down on the social ladder. London's population, for example, included about twenty thousand middle-class families (constituting, at most, one-sixth of the city's population). In this period, the middle classes began to develop distinctive ways of life that set them apart from both the rich noble landowners and the lower classes. Unlike the rich nobles, the middle classes lived primarily in the cities and towns, even if they owned small country estates. They ate more moderately than nobles but much better than peasants or laborers. For breakfast, the British middle classes ate toast and rolls and, after 1700, drank tea. Dinner, served midday, consisted of roasted or boiled beef, mutton, poultry, or pork, and vegetables. Supper was a light meal of bread and cheese with cake or pie. Beer was the main drink in London, and many families brewed their own. Even children drank beer because of the lack of fresh water.

In contrast to the gigantic and sprawling countryseats of the richest English peers, middle-class houses in town had about seven rooms, including four or five bedrooms and one or two living rooms, still many more than the homes of poor agricultural workers. New household items reflected society's increasing wealth and its exposure to colonial imports. By 1700, the middle classes of London typically had several mirrors, a coffeepot and coffee mill, numerous pictures and ornaments, a china collection, and several clocks. Life for the middle classes on the European continent was quite similar, though wine replaced beer in France.

Below the middle classes came the artisans and shopkeepers (most of whom were organized in professional guilds), then the journeymen, apprentices, servants, and laborers. At the bottom of the social scale were the unemployed poor, who survived on intermittent work and charity. Women married to artisans and shopkeepers often kept the accounts, supervised employees, and ran the household. Every home from the middle classes to the upper classes employed servants; artisans and shop-keepers frequently hired them, too. Women from poorer families usually worked as domestic servants until they married. Four out of five domestic servants in the city were female. In large cities such as London, the servant population grew faster than the population of the city as a whole.

Social status in the cities was readily visible. Wide, spacious streets graced rich districts; the houses had gardens, and the air was relatively fresh. In poor districts, the streets were narrow, dirty, dark, humid, and smelly, and the houses were damp and crowded. The poorest people were homeless, sleeping under bridges or in abandoned homes. A Neapolitan prince described his homeless neighbors as "lying like filthy animals, with no distinction of age or sex." In some districts, rich and poor lived in the same buildings; the poor clambered up to shabby, cramped apartments on the top floors.

Like shelter, clothing was a reliable social indicator. The poorest workingwomen in Paris wore woolen skirts and blouses of dark colors over petticoats, bodice, and corset. They also donned caps of various sorts, cotton stockings, and shoes (probably their only pair). Workingmen dressed even more drably. Many occupations could be recognized by their dress: no one could confuse lawyers in their dark robes with masons or butchers in their special aprons, for example. People higher on

Vauxhall Gardens, London
This hand-colored print from the mid-1700s shows the newly refurbished gardens near the Thames River. Prosperous families show off their brightly colored clothes and listen to a public concert by the orchestra seated just above them. These activities helped form a more self-conscious public.
(© Bibliothèque des Arts Décoratifs, Paris, France/The Bridgeman Art Library.)

the social ladder were more likely to sport a variety of fabrics, colors, and unusual designs in their clothing and to own many different outfits. Social status was not an abstract idea; it permeated every detail of daily life.

Public Hygiene and Health Care

The growth of cities created new challenges for public hygiene. Cities were notoriously unhealthy because excrement (animal and human) and garbage accumulated where people lived densely packed together. Paris seemed to a visitor "so detestable that it is impossible to remain there" because of the smell. Even the facade of the Louvre palace was soiled by the contents of night commodes that servants routinely dumped out of windows every morning. Only the wealthy could escape walking in mucky streets, by hiring men to carry them in sedan chairs or drive them in coaches.

After investigating specific cities, medical geographers urged government campaigns to improve public sanitation. Everywhere, environmentalists gathered and analyzed data on climate, disease, and population, searching for correlations to help direct policy. As a result of these efforts, local governments undertook such measures as draining low-lying areas, burying refuse, and cleaning wells, all of which eventually helped lower the death rates from epidemic diseases.

Hospitals and medical care underwent lasting transformations. Founded originally as charities concerned foremost with the moral worthiness of the poor, hospitals gradually evolved into medical institutions that defined patients by their diseases. The process of diagnosis changed as physicians began to use specialized Latin terms for illnesses. The gap between medical experts and their patients increased, as physicians now also relied on postmortem dissections in the hospital to gain better knowledge, a practice most patients' families resented. Press reports of body snatching and grave robbing by surgeons and their apprentices outraged the public well into the 1800s.

Despite the change in hospitals, individual health care remained something of a free-for-all in which physicians competed with bloodletters, itinerant venereal disease doctors, bonesetters, druggists, midwives, and "cunning women," who specialized in home remedies. The medical profession, with nationwide organizations and licensing, had not yet emerged, and no clear line separated trained physicians from quacks. Physicians often followed popular prescriptions for illnesses because they had nothing better to offer. Patients were as likely to die of diseases caught in the hospital as to be cured there. Antiseptics were nearly unknown.

The various "medical opinions" about childbirth highlight the confusion people faced. Midwives delivered most babies, though they sometimes encountered criticism even from within their own ranks. One consulting midwife complained that ordinary midwives in Bristol, England, made women in labor drink a mixture of leek juice and their husbands' urine. By the 1730s, female midwives faced competition from male midwives, who were known for using instruments such as forceps to pull babies out of the birth canal. Women rarely sought a physician's help in giving birth, however; they preferred the advice and assistance of trusted local midwives. In any case, trained physicians were few in number and almost nonexistent outside cities.

Hardly any infectious diseases could be cured, though inoculation against smallpox spread from the Middle East to Europe in the early eighteenth century, thanks largely to the efforts of Lady Mary Wortley Montagu, who learned about the technique while living in Constantinople. After 1750, physicians developed successful procedures for wide-scale vaccination, although even then many people resisted the idea of inoculating themselves with a disease. Other diseases spread quickly in the unsanitary conditions of urban life. Ordinary people washed or changed clothes rarely, lived in overcrowded housing with poor ventilation, and got their water from contaminated sources, such as refuse-filled rivers.

Until the mid-1700s, most people considered bathing dangerous. Public bathhouses had disappeared from cities in the sixteenth and seventeenth centuries because they seemed a source of disorderly behavior and epidemic illness. In the eighteenth century, even private bathing came into disfavor because people feared the effects of contact with water. Fewer than one in ten newly built private mansions in Paris had baths. Bathing was hazardous, physicians insisted, because it opened the body to disease. One manners manual of 1736 admonished, "It is correct to clean the face every morning by using a white cloth to cleanse it. It is less good to wash with water, because it renders the face susceptible to cold in winter and sun in summer." The upper classes associated cleanliness not with baths but with frequently changed linens, powdered hair, and perfume, which was thought to strengthen the body and refresh the brain by counteracting corrupt and foul air.

The New Public Sphere

Cities may have been unhealthy, but they promoted the development of a new public sphere that rested in the first instance on the spread of literacy. City people were more literate than peasants. Protestant countries appear to have been more successful at promoting education and literacy than Catholic countries, perhaps because of the Protestant emphasis on Bible reading. Widespread popular literacy was first achieved in the Protestant areas of Switzerland and in Presbyterian Scotland, and rates were also very high in the New England colonies and the Scandinavian countries. In France, literacy doubled in the eighteenth century thanks to the spread of parish schools, but still only one in two men and one in four women could read and write. Despite the efforts of some Protestant German states to encourage primary education, primary schooling remained woefully inadequate almost everywhere in Europe: few schools existed, teachers received low wages, and no country had yet established a national system of control or supervision.

Despite the deficiencies of primary education, a new literate public arose, especially among the middle classes of the cities. More books and periodicals were published than ever before. England and the Dutch Republic led the way in this powerful outpouring of printed words. The trend began in the 1690s and gradually accelerated. In 1695, the English government allowed the licensing system through which it controlled publications to lapse, and new newspapers and magazines appeared almost immediately. The first London daily newspaper came out in 1702, and in

1709 Joseph Addison and Richard Steele published the first literary magazine, the *Spectator*. They devoted their magazine to the cultural improvement of the increasingly influential middle class. By the 1720s, twenty-four provincial newspapers were published in England. In the London coffeehouses, an edition of a single newspaper might reach ten thousand male readers. Women did their reading at home.

Newspapers on the continent lagged behind and often consisted mainly of advertising with little critical commentary. France, for example, had no daily paper until 1777. The new literate public did not just read newspapers; its members now pursued an interest in painting, attended concerts, and besieged booksellers in search of popular novels. Because increased trade and prosperity put money into the hands of the growing middle classes, the new public sphere began to compete with the churches, rulers, and courtiers as chief patrons of new work. As the public for the arts expanded, printed commentary on them emerged, setting the stage for the appearance of political and social criticism. New artistic tastes thus had effects far beyond the realm of the arts.

Developments in painting reflected the tastes of the new public. The **rococo** style challenged the hold of the baroque and classical schools, especially in France. Like the baroque, the rococo emphasized irregularity and asymmetry, movement and curvature, but it did so on a much smaller, subtler scale. Many rococo paintings depicted scenes of intimate sensuality rather than the monumental, emotional grandeur favored by classical and baroque painters. Personal portraits and pastoral paintings took the place of heroic landscapes and large ceremonial canvases. Rococo

Rococo Painting

This painting by the Venetian artist Rosalba Carriera (1675–1757) is titled *Africa*. The young black girl wearing a turban represents the African continent. Carriera was known for her use of pastels. In 1720, she journeyed to Paris, where she became an associate of Antoine Watteau and helped inaugurate the rococo style in painting. Why might the artist have chosen to paint an African girl? **For more help analyzing this image, see the visual activity for this chapter in the Online Study Guide at** bedfordstmartins.com/huntconcise. (Gemäldegalerie Alte Meister, Staatliche Kunstsammlungen Dresden.)

paintings adorned homes as well as palaces and served as a form of interior decoration rather than as a statement of piety. Its decorative quality made rococo art
an ideal complement to newly discovered materials such as stucco and porcelain,
especially the porcelain vases now imported from China.

Rococo was an invented word (from the French word rocaille, meaning "shell-
work") and originally a derogatory label meaning "frivolous decoration." But the
great French rococo painters, such as Antoine Watteau (1684–1721) and François
Boucher (1703–1770), were much more than mere decorators. Although both
emphasized the erotic in their depictions, Watteau captured the melancholy side of
a passing aristocratic style of life, and Boucher painted middle-class people at home
during their daily activities. Both painters thereby contributed to the emergence of
new sensibilities in art that increasingly attracted a middle-class public.

Music as well as art grew in popularity. The first public music concerts were
performed in England in the 1670s, becoming much more regular and frequent
in the 1690s. City concert halls typically seated about two hundred, but the relatively high price of tickets limited attendance to the better-off. Music clubs provided
entertainment in smaller towns and villages. In continental Europe, Frankfurt organized the first regular public concerts in 1712; Hamburg and Paris began holding
them within a few years. Opera continued to spread in the eighteenth century;
Venice had sixteen public opera houses by 1700, and Covent Garden opera house
opened in London in 1732.

The growth of a public that appreciated and supported music had much the
same effect as the extension of the reading public: like authors, composers could now
begin to liberate themselves from court patronage and work for a paying audience.
This development took time to solidify, however, and court or church patrons still
commissioned much eighteenth-century music. Bach, a German Lutheran, wrote
his St. Matthew Passion for Good Friday services in 1729 while he was organist and
choirmaster for the leading church in Leipzig. He composed secular works (like
the "Coffee Cantata" quoted at the beginning of this chapter) for the public and a
variety of private patrons.

The composer George Frederick Handel (1685–1759) was among the first to
grasp the new directions in music. He began his career playing second violin in
the Hamburg opera orchestra and then moved to Britain in 1710, where he eventually turned to composing oratorios, a form he introduced in Britain. The oratorio
combined the drama of opera with the majesty of religious and ceremonial music
and featured the chorus over the soloists. Handel's most famous oratorio, Messiah
(1741), reflects his personal, deeply felt piety but also his willingness to combine
musical materials into a dramatic form that captured the enthusiasm of the new
public. In 1740, a poem published in the Gentleman's Magazine exulted, "His art so
modulates the sounds in all, / Our passions, as he pleases, rise and fall." Music had
become an integral part of the new public sphere.

But nothing captured the imagination of the new public more than the novel,
the literary genre whose very name underscored the eighteenth-century taste for

novelty. Over three hundred French novels appeared between 1700 and 1730. During this unprecedented explosion, the novel took on its modern form and became more concerned with individual psychology and social description than with the picaresque adventures popular earlier (such as Cervantes's *Don Quixote*). The novel's popularity was closely tied to the expansion of the reading public, and novels were available in serial form in periodicals or from the many booksellers who popped up to serve the new market.

Women figured prominently in novels as characters, and women writers abounded. The English novel *Love in Excess* (1719) quickly reached a sixth printing, and its author, Eliza Haywood (1693?–1756), earned her living turning out a stream of novels with titles such as *Persecuted Virtue, Constancy Rewarded,* and *The History of Miss Betsy Thoughtless*—all showing a concern for the proper place of women as models of virtue in a changing world. Haywood had first worked as an actress when her husband deserted her and her two children, but she soon turned to writing plays and novels. In the 1740s, she began publishing a magazine, the *Female Spectator,* which argued in favor of higher education for women.

Haywood's male counterpart was Daniel Defoe (1660?–1731), a merchant's son who had a diverse and colorful career as a manufacturer, political spy, novelist, and social commentator. Defoe's novel about a shipwrecked sailor, *Robinson Crusoe* (1719), portrayed the new values of the time: to survive, Crusoe had to meet every challenge with fearless entrepreneurial ingenuity. He had to be ready for the unexpected and be able to improvise in every situation. He was, in short, the model for the new man in an expanding economy. Crusoe's patronizing attitude toward the black man Friday now draws much critical attention, but his discovery of Friday shows how the fate of blacks and whites had become intertwined in the new colonial environment.

Religious Revivals

Despite the novel's growing popularity, religious books and pamphlets still sold in huge numbers, and most Europeans remained devout, even as their religions were changing. In this period, a Protestant revival known as **Pietism** rocked the complacency of the established churches in the German Lutheran states, the Dutch Republic, and Scandinavia. Pietists believed in a mystical religion of the heart; they wanted a more deeply emotional, even ecstatic religion. They urged intense Bible study, which in turn promoted popular education and contributed to the increase in literacy. Many Pietists attended catechism instruction every day and also went to morning and evening prayer meetings in addition to regular Sunday services.

Catholicism also had its versions of religious revival. A Frenchwoman, Jeanne Marie Guyon (1648–1717), attracted many noblewomen and a few leading clergymen to her own Catholic brand of Pietism, known as Quietism. Claiming miraculous visions and astounding prophecies, she urged a mystical union with God through prayer and simple devotion. Despite papal condemnation and intense controversy within Catholic circles in France, Guyon had followers all over Europe.

Even more influential were the Jansenists, who gained many new adherents to their austere form of Catholicism despite Louis XIV's harassment and repeated condemnation by the papacy (see page 486). Under the pressure of religious and political persecution, Jansenism took a revivalist turn in the 1720s. At the funeral of a Jansenist priest in Paris in 1727, the crowd that flocked to the grave claimed to witness a series of miraculous healings. Within a few years, a cult formed around the priest's tomb, and clandestine Jansenist presses reported new miracles to the reading public. When the French government tried to suppress the cult, one enraged wit placed a sign at the tomb that read, "By order of the king, God is forbidden to work miracles here." Some believers fell into frenzied convulsions, claiming to be inspired by the Holy Spirit through the intercession of the dead priest. After midcentury, Jansenism became even more politically active as its adherents joined in opposition to crown policies on religion.

> **REVIEW** What were the social and political consequences of the agricultural revolution?

Consolidation of the European State System

The spread of Pietism and Jansenism reflected the emergence of a middle-class public that now participated in every new development, including religion. The middle classes could pursue these interests because the European state system gradually stabilized. Warfare settled three main issues between 1690 and 1740: a coalition of powers held Louis XIV's France in check on the continent; Great Britain emerged from the wars against Louis as the preeminent maritime power; and Russia defeated Sweden in the contest for supremacy in the Baltic. After Louis XIV's death in 1715, Europe enjoyed the fruits of a more balanced diplomatic system, in which warfare became less frequent and less widespread. States could then spend their resources establishing and expanding control over their own populations, both at home and in their colonies.

French Ambitions Thwarted

Lying on his deathbed in 1715, the seventy-six-year-old Louis XIV watched helplessly as his accomplishments continued to unravel. Not only had his plans for territorial expansion been thwarted, but his incessant wars had exhausted the treasury, despite new taxes. In 1689, Louis's rival, William III, prince of Orange and king of England and Scotland (r. 1689–1702), had set out to forge a European alliance that eventually included Britain, the Dutch Republic, Sweden, Austria, and Spain. The allies fought Louis to a stalemate in the War of the League of Augsburg, sometimes called the Nine Years' War (1689–1697), and when hostilities resumed four years later, they finally put an end to Louis's expansionist ambitions.

The War of the Spanish Succession (1701–1713) broke out when the mentally and physically feeble Charles II (r. 1665–1700) of Spain died without a direct heir. The Spanish succession could not help but be a burning issue. Even though Spanish power had declined steadily since Spain's golden age in the sixteenth century, Spain still had extensive territories in Italy and the Netherlands and colonies overseas. Before Charles died, he named Louis XIV's second grandson, Philip, duke of Anjou, as his heir, but the Austrian emperor Leopold I refused to accept Charles's deathbed will. In the ensuing war, the French lost several major battles and had to accept disadvantageous terms in the Peace of Utrecht of 1713–1714 (Map 14.2). Although Philip was recognized as king of Spain, he had to renounce any future claim to the French crown, thus barring unification of the two kingdoms. Spain surrendered its territories in Italy and the Netherlands to the Austrians and Gibraltar to the British; France ceded possessions in North America (Newfoundland, the Hudson Bay area, and most of Nova Scotia) to Britain. France no longer threatened to dominate European power politics.

At home, Louis's policy of absolutism had fomented bitter hostility. Nobles fiercely resented his promotions of commoners to high office. The duke of Saint-Simon complained that "falseness, servility, admiring glances, combined with a dependent and cringing attitude, above all, an appearance of being nothing without him, were the only ways of pleasing him." On his deathbed, Louis XIV gave his blessing and some sound advice to his five-year-old great-grandson and successor, Louis XV (r. 1715–1774): "My child, you are about to become a great King. Do not imitate my love of building nor my liking for war."

After being named regent, the duke of Orléans (1674–1723), nephew of the dead king, revived some of the parlements' powers and tried to give leading nobles a greater say in political affairs. Financial problems plagued the regency as they would beset all succeeding French regimes in the eighteenth century. In 1719, the regent appointed the Scottish financier John Law to the top financial position of controller general. Law founded a trading company for North America and a state bank that issued paper money and stock (without them, trade depended on the available supply of gold and silver). The bank was supposed to offer lower interest rates to the state, thus cutting the cost of financing the government's debts. The value of the stock rose rapidly in a frenzy of speculation, only to crash a few months later. With it vanished any hope of establishing a state bank or issuing paper money for nearly a century.

France finally achieved a measure of financial stability under the leadership of Cardinal Hercule de Fleury (1653–1743), the most powerful member of the government after the death of the regent. Fleury aimed to avoid adventure abroad and keep social peace at home; he balanced the budget and carried out a large project for road and canal construction. Colonial trade boomed. Peace and the acceptance of limits on territorial expansion inaugurated a century of French prosperity.

British Rise and Dutch Decline

The English and Dutch had formed a coalition against Louis XIV under their joint ruler, William III, who was simultaneously stadholder of the Dutch Republic and, with his English wife, Mary (d. 1694), ruler of England, Wales, Scotland, and Ireland. After William's death in 1702, the English and Dutch went their separate ways. Dutch imperial power declined, even though Dutch merchants still controlled a substantial

Map 14.2 Europe, c. 1715
Although Louis XIV succeeded in putting his grandson Philip on the Spanish throne, France emerged from the War of the Spanish Succession considerably weakened. France ceded large territories in Canada to Britain, which also gained key Mediterranean outposts from Spain as well as a monopoly on providing slaves to the Spanish colonies. Spanish losses were catastrophic: Philip had to renounce any future claim to the French crown and give up considerable territory in the Netherlands and Italy to the Austrians.

portion of world trade. English relations with Scotland and Ireland were complicated by the problem of succession: William and Mary had no children. To ensure a Protestant succession, Parliament ruled that Mary's sister, Anne, would succeed William and Mary and that the Protestant house of Hanover in Germany would succeed Anne if she had no surviving heirs. Catholics were excluded. When Queen Anne (r. 1702–1714) died leaving no children, the elector of Hanover, a Protestant great-grandson of James I, consequently became King George I (r. 1714–1727). The house of Hanover—renamed the house of Windsor during World War I in response to anti-German sentiment—still occupies the British throne.

Support from the Scots and Irish for this solution did not come easily because many in Scotland and Ireland supported the claims to the throne of the deposed Catholic king, James II, and, after his death in 1701, his son James Edward. Out of fear of this Jacobitism (from the Latin *Jacobus,* "James"), Scottish Protestant leaders agreed to the Act of Union of 1707, which abolished the Scottish Parliament and affirmed the Scots' recognition of the Protestant Hanoverian succession. The Scots agreed to obey the Parliament of Great Britain, which would include Scottish members in the House of Commons and the House of Lords. A Jacobite rebellion in Scotland in 1715, aiming to restore the Stuart line, was suppressed (Map 14.2, page 543). The threat of Jacobitism nonetheless continued into the 1740s.

The Irish, 90 percent of whom were Catholic, proved even more difficult to subdue. When James II went to Ireland in 1689 to raise a Catholic rebellion against the new monarchs of England, William III responded by taking command of the joint English and Dutch forces and defeating James's Irish supporters. James fled to France, and the Catholics in Ireland faced yet more confiscation and legal restrictions. By 1700, Irish Catholics, who in 1640 had owned 60 percent of the land in Ireland, owned just 14 percent. The Protestant-controlled Irish Parliament passed a series of laws limiting the rights of the Catholic majority: Catholics could not bear arms, send their children abroad for education, establish Catholic schools at home, or marry Protestants. Catholics could not sit in Parliament, nor could they vote for its members unless they took an oath renouncing Catholic doctrine. These and a host of other laws reduced Catholic Ireland to the status of a colony. One British official commented in 1745, "The poor people of Ireland are used worse than negroes." Most of the Irish were peasants who lived in primitive housing and subsisted on a meager diet that included no meat.

The Parliament of Great Britain was soon dominated by the Whigs. In Britain's constitutional system, the monarch ruled with Parliament. The crown chose the ministers, directed policy, and supervised administration, while Parliament raised revenue, passed laws, and represented the interests of the people to the crown. The powers of Parliament were reaffirmed by the Triennial Act of 1694, which provided that Parliament must meet at least once every three years (this was extended to seven years in 1716, after the Whigs had established their ascendancy). Only 200,000 propertied men could vote, out of a population of more than five million people, and not surprisingly, most members of Parliament came from the landed gentry. In fact, a few hundred families controlled all the important political offices.

George I and George II (r. 1727–1760) relied on one man, Sir Robert Walpole (1676–1745), to help them manage their relations with Parliament. From his position as first lord of the treasury, Walpole made himself into first, or "prime," minister, leading the House of Commons from 1721 to 1742. Although appointed initially by the king, Walpole established an enduring pattern of parliamentary government in which a prime minister from the leading party guides legislation through the House of Commons. Walpole also built a vast patronage machine that dispensed government jobs to win support for the crown's policies. Walpole's successors relied more and more on the patronage system and eventually alienated not only the Tories but also the middle classes in London and even the North American colonists.

The partisan division between the Whigs, who had supported the Hanoverian succession and the rights of dissenting Protestants, and the Tories, who had backed the Stuart line and the Anglican church, did not hamper Great Britain's pursuit of economic, military, and colonial power. In this period, Britain became a great power on the world stage by virtue of its navy and its ability to finance major military involvement in the wars against Louis XIV. The founding in 1694 of the Bank of England—which, unlike the French bank, endured—enabled the government to raise money at low interest for foreign wars. By the 1740s, the government could borrow more than four times what it could in the 1690s.

Sir Robert Walpole at a Cabinet Meeting
Sir Robert Walpole and George II developed the institution of the cabinet, which brought together the important heads of government departments. Walpole's cabinet was the ancestor of modern cabinets in Great Britain and the United States. How might discussions in the new coffeehouses (shown in the illustration on page 520) have influenced the kinds of decisions made by Walpole and his cabinet? (The Fotomas Index, U.K./The Bridgeman Art Library.)

By contrast, the Dutch Republic, one of the richest and most influential states of the seventeenth century, saw its power eclipsed in the eighteenth. When William of Orange (William III of England) died in 1702, he left no heirs, and for forty-five years the Dutch lived without a stadholder. The merchant ruling class of some two thousand families dominated the Dutch Republic more than ever, but they presided over a country that counted for less in international power politics. In some areas, Dutch decline was only relative. The Dutch population was not growing as fast as populations elsewhere, for example, and the Dutch share of the Baltic trade decreased from 50 percent in 1720 to less than 30 percent by the 1770s. After 1720, the Baltic countries—Prussia, Russia, Denmark, and Sweden—began to ban imports of manufactured goods to protect their own industries, and Dutch trade in particular suffered. The output of Leiden textiles dropped to one-third its 1700 level by 1740. Shipbuilding, paper manufacturing, tobacco processing, salt refining, and pottery production all dwindled as well. The biggest exception to the downward trend was trade with the New World, which increased with escalating demands for sugar and tobacco. The Dutch shifted their interest away from great-power rivalries toward those areas of international trade and finance where they could establish an enduring presence.

Russia's Emergence as a European Power

The commerce and shipbuilding of the Dutch and English so impressed the Russian tsar Peter I (r. 1689–1725) that he traveled incognito to their shipyards in 1697 to learn their methods firsthand. Known to history as Peter the Great, he dragged Russia kicking and screaming all the way to great-power status. Although he came to the throne while still a minor (on the eve of his tenth birthday), grew up under the threat of a palace coup, and enjoyed little formal education, his accomplishments soon matched his seven-foot-tall stature. Peter transformed public life in Russia and established an absolutist state on the Western model. His **Westernization** efforts ignited an enduring controversy: did Peter set Russia on a course of inevitable Westernization required to compete with the West, or did he forever and fatally disrupt Russia's natural evolution into a distinctive Slavic society?

Peter reorganized government and finance on Western models and, like other absolute rulers, strengthened his army. With ruthless recruiting methods, which included branding a cross on every recruit's left hand to prevent desertion, he forged an army of 200,000 men and equipped it with modern weapons. He created schools for artillery, engineering, and military medicine and built the first navy in Russian history. Not surprisingly, taxes tripled.

The tsar allowed nothing to stand in his way. He did not hesitate to use torture and executed thousands. He allowed a special regiment of guards unprecedented power to expedite cases against those suspected of rebellion, espionage, pretensions to the throne, or just "unseemly utterances against him." Opposition to his policies reached into his own family. When his only son, Alexei, allied himself with Peter's critics, the young man was thrown into prison, where he mysteriously died.

Peter the Great
In this painting by Gottfried Danhauer (1680–1733/7), the Russian tsar appears against the backdrop of his most famous battle, Poltava. The angel holds a laurel wreath, a symbol of victory, over his head. (© Tretyakov Gallery, Moscow, Russia/The Bridgeman Art Library.)

To control the often restive nobility, Peter insisted that all noblemen engage in state service. The Table of Ranks (1722) classified them into military, administrative, and court categories, a codification of social and legal relationships in Russia that would last for nearly two centuries. All social and material advantages now depended on serving the crown. Because the nobles lacked a secure independent status, Peter could command them to a degree that was unimaginable in western Europe. State service was not only compulsory but also permanent. Moreover, the male children of those in service had to be registered by the age of ten and begin serving at fifteen. To increase his authority over the Russian Orthodox church, Peter allowed the office of patriarch (supreme head) to remain vacant, and in 1721 he replaced it with the Holy Synod, a bureaucracy of laymen under his supervision. To many Russians, Peter was the Antichrist incarnate.

With the goal of Westernizing Russian culture, Peter set up the first greenhouses, laboratories, and technical schools and founded the Russian Academy of Sciences. He ordered translations of Western classics and hired a German theater company to perform the French plays of Molière. He replaced the traditional Russian calendar with the Western one,* introduced Arabic numerals, and in 1703 brought out the first public newspaper. He ordered his officials and the nobles to shave their beards and dress in Western fashion, and he even issued precise regulations about the suitable style of jacket, boots, and cap (generally French or German). He published a book on manners for young noblemen and experimented with dentistry on his courtiers.

Peter built a new capital city, named St. Petersburg after him. It symbolized Russia opening to the West. Construction began in 1703 in a Baltic province that had been recently conquered from Sweden. By the end of 1709, forty thousand recruits a year

---

*Peter introduced the Julian calendar, then still used in Protestant but not Catholic countries. Later in the eighteenth century, Protestant Europe abandoned the Julian for the Gregorian calendar. Not until 1918 was the Julian calendar abolished in Russia, at which point it had fallen thirteen days behind Europe's Gregorian calendar.

found themselves assigned to the projects there. Peter ordered skilled workers to move to the new city and commanded all landowners possessing more than forty serf households to build houses there. In the 1720s, a German minister described the city "as a wonder of the world, considering its magnificent palaces . . . and the short time that was employed in the building of it." By 1710, the permanent population of St. Petersburg reached eight thousand. At Peter's death in 1725, it had forty thousand residents.

As a new city far from the Russian heartland around Moscow, St. Petersburg represented a decisive break with Russia's past. Peter widened that gap by every means possible. At his new capital, he tried to improve the traditionally denigrated, secluded status of women by ordering them to dress in European styles and appear publicly at his dinners for diplomatic representatives. Imitating French manners, he decreed that women attend his new social salons of officials, officers, and merchants for conversation and dancing. A foreigner headed every one of Peter's new technical and vocational schools, and for its first eight years the new Academy of Sciences included no Russians. Every ministry was assigned a foreign adviser. Upper-class Russians learned French or German, which they often spoke even at home. Such changes affected only the very top of Russian society, however. The mass of the population had no contact with the new ideas and ended up paying for the innovations either in ruinous new taxation or by building St. Petersburg, a project that cost the lives of thousands of workers. Serfs remained tied to the land, completely dominated by their noble lords.

Despite all his achievements, Peter could not ensure his succession. In the thirty-seven years after his death in 1725, Russia endured six different rulers, including a boy of twelve, an infant, and an imbecile. Recurrent palace coups weakened the monarchy and enabled the nobility to loosen Peter's rigid code of state service. In the process, the status of the serfs only worsened. They ceased to be counted as legal subjects; the criminal code of 1754 listed them as property. They not only were bought and sold like cattle but also had become legally indistinguishable from them. Westernization had not yet touched their lives.

Changes in the Balance of Power in the East

Peter the Great's success in building up state power changed the balance of power in eastern Europe. Overcoming initial military setbacks, Russia eventually defeated Sweden and took its place as the leading power in the Baltic region. Russia could then turn its attention to eastern Europe, where it competed with Austria and Prussia. Formerly mighty Poland-Lithuania became the playground for great-power rivalries.

Sweden had dominated the Baltic region since the Thirty Years' War and did not easily give up its preeminence. In 1700, when Peter the Great formed an anti-Swedish coalition with Denmark, Saxony, and Poland, Sweden's Charles XII (r. 1697–1718) stood up to the test. Still in his teens at the beginning of the Great Northern War, Charles first defeated Denmark, then destroyed the new Russian army, and quickly marched into Poland and Saxony. After defeating the Poles and occupying Saxony, Charles invaded Russia. Here Peter's rebuilt army finally defeated him at the battle of Poltava (1709).

The Russian victory resounded everywhere. The Russian ambassador to Vienna reported, "It is commonly said that the tsar will be formidable to all Europe, that he will be a kind of northern Turk." Prussia and other German states joined the anti-Swedish alliance, and when Charles XII died in battle in 1718, the Great Northern War finally came to an end. By the terms of the Treaty of Nystad (1721), Sweden ceded its eastern Baltic provinces—Livonia, Estonia, Ingria, and southern Karelia—to Russia. Sweden also lost territories on the north German coast to Prussia and the other allied German states (Map 14.3). An aristocratic reaction against Charles XII's incessant demands for war supplies swept away Sweden's absolutist regime, essentially removing Sweden from great-power competition.

Prussia had to make the most of every military opportunity, as it did in the Great Northern War, because it was much smaller in size and population than Russia, Austria, or France. King Frederick William I (r. 1713–1740) doubled the size of the Prussian army; though much smaller than the armies of his rivals, it was the best trained and most up-to-date force in Europe. By 1740, Prussia had Europe's highest proportion of men at arms (1 of every 28 people, versus 1 in 157 in France and 1 in 64 in Russia) and the highest proportion of nobles in the military (1 in 7 noblemen, as compared with 1 in 33 in France and 1 in 50 in Russia).

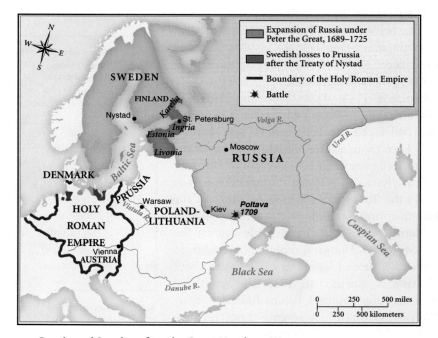

Map 14.3 Russia and Sweden after the Great Northern War, 1721
After the Great Northern War, Russia supplanted Sweden as the major power in the north. Although Russia had a much larger population from which to draw its armies, Sweden made the most of its advantages and gave way only after a great military struggle.

The army so dominated life in Prussia that the country earned the description "a large army with a small state attached." So obsessed was Frederick William with his soldiers that the five-foot-five-inch-tall king formed a regiment of "giants," the Grenadiers, composed exclusively of men over six feet tall. Royal agents scoured Europe trying to find such men and sometimes kidnapped them right off the street. Frederick William, "the Sergeant King," was one of the first rulers to wear a military uniform as his everyday dress. He subordinated the entire domestic administration to the army's needs. He also installed a system for recruiting soldiers by local district quotas. He financed the army growth by subjecting all the provinces to an excise tax on food, drink, and manufactured goods and by increasing rents on crown lands. Prussia was now poised to become one of the major players on the continent of Europe.

During the War of the Polish Succession (1733–1735), Prussia stood on the sidelines, content to watch the bigger powers fight each other. The war showed how the balance of power had changed since the heyday of Louis XIV: France had to maneuver within a complex great-power system that now included Russia, and Poland-Lithuania no longer controlled its own destiny. When the king of Poland-Lithuania died in 1733, France, Spain, and Sardinia went to war against Austria and Russia, each side supporting rival claimants to the Polish throne. After Russia drove the French candidate out of Poland-Lithuania, France agreed to accept the Austrian candidate. In exchange, Austria gave the province of Lorraine to the French candidate, the father-in-law of Louis XV, with the promise that the province would pass to France on his death. France and Britain went back to pursuing their colonial rivalries. Prussia and Russia concentrated on shoring up their influence within Poland-Lithuania.

Austria did not want to become mired in a long struggle in Poland-Lithuania because its armies still faced the Turks on its southeastern border. Even though the Austrians had forced the Turks to recognize their rule over all of Hungary and Transylvania in 1699 and occupied Belgrade in 1717, the Turks did not stop fighting. In the 1730s, the Turks retook Belgrade, and Russia now claimed a role in the struggle against the Turks. Moreover, Hungary, though liberated from Turkish rule, proved less than enthusiastic about submitting to Austria. In 1703, the wealthiest Hungarian noble landlord, Ferenc Rákóczi (1676–1735), raised an army of seventy thousand men who fought for "God, Fatherland, and Liberty"

Austrian Conquest of Hungary, 1657–1730

until 1711. They forced the Austrians to recognize local Hungarian institutions, grant amnesty, and restore confiscated estates in exchange for confirming hereditary Austrian rule.

The Power of Diplomacy and the Importance of Numbers

No single power emerged from the wars of the first half of the eighteenth century clearly superior to the others, and the idea of maintaining a balance of power guided both military and diplomatic maneuvering. The Peace of Utrecht had explicitly declared that such a balance was crucial to maintaining peace in Europe, and in 1720 a British pamphleteer wrote, "There is not, I believe, any doctrine in the law of nations, of more certain truth . . . than this of the balance of power." It was the universal law of gravitation of European politics. This system of equilibrium often rested on military force, such as the leagues formed against Louis XIV or the coalition against Sweden. All states counted on diplomacy, however, to resolve issues even after fighting had begun.

To meet the new demands placed on it, the diplomatic service, like the military and financial bureaucracies before it, had to develop regular procedures. The French set a pattern of diplomatic service that the other European states soon imitated. By 1685, France had embassies in all the important capitals. Nobles of ancient families served as ambassadors to Rome, Madrid, Vienna, and London, whereas royal officials were chosen for Switzerland, the Dutch Republic, and Venice. Most held their appointments for at least three or four years, and all went off with elaborate written instructions that included explicit statements of policy as well as full accounts of the political conditions of the country to which they were posted. The ambassador selected and paid for his own staff. This practice could make the journey to a new post very cumbersome, because the staff might be as large as eighty people, and they brought along all their own furniture, pictures, silverware, and tapestries. It took one French ambassador ten weeks to get from Paris to Stockholm.

By the early 1700s, French writings on diplomatic methods were read everywhere. François de Callières's manual *On the Manner of Negotiating with Sovereigns* (1716) insisted that sound diplomacy was based on the creation of confidence, rather than deception: "The secret of negotiation is to harmonize the real interests of the parties concerned." Callières believed that the diplomatic service had to be professional— that young attachés should be chosen for their skills, not their family connections. These sensible views did not prevent the development of a dual system of diplomacy, in which rulers issued secret instructions that often negated the official ones sent by their own foreign offices. Secret diplomacy had some advantages because it allowed rulers to break with past alliances, but it also led to confusion and, sometimes, scandal, for the rulers often employed unreliable adventurers as their confidential agents. Still, the diplomatic system in the early eighteenth century proved successful enough to ensure a continuation of the principles of the Peace of Westphalia (1648): in the midst of every crisis and war, the great powers would convene and hammer out a written agreement detailing the requirements for peace.

Adroit diplomacy could smooth the road toward peace, but success in war still depended on sheer numbers—of men and muskets. Because each state's strength depended largely on the size of its army, the growth and health of the population increasingly entered into government calculations. The publication in 1690 of the

Englishman William Petty's *Political Arithmetick* quickened the interest of government officials everywhere. Petty offered statistical estimates of human capital—that is, of population and wages—to determine England's national wealth. In 1727, Frederick William I of Prussia founded two university chairs to encourage population studies, and textbooks and handbooks advocated state intervention to improve the population's health and welfare.

REVIEW   What were the consequences of the stabilization of the balance of power in Europe at the start of the eighteenth century?

The Birth of the Enlightenment

Economic expansion, the emergence of a new consumer society, and the stabilization of the European state system all generated optimism about the future. The intellectual corollary was the Enlightenment, a term used later in the eighteenth century to describe the loosely knit group of writers and scholars who believed that human beings could apply a critical, reasoning spirit to every problem they encountered in the world. The new secular, scientific, and critical attitude first emerged in the 1690s, scrutinizing everything from the absolutism of Louis XIV to the traditional role of women in society. After 1740, criticism took a more systematic turn as writers provided new theories for the organization of society and politics, but even by the 1720s and 1730s, established authorities realized they faced a new set of challenges.

The Popularization of Science and the Challenges to Religion

The writers of the Enlightenment glorified the geniuses of the new science and championed the scientific method as the solution for all social problems. One of the most influential popularizations was the French writer Bernard de Fontenelle's *Conversations on the Plurality of Worlds* (1686). Presented as a dialogue between an aristocratic woman and a man of the world, the book made the Copernican, sun-centered view of the universe available to the literate public. By 1700, mathematics and science had become fashionable pastimes in high society, and the public flocked to lectures explaining scientific discoveries. Journals complained that scientific learning had become the passport to female affection: "There were two young ladies in Paris whose heads had been so turned by this branch of learning that one of them declined to listen to a proposal of marriage unless the candidate for her hand undertook to learn how to make telescopes." Such writings poked fun at women with intellectual interests, but they also demonstrated that women now participated in discussions of science.

Interest in science spread in literate circles because it offered a model for all forms of knowledge. As the prestige of science increased, some developed a skeptical attitude toward attempts to enforce religious conformity. A French Huguenot refugee from Louis XIV's persecutions, Pierre Bayle (1647–1706), launched an internationally influential campaign against religious intolerance from his safe haven in the Dutch Republic. His *News from the Republic of Letters* (first published

A Budding Scientist
In this engraving, *Astrologia*, by the Dutch artist Jacob Gole (c. 1660–1723), an upper-class woman looks through a telescope to do her own astronomical investigations. Women were not allowed to attend university classes in any European country, yet the Italian Laura Bassi (1711–1778) still managed to become a professor of physics at the University of Bologna. Because many astronomical observatories were set up in private homes rather than public buildings or universities, wives and daughters of scientists could make observations and even publish their own findings. (Bibliothèque nationale de France.)

in 1684) bitterly criticized the policies of Louis XIV and was quickly banned in Paris and condemned in Rome. After attacking Louis XIV's anti-Protestant policies, Bayle took a more general stand in favor of religious toleration. No state in Europe officially offered complete tolerance, though the Dutch Republic came closest with its tacit acceptance of Catholics, dissident Protestant groups, and open Jewish communities. In 1697, Bayle published the *Historical and Critical Dictionary,* which cited all the errors and delusions that he could find in past and present writers of all religions. Even religion must meet the test of reasonableness: "Any particular dogma, whatever it may be, whether it is advanced on the authority of the Scriptures, or whatever else may be its origins, is to be regarded as false if it clashes with the clear and definite conclusions of the natural understanding [reason]." Although Bayle claimed to be a believer himself, his insistence on rational investigation seemed to challenge the authority of faith. As one critic complained, "It is notorious that the works of M. Bayle have unsettled a large number of readers, and cast doubt on some of the most widely accepted principles of morality and religion." Bayle asserted, for example, that atheists might possess moral codes as effective as those of the devout. Bayle's *Dictionary* became a model of critical thought in the West.

Other scholars challenged the authority of the Bible by subjecting it to historical criticism. Discoveries in geology in the early eighteenth century showed that marine fossils dated immensely farther back than the biblical flood. Investigations of miracles, comets, and oracles, like the growing literature against belief in witchcraft, urged the use of reason to combat superstition and prejudice. Comets, for example, should not be considered evil omens just because such a belief had been passed on from earlier generations. Defenders of church and state published books warning of the dangers of the new skepticism. The spokesman for Louis XIV's absolutism, Bishop Bossuet, warned that "reason is the guide of their choice, but reason only brings them face to face with vague conjectures and baffling perplexities." Human beings, the traditionalists held, were simply incapable of subjecting everything to reason, especially in the realm of religion.

State authorities found religious skepticism particularly unsettling because it threatened to undermine state power, too. The extensive literature of criticism was not limited to France, but much of it was published in French, and the French government took the lead in suppressing the more outspoken works. Forbidden books were then often published in the Dutch Republic, Britain, or Switzerland and smuggled back across the border to a public whose appetite was only whetted by censorship.

The most influential writer of the early Enlightenment was a Frenchman born into the upper middle class, François-Marie Arouet, known by his pen name, Voltaire (1694–1778). In his early years, Voltaire suffered arrest, imprisonment, and exile, but he eventually achieved wealth and acclaim. His tangles with church and state began in the early 1730s, when he published his *Letters concerning the English Nation* (the English version appeared in 1733), in which he devoted several chapters to Newton and Locke and used the virtues of the British as a way to attack Catholic bigotry and government rigidity in France. Impressed by British toleration of religious dissent (at least among Protestants),Voltaire spent two years in exile in Britain when the French state responded to his book with yet another order for his arrest.

Voltaire also popularized Newton's scientific discoveries in his *Elements of the Philosophy of Newton* (1738). The French state and many European theologians considered Newtonianism threatening because it glorified the human mind and seemed to reduce God to an abstract, external, rationalistic force. So sensational was the success of Voltaire's book on Newton that a hostile Jesuit reported, "The great Newton was, it is said, buried in the abyss, in the shop of the first publisher who dared to print him. . . . M. de Voltaire finally appeared, and at once Newton is understood or is in the process of being understood; all Paris resounds with Newton, all Paris stammers Newton, all Paris studies and learns Newton." The success was international, too. Before long, Voltaire was elected a fellow of the Royal Society in London and in Edinburgh, as well as to twenty other scientific academies. Voltaire's fame continued to grow, reaching truly astounding proportions in the 1750s and 1760s (see Chapter 15).

Travel Literature and the Challenge to Custom and Tradition

Just as scientific method could be used to question religious and even state authority, a more general skepticism also emerged from the expanding knowledge about the world outside of Europe. During the seventeenth and eighteenth centuries, accounts of travel to exotic places dramatically increased as travel writers used the contrast between their home societies and other cultures to criticize the customs of European society.

In their travels to the new colonies, visitors sought something resembling "the state of nature"—that is, ways of life that preceded sophisticated social and political organization—although they often misinterpreted different forms of society and politics as having no organization at all. Travelers to the Americas found "noble savages" (native peoples) who appeared to live in conditions of great freedom and equality; they were "naturally good" and "happy" without taxes, lawsuits, or much organized government. In China, in contrast, travelers found a people who enjoyed prosperity and an ancient civilization. Christian missionaries made little headway in China, and visitors had to admit that China's religious systems had flourished for four or five thousand years with no input from Europe or from Christianity. The basic lesson of travel literature in the 1700s, then, was that customs varied: justice, freedom, property, good government, religion, and morality all were relative to the place. One critic complained that travel encouraged free thinking and the destruction of religion: "Some complete their demoralization by extensive travel, and lose whatever shreds of religion remained to them. Every day they see a new religion, new customs, new rites."

Travel literature turned explicitly political in Montesquieu's *Persian Letters* (1721). Charles-Louis de Secondat, baron of Montesquieu (1689–1755), the son of an eminent judicial family, was a high-ranking judge in a French court. He published *Persian Letters* anonymously in the Dutch Republic, and the book went into ten printings in just one year—a best seller for the times. In the book, Montesquieu tells the story of two Persians, Rica and Usbek, who leave their country "for love of knowledge" and travel to Europe. They visit France in the last years of Louis XIV's reign, writing of the king: "He has a minister who is only eighteen years old, and a mistress of eighty. . . . Although he avoids the bustle of towns, and is rarely seen in company, his one concern, from morning till night, is to get himself talked about." Other passages ridicule the pope. Beneath the satire, however, is a serious investigation into the foundation of good government and morality. Montesquieu chose Persians for his travelers because they came from what was widely considered the most despotic of all governments, in which rulers had life-and-death powers over their subjects. In the book, the Persians constantly compare France to Persia, suggesting that the French monarchy itself might verge on despotism.

The paradox of a judge publishing an anonymous work attacking the regime that employed him demonstrates the complications of the intellectual scene in this period. Montesquieu's anonymity did not last long, and soon Parisian society lionized him. In the late 1720s, he sold his judgeship and traveled extensively in Europe, including an eighteen-month stay in Britain. In 1748, he published a widely influential work on comparative government, *The Spirit of Laws*. The Vatican soon listed both *Persian Letters* and *The Spirit of Laws* in its index of forbidden books.

Raising the Woman Question

Many of the letters exchanged in *Persian Letters* focus on women, marriage, and the family because Montesquieu considered the position of women a sure indicator of the nature of government and morality. Although he was not a feminist, his depiction of Roxana, the favorite wife in Usbek's harem, struck a chord with many readers. Roxana revolts against the authority of Usbek's eunuchs and writes a final letter to her husband announcing her impending suicide: "I may have lived in servitude, but I have always been free, I have amended your laws according to the laws of nature, and my mind has always remained independent." Women writers used the same language of tyranny and freedom to argue for concrete changes in their status.

The most systematic of these women writers was the English author Mary Astell (1666–1731), the daughter of a businessman and herself a supporter of the Tory party and the Anglican religious establishment. In 1694, she published *A Serious Proposal to the Ladies,* in which she advocated founding a private women's college to remedy women's lack of education. Addressing women, she asked, "How can you be content to be in the World like Tulips in a Garden, to make a fine *shew* [show] and be good for nothing?" Astell argued for intellectual training based on Descartes's principles, in which reason, debate, and careful consideration of the issues took priority over custom or tradition. Her book was an immediate success: five printings appeared by 1701. In later works, such as *Reflections upon Marriage* (1706), Astell criticized the relationship between the sexes within marriage: "If Absolute Sovereignty be not necessary in a State, how comes it to be so in a family? . . . *If all Men are born free,* how is it that all Women are born slaves?" Her critics accused her of promoting subversive ideas and of contradicting the Scriptures.

The influence of such views should not be overestimated. Most male writers unequivocally stuck to the traditional view of women, which held that women were less capable of reasoning than men and therefore did not need systematic education. Such opinions often rested on biological suppositions. The long-dominant Aristotelian view of reproduction held that only the male seed carried spirit and individuality. At the beginning of the eighteenth century, however, scientists began to undermine this belief. More physicians and surgeons began to champion the doctrine of ovism—that the female egg was essential in making new humans. During the decades that followed, male Enlightenment writers would continue to debate women's nature and appropriate social roles.

REVIEW What were the main issues in the early decades of the Enlightenment?

Conclusion

Europeans crossed a major threshold in the first half of the eighteenth century. They moved silently but nonetheless momentously from an economy governed by scarcity and the threat of famine to one of ever increasing growth and the prospect of continuing improvement. Expansion of colonies overseas and economic development

Mapping the West Europe in 1740
By 1740 Europe had achieved a kind of diplomatic equilibrium in which no one power predominated. But the relative balance should not deflect attention from important underlying changes. Spain, the Dutch Republic, Poland-Lithuania, and Sweden had all declined in power and influence, while Great Britain, Russia, Prussia, and Austria had solidified their positions, each in a different way. France's ambitions had been thwarted, but the combination of a large army and rich overseas possessions made France a major player for a long time to come.

at home created greater wealth, longer life spans, and higher expectations for the future. In these better times for many, a spirit of optimism prevailed. People could now spend money on newspapers, novels, and travel literature as well as on coffee, tea, and cotton cloth. Participants in the growing public sphere avidly followed the latest trends in religious debates, art, and music. Everyone did not share equally in the benefits: slaves toiled in abjection in the Americas; serfs in eastern Europe found themselves ever more closely bound to their noble lords; and rural folk almost everywhere tasted few fruits of consumer society.

Politics, too, changed as population and production increased and cities grew. Experts urged government intervention to improve public health, and states found it in their interest to settle many international disputes by diplomacy, which itself became more regular and routine. The consolidation of the European state system allowed a tide of criticism and new thinking about society to swell in Great Britain and France and begin to spill throughout Europe. Ultimately, the combination of the Atlantic system and the Enlightenment would give rise to a series of Atlantic revolutions.

CHAPTER REVIEW QUESTIONS
1. How did the rise of slavery and the plantation system change European politics and society?
2. Why did the Enlightenment begin just at the moment that the Atlantic system took shape?

For practice quizzes and other study tools, see the Online Study Guide at bedfordstmartins.com/huntconcise.

For primary-source material from this period, see Chapter 17 of *Sources of THE MAKING OF THE WEST,* Third Edition.

TIMELINE

■ **1709** Joseph Addison and Richard Steele publish the first edition of the *Spectator* in England

■ **1703** Peter the Great of Russia begins the construction of St. Petersburg and founds the first Russian newspaper

■ **1699** Turks forced to recognize Habsburg rule over Hungary and Transylvania

1690	1700	1710

■ **1690s** Beginning of the rapid development of plantations in the Caribbean

■ **1694** Bank of England established; Mary Astell's *A Serious Proposal to the Ladies* argues for the founding of a private women's college

■ **1697** Pierre Bayle publishes the *Historical and Critical Dictionary,* detailing errors of religious writers

■ **1713–1714** Peace of Utrecht, following the War of the Spanish Succession (1701–1713)

■ **1714** Elector of Hanover becomes King George I of England

■ **1715** Death of Louis XIV

Suggested References

A new Web site on the slave trade offers the most up-to-date information about the workings of the Atlantic system. The definitive study of the early Enlightenment is the book by Hazard, but many others have contributed biographies of individual figures or studies of women writers.

Bach's Leipzig, 1725–1750: http://www.baroquemusic.org/bachleipzig.html

Black, Jeremy. *European Warfare in a Global Context, 1660–1815.* 2007.

Blackburn, Robin. *The Making of New World Slavery: From the Baroque to the Modern, 1492–1800.* 1997.

Brewer, John. *The Sinews of Power: War, Money, and the English State, 1688–1783.* 1990.

Cracraft, James. *The Revolution of Peter the Great.* 2003.

Handel's Messiah: The New Interactive Edition (CD-ROM). 1997.

Hazard, Paul. *The European Mind: The Critical Years, 1680–1715.* 1990.

*Hill, Bridget. *The First English Feminist: Reflections upon Marriage and Other Writings by Mary Astell.* 1986.

Hunt, Margaret R. *The Middling Sort: Commerce, Gender, and the Family in England, 1680–1780.* 1996.

*Jacob, Margaret C. *The Enlightenment: A Brief History with Selected Readings.* 2000.

Pearson, Roger. *Voltaire Almighty: A Life in Pursuit of Freedom.* 2005.

Slave trade: http://www.slavevoyages.org/tast/index.faces

War of the Spanish Succession: http://www.spanishsuccession.nl/

■ **1721** Treaty of Nystad; Montesquieu publishes *Persian Letters* anonymously in the Dutch Republic; Robert Walpole becomes the first prime minister of Great Britain

■ **1720** Last outbreak of bubonic plague in western Europe

■ **1719** Daniel Defoe publishes *Robinson Crusoe*

■ **1741** George Frederick Handel composes *Messiah*

| 1720 | 1730 | 1740 |

■ **1733** Voltaire's *Letters concerning the English Nation* attacks French intolerance and narrow-mindedness

1733–1735 War of the Polish Succession

Glossary of Key Terms

This glossary of key terms contains definitions of words and ideas that are central to your understanding of the material covered in this textbook. Each term in the glossary is in **boldface** in the text when it is first defined. We have also included the page number on which the full discussion of the term appears so that you can easily locate the complete explanation to strengthen your historical vocabulary.

For words not defined here, two additional resources may be useful: the index, which will direct you to many more topics discussed in the text, and a good dictionary.

Abbasids (272): The caliphal dynasty that came to power in 750. The Abbasids built their capital at Baghdad, where they exercised considerable power over the entire Islamic world until the late ninth century.

absolutism (481): A system of government in which the ruler claimed sole and uncontestable power.

agora (57): The central market square of a Greek city-state; a popular place to gather for conversation.

agricultural revolution (532): Increasingly aggressive attitudes toward investment in and management of land that increased production of food in the 1700s; this revolution developed first in England and then spread to the continent.

Anabaptists (435): Sixteenth-century religious dissenters who believed that humans have free will and that people must knowingly select the Christian faith through rebaptism as adults. They advocated radical separation from society;

though originally pacifist, some chose violent paths to religious renewal.

apocalypticism (29): A religious belief about the end of the world; literally, "uncovering the future."

apostate (207): Literally, "renegade from the faith"; the emperor Julian (r. 361–363), who rejected Christianity and tried to restore traditional religion as the state religion, was given the nickname "the Apostate."

apostolic succession (185): The principle by which Christian bishops traced their authority back to Jesus's Apostles.

Arianism (210): The Christian doctrine named after Arius, who argued that Jesus was "begotten" by God and did not have an identical nature with his Father.

asceticism (213): The practice of self-denial of pleasure (from the Greek *askesis,* "training"), as in the lives of monks; a doctrine for Christians emphasized by Augustine.

Atlantic system (522): The triangular pattern of trade established in the 1700s that bound together western Europe, Africa, and the Americas. Europeans sold slaves from western Africa and bought commodities such as coffee and sugar that were produced by the new colonial plantations in North and South America and the Caribbean.

auctoritas (158): Literally, "moral authority"; the authority derived from respect on which the Roman princeps' power rested.

Augustus (158): The title meaning "divinely favored" that Rome's Senate granted Octavian and that became shorthand for "Roman imperial ruler."

ban (298): The rights to collect taxes, hear court cases, levy fines, and muster men for defense. It was largely understood as a complex of royal rights, but around 1000, local rulers as well as kings began exercising the ban as well.

baroque (469): An artistic style of the seventeenth century that featured curves, exaggerated lighting, intense emotions, release from restraint, and even a kind of artistic sensationalism; like mannerism, it departed from the Renaissance emphasis on harmonious design, unity, and clarity.

Black Death (393): The term historians give to the plague that swept through Europe in 1346–1353.

buccaneers (529): Pirates of the Caribbean who governed themselves and preyed on international shipping.

bureaucracy (486): A network of state officials carrying out orders according to a regular and routine line of authority.

Byzantine Empire (198): Historians' name for the eastern Roman Empire from about 500 to 1453, derived from Byzantium, the original name of Constantinople.

Capetian dynasty (303): A long-lasting dynasty of French kings taking their name from Hugh Capet (r. 987–996).

Carolingian (283): The Frankish dynasty that ruled a western European empire from 751 to the late 800s; its greatest vigor was in the time of Charlemagne (r. 768–814) and Louis the Pious (r. 814–840).

castellan (298): A person who controlled a castle. After around 1000, these castles were the seats of local power in France.

Christ (179): Greek for "anointed one" (the corresponding English word is *Messiah*); in apocalyptic religious thinking, the agent of God sent to conquer the forces of evil.

city-state (8): A state consisting of an urban center exercising political and economic control over the countryside around it.

civilization (3): A way of life that includes political states based on cities with dense populations, large buildings constructed for communal activities, diverse economies, a sense of local identity, and some knowledge of writing.

classicism (511): A style of painting and architecture that reflected the ideals of the art of antiquity; in classicism, geometric shapes, order, and harmony of lines took precedence over the sensuous, exuberant, and emotional forms of the baroque.

Colosseum (171): Rome's giant amphitheater for gladiatorial shows and other spectacles.

commercial revolution (312): The economic transformation of Europe, especially western Europe, from rural to urban and from gift-based to cash-based.

communes (316): Sworn associations of citizens who formed a legal corporate body. Communes were the normal institution of self-government in many medieval towns.

constitutionalism (482): A system of government in which rulers had to share power with parliaments made up of elected representatives.

consumer revolution (530): The rapid increase in consumption of new staples produced in the Atlantic system as well as of other items of daily life, such as mirrors, that were previously unavailable or beyond the reach of ordinary people.

cuneiform (11): The earliest form of writing, invented in Mesopotamia and formed with wedge-shaped characters.

curials (203): The social elite in the Roman Empire's towns who were responsible for collecting taxes for the imperial government and paying for any shortfalls themselves.

debasement of coinage (189): Putting less silver in a coin without changing its face value; practiced during the third-century crisis in Rome, which contributed to inflation.

Delian League (52): The naval alliance headed by Athens after the Persian Wars, and the basis of the Athenian Empire.

dominate (198): Roman rule from Diocletian (r. 284–305) onward; a blatantly authoritarian style of rule; derived from dominus ("master"; "lord") and contrasted with principate (156).

dualism (90): The concept that spiritual being and physical being are separate.

Edict of Milan (204): Constantine and Licinius's proclamation of religious toleration that also expressed their favoring of Christianity.

empire (5): A political unit in which one or more formerly independent territories or peoples are ruled by a single sovereign power.

Enlightenment (522): The eighteenth-century intellectual movement whose proponents believed that human beings could apply a critical, reasoning spirit to every problem. Based on a popularization of scientific discoveries, the movement often challenged religious and secular authorities.

Epicureanism (109): The philosophy initiated by Epicurus of Athens to help people achieve pleasure (meaning an "absence of disturbance") in their lives.

epigrams (105): Short poems covering a variety of themes, especially love, and a favorite genre of Hellenistic women poets.

fealty (296): The promise of faithfulness that a vassal made to his lord.

First Triumvirate (149): The coalition formed in 60 B.C.E. by Gnaeus Pompey, Licinius Crassus, and Julius Caesar (the word *triumvirate* means "a group of three").

friars (347): "Brothers" of the mendicant orders, such as the Franciscans and Dominicans.

Fronde (483): A series of revolts in France, 1648–1653, that challenged the authority of young Louis XIV and his minister Mazarin.

gift economy (258): System of give-and-take that determined most seventh- and eighth-century economic transactions; kings and other powerful people amassed large treasuries and foodstuffs that they distributed at will to mark their power, boost their prestige, and demonstrate their generosity.

Glorious Revolution (504): The events when the English Parliament deposed King James II in 1688 and replaced him with William, prince of Orange, and James's daughter Mary.

Golden Horde (364): The name for the Mongol Empire in Russia.

Gothic (383): A style of architecture characterized by pointed arches, ribbed vaults, and large stained-glass windows.

Great Persecution (204): The violent program initiated by Diocletian in 303 to make Christians convert to traditional religion or risk confiscation of their property and even death.

Great Schism (319, 393): The term *Great Schism* refers to two different periods in the history of the Christian church. The first, in 1054, refers to the separation of the Latin Catholic church and the Greek Orthodox church; the second, to the period from 1378 to 1417, when the church had two and sometimes three popes.

Gregorian reform (319): The movement for church reform—including clerical celibacy and an end to lay investiture—associated with Pope Gregory VII.

guilds (315): Religious, economic, and trade associations. They regulated, protected, and policed their memberships, setting up standards for professional practices.

Hanseatic League (377): A league of northern European cities formed in the fourteenth century to protect their mutual interests in trade and defense.

heliocentrism (472): The view articulated by Polish clergyman Nicolaus Copernicus that the earth and planets revolve around the sun; Galileo Galilei was condemned by the Catholic church for supporting this view.

Hellenistic (86): An adjective meaning "Greek-like" that is today used as a chronological term for the period 323 to 30 B.C.E.

hero cults (61): Religious rituals that people performed at the tombs of extraordinarily famous local men and women to ask for predictions about the future and protection in everyday life.

hierarchy (4): Social system that ranks certain people as more important and more dominant than others; the earliest evidence of social differentiation comes from the Paleolithic period.

hubris (75): The Greek term for excessive arrogance, especially when an over-confident human being goes against the will of the gods.

Huguenots (451): The name given to Calvinists in France after 1560; its linguistic origin remains uncertain.

humanism (415): A literary and intellectual movement that arose in the early fifteenth century to valorize the writings of Greco-Roman antiquity; it was so named because its practitioners studied and supported the liberal arts, or humanities.

humanitas (142): Cicero's ideal of "humaneness," meaning generous and honest treatment of others based on natural law.

Hundred Years' War (393): The long war between England and France, 1337–1453; it produced numerous social upheavals yet left both states more powerful than before.

iconoclasm (252): Literally, "icon breaking"; the destruction of icons, or images of holy people (e.g., Christ, Mary, the saints). Byzantine emperors banned icons from 726 to 787; a modified ban was revived in 815 and lasted until 843.

indulgences (436): In Roman Catholic doctrine, a remission of sin earned by performing certain religious tasks to lessen time in purgatory after death. By the fourteenth century they could be purchased. The Catholic clergy's practice of selling indulgences came under fire during the Reformation.

Inquisition (354): The court of inquiry permanently set up by the church in 1233; its purpose was to ferret out and punish heretics.

Investiture Conflict (320): The conflict between Pope Gregory VII and Henry IV over the right of laymen and even anointed kings to appoint bishops and install them in their offices.

Koine (111): The "common" or "shared" form of the Greek language that became the international language in the Hellenistic period.

ladder of offices (133): The series of Roman elective government offices from quaestor to consul.

law of universal gravitation (474): Newton's law uniting celestial and terrestrial mechanics held that every body in the universe exerts over every other body an attractive force directly proportional to the product of their masses and inversely proportional to the square of the distance between them.

madrasa (283): A school located within or attached to a mosque.

mannerism (469): A late-sixteenth-century style of painting in which a distorted perspective created bizarre and theatrical effects that contrasted with the precise, harmonious lines of Renaissance painting.

manors (289): Great estates consisting (normally) of arable fields, vineyards, meadows, and woodlands, ordinarily owned by a lord (which could as easily be a monastery or a church as a layperson) and cultivated by serfs.

martyr (184): Greek for "witness," designating someone who dies for his or her religious beliefs.

materialism (109): The philosophical doctrine that only things made of matter truly exist and thus denies the existence of the soul or any nonmaterial phenomena.

mercantilism (487): The doctrine that governments must intervene to increase national wealth by whatever means possible.

Merovingian dynasty (261): The dynasty that ruled as kings of the Franks from about 485 to 751.

mestizos (528): People born to Spanish fathers and native American mothers.

metaphysics (90): Ideas about the ultimate nature of reality beyond the reach of human senses.

metics (65): Foreigners granted permanent residency permits in Greek city-states in return for obligations to pay taxes and do military service.

monotheism (21): The belief in only one god, as in Judaism, Christianity, and Islam.

mos maiorum (120): Literally, "the way of the ancestors"; the set of Roman traditional values.

mystery cult (61): Sets of prayers, hymns, ritual purification, sacrifices, and other forms of worship undertaken to gain divine protection; each cult was connected to a particular divinity and centered on initiation into secret knowledge about the divine and human worlds.

Neoplatonism (187): The spiritual philosophy developed by Plotinus (c. 205–270) that was based on Plato's ideas and was very influential among Christian intellectuals.

ostracism (55): Athenian democracy's annual procedure to block tyranny by sending a citizen into exile for ten years by a vote of six thousand citizens in the assembly.

parlements (483): High courts in France (the term comes from the French *parler,* "to speak"). Each region had its parlement; the parlements could not propose laws, but they could review laws presented by the king and refuse to register them (the king could also insist on their registration).

patria potestas (122): Literally, "father's power"; the legal right of a father in ancient Rome to own the property of his children and slaves and to control their lives.

patriarchy (9): Social system in which men exert control over political, social, and economic life.

patron-client system (122): The interlocking network of mutual obligations between Roman patrons (social superiors) and clients (social inferiors).

Pax Romana (156): The period of "Roman peace" under the principate in the first and second centuries C.E.

Peace of God (300): A movement begun by bishops in the south of France first to limit the violence done to property and later (with the Truce of God) to limit fighting between warriors.

Pietism (540): A Protestant revivalist movement that emphasized deeply emotional individual religious experience.

plantations (522): Large tracts of land producing staple crops such as sugar, coffee, and tobacco; farmed by slave labor; and owned by a colonial settler who emigrated from western Europe.

plebiscites (133): Laws passed by the Plebeian Assembly in the Roman republic.

polis (34): The Greek term for an independent city-state based on citizenship.

politiques (453): Political advisers during the French Wars of Religion who argued that compromise in matters of religion—limited toleration for the Calvinists—would strengthen the monarchy.

polyphony (382): Music that consists of two or more melodies performed simultaneously.

polytheism (10): The worship of multiple gods.

praetorian guard (160): The group of soldiers stationed in Rome under the emperor's control; first formed by Augustus.

predestination (442): John Calvin's doctrine that God preordained salvation or damnation for each person before creation; those chosen for salvation were considered the "elect."

principate (156): The political system invented by Augustus as a disguised monarchy with the *princeps* ("first man") as emperor.

proletarians (134): In the Roman republic, the mass of people so poor that males were not eligible to serve in the army.

Protestants (435): Members of the Christian branch that formed when Martin Luther and his followers broke from the Catholic church in 1517; the name was first used in 1529 in an imperial diet by German princes who protested Emperor Charles V's edict to repress religious dissent.

Puritans (444): Strict Calvinists who opposed all vestiges of Catholic ritual in the Church of England.

radical democracy (52): The ancient Athenian system of democracy, established in the 460s and 450s B.C.E., that extended direct political power and participation in the court system to the mass of adult male citizens.

raison d'état (462): French for "reason of state." The political doctrine, first proposed by Cardinal Richelieu of France, that held that the state's interests should prevail over those of religion; Richelieu, for example, allied with the Lutheran king of Sweden even though he himself was a leading official of the Catholic church.

rationalism (42): The philosophic idea that people must justify their claims by logic and reason.

reconquista (319): The Christian conquest of Spain.

redistributive economy (10): A system in which state officials control the production and distribution of goods.

rococo (538): A style of painting that emphasized irregularity and asymmetry, as well as movement and curvature, but on a smaller, more intimate scale than the baroque.

Romanesque (343): The term for the art and architecture in western Europe during the period before around 1150, characterized by monumentality and solidity enhanced by sculpture and painting.

Romanization (175): The spread of Roman law and culture in the provinces of the Roman Empire.

Roman republic (122): A system of government based on shared political decision making and the election of male officials by assemblies organized by social hierarchy; the republic lasted from 509 to 287 B.C.E.

ruler cults (112): Cults that involved worship of a Hellenistic ruler as a savior god.

Sasanid Empire (243): The empire of the Sasanid dynasty of Persia, which lasted from 224 until its conquest by Islamic armies from 637 to 661.

scholasticism (379): The body of theological and philosophical thought of the scholastics, the scholars of the medieval universities.

scientific method (472): A combination of experimental observation and mathematical deduction to determine the laws of nature; it became the secular standard of truth and as such challenged the hold of both the churches and popular beliefs.

serfs (297): Semi-free peasants. Serfs could not legally leave the land they tilled; they owed labor services and either produce or money to their lords. Yet they were not slaves: they had the right to marry, to keep part of their produce, and to remain on the land.

simony (318): Derived from the name of Simon Magus, a magician in the New Testament who offers St. Peter money to have the power to confer the Holy Spirit (Acts 8:9–24), the term came to mean the giving of gifts or money for church offices.

social contract (482): The doctrine found in the writings of Hobbes and Locke that all political authority derives not from divine right but from an implicit contract between citizens and their rulers.

Socratic method (71): Socrates' method of conversation, in which he asked probing questions to make his listeners examine their most cherished assumptions before drawing conclusions.

Sophists (60): Competitive intellectuals and teachers who offered a new form of education and new philosophical and religious ideas beginning about 450 B.C.E.

Stoicism (110): The most influential Hellenistic philosophy, which taught the goal of living a virtuous life in harmony with nature.

struggle of the orders (132): Turmoil between elite Roman families (patricians) and the rest of Rome's population (plebeians) that centered on social and economic issues and resulted in greater sharing of political power between 509 and 287 B.C.E.

subjectivism (69): The belief, especially associated with the Sophist Protagoras, that there is no absolute reality behind and independent of appearances.

successor kings (99): Alexander's commanders (Antigonus, Seleucus, and Ptolemy) who took over portions of his empire to create personal monarchies after his death.

summa (342): A scholastic treatise that characteristically took up a topic and explored it exhaustively, resulting in a "summary" of all opinions and their resolution.

symposia (singular: symposium) (65): Drinking parties for Greek men with entertainment ranging from philosophical conversation to hired female companions.

tetrarchy (200): Literally, "rule by four"; devised by Diocletian to put into practice his principle of subdivision of power in ruling the Roman Empire.

tithe (297): A tax, taken by the church, equivalent to one-tenth of the parishioner's annual income.

Treaty of Verdun (288): The treaty that, in 843, split the Carolingian Empire into three parts; its borders roughly outline modern western European states.

Umayyad caliphate (244): The successors of Muhammad who traced their ancestry to Umayyah, a member of Muhammad's tribe. The dynasty lasted from 661 to 750.

ummah (240): The community of believers in Islam.

vassals (294): Free warriors who pledged homage and fealty to a lord, thereby creating a bond that implied mutual obligations, among them to fight for one another.

wergild (224): Under Frankish law, money or goods a murderer had to pay as compensation for his crime; most went to the victim's kin, but the king received about one-third.

Westernization (546): The effort, especially in Peter the Great's Russia, to make society and social customs resemble counterparts in western Europe, especially France, Britain, and the Dutch Republic.

Additional Acknowledgments

Chapter 1, page 16: Figure 1.2: "Egyptian Hiero-glyphs." Print of Egyptian hieroglyphs chart from *Detail of Book of the Dead—18th Dynasty Tomb of Thutmosis III, Valley of the Kings.* Reprinted by permission of Bridgeman/Art Resource, NY.

Chapter 5, page 189: Taking Measure: "The Falling Value of Roman Imperial Coinage, 27 B.C.E.–300 C.E." From *The Archeology of the Roman Economy* by Kevin Greene. Copyright © 1990. Reprinted by permission of The University of California Press via Rightslink.

Chapter 8, page 296: Taking Measure: "Sellers, Buyers, and Donors, 800–1000." Graph created by Lluís de Figueras, featured in *Dot et douaire dans le haut moyen âge* by F. Bougard, L. Feller, and R. Le Jan, eds. Copyright © 2002. (École française de Rome Service des publications, 2002, 193, Table 1.) Reprinted by permission of the French School of Rome.

Chapter 9, page 345: Figure 9.3: "Floor Plan of a Cistercian Monastery." Adaption of three figures (8a, 8b, and 8c) from page 75 in *Monasteries of Western Europe* by Wolfgang Braunfels, Thames & Hudson Ltd., London.

Chapter 10, page 360: Taking Measure: "Sentences Imposed by an Inquisitor, 1308–1323." From *Portraits of Medieval and Renaissance Living: Essays in Memory of Dave Herlihy* by Samuel K. Cohn Jr. and Steven A. Epstein. Copyright © 1996. Reprinted with permission from the University of Michigan Press. **Page 385:** Figure 10.1: "Elements of a Gothic Cathedral." After image in *Dictionnaire raisonné de l'architecture française du XIe au XVIe siècle* (Paris 1859–1868) by Eugène Emmanuel Viollet-le-Duc. Copyright © Calmann & King (London). Reprinted by permission of Laurence King Publishing, Ltd.

Chapter 12, page 463: Taking Measure: "The Rise and Fall of Silver Imports to Spain, 1550–1660." From Chart 1, "Total Imports of Treasure in Pesos (450 Maravedis) by Five-Year Intervals," page 35, in *American Revolution and the Price Revolution in Spain, 1501–1650,* edited by Earl J. Hamilton. Courtesy of Harvard University Press.

Chapter 13, page 491: Taking Measure: "The Seventeenth-Century Army." From *Armées et sociétés en Europe de 1494 à 1789* by André Corvisier. (1976, page 126). Courtesy Presses Universitaires de France.

Chapter 14, page 525: Figure 14.1: "African Slaves Imported into American Territories, 1701–1800." Adapted from *The Atlantic Slave Trade: A Census* by Philip D. Curtin. Copyright © 1969 by the Board of Regents of the University of Wisconsin System. Reprinted by permission of The University of Wisconsin Press. **Page 532:** Taking Measure: "Relationship of Crop Harvested to Seed Used, 1400–1800." Adapted from Figure 2.8, page 56, in *World Trade Since 1431: Geography, Technology, and Capitalism* by Peter J. Hugill. Copyright © 1993 The Johns Hopkins University Press. Reprinted with permission of The Johns Hopkins University Press.

Index

A note about the index:
Names of individuals appear in boldface.
Letters following pages refer to:
(i)   illustrations, including photographs and artifacts
(f)   figures, including charts and graphs
(m)   maps
(n)   footnotes